Simone Mollea

Humanitas in the Imperial Age

From Pliny the Younger to Symmachus

DE GRUYTER

The publication of this volume was made possible through the financial support of the *Patrum Lumen Sustine* foundation in Basel.

www.patrumlumensustine.com

ISBN 978-3-11-150088-1
e-ISBN (PDF) 978-3-11-151050-7
e-ISBN (EPUB) 978-3-11-151132-0
ISSN 2943-2391
DOI https://doi.org/10.1515/9783111510507

Library of Congress Control Number: 2024937231

Bibliographic information published by the Deutsche Nationalbibliothek
The Deutsche Nationalbibliothek lists this publication in the Deutsche Nationalbibliografie; detailed bibliographic data are available on the internet at http://dnb.dnb.de.

Cover image: Detail of Helios Metope (Redrawing), Temple of Athena, Troy.
© Nastasic/DigitalVision Vectors/Getty Images
Typesetting: Integra Software Services Pvt. Ltd.
Printing and binding: CPI books GmbH, Leck

www.degruyter.com

Simone Mollea
Humanitas in the Imperial Age

LUMINA

———

Leitbegriffe der griechischen und römischen Kultur und ihre Rezeption

herausgegeben von der Stiftung
Patrum Lumen Sustine (Basel)
Verantwortlicher Reihenherausgeber: Gregor Vogt-Spira

Band 1

To Elena and Edo
May *humanitas* guide your minds and your hearts

Flavio Gagnor, summo humanitatis magistro
In memoriam

Zu dieser Reihe

Die Reihe *LUMINA* versammelt Untersuchungen zu Leitbegriffen der griechischen und römischen Kultur der Antike und ihrer Rezeption. Das Interesse gilt einerseits der historischen Alterität der Konzepte; ebenso wird ihre spätere Transformation in den Blick genommen. Die Reihe sucht damit einen Beitrag zum Verständnis von zentralen Begriffen zu leisten, in denen sich Grundanschauungen verdichten, die für die antiken Kulturen leitend sind und die oftmals über komplexe Rezeptionsprozesse bis in die Moderne wirken.

Für die Herausforderung, sich dem historischen Sinngehalt eines Begriffs oder Konzepts anzunähern und zu internen Kategorien der antiken Kulturen vorzudringen, ist eine Fülle von methodischen Ansätzen entwickelt worden, wobei die nationalen Wissenschaftskulturen zum Teil sehr unterschiedliche Wege gegangen sind. Die neue Reihe steht der ganzen methodischen und inhaltlichen Pluralität, die mit der Frage nach Leitbegriffen verbunden ist, offen. Sie ist dabei explizit interdisziplinär angelegt und bietet darüber hinaus Raum für kulturvergleichende Perspektiven.

Viele dieser Begriffe und Konzepte haben sich, als sich zu Ende der Frühen Neuzeit der Stellenwert der Antike und der Modus des Rückbezugs wandelten, auch selbst tiefgreifend verändert, und in der Regel sind es diese neuen Bedeutungen, die heute die Vorstellungen prägen. Daraus erwächst ein Spannungsfeld, das der Frage nach Leitbegriffen der griechischen und römischen Antike eine Relevanz über die Altertumswissenschaft hinaus verleiht und sie auch für andere Disziplinen von Interesse werden lässt. Denn die bisweilen provozierende Alterität eines antiken Leitbegriffs führt aus der scheinbaren Vertrautheit, was unter einem bestimmten Konzept zu verstehen sei, heraus: Die Erkenntnis des historischen Gegenstands ermöglicht damit zugleich reflexive Distanz zu versteckten Implikationen gegenwärtigen Begriffsgebrauchs.

Im Zentrum der Reihe steht eine interdisziplinäre Symposiumsserie, die durch Monographien und Sammelbände ergänzt wird. Herausgebende Institution ist die Stiftung *Patrum Lumen Sustine* (*PLuS*) in Basel, in deren Auftrag auch die Symposiumsserie konzipiert wird. Monographien und Sammelbände, die darüber hinaus für die Aufnahme vorgeschlagen werden, unterliegen einem Peer-Review-Verfahren.

Gregor Vogt-Spira
Reihenherausgeber

Zu diesem Band

Dass bei Gründung der neuen Reihe die Studie von Simone Mollea zu *humanitas* soeben erfolgreich das Peer-Review-Verfahren in der anderen Reihe der *PLuS*-Stiftung (*CICERO. Studies on Roman Thought and Its Reception,* ebenfalls im Verlag De Gruyter) durchlaufen hatte, ist ein glücklicher Zufall. Denn angesichts des Themas, das nicht zuletzt durch die Untersuchung von Richard Reitzenstein aus dem Jahr 1907 einen prominenten Platz in der beginnenden Diskussion um Leitbegriffe der griechischen und römischen Kultur hat, erscheint diese Arbeit besonders geeignet, die neue Reihe zu eröffnen. Für die freundliche Zustimmung sei dem General Editor von *CICERO* und Präsidenten der Stiftung *PLuS*, Ermanno Malaspina, ebenso wie dem Autor Simone Mollea gedankt.

Gregor Vogt-Spira
Reihenherausgeber

Acknowledgements

This book should have come out much earlier, but now that it does, I have not only understood – I hope – but also experienced what *humanitas* is about. Three years of teaching at Scuola media (students aged 11 to 14) Don Bosco Cumiana, not far from Turin, two of which during the Covid-19 pandemic, as well as four at the Università della Svizzera italiana have taught me that education (παιδεία) and philanthropy (φιλανθρωπία), two concepts that will be mentioned repeatedly throughout the course of this study, are, or should actually be, inseparable. As Seneca says, *homines dum docent discunt*, and what I have learnt from my former pupils in Cumiana and students in Lugano is incalculable and certainly worth a delay in publishing a book.

This study is a considerably revised and expanded version of my PhD thesis. Many debts of gratitude I have incurred since I decided to move to Warwick for my doctoral studies. Andrew Laird was the first to support my research project and to encourage me to broaden my horizons. After his early departure to the States, Victoria Rimell kindly accepted to take over from him: it is hard to do justice to the fundamental role she played in helping me not only improve – indeed reshape at times – my thesis at all stages and levels, but also mature as a scholar and teacher. Fortunately, this handover was facilitated by the constant presence of another supervisor, Maude Vanhaelen, whose always thought-provoking feedback turned out to be essential to improve my thesis.

Compared to the thesis, this book shows some new chapters and sections as well as clearer ideas – I hope – about several key issues concerning *humanitas*, as is the case with the relationship between the adjective *humanus* and the noun *humanitas*: I am grateful to my examiners, Matthew Leigh and Roger Rees, for recommending both these two kinds of improvements, and to Lucie Pultrová for sharing with me the results of her research on comparatives in Latin. On single chapters or sub-chapters I have benefited from the expertise of many scholars and colleagues whom I met at conferences in Athens, Coimbra, Edinburgh, Leicester, Lugano, Lisbon, Paris and Turin. A couple of lectures on Cicero's *Pro Archia* – one at the *Certamen Ciceronianum Arpinas* 2022 and another during the course of Latin Language and Literature held by Andrea Balbo at the University of Turin in Winter 2022 – have helped me understand to what a great extent this oration sums up the essence of *humanitas*. Michael Winterbottom gave me precious advice on improving the chapter on [Quintilian's] *Major* and *Minor Declamations*, and two anonymous reviewers induced me to rethink relevant parts of the general introduction and conclusion. While working in the Classics Library of the University of Turin during off-term times in Warwick and on a daily basis afterwards, I have been able to discuss research issues with Ermanno Malaspina and my very dear friend Elisa Della Calce, both great experts of a concept of value which is in close relation with *humanitas, clementia.* To the former also go my deepest thanks for what he has taught me since we first met about ten years ago as well as for reading with unrivaled carefulness and commenting on a draft of this book. Gregor Vogt-Spira has kindly agreed to welcome this book in the new *Lumina* series which he edits; in addition, he has given me invaluable insights into Roman comedy and Rome's relationship with the Greek world, making me avoid serious mistakes: to him goes my deepest gratitude. Philip Barras, whose generosity can only be equalled by his learning, also on this occasion has burdened himself with polishing my English, while Torben Behm's and Ulla Schmidt's help with the editing of this manuscript has been most precious. But, above all, I am grateful to Andrea Balbo: as well as accompanying my life with the care of a father rather than a supervisor, he first introduced myself to the idea *humanitas*, then took an eagle eye from the beginning until the end of this work, eventually was the first to read its complete draft, thereby enabling me to avoid many errors and inconsistencies. Elena Polastri, one of my former pupils in Cumiana and a green classicist, has kindly helped me with the indexes. Last but not least, all lecturers, my colleagues and friends in the Warwick Department of Classics and Ancient History have not only tolerated my papers on *humanitas* during work-in-progress seminars giving important advice, but – most importantly – have made a marvellous and unforgettable experience of my days in Warwick. To all of them, as well as to the librarians of the Warwick and Turin libraries, go my deepest thanks. Needless to say, none of the aforementioned are responsible for any remaining deficiencies or mistakes, which are only my fault.

Part of the Apuleius section has already been published in S. Mollea, Huma-nitas*: a Double-edged Sword in Apuleius the Orator*, in: Andreas N. Michalopoulos, Andreas Serafim, Flaminia Beneventano Della Corte and Alessandro Vatri (eds.), *The Rhetoric of Unity and Division in Ancient Literature*, Trends in Classics – Supplementary Volumes, 108, De Gruyter, pp. 373–386.

While I was working on this book, the *Associazione Internazionale di Studi Tardoantichi* (AIST) awarded a *premio alla ricerca* to my thesis, thus encouraging the continuation of my research: to the members of the Assessment Committee goes therefore my most sincere gratitude.

Without the moral support of my family and my wife Sara, who has tolerated quite a few moments of nervousness, and the economic support of CADRE, which awarded me an AHRC scholarship, and SERICA (Sino-European Religious Intersections in Central Asia. Interactive Texts and Intelligent Networks), that funded my postdoctoral research at the University of Turin, all this would have been impossible and this book would not exist.

Preface

This book investigates one of the most polysemic Latin words I know of, *humanitas*, and, subordinately, the adjective from which it derives, *humanus*. While after the introduction the second chapter briefly retraces the history of *humanitas* from its origins, the book as a whole focuses on the uses of these two words in the pagan literary texts from the Trajanic (late first century CE) to the Theodosian age (late fourth century CE). My aim is to explore the extent to which the different meanings usually attributed to *humanitas* by dictionaries (roughly 'human nature', 'education and culture', 'philanthropy') are much more nuanced and in continuous relation with one another, and how the use of *humanitas* by some authors often performs clear rhetorical and/or ideological strategies. This book is therefore not only a lexicographical study, but pays careful attention to the wider historical and cultural contexts in which *humanitas* was used. In this respect, the study of the evolution of the word provides a new and interesting insight into wider issues of authorship, political and social changes, as well as ideological appropriations. More specifically, the use of *humanitas* reveals the ways in which Roman authors considered themes that were at the core of their conception of culture and civilization, such as the relationship between being learned and behaving morally, the ideas of moral nobility and clemency, the notion that a value concept can distinguish one category of men from another, or even one historical period from another. These themes, which remain central to later periods – from the Middle Ages to the present day – are crucial to understanding how a civilization constructed itself and changed over time.

In the light of the above, this book might be of interest to a wide range of people. Historians of ideas and philosophers will find a philologically solid basis for determining the historical and cultural premises of concepts such as Humanism, Posthumanism, Humanismus, Humanisation, Dehumanisation etc. Scholars and students of Latin literature will find interpretations of several authors and works (or parts of them), as well as discussions of issues for which *humanitas* itself or passages in which it crops up can be relevant. Classical philologists might be interested too, for all *humanitas*-connected passages that are affected by textual uncertainties are discussed in the light not only of each and every author's *usus scribendi*, but also of the history of the uses of the term *humanitas* according to genre, period, and overall context. Last but not least, the rhetorical dialectic between *humanitas*, *clementia* and other value concepts can help historians better define the imperial ideology – both on public and private levels – at different stages of its long history.

This book was virtually finished by the end of 2022, but then the delay in the peer review and editorial processes have postponed its publication. Because of the considerable amount of authors and works dealt with, I was able to add only scant references to scholarly works published after 2022.

Contents

I Laying the Foundations

Appendices

I Laying the Foundations

1 Introduction

> Oltre dunque al fenomeno storico che siamo soliti indicare con tale termine, e talora sovrappo-nendosi o intrecciandosi a quello, talora, al contrario, prescindendone del tutto, programmati-camente o meno, si parla oggi d'"umanesimo civile", d'"umanesimo politico", d'"umanesimo integrale", d'"umanesimo solidale", d'"umanesimo fraterno", d'"umanesimo marxista", d'"uma-nesimo ateo", d'"umanesimo esistenzialistico", d'"umanesimo antropocentrico", d'"umanesimo teocentrico", d'"umanesimo nuovo", d'"umanesimo moderno", d'"umanesimo cristiano", d'"u-manesimo reale", d'"umanesimo critico", d'"umanesimo ecologico", d'"umanesimo planetario", d'"umanesimo evoluzionistico", d'"umanesimo digitale", d'"umanesimo interculturale", d'"u-manesimo secolare", d'"umanesimo rigenerato" e persino d'"umanesimo fascista", d'"umane-simo nazista", e d'"umanesimo alla conquista del *business*."[1]

The *enumeratio* – or even *accumulatio* on this occasion – is a very effective figure of speech, as Miraglia knows well. It is sufficient to take a quick look at all the aforementioned labels, in which *humanism* constitutes the first element to under-stand how pervasive this word is in today's thought and, consequently, world. And, what is more, that list is anything but exhaustive. For what about concepts like *antihumanism*, *posthumanism* and *transhumanism*, for instance? They affect art and philosophy, but also science fiction, computer games and other fields. And in addition to *humanism*, the root *human-* is used to coin several other words and relative concepts which are crucial to the twenty-first century and to these years in particular. While I am writing these pages, Ukraine, Israel and other countries are theatres of wars which utterly disregard those *humanitarian* princi-ples that international treaties usually invoke and that should impede certain atrocities instead of leading to the phenomenon of *dehumanisation*. And any reader who, like myself, likes to start reading a book from its acknowledgements section will have noticed that I am a supporter of what can be broadly speaking defined as *humanistic education* (also known as person-centered education) – al-though this label might sound a bit old-fashioned today. Needless to say, by *hu-manistic education* I do not mean that sort of teaching which is imparted – almost all over the world – in the faculties of *Humanities*, but I refer to the kind of educa-tion which is centred on each and every student and on establishing an intimate, profound and, why not?, *humane* relationship with them.

Clearly, all these words and concepts did not come out of the blue. No doubt the term humanism is immediately associated with Renaissance, but the Renais-sance humanism of fourteenth–sixteenth centuries is only an intermediate step – however crucial it was – in the long history of Western *human*-related society

---

1 Miraglia 2019, 13–16 (with notes 3 to 27 with bibliographical references to all these expressions).

and culture. Alongside and after it comes, to remain in the field of *human*-related concepts and epochs, the eighteenth- and nineteenth-centuries German *Neuhumanismus*, which aimed at restoring the cultural splendour of the Renaissance by paying special attention to classical philology and the study of antiquity. And in the early twentieth century, again in Germany, Werner Jaeger became the herald of the so-called Third Humanism, yet again a cultural movement which was oriented towards classical antiquity.[2] The other concepts mentioned above came later in the twentieth and twenty-first centuries. Yet the label 'Renaissance humanism' did not come out of the blue either, and numerous studies have long shown that this cultural revolution which followed the Middle Ages is named after the Latin word *humanitas* as it was conceived of by Cicero.[3] But this also means that all the concepts which I have mentioned so far ultimately derive from an ideal which was born at the beginning of the first century BCE. So what happened to *humanitas* during the fourteen centuries which separate Cicero from the Renaissance humanism? As we shall see, the major part of the history of *humanitas* has yet to be investigated, and this book will try to throw some light on part of it, focusing on the pagan authors from the late first to the late fourth century CE.

The choice of this span of time is not only due to the paucity of studies devoted to *humanitas* across these centuries and therefore asks for some clarification, especially because periodisations always imply some degree of artificiality, and depend on various aspects: literature, politics, history, evolution of ideas and semantics of words, for instance, do not necessarily run in parallel, and this is a problem for a study which is around a word, *humanitas*, whose polysemy is influenced by both the historical, socio-political contexts and the different genres of texts – mainly literary – in which it is employed. Add to this the fact that scholarly trends, often related to national traditions, have proposed different periodisations for Latin literature, which on the one hand confirm the artificiality of such partitions and, on the other, make it more difficult to establish firm starting and arrival points for scholarly works which span several authors belonging to different ages.

The starting point of this research is represented by the Trajanic age, because, after being eclipsed by other value concepts during the Neronian and, even more, the Flavian age, under the Emperor Trajan *humanitas* first reacquired

---

2 On all these and other forms of humanisms cf. especially Toussaint 2008; Sola 2016. A brief but useful survey is provided by Giacomelli/Givone 2019.
3 Cf. below, pp. 61–62.

socio-political predominance, as emerges in particular from Pliny the Younger's oeuvre. In light of this, it would be less proper to start either earlier with the Flavian or later with the age of Hadrian, that is, after 69 or 117 CE respectively, according to two watersheds that have found ample consensus among historians of Latin literature.[4]

Likewise, also the chronological point of arrival has not been chosen by chance. To begin with, *humanitas* saw a new, the last pagan, revival during the reign of Theodosius and, what is more, by showcasing several analogies with its use during the age of Trajan. This appears as less surprising if one considers that students of both ancient history and literature have acknowledged that Roman *Weltanschauung*, or, in English, worldview, changed radically at the turn of the fifth century.[5] Symbolically, this sort of revolution is marked by the Visigoths' Sack of Rome on 24 August 410 CE,[6] which both pagans and Christians considered the beginning of a new era in which Rome could no longer be the *caput mundi* guarantor of political as well as ideological unity.[7] But at the same time, the reign of Theodosius and, in the literary field, the figure of Symmachus are representative of the last epoch for which it can make sense to distinguish between Christian and pagan Latin literature.[8] For if on the one hand it is true that, as Cameron observes, pagans and Christians, until the age of Symmachus at least, shared the same classical culture, since "it was the only culture there was",[9] on the other

---

4 Cf. B. Gibson 2005, 69–70. On the Trajanic age as a possible watershed in the history of Latin literature cf. also below, p. 81.
5 Cf. *e.g.* the recent Gasti 2020, 19. Cf. also Schanz 1959[2], 6, for whom at the turn of the fifth century there is a radical change in the Christian spirit (*des christlichen Geistes*) thanks to Augustine.
6 Cf. Brown 1971, 112: "In 410, the Visigothic king, Alaric, sacked Rome. It is fashionable to regard these barbarian invasions are inevitable. Contemporaries, however, did not enjoy the detachment and the hindsight of the modern historian." Cf. also Conte 1994, 625; Drake 2016[2], 1; Gasti 2020, 17; Gassman 2020, 175–176; Berger/Fontaine/Schmidt 2020a, 2.
7 Cf. Brown 1971, 120: "The myth of Rome that was to haunt medieval and Renaissance men – *Roma aeterna*, Rome conceived of as the natural climax of civilization, destined to continue forever – was not created by the men of the classical Roman empire: it was a direct legacy of the heady patriotism of the late fourth-century Latin world." Cf. in fact Gassman 2020, 15 (with reference to late-fourth-century authors, both Christian and pagan): "Rome still stood at the centre of their imaginative universe."
8 Cf. for example the recent Berger/Fontaine/Schmidt 2020a and Berger/Fontaine/Schmidt 2020b, the former devoted to pagan, the latter to Christian literature during the reign of Theodosius. Cf. also Schanz 1959[2], 127 (with reference to Symmachus): "Dass das Heidentum reif für den Untergang war, zeigt diese an Gedanken so arme, nur in Phrasengeklingel sich ergehende Briefsammlung, der eine christliche Literatur gegenübertrat, reich an gärenden Ideen."
9 Cameron 2011, 398. Cf. also Marrou 1948, 120–122; 137; Berger/Fontaine/Schmidt 2020a, 7–8. Brown 1971, 32 puts it in different terms: "It is not surprising, therefore, that pagans and Christi-

hand it is no less true that the religious creed – whether pagan or Christian – of each and every Latin author until that time shines through and/or influences their works, when it is not their kernel.[10] By contrast, "the fifth century witnessed the definitive adoption of secular learning by Christianity", and this could only happen because the religious dispute was won and pagan literature could no longer be a menace.[11] But at the same time, this also implies that from the fifth century onwards at least a Christian substratum is usually to be taken for granted in any Latin literary text.

Against this background, *humanitas* overall emerges in the pagan Latin literature from the second to the fourth century as a multifaceted concept which aims to defend the essence of being Roman from external threats, mainly coming from Christians and barbarians, by evoking – more or less explicitly – Rome's glorious republican, and therefore pagan, splendour.

In the case of Christian authors, instead, although we already possess some studies devoted to *humanitas* in the works of Lactantius, Ambrose, Ennodius and others,[12] a deep and extensive research is still a desideratum. Yet from the very little I have so far looked into, I have the impression that such a study might reveal interesting aspects and rhetorical strategies on Christian authors' part too. Moreover, as Marrou put it:

> Pour pouvoir être chrétien, il faut d'abord être un *homme*, assez mûr sur le plan proprement *humain* pour pouvoir poser un act de foi et des acts *moraux* (c'est un fait, historiquement et ethnographiquement constaté: le christianisme exige un minimum de *civilisation*). (my emphases)[13]

'Human being', 'humane', 'moral' and 'civilization': since this book will show that all these concepts, which have always been crucial in Western culture, are at the core of the idea of *humanitas* in pagan authors, we can be sure that also a book on *humanitas* in Christian authors would be rewarding.

---

ans fought so virulently throughout the fourth century as to whether literature or Christianity was the true paideia, the true education: for both sides expected to be saved by education." For a state of research and further bibliography cf. Gassman 2020, 4–5.
10 Cf. Brown 1971, *passim.*
11 Markus 1974,1.
12 Cf. *e.g.* Sellmair 1948; Hiltbrunner 1994a, 737–747 (on Christian authors); Høgel 2015, 85–97; Mollea 2022b.
13 Marrou 1948, 134.

1.1 *Humanitas*: State of Research

Probably because its modern derivatives, as we have just seen, play an important role in today's society, the debate over Latin *humanitas* is more alive than ever in contemporary scholarship.[14] The main general points of discussion concerning this value concept will be addressed in detail in the following sections of this introduction, but since they all originated throughout the course of the numerous studies around *humanitas* in the twentieth century, it will be useful to retrace briefly the history of scholarship on this concept of value.[15]

We have just observed that in the modern age the word *humanitas* was very productive in Germany, where it led to the *Neuhumanismus* and Third Humanism; it will therefore come as unsurprising that the first studies on Latin *humanitas* also come from the German world. A good starting point is provided by Schneidewin, whose book yet moves from the modern idea of humanity (*Humanität* in German) rather than from Latin *humanitas*, and whose main weakness, as Mayer already stressed, lies in the very fact of overlapping *Humanität* and *humanitas*.[16] Thus, we read therein that humanity corresponds to the worldview and moral programme of the elite of Roman society from the Scipionic Circle until Cicero's day, and that Cicero's work represents the fundamental mirror of ancient humanity.[17] According to Schneidewin, *Humanität* has no Greek forerunner nor it is influenced by any particular philosophical school. The features of, and topics which will be central to, the twentieth-century discussion of Roman *humanitas* are already there: an inward or outward perspective – from a modern idea to the ancient materialisation of it or, conversely, from the ancient words to their profound meanings and implications –; the origins of this idea – Greek or Roman and the possible role of mediation played by the Scipionic Circle –; the prominence of Cicero and, by more or less explicit implication, the limited relevance of later Roman authors; the relationship between *humanitas*, liberal studies, culture and civilization, and a possible elitist conception of this concept of

---

14 Prost 2006; Stroh 2008; Romano 2014; Høgel 2015; Vesperini 2015; Sola 2016; Miraglia 2019 are the most recent contributions in this field to take the cue from, or refer to, the importance of modern derivatives of *humanitas*.

15 It is worth stressing that I am not going to look at all the studies on *humanitas* in this summary, as some works which are particularly relevant for the authors whom I focus on in this book will be dealt with in the proper section(s). Likewise, further details about the studies by most of the authors who are cited in this summary will emerge throughout the course of the present book.

16 Schneidewin 1897; Mayer 1951, 1.

17 Schneidewin 1897, 445 and 18 respectively.

value.[18] Most of Schneidewin's ideas were endorsed by Reitzenstein, the main difference between the two lying in the fact that the latter believed that Panaetius and, consequently, Stoic philosophy developed a conception of human being which was fundamental to the birth of the idea of *humanitas*.[19]

Around those same years in France Boissier devoted a couple of articles to the notion of *humanitas* and stressed that while the noun takes on meanings which tend to be very different from one another, yet one sole notion unites them: they all originate from the relationships among men.[20] Moreover, Boissier highlighted that several other value concepts come into contact with *humanitas,* and that in the case of Cicero in particular, the pairing of *humanitas* with other abstract nouns helps us understand its meaning.[21] Also of relevance is that Boissier identified *humanitas* with a cult of literature which results in social usefulness.[22] But perhaps most importantly, we owe to both Boissier and Reitzenstein the notion that the socio-cultural and political importance of the concept *humanitas* began to decline with the Augustan age. This has been taken as a postulate since, and, apart from very few exceptions, still jeopardises studies on *humanitas*.[23]

---

18 As words like civilization, culture and liberal studies recur often in this book, some clarifications on what I mean by them are in order straight away. I am well aware of the discussions words like culture and civilization have raised since the nineteenth century, especially in the anthropological and archeological fields. For reasons of length, however, I am not going to look into studies such as Tylor's, Malinowski's, Spengler's and Geertz's, to name but a few. The reader in search of details about their theories can after all easily find accurate summaries in any good handbook of (cultural) anthropology. Yet when I use the term culture in this book, I broadly mean to indicate what Tylor expressed back in 1871, that is: "the complex whole which includes knowledge, belief, art, law, morals, custom, and any other capabilities acquired by man as a member of society" (Tylor 1871, 1). Although Tylor regards culture and civilization as synonyms, by civilization I indicate what the entry in the *Oxford English Dictionary* displays in section 3 a, that is, "the state or condition of being civilized; human cultural, social, and intellectual development when considered to be advanced and progressive in nature." On civilization in antiquity cf. *e.g.* Blundell 1986; Scherr 2023, 4–7, 10 and *passim* (with up-to-date bibliography). Lastly, by liberal arts / liberal studies I by and large follow Cicero's definition at *De oratore* 3.127: *has artis, quibus liberales doctrinae atque ingenuae continerentur, geometriam, musicam, litterarum cognitionem et poetarum atque illa, quae de naturis rerum, quae de hominum moribus, quae de rebus publicis dicerentur* ("the arts which are the basis for liberal education (mathematics, music, the study of literature and poetry), or the doctrines on the nature of the universe, human behavior, and the affairs of state", trans. May/Wisse 2001, adapted), on which cf. more in detail below, pp. 55–56.
19 Cf. Reitzenstein 1907.
20 Cf. Boissier 1906, 765.
21 Cf. Boissier 1906, 763.
22 Cf. Boissier 1907, 115.
23 Cf. *e.g.* Høgel 2015.

With the work of Immisch *humanitas* was for the first time closely linked to Greek φιλανθρωπία: unlike his former colleagues, Immisch believed in fact that *humanitas* was the Latin translation of the Greek word.[24] Lorenz's study on φιλανθρωπία, on which we will focus in greater detail later, by and large agrees on this point, although it also highlights differences between the Greek and the Latin word.[25]

In 1928 Zucker's attempt might have broaden the horizons of the studies on *humanitas* by focusing on later ages: he was in fact the first to spotlight the importance of *humanitas* in Pliny the Younger, but only as far as *Ep.* 8.24 is concerned.[26] Yet his attempt long remained a drop in the ocean.

A broadening in this field of studies took place one year later, not in terms of chronology, but in terms of the relationship between *humanitas* and other value concepts. Following in Reitzenstein's footsteps and therefore reiterating the ideas that the Greeks did not have any single word which was analogous to *humanitas* and that only Panaetius' conception of man led to the overlapping of the ideas of *Bildung* (education) and *Milde* (clemency) in the word *humanitas*, in 1929 Harder added that another Latin concept, that of *clementia*, was a forerunner of *humanitas*. Moreover, he maintained that Cicero's understanding of *humanitas* was influenced by Rome's foreign policy.[27]

Despite the numerous contributions that have dealt with it over the last 120 years, all the issues concerning the relationship of *humanitas* with Greek culture have not yet found answers on which all scholars agree – and probably will never do. It is therefore unsurprising that a couple of years after Harder's paper, in the introduction to his study on Erasmus' *humanitas*, Pfeiffer denied any connections between this Latin term and the Greek ἄνθρωπος as well as the influence of any philosophical strand of thought on it. By contrast, he accepted the idea that *humanitas* subsumed the Greek notions of παιδεία and φιλανθρωπία and, what is more relevant, he stressed the role of *humanitas* in softening rigidity and severity in the ethical as well as in the judicial sphere.[28]

In the late thirties of the twentieth century Nybakken put an end to the German monopoly – apart from the early case of Boissier – over studies on Roman *humanitas*. He too agreed that *humanitas* was fostered in the Scipionic Circle and

---

24 Cf. Immisch 1911, 6.

25 Cf. Lorenz 1914, on which more below, pp. 27–31.

26 Cf. Zucker 1928.

27 Cf. Harder 1929 and also Harder 1934. On the relationship between *humanitas* and *clementia* cf. below, pp. 38–40.

28 Cf. Pfeiffer 1931, 3. The notion that *humanitas* has to do with law is already in Reitzenstein 1907, 24 n. 3 and Harder 1929, 301–302; 1934, 65–66.

that was "most adequately expressed in literary form by Cicero."[29] He also added that *humanitas* subsumes both the ideas of humanism and humanitarianism, and rests largely on Greek philosophy. What is more, Nybakken reiterated Boissier's and Reitzenstein's idea of the loss of importance of *humanitas* after the republican age by peremptorily stating that *humanitas* "dropped after Cicero's death and not revived until the Renaissance and later humanistic periods."[30]

In the decade which followed, studies by Klingner and, above all, Prete stressed the importance of *humanus* and *humanitas* in the comedies by Plautus and, even more, Terence, thereby strengthening the relationship of this *Wertbegriff* with the Scipionic Circle and, consequently, the Greek world and the playwright Menander in particular.[31] In short, the 'new', more lenient and benevolent conception of man that emerges from Terence finds its roots in Terence's Greek model Menander. It is therefore clear that in this context *humanitas* was mainly conceived as φιλανθρωπία.

During those same years, Pohlenz suggested in passing that *humanitas* was to be taken as the sum of the Greek concepts of παιδεία and φιλανθρωπία, and something analogous can be found in Snell, who also stressed the influence of Stoic philosophy on the development of this Roman concept of value.[32] Unfortunately this claim, whose implications were in my view potentially decisive, was long neglected by scholarship on *humanitas*, at least until Stroh reformulated it in a more articulated way.[33] In the case of Snell, Mayer even went as far as to claim that he wanted to show that his thesis was wrong.[34]

As we have seen, until the late forties of the past century studies on *humanitas* focused mainly on Cicero and, to a lesser degree, on Terence. Something unusual, not to say revolutionary, might have happened in 1948, when Sellmair published a book titled *Humanitas Christiana*. Yet, when one reads it, one finds out that the noun *humanitas* itself does not play any relevant role, with the title only indicating a study on the humane attitude by some Christian authors.[35]

Eventually, in 1949, studies on *humanitas* did broaden their horizons. The article on Cicero and Varro by Riposati, following Gellius' 13.17, also acknowledged

---

29 Nybakken 1939, 396.
30 Nybakken 1939, 396.
31 Cf. Prete 1944; Klingner 1947; Prete 1948.
32 Pohlenz 1947, 451; Snell 1953², 249–255.
33 Stroh 2008. It is nonetheless to stress that Stroh too is still neglected or underestimated: more below, p. 14.
34 Mayer 1951, 5.
35 Cf. Sellmair 1948.

some importance to Varro,[36] whereas in the same year Büchner dealt with Cornelius Nepos' *Life of Atticus*, which he regarded as utterly guided by the idea *humanitas*.[37] Büchner also stressed the connection between *humanitas* and *pietas* in this biography and reached the conclusion that while the former concerns the relationship of a learned person with any other man, the latter implies kinship.[38]

The return to Cicero was marked by Mayer's impressive work, a dissertation which took into account all of the Ciceronian instances of *humanus* and *humanitas*.[39] The analysis is by and large divided into three parts: the first one looks at *humanitas* in private contexts, the second at its use in public and political situations, while the third investigates the occurrences which pertain to the cultural and philosophical sphere. Quite expectedly, the analysis also highlights the relationship between *humanitas* and other important concepts, such as *clementia*, *doctrina*, *lenitas*, *liberalitas*, *mansuetudo*, *urbanitas*, etc.

An important novelty in the studies on *humanitas* dates to 1960, when Honig looked in depth at the meanings of this word in the judicial sphere and, more in detail, in the legislation of the late Empire, when, according to him, laws became milder, more humane than before.[40] He paid special attention to the *Theodosian Code* and was the first to show the importance of this *Wertbegriff* after the political crisis of the third century CE.[41]

One year later, the already mentioned Büchner returned on *humanus* and *humanitas*, and stressed for example that these two words, when *emphatisch gebraucht*, always take on positive connotations.[42] Furthermore, he observed that the noun *humanitas* appeared only in the first century BCE because the notion of abstraction itself came after the idea of concreteness, that the value is typically Roman – he too believed that it originated in the Scipionic Circle – and that it is *etwas Unphilosophisches*.[43] Eventually, Büchner reiterated the notion that the importance of *humanitas* began to decline in the Augustan age and denied that we can find a *Bildungstheorie* based on the idea of *humanitas* in later Latin authors.[44]

---

36 Cf. Riposati 1949.
37 Cf. Büchner 1949, 102–103.
38 Cf. Büchner 1949, 107 and 112. On the important discussion of the relation between *humanitas* and *doctrina* as it emerges at *Life of Atticus* 4, cf. below, pp. 62–63.
39 Mayer 1951.
40 For the sake of honesty, some importance to the concept of *humanitas* in Roman law had already been attributed at least by Guarneri Citati 1927, s.v. *humanitas* and Schulz 1934, 130, but theirs are not studies explicitly devoted to this value concept in the legal sphere.
41 Cf. Honig 1950. For further details cf. below, p. 215.
42 Büchner 1961, 637.
43 Büchner 1961, 638 and 640.
44 Büchner 1961, 643 and 645.

In contrast with Büchner's recent claim, which explicitly underestimated the role of *humanitas* in Pliny the Younger's work, in 1961–1962 Bolisani devoted the first in-depth study to his *humanitas* and highlighted its importance in Pliny's worldview.[45] Notwithstanding, Bolisani did not succeed in establishing the crucial role of this author in the history of *humanitas* once and for all, as will become clearer in the section on Pliny.[46]

In 1963 the entry on *humanitas* in Hellegouarc'h's *Le vocabulaire latin des relations et des partis politiques sous la république* clarified the importance of this value concept in the political life of the late republic,[47] while joint attention to Cicero and the judicial sphere is what characterised J. Schneider's dissertation in 1964.[48] In the first part of his work, he investigated the relationship between *humanitas* and law in the scopes of slavery (*seruitus*), kinship (*cognatio*) and friendship (*amicitia*) as it emerges from Cicero's oeuvre. In the second half he first turned to the same relationship as it materialises between citizens in private law, and then looked at public law, both in foreign and domestic policies.

If we exclude Plautus, Terence, Cicero and, to a lesser degree, Cornelius Nepos, we do not find specific analyses of the concept of *humanitas* in other authors until 1967. Curiously enough, in this same year two important studies on authors of the first century CE appeared, those by Lipps and Rieks. Lipps investigated the idea of human being and humanity as it emerges from the works of Seneca, Lucan, Persius, Petronius, Curtius Rufus and Velleius Paterculus. His analysis took into account not only the instances of *humanus* and *humanitas*, but also those of *homo*.[49] The same approach and methodology characterised the work by Rieks, but the authors he analysed are at times different from those investigated by Lipps. Rieks did look at *homo*, *humanus* and *humanitas* in Velleius Paterculus, Seneca, Petronius, Lucan and Persius, but also added Vitruvius, Ovid, Manilius, Valerius Maximus, Phaedrus, Statius and Pliny the Younger.[50] Despite their efforts and results, they did not succeed completely in dismantling the prejudice according to which after Cicero there was no true cultural and socio-political programmes based on *humanitas*.

Another important step in the history of the studies on *humanitas* is represented by the entry in *Aufstieg und Niedergang der römischen Welt*, written by Schadewaldt in 1973. As is typical of the contributions in *ANRW*, Schadewaldt's too

---

45 Cf. Bolisani 1961–62.
46 Cf. below, pp. 83–115.
47 Cf. Hellegouarc'h 1963, 267–271.
48 Cf. J. Schneider 1964.
49 Cf. Lipps 1967.
50 Cf. Rieks 1967.

provided a state of research, but also offered new insights into this word, which was famously regarded as "schillernd wie ein Chamäleon".[51] *Humanitas* is ultimately conceived as what can be found in the human beings and belongs to them, but also what identifies their imperfections and, as a consequence, tolerance and compassion of a human being towards their fellows.[52] Furthermore, *humanitas* stands to indicate the fulfilment of true human being through encyclopedic learning (or *studia humanitatis*).[53] Importantly, Schadewaldt highlighted that this is not an absolute value concept, but its meanings and implications depend on the historical and social situations in which it is used.[54]

In the same 1973 Jocelyn wrote an article that should have downsized the relevance of *humanitas* in Terence's oeuvre, as it showed that the famous line 77 of the *Heautontimoroumenos* (*homo sum: humani nil a me alienum puto*) had in fact little to do with the nobility of the concept as it emerges in first-century BCE Latin literature.[55] Yet this contribution has not been as influential as it would deserve.[56]

The often cited Gellius, *Noctes Atticae* 13.17 was first analysed in depth only in 1986 thanks to a contribution by Kaster, which I will deal with in the subchapter on Gellius;[57] while in 1993 Veyne stressed the role played by *humanitas* in defining Romanness and, consequently, non-Romanness and barbarity.[58] This inevitably leads to the complex discourse concerning Roman imperialism, as is made more explicit in a contribution by S. Braund.[59] In cases such as these, texts like Caesar's *De Bello Gallico* 1.1 and Tacitus' *Agricola* 21, whose importance was often underestimated in previous studies, become crucial, as we will see in greater detail in due course.[60]

In 1994 then, Hiltbrunner wrote the entry on *humanitas* in the *Reallexikon für Antike und Christentum*, but the title itself – *Humanitas* (φιλανθρωπία) – reveals that *humanitas* is mainly understood in terms of the Greek φιλανθρωπία and – the author maintained – only with the appearance of the phrase *studia humanitatis* in Cicero it began to include the meaning of παιδεία, a meaning that it retained seldom.[61] On the other hand, however, Hiltbrunner was the first to actually broaden the chronological limits traditionally imposed to studies on *humanitas*:

---

51 Schadewaldt 1973, 44.
52 Cf. Schadewaldt 1973, 44.
53 Cf. Schadewaldt 1973, 45 and 60.
54 Cf. Schadewaldt 1973, 47 and 49.
55 Cf. Jocelyn 1973. Cf. also below, pp. 47–50.
56 Cf. below, p. 47.
57 Cf. Kaster 1986 and below, pp. 169–173.
58 Cf. Veyne 1993.
59 Cf. S. Braund 1997.
60 Cf. below, pp. 64; 118–124.
61 Cf. Hiltbrunner 1994a, 729–730.

his entry goes so far as to touch upon Drepanius (*Pan. Lat.* 2.20),[62] including Fronto, Gellius, legal texts from the second and third centuries CE as well as several Christian authors.[63] Yet the length of a dictionary entry prevented him from investigating the role of *humanitas* within each and every single author in depth, and when it comes to the imperial age from the first century, his focus is rather on Christian than on pagan authors.

The new millennium was inaugurated by a monograph by Bauman in which *humanitas* is connected with the aim of pinpointing the presence of the notion of human rights in ancient Roman society.[64] But a few years later the horizons of *humanitas* studies are further broadened by a contribution in which Maróti shifted the focus from literary to epigraphic texts and showed that the term *humanitas* can also be used to refer to, and actually mean, subsistence.[65]

As I have already suggested, Stroh's 2008 article is in my view decisive, as it eventually explained the way the Greek concepts of παιδεία and φιλανθρωπία are intertwined in Roman, Ciceronian *humanitas*. Because of its importance, I am going to deal with it in greater detail in another section of this introduction. For the moment, however, I should like to stress that it has often been utterly neglected in recent scholarship on *humanitas* – a great shame![66]

Two important studies appeared in 2015. Høgel's monograph looked in particular at the argumentative use of the concept of the humane from the origins up to the Renaissance, but neglected most of the Latin literature between the late first century CE and the fourteenth century in the belief that "in the centuries after Seneca and Pliny, various other writers use the humane, but few with any argumentative purpose or clear agenda".[67] Vesperini was instead the first to analyse *humanitas* from a pure anthropological perspective, and the conclusion he reached seems to confirm the thesis according to which *humanitas* indicates the human being's capacity to be social – ultimately something which has to do with φιλανθρωπία – and this is not provided by nature but by education (παιδεία).[68]

In the years which followed other studies on *humanitas* have appeared, but in some cases they did not add much to the picture, while on other occasions

---

62 Hiltbrunner 1994a, 733. On Drepanius cf. below, pp. 295; 300–301.
63 Cf. Hiltbrunner 1994a, 734 (on Fronto and Gellius), 735–737 (on legal texts), 737–747 (on Christian authors).
64 Cf. Bauman 2000.
65 Cf. Maróti 2002–2003.
66 Cf. Stroh 2008, and below, p. 16. Elice 2017, 264 only quotes Stroh 2008 with regard to the role of the Scipionic Circle in founding the idea of *humanitas*; Høgel 2015 and Vesperini 2015 seem to ignore him altogether.
67 Høgel 2015, 83.
68 Cf. Vesperini 2015.

their focus was on singular authors and will therefore be discussed in the relevant sections of this book.

Some points should have emerged clearly from this summary of the history of *humanitas* over the past 120 years or so. To begin with, some crucial issues are still open and discussed, as is the case of the Greek or Roman origins of *humanitas*, or of the meanings of *humanitas* and the way they are interconnected. To these, I would add the relationship between *humanus* and *humanitas*, which, by implication of its immediate opposites *inhumanus* and *inhumanitas*, also leads to the way *humanitas* relates to other concepts of value, a topic which, as we have seen, has naturally attracted scholars' attention, but on which there is still much to say. Finally and crucially, whatever the viewpoint from which it has been looked at – educational programme, human rights, idea of the humane or other – the imperial age from the late first century has mostly been disregarded in studies explicitly devoted to *humanitas*. As I hope this book shows, expanding the analysis of *humanus* and *humanitas* on imperial authors and therefore gaining an ampler picture also helps us address and throw new light on all the aforementioned issues.

1.2 *Humanitas*: The (Impossible?) Search for a Definition

The first issue I want to focus on concerns the definition of *humanitas*. This is a problematic word onto which modern scholars often project their own understanding of what 'human' and 'educated' might mean – just think of Schneidewin's pioneering study in the late nineteenth century.[69] In addition, many studies have been criticised for their 'tired repetitiveness'.[70] As we have seen, it is also difficult to find firm points of reference in the existing scholarship, both in terms of methodology and concrete results. A (too) strict approach, which is epitomised in dictionary entries, has led to the division of *humanitas* into different clusters of meanings – it is sufficient to recall that Hiltbrunner's entry in the *Reallexikon* right from the title regards *humanitas* as an equivalent of φιλανθρωπία.[71] The partition I find more convenient despite Balbo's objection of oversimplification[72] can be found in the *Oxford Latin Dictionary* entry, and distinguishes three main semantic areas: 1) human nature or character; 2) the quality distinguishing civilized men from savages or

---

69 Cf. above, p. 7.
70 Narducci 1981, 179.
71 Cf. above, pp. 13–14.
72 Balbo 2012, 67 does not go too much into detail, but stresses that in this partition the semantic complexity of *humanitas* is "dumbed down" as the entry "sticks to generalities."

beasts, civilization, culture; 3) humane character, kindness, human feeling.[73] While it lacks the higher degree of detail found in the *TLL* or *L&S*,[74] the *OLD* approach has the merit of following in the footsteps of a native speaker of Latin, Aulus Gellius, who was the first to raise the problem of defining *humanitas* in the second century CE.[75] On the basis of this or analogous categorisations, many studies have sought to fix the exact meaning of *humanitas* on case-by-case criteria, often focusing on a single author.[76] Yet, as I have already hinted, in 1947 Pohlenz suggested in passing that *humanitas* was to be taken as the sum of those definitions which form points 2 and 3 of the *OLD* entry, and which Gellius, resorting to Greek values, referred to as παιδεία and φιλανθρωπία respectively.[77] The potential implications of this statement were long neglected or underestimated, until Stroh reformulated this principle, arguing that the idea of φιλανθρωπία originated from that of παιδεία: in short, being benevolent towards other fellow human beings is (or can be) a consequence of being learned, and education is ultimately useless unless it contributes to moral improvement.[78] As I will suggest in this book, a possible solution to understanding the intricate nature of *humanitas* should take the cue from, and expand on, Pohlenz's and Stroh's intuitions.

Veyne sums up what has induced *humanitas*-scholarship to try to pigeonhole occurrences of this word: "The reader can rest assured that I am as leery as he or she of the word *humanitas*. The term is both vague and laudatory."[79] What has always disturbed scholars, whether or not they declare it, is the same aspect which has always fascinated them, the polysemy of *humanitas*, which easily re-

---

73 For an overview of the other dictionary-styled entries on *humanitas* cf. S. Braund 1997, 16–18; Balbo 2012, 65–69.
74 The *TLL* entry (6.3.3075.5–3083.56) distinguishes between a general and an emphatic meaning of *humanitas*. The general meaning is in turn divided into human nature (for example as opposed to divine nature: 3075.29–3076.47), idea of man (3076.48–59), mankind (3076.60–3077.7) and also includes instances in which *humanitas* is used as a synonym of the adjective *humanus* (3077.8–19). The emphatic meaning refers instead to those occurrences in which *humanitas* characterises what is worthy of man: on these occasions *humanitas* is linked to other concepts of value like *prudentia* (3077.29–36), *dignitas, honestas* (3077.75–3078.6), *elegantia* (3078.7–28), *comitas, clementia, benignitas* (3079.1–3082.18), *hospitalitas* (3082.19–55), *munificentia* and *largitas* (3082.56–76) but also *eruditio, doctrina* and *urbanitas* (3078.32–84). *L&S*'s entry is very close to the *TLL*'s.
75 On *humanitas* in Gellius cf. below, pp. 158–174.
76 Without aiming at (impossible) completeness, I think of works such as Mayer 1951; Lipps 1967; Rieks 1967 or Schadewaldt 1973, on which cf. above, pp. 11–13. Further examples will emerge in the next chapters.
77 Pohlenz 1947, 451. Cf. also Snell 1953², 249–255; J. Schneider 1964, 120; Boyancé 1970b, 6.
78 Stroh 2008.
79 Veyne 1993, 342.

sults in vagueness and ambiguity. As a result, many scholars have felt the need to 'overcome' the vagueness of the word by forcing it into rigid meanings, which are themselves ideologically charged. Yet, as I will show, such a strategy leads to results that are inconclusive, for the vagueness of *humanitas* cannot simply be resolved and several Latin authors themselves purposely exploited the polysemy of this word.

Let me return to the *OLD* entry and imagine putting it under a microscope which can zoom either in or out. When we magnify our subject, which is what scholars usually do, it will be clear that *humanitas* is about being human and possessing the qualities which make human beings worthy of being called so, qualities which can be acquired through education and lead to the (modern) ideas of culture and civilization. What such an education and culture consist in is likely to depend on the historical period and socio-political condition, or else on the subjectivity of any single person, but one might think of literature, the so-called liberal arts in general, religion, law, and possibly many others.[80] Moreover, there is a further aspect of *humanitas*, that which relates to kindness, and which can materialise in hospitality, generosity, clemency, or, more simply, sympathy towards 'the other', whether a foreigner, enemy, or a lower-, equal- or higher-ranking person.

Yet we should also zoom out and avoid considering those three main meanings as compartmentalised. What emerges is that this strikingly broad spectrum of meanings originates from one and the same word. And if this is obviously not unique to this term, my objective is to attempt to understand how and to what extent these meanings relate to one another, and to show that it is much more proper as well as more effective to consider that these various meanings can often be simultaneously present in occurrences of the word *humanitas*. Zooming out is to take distance from the case-by-case perspective and adopt the work-by-work or author-by-author approach. This does not simply mean focusing on single authors only – there would be nothing new in this respect – but rather to understand whether and when there is a logic behind the use of *humanitas* in a given work, and whether such a use responds to a specific purpose, or produces certain effects. This change of tack turns out to be crucial, for it reveals the rhetorical strategies which underpin most authors' use of this word. More precisely, the main result of this approach is to show that the authors under investigation tend to use the word *humanitas* to unite as well as to differentiate between categories of people, as might be implicitly suggested by the second *OLD* definition of

---

80 On the understanding of civilization and culture throughout the course of this book cf. above, p. 8. n.18.

humanitas ('the quality distinguishing civilized man from savages'), especially if we bear in mind that the Roman upper classes usually regarded themselves as the true men. It is important to remark straight away that these categories are not fixed, but depend on the situation, the cultural climate, and the specific aims of the writer.

1.3 Studying *Humanitas* in the Imperial Age

The need to investigate *humanitas* as a nexus of interrelated connotations that concern important cultural-political discourses seems to me to pertain especially to the main pagan authors of the imperial period. As I will make clear later on, these authors inevitably had to engage with the previous history of *humanitas* and the rhetorical, historical and, above all, political and ideological connotations the word had acquired. Indeed, as the second chapter of this book will show, by the end of the first century CE the history of *humanitas* had already gone through different stages – from the heyday in the Ciceronian age to a gradual downfall, both in terms of quantity and polysemy of the occurrences, which began under Augustus and (provisionally) ended with Domitian's death in 96 CE. To some degree, therefore, studies such as those by Boissier, Reitzenstein and Nybakken hit the mark when highlighting the socio-political and cultural loss of importance of *humanitas* after the end of the republican age.[81] Yet the main problem of their contributions is that they did not look beyond the Augustan or the Neronian, Flavian ages at the latest, when, as figures too show, the frequency of the use of the noun *humanitas* increased again.[82] In fact, the pattern of ups and downs continued in the ages which followed, so that a Theodosian author like Symmachus made use of a kind of *humanitas* which carried with it the multi-layered history of its various uses until the late fourth century CE. Furthermore, since I have already explained why the Theodosian age marks the endpoint of this research,[83] and because it bears some resemblance to the Trajanic age, especially as a consequence of Theodosius' admiration for Trajan,[84] it will come as unsurprising that Pliny the Younger is the first while Symmachus is the last author I focus on. And after all, as some scholars have ar-

---

81 Cf. above, pp. 8–10.
82 On the frequency of *humanitas* from the republican age up to the late fourth century CE cf. below, pp. 41–44.
83 Cf. above, pp. 5–6.
84 Cf. below, pp. 224–226.

gued and this book should show further, in many respects (style and socio-political function above all) Symmachus relates very closely to Pliny the Younger.[85]

The benefits to this analysis are numerous and span socio-political, judicial, historical and educational fields. In works which have explicit socio-political aims, such as Pliny's *Panegyricus* and *Letters*, Ausonius' *Gratiarum actio* or Symmachus' oeuvre, the use of *humanitas*, especially as it seems to replace another concept of value like *clementia*, is likely to express a willingness to mark discontinuity between past and present political climates. If we then consider that *humanitas* is often understood by Pliny and Symmachus as Ciceronian, and as associated with late republican Rome, the message may even imply that their age is (or should be) more inclined to guarantee freedoms, as more associated with republican values than the previous one(s).[86] In different ways, attitudes towards *humanitas* in historians such as Tacitus, Ammianus, or the 'minor' historians of the fourth century reflect these changes of values. On other occasions, for example Apuleius' *Apologia* and *Metamorphoses*, Eumenius' *Oratio pro instaurandis scholis* and, to a lesser degree, some declamations, *humanitas* was instead perceived as an excellent weapon of persuasion in oratorical contexts, again following in Cicero's footsteps, especially in his *Pro Archia*. Moreover, a learned man like Gellius tried to restore, through the concept of *humanitas*, what he regarded as the best educational system in opposition to the grammarians' widespread but low-quality teaching. Finally, Firmicus Maternus and the author of the *Asclepius* display their own, singular understandings of *humanitas*, which are in tune with the particular genres of their works as well as by their being in close relationship with Greek models.

In the following sections of this introduction, after adding some methodological remarks, I shall first deal with the ancient texts which discussed the meanings of *humanitas* and influenced the twentieth-century compartmentalising approach to this concept of value. These texts bring into play the Greek concepts of παιδεία and φιλανθρωπία, whose connotations I will briefly explore. I will then discuss the origins of *humanitas*. Finally, I will outline the structure of the main part of the book.

---

85 Cf. below, pp. 314–315.
86 On the general attempt to recover republican values during the Trajanic age and in Pliny the Younger in particular cf. Gowing 2005, 121–122, where crucial is Pliny's expression *libertas reddita* of *Pan.* 58.3.

1.4 Some Methodological Remarks

I have been emphasising that the term *humanitas* is characterised by consistent polysemy, which is exploited differently according to authors, works, and contexts. It is my contention that any investigation of this multifaceted concept should work outwards, having the occurrences of the term *humanitas* itself as a starting point and exploring its significance in context. Once separated off from its context and studied in isolation, *humanitas* can mean anything and nothing. Most recent studies on *humanitas* agree with this methodological principle; however some, and especially earlier ones, do not.[87] We can therefore encounter studies on *humanitas* in authors who did not use, and often could not have used the word *humanitas* in the works which have come down to us. Such is the case, for example, in contributions studying the *humanitas* of some poets who wrote hexameters:[88] the sequence of two long syllables followed by one short and then another long syllable (*hūmānĭtās*) simply does not fit any hexametric verse. *Humanus* does fit the hexameter, but, as I shall clarify below, it can hardly be seen as an exact equivalent of *humanitas*. It is therefore impossible to understand the connotations authors who did not use the word *humanitas* would have given to this word. I by no means want to disregard these studies altogether: I simply want to say that they cannot play a key role in an analysis of Roman *humanitas*. Accordingly, this book deals with prose authors only.

Some comment on translation. In the course of this book, I consider a great many Latin texts in their literary, cultural and political contexts, some of which are of considerable length. To make it easier for readers who are little or not at all skilled in Classical languages to follow the discourse, I have provided all Greek and Latin texts with English translations, but because of the evident problems of conveying the multiple, ever-transforming meanings of *humanitas* without paraphrasing at length, or misleading my readers with inadequate single synonyms, I have most of the times left the word *humanitas* untranslated. These problems are exacerbated when in many cases *humanitas* is paired with other value concepts or other terms whose meanings are in turn influenced by their being associated with *humanitas*. I give here just one example. In the case of Eumenius' panegyric, discussed in Chapter 6, we encounter the pairing of *humanitas* and *uirtus*. Taken

---

87 Recent studies working outwards include Prost 2006; Stroh 2008; Oniga 2009; Balbo 2012; Høgel 2015; Vesperini 2015; Elice 2017; Boldrer 2021. Others will be mentioned in the next chapters. Büchner 1958; in part Lipps 1967, cf. *e.g.* 99–100; Rieks 1967 – cf. in particular 24; Nussbaum 1971; Girotti 2017 and others work instead inwards, moving from a questionable, pre-conceived idea of *humanitas*.

88 Cf. *e.g.* Büchner 1958 and Nussbaum 1971 on Horace's; Lipps 1967, 70–121 on Lucan's and Persius'; or Rieks 1967, 39; 50; 217 on Ovid's, Manilius' and Statius' *humanitas*.

alone, *uirtus* is no less polysemic than *humanitas*, but the context and the pairing with *humanitas* make clear that *uirtus* exalts the emperor's military prowess, while *humanitas* underscores his care for education and culture. The one value concept clarifies the other, and vice versa. On occasions such as this I have sometimes left untranslated also the Latin words which are paired with *humanitas*.

In order to understand the meaning of *humanitas* in context, analysing the words with which it is paired or to which it is opposed is often necessary. Yet some clarification is in order, especially because Høgel claims: "Many studies have [. . .] tried to derive the meaning of *humanitas* by searching for its relationship to other virtues. This is a difficult procedure and threatens to make nothing but a list of partially equivalent positive virtues."[89] While I agree that the presence of *humanitas* within lists of value concepts is usually of little help in terms of our understanding, this is often not the case when *humanitas* is paired with one single word (or two at most). To simply disregard the cases of pairing would be to ignore one major feature of the Latin language, its propensity to resort to synonymic dittologies: in order to convey a given idea as clearly as possible, two potentially synonymous, or, better, quasi-synonymous terms are paired together. This practice becomes particularly significant and helpful when the meaning of one of the two words, or both, would be ambiguous if taken alone: the passages from Gellius and Nonius quoted below make it clear that this is the case with *humanitas*, and that its ambiguity was already perceived by native Latin speakers.[90]

1.5 *Humanitas*: Ideological Components and Other Issues

As the initial state of research should have made clear, the question of the origins of *humanitas* is complicated and long-debated. To recap. Scholars disagree on what is to be seen as the first appearance of this value concept in Latin texts: do we need to stick to the very occurrences of the word *humanitas* or can instances of *humanus* express the same meaning as the noun? Closely related to this is a second question: is *humanitas* a typically Roman ideal or was it imported from Greece? I have already expressed my opinion on both these questions elsewhere,[91] but will reiterate them and, especially as far as the first one is concerned, starting from the subsection on Terence (2.1), this book will bring new evidence in favour of the substantial independence of the noun from the adjective.

---

89 Høgel 2015, 39.
90 Cf. below, pp. 24–25.
91 Cf. Mollea 2018b and Mollea 2023b.

1.5.1 *Humanus* and *Homo*

Humanus was originally a purely relational adjective that was coined to mean *hominis-hominum* / 'of man-men', but at some point developed an evaluative dimension and came to indicate what was worthy of the 'true' man, or, more etymologically, what was 'worthier' of man. I said more etymologically because evidence shows that it is rather in its comparative and superlative forms that the adjective *humanus* reveals its evaluative dimension. And, as Pultrová's very recent studies on comparatives in Latin show, there is a very tight connection between the gradability of an adjective and its capacity to give birth to abstract nouns.[92] As a result, we perceive that the abstract *humanitas*, which ultimately epitomises the qualities which make man worthy of being so called, is also rendered through comparatives and superlatives of *humanus* – which are employed only occasionally by the way – but rarely, and in particular contexts, by its positive form.

A fortiori, therefore, this book will not investigate the noun *homo*, and this is not due to the arguments put forward by modern linguistics.[93] For Giustiniani's following words would provide a satisfying objection against those theories: "Although modern linguists may question whether Latin *ŏ* can change into *ū*, both terms have been regarded as related to one another since antiquity, which is what matters here."[94] Yet while I do admit that *homo* and *humanus* / *humanitas* are linked to each other, those same antique sources invoked by Giustiniani also warn us against exceeding in drawing this parallelism. Cf. for example Pliny the Elder:

---

92 Cf. Pultrová 2019 and Pultrová 2022.

93 As we have seen (cf. above, pp. 12–13), some previous studies on *humanitas* also deal with the occurrences of *homo*. Needless to say, the distance from *humanitas* would increase further and, at any event, it is difficult to imagine that a word like 'man' could usually carry ideological and ethical components. Furthermore, despite the intuitive connection of *humanus* / *humanitas* with *homo* (cf. *e.g.* Val. Max. 5.1. *praef.*, accepting Badius' conjecture *homine* – on which I am sceptical – instead of *numine*, or Ter. *Haut.* 77; further examples in Elice 2017, 287) the problem of their relationship is complicated further by the passage from *ŏ* of *hŏmo* to *ū* of *hūmanus*, which glottologists have yet to explain: cf. Ernout/Meillet 2001⁴, 298; De Vaan 2008, 288; it is methodologically unsustainable to claim that we should accept the derivation of *humanus* from *homo* on the grounds that it is attested in ancient sources, as proposed by Walde/Hofmann 1938, 663–664, who then added: "erklärungsbedürftig ist lediglich (!) das ū." But the easiest explanation is that ancient sources – cf. Maltby 1991, s.v. *homo* for a complete list of these sources – produced a case of false etymology. Isidore of Seville (*Orig.* 10.116) inverts the reasoning and makes *homo* derive from *humanitas*, but the glottological problem does not change. I will return to this issue in the sub-chapters on Pliny and Gellius.

94 Giustiniani 1985, 167.

Nec ignoro ingrati ac segnis animi existimari posse merito si obiter atque in transcursu ad hunc modum dicatur terra omnium terrarum alumna eadem et parens, numine deum electa quae caelum ipsum clarius faceret, sparsa congregaret imperia ritusque molliret et tot populorum discordes ferasque linguas sermonis commercio contraheret ad colloquia et humanitatem homini daret, breuiterque una cunctarum gentium in tot orbe patria fieret. (*HN* 3.39)

I am well aware that I may with justice be considered ungrateful and lazy if I describe in this casual and cursory manner a land which is at once the nursling and the mother of all other lands, chosen by the providence of the gods to make heaven itself more glorious, to unite scattered empires, to make manners gentle, to draw together in converse by community of languages the jarring and uncouth tongues of so many nations, to give humankind civilization (*humanitatem homini*) and in a word to become throughout the world the single fatherland of all the races. (trans. S. Braund 1997)

The land which is said to give humankind civilization (*humanitatem homini*) is the Italian peninsula, and while this passage, whose imperialistic tone is undeniable,[95] may also be used to counter the texts in which Greece is regarded as the dispenser of *humanitas* – although of course one might object that Rome inherited this role from Greece –[96] what I want to stress is that Pliny makes it clear that being man is something utterly different from possessing *humanitas*. Rather, what he implies is that man, in order to become worthy of being so called, needs to acquire *humanitas*, but this cannot be taken for granted.

An opposition between *homo* and *humanitas* can also be found in one of the 'founders' of *humanitas*, Varro, who at *De lingua Latina* 8.31 observes: *quod aliud homini, aliud humanitati satis est; quoduis sitienti homini poculum idoneum, humanitati <ni>si bellum parum*, "for one thing is enough for man (*homini*), and quite another thing satisfies human refinement (*humanitati*): any cup at all is satisfactory to a man (*homini*) parched with thirst, but any cup is inferior to the demands of refinement (*humanitati*) unless it is artistically beautiful" (trans. Kent 1938, slightly adapted). A striking difference emerges here: like all other animals, man only has survival needs, whereas *humanitas* has greater demands, like that of beauty for instance. And as with the previous Plinian instance, here again it is clear that there is no automatic shift from *homo* to *humanitas*. Quite on the contrary, as Leonardis puts it: "la natura degli *humani* contempla qualcosa in più rispetto a quella dei semplici *homines*, dai quali i primi si differenzierebbero in quanto «raffinati», ovvero dotati di *humanitas*."[97]

---

95 Cf. S. Braund 1997, 23.
96 Cf. S. Braund 1997, 23. More on this passage and its relationship with the idea of civilization in Scherr 2023, 325–334.
97 Leonardis 2018, 526.

And in a famous passage of his *De republica* on which we will return later on, Cicero's Scipio firmly states that "only those who are skilled in the specifically human arts are worthy of the name of men" (*appellari ceteros homines, esse solos eos, qui essent politi propriis humanitatis artibus*, trans. Rudd 1998, slightly adapted).[98] He therefore makes explicit the relationship between *homo* and *humanitas*, but at the same time also reinforces the idea that the human being is not intrinsically, ontologically worthy of being so called: this happens only when common man possesses those arts that are appropriate for him. By contrast, those men who do not possess or share *humanitas*, whether they are noblemen, humble people or barbarians, threaten to return Rome to a barbarian, pre-civilized past.[99]

In the light of the above, the occurrences of *homo* will not be at the core of this research, although it is obvious that this noun crops up from time to time.

1.5.2 Greek or Latin *Humanitas*?

As for the issue concerning the origins of *humanitas*, before looking at it in detail, it is necessary to return to the core meanings and nuances conveyed by the word *humanitas*, starting from the ancient debate around it.

The first definition of *humanitas* is provided in the second century CE by Aulus Gellius at *Noctes Atticae* 13.17.1:

> Qui uerba Latina fecerunt quique his probe usi sunt, humanitatem non id esse uoluerunt, quod uolgus existimat quodque a Graecis φιλανθρωπία dicitur et significat dexteritatem quandam beniuolentiamque erga omnis homines promiscam, sed humanitatem appellauerunt id propemodum quod Graeci παιδείαν uocant, nos eruditionem institutionemque in bonas artis dicimus.

> Those who have spoken Latin and have used the language correctly do not give to the word *humanitas* the meaning which it is commonly thought to have, namely, what the Greeks call φιλανθρωπία, signifying a kind of friendly spirit and good-feeling towards all men without distinction; but they gave to *humanitas* about the force of the Greek παιδεία; that is, what we call *eruditionem institutionemque in bonas artes*, or 'education and training in the liberal arts.' (trans. Rolfe 1927)

To explain *humanitas*, Gellius brings into play the two Greek concepts of παιδεία and φιλανθρωπία. For the sake of clarity, he then gives other possible synonyms of these Greek concepts, defining φιλανθρωπία as *dexteritas* and *beniuolentia*, and

---

98 Cic. *Rep.* 1.28. Cf. below, pp. 49–50.
99 Cf. Gildenhard 2010, 211.

παιδεία as *eruditio* and *institutio in bonas artis.* He also expresses his own personal opinion on the meaning of the term: according to him, παιδεία is the correct meaning of *humanitas* while φιλανθρωπία is the wrong one. Gellius' preference can be explained in relation with the aims and the specific cultural context of his work, as we will see in detail in the Gellius section (4.2). More importantly, this statement signals that both senses of the word *humanitas* were attested in the literature of the time. Further and most precious confirmation comes from the later grammarian Nonius (fourth century CE), who nuances Gellius' definition at *De compendiosa doctrina* 1.255 (pp. 73–74 Lindsay):

> Humanitatem non solum, uti nunc consuetudine persuasum est, de beniuolentia, dexteritate quoque et comitate ueteres dicenda putauerunt, quam Graeci φιλανθρωπίαν uocant; sed honestorum studiorum et artium adpetitum, quod nulli animantium generi absque hominibus concessa sit. Varro Rerum humanarum [lib.] I Praxiteles, qui propter artificium egregium nemini est paululum modo humanior<i> ignotus.

> The ancients believed that, unlike what custom has now convinced us of, *humanitas* was not only to be invoked to indicate a kind of friendly spirit and kindness, namely what the Greeks call φιλανθρωπία. In contrast, it also indicated the desire of noble studies and noble arts, which were only conceded to man among all animal species. Varro, in the first book of his *Human Antiquities*, says: "Praxiteles, who, because of his surpassing art, is unknown to no one of any liberal culture (*humaniori*)."

The example taken from Varro's *Rerum humanarum libri*,[100] the same which we also read at *Noctes Atticae* 13.17.3, confirms that Nonius is following Gellius closely. However, the addition of *comitas* to the Latin equivalents of φιλανθρωπία, the absence of the terms παιδεία, *eruditio*, and *institutio*, and their replacement with *honestorum studiorum et artium adpetitum* guarantees that in this passage at least Nonius is not to be regarded as a pedestrian epitomator of Gellius. This consideration becomes all the more important when we consider that, unlike his predecessor, Nonius does not express a preference for one meaning of the word *humanitas* over the other. As a consequence, it is legitimate to state that Nonius attests even more firmly than Gellius the co-existence of the two meanings of *humanitas*. At the same time, both authors make clear that their considerations are not to be taken as grounded in, or exclusively pertinent to, the historical period in which they were writing. The presence of a fragment by Varro testifies to their campaign towards an ideally atemporal dimension of the Latin language, which is clearly in contrast with how language actually evolved, and which aimed at exalting the last authors of the republican or those of the Augustan age. As far as vocabulary is concerned, therefore, all later authors should employ the words in

---

100 Varro *Fr.* 1 Mirsch.

the same way and with the same meaning as their unrivaled predecessors. Gellius' criticism of his contemporaries who misused the term *humanitas* is based on this assumption.

Once it is established that φιλανθρωπία and παιδεία are the meanings that Roman men of learning gave to the word *humanitas*, I hope to show that Gellius' and, above all, Nonius' statements stand up to scrutiny, at least partly. For φιλανθρωπία and παιδεία are the two main components of the word *humanitas* that will be the object of discussion. However, it is important to emphasise again that there is sometimes, not to say often, a fine line between the two, so much so that the ideas of φιλανθρωπία and παιδεία can even overlap in Latin occurrences of *humanitas*. As I have already hinted, this principle of multi-layering, which is in my view crucial to our understanding of Roman *humanitas*, and consequently, of the Roman worldview, is less well established in scholarship. Stroh is unusual in explaining the process through which φιλανθρωπία and παιδεία are connected to one another:

> Iam uidemus igitur ex aliqua parte quomodo illae duae notiones φιλανθρωπίας et παιδείας ortae interque se commixtae sint. Atque initio humanitas non est illa quidem, si stricte interpretamur, eadem atque φιλανθρωπία, i.e. amor hominum et mansuetudo, sed magis communis natura humana, quam cum homo in altero esse sentit, a crudelitate auocatur, ad mansuetudinem misericordiamque commouetur. Postea per metonymiam quandam nomen humanitatis ipsam uirtutem declarat, quae plerumque mansuetudo aut clementia est, interdum etiam urbanitas et facilitas morum. Sed quia illa urbanitas litteris potissimum augeatur, ipsae quoque litterae uel artes, quibus παιδεία constat, humanitatis nomine dici possunt.[101]

Stroh spotlights well the two lines along which this process develops: from a chronological standpoint, the φιλανθρωπία meaning of *humanitas* precedes the παιδεία meaning; from a logical standpoint, the παιδεία meaning enhances φιλανθρωπία. In other words, if it is true that occurrences of *humanitas* (roughly) standing for φιλανθρωπία predate the first instances of *humanitas* meaning παιδεία, it is also true that, from Cicero onwards at least, education, liberal arts, and literature can be seen as (*the*) prerequisites for gaining access to the ideal of φιλανθρωπία. By the same token, this might also imply that to be a learned man is not necessarily to possess *humanitas*, for learning and education are not to be seen as ends in themselves. Therefore, the equation between possessing *humanitas* and being well-educated is only valid as long as education leads to a morally impeccable behaviour towards other fellow human beings. In the light of all this, it should not be difficult

---

101 Stroh 2008, 551–552.

to figure out that instances of *humanitas* in which the philanthropic meaning is predominant can also carry the educational component in the background.

At this point, the recurrent recourse to two different Greek concepts to express just one Roman value will have suggested that *humanitas* has no perfect equivalent in Greek. This in turn may already lead to the conclusion that *humanitas* so conceived was born and found its cultural premises in Rome. Although this is ultimately my belief, the solution to this issue is not so straightforward, and requires further analysis. For first, I would like to look briefly at the Greek use of φιλανθρωπία and παιδεία. I do not intend to provide a detailed analysis of the occurrences of these two concepts in Greek texts: in the case of φιλανθρωπία we already possess such studies; in the case of παιδεία, although several scholars have dealt with this concept, a thorough investigation of the instances of the word itself is to my knowledge still a *desideratum*, and it is beyond the scope of this book. I shall therefore limit myself to a summary whose aim is to provide sufficient background to address the problem of the origins of *humanitas*.

1.5.2.1 Φιλανθρωπία

Gellius'[102] and Nonius' conception of φιλανθρωπία as *beniuolentia* as well as Festugière's authoritative definition of this term as "a general disposition to benevolence and to act well towards men" ultimately find their roots in the pseudo-Platonic *Definitions*: Φιλανθρωπία ἕξις εὐάγωγος ἤθους πρὸς ἀνθρώπου φιλίαν· ἕξις εὐεργετικὴ ἀνθρώπων· χάριτος σχέσις· μνήμη μετ'εὐεργεσίας (412e: "the easy-going character state of being friendly to people; the state of being helpful to people; the trait of gratefulness; memory, together with helpfulness", trans. Hutchinson 1997).[103] As is typical of compilatory works of this kind, abundance of quasi-synonyms serves the purpose of clarifying the word under investigation and its contexts of application. Even beyond this definition, the etymology of the word is clear: it combines the root of the verb φιλέω ('to love') with ἄνθρωπος ('man / human being'), thereby meaning 'benevolence towards men'.[104] But if in the wake of derivatives of φιλανθρωπία in modern languages we are likely to take for granted that such a behaviour or attitude is not only displayed *towards* men but also *by* men, this is not true of the first attested instances of φιλανθρωπία in ancient Greek. As Lorenz probably showed for first, these date back to fifth-century Athens, and are to be found in Aeschylus' *Prometheus Bound* 11 and 28 (φιλανθρώπου δὲ παύεσθαι τρόπου, "to stop his habit of

---

102 In tracing the history of φιλανθρωπία I mainly follow De Romilly 2011[2]. A rich bibliography on this topic can be found in Sulek 2010, 386. Cf. also Bettini 2019, 92–94.
103 Festugière 1949, 301.
104 Cf. Chantraine 1968 s.v. ἄνθρωπος.

favouring mankind", and τοιαῦτ'ἐπηύρου τοῦ φιλανθρώπου τρόπου "such is your reward for your habit of favouring mankind", trans. Collard 2008), and in Aristophanes' *Peace* 392–394 (ὦ φιλανθρωπότατε καὶ μεγαλοδωρότατε δαιμόνων, "O God most generous towards men").[105] In both cases gods are said to be φιλάνθρωποι towards humans, and, as De Romilly puts it, "il s'agit donc d'un acte de générosité venu du dehors aider l'espèce humaine; et ceci restera la valeur originelle du terme."[106] In fact, as she goes on to explain (45–46), analogous uses of the word can be found in Xenophon and Plato, which also means that this concept acquired a philosophical dimension.[107] In Xenophon's *Oeconomicus* then, φιλανθρωπία is also acknowledged to be an art which helps the human race, as is the case of agriculture (15.4: Νῦν τοίνυν, ἔφη, ὦ Σώκρατες, καὶ τὴν φιλανθρωπίαν ταύτης τῆς τέχνης ἀκούσῃ, "Now therefore, Socrates – he said – also listen to the philanthropy of this art").[108]

At some point – although it is not clear how and when – φιλανθρωπία mainly came to characterise relationships among human beings, thereby losing its divine component. Xenophon and Plato testify to this shift in meaning, which is embodied in the figure of Socrates at *Memorabilia* 1.2.60 and *Euthyphro* 3d. By resorting to a comparison between these two occurrences, Lorenz endeavoured to explain the shift from gods to men as possessors of φιλανθρωπία on the grounds that the Athenian philosopher would be the perfect 'intermediary' between the two categories.[109] More specifically, Lorenz argues that at *Euthyphro* 3d Socrates is playfully pretending to be acting like a god when attributing a divine virtue like φιλανθρωπία to himself: ἐγὼ δὲ φοβοῦμαι μὴ ὑπὸ φιλανθρωπίας δοκῶ αὐτοῖς ὅτιπερ ἔχω ἐκκεχυμένως παντὶ ἀνδρὶ λέγειν, οὐ μόνον ἄνευ μισθοῦ, ἀλλὰ καὶ προστιθεὶς ἂν ἡδέως εἴ τίς μου ἐθέλει ἀκούειν ("I'm afraid that my liking for people makes them think that I pour

---

105 Lorenz 1914, 9. More in-depth discussion of these occurrences in Sulek 2010, 387–389. Cf. also Tromp de Ruiter 1931, 273–274, who also has a point in claiming that the idea of φιλανθρωπία can already be found in Homer. Consider for instance *Il.* 6. 12–15: Ἄξυλον δ' ἄρ' ἔπεφνε βοὴν ἀγαθὸς Διομήδης / Τευθρανίδην, ὃς ἔναιεν ἐϋκτιμένῃ ἐν Ἀρίσβῃ / ἀφνειὸς βιότοιο, φίλος δ' ἦν ἀνθρώποισι. / πάντας γὰρ φιλέεσκεν ὁδῷ ἔπι οἰκία ναίων ("Diomedes then slew Axylos / Teuthninides from the walled town Arisbe. / A rich man and kindly, he befriended all who passed his manor by the road", trans. Fitzgerald 1974). Cf. also Hügli/Kipfer 1989, 543.
106 De Romilly 2011², 45. Cf. also Nikolaïdis 1980, 351: "The first basic difference between philanthropía and humanitas is that, whereas the former is connected with the gods right from the beginning, the latter is never associated with the Divine". On the relationship between *humanitas* and the Divine (or *diuinitas*), cf. below, pp. 85; 323; 328; 336.
107 Xen. *Mem.* 4.3; Plato *Symp.* 189d and *Leg.* 713d. Cf. also Lorenz 1914, 10–11; Hügli/Kipfer 1989, 543. On φιλανθρωπία in Plato cf. also Hiltbrunner 1994a, 715; Sulek 2010, 390–392.
108 Cf. Tromp de Ruiter 1931, 281.
109 Lorenz 1914, 14.

out to anybody anything I have to say, not only without charging a fee but even glad to reward anyone who is willing to listen", trans. Grube 1974).[110] This reading is corroborated by Xenophon's *Memorabilia* 1.2.60, where Socrates is said to be δημο-τικός ('friend of the populace') καὶ φιλάνθρωπος for roughly the same reasons as in Plato's *Euthyphro* (which would also suggest that this was a topos among Socrates' pupils). De Romilly endorsed Lorenz's thesis and Sulek has brought new arguments in support of it, claiming that *"philanthrôpía* [. . .] maintains its close association with divinity in *Euthyphro,* in terms of distinguishing the nature of Socrates' rela-tionship with his *daemon* or divine sign from that of Euthyphro."[111] Nevertheless, like Tromp de Ruiter, I am hesitant to embrace Lorenz's interpretation that Socra-tes' words allude to a comparison between himself and gods.[112] First, expressed in these terms, such an allusion would hardly be grasped. Secondly, even if in a couple of previous instances φιλανθρωπία pertains to gods, this is not sufficient to conclude that it was conceived as the prerogative of divine entities only. On the other hand, Sulek's argument, however convincing in principle, is too vague. That said, I do not deny the pivotal role of Socrates, who really is the first man said to possess φιλανθρωπία in the Greek works which have come down to us, but I would not push the reasoning further.

Regardless of the persuasiveness of Lorenz's reasoning, from Plato and Xeno-phon down to the fourth century BCE, φιλανθρωπία often refers to a human atti-tude, or, better, a human virtue which has to be displayed towards other men to concretise itself, especially in Athenian society.[113] At the beginning, it maintains its noblest and most exclusive meaning, and also applies to politics. Judges, laws and, *a fortiori*, sovereigns must be guided by φιλανθρωπία.[114] In this respect, Xenophon's *Cyropaedia* and Isocrates' *Panegyricus* are cases in point.[115] As a consequence, it comes as no surprise that we find it at times linked with ἔλεος ('clemency').[116] For his part, Aristotle sets himself in Xenophon's footsteps, and regards φιλανθρωπία as

---

110 Lorenz 1914, 14.

111 De Romilly 2011², 46–47; Sulek 2010, 392. Cf. De Romilly 2011², 47: "on voit par ce rapproche-ment comment on pouvait user d'une exagération souriante et délibérée pour comparer un acte de générosité à la bonté divine."

112 Tromp de Ruiter 1931, 275.

113 Lorenz 1914, 25; 29; Tromp de Ruiter 1931, 288–290; De Romilly 2011², 48. See De Romilly 2011², 97–112 for more on the idea of *douceur* in Athens.

114 Cf. Lorenz 1914, 15–21; Hügli/Kipfer 1989, 544. Some references can also be found in De Ro-milly 2011², 49 nn. 4, 5 and 6; Sulek 2010, 393. Cf. also Tromp de Ruiter 1931, 284; Hiltbrunner 1994a, 716.

115 Cf. Lorenz 1914, 15–16; Tromp de Ruiter 1931, 277–281; Hügli/Kipfer 1989, 544; Sulek 2010, 392–393.

116 Cf. Lorenz 1914, 22; Tromp de Ruiter 1931, 286.

'an innate characteristic of a person or thing that causes them to be attracted to human beings'.[117] But it is also the case that in the cultural milieu of the Sophistic as well as in a figure like Isocrates some scholars have seen glimpses of the influence of education, that is, of παιδεία, on φιλανθρωπία or a philanthropic attitude,[118] despite the fact that the two terms themselves are not found next to each other, and often just one or even neither of them is mentioned. In this respect, a relevant example they provided is by the Stoic philosopher Chrysippus of Soli (third century BCE – Chrysippus' words are referred by Diogenes Laertius at 2.70): ἄμεινον ἔφη ἐπαιτεῖν ἢ ἀπαίδευτον εἶναι· οἱ μὲν γὰρ χρημάτων, οἱ δ' ἀνθρωπισμοῦ δέονται ("It is better to be a beggar than to be uneducated: the former lacks wealth, the latter lacks humanity"). The general message seems in effect to be clear; φιλανθρωπία, however, is replaced by the rare ἀνθρωπισμός, whose relationship to ἄνθρωπος is evident, but that lacks the fundamental component of φιλέω.

Moreover, φιλανθρωπία becomes one of the values of everyday life which characterise the 'honest man'.[119] On the other hand, its diffusion as well as its applicability to different aspects of life also account for the weakening of its meaning in the period which followed, when φιλάνθρωπος said of a speech meant little more than 'pleasant',[120] and φιλανθρωπία also came to indicate 'kindness', as in Menander, or even 'hospitality'.[121] In the third century BCE then, φιλανθρωπία also stands for private generosity.[122] Furthermore, φιλανθρωπία began to be expressed more in words than in deeds, as is the case with Philip II of Macedon in Demosthenes' *De corona* 231.[123] Still later, in inscriptions, in Polybius' work as well as in the Roman age in general, φιλανθρωπία becomes more and more clichéd, and generally pertains to the diplomatic world.[124] As an alternative, it could indicate 'salary' or 'compensation', or even 'benefits'.[125] Needless to say, this was the main trend, but instances of the word maintaining its original meaning

---

117 Sulek 2010, 394. On φιλανθρωπία in Aristotle cf. also Lorenz 1914, 37–39; Hügli/Kipfer 1989, 544–545.
118 Cf. Hügli/Kipfer 1989, 544.
119 De Romilly 2011², 50.
120 De Romilly 2011², 50. Hügli/Kipfer 1989, 544 highlight the stress on the educational component of a λόγος which is regarded as φιλάνθρωπος.
121 Sulek 2010, 394 on Menander; Lorenz 1914, 32; De Romilly 2011², 230 on hospitality. On the weakening of the meaning of φιλανθρωπία cf. also Tromp de Ruiter 1931, 291–292.
122 Sulek 2010, 395.
123 Tromp de Ruiter 1931, 291; De Romilly 2011², 50; Sulek 2010, 393. Cf. also Tromp de Ruiter 1931, 291 on Isocrates 15.133.
124 Tromp de Ruiter 1931, 292–294; Hügli/Kipfer 1989, 545; Hiltbrunner 1994a, 725 – on Polybius; De Romilly 2011², 51.
125 Cf. Lorenz 1914, 35; Tromp de Ruiter 1931, 288–289; Sulek 2010, 395.

and momentum can also be found beyond the fourth century BCE,[126] for example in the already mentioned Menander, in Philo of Alexandria's Περὶ φιλανθρωπίας or in Plutarch's work.[127] According to De Romilly, Plutarch even ends up identifying the broader idea of what she calls *douceur* (of which φιλανθρωπία is one crucial component) with the idea of civilization itself, which is in turn regarded as the prerogative of Greece.[128] Among Christians, φιλανθρωπία is at times considered a quality of Jesus Christ.[129]

1.5.2.2 Παιδεία

In linguistic terms, παιδεία is a verbal noun which derives from παιδεύω ('bring up a child', 'train and teach', 'educate' according to *LSJ*) and therefore stands for 'education', 'formation', but also for what education produces, 'culture'.[130] As I have mentioned, a thorough analysis of the instances of this word in ancient Greek literature has to my knowledge not yet been undertaken, and Jaeger's authoritative statement at the beginning of his masterpiece *Paideia* warns scholars against undertaking it:

> It would seem obvious for us to use the history of the word *paideia* as a clue to the origins of Greek culture. But we cannot do so, since the word does not occur before the fifth century. That is of course merely an accident of transmission. If new sources were discovered, we might well find evidence of its occurrence at an earlier date. But even then we should be none the wiser; for the earliest examples of its use show that at the beginning of the fifth century it still had the narrow meaning of 'child-rearing' and practically nothing of its later, higher sense.[131]

Havelock's definition of the Homeric works as a 'tribal encyclopedia', that is, as a tribal, circular, comprehensive παιδεία, is in tune with this argument.[132] Because of the numerous descriptions and prescriptions of events and rituals belonging to the everyday life of Homeric society, Havelock, through the lens of Plato, therefore views the *Iliad* and *Odyssey* as founding texts not only of Greek culture, but also of Greek education. Yet without the term παιδεία, 'culture', being mentioned

---

126 Sulek 2010, 395.

127 On φιλανθρωπία in Menander cf. Hügli/Kipfer 1989, 545; De Romilly 2011[2], 202–203, according to whom in the Greek playwright φιλανθρωπία takes on a meaning very close to Latin *humanitas*; on Philo cf. Tromp de Ruiter 1931, 294–295; Hügli/Kipfer 1989, 545–546; Hiltbrunner 1994a, 723; on Plutarch Tromp de Ruiter 1931, 295–300; Hügli/Kipfer 1989, 545–546.

128 De Romilly 2011[2], 305.

129 Tromp de Ruiter 1931, 301–302: cf. *Act. Ap.* 27.3; *Ep. Tit.* 3.4; Origenes *Comm. in Johan.* 1.20.121.

130 Cf. Chantraine 1974 s.v. παῖς.

131 Jaeger 1946[3], 4.

132 Havelock 1963, 66; *passim*.

throughout, these two works would not play any role in a history of the word παιδεία.

Indeed, the first instance of παιδεία is to be found in an elegy by Theognis (2.1305–1310), and Jaeger's statement above turns out to be even optimistic on closer inspection, for παιδεία simply means 'boyhood' on this occasion. However, we encounter the idea of 'child rearing' in Aeschylus' *Seven against Thebes* (467 BCE) when in his opening speech Eteocles also praises Thebes for accepting the toil of bringing up its children (ll. 17–18: ἥ γὰρ νέους ἕρποντας εὐμενεῖ πέδῳ, / ἅπαντα πανδοκοῦσα παιδείας ὄτλον, "when you came to her as new children, and on her kindly soil she bred you to found homes [. . .] for our present need", trans. Collard 2008), as well as in Thucydides' comparison of the different upbringings of Athenians and Spartans (2.39.1: καὶ ἐν ταῖς παιδείαις οἱ μὲν ἐπιπόνῳ ἀσκήσει εὐθὺς νέοι ὄντες τὸ ἀνδρεῖον μετέρχονται, ἡμεῖς δὲ ἀνειμένως διαιτώμενοι οὐδὲν ἦσσον ἐπὶ τοὺς ἰσοπαλεῖς κινδύνους χωροῦμεν, "In education also they follow an arduous regime, training for manliness right from childhood, whereas we have a relaxed lifestyle but are still just as ready as they to go out and face our equivalent dangers", trans. Hammond 2009). To be sure, Jaeger was right in claiming that these instances display a 'weaker', 'less noble' meaning of παιδεία, but he probably underestimated the fact that the foundation of Plato's (and others') nobler idea of this word lies in these very first occurrences. Compare Plato's juvenile dialogue *Crito*, in which Socrates has the Laws of Athens ask him several, mainly rhetorical, questions, one of which is: Ἀλλὰ [scil. μέμφῃ] τοῖς περὶ τὴν τοῦ γενομένου τροφήν τε καὶ παιδείαν ἐν ᾗ καὶ σὺ ἐπαιδεύθης; ἢ οὐ καλῶς προσέταττον ἡμῶν οἱ ἐπὶ τούτῳ τεταγμένοι νόμοι, παραγγέλλοντες τῷ πατρὶ τῷ σῷ σε ἐν μουσικῇ καὶ γυμναστικῇ παιδεύειν; (50d: "[do you find anything to criticize] in those of us concerned with the nurture of babies and the education that you too received? Were those assigned to that subject not right to instruct your father to educate you in the arts and in physical culture?", trans. Grube 1974). The meaning of this occurrence of παιδεία is ultimately analogous to the Aeschylean and Thucydidean ones, the only difference lying in the addition of τροφή, 'food', which allows Plato to distinguish between 'physical' and 'spiritual' forms of nourishment, τροφή and παιδεία respectively. Yet Plato employed this term at least 135 other times across his work – only the fifth-century CE theologian Theodoretus of Cyrus seems to have used it more often – and in such a way as to expand its original meaning. In the *Republic* for instance, Plato investigates it in detail, seeks to define what its components are, and claims: Τίς οὖν ἡ παιδεία; ἢ χαλεπὸν εὑρεῖν βελτίω τῆς ὑπὸ τοῦ πολλοῦ χρόνου ηὑρημένης; ἔστιν δέ που ἡ μὲν ἐπὶ σώμασι γυμναστική, ἡ δ' ἐπὶ ψυχῇ μουσική (376e: "What will their education be? Or is it hard to find anything better than that which has developed over a long period – physical training for bodies and music and poetry for the soul?", trans. Grube/

Reeve 1974). Παιδεία has therefore come to include both gymnastics and the arts of the Muses – *mens sana in corpore sano,* as Juvenal 10.356 would later paraphrase it. But there is more: to know the arts of the Muses is to possess what we call culture. In other words, Plato bridged the gulf between what Jaeger called the narrow and the higher meanings of this word. Jaeger himself stressed this fundamental role played by Plato, and also added that Plato had been the first to 'theorise' a concept which ends up covering "the artist's act of plastic formation as well as the guiding pattern present to his imagination, the *idea* or *typos*."[133] Yet Plato was not alone. Along with him, the Sophists, Isocrates and Xenophon established the conception of παιδεία as ideal perfection of mind and body, which mainly resulted from "a genuine intellectual and spiritual culture",[134] and which was destined to express one of the main features of Hellenism in the centuries which followed.

During one later period and cultural climate in particular, the role of παιδεία was again crucial: this is the so-called Second Sophistic of the second century CE, a cultural movement which also influenced the works and thought of Apuleius, Gellius and Fronto, and is therefore of special relevance to this book. One of the main exponents of this movement, Dio Chrysostom, provides a twofold definition of παιδεία in his fourth discourse *On Kingship.* Worried by Diogenes the Cynic's questions, Alexander the Great, the second protagonist of this dialogue, asks the philosopher who imparts the art of kingship. Diogenes replies that only Zeus can teach this art, and the discussion seamlessly shifts to education (29–33). There are two kinds of education (διττή ἐστιν ἡ παιδεία), says the philosopher: one comes from Heaven, the other is human (ἡ μέν τις δαιμόνιος, ἡ δὲ ἀνθρωπίνη). Most people believe that the latter is the true education, and that it consists in reading and knowing as much literature as possible (καὶ νομίζουσι τὸν πλεῖστα γράμματα εἰδότα [. . .] καὶ πλείστοις ἐντυγχάνοντα βιβλίοις, τοῦτον σοφώτατον καὶ μάλιστα πεπαιδευμένον). Yet this kind of education does not prevent people from being disreputable men. By contrast, the second form of education, which is called not only παιδεία, but also ἀνδρεία or μεγαλοφροσύνη, originates from Zeus and makes men noble and brave. Those who possess this second, true and complete παιδεία, concludes the philosopher, can easily acquire the first one. The true παιδεία thus combines cultural and moral components (although the idea of φιλανθρωπία remains distant), but, compared with Stroh's explanation of *humanitas* above, the logic is significantly inverted: the moral qualities can be complemented by literature and culture in general, but it is not a 'humanistic' education which can favour the development of morality.

---

133 Jaeger 1946³, xxiii.
134 Jaeger 1946³, 286.

Nor is παιδεία less important to the thought of the second major exponent of the Second Sophistic, Aelius Aristides. If the term itself already appears 31 times in Dio's oeuvre, it appears, excluding spurious works, as many as 38 times in Aelius Aristides'. I shall return to this figure in the next section. For the moment, I limit myself to anticipating that his particularity lies in the fact that he paired παιδεία with φιλανθρωπία, thereby combining the two main values upon which *humanitas* was based.

1.6 The Origins of *Humanitas*

Now that we have reached a better understanding of the meanings and nuances of the two Greek concepts that Gellius and Nonius associated with *humanitas*, we can address the problem of the origins of this value term. Ancient sources agree in acknowledging that *humanitas* was born in Greece, more precisely in Athens.[135] Cicero reiterates this several times, for example in *Ad Quintum fratrem* 1.1.27 and in *Pro Flacco* 62. In congratulating his brother, recently appointed as propraetor of Asia, Cicero both stresses the honour of governing such a prestigious province and gives him some advice on how to carry out his duties:

> Quod si te sors Afris aut Hispanis aut Gallis praefecisset, immanibus ac barbaris nationibus, tamen esset humanitatis tuae consulere eorum commodis et utilitati salutique seruire; cum uero ei generi hominum [*scil.* Graecorum] praesimus non modo in quo ipsa sit sed etiam a quo ad alios peruenisse putetur humanitas, certe iis eam potissimum tribuere debemus a quibus accepimus. (*QFr.* 1.1.27)[136]

> If the luck of the draw had sent you to govern savage, barbarous tribes in Africa or Spain or Gaul, you would still as a civilized man (*humanitatis tuae*) be bound to think of their interests and devote yourself to their needs and welfare. But we are governing a civilized race, in fact the race from which civilization (*humanitas*) is believed to have passed to others, and assuredly we ought to give its benefits above all to those from whom we have received it. (trans. Shackleton Bailey 2002)

While here Cicero is rather vague in regarding all Greeks as 'founders' of *humanitas*, in the oration he pronounced in 59 BCE in defence of Lucius Valerius Flaccus, who was charged *de repetundis*, this merit is restricted to the Athenians: *Adsunt*

---

135 Cf. S. Braund 1997, 21–22. Cf. also Edelstein 1967, 132; Scherr 2023, 2 and n. 7, 81–85, 270–290 (with relevant bibliography) on Athens as birthplace of civilization.
136 Cf. J. Schneider 1964, 97: "O. Flemming sieht in ihm [scil. im Begriff *humanitas*] die zentrale Mitte des gesamten Briefes." Flemming's assertion is on page 62 (J. Schneider on n. 54). On this passage cf. also Scherr 2023, 303–305.

Athenienses, unde humanitas, doctrina, religio, fruges, iura, leges ortae atque in omnis terras distributae putantur ("Here present are men from Athens, where men think *humanitas*, learning, religion, grain, rights, and laws were born, and whence they were spread through all the earth", trans. Lord 1953).[137]

More than a century and a half later, Pliny the Younger wrote to his friend Maximus a letter which, as scholarship has pointed out, closely echoes *Ad Quintum fratrem* 1.1, not least in its use of *humanitas*.[138] Like Cicero's brother, Maximus too was sent to govern the province of Achaia, probably as *corrector* (a special commissioner, appointed from the time of Trajan onward, to supervise the finances of a *libera ciuitas*):

> Cogita te missum in prouinciam Achaiam, illam ueram et meram Graeciam, in qua primum humanitas litterae, etiam fruges inuentae esse creduntur; missum ad ordinandum statum liberarum ciuitatum, id est ad homines maxime homines, ad liberos maxime liberos, qui ius a natura datum uirtute meritis amicitia, foedere denique et religione tenuerunt. (*Ep.* 8.24.2)

> Bear in mind that you have been dispatched to the province of Achaia, which is the true and genuine Greece in which *humanitas*, literature, and agriculture too are believed to have been first invented. Remember that you have been sent to order the condition of free states, dispatched in other words to men who are men in the highest sense, to free citizens, free in the highest sense, who have maintained the rights which nature bestowed on them by virtue of their excellence, merits, political friendships, treaty, and finally religious devotion. (trans. Walsh 2006)

I will deal further with this letter in the Pliny section. For the moment, we need to take note of the fact that the agreement of Cicero, Pliny, and also, implicitly, Gellius on the Greek origins of *humanitas* has not been sufficient to persuade much modern scholarship. Why? The answer is rather simple: investigations of *humanitas* reveal that the Greeks did not have any single word which could cover the polysemy of this Latin term. Or, if we wish to push this reasoning one step further, the absence of a noun with all these characteristics would reveal the lack

---

137 Cf. also Cic. *Sen.* 1; *Leg.* 2.36. *Pro Flacco* 62 might in part echo Isocrates' *Panegyricus* 47–50, where the invention of philosophy and eloquence, and their educative impact, are attributed to the Athenians. In fact: Τοσοῦτον δ' ἀπολέλοιπεν ἡ πόλις ἡμῶν περὶ τὸ φρονεῖν καὶ λέγειν τοὺς ἄλλους ἀνθρώπους, ὥσθ' οἱ ταύτης μαθηταὶ τῶν ἄλλων διδάσκαλοι γεγόνασιν, καὶ τὸ τῶν Ἑλλή- νων ὄνομα πεποίηκεν μηκέτι τοῦ γένους, ἀλλὰ τῆς διανοίας δοκεῖν εἶναι, καὶ μᾶλλον Ἕλληνας καλεῖσθαι τοὺς τῆς παιδεύσεως τῆς ἡμετέρας ἢ τοὺς τῆς κοινῆς φύσεως μετέχοντας (50: "And so far has our city distanced the rest of mankind in thought and in speech that her pupils have become the teachers of the rest of the world; and she has brought it about that the name 'Hellenes' suggests no longer a race but an intelligence, and that the title 'Hellenes' is applied rather to those who share our culture than to those who share a common blood.", trans. Norlin 1928).
138 Cf. above all Zucker 1928.

of a single, albeit composed, concept in Greek mentality and worldview.[139] I ultimately agree with this conclusion, but it is my conviction that the issue deserves further attention.

We might approach this problem differently: because Gellius mentions both παιδεία and φιλανθρωπία, two values which are apparently distant from one another, and because there is abundant evidence that these two ideas co-exist in *humanitas*, to look for pairings of these two words in Greek texts goes some way towards verifying if the Greeks perceived any close relationship between παιδεία and φιλανθρωπία. I sum up here the results of this investigation:[140] if we exclude the literature of the Byzantine age, παιδεία and φιλανθρωπία only appear together three times, once in a fragment of Diodorus Siculus which has come down to us thanks to Constantine VII Porphyrogenitus' *De uirtutibus et uitiis* (tenth century CE) and twice in orations by Aelius Aristides (3.382 and 29.33 Lenz/Behr). The occurrence at Diodorus 37.8.2 (= Const. Exc. 2(1), p. 317 = Posidon. *Fr.* 215 Theiler) concerns one of Sempronius Asellio's advisors, who, also thanks to his παιδεία and φιλανθρωπία, played a key role in helping the probable governor of Sicily of 96 BCE to restore the ruined island. Yet this passage involves doubts about authorship and periods of composition, which makes any argument concerning it highly speculative.[141] By contrast, the case of Aelius Aristides might be of special relevance, for he lived and wrote in the second century CE in the Second Sophistic, of which he was perhaps the most important exponent. Chapter 4, which looks at the figures of Gellius and Apuleius in particular, explores the key role played by Latin *humanitas* within that cultural milieu, and it would be tempting to consider Aelius Aristides' simultaneous use of παιδεία and φιλανθρωπία as an attempt to translate *humanitas* (back?) into Greek.

Is it possible to explain, if not reconcile, these inconsistencies, that is, the fact that many Latin authors speak of a Greek *humanitas* despite the fact that an exact Greek equivalent of this term does not exist? Let us return to the Latin texts above. Of all the Ciceronian and Plinian passages which explicitly regard *humanitas* as a Greek invention, *Pro Flacco* 62 is perhaps the most useful for understanding what is meant by *humanitas* in this context. In the list of the Greek inventions, *humanitas* takes pride of place, followed by education/learning (*doctrina*), religion (*religio*), agriculture (*fruges*), and laws (*iura, leges*). This is not due to the fact that *humanitas* is more important than the other elements of the series;

---

139 Cf. Nikolaïdis 1980, 354.

140 For more details cf. Mollea 2018b.

141 In addition to the problems posed by the fact that we face a case of indirect tradition, Theiler attributed this fragment to the Stoic philosopher Posidonius, but in previous editions of Posidonius Edelstein/Kidd and Jacoby had not. More on this in Mollea 2018b, 150.

rather, it is because *humanitas* can encompass all of them. Yet the notion that it is potentially all-encompassing implies a certain degree of ambiguity, an ambiguity which is nevertheless limited, when necessary, by the authors' habit of pairing *humanitas* with more specific, less ambiguous terms. We will see throughout the course of this study that most, not to say all, of the elements that Cicero names at *Pro Flacco* 62 appear elsewhere in conjunction with *humanitas*, in order to help the reader understand case by case the nuances that this word takes on in a particular passage. Accordingly, in this Ciceronian oration the simultaneous presence of so many elements clearly has rhetorical ends – this figure of speech is called *enumeratio* – but more importantly for my point, it indicates that *humanitas* is to be understood in its broadest and highest senses of 'civilization' and 'human culture', which are the results as well as the sum of education, religion, and so on. This idea of civilization, Cicero says, was born in Greece, and this has been a widely held belief in Western society since. On the other hand, however, I cannot think of any ancient Greek word which could render this Ciceronian instance (and idea) of *humanitas* as civilization, while we might easily find Greek words that can translate the other items of the above list.

In the light of this, I would suggest that the problem can be resolved as follows: by claiming that *humanitas* was born in Greece, Cicero and Pliny refer to those elements of Greek, or more precisely, of Athenian origin which, taken together, express the notion of human civilization. It is telling that the Greeks themselves would not have any single word to express this concept. Evidently, they – and the Athenians in particular – did not feel the need to elaborate such a concept formally: that their society was the acme of human realisation, whether in social, cultural or political terms, was simply a given to them. And also a given must have been the fact that the (combination of the) ideals of παιδεία and φιλανθρωπία played a crucial role in defining the features of their perfect model of human society. Conversely, by presenting *humanitas* as a Greek invention, it looks as though Latin authors also sought to legitimise and ennoble what was in fact their own great contribution to humankind. Yet when we look at other occurrences of *humanitas* and realise that παιδεία and φιλανθρωπία are ultimately the main, or simply the most common and the most apparent, components of *humanitas* and that, unlike what occurs in Greek culture, they are inevitably connected with one another, the distance between the Roman and Greek mentality increases further. Briefly, it is legitimate to consider the Greeks as the inventors of the elements which constitute the idea of *humanitas*, but the Romans were the first to combine these elements, to regard them as interwoven, and to call the sum of them by just one name.[142]

1.7 *Humanitas* and Other Value Concepts

As we have just seen and will become clearer in the course of this book, the study of this concept of value often calls into play other *Wertbegriffe* or abstract concepts, to which are in turn devoted specific studies. In addition to the habit of Latin authors of juxtaposing other nouns to *humanitas* to define better the nuances it takes on occurrence by occurrence, there are in particular two abstract concepts whose history is inevitably linked to that of *humanitas*: *clementia* and *superbia*. The former can at times be seen as a partial synonym, or, better, as a hyponym, of *humanitas* and establishes an important dialectical relationship with it, whereas the latter is rather to be regarded as one of its opposites.[143] As both of them will crop us often throughout this study, it can be useful to provide some remarks straight away.

1.7.1 *Clementia*

A clear and bibliographically updated synthesis of the history of *clementia* from its first occurrences until the end of the first century CE has very recently been provided by Della Calce, from which I draw heavily in what follows.[144] Like the case of *humanitas*, *clementia* too has raised some questions on which scholars are not yet in agreement. One, in particular, concerns the so called *clementia Caesaris*, that is, the role of the term *clementia* with the figure of Julius Caesar. We will return on this issue in a while. For the moment, it is worth stressing that the first instances of words coined on the root of *clementia*, like *clemens* or *(in)clementer*, appeared in the works of Plautus, while the noun itself was first used by Terence (*Ad.* 861). Its first occurrences broadly indicate the idea of mildness, also applying to hills or weather conditions. Yet this meaning was not exclusive: as Malaspina

---

142 Cf. Schneider 1964, 120 with reference to Cicero, *QFr.* 1.1: "Geist, Politik und Recht [. . .] stellen eine unauflösbare Einheit dar. Wir haben also hier, wo das griechische Element im humanitas-Begriff so stark in Erscheinung tritt, es trotzdem mit einer genuin römischen Vorstellung zu tun."
143 On *humanitas* as hyponym of *clementia* cf. Harder 1934, 64–74; Hellegouarc'h 1963, 268; Lipps 1967, 43 and 60; Rieks 1967, 70–79 and Mineo 2006, 73.
144 Cf. Della Calce 2023, 19–21.

has shown, in Plautus some instances of the adjective and adverb are also related with the idea of politeness.[145] Furthermore, in the years which followed, *clementia* also took on an ethical-political dimension, which gradually became prevalent, so much so that "the invocation and celebration of the emperor's *clementia* became increasingly forthright, indeed blunt, as the first century [*scil.* CE] progressed"[146]: it is in this very respect that its relationship with *humanitas* becomes in my view crucial, especially from the late first century CE onwards. Regardless of the reasons for which Cicero often attributed the noun *clementia* to Julius Caesar, while Caesar himself was very careful in using it, it is evident that it became an imperial virtue right from Augustus, since it appears – alongside *uirtus*, *iustitia* and *pietas* – in the famous *clipeus aureus* the Senate dedicated to him in 27 BCE. The step from being considered an imperial to a tyrannical value was a short one, and the gap was involuntarily bridged by Seneca. When he devoted to Nero his treatise *De clementia* he could not know that what he regarded as a noble virtue would end up being associated with the name of an emperor who was far from showing himself as clement, especially in the last period of his reign. The result was therefore that the term *clementia* was looked at with suspicion after the Neronian age, so much so that Statius needed to reinvent it in the *Thebaid*. Instead of using *clementia* to refer to forgiveness, Statius conferred a more general philanthropical dimension upon it, which came to indicate a value through which to help the oppressed.[147] Yet, Domitian too turned out to be remembered as a tyrant in Roman cultural memory, and right from the time of his successor Trajan. It therefore comes as unsurprising that an author of the Trajanic age like Pliny recovered a value concept which on the one hand implied the idea of philanthropy as in Statius's understanding of *clementia*, but on the other hand was likely to remind people of the ideal, or, perhaps better, idealised years of the late Roman republic, when Cicero had used *humanitas* as a value concept that could reinforce Roman society in a time of crisis also because it theoretically transcended social class distinctions and privileges.[148] Likewise, we shall observe that something analogous happened towards the end of the fourth century CE, when *clementia*, after a sort of revival, ended up being used as an honorific title, whereas *humanitas* was once again considered as a possible binding value within

---

[145] Cf. *Epid.* 205; *Merc.* 952; *Mil.* 695; 1098; 1252; *Poen.* 1323; 1373; *Pseud.* 27; *Rud.* 114; 734; *Stich.* 531; *Trin.* 827; *Truc.* 273; 604–605; on which Malaspina 2009, 42 states that they refer to the "sfera del vivere quotidiano, dei rapporti interpersonali e di quella che oggi chiameremmo 'buona educazione'".

[146] Dowling 2006, 181. Cf. also Braund 2009, 32.

[147] Cf. Burgess 1972, 345–348; Bessone 2011, 23–24; Della Calce 2023, 21.

[148] On Cicero's *humanitas* cf. below, pp. 52–62; on Pliny's pp. 83–115.

Roman society, although rather as a prerogative of the pagan senatorial class, as emerges from the writings of Symmachus.[149] In sum, we can conclude that the rhetorical and political dialectic between *clementia* and *humanitas* characterised quite a few periods between the first century BCE and at least the fourth century CE, as we will see in greater detail in the course of this book.

1.7.1.1 The Dialectic *Humanitas – Clementia* from a Computational Linguistic Perspective

What I called above a pattern of ups and downs in relation to the frequency of the use of the word *humanitas* throughout the ages clearly applies to *clementia* as well.[150] To appreciate better the proportion of the dialectic relation between these two words, a tool which permits a comparison of their frequencies at one and the same time or within single works or authors would be of most valuable. Unfortunately, as far as I know, such a tool for Latin language does not exist yet. Gardner's *Frequency Dictionary of Classical Latin Words* is useless in this respect, whereas very recently Spinelli has published *The Diachronic Frequency of Latin Words. A Computational Dictionary*, which promises to be much useful, but whose first volume is to my regret limited to letter A.[151] Digital databases of Latin corpora either do not allow this kind of research or their corpora of Latin texts do not (permit us to) match the corpus and the period of time I consider throughout this research. This is the case, for instance, with *Perseus*, the *Packard Humanities Institute (PHI) Latin Texts, Corpus Corporum* and others whose use is no doubt of help, but not *per se* sufficient to lead to exhaustive results. Yet it is my contention that some attempts, albeit partial, can be made, and, although their results will undoubtedly be improvable, they nonetheless contribute to sketching a picture of the situation.

First of all, it is necessary to distinguish between the frequency of a word based on the total number of different words (*types*) a given text is made of, and the frequency of a word based on the total number of words, regardless of possible repetitions (*tokens*). To give an example, take the famous *O tempora! O mores!*: there are three types (*o*, *tempora* and *mores*), but four tokens (*o* appears twice). Thus, *o* constitutes 50% of the tokens of the phrase, but only 33% of the types: percentages aside, in the first case the relevance of *o* is very high, as it appears twice as much as the other elements (whose percentage of appearance is in fact 25% each); by contrast, when we speak in terms of types, 33% is also the fre-

---

149 Cf. below, pp. 273–315.
150 Cf. above, p. 18.
151 Cf. Gardner 1970 and Spinelli 2022.

quency of appearance of *tempora* and *mores*, and therefore the relevance of *o* is almost negligible.

If we worked on *types*, because of the inflected nature of Latin and of this research itself, some words should be excluded from the calculation as semantically irrelevant – *e.g.* connectives, forms of the verb *esse* that appear in perfect passive, passive periphrastic, active periphrastic, numbers, pronouns etc. On the other hand, however, this kind of selection implies a high level of arbitrariness if not conducted carefully, and, as far as I know, the digital tools we can benefit from do not guarantee such accuracy. It follows that we can work on quite a safe ground only as long as we look at the relationship between the frequency of *humanitas* and *clementia* in terms of *tokens*. For all the limitations this research can have, it nonetheless offers some results from a comparative perspective.[152]

I take advantage of some corpora offered by *Perseus* that I consider relevant to this research, and report in the two charts on pages 42–43 the frequency of *humanitas* and *clementia* as if each of the corpora were composed of 10,000 tokens. The first chart does not take into account Seneca's *ad Polybium* and *De clementia*, since, as the second chart reveals, the presence of *clementia* therein is so high that the differences among all the other corpora become difficult to be perceived graphically.

It is clear that, during the late republican age, *humanitas* largely prevails over *clementia*, whereas in the Augustan age the trend is inverted. In Valerius Maximus' *Facta et dicta memorabilia*, that is, during the age of Tiberius, the two broadly run in parallel, although one single text is not that relevant statistically. In the case of Seneca, *clementia* overrides *humanitas* by far in the *Consolatio ad Polybium* and in the *De clementia*, but things change in his latest works. During most part of the Flavian age *clementia* returns to prevail, but in Quintilian *humanitas* appears again more often. In the authors of the Trajanic era, *humanitas* prevails in Pliny the Younger and Tacitus' *Agricola* and *Germania*, but in the *Historiae* and *Annales* there is only *clementia*, and quite often. From Apuleius onwards then, *humanitas* takes the lead and *clementia* sometimes appears very rarely or does not appear at all.

———

152 Further improvement to this research might come from the application of the so called Zipf's law (and its offshoots), a formula that explains in mathematical terms the distribution of words in a given corpus, assigning a precise ranking to each and every word within that corpus. Yet on the one hand I think that the simple comparison of frequencies I show here is already telling in terms of explaining graphically the dialectic between *humanitas* and *clementia* over time and, on the other hand, I am not sure the tools we possess would make feasible and reliable the application of the Zipf's law to the present research in the light of the ample chronological spectrum and, at the same time, comparative approach to Latin texts it requires. For an overview of Zipf's law and other possible computational linguistic models as well as of the possible explanations to the validity of the law cf. at least Piantadosi 2014.

Table 1: *Humanitas vs. clementia (without ad Polybium and De clementia).*

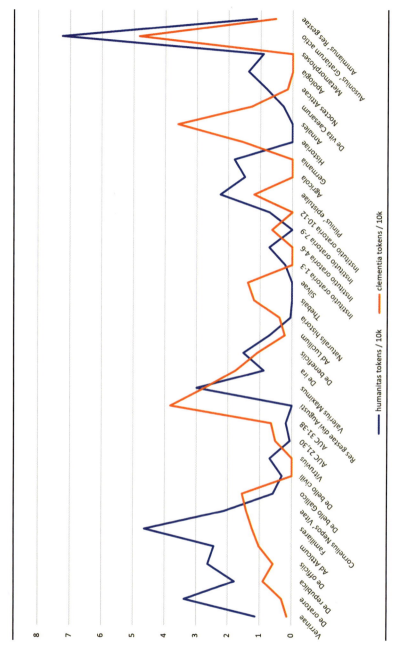

Table 2: *Humanitas* vs. *clementia*.

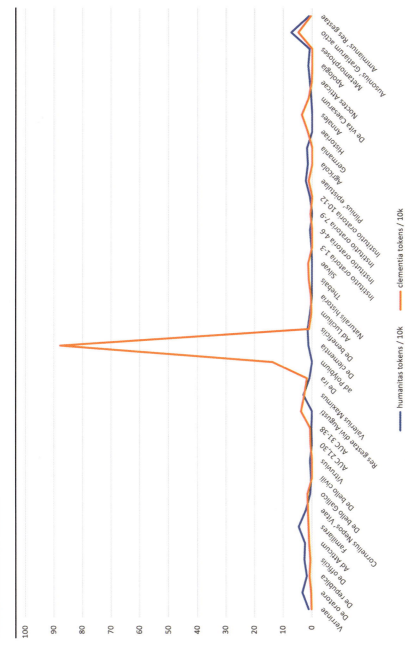

These are the data, but they are partial and, at any event, only tell a tiny part of the story. As we know, words change frequency, meanings and contexts of use for many reasons – and this can be explained rather in terms of sociolinguistics than computational linguistics. I have already anticipated that in the case in question it is likely to be due to sociopolitical reasons, and the development of this book should make this clearer.

1.7.2 *Superbia* (and *Inhumanitas*)

While the fact that there was some relationship between *humanitas* and *clementia* has long been acknowledged, this is not the case with *superbia*. It is sufficient to stress that in Baraz's recent monograph on *superbia* and other words that can be used to express the idea of pride in Latin the word *humanitas* does not appear at all.[153] Yet, it is some authors themselves who explicitly oppose *humanitas* to *superbia*, the first one probably being Phaedrus. The beginning of 3.16, a fable whose protagonists are a cicada and an owl, reads in fact: *Humanitati qui se non accommodat / plerumque poenas oppetit superbiae* ("Those who do not conform to *humanitas*, mostly pay the penalty of their haughtiness"), where it is worth noting in passing that Phaedrus' iambic senarius offers the unusual opportunity to meet the noun *humanitas* in poetry.[154] As for the relationship between *humanitas* and *superbia*, Rieks rightly stressed that the one is opposed to the other, but did not push his analysis further and later scholars of *humanitas* seem to have ignored it altogether.[155]

Some time later, Seneca expressed the opposition between *humanitas* and *superbia* in perhaps even clearer terms. In *Ep.* 88, a letter which is decisive to understand Seneca's role in the history of *humanitas*, as will be made clear later, on paragraph 30 we read: *Humanitas uetat superbum esse aduersus socios, uetat amarum* ("*Humanitas* is the quality which stops one being arrogant towards one's fellows, or being acrimonious", trans. Campbell 1969).[156]

But it is probably thanks to Pliny the Younger that we can best understand why these two abstract concepts are opposed to each other. At *Pan.* 3.4, yet again a passage which will be necessary to investigate further in the relevant section on Pliny's *humanitas*, the just nominated consul claims: *Non enim periculum est, ne,*

---

153 Cf. Baraz 2020.

154 Cf. Rieks 1967, 85.

155 Cf. Rieks 1967, 85. Høgel 2015, 74 for one mentions Phaedrus 3.16.1–2, but does not pay any attention to the relationship between *humanitas* and *superbia* therein.

156 On Seneca's *Ep.* 88 cf. below, p. 68.

cum loquar de humanitate, exprobrari sibi superbiam credat ("There is no danger that in my references to his *humanitas* he will see a reproach for arrogance", trans. Radice 1975).[157] The person Pliny is talking about is clearly emperor Trajan, and this is the deciding factor. If we think about the etymologies of the words *humanitas* and *superbia* in fact, we will realise that the contrast is absolutely logical and, on the other hand, that in this passage *humanitas* probably takes on a meaning most in keeping with its etymology. Indeed, *superbia* derives from *super* ('above', 'in higher position') and thus refers to that feeling of superiority which leads some people to look down on others – it may be worth mentioning in passing that the gods, whose dwelling is on the highest mountain in the world, Mount Olympus, are often called *Superi* in Latin.[158] In contrast, *humanitas* derives – via *homo*? – from *humus* ('earth', 'ground'), to characterise the worldly, earthly nature of man and what is typical of him.[159] Accordingly, although it might seem obvious for an emperor to be characterised by *superbia*, the greatness of Trajan in Pliny's view lies in the fact that he is instead guided by *humanitas*.[160]

Thus *superbia* stands out as *humanitas*' main opposite, especially during the imperial age on which I focus in this book. Indeed, the closest etymological opposite of *humanitas* is *inhumanitas*, but its destiny is curious: after appearing ten times in Cicero, twice in Seneca the Elder's *Controuersiae* and three times in Seneca the Younger, it completely disappears in the pagan authors I investigate here.[161] By contrast, Christian authors continue to use *inhumanitas* ceaselessly. Things differ instead when it comes to *inhumanus*, which can be found in Ps.-Quintilian's declamations as well as in Martial, Apuleius, Gellius et al., although its occurrences are not that many. Yet, as I have already hinted, the history of *humanus* and that of *humanitas* do not and cannot run utterly in parallel, and the same seems to apply to *inhumanus* and *inhumanitas*.[162]

---

157 On this passage cf. below, pp. 87–88.
158 Cf. Ernout/Meillet 2001⁴ s.v. *super*; De Vaan 2008, 601.
159 Cf. Meillet 1921, 275 and 279–280; Walde/Hofmann 1938, s.v. *humanus*; De Vaan 2008, 288. Compare also *Pan.* 24.5: *te ad sidera tollit humus ista communis et confusa principis uestigia* ("you are lifted to the heavens by the very ground we all tread, where your imperial footsteps are mingled with our own", trans. Radice 1975). On the problems concerning the relationship between *homo* and *humanus* cf. above, pp. 22–24.
160 For further details cf. below, pp. 88–89.
161 Yet Tiberius Claudius Donatus (late fourth–early fifth century CE) employs *inhumanitas* several times in his *Interpretationes Vergilianae*.
162 Cf. above, p. 22.

2 *Humanitas* from the Republican Age to that of Domitian

This chapter retraces the history of *humanitas* from its beginnings in first-century republican Rome until the reign of Domitian (81–96 CE). As this period is not the focus of this research, I will not investigate all the occurrences of the word in each work and author, but shall limit myself to touching upon the most important episodes of the early history of this value concept. In particular, I will pay attention to those cases which are of greater consequence for the understanding of the use of *humanitas* by the later authors who are at the core of this book, from Pliny the Younger to Symmachus.

Although because he paid much attention to human nature and feelings many scholars have associated this value concept with the playwright Terence, whose works date to 166–160 BCE, the word *humanitas* is not attested in Terence or in any authors of this period, but is first used in the *Rhetorica ad Herennium* (early first century BCE). From this point onwards Cicero's role in the development of the term is crucial, as it is Cicero who invests *humanitas* with the educational connotations which will characterise it for many periods of time, not least in Renaissance humanism. Moreover, Cicero's *Pro Archia* highlights how the Romans themselves exploited the polysemy of *humanitas*. Varro, Caesar, Cornelius Nepos, Vitruvius and Livy demonstrate the extent to which Cicero's understanding of *humanitas* took root. Yet the Tiberian age saw a change of trend, and Valerius Maximus paired *humanitas* with *clementia*, thereby implicitly confining the former to its philanthropic connotations, as if ignoring, or even writing against, Cicero's 'revolution'. The histories of *humanitas* and *clementia* in the years that followed suggest that the two worked in parallel, the former being considered a republican value (which was often rejected), the latter the virtue *par excellence* of the emperor. In particular, this happened in the Neronian age thanks to Seneca: he explicitly rejected the relationship between *humanitas* and the liberal arts, which had been at the core of the republican idea of the *uir bonus*, and wrote in the *De clementia* that the key virtue of the new Neronian age was *clementia*. Nero's cruel behaviour, however, ended up compromising the notion of clemency and the word *clementia* itself, which were thenceforth regarded by many as another aspect of tyranny. Statius seems to have been well-aware of this, and consequently reformulated the traditional notion of *clementia* before attributing it to Domitian. Yet his efforts were in vain, for Domitian turned out to be a second Nero, so that *clementia* was compromised once again. Accordingly, as we shall see in the next chapter, when Trajan became emperor, Pliny the Younger avoided praising his *clementia* and restored the Ciceronian concept of *humanitas* (which not even a

Ciceronian author like Quintilian had been able to preserve) to mark the beginning of a new, more democratic age.[1]

2.1 *Humanitas* before *Humanitas*: The Debated Case of Terence

The first occurrence of the word *humanitas* in Latin literature is to be found in the early-first-century BCE rhetorical treatise known as *Rhetorica ad Herennium*. Yet much scholarship has regarded the second-century playwright Terence as a sort of founder of Latin *humanitas*. This is mainly due to two reasons. First, presumably influenced by the reading of Cicero's *De re publica* or *De officiis*, many scholars have thought that *humanitas* was born in the so-called Scipionic Circle, of which Terence would have been one of the main members.[2] Secondly, Terence has seemed to be the first Latin author to pay significant attention to man and to what is *humanus*. I want to focus my attention on this second point first.

Despite the efforts of some scholars to provide comprehensive investigations of Terence's alleged *humanitas*,[3] if a verse such as *homo sum: humani nil a me alienum puto* ("I am a man, and nothing pertaining to man I deem extraneous to me", *Heaut.* 77) had not been cited often in antiquity and come down to us, Terence would have hardly played any role in discussions on Roman *humanitas*.[4] The reason is plain: as Traina justly put it, referring to this line, "l'umanità vi ha riconosciuto la formula definitiva di ogni umanesimo."[5] Yet, as Jocelyn argued, this is to overstate the case, and a close reading of the conversation between the two neighbours, Chremes and Menedemus, makes it clear that Terence's goal was far less ambitious:[6]

---

1 On the idea of democracy as related to Trajan's revival of freedom according to Pliny cf. above, p. 19.

2 Cf. *e.g.* Schneidewin 1897, 22; Reitzenstein 1907; Harder 1929; Pfeiffer 1931; Harder 1934; Schadewaldt 1973, 46 or, in more recent times, Høgel 2015, 35–36; Elice 2017, 264 and, more cautiously, Ferrary 2014², 516. *Contra*, against the influence of the Scipionic Circle on the birth of *humanitas* cf. for example Snell 1953², 254.

3 Cf. Prete 1944; Comerci 1994; Oniga 2016; Elice 2017, 260–269; Boldrer 2021. Cf. also, albeit on a smaller scale, S. Braund 1997, 19; Leigh 2004, 313–314.

4 Cf. Mollea 2023b, 11–12.

5 Traina 1969³, 124.

6 Jocelyn 1973. On the 'autonomous' life of Terence's line cf. also Lefèvre 1994, 26–56. I do not agree with opinions such as Elice's 2017, 268–269, according to whom Terence's line is decontextualized in the *Heautontimoroumenos* itself – can we really claim that Terence misplaced this line and should have put it in a nobler context?

{CH.} Numquam tam mane egredior neque tam uesperi
domum reuortor quin te in fundo conspicer
fodere aut arare aut aliquid ferre denique.
Nullum remitti' tempu' neque te respicis.
Haec non uolŭptati tibi ĕsse sati' certo scio. At
enĭm dices "quantum hic operi' fiat paenitet."
Quod in opere faciundo operae consumis tuae,
si sumas in ĭllis exercendis, plus agas.
{ME.} Chreme, tantumne ab re tuast oti tibi
aliena ut cures ea quae nil ad te attinent?
{CH.} Homo sum: humani nil a me alienum puto.
Vel me monere hoc uel percontari puta:
rectumst ego ŭt faciam; non est tĕ ŭt deterream.

(*Haut.* 67–79)

{CH.} However early in the morning I go out, and however late in the evening I return home, I see you either digging, or plowing, or doing something, in fact, in the fields. You take respite not an instant, and are quite regardless of yourself. I am very sure that this is not done for your amusement. But really I am vexed how little work is done here. If you were to employ the time you spend in laboring yourself, in keeping your servants at work, you would profit much more.

{ME.} Have you so much leisure, Chremes, from your own affairs, that you can attend to those of others — those which don't concern you?

{CH.} I am a man, and nothing that concerns a man do I deem a matter of indifference to me. Suppose that I wish either to advise you in this matter, or to be informed myself: if what you do is right, that I may do the same; if it is not, then that I may dissuade you. (trans. Riley 2013)

There are no human, humane or ethical implications here; it is all about curiosity, and not even positive curiosity.[7] Nevertheless, there is no doubt that verse 77 could be in tune with, and perfectly embodies, a philanthropic ideal of *humanitas* which authors such as Cicero or Seneca evidently possessed. It is therefore due to their – and, later on, Augustine's, Ambrose's and Julianus Pomerius' – citations of this verse that it gradually began to be regarded as a sort of manifesto of pagan (and then Christian) *humanitas*.

---

7 Cf. Leigh 2013, 64–65: "Chremes' words at v. 77 have taken on a life of their own and are often evoked as an encapsulation of scholarly *humanitas*. [. . .] Yet in the context of the play as a whole what they betray is precisely his status as a busybody." Bettini 2019, 103–107 acknowledges Chremes' curious behavior, but also regards it as a sign of *humanitas*, which, on this occasion, would consist in showing interest for other fellow human beings. Cf. also Braund 1997, 19 and, for an overview which includes bibliographical references to previous discussion of this issue, Lefèvre 1994, 68–71.

But Cicero also fostered the idea of a Terentian *humanitas* in another way, that is, by promoting the existence of the so-called Scipionic Circle, a sort of cultural Philhellenic society which flourished around the figure of Publius Cornelius Scipio Aemilianus in the second century BCE.[8] *Humanitas* would therefore be seen as one of the Greek ideas and habits that the members of the Scipionic Circle sought to introduce to Rome – recall the Ciceronian passages about the Greek origin of *humanitas*.[9] Works such as the *De officiis* or *Laelius de amicitia* are clearly connected with that milieu: the former has its model in the Stoic philosopher Panaetius' Περὶ τοῦ καθήκοντος, while the latter is even named after another member of that club, the wise man Laelius. But nowhere is the relationship between the Scipionic Circle and *humanitas* clearer than in Scipio's own speech in *De re publica* 1.28:

> Quis uero diuitiorem quemquam putet quam eum, cui nihil desit, quod quidem natura desideret, aut potentiorem quam illum, qui omnia, quae expetat, consequatur, aut beatiorem, quam qui sit omni perturbatione animi liberatus, aut firmiore fortuna, quam qui ea possideat, quae secum, ut aiunt, uel e naufragio possit ecferre? Quod autem imperium, qui magistratus, quod regnum potest esse praestantius quam despicientem omnia humana et inferiora sapientia ducentem nihil umquam nisi sempiternum et diuinum animo uolutare? Cui persuasum sit appellari ceteros homines, esse solos eos, qui essent politi propriis humanitatis artibus.

> Who would think anyone richer than the man who lacks nothing – nothing, at least, that is required by nature, or anyone more powerful than the man who obtains all he desires, or anyone more blessed than the man who is free from emotional disturbance, or anyone more secure in his prosperity than the man who possesses everything that he could, as they say, take with him from a shipwreck? What power, what office, what kingdom can be more desirable than the ability to look down on all things human, ranking them lower than wisdom, and never turn over in one's mind anything except what is divine and eternal, or the conviction that, while others are called men, only those who are skilled in the specifically human arts (*humanitatis artibus*) are worthy of the name? (trans. Rudd 1998)

There can be little doubt that the expression *humanitatis artes* is to be understood as a synonym of *liberales artes*, to which Cicero, as we have seen, resorts in the *De*

---

8 Cf. Strasburger 1966, 61: "In der Tat ist die Annahme griechischer Bildung durch die römische Oberschicht im 2. und 1. Jh. v. Chr. ja auch ein Vorgang von größter weltgeschicht licher Wirkung. Aber die Sonderrolle, die man Scipio Aemilianus und seinem Kreise in ihm zugewiesen hat, läßt sich wissenschaftlich nicht begründen. Sie hätte sich, beim Stande des Quellenmaterials, niemals entwickeln können, hätte man nicht poetische Fiktionen Ciceros in die Kombination einbezogen, die dieser selbst deutlich als solche kennzeichnet."
9 Cf. above, pp. 34–38.

oratore.[10] After all, as scholars have long noticed, the *De republica* and *De oratore* are to be seen as two sides to the same coin, and ultimately both contribute to portraying the image of a good politician.[11] And as will be made clearer in the section devoted to him, Cicero regards as fundamental for a good citizen, and, even more so, for a good politician, the training in the liberal arts. In the passage under investigation, this notion is further emphasised by the past participle *politi*, with the verb *polio* evoking the idea of bringing to a refined state, certainly with reference to intellectual and moral stature in this case.[12] And unsurprisingly the same happens in a passage of the *De oratore*, in which we come across once again the names of Scipio and Laelius: *et certe non tulit ullos haec ciuitas aut gloria clariores aut auctoritate grauiores aut humanitate politiores P. Africano, C. Laelio, L. Furio, qui secum eruditissimos homines ex Graecia palam semper habuerunt.* (2.154: "Also, this community has certainly produced none of more splendid renown or more venerable authority or more refined humanity than Scipio Africanus, Gaius Laelius, and Lucius Furius, and they were always openly in the company of the most learned men from Greece.", trans. May/Wisse 2001). At *Rep.* 1.28 therefore, *humanitas* is central to Scipio's message, and is regarded as a, if not *the*, fundamental quality that a ruler should possess. In sum, because of Cicero's multiple quotations of *Haut.* 77 and because of the centrality he accords to *humanitas* within the Scipionic Circle, it becomes evident why so many scholars have maintained that Terence was instrumental in developing the concept of Roman *humanitas*, despite this word never appearing in Terence's work. While most scholarship on Terence is persuasive in showing Terence's attention to the nature of the human and, at times, his loaded use of the adjective *humanus*, it is not the case that he is concerned with *humanitas* as such.[13]

2.2 The Beginning: The *Rhetorica ad Herennium*

The true starting point for the history of the word *humanitas* is the *Rhetorica ad Herennium*, which also provides breeding ground for future orators' usage of this value concept. As many as three times *humanitas* is paired with *misericordia*, and, most importantly, on one occasion the anonymous author of the treatise even recommends that lawyers defending their clients appeal to these value con-

---

10 Cf. above, p. 8, and further below, p. 55.
11 Cf. Klingner 1952², 90; Boyancé 1970b, 183, 233; Volk 2021, 84 and Zetzel 2022.
12 Cf. the point 3 in the entry on *polio* in the *OLD* and *TLL* 10.1.2532.39–55. On *humanitas* in Cicero's *De republica* cf. also Della Calce/Mollea 2023.
13 Cf. above, p. 10. Further in Mollea 2023b, 11–12.

cepts, and that prosecutors too should respond by emphasising the very same concepts:

> Loci communis in his causis: accusatoris contra eum, qui cum peccasse confiteatur, tamen oratione iudices demoretur; defensoris, de humanitate, misericordia: uoluntatem in omnibus rebus spectari conuenire [. . .] His [scil. defensoris] locis omnibus ex contrario utetur is, qui contra dicet, cum amplificatione et enumeratione peccatorum. (*Rhet. Her.* 2.24 and 2.26)[14]

> Commonplaces in these causes are the following: that of the prosecutor against one who confesses a crime, yet holds the jurors up by prolix speech-making; for the defence, on *humanitas* and pity, that it is the intention which should always be considered [. . .] All these commonplaces, reversed, will be used by the adversary, what will also amplify and recount the defendant's transgressions. (trans. Caplan 1954)

Unfortunately, we do not possess any one true Roman indictment with its related defensive oration, let alone one centred on *humanitas* and *misericordia*. Yet this same strategy, in which *humanitas* ultimately acts as a double-edged sword, is to be found in the mock trial which takes place in Apuleius' *Metamorphoses* 3, as we will see in Chapter 4.[15]

As Høgel points out, the other two instances of *humanitas* within the *Rhetorica*, 4.12 and 4.23, have to do with man's correct conduct in warfare.[16] More specifically, 4.12 regards those who are guilty of treason as devoid of *humanitas* (*derelictos homines ab humanitate*), while at 4.23 *humanitas* can increase peace (*ut possit . . . pacem humanitas augere*).

Overall, *humanitas* emerges from the *Rhetorica ad Herennium* as a philanthropic value,[17] but, at the same time, as a value which can carry with it the notions of inclusion and / vs. exclusion, and which can be rhetorically manipulated. According to Høgel, the possibility that some people might be devoid of *humanitas* allows for two different interpretations: either it means that they ignore the principles of *humanitas*, or that they are even excluded from the human realm.[18] Yet there is exclusion (or inclusion, if we change standpoint) either way, and one is simply consequence of the other. In the first case, the exclusion is theoretical: the poor, substandard intelligence and / or sensitivity of some people means that they cannot understand the implications of their own existence and of their being human – compare the Socratic idea that those who do evil do so because they lack knowledge of goodness. If we then take this argument to the extreme, these

---

14 Cf. also *Rhet. ad Her.* 2.50, where also *clementia* is paired with *humanitas* and *misericordia*.
15 Cf. below, pp. 147–156.
16 Høgel 2015, 37–38.
17 Cf. Hiltbrunner 1994a, 726.
18 Høgel 2015, 39.

people end up being considered unworthy of the label 'human beings', and are therefore excluded from the notion of human society. And despite the apparent differences, an analogous process takes place in the case of trials: whether the defence or the prosecution appeals to the judges' *humanitas*, the aim is to seek to persuade them that the accused deserve or do not deserve to be considered human beings worthy of this definition, and that they be treated accordingly. Moreover, all this implies that *humanitas* is not seen as an innate quality; or, if it is innate, that it must be preserved accurately because it can (easily?) vanish.

2.3 Cicero and the Heyday of *Humanitas*

It would be over-simplistic to claim that Cicero's most prominent role in the long history of the word *humanitas* lies in the fact that he employed the term far more often than any other pagan Latin author, that is, more than 200 times in the works which have come down to us. Granted, this means that this word was of extraordinary importance to his thought and worldview, but it is not sufficient to explain the opposite, that is, why Cicero is important to the study of *humanitas*. The exceptionality of Cicero is that *humanitas* spans all his works, whether they are orations, treatises or letters; or, to put it differently, whether the context is public or private, official or unofficial, and eventually, whether the style is formal or informal. Nor is this a word which appears only in works which date to certain periods of his life: it can be found in the *Pro Quinctio* and *Pro Roscio Amerino*, the first orations he delivered between 81–80 BCE, as well as in the *Philippicae*, which ultimately brought about his violent death in 43 BCE.[19] But perhaps most importantly, Cicero was the first to use the word *humanitas* to suggest a vast range of possible meanings and nuances. Accordingly, *humanitas* comes up in the majority of studies on Cicero's thought, and, by the same token, most studies on *humanitas* deal with, or focus on, Cicero.[20] I limit myself here to a brief discussion of those which seem to me to be two crucial Ciceronian contributions to the long history of *humanitas*: first, that, as far as we can know, Cicero was the first to conceive and then exploit the polysemy of *humanitas*, which he did for rhetorical, oratorical and socio-political ends; secondly and consequently, that through *humanitas* Cicero ultimately gave mankind the modern notion of the Humanities. These two

---

19 Cf. Høgel 2015, 47. On *humanitas* in the *Pro Roscio Amerino* cf. Hiltbrunner 1994a, 727.
20 Most important (and recent) contributions on Cicero's *humanitas* include Hiltbrunner 1994a, 727–730; Stroh 2008; Altman 2009; Gildenhard 2010, 201–217; Altman 2016; Høgel 2019.

aspects are closely intertwined with each other, as a focus on the oration in defence of Archias in connection with other Ciceronian works will show.

2.3.1 The Educational Path of the *Pro Archia*: From παιδεία to φιλανθρωπία

Cicero lived through an age of major socio-political changes. The destruction of Carthage in 146 BCE had freed Rome from her greatest external enemy, but, paradoxically, had also exposed her to an even greater danger, the greed and corruption of her upper echelons. As Sallust's *Bellum Iugurthinum* suggests, once the *metus hostilis* which had long bound together Roman society suddenly vanished, personal interests had the upper hand. This fragmentation led to a strong decrease of the overall power of the nobility as well as to internal socio-political instability. The conspiracy of Catiline in 63 BCE, when Cicero himself was consul and had to fight this revolt, marks the climactic point of such instability. To invert this trend, that would end up bringing about the fall of the republic, Cicero believed that a new form of education which might induce Roman youth to fight for the State was needed. After all, he was well aware that the *antiqui mores* / *mos maiorum* that Ennius had regarded as the backbone of the Roman republic were no longer sufficient to serve this purpose:

> "Moribus antiquis res stat romana uirisque,"[21] quem quidem ille uersum uel breuitate uel ueritate tamquam ex oraculo mihi quodam esse effatus uidetur. Nam neque uiri, nisi ita morata ciuitas fuisset, neque mores, nisi hi uiri praefuissent, aut fundare aut tam diu tenere potuissent tantam et tam fuse lateque imperantem rem publicam. Itaque ante nostram memoriam et mos ipse patrius praestantes uiros adhibebat, et ueterem morem ac maiorum instituta retinebant excellentes uiri. Nostra uero aetas cum rem publicam sicut picturam accepisset egregiam, sed iam euanescentem uetustate, non modo eam coloribus eisdem, quibus fuerat, renouare neglexit, sed ne id quidem curauit, ut formam saltem eius et extrema tamquam liniamenta seruaret. Quid enim manet ex antiquis moribus, quibus ille dixit rem stare Romanam? Quos ita obliuione obsoletos uidemus, ut non modo non colantur, sed iam ignorentur. Nam de uiris quid dicam? Mores enim ipsi interierunt uirorum penuria, cuius tanti mali non modo reddenda ratio nobis, sed etiam tamquam reis capitis quodam modo dicenda causa est. Nostris enim uitiis, non casu aliquo, rem publicam uerbo retinemus, re ipsa uero iam pridem amisimus. (Aug. *De civ. D.* 2.21 = Cic. *Rep.* 5.1–2)

> "On ancient customs and old-fashioned men the state of Rome stands firm." The compactness and truth of that line are such that the poet who uttered it must, I think, have been prompted by an oracle. For neither the men on their own (in a state which lacked such a moral tradition) nor the state on its own (without such men in charge) could have founded or long maintained so great and wide-ranging an empire. Long before living memory our

---

21 Enn. *Ann. fr.* 156 Skutsch.

ancestral way of life produced outstanding men, and those excellent men preserved the old way of life and the institutions of their forefathers. Our generation, however, after inheriting our political organization like a magnificent picture now fading with age, not only neglected to restore its original colours but did not even bother to ensure that it retained its basic form and, as it were, its faintest outlines. What remains of those ancient customs on which he said the state of Rome stood firm? We see them so ruined by neglect that not only do they go unobserved, they are no longer known. And what shall I say of the men? It is the lack of such men that has led to the disappearance of those customs. Of this great tragedy we are not only bound to give a description; we must somehow defend ourselves as if we were arraigned on a capital charge. For it is not by some accident – no, it is because of our own moral failings – that we are left with the name of the Republic, having long since lost its substance . . . (trans. Rudd 1998)

As Pagnotta has recently observed:

Tra intransigenza e lassismo educativo Cicerone scelse una terza via per cercare di recuperare un'egemonia sulla nuova generazione, quella di un discorso 'paideutico' indirizzato ai più giovani che sostituiva la semantica del rigido giudizio e della colpa, propri dell'*antiquus mos*, con l'indulgente semantica della comprensione empatica propria di quell'*humanitas* che avrebbe dovuto rappresentare, nell'intento dell'Arpinate, la chiave d'accesso all'animo di quei molti giovani che egli si augurava di poter richiamare alla causa della difesa della *res publica*.[22]

Written in the aftermath of the conspiracy of Catiline, the oration *Pro Archia* seems to lay the foundations of this programme.

Cicero took on the defence of poet Aulus Licinius Archias, accused in 62 BCE of usurping Roman citizenship, being well aware of the paucity of evidence he could resort to and thus resolved that he should turn his defence speech into a praise of poetry and of the liberal arts, which, in his opinion, Archias splendidly embodied. The core message is that the Roman people should pride themselves on Archias' willingness to be considered a Roman citizen even in the remote case that he did not meet all citizenship requirements, for such a great poet can only confer prestige onto the city. But perhaps more importantly, the *Pro Archia* represents a short educational path through which Cicero makes it clear not only that *humanitas* needs to be a mix of both παιδεία and φιλανθρωπία, but also that the former must lead to the latter, for education and culture would be insufficient if they did not lead to moral improvement. Or, to put it another way, παιδεία cannot be an end in and by itself. Let us undertake this path with Cicero, starting from the exordium of the *Pro Archia*, which on § 2–3 reads:

---

22 Pagnotta 2022, 72–74.

Omnes artes quae ad humanitatem pertinent habent quoddam commune uinclum et quasi cognatione quadam inter se continentur. Sed ne cui uestrum mirum esse uideatur, me in quaestione legitima et in iudicio publico, cum res agatur apud praetorem populi Romani, lectissimum uirum, et apud seuerissimos iudices, tanto conuentu hominum ac frequentia hoc uti genere dicendi quod non modo a consuetudine iudiciorum uerum etiam a forensi sermone abhorreat, quaeso a uobis ut in hac causa mihi detis hanc ueniam accommodatam huic reo, uobis, quem ad modum spero, non molestam, ut me pro summo poeta atque eruditissimo homine dicentem hoc concursu hominum litteratissimorum, hac uestra humanitate, hoc denique praetore exercente iudicium, patiamini de studiis humanitatis ac litterarum paulo loqui liberius, et in eius modi persona quae propter otium ac studium minime in iudiciis periculisque tractata est uti prope nouo quodam et inusitato genere dicendi.

For all branches of culture (*Omnes artes quae ad humanitatem pertinent*) are linked by a sort of common bond and have a certain kinship with one another. Some of you may also be surprised that, in a statutory court and at a public trial, when a case is being heard before a praetor of the Roman people, a most excellent man, and before the most principled jurors, and with such a large crowd of listeners, I should be using a manner of speaking which is out of keeping not only with the tradition of the courts but also with the customary style of forensic pleading. If this is so, then I beg of you that you will grant me an indulgence in this trial which is appropriate to this defendant here, and, I trust, not disagreeable to you – that you will allow me, speaking as I am on behalf of an eminent poet and a most learned man and before this crowd of highly educated people, this civilized jury (*hac uestra humanitate*), and such a praetor as is now presiding, to speak rather more freely on cultural and literary matters (*de studiis humanitatis ac litterarum*), and, as befits the character of a man who because of his life of seclusion and study has had very little to do with the hazards of the courts, to employ a somewhat novel and unconventional manner of speaking. (trans. Berry 2000)

To begin with, what are the *omnes artes quae ad humanitatem pertinent*? A clear answer is provided by *De oratore* (55–54 BCE) 3.127: *has artis, quibus liberales doctrinae atque ingenuae continerentur, geometriam, musicam, litterarum cognitionem et poetarum atque illa, quae de naturis rerum, quae de hominum moribus, quae de rebus publicis dicerentur* ("the arts which are the basis for liberal education – mathematics, music, the study of literature and poetry –, or the doctrines on the nature of the universe, human behavior, and the affairs of state", trans. May/Wisse 2001, adapted).[23] As is evident, this definition of the liberal arts binds together educational (*geometria, musica, litterae*) and moral (*hominum mores*) aspects, something we will soon see happening in the *Pro Archia* as well.[24] Moreover, the cross-reading of this passage with *Pro Archia* 2–3, *Pro Flacco* 62 and further passages we shall encounter later on makes it also clear that there is a tight bond not only between *humanitas* and *artes*, but between *humanitas, artes*

---

23 On Cicero's understanding of the *artes liberales* cf. above all Tempest 2020.
24 Remember that the adjective *moral* comes from Latin *mos, moris*.

and *doctrina*.[25] *Doctrina* clearly derives from *doceo*, 'to teach' and it is therefore natural that ancient Latin-Greek lexica identify it with μάθησις or διδαχή.[26] To find a logic which links these three elements in the light of our Ciceronian texts, we may say that the *artes* are the subjects that need to be studied, *doctrinae* allude to the important contents or teachings one can find in those subjects, and *humanitas* is what one reaches mainly thanks to them.

Before moving on, I also want to highlight Cicero's strategy of ideologically binding together the judges, the defendant and himself through the ideal of *humanitas* that they share, thereby also excluding those such as Archias' accusers who do not understand its importance.[27] It is in fact thanks to the fact that they already possess the notion of *humanitas* as culture (*hac uestra humanitate*) that the judges can bear and appreciate a discourse on it (*patiamini de studiis humanitatis ac litterarum paulo loqui liberius*).[28] As Nesholm puts it:

> Cicero has drawn the jurors into this exclusive group, defined by Archias and himself. This new flattery serves to make the central point of the speech, namely that they are so well suited to perform their civic and legal function precisely because they have benefited from literary education. The compliment to their cultured sophistication inherently requires that they recognize Archias' contribution to Rome and therefore include him in their ranks.[29]

I have argued in the Introduction that at *Pro Flacco* 62 laws (*iura*) are to be seen as a hyponym of *humanitas*. Nesholm's argument here provides another point of view from which to look at the relationship between *humanitas* and justice: *humanitas* is a prerequisite for justice. We will see in due course that there are other ways in which these two concepts are connected, especially when we turn to the philanthropic side of *humanitas*, which remains only implicit until the end of the *Pro Archia*, but is adumbrated from § 12 onwards, to which we shall turn in a moment. Before, we need to answer a question: how is it that some people possess *humanitas* and others do not? Does that depend on natural predisposition or has it to do with education?

In the early *Pro Roscio Amerino* (80 BCE), for instance, Cicero made it clear that *humanitas* can be accorded by nature, but also added that the *studium doctri-*

---

25 On *Pro Flacco* 62 cf. above, pp. 34–38.
26 Cf. *TLL* 5.1.1784.2–4.
27 On the importance of *humanitas* as element of inclusion or exclusion cf. also S. Braund 1997.
28 For further details on this strategy cf. Mollea 2022, 242–246, with further bibliography.
29 Nesholm 2010, 481. Cf. also Panoussi 2009, 521; Høgel 2015, 60. The notion that the protagonists of this trial are bound by their adherence to the ideal of *humanitas* can be found *in nuce* in von Albrecht 1969, 421–422.

nae, namely education, can improve it.[30] The word *studium* thus seems to play a key role, as is made even clearer by the phrase *studia humanitatis* we find in *Pro Archia* 3. While we will see in the next sub-chapter the influence this expression had on the birth of Renaissance Humanism as well as, consequently, on the category of the Humanities, it is worth stressing that Cicero employed it rarely: in addition to the occurrence in the *Pro Archia*, only at *Pro Murena* 61 and *Pro Ligario* 12.[31] Yet despite this rarity, it is telling that we shall also encounter this phrase when dealing with Pliny the Younger and Gellius, possibly the two authors from the early imperial age who best understood and reemployed Cicero's conception of *humanitas*.[32] Indeed, the continuation of the *Pro Archia* makes explicit what the expression *studia humanitatis* implies, that is, that *humanitas* can be learnt. Read *Pro Archia* 4:

> Nam ut primum ex pueris excessit Archias, atque ab eis artibus quibus aetas puerilis ad humanitatem informari solet se ad scribendi studium contulit, primum Antiochiae – nam ibi natus est loco nobili – celebri quondam urbe et copiosa, atque eruditissimis hominibus liberalissimisque studiis adfluenti, celeriter antecellere omnibus ingeni gloria contigit.

> As soon as Archias had grown out of childhood and those studies which mould the years of boyhood with an outline of culture (*humanitatem*), he devoted himself to literary composition. At Antioch, first of all, then a bustling and wealthy city and overflowing with liberal culture and men of the greatest learning (and where he was born, to high-ranking parents), he quickly began to outshine everybody else by his exceptional talents. (trans. Berry 2000)

This passage, which tells us about Archias' youth, puts together the aforementioned arts (*artibus*), the *humanitas* that should originate from the study of those arts (*quibus aetas puerilis ad humanitatem informari solet*), as well as the activity of writing literary texts (*scribendi studium*). It becomes therefore clear that this kind of *humanitas* can be acquired through education.[33] From Cicero's time onwards, we need to take into account this potential educational substratum every time we encounter the word *humanitas*: sometimes this will be more evident,

---

30 Cf. *Rosc. Am.* 46: *natura certe dedit, ut humanitatis non parum haberes* [. . .] *eo accessit studium doctrinae* ("Nature conceded that you had no little *humanitas* [. . .] and learning improved it"). On this passage cf. Mayer 1951, 36–37, with further Ciceronian instances where *humanitas* has to do with innate attitude, and Mollea 2023c, 42.

31 Hiltbrunner 1994a, 729 rightly adds to the list *Pro Ligario* 12, usually neglected by scholars because other genitives depending on *studia* precede *humanitatis*: *studia generis ac familiae uestrae uirtutis, humanitatis, doctrinae, plurimarum artium atque optimarum nota mihi sunt* ("the ardour of your family and your household for virtue, for enlightenment (*humanitatis*), for learning, and for many high and noble accomplishments – all this is known to me", trans. Watts 1964).

32 Cf. below, pp. 90; 166–167.

33 Cf. Panoussi 2009, 521 with regard to the *Pro Archia*.

sometimes less; at times then it might be utterly absent, but it is telling that Seneca feels the need to specify that his understanding of *humanitas* disregards its relationship with the *artes* altogether, as we shall see in detail in a moment. Conversely, there is no evidence that the educational component of *humanitas* existed before Cicero's day, and this is another reason why scholars should be cautious about speaking of Terence's or other pre-Ciceronian authors' *humanitas*.

Also of interest is the relationship between *humanitas* and the active practice of writing which emerges from *Pro Archia* 4. An interesting parallel is provided by Pliny the Elder at *Naturalis Historia* 13.68: *Nondum palustria attingimus nec frutices amnium; prius tamen quam digrediamur ab Aegypto, et papyri natura dicetur, cum chartae usu maxime humanitas uitae constet, certe memoria* ("We have not yet touched on the marsh-plants nor the shrubs that grow by rivers. But before we leave Egypt we shall also describe the nature of papyrus, since our civilization or at all events our records depend very largely on the employment of paper", trans. Rackham 1960). Maurizio Bettini has recently observed:

> Condurre una vita civile, degna di esseri che possano essere definiti uomini, presuppone l'uso della carta, della scrittura: in una parola, la pratica della cultura. La *humanitas vitae* di Plinio, che ha come propria base la *charta*, la membrana di papiro destinata alla scrittura, ci pare una formula tanto sintetica quanto perfetta per descrivere un incontro, nello stesso tempo linguistico e antropologico, da cui ha preso vita una nozione che la civiltà europea successiva ha fatto propria e ha ulteriormente sviluppato.[34]

The importance of Archias, and, more generally, of the oration in his defence becomes therefore even greater if we understand that through the act of being a poet – but we can be sure that in Cicero's view the same applies to all literary genres and oratory above all – Archias is himself preserver and herald of the ideal of *humanitas*.

As I said, the idea that *humanitas* also implies a philanthropic attitude can be read through the lines from *Pro Archia* 12, where Cicero makes it clear that the *studia humanitatis* cannot be an excuse for disregarding Rome's common interests. He says:

> Ego uero fateor me his studiis [*scil.* humanitatis] esse deditum: ceteros pudeat, si qui se ita litteris abdiderunt ut nihil possint ex eis neque ad communem adferre fructum, neque in aspectum lucemque proferre: me autem quid pudeat, qui tot annos ita uiuo, iudices, ut a nullius umquam me tempore aut commodo aut otium meum abstraxerit, aut uoluptas auocarit, aut denique somnus retardit?

---

34 Bettini 2019, 98.

Yes, I for one am not ashamed to admit that I am devoted to the study of literature. Let others be ashamed if they have buried their heads in books and have not been able to find anything in them which could either be applied to the common good or brought out into the open and the light of day. But why should I be ashamed, gentlemen, given that in all the years I have lived my private pastimes have never distracted me, my own pleasures have never prevented me, and not even the need for sleep has ever called me away from helping anyone in his hour of danger or of need? (trans. Berry 2000)

At the beginning of this speech (*Pro Archia* 1), Cicero had explicitly acknowledged his gratitude and debts to Archias, claiming that both his knowledge and oratorical skills are ultimately Archias' merit. And on these very grounds he said he had to take on Archias' defence during this trial. The connection between being learned and employing knowledge to help others was therefore already implicit, but on § 12 Cicero turns this message into an explicit accusation of those who ignore that the *studia humanitatis* are useless unless they serve a superior purpose, for example that of helping others.[35] The *peroratio* of the *Pro Archia* will enable us to perfectly close this reasoning.

In the Introduction I quoted a rather long passage by Stroh which explains the logical connection between the two main ideas expressed by *humanitas*, that is, παιδεία and φιλανθρωπία.[36] That the *Pro Archia* is paradigmatic in displaying this relationship becomes crystal clear at the end of this educational path, on § 31, which reads:

Quae cum ita sint, petimus a uobis, iudices, si qua non modo humana, uerum etiam diuina in tantis ingeniis commendatio debet esse, ut eum qui uos, qui uestros imperatores, qui populi Romani res gestas semper ornauit, qui etiam his recentibus nostris uestrisque domesticis periculis aeternum se testimonium laudis daturum esse profitetur, estque ex eo numero qui semper apud omnis sancti sunt habiti itaque dicti, sic in uestram accipiatis fidem, ut humanitate uestra leuatus potius quam acerbitate uiolatus esse uideatur.

Under these circumstances, gentlemen, if you consider that talents such as his deserve the blessing not only of men, but of the gods as well, then I entreat you to take him under your protection. He is a man who has always done honour to you, to your generals, and to the achievements of the Roman people, who has undertaken to give an everlasting testimonial of praise to these civil dangers which you and I recently faced together, and who follows

---

35 Cf. Boyancé 1970b, 101: "S'il lui [*scil.* Ciceron] arrivait, comme dans le *Pro Archia*, de faire l'éloge des études, de la poésie, de la littérature, il lui fallait adapter ces éloges à son auditoire et aux conceptions traditionelles de la politique romaine. Il ne pouvait les justifier qu'en mettant les études, la littérature au service des valeurs morales et sociales en honneur dans la cité et il atteste au § 12 que peuvent bien rougir, dans leur goût des lettres, ceux qui n'en ont rien tiré qui puisse servir l'utilité commune et se produire au grand jour."
36 Cf. above, p. 26.

that calling which has always been declared and believed by all men to be sacred: let him therefore be seen to have been rescued by your *humanitas* rather than injured by your severity. (trans. Berry 2000)

Compared with the exordium, it is clear that Cicero plays on the manifold aspects of *humanitas*, especially when reemploying the expression *uestra humanitate* with regard to the judges: at § 3 it exalted their literary education, while here it pleads for mercy, that is, appeals to the judges' benevolent attitude towards the defendant. To put it more simply, the first instance might be translated by and large as παιδεία, whereas φιλανθρωπία is far more appropriate for the second one. After all, the play on words, or the paronomasia, between *humanitate* [. . .] *leuatus* and *acerbitate uiolatus* only works as long as the meaning of *humanitas* can be opposed to that of *acerbitas* ('severity', 'cruelty'). And yet it is no coincidence that Cicero used at the end of his speech the same term he had used at the beginning: the polysemy of *humanitas* allows him to remind the jury that to be learned is to understand their fellow human beings and the situations in which they find themselves. This, at times, turns into being benevolent, at least towards those people like Archias who are worthy of receiving benevolence.

The paradigmatic case of the *Pro Archia* in highlighting and interconnecting the main meanings and aspects of *humanitas* seems to me to be unparalleled in Cicero's oeuvre. Yet, albeit on a smaller scale, an analogous dialectic between the meanings of *humanitas* can be observed in the letter to Cicero's brother Quintus already discussed in the Introduction.[37] I quote again the crucial point: *cum uero ei generi hominum* [scil. *Graecorum*] *praesimus non modo in quo ipsa sit sed etiam a quo ad alios peruenisse putetur humanitas, certe iis eam potissimum tribuere debemus a quibus accepimus* (*QFr.* 1.1.27: "But we are governing a civilized race, in fact the race from which civilization is believed to have passed to others, and assuredly we ought to give its benefits above all to those from whom we have received it", trans. Shackleton Bailey 2002). It also emerges, from the other passages analysed in the Introduction, that when Cicero speaks of the Greeks as purveyors of *humanitas*, he has in mind the idea of culture broadly understood.[38] But when he then admonishes Quintus, whose duty it is to rule over the Greeks, that the Romans should treat them with the very *humanitas* they had learnt from Greece, he clearly means something else, namely that the Roman invaders ought to be-

---

37 Cf. above, p. 34. Prost 2006, 40 speaks of a 'bidirectional theory' of *humanitas* with regard to this letter.
38 Cf. above, pp. 34–38.

have humanely and benevolently towards the subjugated Greeks.[39] Yet again, by exploiting two different aspects of a same word, Cicero is able to maximise rhetorical effectiveness.

2.3.2 The *Pro Archia* and the Birth of the Humanities

Because of its content as well as the history of its reception,[40] the *Pro Archia* also played a crucial role with regard to "one of the most important of Cicero's own discoveries [. . .]: 'the humanities' understood as 'the distinctive arts of mankind'."[41] After the Middle Ages, it is on these arts that the cultural revolution which took the name of Renaissance Humanism laid its foundations.[42] At the same time, the very term Humanism originates from the expression *studia humanitatis* of *Pro Archia* 3.[43]

The *Pro Archia* had been unknown to the Western Middle Ages and was recovered in Liège, Belgium, by Petrarch only in 1333. It nonetheless took a few more years before the phrase *studia humanitatis* was employed once again since antiquity by Coluccio Salutati in 1369. And almost one more century it took before the expression became widespread "to denominate a well-defined cycle of disciplines."[44] These included "grammar, rhetoric, poetry, history, and moral philosophy", that is, more or less those listed at *De oratore* 3.127 quoted above.[45] Indeed, Cicero had also used another very fortunate expression to call them, namely *artes liberales*, which is first attested in *De inuentione* 1.35. What matters the most, however, is that this list of disciplines reproduces by and large Plato's idea of παιδεία as outlined in the Introduction.[46] And at the end of the Italian Quattrocento, the greatest advocate of Platonism in the Renaissance, Marsilio Ficino, writes a letter to Tommaso Minerbetti which enables us to square the circle, because "Ficin y exalte l'*humanitas* en trois sens distincts avant lui: douceur, unité de l'homme et

---

39 I note in passing that Boyancé 1970a, 8 observed that Cicero's amplest employ of *humanitas* as φιλανθρωπία is to be found in his collection of letters.
40 On the reception of the *Pro Archia* after its discovery by Petrarch cf. Kohl 1992; Reeve 1996, 21–26.
41 Altman 2016, 22.
42 Cf. above, pp. 3–4.
43 For the state of research on the importance of the expression *studia humanitatis* in the Renaissance cf. Baker 2015, 1–35. Cf. also Reeve 1996, 21–22.
44 Kohl 1992, 186.
45 Kristeller 1961[2], 110. Cf. also Kohl 1992, 186 and above, pp. 8; 55.
46 Cf. above, pp. 32–33.

humanités littéraires."[47] In other words, whether because it took some time to digest Cicero's message or because Platonic as well as Hermetic texts, which Ficino translated into Latin, helped him understand it to the core, the simultaneous polysemy[48] of *humanitas* was eventually recovered and laid the foundations for future developments of this concept until the birth of the Humanities, of nineteenth-century German *Humanismus* etc.[49]

2.4 Other Republican Instances

If the idea of the humanities so conceived can be seen to derive from Ciceronian coinages like *studia humanitatis* and *artes liberales*, the notion of *humanitas* as educationally connoted was apparently widespread in the Caesarian age. Yet the works which have come down to us from this period seem to suggest that none of these authors regarded *humanitas* as an ideal that was crucial to a socio-political project as it was for Cicero.

The copious work of Varro has mostly perished, but *Res Rusticae* 1.17.4 clearly shows that Gellius was right in regarding him, alongside Cicero, as a purveyor of *humanitas*-παιδεία: *qui praesint esse oportet, qui litteris <atque> aliqua sint humanitate imbuti, frugi, aetate maiore quam operarios, quos dixi* ("They ought to have men over them who know how to read and write and have some little education (*humanitate*), who are dependable and older than the hands whom I have mentioned", trans. Hooper/Ash 1934).Varro is reporting the opinion of the third-century Greek writer Cassius about the correct hierarchy in estate management. The slaves who work in the estates, claims Cassius, should have men over them who have some education. Two remarks are in order: first, that *humanitas* is to be taken as education here is made all the more clear by the pairing with *litterae*; secondly, Varro was probably translating from Greek, and it is therefore easy to imagine that *humanitas* replaces παιδεία.[50]

Something analogous can be found in Cornelius Nepos' *Vita Attici* 4.1, where *humanitas* is paired with *doctrina*. The passage merits quoting at length (especially because it will be recalled when looking at Pliny's *Epistula* 8.24.2 and at Tacitus' *Agricola* 21):[51]

---

47 Toussaint 2008, 55. The text of Ficino's letter *De humanitate* to Minerbetti can be found in Toussaint 2008, 54 n. 13.
48 Cf. Toussaint 2008, 49.
49 Cf. above, pp. 3–4.
50 On this passage cf. also Leonardis 2018, 527. On Varro's *humanitas* cf. also above, p. 23.
51 Cf. below, pp. 99–102 and pp. 118–124 respectively.

Huc ex Asia Sulla decedens cum uenisset, quamdiu ibi fuit, secum habuit Pomponium, cap-
tus adulescentis et humanitate et doctrina. Sic enim Graece loquebatur, ut Athenis natus
uideretur; tanta autem suauitas erat sermonis Latini, ut appareret in eo natiuum quendam
leporem esse, non ascitum. Idem poemata pronuntiabat et Graece et Latine sic, ut supra
nihil posset addi.

When Sulla, on his way back from Asia, came to Athens, he kept Pomponius by him as long
as he was there, captured by the young man's qualities of *humanitas* and learning. He spoke
Greek so well that he seemed a native Athenian; so agreeable was his Latin that its charm
seemed somehow inborn, not acquired. He also delivered poetry, both in Greek and in
Latin, so well that there was nothing further to be added. (trans. Horsfall 1989)

Narducci suggests that there is a sort of opposition between *humanitas* and *doctrina*, the former referring to Atticus' innate graceful Latin, the latter to his ability
to recite poems both in Greek and Latin.[52] But I am sceptical. To begin with, *humanitate et doctrina* might be understood as one of those quasi-synonymous pairings in Latin where the second item, *doctrina*, serves to clarify the polysemic
humanitas.[53] Furthermore, given its undeniable relation with education and
learning (especially in this very passage), it seems rash to identify *humanitas* with
the notion of innateness.[54] After all, Nepos also says that Atticus spoke Greek so
well that he seemed to have been born in Athens, but this can only aim to emphasise his statement. In view of the above, and of the fact that at 3.3 Nepos had associated both *humanitas* and *doctrina* with the city of Athens,[55] I would therefore
argue that we should read the two terms in positive interaction rather than in
opposition also at 4.1, where it is stressed that good, actually excellent, knowledge
of languages and poetic ability reveal, or are components of, both *humanitas* and
doctrina.[56]

Similarly we can interpret Julius Caesar's *De Bello Gallico* 1.47, in which Valerius Procillus is regarded as a young man *summa uirtute et humanitate*, and immediately afterwards is praised for his knowledge of the Gaulish tongue (*propter*

---

52 Narducci 1981, 178–179.
53 Cf. above, p. 21.
54 A sort of middle way is provided by Büchner's reading: despite suggesting the idea of an opposition between natural attitude (*humanitas*) and education (*doctrina*) (Büchner 1949, 106), he
claims "*humanitas*, eigentliches höheres menschliches Wesen, und *doctrina* in den Schriften nie-
dergelegte Lehre, sind offenbar nicht dasselbe, gehören aber zusammen." (Büchner 1949, 105). Cf.
also Büchner 1949, 116.
55 *Hoc specimen prudentiae, quod, cum in eam se ciuitatem contulisset, quae antiquitate, humanitate doctrinaque praestaret omnes,* ** *unus ei fuerit carissimus* ("On the other hand, it was a sign
of his wisdom that when he moved to the city which excelled all others in its antiquity, its culture, and its learning, he was uniquely dear to it", trans. Horsfall 1989).
56 Cf. Büchner 1949.

linguae Gallicae scientiam) along the same lines. In the light of Cornelius Nepos' and later authors' instances which draw close connections between *humanitas* and proficiency in languages, I am inclined to take Caesar's emphasis on Procillus' excellent Gaulish as a clarification of one of the aspects of *humanitas* as he conceives it, as well as a nice way of thinking about the broader community of humanity.

Yet Caesar is usually mentioned in *humanitas*-studies because of another occurrence, that at the beginning of his *De Bello Gallico* (1.1.3):

> Horum omnium fortissimi sunt Belgae, propterea quod a cultu atque humanitate prouinciae longissime absunt minimeque ad eos mercatores saepe commeant atque ea, quae ad effeminandos animos pertinent, important proximique sunt Germanis, qui trans Rhenum incolunt, quibuscum continenter bellum gerunt.

> Of all these, the Belgae are the bravest, for they are furthest away from the civilization and *humanitas* of the Province. Merchants very rarely travel to them or import such goods as make men's courage weak and womanish. They live, moreover, in close proximity to the Germans who inhabit the land across the Rhine, and they are continually at war with them. (trans. Hammond 1996, slightly adapted)

The reason why the Belgae are regarded as the bravest and strongest Gallic people is because they are the farthest from the *cultus* and *humanitas* of the Roman provinces: this is a strong statement, which might imply an indirect criticism of the Roman idea of civilization, that is, of *humanitas*, as observed by some scholars.[57] Yet I would not overstate the case: Caesar might well claim that (Roman) civilization would make the Belgae less brave, but why should he attack expansionism and the related idea of civilizing barbarians at the beginning of a work like *De Bello Gallico*, whose main aim throughout, as is evident, is to exalt such concepts?[58] Moreover, I would stress that the most polemical part of the statement concerns traders and the products they sell, which can make men effeminate: this second part, however, is neither directly related to, nor a consequence of, the first half, as the coordinating conjuction *-que* (*minimeque*) reveals.

---

[57] Cf. recently Høgel 2015, 73. Vesperini 2015 is more cautious, generally speaking of *humanitas* as a vice. Kraner/Dittenberger/Meusel 1960, 80–81 stressed that this passage might be understood in different ways: "Diese Worte können im eigentlichen Sinne genommen werden („sie wohnen am weitesten entfernt von der aüßerlich verfeinerten (*cultu*) und geistig gebildeten (*humanitate*) provincia"); sie können aber auch bedeuten: sie stehen der Verfeinerung und Bildung der Provinz ganz besonders fern, und mancher römische Leser hat die Worte gewiß in dem ersten, mancher in dem zweiten Sinne genommen." On the meaning of *humanitas* in this passage cf. also Scherr 2023, 140: "Die Zivilisation, formuliert als *cultus* und *humanitas*, wird dabei mit Weiblichkeit als Chiffre der Weichheit assoziiert."

[58] On Caesar's civilizing role cf. Scherr 2023, 139–161 (with rich bibliography).

2.5 The Augustan Age: Vitruvius and Livy

As I mentioned in the Introduction, we have far fewer occurrences of the word *humanitas* from the Augustan than from the Ciceronian (or Caesarian) age. Granted, the fact that the large majority of Augustan literature is in verse contributed to this phenomenon; still, figures remain low: three occurrences in as many as 35 books of Livy, four in Vitruvius' *De Architectura* and none in Augustus' *Res Gestae*. We also note a decline in the exploitation of the polysemy of the word, especially in Vitruvius' treatise, in which all four instances evoke the notion of civilization.[59] Livy is a partial exception, because each instance takes on different nuances.

Of the four Vitruvian occurrences let me quote 2.1.6 and 9 *praef.* 2. The former is one of the best definitions of *humanitas* as the achievement of the higher level of civilization, the climax of a process which, according to Vitruvius, begins with building construction and continues with other arts and disciplines: *ex fabricationibus aedificiorum gradatim progressi* [scil. *homines*] *ad ceteras artes et disciplinas, e fera agrestique uita ad mansuetam perduxerunt humanitatem* ("so from the making of buildings they progressed, step by step, to the other arts and disciplines, and thus they led themselves out of a rough and brutish life into gentle *humanitas*", trans. Rowland 1999). 9 *praef.* 2 instead is another instance which, like Cicero's *Pro Flacco* 62, associates *humanitas* with law: *e quibus* [scil. *gentibus / hominibus*] *qui a teneris aetatibus doctrinarum abundantia satiantur, optimos habent sapientiae sensus, instituunt ciuitatibus humanitatis mores, aequa iura, leges, quibus absentibus nulla potest esse ciuitas incolumis* ("And those who from an early age enjoy an abundance of learning develop the best judgment, and in their cities they have established civilized customs (*humanitatis mores*), equal justice, and those laws without which no community can exist safely", trans. Rowland 1999).

As for Livy, if we bear in mind the three main meanings of *humanitas* as classified in the *OLD*, all three of them can be found in his historical work.[60] The rarest one, that of human nature, relates to the Pleminius affair at 29.9.6: Pleminius, Scipio's legatus at Locri, is beaten by two tribunes, who thereby neglect not only his official role of magistrate, but also his human nature (*sine respectu non maiestatis modo sed etiam humanitatis*). Like Cicero, Livy seems to draw a connection between this broad idea of man, and education as a means to accomplish it. This becomes clear thanks to the dittology *humanitatis doctrinarumque* at 37.54.17, where the Rhodian ambassadors even state before the Roman senate that the Greeks' high, unrivaled level of education should be sufficient reason for them to

---

59 Cf. Vitr. 2 *praef.* 5; 2.1.6; 2.8.12; 9 *praef.* 2.
60 More in detail on Livy's *humanitas* in Della Calce/Mollea 2022.

deserve freedom. Finally, there is also the philanthropic component, as emerges from 37.7, where *humanitas* is paired with *dexteritas*. I will return to this passage in the section on Gellius (4.2), because on that occasion Gellius mentions *dexteritas* as a Latin equivalent of φιλανθρωπία while attacking those who give to *humanitas* the meaning of φιλανθρωπία.[61]

2.6 Valerius Maximus and the Pairing of *Humanitas* and *Clementia*

One author from the Tiberian age is of particular importance to the development of this study, Valerius Maximus. Book 5 of his *Facta et dicta memorabilia* opens up by associating *humanitas* with *clementia*:

> Liberalitati quas aptiores comites quam humanitatem et clementiam dederim, quoniam idem genus laudis expetunt? Quarum prima inopia, proxima occupatione, tertia ancipiti fortuna praestatur, cumque nescias quam maxime probes, eius tamen commendatio praecurrere uidetur, cui nomen ex ipso numine quaesitum est. (Val. Max. 5.1 *praef.*)

> What more suitable companions could I provide for generosity than *humanitas* and *clementia*, since they aim at the same kind of glory? The first of these is shown to those who are poor, the second to those who are in trouble, the third to those whose luck has turned against them. And though you would not know which to praise the most, it seems to me that the one that derives its name from an actual god must surpass the others in our approval. (trans. Walker 2004)

As Rieks rightly notices, the philanthropic component of *humanitas*, which was not predominant in Cicero, appears to have become exclusive in Valerius Maximus.[62] Judging from the *exordium* of this chapter, in fact, while it is clear that *humanitas* and *clementia* pertain to the same sphere and yearn for the same kind of praise, it is also evident that they are not the same thing: *clementia* assists people in dangerous fortune (*ancipiti fortuna*), *humanitas* on other unclear, but probably more general, occasions which generate preoccupation (*occupatione*).[63] If *anceps fortuna* is therefore to be seen as a specific case of *occupatio*, Rieks is right in claiming that

---

61 Cf. above, pp. 24–25 and below pp. 159–161; 168–172.
62 Rieks 1967, 69. On *humanitas* in Valerius Maximus cf. also Høgel 2015, 71–72; on *clementia* and *humanitas* in Valerius Maximus cf. Dowling 2006, 181–184.
63 The phrase *proxima occupatione* [. . .] *praestatur* is nebulous, and has induced scholars to make conjectures: Shackleton Bailey for instance suggested *occasioni* (which however obliges to make further changes to the period). The main problem is that *occupatio* is usually employed to refer to an unspecified occupation (cf. *OLD* s.v. *occupatio* and *TLL* 9.2.381.73–382.84), and the fact

overall *clementia* emerges as a subcategory of *humanitas*, a notion which becomes crucial once it is made clear in what terms this subcategorisation is to be conceived.[64] Broadly speaking, *clementia* is not to be understood as the philanthropic component of *humanitas*, but as a part of this philanthropic component (ultimately, it is a subcategory of a subcategory of *humanitas*): indeed, *clementia* also implies a downward relationship between the one who concedes and the one who benefits from it.[65] In other words, the giver of *clementia* should be ranked more highly or seen in a position of strength. This dependence of *clementia* on *humanitas* is crucial to Valerius Maximus' conception of both these value concepts, and, in particular, it helps us understand why it can also happen that they are used as synonymous, as is made clear by the case of Pompey's behaviour towards the Armenian king Tigranes, at first designated as *clementia* (5.1.9) and one paragraph later as *humanitas* (5.1.10).[66] Although at 5.1 *praef.* these two value concepts are said to relate to different circumstances, the notion that *clementia* is a subcategory of *humanitas* enables them at times to be used as synonyms without raising any contradictions. Nevertheless, it is clear that Valerius' understanding of *humanitas* as an exclusive philanthropic value implies that he is impoverishing it through the removal of its educational, Ciceronian component. By the same token, "Valerius attests to the expansion of *clementia* as an increasingly important virtue in popular ethics."[67] As we are about to see, Seneca will bring both these tendencies to the extreme with his *Epistulae ad Lucilium* and *De clementia* respectively.

2.7 Seneca: *Humanitas*, *Clementia* and Tyranny

After a long-lasting tendency to overemphasise the importance of *humanitas* in Seneca's thought, Høgel has rightly tried to put things into perspective.[68] Yet, I argue, he overstates the case when he claims that Seneca's "overall approach to

---

that this would be the sole occurrence in Valerius Maximus does not facilitate the understanding of what it really means on this occasion.

64 Rieks 1967, 70–79. More generally on the dialectic between *humanitas* and *clementia* cf. above, pp. 40–44.

65 Sen. *Clem.* 2.3.1: *clementia est* [. . .] *lenitas superioris aduersus inferiorem in constituendis poenis* ("Mercy is [. . .] leniency on the part of a superior towards an inferior in imposing punishments", trans. Cooper/Procopé 1995). Cf. Konstan 2005, 339.

66 Cf. Rieks 1967, 75.

67 Dowling 2006, 184.

68 Høgel 2015, 76–83, ignored by Elice 2017. Cf. previously Lipps 1967, 17–69; Rieks 1967, 89–137; Balbo 2012, 69–81 (with further bibliography) and, more recently, Laudizi 2021, who seems to ignore all this debate.

the concept was to avoid it", and does not pay sufficient attention to *clementia* as a counterpart of *humanitas*.[69] The 27 occurrences of the terms *humanitas* and *inhumanitas* in Seneca's oeuvre seem too many to justify Høgel's view: he did not shun it, but rather deprived it of a fundamental aspect, its Ciceronian, educational and cultural component. This is made clear in *Ep.* 88.30, where *humanitas*, which is regarded as a positive value as usual, is separated from the *studia liberalia* (the Ciceronian *artes liberales*), which do not have the power to morally improve human beings:

> Humanitas uetat superbum esse aduersus socios, uetat amarum; uerbis, rebus, adfectibus comem se facilemque omnibus praestat; nullum alienum malum putat, bonum autem suum ideo maxime quod alicui bono futurum est amat. Numquid liberalia studia hos mores praecipiunt?

> Humanity is the quality which stops one being arrogant towards one's fellows, or being acrimonious. In words, in actions, in emotions she reveals herself as kind and good-natured towards all. To her the troubles of anyone else are her own, and anything that benefits herself she welcomes primarily because it will be of benefit to someone else. Do the liberal studies inculcate these attitudes? No. (trans. Campbell 1969)

The gulf between Cicero, who identifies *humanitas* with the liberal arts, and Seneca, who does not draw any connections between them, could hardly be greater. And yet in explicitly denying the link between *humanitas* and the liberal arts, Seneca establishes a dialectic relationship with Cicero. The main reason of their opposite conception of *humanitas* must lie in the different socio-political contexts in which Cicero and Seneca lived. Unlike the other authors we have so far mentioned – with the exception of Julius Caesar – Cicero and Seneca also played a fundamental role in the political life of their days, and their political commitment is very often reflected in their works. As we saw above, Cicero's understanding of *humanitas* was based on the assumption that this concept, educational and consequently ethical, would foster wider participation in politics by creating a new, trans-social, category of *boni*. These, and not the traditional nobility, would save the Roman Republic. Clearly his project failed, and Octavian inaugurated a new political era, the principate. By the time of the *Epistulae ad Lucilium*, which were written when Nero's tyrannical turn was reaching its acme, this new form of government was mature.[70] It was therefore clear to each and every Roman citizen that all the power was concentrated in one man's hands. In Seneca's view, *humanitas*

---

69 Høgel 2015, 77, on which cf. the reservations expressed in Mollea 2016.
70 On the date of the *Epistulae ad Lucilium* cf. Mollea 2019 and Mollea 2023a, 13–17, with up-to-date state of research.

did remain a moral quality – and actually the word is much more frequent in Seneca's latest works like *De beneficiis* and *Epistulae* than in the earlier ones – but its educational component would be socio-politically useless, for no citizen could hope to gain political influence merely by relying on a higher level of education.[71] Moreover, I suspect that the negative example of Nero influenced Seneca in denying ethical importance to the liberal arts: this emperor was extraordinarily imbued with literature and a writer himself, but this fact did not prevent him from being extraordinarily cruel as well.

Seneca had actually tried to replace the republican *humanitas* with a political virtue which seemed more fitting to the new imperial climate, *clementia*. The choice of this concept was probably suggested by Cicero himself. In the so-called Caesarian orations (*Pro Marcello, Pro Ligario, Pro rege Deiotaro*), Cicero created, or at least contributed to, the myth of the *clementia Caesaris*. Perceiving the Republic's tyrannical turn under Julius Caesar, he evidently thought that "the policy of 'mildness' was the best solution *sub tyranno*, or at least the less bad".[72] Moreover, by Seneca's time *clementia* was included among the *uirtutes imperatoriae*.[73] Like Cicero's attempt with *humanitas*, Seneca's with *clementia* was also destined to fail, but it is worth noting that the alternation of these two concepts would be central to political rhetoric in the centuries which followed, at least until the late fourth, as we shall see.

Some years before writing the *Epistulae ad Lucilium*, Seneca had sought to influence Nero's policy in many ways, not least by addressing him in the *De clementia*.[74] According to Lana, Seneca's main aim in this treatise was to provide a theoretical justification for the principate.[75] Malaspina has then expanded on this premise by highlighting three aspects which characterised Seneca's political thought as it emerges from the *De clementia*.[76] First, the emperor is a person whose absolute power is legitimate. He exercises his power by limiting himself spontaneously, and by administering justice with mildness, despite having the right to do so severely and with impunity. Secondly, this mild behaviour derives from only one virtue, the emperor's *clementia*. Even taken alone, this virtue is the

---

71 Cf. Laudizi 2021, 340–341 (with particular reference to Seneca's *Ep.* 115.3).

72 Malaspina 2009, 49. Cf. also Konstan 2005, 340–341.

73 Malaspina 2009, 62.

74 On the protreptic function of Seneca's *De clementia* cf. for example S. Braund 2009, 1, according to whom this is a "complex hybrid between different models: didactic kingship treatise addressed to a new ruler, panegyrical oration, and philosophical disquisition on one of the classic virtues of a ruler." Cf. also Bartsch 2006, 183–229 (186 in particular).

75 Lana 1955, 213–222. This theory has been endorsed by the majority of Senecan scholars: cf. Malaspina 2009, 36 n. 63 for the relevant bibliography.

76 Malaspina 2009, 36.

distinctive feature of the good monarch, and to possess it is to possess all other virtues, which are regarded as ancillary.[77] The third aspect, which is perhaps the most problematic one, is that the emperor is compared to the Stoic *sapiens*. In other words, there would be a shift from the political to the philosophical and moral dimension. This topic should have been central to Book 2, but it is no coincidence that Seneca left off after writing only a few paragraphs of this book.[78] In particular, the equation between emperor and Stoic sage could have been considered a downgrade by Nero, and in any case Seneca could not find any philosophical support for the prevalence of one imperial virtue over the others.[79]

Yet regardless of this theoretical issue, the value Seneca had chosen to epitomise the imperial virtues had well-defined features. First, as I have already mentioned, unlike *humanitas*, *clementia* implies a downward, unilateral relationship between giver and recipient.[80] Secondly, to expand on Malaspina's second point, regardless of the different specific interpretations of *Clem.* 2.7.3, here Seneca claims that *clementia* "has freedom in decision": as the author himself makes it clear, this statement is to be understood in positive terms, meaning that this value concept should induce the emperor to mitigate judicial verdicts, which might be at times too severe.[81] Yet this same claim also implies the notion of arbitrariness in the legal sphere, as well as the idea that *clementia*, and consequently the emperor who possesses it, is above the law.[82] The continuation of the passage (*ex aequo et bono iudicat*) suggests that Seneca conceived this superiority in moral terms, almost putting *clementia* on the same level as *aequitas*;[83] but an *ex post facto* reading rather shows that Nero exercised his freedom *not* to concede *clementia*, and to do whatever he wanted, regardless of laws. In other words, *clementia* is to be seen as the only check on unlimited power, but when an em-

---

77 Cf. also Malaspina 2009, 61.

78 Cf. also Malaspina 2003 for a survey of research on the theoretical problems posed by Seneca's *De clementia*.

79 Cf. Malaspina 2009, 61–63.

80 Cf. above, p. 67 n. 65.

81 *Clementia liberum arbitrium habet; non sub formula, sed ex aequo et bono iudicat; et absoluere illi licet et, quanti uult, taxare litem. Nihil ex his facit, tamquam iusto minus fecerit, sed tamquam id, quod constituit, iustissimum sit* ("Mercy has a freedom of decision. It judges not by legal formula, but by what is equitable and good. It can acquit or set the damages as high as it wishes. All these things it does with the idea not of doing something less than what is just but that what it decides should be the justest possible", trans. Cooper/Procopé 1995). Cf. Malaspina 2003, 146 on the different readings of 2.7.3 and S. Braund 2009, 70; 419. On the relationship between *humanitas* and *iustitia* cf. below, pp. 97–98; 283; 288–289.

82 Cf. Borgo 1985, 27.

83 On *aequitas* cf. below, pp. 288–289.

peror lacks *clementia*, he is likely to become a tyrant.[84] This was certainly the case with Nero, whose image, as it has come down to us from antiquity, does not at all epitomise the idea of clemency – let alone that of Stoic *sapientia*. On the contrary, the association of Seneca's *De clementia* with an emperor who lacked *clementia* probably ended up compromising the very idea of *clementia* itself. Neither analogous attempts at educating the monarch and at theoretically justifying the principate, nor such a strong emphasis on the importance of *clementia* as the sole imperial virtue returned after Seneca.[85] Under Domitian, Statius represented a unique exception in giving importance to *clementia*, as we shall see in the next section. Seneca's treatise therefore marked a turning point in the history of this value concept.

2.8 The Flavian Age and a Second Nero

After the reign of Nero and after Seneca's writings, new emphases emerged in the significance accorded to *humanitas* and *clementia*, as represented in our extant sources: the former had lost its main Ciceronian and republican component, while the latter become synonymous with tyranny.[86] The Flavian age reveals both these trends: there seems to be no place for Ciceronian *humanitas*, and *clementia* will be even more compromised at the end of the reign of Domitian. The role and the nuances of *humanitas* in Quintilian's *Institutio oratoria* and of *clementia* in Statius' *Thebaid* are symptomatic of these two tendencies respectively.

To Quintilian Cicero was the model *par excellence*, both as an orator and writer. His style is clearly Ciceronian, and so is his idea of the orator as *uir bonus dicendi peritus*, a man who combines moral qualities with encyclopaedic knowledge – in a word, a man who possesses what Cicero calls *humanitas*. In the light of this, it is all the more surprising that none of the seven occurrences of *humanitas* in Quintilian's treatise evoke the notions of *doctrina* or liberal arts.[87] In the 'library of the orator' in *Institutio oratoria* 10.1, Quintilian attacks Seneca and his style, but also claims that young people seem to read him exclusively (10.1.125: *tum autem*

---

84 Cf. Syme 1958, 414, although with reference to Julius Caesar: "To acquiesce in the 'clementia Caesaris' implied a recognition of despotism."

85 Cf. Malaspina 2009, 74–75.

86 On clemency in Julio-Claudian Rome cf. Burgess 1972, 341: "It seems probable that during the Julio-Claudian principate there were people at Rome, Stoics and Republicans perhaps, for whom *clementia* was a symbol of the imperial tyranny." Cf. also Dowling 2006, 215.

87 Cf. Balbo 2012, 81–82. Cf. however 12.11.5–6, where the educational aspect does seem to shine through: below, pp. 248–249.

solus hic fere in manibus adulescentium fuit. "Yet he alone was almost in each and every young man's hands"). This is telling, because it explains why Seneca was so influential, and whether or not he was aware of this, Quintilian also appears to have been influenced, at least in his understanding of *humanitas*.[88]

Statius' *Siluae* and *Thebaid* are the other side of the same coin. Statius regarded *clementia* as a crucial virtue, but was also well-aware of the tyrannical connotations it carried, especially after the years of Nero.[89] Thus, as Burgess has stressed, he reinvented *clementia* by adding a third part to the traditional dual relationship between the inferior and the superior, that is, another superior.[90] In this new conceptualisation the roles of victimising and, at the same time, indulgent part no longer belong to the same referent, for one superior plays the negative, the other one the positive role. Outside the metaphor of the *Thebaid*, the new superior *par excellence*, who is not victimising but only a bestower of *clementia*, must be the emperor, Domitian. In the *Siluae*, this becomes explicit,[91] and a passage by Suetonius (*Dom.* 11) gives us further hints as to why *clementia* was 'officially' associated with Domitian during his lifetime, and why it was distrusted after his death: *numquam tristiorem sententiam sine praefatione clementiae pronuntiauit* ("he would never pronounce an especially dreadful sentence without first talking of clemency", trans. Edwards 2000). But with Suetonius we have reached the age of Trajan and Hadrian, which I shall investigate in detail in the next chapter.

2.9 *Humanitas* in the Centuries First BCE–First CE: Final Remarks

The first two centuries in the long history of *humanitas* were crucial for future uses and perceptions of this term. Cicero played the fundamental role in making *humanitas* as loaded and multifaceted a value concept as it was in the final years of the Roman Republic. The juxtaposition of the educational and ethical aspect, and the broader idea of civilization resulting from the simultaneous presence of these two aspects, all potentially encapsulated within one single word, had no precedents in Greek or in Roman thought. Furthermore, Cicero invested *humani-*

---

88 As we will see later on, the discourse is quite different as regards [Quintilian's] *Minor* and *Major Declamations*.
89 More generally, cf. Tuck 2016, 110: "A crucial element of the Flavian 'message' lay in the denigration of Nero."
90 Burgess 1972, 345. Doubtful on this Konstan 2005, 339 n. 4.
91 Cf. *Silu.* 3.4.73–77 with Burgess 1972, 345–346. Cf. also Bessone 2011, 23.

tas with strong political connotations, condensing into this word his message that the survival of the Republican system could only lie in the general consensus of the *boni homines*, that is, those who, thanks to the principles of *humanitas* they have assimilated, can really "serve the best interests of the *res publica*".[92] Both *humanitas* and this new category of people therefore potentially transcended traditional social-class distinctions, and this would make of *humanitas* a 'republican' connoted term thenceforth. In this respect, it is no coincidence that Pliny the Younger exalted Trajan's *humanitas* after the despotic years of Domitian, thereby suggesting that an age inspired by more freedom had just begun.

The clear-cut distinction between possessors and non-possessors of *humanitas* could also be exploited in judicial, and, more generally, oratorical contexts, as Cicero did in the *Pro Archia* and other orations. In doing so, he also followed in the footsteps of the *Rhetorica ad Herennium*, which had already highlighted the importance of the *humanitas* argument in trials. With the advent of the principate, oratory witnessed a period of decadence, as testified for example by Quintilian and Tacitus. Yet Cicero remained the model of the perfect orator, and it comes as no surprise that later imperial authors like Apuleius, Eumenius, and, at times, the declaimer(s) followed his example and gave prominence to the *humanitas* argument in oratorical contexts.

During the early imperial age, however, *humanitas* must have been perceived as too Ciceronian a value, and "throughout the early imperial period Cicero is in many respects equated with the Republic and its demise."[93] It follows that the first author after Cicero to openly deal with political theory, Seneca, preferred *clementia* over *humanitas*, especially before realising that his project of educating Nero was a failure. Because of its features, among which its implying a downward relationship between bestower and recipient, *clementia* appeared as far more suitable to the new political climate, when all power was concentrated in one man's hands. In the *Epistulae ad Lucilium* then, Seneca explicitly denied any relationships between *humanitas* and the liberal arts, and this contributes to dismantling the theoretical validity of Cicero's socio-political project.[94] Yet figures reveal that at the same time Seneca was also more careful in resorting to the term *clementia.*

Seneca freed *humanitas* of its Ciceronian accrescences, and also influenced a Ciceronian author like Quintilian in this respect. Yet the age of Domitian cele-

---

92 Lacey 1970, 11. Cf. also Lacey 1970, 14: "It was always in fact a cardinal point in Cicero's thought that *boni* were those who supported the rule of law, and hence the rule of *otium* – civil peace."

93 Gowing 2005, 110.

94 On the notion that Cicero was not perceived as a political model throughout the major part of the first century CE cf. Gowing 2005, 110 and n. 20 for further bibliography.

brated once again the emperor's *clementia*, but in fact, like Nero, Domitian proved not at all clement. Also in this respect, therefore, the two last representatives of their dynasties seem to confirm Boyle's notion that the Flavian dynasty oddly re-iterates the Julio Claudian.[95]

2.10 From Trajan to Theodosius, from Pliny to Symmachus

Having sketched out the key issues at stake and after taking a rather quick look at the first two centuries in the history of *humanitas*, I now turn to providing a short chronological outline of the main part of this book.

Despite the relatively high number of studies on *humanitas* in Pliny the Younger, I have chosen him as the true starting point for this book because he played a watershed role in the history of this value concept. When Trajan became emperor after the short reign of Nerva, the dreadful image of Domitian was still far too vivid in people's minds, and the concept of *clementia*, associated both with him and the previous tyrant Nero, was compromised: this, at least, is what emerges from our elite sources, who wanted to distance themselves from the previous dynasty, probably to show support for the new emperor. Therefore, whether or not he was the first to do so, when in 100 CE he delivered his *Panegyricus* on Trajan, Pliny the Younger restored the republican-, Ciceronian-connoted *humanitas* to characterise the 'revolutionary' attitude of the new emperor. Through *humanitas*, Trajan emerges as a *primus inter pares* rather than a tyrant, and the polysemy of this single word allows Pliny to compare, more or less explicitly, the numerous qualities of this emperor to the vices of Domitian. This role of *humanitas* in the *Panegyricus* is corroborated by its use in the *Letters*, where Pliny makes all the more clear that this value concept transcends social class distinctions, and is therefore very apt to promote a new climate of mutual respect and collaboration among Roman citizens.

I devote the main part of Chapter 3 to Pliny, and conclude the chapter with two sections on Tacitus and Suetonius respectively. Overall, it is my contention that their historical and biographical works represent a sort of photographic negative of Pliny's texts, for both Tacitus and Suetonius do not associate *humanitas* with any first-century emperor, and imply that *humanitas* does not play any role in first-century society as they portrayed it. In Tacitus' *Annals* and *Histories* there is no occurrence of the word *humanitas* at all, whereas in Suetonius' *Caesars* the only two instances in the *Life of Tiberius* only reveal the emperor's lack of the values *humanitas* represents. Tacitus, however, has two very interesting occur-

---

95 Boyle 2003, 5–6. Cf. also Gowing 2005, 104.

rences of *humanitas* in his 'minor' works, one in the *Agricola* and one in the *Germania*. The *Agricola* instance in particular is usually regarded as evidence for Tacitus' criticism of hypocritical and false uses of Roman *humanitas*, here interpreted as the civilization which the Romans try to inflict on the world. Yet I seek to show that a close reading of *Agricola* 21 rather reveals Tacitus' extraordinarily broad, and at the same time suspicious, conception of *humanitas*, which has both positive and negative aspects. The second occurrence, at *Germania* 21.3, is somehow complementary to the *Agricola* one, and shows that also the barbarians could have their own idea of civilization: it is less sophisticated than the Romans', but also less prone to fall into vice.

In Chapter 4 I turn to the Antonine age. Apuleius' conception of *humanitas* looks rather flat, devoid of the polysemy observed in Pliny and Tacitus' *Agricola*. In short, he might be included in the category of those whom Gellius blamed for (mis-)understanding *humanitas* as φιλανθρωπία. Yet his use of the *humanitas* argument in judicial contexts is masterly. In the *Apologia*, he exploits *humanitas*, alongside higher education, to create a bond between the proconsul Maximus, who is also the judge of the trial, his predecessor and himself which separates them from the rude throng and the accusers. But in the mock trial of *Metamorphoses* 3 Apuleius' rhetorical and oratorical skills reach a perhaps higher level of perfection, because *humanitas* even becomes a double-edged sword: the defendant Lucius seeks to employ it in pretty much the same way as Apuleius himself had done in the *Apologia*, but the accusers resort to the same argument, which, cleverly handled, would probably persuade the judges that they deserve to be treated with *humanitas* more than Lucius. Unfortunately, the fiction of the trial is interrupted and the reader will never know of its outcome.

Unsurprisingly, *humanitas* is conceived in educational terms in Aulus Gellius' *Noctes Atticae*, the focus of the next section of Chapter 4. As well as analysing in depth the well-known passage at 13.17, which, as we have seen, is central to all studies on *humanitas*, I show how Gellius' interest in *humanitas* is not limited to linguistic reasons. Instead, the very cultural programme he proposes throughout his work, and whose guidelines he sets forth in the preface, is based on the restoration of this value concept, which, like Cicero, he regards as closely linked to the liberal arts. In a way, Gellius' use and understanding of *humanitas* also functions to include and exclude: those who intend to follow his teaching will be separated from those who follow the grammarians', the main target of his oeuvre.

The last, brief section of Chapter 4 is devoted to Fronto, who, unlike his pupil Gellius, seems to be wary of the word *humanitas*. The hypothesis I put forward is that his theory of language led him to prefer less polysemic words to express the ideas potentially implied by *humanitas*. In particular, he favoured the Greek φιλοστοργία.

Chapter 5 investigates the role of *humanitas* within [Quintilian's] *Minor* and *Major Declamations*. The school-related character of these two collections is in tune with the (little) argumentative use of this *Wertbegriff* in some declamations, which turns out to be far less sophisticated than in the cases of Cicero and Apuleius. Yet the declamations in which *humanitas* appears corroborate Gellius' criticism of his contemporaries – and of teachers in particular – by displaying a meaning which is mainly, if not exclusively, connoted in philanthropic terms.

In Chapter 6 I focus on the sole work of third-century pagan Latin literature in which *humanitas* plays a key role, Eumenius' *Oratio pro instaurandis scholis*. Along the lines sketched out in Cicero's *Pro Archia*, the rhetor Eumenius both exploits the polysemy of this word and exalts the governor's and the emperor's *humanitas* to persuade them to rebuild the famous *scholae Maenianae* of Augustodunum (today's Autun), a place in central Gaul where the values expressed by *humanitas* could perpetuate themselves thanks to the excellence of its teaching.

To another exception is devoted Chapter 7, which instead looks at the sole pagan work of the Constantine age in which *humanitas* plays some role, that is, Firmicus Maternus' *Mathesis*. This astrological treatise is of particular interest for the history of this value concept for it consistently displays a conception of *humanitas* as civilization that, curiously but logically on closer inspection, utterly overlooks its expected educational dimension. Indeed – Firmicus shows – the presence or absence of civilization depends on and derives from the stars, education having little power in comparison.

My investigation of *humanitas* concludes with late fourth-century authors, Ammianus, some 'minor' Roman historians, Ausonius and Symmachus. In the first part of Chapter 8, I show that, unlike Tacitus, one of his models, Ammianus makes ample use of the word *humanitas*, but like him, he does not recognise this value concept as characteristic of the ages he examines, let alone a quality of the emperors who are protagonists of his *Historiae*. Sometimes he associates *humanitas* (which he primarily conceives as morally connoted, as benevolence or indulgence) with emperors, but only to show that their *humanitas* is feigned, or that they lack *humanitas* despite having good moral examples to follow. From this perspective, it is telling that the term *humanitas* is never mentioned in relation to Julian the Apostate, Ammianus' favourite emperor. More generally, Ammianus' use of *humanitas* betrays both his role of soldier and the influence of Greek historiography over his style, which lead him to pay special attention to the moral behaviour of emperors, chieftains, soldiers and enemies, and to emphasise when they are, or are not, humane.

A rather short survey of the role of *humanitas* within Eutropius, Aurelius Victor and his *corpus*, as well as in the *Historia Augusta* ends up serving as a sort of corollary to Ammianus. Specifically, *humanitas* is mentioned very rarely in these works, which on the one hand recalls us that historians tend to eschew the word *humanitas*, but on the other hand indirectly offers an explanation for this: historiographers are not used to speaking of *humanitas* because they see little concrete evidence of it during the periods on which their narrations focus.

But something different seemed to happen when Theodosius I ascended the throne, as anticipated by Ausonius' *Gratiarum actio* to Gratian. In this oration yet again *humanitas* crops up quite often and also reacquires an educational dimension. After all, Ausonius, a Ciceronian as well as Gratian's teacher, expectedly exalts the importance of education when delivering his official discourse, and it is not to rule out the hypothesis that the *Gratiarum actio* itself contributed to the socio-political renaissance of *humanitas* in the Theodosian age.

The last part of Chapter 8, whose protagonist is Symmachus, brings us back to the beginning of this book. As I shall show, Theodosius I's efforts to appear as a new Trajan are mirrored by Symmachus' role of purveyor of *humanitas*, which very much recalls Pliny's role in the Trajanic age. After a period in the fourth century when *clementia* had again become a mainstream concept, but was also linked to the political crisis prior to Theodosius' ascension to the throne as well as to the dark images of bad emperors, it seems to have been replaced by *humanitas*, thereby reiterating the same pattern observed for the late first century. In Symmachus' oeuvre yet again *humanitas* emerges as linking value within Roman society, especially within the upper classes which help the emperor to govern the empire.

From the socio-political perspective, it is fitting that the path of *humanitas* which starts from Pliny the Younger during the age of Trajan ends with Symmachus under Theodosius. Yet, before the conclusion, the true last chapter of this book is devoted to the *Asclepius*, a work of its own whose characteristics make it difficult to categorise. It is not only because of the doubts concerning its dating that I have decided to put it at the end of this study, but also because the role that *humanitas* plays in it has little to do, if anything, with the rest of the story. But on the other hand it contributes to showing to what a great extent *humanitas* is polysemic.

In sketching this outline, I have always referred to the noun *humanitas*, completely neglecting the adjective *humanus*. Although each chapter contains minor sections on *humanus*, I will show throughout that *humanus* only occasionally takes on the rich, multi-faceted meaning of *humanitas*, thus confirming what I have mentioned earlier on, namely that this usually happens when the adjective is in its comparative or superlative form.[96]

---

96 Cf. above, p. 22.

II Pagan *Humanitas* in the Imperial Age

3 A New Apogee of *Humanitas* in the Trajanic Age: Pliny the Younger, Tacitus and Suetonius

As the frequency of these two words as well as the analysis brought forward in the previous chapters reveal,[1] for about half a century *clementia* was more invoked a value concept than *humanitas*, especially in the public, official sphere, for which the literary works we deal with in this book are a good touchstone. Yet, at the beginning of the Trajanic age, *humanitas* recovered the significance it had had in Cicero's political thought thanks to Pliny the Younger. Despite all attempts at denigrating, and distancing themselves from, the figure of Nero, the emperors of the Flavian dynasty saw all their efforts vanish because of Domitian, who was long regarded as a second Nero after his death.[2] Recent scholarship has expressed doubt as to whether 96 CE can be considered a watershed in Latin literature; as far as the concepts of value are concerned, however, a significant transformation certainly took place.[3] In particular, by the end of Domitian's reign, *clementia*, which had played a key role (albeit in vain) in the ideology of the Neronian age, and which had been reinvented by Statius at the time of the last Flavian emperor, appears to have been looked at with suspicion once again.[4] In this sense, the arguments put forward by Benferhat, following Charlesworth and others, are convincing and merit being summarised here.[5] As Benferhat points out, there are very few occurrences of *clementia* in the authors of the Trajanic age such as Suetonius and Pliny the Younger, and in the *Panegyricus* in particular the author seems to be wary of Domitian's false clemency. As a consequence, it is unsurprising that the term is employed only once with reference to Trajan (*Pan.* 35.1). Conversely, it appears quite often in Tacitus: once in the *Dialogus de oratoribus*, seven times in the *Historiae* and 27 in the *Annales*. Yet all these instances mainly seem to high-

---

1 Cf. above, pp. 40–44.

2 On the denigration of Nero as a fundamental component of Flavian image-making cf. Tuck 2016; on Domitian as a second Nero cf. Zissos 2016b.

3 Cf. König/Whitton 2018, 9: "Whether 96 really did inaugurate a literary revival, then, and how long it lasted, are questions we can hardly answer." In this respect, previous scholarship had been less cautious, and Coleman 1990, 38 for instance claimed that 96 "does not represent a dramatic transformation for Latin literature, although neither was the change negligible." Cf. also Wallace-Hadrill 1984, 200 and Dihle 2013, 213–215. Further bibliography in König/Whitton 2018, 6 n. 24.

4 Cf. above, p. 39.

5 Benferhat 2011, 185 n. 212; Charlesworth 1937, 112–113. Cf. also Syme 1958, 414; Burgess 1972, 340–341; Benferhat 2011, 197. Further supporters of *clementia* as a concept which reveals despotic power are mentioned in Konstan 2005, 337–339.

light the historian's hostility towards what has become the *clementia principis* as opposed to the former *clementia populi Romani*. In other words, what had once been the virtue of a great people which was able to show mercy towards the conquered enemy came to symbolise the cruelty and arbitrariness of a tyrant.[6] The same holds true with regard to Suetonius' usage of *clementia*.[7] As Burgess remarks, "Suetonius laid great emphasis on the *clementia* of the emperors, and by concentrating on pardon not for serious offences but for personal insults and trivialities he presents the emperors, apart from Vespasian, as malevolent tyrants."[8] Moreover, despite an image of *Clementia* appearing on coins of 99–100 CE, *clementia* is not included among Trajan's official virtues. In sum, by Trajan's day *clementia* "had become too much a despotic quality [. . .] and it could return again under Hadrian or under later emperors in an altered form as *Clementia Temporum*."[9]

As I argue in what follows, while *clementia* progressively lost its political significance, *humanitas* took its place and also started to embody part of the meaning *clementia* once had. This is first and foremost shown by Pliny, who seems to have understood *humanitas* as Cicero had done, that is, as an ideal which roughly intermingles superior education (the Greek παιδεία) with a benevolent disposition towards humans *qua* humans (the Greek φιλανθρωπία). As I shall show in the first section of this chapter, in the *Panegyricus* the term *humanitas* plays an analogous central role to that played by *clementia* in Seneca's *De clementia*, which can be regarded as a forerunner of the Latin panegyrics – Pliny's in particular –, and Statius' *Siluae* and *Thebaid*. And while Nero and Domitian are either characterised by or encouraged to pursue *clementia*, *humanitas* epitomises the values which differentiate Trajan from his predecessor(s). However, unlike *clementia*, *humanitas* is not an exclusive prerogative of the ruler: it is a value that can and should be possessed by the entire Roman intellectual and political elite that we get to know from Pliny's *Epistulae*. In a way, we could say that *humanitas* is at the

---

6 Cf. Benferhat 2011, 201. Cf. also Burgess 1972, 341: "This master of irony and innuendo [*scil.* Tacitus] uses *clementia* to great effect in his charcterization of the Julio-Claudian emperors; furthermore, he represents it as a basically imperial prerogative, and it is a short step from here to its use as a propaganda word in anti-imperial sources, a word symbolizing the despotism of the emperors", and Borgo 1985, 48–51. *Contra* Konstan 2005, 344.
7 It must be borne in mind that scholars such as Wallace-Hadrill 1984 maintain that *clementia* played an important role in Suetonius' *Caesares*. But first, this is not to deny that the number of occurrences of this word is rather low (eight instances of *clementia* and two of *clemens*); secondly and crucially, this concept is always used with reference to emperors of the first century CE (Augustus, Tiberius, Nero, Vitellius, Vespasian and Domitian). I will deal with this issue in more detail in the section on Suetonius: cf. below, pp. 127–132.
8 Burgess 1972, 341. On *clementia* in Suetonius cf. also Borgo 1985, 44; 50–52.
9 Charlesworth 1937, 113.

core of the cultural, social and political renaissance that not only Pliny, but also the Roman *nobilitas* and, presumably, Trajan himself, hope will follow the dark age of Domitian's tyranny.[10]

In the light of this, it is perhaps unsurprising that in Tacitus and Suetonius the term is differently nuanced and appears rarely. After all, most of what has survived of their works, that is, Tacitus' *Annales* and *Historiae* and Suetonius' *De uita Caesarum*, deal with the history of the Principate until Domitian, whereas *humanitas* was rather a republican, Ciceronian concept which Pliny (and Trajan?) were trying to reintroduce. Yet because of their rarity the very few occurrences of the word in their oeuvre are worth investigating. Accordingly, the second section of this chapter will be devoted to Tacitus, in whose work the term *humanitas* is found only twice: once in the *Agricola* and once in the *Germania*. As we will see, these two occurrences take on different nuances. Of the two, the instance in the *Agricola* is striking and merits discussion at length, because here *humanitas*, which roughly stands for 'civilization', becomes closely related to Tacitus' attitude towards Roman imperialism.

As for Suetonius, the topic of the third and last section of this chapter, *humanitas* only appears twice in the *Vita Tiberii*. As is the case with *Agricola* 21, the term itself is positively connoted but the contexts in which *humanitas* is mentioned seem to warn against the possible risks provoked either by the misuse of this concept or, on the contrary, by its total absence.

Brief subsections at the end of the analysis of *humanitas* in each author are devoted to *humanus* and its adverbial derivatives. As will soon be clear, the adjective is very often deprived of the ideological values carried by the noun, so much so that the meanings of *humanitas* and *humanus* rarely overlap.

3.1 Pliny the Younger: Refounding Imperial Rome in the Name of *Humanitas*

There can be little doubt that in Pliny the Younger's view the idea of *humanitas* was meant to be at the core of the cultural, social and political renaissance that he hoped would follow Domitian's death. Holding a prominent post at Trajan's court and, consequently, in Trajanic society, Pliny did not want to miss the opportunity to try to influence the world in which he lived. This he certainly did in the

---

10 As Geisthardt 2015, *passim* persuasively shows, Pliny's and Tacitus' works tend to reflect not only their own views, but those of the senatorial class to which they belong. Cf. also Sonnabend 2002, 174: "Die Perspektive des Tacitus war die des Senats, die Perspektive Suetons war die des kaiserlichen Hauses."

Panegyricus and *Epistulae*, the only works which have come down to us. *Humanitas* is a recurrent word in both these works, and this fact is significant. First, after the tyranny of a man who considered himself a second Jupiter, the *humanitas* of his successor made it clear that times had changed and the emperor was again a man among men. Secondly, to restore such an important Ciceronian, republican concept was to indicate the lines along which the Trajanic 'revolution' could take place, that is, by combining education, knowledge and culture with a benevolent attitude towards one's fellow human beings.[11] To best appreciate how Pliny employed this *humanitas* argument, let us look at his works in greater detail, starting with the *Panegyricus*.

3.1.1 The *Panegyricus*

As Innes and others remark, Pliny calls *gratiarum actio* what we usually call *Panegyricus*, that is, the speech he gave in praise of Trajan before the Senate in September 100 CE when he was appointed consul, of which a revised version has come down to us.[12] Although this is the first imperial panegyric we are aware of, Ciceronian orations such as *Pro Marcello* and *Pro Archia* as well as Seneca's *De clementia* can to some extent be considered its precedents and perhaps models, especially with regard to the custom of listing the virtues which characterise the subject of praise.[13] Roche has listed and counted the occurrences of the main virtues of Trajan that Pliny mentions in the *Panegyricus*.[14] Yet his otherwise useful quantitative analysis ends up underestimating the key role that *humanitas* plays in this speech. Compared to *modestia, moderatio, fides, reuerentia, cura, labor, liberalitas, securitas, pudor, pietas, benignitas* and *maiestas*, which all appear ten times or more, the seven occurrences of *humani-*

---

11 Cf. Boyancé 1970b: "En donnant à Rome son œuvre littéraire et philosophique, Cicéron lui [*scil.* Pline le Jeune] a enseigné l'*humanitas* et il a établi les bases de l'unité des hommes de l'empire."
12 Innes 2011, 67. Cf. also Radice 1968, 166. The date is certain, and Pliny himself informs us of his revision of the speech in *Ep.* 3.18. Cf. also *Ep.* 3.13. Recent studies have suggested that it was published "half a dozen years or more after he [*scil.* Pliny] gave his consular thanksgiving in the senate" (Whitton 2019, 340). Cf. also Woytek 2006.
13 Cf. Radice 1968, 170; Picone 1978, 133 and n. 68 for further bibliography; Levene 1997, 67–77; Manuwald 2011. Casapulla 2019 highlights possible elements of originality that distinguish Pliny's *Panegyricus* from previous *gratiarum actiones*.
14 Roche 2011, 8–9.

tas might at first sight suggest that this concept plays a secondary role, but nothing is further from the truth.[15] As ever, figures need interpretation.

To begin with, *humanitas* is a key element in perhaps the most important part of this *gratiarum actio*, its opening, when a sort of *captatio beneuolentiae* is needed. Following the old precept *Ab Ioue principium*, the *Panegyricus* opens up by invoking the gods and stating that Trajan is very similar to any one of them (§ 1.3: *dis simillimus princeps*). Yet, unlike his predecessor Domitian, he behaves and rules like a man among men – and this is his most extraordinary quality (2.4: *et hoc magis excellit atque eminet, quod unum <ille se> ex nobis putat nec minus hominem se quam hominibus praeesse meminit*, "and his special virtue lies in his thinking so, as also in his never forgetting that he is a man himself while a ruler of men", trans. Radice 1975).[16] The term *humanitas* has not yet been mentioned, but it is sufficiently clear that the theme of Trajan's humanness, or, more generally, of his human qualities, will be at the core of the speech. This becomes explicit soon, when at 2.7 *humanitas* is strikingly opposed to *diuinitas*: *Quid nos ipsi? Diuinitatem principis nostri an humanitatem, temperantiam, facilitatem, ut amor et gaudium tulit, celebrare uniuersi solemus?* ("What about us? Is it the divine nature of our prince or his *humanitas*, his moderation and his courtesy which joy and affection prompt us to celebrate in a single voice?", trans. Radice 1975). This juxtaposition, albeit rare, is not new in the literature of Pliny's day, for Cicero had regarded *diuinitas* as superior to *humanitas*, identifying the former with the (high) qualities of the gods, the latter with the (lower) qualities of human beings.[17] In contrast, not only does this passage seem to put humanness and divinity on the same level, but it implicitly suggests that *humanitas* could even be more important, at least for an emperor.[18] As Rees puts it, Trajan's "simple *humanitas* sets him apart from the arrogance of former emperors and is clearly presented as being of great credit to him. Trajan is not a god, is not called a god and does not want to be treated as a god."[19]

Pliny also innovatively opposes *temperantia* and *facilitas* to *diuinitas*, probably to stress further this novel way of reading the relationship between *humanitas* and *diuinitas*. Indeed, Pliny's originality only consists in creating this polarity – the

---

15 On the importance of *humanitas* in Pliny's *Panegyricus* cf. also Rieks 1967, 244–248; S. Braund 2012², 93; 98.

16 Cf. Feldherr 2019, 403: "By this point [*scil.* after *dis simillimus* at 1.3] Trajan's title perfectly encapsulates the guiding theme of Pliny's praise, that Trajan is most divine because most deeply embedded in human institutions".

17 Cf. Cic. *De or.* 2.86.

18 Cf. Feldherr 2019, 398. On this passage in general cf. also Cova 1978, 108.

19 Rees 2001, 163. Indeed, Rees 2001, 163–164 also shows that other places in the *Panegyricus* would equate Trajan to a god (cf. Levene 1997, 78–83), and yet Pliny's rhetoric manages to hide this aspect. Cf. also Busti 2019; Wood 2019.

triad *humanitas, temperantia* and *facilitas* echoes Cicero's *Pro lege Manilia* 36, where *innocentia, fides* and *ingenium* complete the list of the qualities that leaders and generals should possess.[20] Of the two, *facilitas* in particular is paired with *humanitas* quite often in Cicero (*De or.* 2.362; *Off.* 1.90; *Fam.* 3.10.10 and 13.24.2) and once in Quintilian (at 11.1.42 in a list of those values which make an orator appeal to the audience), and Hellegouarc'h even regards it as an aspect of *humanitas.*[21] Yet if we accept his definition, *facilitas* is to be seen as the act of a person of higher rank who strives to understand the situation of a subordinate person and does not show *superbia* towards them. Certainly, as other Plinian passages will show, *humanitas* transcends social distinctions, so that in the passage under investigation *facilitas* may serve the purpose of counterbalancing the situation: if *humanitas* casts Trajan down from Olympus, *facilitas* reminds the audience that the emperor is nonetheless in a higher position. The addition of *temperantia*, which appears rarely in Pliny but is at the heart of Tacitus' political message according to Benferhat, and which refers to the ability to restrain passions and instincts according to Hellegouarc'h, thus standing for moderation in political contexts, somehow reiterates the superiority of an emperor who is no longer a god, but is still the emperor.[22]

No sooner has Pliny started mentioning these virtues of Trajan than, in the improvisation he simulates of the speech, he immediately realises that to talk about virtues is to risk undermining the genuineness of his speech. In fact, previous emperors, not least Domitian, had been praised for their virtues too. They had probably been praised insincerely, but still praised. This leads us to Bartsch's emphasis on the practice of doublespeak in imperial literature, that is, the custom of praising someone to blame them, of listing their virtues to indicate that they lack these virtues.[23] To avoid this ambiguity, Pliny feels the need to stress that he is improvising his speech, for he takes it that improvisation is synonymous with

---

20 Cf. Benferhat 2011, 293: "Pline choisit trois termes cicéroniens qui désignent des qualités propres aux hommes: la conscience d'appartenir à la communauté humaine, la lutte victorieuse de la raison contre les plaisirs, un contact facile."

21 Hellegouarc'h 1963, 216.

22 Benferhat 2011, 291–308; Hellegouarc'h 1963, 259. Cf. Benferhat 2011, 292: "[La *temperantia*] est un mélange du trop peu et du pas assez qui doit servir de règle dans la vie dans toutes ses dimensions, y compris politique."

23 Bartsch 1994. Cf. also Bartsch's theory of the praise/blame axis: "that is, the tendency for terms of praise and blame to be liable to slippage and thus to mean their opposites or their negative counterparts on one or another evaluative axis separating good qualities from bad" (1994, 170).

sincerity. (It does not seem to matter to Pliny that in claiming that he was improvising, he was presumably telling one of his biggest lies ever.) Compare 3.1:

> Igitur quod temperamentum omnes in illo subito pietatis calore seruamus, hoc singuli quo-
> que meditatique teneamus, sciamusque nullum esse neque sincerius neque acceptius genus
> gratiarum, quam quod illas acclamationes aemulemur, quae fingendi non habent tempus.

> This moderation, then, which we have all maintained in the sudden surge of our affection,
> we must individually try to keep in our more studied tributes, remembering that there is no
> more sincere nor welcome kind of thanks than that which most resembles the spontaneous
> acclamation which has no time for artifice. (trans. Radice 1975)

There follows (3.4) a long list of virtues that Pliny attributes to Trajan against
their opposites:

> Non enim periculum est, ne, cum loquar de humanitate, exprobrari sibi superbiam credat,
> cum de frugalitate, luxuriam, cum de clementia, crudelitatem, cum de liberalitate, auari-
> tiam, cum de benignitate, liuorem, cum de continentia, libidinem, cum de labore, iner-
> tiam, cum de fortitudine, timorem.

> There is no danger that in my references to his *humanitas* he will see a reproach for arro-
> gance; that he will suppose I mean extravagance by modest expenditure, and cruelty by for-
> bearance; that I think him covetous and capricious when I call him generous and kind,
> profligate and idle instead of self-controlled and active, or that I judge him a coward when I
> speak of him as a brave man. (trans. Radice 1975)

Both in terms of *humanitas* and in the framework of the *Panegyricus* section 3.4
plays a key role. As Bartsch points out, this passage is of crucial importance in that
it represents Pliny's official declaration that there is no doublespeak in his panegyric.[24] After a long time, hidden and public transcripts can again coincide,[25] and no
doubt this happens because the emperor deserves to be praised (*nam merenti gratias agere facile est*) and would not have any reasons to take offence and see a reproach for the opposites of the praised virtues.[26] Among these virtues, *humanitas*,
coming at the very beginning of the list, clearly has a prominent position. Moreover, this word has already been mentioned twice, and we are still at the very beginning of a speech which runs to 95 sections in total. But it is also the case that

---

24 Bartsch 1994, 156–157.
25 Bartsch 1994, 162.
26 Bradley 1991, 3719 does see in this passage a kind of reproach, but not for Trajan's vices,
rather for Domitian's: "Trajan thus benefits in the 'Panegyricus' at Domitian's expense because if
the present emperor is the epitome of imperial virtues, the last Flavian embodies all the vices
that, by their existence, those virtues presupposed."

this passage helps us infer another characteristic of *humanitas* I have already discussed in the introduction: when it comes to defining it as a virtue, its opposite is not only represented by the obvious *inhumanitas*, but also by *superbia*.[27] In a way, the contrast between *superbia* and *humanitas* at 3.4 echoes and completes that between *diuinitas* and *humanitas* at 2.7: while here at 3.4 it is clearly ethical, at 2.7, in counterposing divine and human nature, it is ontological. Yet in historical terms the comparison is always the same: while Trajan possesses *humanitas*, Domitian is not only characterised by *diuinitas*, but also by *superbia* (*Pan.* 48).[28] After all, as Baraz has remarked, although the poetic panegyric tradition of the Flavian Age admits a positive conception of pride, "the prose panegyrics, beginning with Pliny the Younger's spirited attacks on the recently dispatched Domitian, are committed to linking pride to tyranny, continuing the line that begins with Tarquin the Proud."[29]

In addition to the ontological and ethical points of view, there is a third perspective from which to understand *humanitas*: we might call it the public, 'official' or hierarchical value of *humanitas*, to which we shall return later. This aspect of *humanitas* too can be grasped in the opening sections of the *Panegyricus. Pan.* 4.6 reads: *At principi nostro quanta concordia quantusque concentus omnium laudum omnisque gloriae contigit! Vt nihil seueritati eius hilaritate, nihil grauitati simplicitate, nihil maiestati humanitate detrahitur!* ("Contrast our prince, in whose person all the merits which win our admiration are found in complete and happy harmony! His essential seriousness and authority lose nothing through his candour and good humour; he can show *humanitas* but remain a sovereign power", trans. Radice 1975). So the contrast is now between *humanitas* and *maiestas*. Like *diuinitas* and *superbia*, *maiestas* too, at least originally, was linked to gods and religion in general, and essentially referred to the superiority of the gods over mortals.[30] Yet ever since the Republican age *maiestas* also evoked superiority in general, whether it was physical, social or political – in this sense, the root of *maior* is the determinant.[31] It usually characterised the Romans – their magistrates and generals in particular – and the superiority of the Romans over all other peoples.[32] Consequently, the charge of *maiestas* generally referred to vio-

---

27 Cf. above, pp. 44–45.

28 On the implicit comparison between Trajan's *humanitas* and Domitian's *diuinitas* (and *maiestas*) cf. also Hiltbrunner 1994a, 733, although discussion here is very concise.

29 Baraz 2020, 261–262. More generally on the relationship between *humanitas* and *superbia* cf. above, pp. 44–45.

30 Cf. Hellegouarc'h 1963, 315 n. 6 and 7 for a list of the occurrences; Drexler 1956, 196. More in detail d'Aloja 2011, 16–27.

31 Cf. Hellegouarc'h 1963, 314–315; d'Aloja 2011, 240.

32 Cf. Drexler 1956, 196; Hellegouarc'h 1963, 317–318.

lation of the Roman magistrates' authority.[33] As we have already seen, in Livy 29.9.6, Pleminius, Scipio's hated legatus of Locris, is said to be beaten by the Locrians *sine respectu non maiestatis modo sed etiam humanitatis*, where we notice the contrast between Pleminius' official role of representative of the *maiestas populi Romani* and, despite all his faults, his nature and rights as a human being (*humanitas*).[34] Applied to the case of Trajan, *maiestas*, which we have seen to be one of the most frequently mentioned values in the *Panegyricus*, thus refers to that superior political power which every emperor possesses[35] – and yet Trajan is such a great emperor that he does not need to worry that his *maiestas* might be diminished by his *humanitas*.

The richness of these first paragraphs of the *Panegyricus* requires some summary here. Despite Roche's data, we have only reached paragraph 4 of the *Panegyricus* and Pliny has already mentioned Trajan's *humanitas* three times, one of which at the very beginning of the long list of the emperor's virtues that we read at 3.4, a paragraph whose centrality has already been shown. In addition, Pliny has so far opposed *humanitas* to three concepts which belong to three different spheres: ontological (*diuinitas*), ethical (*superbia*) and political (*maiestas*). Needless to say, this implies that *humanitas* too, thanks to its polysemy, can belong (at the very least) to these three spheres. But it is also worth stressing that, while the first two comparisons are presented by Pliny as antithetical so that the presence of one element excludes the other (so either we have *diuinitas* or *humanitas*, either *superbia* or *humanitas*), *humanitas* and *maiestas* seem instead to be allowed to coexist.[36] If we wanted to look for a rational explanation, we might perhaps conjecture that this difference is due to the fact that in Pliny's view ontology and ethics are not used to accepting compromise, while politics is all about compromise. Accordingly, the best ruler is he who is able to maintain all his social and political prerogatives without showing haughtiness and making the people feel his superiority; or he who has received supreme power from the gods but does not forget the most important value of all, *humanitas*; or else, to borrow Pliny's own words, the best ruler is one who can mix two utterly different things, *securitatem olim imperantis et incipientis pudorem* (24.1: "a beginner's modesty and the

---

33 Cf. Drexler 1956; Hellegouarc'h 1963, 319.

34 On this Livian occurrence of *humanitas* with reference to Pleminius cf. Della Calce/Mollea 2022, and above, p. 65.

35 As d'Aloja 2011, 151; 246–247 remarks, in the imperial age *maiestas* almost becomes a prerogative of the emperor.

36 On the coexistence of *humanitas* and *maiestas* at *Pan.* 4.6 cf. also d'Aloja 2011, 165. On the importance of anthithesis to highlight Trajan's virtues in the *Panegyricus* cf. S. Braund 2012², 96; Feldherr 2019, 392–394 and, above all, Rees 2001.

assurance of one long accustomed to command", trans. Radice 1975). Such a goal can also be achieved through facial expression: *manet imperatori quae prius oris humanitas* (24.2: "your lips keep their old *humanitas* now you are emperor", trans. Radice 1975). Interestingly, this suggests that *humanitas* can be perceived visually: although we shall look at this aspect in more detail when focusing on the *Epistulae*, we shall also find this same idea in the last occurrence of *humanitas* in the *Panegyricus* (71.5).[37] For the moment, it is sufficient to stress that in attributing this good balance of imperial and human characteristics to Trajan, we can assume that Pliny was also urging the emperor to continue to behave in this manner.

There is, however, a fourth aspect of *humanitas*, which underlies and facilitates its ethical and political features: Pliny introduces this educational component at 47.3, that is, in the middle of his panegyric, while lauding Trajan's restoration of the liberal arts: *An quisquam studia humanitatis professus non cum omnia tua tum uel in primis laudibus ferat admissionum tuarum facilitatem?* ("Every lover of culture (*studia humanitatis*) must applaud all your actions, while reserving his highest praise for your readiness to give audiences", trans. Radice 1975). With the phrase *studia humanitatis* Pliny really proves to be Ciceronian.[38] No one else before him resorted to such an expression, except Cicero. As we have seen, particularly significant for the history of the term *humanitas* and its success in Renaissance humanism is the instance in his *Pro Archia* 3, but its first appearance is to be found in *Pro Murena* 61 (63 BCE).[39] *Studia humanitatis* evidently refers to culture, liberal studies, education, and therefore evokes the Greek idea of παιδεία.[40] Granted, as a man of letters Pliny has personal interests in the emperor's fostering of the liberal arts, but, as with Cicero, it would be a mistake to assume that the *studia humanitatis* are to be seen as an end in themselves. Rather, they represent a point of departure on which to build a civilized society which is worthy of this name, that is to say, a society which is governed by sound political and ethical principles – and these principles too, as we have seen, can be expressed through the term *humanitas*. By contrast, the preceding era, that is to say, that of Domitian, was characterised by *immanitas*, which alongside *superbia* and *inhumanitas*, stands in opposition to *humanitas*. In fact, what immediately precedes 47.3 reads:

---

37 On *Pan.* 71.5 cf. below, pp. 93–95.
38 On Pliny's Ciceronianism see R. Gibson/Morello 2012, 296–297 with further bibliography. According to Méthy 2007, 295: "l'influence de Cicéron sur la pratique littéraire de Pline, reconnue et revendiquée comme telle, n'est plus à démontrer."
39 For the relevant bibliography cf. above, pp. 57; 61.
40 More in detail on the expression *studia humanitatis* above, p. 57.

Quid uitam? Quid mores iuuentutis? Quam principaliter formas! Quem honorem dicendi magistris, quam dignationem sapientiae doctoribus habes! Vt sub te spiritum et sanguinem et patriam receperunt studia! Quae priorum temporum immanitas exsiliis puniebat, quum sibi uitiorum omnium conscius princeps inimicas uitiis artes non odio magis, quam reuerentia, relegaret. At tu easdem artes in complexu, oculis, auribus habes. Praestas enim, quaecunque praecipiunt, tantumque eas diligis, quantum ab illis probaris. (*Pan.* 47.1–2)

As for the lives and characters of the young – how you are forming them in true princely fashion! And the teachers of rhetoric and professors of philosophy – how you hold them in honour! Under you the liberal arts are restored, to breathe and live in their own country – the learning which the barbarity of the past punished with exile, when an emperor acquainted with all the vices sought to banish everything hostile to vice, motivated less by hatred for learning as by fear for its authority. But you embrace these very arts, opening arms, eyes and ears to them, a living example of their precepts, as much their lover as the subject of their regard. (trans. Radice 1975)

That in this passage Trajan is (more or less tacitly) compared to Domitian seems obvious and has already been noticed.[41] Other Plinian as well as Tacitean passages support this view.[42] *Immanitas* too plays a role in this respect, as in *Ep.* 4.11.6 *immanitate tyranni* is explicitly referred to Domitian and no doubt the referent does not change in the case of *immanissima belua* of *Pan.* 48.3.[43] Nor is *Pan.* 47 the only time when *humanitas* is opposed to *immanitas*. The most relevant precedent is represented by a passage in Cicero's *De officiis* which deals, needless to say, with tyranny. Speaking of Phalaris, tyrant of Akragas, today's Agrigento, in Sicily, Cicero says:

Nam quod ad Phalarim attinet, perfacile iudicium est. Nulla est enim societas nobis cum tyrannis et potius summa distractio est, neque est contra naturam spoliare eum, si possis, quem est honestum necare, atque hoc omne genus pestiferum atque impium ex hominum communitate exterminandum est. Etenim, ut membra quaedam amputantur, si et ipsa sanguine et tamquam spiritu carere coeperunt et nocent reliquis partibus corporis, sic ista in figura hominis feritas et immanitas beluae a communi tamquam humanitatis corpore segreganda est. (Cic. *Off.* 3.32)

Now it is very easy to make a judgement in the case of Phalaris. For there can be no fellowship between us and tyrants – on the contrary there is a complete estrangement – and it is not contrary to nature to rob a man, if you are able, to whom it is honourable to kill. Indeed, the whole pestilential and irreverent class ought to be expelled from the community of mankind. For just as some limbs are amputated, if they begin to lose their blood and their life, as it were, and are harming the other parts of the body, similarly if the wildness and mon-

---

41 Cf. Whitton 2019, 364.
42 Cf. Whitton 2019, 364 n. 151.
43 On *immanissima belua* and the Ciceronian ring of this image, used with reference to Verres and Mark Antony for instance, cf. Blair 2019, 433–434.

strousness of a beast appears in human form, it must be removed from the common humanity, so to speak, of the body. (trans. Atkins 1991)

Alongside Cicero's *De republica* 2.48, we find here one of the first passages in
Latin literature where beasts' wildness (*feritas et immanitas beluae*) is synonymous with human barbarity (*in figura hominis*) in opposition to civilization (*humanitatis corpore*).[44] And given the importance and success of Cicero's *De officiis*,
it will not be too far off to think that Pliny the Younger had this passage in mind
when identifying the tyrant Domitian with *immanitas* and Trajan with *humanitas*.
But what is the exact meaning of *immanitas*? *Immanitas* derives from the adjective *immanis*, which is in turn the negative form of *manis / manus*, meaning
bonus.[45] This means that there is no etymological relationship whatsoever between *humanitas* and *immanitas*, and their being counterposed is probably due
to two reasons: first, they sound similar; second, the former has a positive, the
latter a negative meaning. In other words, they give birth to a paronomasia, a figure of speech Cicero seems to like, as we have already seen in the closure of his
Pro Archia.[46]

Returning to Pliny's *Panegyricus*, it is worth stressing that, despite the different nuances we have already noticed *humanitas* takes on therein, its polisemy
has not been fully exploited yet, for in this work this concept also has a 'social'
aspect. Just after praising Trajan's care for intellectuals, Pliny turns to the emper-
or's behaviour during banquets (which have always offered intellectuals occasions to meet and discuss literary issues after all). In this context, Trajan is said
always to be very kind to his fellow diners:

> Num autem serias tantum partes dierum in oculis nostris coetuque consumis? Non remissio-
> nibus tuis eadem frequentia eademque illa socialitas interest? Non tibi semper in medio
> cibus semperque mensa communis? Non ex conuictu nostro mutua uoluptas? Non prouocas
> reddisque sermones? Non ipsum tempus epularum tuarum, cum frugalitas contrahat, exten-
> dit humanitas? (*Pan.* 49.4–5)

---

44 On Cicero's *Rep.* 2.48 cf. Della Calce/Mollea 2023. Following Muretus and some *codices recentiores*, I read *humanitatis corpore* instead of *humanitate corporis*. Despite printing the latter *lectio*, in his OCT edition Winterbottom 1994, 121 glossed Muretus' choice with the words *fort(asse)
recte* and also Dyck 1996, 535 endorses it. I take it that *humanitatis corpus* refers to the whole
civilized society, from which uncivilized elements should be removed. On the opposition *humanitas / immanitas* cf. also *Off.* 1.62.
45 Cf. Macr. *Sat.* 1.3.13: "*Lanuuini mane pro bono dicunt*", with Ernout/Meillet 2001[4], 384; De Vaan
2008, 364.
46 Cf. above, pp. 59–60.

> Nor is it only the working hours of your day which you spend in our midst for all to see; your leisure hours are marked by the same numbers and friendliness. Your meals are always taken in public and your table open to all, the repast and its pleasures are there for us to share, while you encourage our conversation and join in it. As for the length of your banquet, polite manners (*humanitas*) prolong what frugality cut short. (trans. Radice 1975)

Here the emperor's *humanitas* balances out his *frugalitas* (roughly 'sober habits', 'frugality'), thus prolonging the banquet. This implicit comparison further stresses the importance of *humanitas* if we remember that at the beginning of this panegyric Pliny also considered *frugalitas* to be one of the virtues a good ruler should possess.[47] 'Polite manners', 'courtesy', 'kindness' are of course acceptable translations, but – as is often the case when dealing with the term *humanitas* – none of them are very telling about what *humanitas* implies. Also, they may suggest that the emperor was only worried about appearing (rather than being) kind and polite. To some extent this might be true. Yet if we think *humanitas* in terms of φιλανθρωπία, we cannot rule out the hypothesis that Trajan really felt the need to spend time among his friends.[48] In other words, not only do Trajan's fellow diners benefit from his *humanitas*, but the emperor himself benefits from his own *humanitas*. As Susanna Braund has persuasively showed in fact, his sociable attitude towards feasting is another aspect of his being a good ruler, who "advertises his *humanitas* by his communality and especially by his commensality" while "[i]solation and inaccessibility [also during banquets] are classic marks of the 'bad' ruler."[49] The (implicit) contrast with Domitian, who was not accessible, is again significant:[50] fortunately, the times when Statius had the feeling of dining in the presence of Jupiter when at Domitian's table now seem distant.[51]

In the wake of this (implied) contrast with Domitian as well as of the opposition between *humanitas* and *superbia* at 3.4, the final occurrence of *humanitas* in the *Panegyricus* reiterates and strengthens the idea that Trajan must also be praised for not looking down on his people, despite having the opportunity to do so. *Pan.* 71.4–6 could not be a more peremptory confirmation of this:

---

47 Cf. *Pan.* 3.4 above. *Frugalitas* is here opposed to *luxuria*. The comparison between *Pan.* 3.4 and 49.6 seems to confirm that Maguinness 2012[2], 269 is right in claiming that *frugalitas* and *humanitas* are not incompatible and thus Pliny is not contradicting himself at 49.6. We will meet the theme of *humanitas* during banquets as a virtue of the good ruler again during this study: cf. below, pp. 188–189.

48 On the importance for an emperor of having good friends cf. *Pan.* 85.

49 S. Braund 1996, 51 and 45.

50 Cf. S. Braund 1996, 44: "One of the most striking things about this passage [*scil. Pan.* 49.4–6] is that Pliny articulates his praise of Trajan through contrast with Domitian, unnamed but unmistakable."

51 Cf. *Silu.* 4.2.10–12 and B. Gibson 2011, 121–122. Cf. also Juvenal's *Satire* 4.

Nam, cui nihil ad augendum fastigium superest, hic uno modo crescere potest, si se ipse summittat securus magnitudinis suae. Neque enim ab ullo periculo fortuna principum longius abest quam humilitatis. Mihi quidem non tam humanitas tua quam intentio eius admirabilis uidebatur. Quippe, cum orationi oculos, uocem, manum commodares, ut si alii eadem ista mandasses, omnes comitatis numeros obibas.

For when a man can improve no more on his supreme position, the only way he can rise still higher is by stepping down, confident in his greatness. (There is nothing the fortune of princes has less to fear than the risk of being brought too low.) For me, even your *humanitas* seemed less remarkable than your anxiety to make it felt. In adapting your expression, your voice and gestures to your words, as if this was some commission you had to entrust to another, you ran through the whole gamut of politeness. (trans. Radice 1975)

Trajan's *humanitas* is not considered as admirable (*admirabilis*) as his anxiety to make it felt. This suggests that for an emperor, as well as for other statesmen, the emphasis is not only on possessing *humanitas*, but also on flaunting it – and this is another good thing about Trajan according to Pliny. Evidently, attention to the emperor's body language (*oculos uocem manum*), which we have already noticed at 24.2, reveals Pliny's interest in, and practice of, oratory and poetry, as we will see the *Epistulae* show in greater detail.[52]

In this passage *humanitas* is rendered by 'courtesy' in Radice's original translation, but the sense of the sentence is more probably that Pliny appreciates Trajan's attempt to be seen as a humble man more than his simple lack of haughtiness. The emperor is thus praised not only because he does not show haughtiness, but also because he attempts to reach the common man's level.[53] In this sense, the fact that here the discussion of *humanitas* comes right after a sentence centred on *humilitas* is of particular interest. Unlike *humanitas*, whose derivation from the root of *humus* is indirect, *humilitas* derives directly from *humus*.[54] Yet despite this etymological relationship, their meanings are at opposite poles: while *humanitas* tends always to be positive, *humilitas* is generally negative, mainly standing for 'insignificance', 'unimportance', 'lowness of rank', 'degradation'.[55] This applies not only to Latin authors in general, but also to Pliny in particular. Of the other two instances of *humilitas*, one refers to the degradation of the senate when heaping excessive praise on the ex-slave Pallas (*Ep.* 8.6.15), the other to those bad emperors who are only able to win over their people's love by displaying humility or submissiveness

---

52 Cf. above, p. 90. The part of the sentence from *Quippe, cum orationi* to *mandasses* has raised some doubts among scholars: See the relevant discussion in B. Gibson 2019, 258–260.
53 Cf. Cova 1978, 108–109; Wallace-Hadrill 1982, 42–43; S. Braund 2012[2], 93.
54 On the etymology of *humanitas* cf. above, pp. 22; 45.
55 Cf. the entry on *humilitas* in the *OLD* and *TLL* 6.3.3115.80–3118.20.

(*Pan.* 4.5).[56] Therefore, in view of this implicit comparison with *humilitas* at *Pan.* 71.5, it looks as though *humanitas* can also be regarded as the right compromise between the high extremes *superbia* and *diuinitas* on the one hand, and the low extreme *humilitas* on the other.

To summarise, the general image we get from Pliny's use of *humanitas* in the *Panegyricus* is that of a balanced value which has its roots in education and culture. However, following Cicero, Pliny does not consider education as an end in itself. The emperor needs to be a learned man, but, whatever the level of learning he can reach, that would be useless if it did not give rise to those ethical and then political sentiments which prevent him from being haughty and considering himself like a god. After all, Domitian was probably more learned than his successor, but he stopped at the first step, without understanding that learning was merely a precondition.[57] When opposing Trajan's *humanitas* to *diuinitas* and *superbia*, Pliny was therefore probably alluding to Domitian, and at the same time he was also telling the new emperor that in following *humanitas* he would avoid the main vices of his predecessor. As S. Braund has suggested, *humanitas* is therefore to be regarded (also) as the common denominator between praise and protreptic.[58]

Yet Pliny was very accurate in choosing *humanitas*. Being well aware that, under a good emperor, the Roman intelligentsia would have the chance to reacquire power and contribute to the rebuilding of society, he must have regarded *humanitas* as a possible *trait d'union* between Trajan and his court. After all, the good thing about *humanitas* is that it is not, by definition as it were, a prerogative of any social class in particular, unlike *clementia* for example, which we have seen was instead possessed only by those people who had a superior power. All this, along with further nuances of *humanitas*, emerges well from Pliny's *Epistulae*, to which we now turn.

3.1.2 The *Letters*

In the ten books of his *Epistulae*, presumably written between 96 CE (or 97/98) and 113 CE, that is to say mainly if not exclusively under the reign of Trajan, we can

---

56 Also worth noting in the case of *Pan.* 4.5 is the fact that some *codices recentiores* wrongly read *humanitate* instead of *humilitate* (*reuerentiam ille terrore, alius amorem humilitate captauit*).
57 Cf. Coleman 1990, 19: "the tyrant Domitian, an author himself, had actively sponsored literary creativity, whereas Trajan, *optimus princeps*, seems to have been the least literary of emperors."
58 S. Braund 2012², 98.

count 14 instances of the term *humanitas*.[59] Along the established lines of under-standing *humanitas* as either φιλανθρωπία or παιδεία, Méthy claims that in most cases the idea of φιλανθρωπία seems to be prominent.[60] Even though the same can hold true to some extent with regard to the *Panegyricus*, we have seen that it would be simplistic to reduce Pliny's use of *humanitas* there just to this idea. By the same token, it would be rash to take that for granted in the *Epistulae*, which on the contrary display further nuances, if not meanings, that the word can take on according to Pliny.[61] For the sake of continuity, let us begin with those letters in which *humanitas*, like in the *Panegyricus*, has to do with the role of the emperor.

If one recalls the 'social' aspect of *humanitas* I mentioned with regard to *Pan.* 49.4–5, where this value urges the emperor to prolong the banquets, *Ep.* 6.31.14 seems to lead to the climax of this aspect.[62] Indeed, here Trajan's *humanitas* even takes the shape of generosity in giving gifts to his guests when they leave: *Summo die abeuntibus nobis (tam diligens in Caesare humanitas) xenia sunt missa* ("On the final day as we departed we were sent guest-presents; such is the solicitous *humanitas* shown by the emperor", trans. Walsh 2006). This letter, which Pliny wrote to an otherwise unknown Cornelianus in 107 CE after Trajan's return from Dacia, seems therefore to confirm both that Pliny had been sincere in praising the emperor's kindness at *Pan.* 49.4–5 and that Trajan maintained the same kind attitude during banquets throughout the entire course of his reign.[63]

But it is also towards his soldiers that Trajan seems to be particularly keen on showing his *humanitas*.[64] This is what we learn from *Ep.* 10.106, which is suffi-ciently short to quote in full:

> Rogatus, domine, a P. Accio Aquila, centurione cohortis sextae equestris, ut mitterem tibi libellum per quem indulgentiam pro statu filiae suae implorat, durum putaui negare, cum scirem quantam soleres militum precibus patientiam humanitatemque praestare.

---

59 On the chronology of the letters cf. Sherwin-White 1966, 20–41; 62–65; 529–532; Marchesi 2008, 12 and n. 1, and, above all, Bodel 2015, 42–108, who provides a useful overview of the different chronologies proposed by previous scholars.

60 Méthy 2007, 250.

61 In this sense, Malaspina 2019, 137 looks far more careful: "toutefois, il [scil. Pline] suit les posi-tions de Cicéron et, dans son *temperamentum*, il ne propose pas de classifications rigides entre l'*humanitas* comme culture et l'*humanitas* comme humanité."

62 Cf. Bütler 1970, 117, who already links the occurrence of *humanitas* at *Ep.* 6.31.14 to that of *Pan.* 49.4–5; Whitton 2019, 355–356.

63 On the date of this letter as well as on the problem of identifying Cornelianus cf. Sherwin-White 1966, 391.

64 Cf. Méthy 2007, 269.

> When I was asked, my lord, by P. Accius Aquila, a centurion in the sixth mounted cohort, to send to you a petition through which he begs your generosity on behalf of the status of his daughter, I thought it harsh to refuse, since I was aware how much forbearance and *humanitas* you regularly show to the pleas of soldiers. (trans. Walsh 2006)

Publius Accius Aquila – the *tria nomina* immediately reveal that he was a Roman citizen – had probably married a *peregrina* (foreign woman), which explains why his daughter lacked Roman citizenship. Given that this letter is addressed to the emperor, its flattering tone is to be expected and it reminds us of the tone of the *Panegyricus*. In acknowledging the emperor's *humanitas* and *patientia*, which are here juxtaposed for the first time in Latin literature, Pliny actually urges him to put such virtues into practice. Indeed *patientia*, presumably to be understood as tolerance, patience on this occasion, is not necessarily a virtue. However, I postpone this discussion to the section on Apuleius' *Apologia*, for *patientia* plays a more significant role in that context.[65] For the time being, it is enough to say that Trajan's positive response (10.107: *cuius* [scil. *Aquilae*] *precibus motus dedi filiae eius ciuitatem Romanam*, "In response to his pleas, I have granted Roman citizenship to his daughter", trans. Walsh 2006) confirms that he does possess *humanitas* and *patientia*, at least in this situation.

So much for *humanitas* with regard to Trajan. However, as I hinted at before, the success of this value-term in Pliny's view seems to be due, among other aspects, to its transcending certain distinction of social class, and, in particular, to its being shared by the emperor and the upper classes of Rome. Like the emperor, also the members of his entourage could – and often did – hold posts which involved the direct exercise of political power, especially abroad. *Humanitas* was one of the virtues they had to display.[66] According to Pliny, Calestrius Tiro did so at the time of his proconsulship of Baetica:

> Egregie facis (inquiro enim) et perseuera, quod iustitiam tuam prouincialibus multa humanitate commendas; cuius praecipua pars est honestissimum quemque complecti atque ita a minoribus amari, ut simul a principibus diligare. Plerique autem dum uerentur ne gratiae potentium nimium impertire uideantur, sinisteritatis atque etiam malignitatis famam consequuntur. (*Ep.* 9.5.1–2)[67]

> You are doing splendid work (for I am taking soundings). Carry on the good work in administering your justice to the provincials in that most civilized way (*multa humanitate*). One principal branch of which virtue is to distinguish merit in every degree: this wins you the

---

65 Cf. below, pp. 140–141.
66 Cf. Wallace-Hadrill 1982, 42: "In the exercise of power, it was provincial government that especially called on qualities like *comitas, facilitas* and *humanitas*."
67 This letter probably dates to 107–108 CE: cf. Sherwin-White 1966, 484.

affection of the lesser citizens, and at the same time the regard of the leading men. Many people, in their fear that they may bestow too many favours on the powerful, gain a reputation for bad manners and even ill-will. (trans. Walsh 2006, adapted)

This passage interestingly establishes a relation between *humanitas*, whose nuances here we have yet to delineate, and *iustitia*. In particular, to claim that justice should be administered with *humanitas* might lead to the conclusion that justice alone is not enough, a strong statement which would call for an explanation. Hellegouarc'h points out that in the *De officiis* Cicero went so far as to regard *iustitia* as the most important virtue, upon which Roman society as a whole was based.[68] So is Pliny somehow contradicting his beloved Cicero? This does not seem to be the case. To begin with, in a very short letter to Trajan (10.86b), Pliny himself recommends Fabius Valens to the emperor for his *iustitia* and *humanitas*, thus implying that there is no contrast between the two. But also Cicero juxtaposes *iustitia* and *humanitas* when listing the values which best fit the head judge (along with *fides* and *grauitas*) at *Pro Milone* 22. And the same holds true for Seneca (*Dial.* 4.28.2 and 9.10.6), although at *Ben.* 3.7.5 he counterposes the role of the judge (*iudex*), who has to judge according to laws, to that of the referee (*arbiter*), who can instead modify his verdict on the base of his *humanitas* or *misericordia* (*non prout lex aut iustitia suadet, sed prout humanitas aut misericordia inpulit*).[69] Yet not even this passage calls *iustitia* into question, for Seneca claims to prefer a judge over a referee in case of judicial inquiries. The figure of the referee appears however to be comparable to that of a provincial governor like Calestrius Tiro: while *iustitia* must set the guidelines, *humanitas* provides common sense, compassion and mental flexibility, all of which are important, if not fundamental, in the passage from legal theory to practice, that is to say, from the theoretical conception of justice to its application in contexts where different human beings belonging to different social classes are involved. This is the reason why Pliny says that this *humanitas* mainly consists in becoming the friend of every honest man, from those of humble extraction (*minores*) to the nobles (*principes*). As we saw in the *Panegyricus*, *humanitas* often implies steering a path between opposites.

But there is a special circumstance in which *humanitas* really becomes a requisite for a provincial governor, namely when this magistrate is appointed as pro-

---

68 Hellegouarc'h 1963, 266. Cf. Cic. *Off.* 3.28 and 1.20, with Benoist/Gangloff 2019, 21–22. On *Off.* 1.20 and its relationship with the idea of *aequitas*, which we shall see Symmachus for one linking to *humanitas*, cf. Vogt-Spira 2014, 52–54; Mantovani 2017, 51–53 and below, pp. 288–289.
69 Cf. also the relationship between *clementia* and *iustitia* in Seneca: above, p. 70. Much later, at *Diuinae Institutiones* 3.9.19, Lactantius will equate *humanitas*, *iustitia* and *pietas*, almost regarding the three as synonyms.

consul of Achaea. As we saw in the Introduction, Greece was regarded by the Romans as the birthplace of *humanitas*. In this respect, the importance of Pliny's letter to Maximus (*Ep.* 8.24.2) has already been pointed out, but it now merits further examination.[70] Let us recapitulate. A certain Maximus, about whom we do not know so much, is about to become the annual proconsul of Achaea. Pliny gives him some advice on how to best carry out his duties.[71] The exhortation begins as follows:

> Cogita te missum in prouinciam Achaiam, illam ueram et meram Graeciam, in qua primum humanitas litterae, etiam fruges inuentae esse creduntur; missum ad ordinandum statum liberarum ciuitatum, id est ad homines maxime homines, ad liberos maxime liberos, qui ius a natura datum uirtute meritis amicitia, foedere denique et religione tenuerunt.

> Bear in mind that you have been dispatched to the province of Achaia, which is the true and genuine Greece in which *humanitas*, literature, and agriculture too are believed to have been first invented. Remember that you have been sent to order the condition of free states, dispatched in other words to men who are men in the highest sense, to free citizens, free in the highest sense, who have maintained the rights which nature bestowed on them by virtue of their excellence, merits, political friendships, treaty, and finally religious devotion. (trans. Walsh 2006)

To begin with, in the list of the Greek 'inventions' *humanitas* comes first – and, as we will see shortly, it probably implies or includes the elements that Pliny mentions later in the paragraph. Given Pliny's philhellenism, which shines through frequently in his work and very much in this letter, the prominent position of a word which we have seen characterising the *optimus princeps* Trajan cannot pass unnoticed. On the contrary, we might argue that this value is seen as central to the emperor and Roman society for the very reason that it had been the founding value of Greek society, admiration for which Pliny discloses several times.[72]

Ciceronian model aside,[73] this letter seems to express a meaning of *humanitas* which is very close to that of Tacitus' *Agricola* 21, to which we will turn in the next section of this chapter. By saying *in qua* [scil. *Graecia*] *primum humanitas litterae, etiam fruges inuentae esse creduntur*, Pliny seems to imply that neither literature (*litterae*) nor agriculture (*fruges*) can be considered synonyms of or, in

---

70 Cf. above, p. 35.

71 On Maximus cf. Sherwin-White 1966, 477. The date of the letter cannot be established with certainty, but Sherwin-White 1966, 477 seems to exclude that it was written before 104–105 CE.

72 On Pliny's philhellenism in the *Epistulae* cf. Rees 2014, 109–112 (with further bibliography). By contrast, there is almost total lack of Greekness in the *Panegyricus*, presumably because Pliny tries to distance "his speech from the reputation for debased, hackneyed, extorted, insincere praise he could neatly align with the Greek associations of Flavian rhetoric" (Rees 2014, 122).

73 Cf. above, p. 35.

the case of *fruges* at least (*etiam* marks a hiatus between the first two elements and *fruges*), hyponyms of *humanitas*: these three elements appear as distinct.[74] The consequences for our understanding of the term are relevant. Most interpretations of this passage claim that here *humanitas* stands for 'civilization',[75] but who would not consider the birth of agriculture as a milestone in the process of civilization?[76] The myth of Prometheus and Epimetheus in Plato's *Protagoras* (322a) is clear evidence of this:[77]

Ἐπειδὴ δὲ ὁ ἄνθρωπος θείας μετέσχε μοίρας, πρῶτον μὲν διὰ τὴν τοῦ θεοῦ συγγένειαν ζῴων μόνον θεοὺς ἐνόμισεν, καὶ ἐπεχείρει βωμούς τε ἱδρύεσθαι καὶ ἀγάλματα θεῶν· ἔπειτα φωνὴν καὶ ὀνόματα ταχὺ διηρθρώσατο τῇ τέχνῃ, καὶ οἰκήσεις καὶ ἐσθῆτας καὶ ὑποδέσεις καὶ στρωμνὰς καὶ τὰς ἐκ γῆς τροφὰς ηὕρετο.

It is because humans had a share of the divine dispensation that they alone among animals worshipped the gods, with whom they had a kind of kinship, and erected altars and sacred images. It wasn't long before they were articulating speech and words and had invented houses, clothes, shoes, and blankets, and were nourished by food from the earth. (trans. Lombardo/Bell 1997)

Granted, *humanitas* seems at first glance to be conceived as something which is more related to *litterae*, maybe a sort of hypernym, and thus to cultural and educational aspects.[78] Or, to put it another way, it would seem that Pliny's interpretation of civilization exclusively rests on educational bases. Yet, as often with *humanitas*, it would probably be simplistic to reach such a conclusion. True, education (*litterae*) is there and can be the precondition, so to speak, but then Pliny lists other elements that may ultimately fall under the label 'civilization'. Pride of place goes to *libertas* (*liberarum ciuitatum, liberos maxime liberos*), which of

---

74 Following Merrill 1919, 375, Lefèvre 2009, 172 believes that in this passage *litterae* stands for 'letters of the alphabet', thus alluding to the myth of Palamedes. In this way, the allusion to the myth of Triptolemos through the alleged invention of agriculture (*fruges*) would be counterbalanced. Of course this interpretation is possible, but on the one hand the third item, *humanitas*, would still lack any clear reference to another myth; on the other, the letters of the alphabet would simply represent the first stage of literature.
75 Cf. Bolisani 1961–62, 63.
76 On agriculture as a fundamental element in the process of civilization cf. in particular Edelstein 1967, 44; Müller 2003, *passim*.
77 On this myth, its variations and its relationship to the notion of civilization cf. at least Edelstein 1967, 21–24, 86. More generally on ancient myths of civilization cf. Zago 2012, with rich bibliography.
78 Cf. Cova 1972, 33; 1978, 111.

course took on different nuances in the idealised Athens and in Trajanic Rome,[79] but also law (*ius*), virtue (*uirtus*), friendship (*amicitia*), treaties (*foedera*) and religion (*religio*) are mentioned. In other words, we might perhaps say that here *humanitas* is not only the presupposition, but also the theoretical and abstract ideal, whose explanation, but also materialisation, is illustrated by the aforementioned elements, which in the end involve relationships either among men or between men and gods. Since Greece was the first to understand the importance of this multifaceted concept, it follows that it deserves admiration and has the right to be treated accordingly by any man who exercises power there. This is the message that Pliny seems to convey to Maximus, the same message that Cicero had conveyed to his brother Quintus.[80]

After all, governors, politicians, public officials and the like must not let power go to their heads, irrespective of the post they hold and where they exercise it. The case of Claudius Pollio makes this clear. *Ep.* 7.31.3 is a letter of recommendation (*commendaticia*) in which Pliny asks his friend Cornutus Tertullus, *curator Aemiliae* when the letter was written, to accept Pollio's friendship.[81] To this end, Pliny praises Pollio for preserving intact his reputation for *humanitas* despite holding various posts: *numquam officiorum uarietate continuam laudem humanitatis infregit* ("never in the wide range of his offices he breached his unbroken reputation for *humanitas*", trans. Walsh 2006).[82]

It will not have passed unnoticed that the cases of Calestrius Tiro, Pollio and partly Maximus all remind us of what I have defined earlier as the 'official' aspect of *humanitas*. Like the emperor, his magistrates too need to be humane in exercising their power; and like the emperor, they too can rely on the 'educational' aspect of *humanitas* to enhance their humaneness. At times, this aspect can even emerge in an extraordinary manner, as is the case with Arrius Antoninus, one of the most influential men under Nerva's reign.[83] Pliny seems to appreciate his literary talent even more than his public career and, in particular, he exalts Antoninus' Greek epigrams and iambic mimes:

Quantum ibi humanitatis uenustatis, quam dulcia illa quam amantia quam arguta quam recta! Callimachum me uel Heroden, uel si quid his melius, tenere credebam; quorum

---

79 Cf. R. Gibson 2019, 461: "The freedom enjoyed by the Greeks of Achaea is a mere residue, the 'name and shadow' of *libertas*, and one that can easily be swapped for slavery."
80 On Cicero's letter to Quintus cf. above, pp. 34; 60.
81 Cf. Sherwin-White 1966, 440. The letter was presumably written after 100 CE.
82 Cf. Cova 1978, 113.
83 On Arrius Antoninus see Sherwin-White 1966, 267 with further bibliographical references; Méthy 2007, 169–171.

tamen neuter utrumque aut absoluit aut attigit. Hominemne Romanum tam Graece loqui? Non medius fidius ipsas Athenas tam Atticas dixerim. (*Ep.* 4.3.4–5)

What *humanitas*, what charm they embody, how agreeable and affecting they are! What clarity, what propriety lie in them! I thought that I was handling Callimachus or Herodas, or such as is better than these – yet neither of these poets wrote, or sought to write, poetry in both genres. To think that a Roman can be so at home in Greek! I could swear that Athens herself could not be so Attic! (trans. Walsh 2006)

For the first time in the Latin texts which have come down to us, *humanitas* is paired with *uenustas* (charm), and in this context they seem to be two sides of the same coin. Bearing in mind that these two concepts are employed with regard to 'Callimachean' poems, it looks as though the latter points to the outward appearance of these poems, that is, to their beauty, their rhythm or grace, while the former alludes to what facilitates it, that is, to the author's education and culture which emerge there.[84] Therefore, what are two – perhaps *the* two – cornerstones of Hellenistic and Callimachean poetics, namely erudition and stylistic sophistication, seem to be mirrored in *humanitas* and *uenustas* respectively.[85]

Moreover (and importantly), like *Ep.* 8.24.2, this letter draws a link between *humanitas* and Greek culture. If, as I have argued, Pliny's broadest idea of *humanitas* as civilization in the letter to Maximus rests mainly, though by no means exclusively, on literature and culture (*litterae*), it is thanks to this 'Greek' *humanitas* that Antoninus is so learned that he is able to write in Greek better than the most erudite Greek poets (at least according to Pliny). After all, if the Greek idea of civilization is to be taken as the model *par excellence*, so are its components, first and foremost literature. Compare Hoffer, with reference to Pliny's thought: "It is no shame for Romans to be imitators of the great cultural tradition of their conquered Greek subjects if they know and use Greek as well as, or better than, the Greeks."[86]

---

84 Cf. also Rieks 1967, 238; Bütler 1970, 109; Méthy 2007, 251. *Venustas* is also attributed to the poems of Sentius Augurinus at *Ep.* 4.27.1 and of Vergilius Romanus at 6.21.4. Roller 1998, 286 rightly considers it to be typical of Catullan (and thus Callimachean) poetry.
85 In *Ep.* 7.9 Pliny himself explains why writing these short, low poems (*lusus*) can be beneficial. Because of the strict norms writing poems requires, this exercise will also improve prose style, which is fundamental to any publicly engaged man. And since short poems do not take up too much time, they can be written during the very few moments of idleness (*otium*) a busy man can have. Cf. Hershkowitz 1995, 169–171; Gamberini 1983, 89 and 99; Roller 1998, *passim* – 282–283 on *Ep.* 4.3. For a wider discussion of Pliny's attitude towards poetry cf. Gamberini 1983, 82–121; Roller 1998; Marchesi 2008, 53–96; Janka 2015. Needless to say, Pliny was not the only one to link poetry to oratory, so to speak: further discussion in Fantham 1982, 259–261; Hershkowitz 1995, 171–173; Cavarzere 2011, *passim*, with rich bibliography.
86 Hoffer 1999, 38. Cf. also Swain 2004, 9.

This same poetic atmosphere permeates *Ep.* 5.3. Here Pliny writes to the lawyer Titius Aristo about his own poems. In what might be considered as a sort of apology for his poetic activity, Pliny lists several great Roman men of the past who combined public life with literary endeavour. At some point (5.3.9–10), Pliny stresses the importance of public readings, which give the author a chance to benefit from the audience's judgement: *Multa etiam a multis admonetur, et si non admoneatur, quid quisque sentiat perspicit ex uultu oculis nutu manu murmure silentio; quae satis apertis notis iudicium ab humanitate discernunt* ("Further, he receives numerous suggestions from numerous people, and even if he does not, he observes the reactions of individuals from their facial expressions, eyes, nods, applause, murmurs, and silences, for these offer sufficiently clear indications of the difference between their judgements and their *humanitas*", trans. Walsh 2006). When applied to arts, *iudicium* is that taste which becomes the faculty of judging the quality of a work or performance, and then the judgement itself.[87] The assumption here is that the audience's *humanitas* mitigates a judgement that would probably be negative – or at least this is what Pliny's modesty seems to suggest.[88] The verb *discerno*, which 'divides into two parts' (*in duas partes diuidit*) according to Isidore of Seville's authoritative formulation, leaves little room for doubts in creating this conceptual opposition.[89] *Humanitas* is therefore to be seen as a positive attitude toward a fellow poet whose (low-level?) works deserve sympathy rather than criticism.[90] The Greek idea of φιλανθρωπία comes to mind, but it is tempting to say that this is also a consequence of being well-educated, as Pliny's audience for sure was.

The most interesting thing about this passage is, however, represented by that which permits us to distinguish frank judgement from friendly benevolence: in a nutshell, body language. We have already noticed in the *Panegyricus* that *humanitas* can be physically perceived, but never in Latin literature before *Ep.* 5.3.9–10 are all these physical elements and gestures asyndetically listed together: *uultu oculis nutu manu murmure silentio.*

As in the *Panegyricus*, Pliny's attention towards bodily attitudes probably reveals the experience of an orator and statesman who is used to observing reactions of judges and audience during trials or public speeches, as well as to modifying his behaviour accordingly.[91] Analysing this issue in depth is beyond

---

87 Cf. *TLL* 7.2.615.76–616.27.
88 Cf. Rieks 1967, 229–230.
89 Cf. Isid. *Diff.* 1.151 and *TLL* 5.1.1296.12–1304.47. Cf. also Roller 1998, 294–295; Méthy 2007, 193–196; 254.
90 Cf. also Bolisani 1961–62, 62.
91 Cf. Gamberini 1983, 98.

the scope of this project, but a passage of the *Institutio oratoria* where Quintilian stresses the importance of gesture for an orator should be sufficient to make the argument clearer:

> Quid autem quisque in dicendo postulet locus paulum differam, ut de gestu prius dicam, qui et ipse uoci consentit et animo cum ea simul paret. Is quantum habeat in oratore momenti satis uel ex eo patet, quod pleraque etiam citra uerba significat. Quippe non manus solum sed nutus etiam declarant nostram uoluntatem, et in mutis pro sermone sunt, et saltatio frequenter sine uoce intellegitur atque adficit, et ex uultu ingressuque perspicitur habitus animorum, et animalium quoque sermone carentium ira, laetitia, adulatio et oculis et quibusdam aliis corporis signis deprenditur. Nec mirum si ista, quae tamen in aliquo posita sunt motu, tantum in animis ualent, cum pictura, tacens opus et habitus semper eiusdem, sic in intimos penetret adfectus ut ipsam uim dicendi nonnumquam superare uideatur. (11.3.65–67)

> I postpone for the moment, however, the question of what is required for particular oratorical contexts, in order to speak first of Gesture, which itself conforms to the voice and joins it in obeying the mind. The importance of Gesture for an orator is evident from the simple fact that it can often convey meaning even without the help of words. Not only hands but nods show our intentions; for the dumb, indeed, these take the place of language. A dance too is often understood and emotionally effective without the voice; mental attitudes can be inferred from the face of the walk; and even dumb animals reveal their anger, joy, or wish to please by their eyes or some other bodily signal. Nor is it surprising that these things, which do after all involve some movement, should have such power over the mind, when a picture, a silent work of art in an unvarying attitude, can penetrate our innermost feelings to such an extent that it seems sometimes to be more powerful than speech itself. (trans. Russell 2001)

Speaking of non-spoken language, here Quintilian explicitly connects oratorical gesture to painting (*pictura*) rather than to poetry, whereas at *Institutio oratoria* 1.11.3 he draws an explicit comparison between orator and comedian (*comoedus*).[92] And, as we have seen, in *Ep.* 7.9 Pliny himself admits that there is a relation between poetry and oratory.[93] Going back to the letter to Titius Aristo, the

---

92 Cf. also the Horatian maxim *ut pictura poesis* (*Ars P.* 361). On the importance of gesture in Quintilian and in Roman oratory cf. Fantham 1982; Dutsch 2002; Hall 2004; Nocchi 2013, 117–148. However, an important caveat is added by Cavarzere 2011, 222: "Il gesto, per Quintiliano e per la retorica antica, coopera sì alla strutturazione logica e ritmica del discorso, ma ne è quasi parassitario; perché altro non fa che tradurre visivamente la segmentazione presente nella catena parlata e che è piuttosto il frutto della *pronuntiatio* vocale, quale era già stata pianificata al momento dell'*inuentio*." Quintilian also believes that a comedian can be an excellent teacher for the future orator, especially at the beginning of his training: cf. Nocchi 2013, 135–137.
93 Cf. above, p. 102 n. 85.

importance that Pliny grants to body language in this case is that, unlike vocal language, it cannot deceive.[94]

To sum up, *Ep.* 4.3 and *Ep.* 5.3 show two different ways in which *humanitas* can be connected to poetry: in the first case it stands to characterise the erudition of the author which emerges from the poems, while in the second case it represents the benevolent attitude of the audience towards authors who do not live up to expectations. But both these circumstances refer to social contexts such as literary circles which must have played a key role in the everyday life of high society, offering either a form of entertainment or occasions to talk about politics or any other topic. Moreover, these letters suggest the pervasiveness of *humanitas* in Roman society, especially within its upper echelons.

Although he did not belong to the Roman political elite and although poetry was probably not among his main interests, no doubt also the Stoic philosopher Euphrates played a role in enlivening the cultural life of Rome, so much so that Pliny considered him as the living proof of the flourishing of the liberal arts in the empire: *Si quando urbs nostra liberalibus studiis floruit, nunc maxime floret. Multa claraque exempla sunt; sufficeret unum, Euphrates philosophus* (*Ep.* 1.10.1–2: "Liberal studies in this city of ours are flourishing as splendidly as ever before. There are many outstanding examples of this, but it would be enough to cite one, the philosopher Euphrates", trans. Walsh 2006).[95] In this letter, addressed to the otherwise unknown Attius Clemens, Pliny also describes his first meeting with Euphrates as follows: *Hunc ego in Syria, cum adulescentulus militarem, penitus et domi inspexi, amarique ab eo laboraui, etsi non erat laborandum. Est enim obuius et expositus plenusque humanitate, quam praecipit* (*Ep.* 1.10.2: "When I was serving in the army in Syria as a mere youth, I became closely acquainted with him – indeed, in his home. I worked hard to win his affection, though the effort was superfluous, for he is accessible and straightforward, and entirely practises the *humanitas* which he preaches", trans. Walsh 2006).[96] To win Euphrates' affection was thus anything but difficult, because he was easy (*obuius*) and frank (*expositus*), but also full of *humanitas*. But how to translate the term – kindness, courtesy, sympathy? *Humanitas* here can easily imply all of these ideas, but, as Rieks suggests, it is difficult to refrain from connecting it to the *liberalia studia* men-

---

94 Cf. also Roller 1998, 295. But this cannot be taken as a rule. On the contrary, Quintilian divides gestures into two types: natural ones and imitative ones (*Inst.* 11.3.88–89). He then remarks that gesture should be measured and in tune with the speech, otherwise its artificiality would be perceived (*Inst.* 11.3.89). On this issue cf. Nocchi 2013, 129–133.

95 More on the figure of Euphrates in Sherwin-White 1966, 108–109; Pausch 2004, 133–141.

96 Cf. Pausch 2004, 134: "ein zentraler Akzent in seiner [i.e. Pliny's] Charakterisierung des Euphrates darauf liegt, daß dieser sein Leben in Übereinstimmung mit seiner Lehre fuhrt."

tioned in the opening of the letter and the more general context, in which Euphrates' most praised talents derive from his superior education:[97]

> Quantum tamen mihi cernere datur, multa in Euphrate sic eminent et elucent, ut mediocriter quoque doctos aduertant et adficiant. Disputat subtiliter grauiter ornate, frequenter etiam Platonicam illam sublimitatem et latitudinem effingit. Sermo est copiosus et uarius, dulcis in primis, et qui repugnantes quoque ducat impellat. (*Ep.* 1.10.5)[98]

> However, to such insights as are granted to me the many qualities in Euphrates are so outstanding and crystal-clear that even moderately learned men are attracted and struck by them. In argument, he is precise, earnest, and elegant, and often he even achieves the grandeur and sweep of a Plato. In discussion he is fluent, wide-ranging, and particularly charming, the sort of person who can lead on and impress even those who confront him. (trans. Walsh 2006)

Rieks also claims that Euphrates emerges from Pliny's portrait of him as embodying that ideal Panaetian and thus Stoic humanity which shines through Cicero's *De officiis*, while on the contrary Bütler denies the influence of any particular philosophical strand of thought on Pliny's *humanitas*, not least in the case of Euphrates.[99] Irrespective of what position one takes on Pliny's attitude towards philosophy, it would seem quite counterproductive to attribute all the importance Pliny gives to *humanitas* to a sectarian ideal which would hardly meet with wide approval.[100] Accordingly, it is unsurprising that none of his occurrences of *humanitas* have a direct link with Stoicism or other philosophies, let alone in *Ep.* 1.10.2. At any rate, what is particularly relevant in this letter is that it makes it explicit that *humanitas* can be taught (*quam praecipit*). On the one hand, this seems to confirm the interpretation that *humanitas* can have educational implications even when it does not seem to at first sight. On the other hand, the potential to acquire this ideal (rather than being given it at birth) will have been one of the reasons why Pliny, in Cicero's footsteps, relied on it to promote the social and political 'renaissance' after Domitian's death.[101]

In the case of the senator Voconius Romanus, a well-educated friend of Pliny's, the connection between the notions of φιλανθρωπία and education is perhaps tighter.[102] In *Ep.* 8.8 Pliny describes the source of the Clitumnus, which em-

---

97 Rieks 1967, 240.
98 Cf. also Bolisani 1961–62, 63–64.
99 Rieks 1967, 240; Bütler 1970, 115–116.
100 On Pliny's relationship to philosophy cf. above all Malaspina 2019.
101 On Euphrates' *humanitas* cf. also Cova 1978, 112; Malaspina 2019, 137.
102 Pliny himself calls Romanus *doctissimus uir* in *Ep.* 3.13.5. On Romanus cf. Sherwin-White 1966, 93.

bodies the idea of the *locus amoenus*. At the very end of this letter (8.8.7), Pliny remarks that this wonderful place is not only a source of pleasure, but also offers the possibility of learning something:

> In summa nihil erit, ex quo non capias uoluptatem. Nam studebis quoque: leges multa multorum omnibus columnis omnibus parietibus inscripta, quibus fons ille deusque celebratur. Plura laudabis, non nulla ridebis; quamquam tu uero, quae tua humanitas, nulla ridebis.
>
> In short, there is no aspect which will not afford you pleasure. For you will also have things to study; you will read many inscriptions written by many hands on all the pillars and on all the walls, which hymn the waters and the god. Several of them you will praise, and a few will make you laugh. But such is your *humanitas* that you will not laugh at them. (trans. Walsh 2006)

Some of these inscriptions must have been funny – because of their content? Because of their bad style? We will never know. But again, as in *Ep.* 5.3 discussed above, people who possess *humanitas* do not make fun of other human beings.[103] Nor do they abandon themselves to joy with excess: it is true that they enjoy themselves (*capias uoluptatem*) while learning (*studebis*), but their *humanitas* seems to guarantee composure.[104] In sum, Romanus ought to visit this place because he could increase his *humanitas*-παιδεία by learning something new, but at the same time his *humanitas*-φιλανθρωπία, which is already the result of his education (i.e. of his *humanitas*-παιδεία), will prevent him from resorting to mockery.[105]

Ep. 8.22 probably represents the climax of this nuance of *humanitas*. Here Pliny discusses ethical matters with another senator, Rosianus Geminus; in particular, he provides a definition of what constitutes a truly good and faultless man (8.22.2): *Atque ego optimum et emendatissimum existimo, qui ceteris ita ignoscit, tamquam ipse cotidie peccet, ita peccatis abstinet tamquam nemini ignoscat* ("For my own part, I regard as best and most unblemished the character who is indulgent to the faults of others as if he were guilty of them day after day, yet eschews faults as though he would forgive none of them", trans. Walsh 2006).[106] When it comes to explaining what or who has provoked him to write on such themes, however, Pliny's response reads as follows (8.22.4):

> Nuper quidam — sed melius coram; quamquam ne tunc quidem. Vereor enim ne id quod improbo consectari carpere referre huic quod cum maxime praecipimus repugnet. Quisquis

---

103 Cf. Bolisani 1961–62, 63.
104 On the relation between pleasure and learning in this letter cf. Lefèvre 2009, 272.
105 On Pliny's *humanitas* in this letter cf. also Rieks 1967, 230–231; Bütler 1970, 115; Lefèvre 2009, 290.
106 Cf. Méthy 2007, 51; Lefèvre 2009, 289. On Geminus cf. Sherwin-White 1966, 402.

ille qualiscumque sileatur, quem insignire exempli nihil, non insignire humanitatis plurimum refert.

The other day a certain person – but I had better tell you of him face to face, or rather not even then; for I fear that my condemnation of such persecution, sniping, and judgement which I condemn may militate against the precept which I particularly lay down. So I must make no mention of the man's identity and his character, for to reveal him offers no useful lesson, and to refrain from exposing him is the greatest mark of *humanitas*. (trans. Walsh 2006)

The reason why he refrains from telling the name of the man he has in mind is by now evident, at least in terms of Pliny's *humanitas*: like his model Euphrates, he has learnt to attack vices, not individuals.[107] The viewpoint is clearly that of a (self-appointed) teacher of ethics who has a specific idea of his duty to provide good moral examples.[108] Whatever goes beyond this aim (*exempli nihil*), is of little use, or even counterproductive. On the contrary, showing respect, pity or sympathy towards every kind of man is an additional teaching, if not the main one, of Pliny's *humanitas*. We have already seen how this aspect of *humanitas* is central to the *Panegyricus* and to those *Epistulae* where there is a clear distinction of ranks between the person who possesses *humanitas*, that is the emperor, and those who benefit from his *humanitas*, namely the court and the Roman people as a whole. Likewise, other instances of *humanitas* in the *Epistulae* show this ideal at work among peers, thereby confirming the notion that there is no need for a downward relationship between the bestower of *humanitas* and its beneficiary: this is certainly the case in *Ep.* 5.3 and probably in *Ep.* 8.22 as well.

But there are also cases in which the person of higher rank showing *humanitas* is not the emperor. For example, *humanitas* can be shown by a lawyer towards a defendant whose case no one else would take on, as happens in *Ep.* 6.29.2 – and this is one of the reasons why the Stoic philosopher Thrasea suggested such cases should be undertaken: *Cur destitutas* [scil. *causas*]*? Quod in illis maxime et constantia agentis et humanitas cerneretur* ("Why those without an advocate? Because in these above all both the resolve and the *humanitas* of the speaker were demonstrated", trans. Walsh 2006).[109] First, it must be noted that once again Pliny reveals all his Ciceronianism, for an analogous message can be found at *De officiis* 2.51: *Nec*

---

107 *Ep.* 1.10.7: '*Vitae sanctitas summa; comitas par: insectatur uitia non homines, nec castigat errantes sed emendat.*' Cf. also Rieks 1967, 234–235; Bütler 1970, 110. On Euphrates cf. also above, pp. 105–106.
108 The style and content of this letter reminds the reader of Seneca's *Epistulae ad Lucilium*, where *exempla* are central.
109 Cf. Rieks 1967, 235; Cova 1978, 113.

tamen, ut hoc fugiendum est, item est habendum religioni nocentem aliquando, modo ne nefarium impiumque defendere. Vult hoc multitudo, patitur consuetudo, fert etiam humanitas ("But, on the other hand, though that must be avoided, still scruples should not prevent us from occasionally defending a guilty man, provided he is not wicked and impious. The masses want it; custom permits it; *humanitas* tolerates it", trans. Atkins 1991).[110] Secondly, Pliny's *Ep.* 6.29.2 provides little context, but the juxtaposition of *humanitas* with *constantia* may help us better define this instance of *humanitas*. To begin with, the noun *constantia* appears no fewer than 23 times in Pliny's oeuvre. Sometimes, it refers as in this passage to one of the qualities a good lawyer should possess: *Nam pater ei Erucius Clarus, uir sanctus antiquus disertus atque in agendis causis exercitatus, quas summa fide pari constantia nec uerecundia minore defendit* ("For his father is Erucius Clarus, a man of integrity, old-fashioned manners, eloquence, and long practice in handling cases in the courts, which he defends with the utmost probity and a similar tenacity, yet with equal moderation", trans. Walsh 2006).[111] In this last case, the pairing with *fides* (*summa fide pari constantia*), which is common ever since Republican literature, makes it clear that in such contexts Pliny regards *constantia* as the attitude of remaining faithful to one's principles or decisions.[112] Accordingly, in the wake of Cicero, to show both *constantia* and *humanitas* in a trial is to remain faithful to the principle of the right of defence which should be guaranteed to each and every human being, irrespective of their social condition as well as of their probable guilt. But also of note here is that the lawyer, like the emperor in the *Panegyricus*, not only needs to possess *humanitas*, but also to display it (*quod . . . maxime . . . humanitas cerneretur*).

Similarly, in *Ep.* 5.19.2, Pliny uses the word *humanitas* to characterise his attitude toward his freedman (*libertus*) Zosimus, recently hit by illness: *Quod si essem natura asperior et durior, frangeret me tamen infirmitas liberti mei Zosimi, cui tanto maior humanitas exhibenda est, quanto nunc illa magis eget* ("But even if I were by nature harsher and more unsympathetic, my freedman Zosimus' illness would deeply distress me, and I must show him *humanitas* all the greater now that he is in need of it", trans. Walsh 2006). A hint of educational aspect can be found in this context as well, but, surprisingly, on the side of the beneficiary Zosimus, an honest (*probus*), serviceable (*officiosus*) and liberally educated (*litteratus*) man.[113] From a certain point of view, Zosimus seems to deserve to be treated with *humanitas* because he already shares the ideal of *humanitas*.

---

110 More on this in Mollea 2022a, 233–234 and *passim*.
111 *Ep.* 2.9.4. Cf. also 5.13.2 and 9.13.19.
112 Cf. Hellegouarc'h 1963, 284 on this meaning of *constantia* in the Republican age.
113 *Ep.* 5.19.3. On *humanitas* in *Ep.* 5.19 cf. also Bolisani 1961–62, 64–65; Lefèvre 2009, 181–182; 190–192.

But sometimes *humanitas* toward slaves and freedmen can be comforting and bothersome at once. This is what Pliny feels as he writes *Ep.* 8.16.1–3:

> Solacia duo nequaquam paria tanto dolori, solacia tamen: unum facilitas manumittendi (uideor enim non omnino immaturos perdidisse, quos iam liberos perdidi), alterum quod permitto seruis quoque quasi testamenta facere, eaque ut legitima custodio. Mandant rogantque quod uisum; pareo ut iussus. Diuidunt donant relinquunt, dumtaxat intra domum; nam seruis res publica quaedam et quasi ciuitas domus est. Sed quamquam his solaciis adquiescam, debilitor et frangor eadem illa humanitate, quae me ut hoc ipsum permitterem induxit.

> I have two consolations, which though in no way commensurate with the overwhelming grief, are none the less consolations. The first is my readiness to grant them their freedom (I seem not to have lost them wholly before their time, when they were free as I lost them), and the second is my permitting those who remain slaves to make a sort of will; such documents I guard as if they are legal. The slaves issue their instructions and requests according to their wishes, and I fall in with them as though under orders. They allocate, bestow, and bequeath their possessions, with the proviso that they are confined to the household, for the household is for slaves a sort of republic and citizen-state. But though these consolations ease my mind, I am badly affected and heartbroken, owing to the same *humanitas* which led me to grant that concession. (trans. Walsh 2006)

Thus *humanitas* can also appear as a conflicting force. On the one hand, it looks as if Pliny realises that being too benevolent and generous towards slaves could be risky, probably because it would disrupt the balance of power. Nor would such benevolence guarantee his slaves' devotion. In *Ep.* 3.14.5, in informing Acilius that Larcius Macedo has been killed by some slaves of his, Pliny bitterly ponders: *Vides quot periculis quot contumeliis quot ludibriis simus obnoxii; nec est quod quisquam possit esse securus, quia sit remissus et mitis; non enim iudicio domini sed scelere perimuntur* ("You realize to what dangers and insults and derision we are exposed. No man can remain untroubled because he is relaxed and gentle, for masters are murdered through wickedness rather than considered judgement", trans. Walsh 2006).[114] But on the other hand, the ethical obligations which bind Pliny to all other human beings as humans seem to be overwhelming. Furthermore, as Pliny reveals in the next paragraph of *Ep.* 8.16, there cannot be room for doubt: *Hominis est enim adfici dolore sentire, resistere tamen et solacia admittere, non solaciis non egere* (*Ep.* 8.16.4: "for it is part of being human to be assailed by grief and to have feelings, but to struggle against them and to acknowledge consolations rather than to have no need of them", trans. Walsh

---

114 Cf. Lefèvre 2009, 183–186.

2006).[115] The overall message of this letter can be a little surprising, especially when compared to a Stoic consideration such as the one we read in Cicero's *De finibus bonorum et malorum* 2.95:

> Potius ergo illa dicantur, turpe esse, uiri non esse debilitari dolore, frangi, succumbere. Nam ista uestra [i.e. Epicurean]: 'Si grauis, breuis; si longus, leuis' dictata sunt. Virtutis, magnitudinis animi, patientiae, fortitudinis fomentis dolor mitigari solet.

> Better, then, to say that it is shameful and pathetic to succumb, crushed and broken, to pain. Your maxim "Short if it is severe; light if it is long" makes a nice jingle. But virtue, highmindedness, courage and endurance are the real remedies for the alleviation of pain. (trans. Woolf 2001)

Rather than stressing Pliny's non-Stoic tendency, however, this comparison has the result of revealing the humane as well as the human character of his *humanitas*.[116] As Trisoglio puts it: "Il suo [i.e. Pliny's] ideale dell'*humanitas* si rivela come permeato di una sensibilità che implica il dolore, ammette il conforto e brama una carezzevole compassione altrui."[117]

In terms of a diachronic evolution of the relationship between masters and slaves, Bolisani is therefore right in stressing the striking contrast between Pliny's *Ep.* 8.16 and a passage by Cato the Elder in which the sickness and death of slaves are regarded as a material loss for their masters – and sick slaves are therefore to be sold:[118]

> Pecus consideret. Auctionem uti faciat: uendat oleum, si pretium habeat; uinum, frumentum quod supersit, uendat; boues uetulos, armenta delicula, oues deliculas, lanam, pelles, plostrum uetus, ferramenta uetera, seruum senem, seruum morbosum, et si quid aliut supersit, uendat. Patrem familias uendacem, non emacem esse oportet. (*Agr.* 2.7)[119]

> Look over the live stock and hold a sale. Sell your oil, if the price is satisfactory, and sell the surplus of your wine and grain. Sell worn-out oxen, blemished cattle, blemished sheep, wool, hides, an old wagon, old tools, an old slave, a sickly slave, and whatever else is superfluous. The master should have the selling habit, not the buying habit. (trans. Hooper/ Ash 1934)

---

115 On this passage cf. also Rieks 1967, 250; Cova 1978, 94–95; Méthy 2007, 220 and n. 62; Lefèvre 2009, 187–188.
116 On the anti-Stoic character of this letter cf. Lefèvre 2009, 188. More generally on the relation of Pliny's *humanitas* with philosophy cf. Malaspina 2019, 136–137.
117 Trisoglio 1971, 418.
118 Bolisani 1961–62, 65–66.
119 Cf. also Cic. *Att.* 1.12.4 and Bütler 1970, 112.

It is hard to establish whether this radical change of perspective is due to the increasing diffusion of *humanitas* after Cato's day, or, conversely, if such a theoretical revolution ended up being labelled as *humanitas*.[120] Perhaps this question is futile. What is certain is that in Pliny's view *humanitas* was a multifaceted (political, ethical, ontological, literary) value of Greek inspiration that a good emperor like Trajan and the ruling class of Rome had to possess and show in every aspect of their life, differently nuanced according to circumstances, towards all men without distinction, from nobles to slaves, from Romans to non-Romans (Greeks in particular).[121] To put it another way, if a renaissance could follow the age of Domitian, Pliny believes it had (also) to be in the spirit of *humanitas.*

3.1.3 *Humanus* in Pliny the Younger

In Pliny's *Panegyricus* and ten books of *Epistulae* there are 22 instances of the adjective in total, the neuter form is never used as a noun and *inhumanus* never appears.

Yet Pliny employs both comparatives and superlatives. This is the case, for instance, of *Ep.* 2.3.8. Pliny praises the sophist Isaeus' gift of eloquence and urges his friend Maecilius Nepos to hear him at least once, because ἀφιλόκαλον *inlitteratum iners ac paene etiam turpe est non putare tanti cognitionem qua nulla est iucundior, nulla pulchrior, nulla denique humanior* ("To fail to regard as worthwhile an acquaintance which is as pleasant, charming, and civilized (*humanior*) as can be, is an attitude which is malappris, uneducated, sluggish, and virtually degrading", trans. Walsh 2006).[122] As Rieks and Bütler rightly observe, the context leaves little doubt that *humanior* takes on educational nuances.[123] In other words, such experience would feed Nepos' *humanitas,* probably in the way the sources of the Clitumnus can feed Romanus', as we have already seen.[124]

---

120 Some scholars have observed that, when dealing with slaves, *humanitas* can be complemented by self-interest. For example, Hopkins 1978, 118 has claimed that "the prospect of becoming free kept a slave under control and hard at work, while the exaction of a market price as the cost of liberty enabled the master to buy a younger replacement." On this theme cf. also Bonelli 1994, 142 and n. 4 for further bibliography. Although it does not contain the word *humanitas,* Seneca's letter 47 represents perhaps the best previous example of this 'new' attitude towards slaves. And after all, from its very beginning, it stresses the human character of slaves: *'Serui sunt'. Immo homines* ("They are slaves. No, they are men").
121 In this sense, Bury 1989, 59; Méthy 2007, 25; Lefèvre 2009, 171; 176; 294 are right in highlighting the overlap of παιδεία and φιλανθρωπία in Pliny's *humanitas.*
122 On Iseus cf. Sherwin-White 1966, 147–148; Anderson 1993, 19–20; Pausch 2004, 130–132.
123 Rieks 1967, 227–228; Bütler 1970, 108.
124 Cf. above, pp. 106–107.

One of the two superlatives (*Pan.* 59.3) and the comparative of *Ep.* 8.24.9 again remind us of a previously analysed connotation of *humanitas* in Pliny – the one that relates to the relationship between a ruler and his people, as we saw in particular in the *Panegyricus*.[125] So at *Pan.* 59.3 Trajan is said to have been *iustissimus, humanissimus, patientissimus* during his second consulate, in which we also find the juxtaposition of *iustitia* and *patientia*, which are often linked with *humanitas*.[126] As for the comparative at 8.24.9, this is the letter to Maximus that I have analysed above, in which *humanitas* at the outset stands for (Greek) 'civilization'. Towards its close, Pliny urges his friend to behave in his proconsulship of Achaea no worse than he did in his previous proconsulship in Baetica. As one would expect, the reason for this mainly lies in the Greeks' cultural and moral superiority, which emerges throughout the course of the entire letter:

> Quo magis nitendum est ne in longinqua prouincia quam suburbana, ne inter seruientes quam liberos, ne sorte quam iudicio missus, ne rudis et incognitus quam exploratus probatusque humanior melior peritior fuisse uidearis, cum sit alioqui, ut saepe audisti saepe legisti, multo deformius amittere quam non adsequi laudem.

> So you are to strive all the more not to appear to have been more civilized (*humanior*), more efficient, and more experienced as an official in that distant province than in this one closer to Rome, nor among that subject people than among free men, nor when chosen by lot than here specially selected, nor when inexperienced and unknown than well tried and approved. For in general, as we have often heard and we often read, it is much more humiliating to lose a reputation than to fail to win it. (trans. Walsh 2006)

Lefèvre comments: "Mit ihnen [d.h. παιδεία und φιλανθρωπία] rahmt Plinius den [8,24] Brief, indem er *humanitas* als παιδεία an den Anfang (2), *humanus* (*humanior*) als φιλάνθρωπος an den Schluß (9) stellt."[127] Although the occurrence of *humanitas* at 8.24.2, as I have shown, is probably more nuanced than it appears in Lefèvre's analysis, the passage suggests that, in Pliny's mind, Maximus ought to be particularly humane for the very reason that he is going to govern the homeland of *humanitas*. Once again the parallelism with Cicero's letter to Quintus is striking.[128]

Also of interest is the case of the other superlative, which is again to be found within a letter dealing with poetry and literature. Writing to his friend Arrianus, Pliny states:

---

125 Cf. above, pp. 87–89 and 93–95 in particular.
126 Cf. above, p. 97–98 and below, pp. 140–141; 283; 288–289.
127 Lefèvre 2009, 171.
128 Cf. above, pp. 34 and 60.

Vt in uita sic in studiis pulcherrimum et humanissimum existimo seueritatem comitatem-
que miscere, ne illa in tristitiam, haec in petulantiam excedat. Qua ratione ductus grauiora
opera lusibus iocisque distinguo. (*Ep.* 8.21.1–2)

As in life, so in literature I regard it as the most handsome and civilized (*humanissimum*)
thing to mingle the serious with the genial, so that the first does not lapse into melancholy,
nor the second into wantonness. This is the rationale which leads me to intersperse more
serious works with playful and sportive ones. (trans. Walsh 2006)

Paired with *pulcherrimum, humanissimum* appears to convey a value that is worthy of the highest kind of man – the reader will remember the *homines maxime
homines*, that is the Greeks, of *Ep.* 8.24 – to steer a path between opposite activities as well as opposite virtues. In such a context, it is hard to establish to what
extent education, culture, philanthropy and the like contribute to defining *humanissimum*. Certainly, as we have already seen, the best men should possess all
these values, which can all fall under the (Plinian) label of *humanitas*. Also, as is
made clear by the case of *humanitas* in the *Panegyricus*, this value-term has to do
with balance and moderation, which Pliny seems to have understood as being a
necessity in study as well as in life.[129] In life in particular, *seueritas* and *comitas*
are two opposite qualities, and a good balance of both is especially important to
the way in which people of higher rank behave towards people of lower rank –
an emperor towards his subjects, for instance.[130]

But when *humanus* is paired with *figura, fragilitas, genus, natura, res,* or *sanguis*, that is, when it appears in its pure relational meaning, standing for *hominis*,
it loses much of its connection with *humanitas*, as we will note with most other
authors.[131]

Two cases that might seem to counter what I have just claimed are yet to be
investigated. In *Ep.* 4.14.10, Pliny maintains that the phrase *habes quod agas* ("You
have something else to do") is a polite way (*molle et humanum*) to express dislike
of his poems: the context and the meaning are almost the same of *humanitas* in
Ep. 5.3, that is to say that whoever reads or listens to poems by amateurs should
be tolerant in case such poems turn out to be of low quality.[132] But *molle et humanum* should also be a *solacium* ('form of consolation') for a friend who has lost
his daughter, as is the case of *Ep.* 5.16.10, where φιλανθρωπία probably takes the

---

129 Cf. Rieks 1967, 230; Bütler 1970, 107.
130 Cf. above, pp. 85–95.
131 On this frequent lack of meaningfulness of *humanus* in Pliny cf. also Cova 1978, 108; Méthy
2007, 26–27; 249.
132 Cf. Rieks 1967, 229; Bütler 1970, 115 and above, pp. 103–104.

shape of sympathy or compassion.[133] In both these instances *humanus* appears in its positive grade, but at the same time it seems to have connections with *humanitas*: does this come into conflict with the thesis that Latin authors usually resort to comparatives and superlatives of *humanus* when they want to render *humanitas*? I do not think so. Quite opposite, it is my contention that these two occurrences contribute to supporting my theory, for in both cases *humanum* does not stand alone but is paired with *molle*, as if Pliny felt a need to clarify what would otherwise be left unclear. In other words, the presence of *mollis* is like an alternative to the use of a comparative. After all, we observe something analogous with *humanitas* itself, whose polysemy induces several authors to pair it with other abstract concepts that clarify its nuances case by case.

3.2 Tacitus: Is the Absence of *Humanitas* a Photographic Negative?

A very good friend of Pliny's, Tacitus also belonged to the social and political elite of Rome, both in the age of the hated Domitian and in that of the *optimus princeps* Trajan. From a certain viewpoint, he may be considered Pliny's *alter ego*, for he too hoped to contribute to Rome's renaissance under Trajan, but with a significant methodological difference: while Pliny resorted to a 'positive' approach, Tacitus resorted to a 'negative' one. This assertion clearly calls for an explanation. As we have seen, through his *Panegyricus* and *Epistulae*, Pliny was trying to reflect if not propose new cultural and social values – among which *humanitas* – in order to restore Rome's past splendour. Conversely, Tacitus' historical work, which reminded people of the nastinesses perpetrated in the first century of the Roman Empire, posits itself as a sort of admonishment to contemporary and future generations, which should not repeat the errors of their predecessors. In this sense, the opening of the *Historiae*, 1.2 in particular, is eloquent, for here Tacitus' tone is dramatic and ominous. For Tacitus' teaching to be effective, however, there must be room for hope, and hope is represented by either the new emperors Nerva and Trajan (1.1) or the very few virtuous figures who lived under bad emperors (1.3). To the latter category, we might add, also belonged Tacitus' father-in-law Agricola,[134] to whom the historian dedicated his monograph *Agricola*, and those who had not been corrupted by Roman imperial society, as is the case with the Germani, whom Tacitus generally praised in the *Germania*.

---

133 On this passage cf. also Rieks 1967, 239; Bütler 1970, 114; Cova 1978, 94; Lefèvre 2009, 216.
134 On the historical figure of Agricola cf. the recent Sailor 2023.

In these two works, as Syme was among the first to note, we encounter the only two Tacitean occurrences of the term *humanitas*.[135] Such rarity is at least curious, especially in the light of the pervasive use of this concept in the works which have come down to us of Tacitus' contemporary Pliny. Syme puts it down to the ethical and rhetorical connotations of this word, which is not so far from saying that Tacitus disliked this word because of its Ciceronian flavour.[136] Along with or as an alternative to this argument, other scholars, Bauman for one, have pointed out that *humanitas* is not a prominent concept in Roman historiography: there are no occurrences of the term in Sallust and only three in Livy, as we have seen.[137] On a different tack then, Benferhat believes that the sentiment of human solidarity expressed by (Ciceronian) *humanitas* is simply unknown to Tacitus.[138] In my view, all the aforementioned arguments somewhat contribute to explaining Tacitus' discomfort in using the term, but it is my contention that there is more at stake, and that Tacitus deliberately avoided the term because of his 'negative' approach. As has been made clear in Chapter 2, the first century CE saw a decline in the use of *humanitas* and of the exploitation of its polysemy, possibly on account of its Ciceronian, that is republican, inflections. Accordingly, the fact that this 'lack' of *humanitas* in first-century history, especially among the emperors, is mirrored in the lack of *humanitas* in the narration of the first-century history seems to be utterly consistent. As it seems to me, this is but one of "Tacitus' repeated efforts to highlight the discontinuity between Republic and Principate", which are in turn "an attempt to reveal the autocracy of the Principate and to emphasize that he is a historian writing after the fall of *libertas*."[139] As a countercheck, we could reiterate what has been said in the introduction to this chapter, that *clementia*, which played an important role in the first century, is recurrent in Tacitus' oeuvre as well – even if one endorses Syme's opinion that Tacitus refers to it only ironically – while, on the contrary, it is very rare in Pliny.[140] Also consistent with what I have been suggesting so far is that in Tacitus *humanitas*, as well as never appearing in the 'true' historical works, never refers to individuals, but only to peoples: in the *Agricola*, to the Romans as a whole and consequently to the Britons; and in the *Germania*, to the Germani. Accordingly, it cannot go unnoticed that there is also a significant decentralisation of *humanitas* from the Athenian – Roman axis.

---

135 Syme 1958, 712 and 714.
136 Syme 1958, 712.
137 Bauman 2000, 30 and 36. On *humanitas* in Livy cf. above, pp. 65–66.
138 Benferhat 2011, 97.
139 Strunk 2017, 3.
140 Syme 1958, 414. *Contra* Konstan 2005, 344.

Yet despite the rarity of the word *humanitas*, or rather *because of* its rarity, the two instances in Tacitus become all the more interesting. Its use in the *Agricola* in particular, which I shall analyse first, brings into play Tacitus' attitude towards Roman imperialism. But before lingering a while over this occurrence, let me devote a few sentences to describing the *Agricola*, a hybrid work in a genre of its own.

3.2.1 The *Agricola*

Presumably written in 98 CE, this *uita*, as the author himself calls it (1.4), is at once a biography and a *laudatio funebris* of Tacitus' father-in-law, a history of Domitian's campaign in Britain and an ethnographic study of the Britons.[141] It therefore comes as no surprise that Tacitus' models vary throughout the course of the *Agricola*: the description of Agricola's youth recalls the upbringing of Catiline, Jugurtha or Marius as had been narrated by Sallust; the important speeches of Calgacus and Agricola have the 'Livian' flavour of those of Scipio and Hannibal; Cicero's consolation for the death of Crassus no doubt influenced Tacitus' for the death of his father-in-law.[142] Most importantly perhaps, the variety of genres is reflected in the ambiguities about its political message, which seems to waver between pro-Trajanic propaganda and a manifesto of anti-imperialism. Whitmarsh suggests that these two ideological aspects are both constitutive of the *Agricola*, and in constant dialogue with one another.[143] While it exceeds the aims of this study to determine what ideo-

---

141 On the date of the *Agricola* cf. *Ag.* 3.1 and 44.5 with discussion in Forni 1962, 14; Sage 1990, 854–855; Soverini 2004, 6–7. Beck 1998, 72–101 opts for a later publication (late 98 CE–early 99 CE). More recent scholarship tends to deem the problem of the genre of the *Agricola* pointless: cf. Beck 1998, 65; Soverini 2004, 10–11; Birley 2009, 49; Sailor 2012, 37. During the nineteenth and twentieth centuries however, most debate over this work actually focused on this issue: for a synthesis of the various opinions cf. Soverini 2004, 10–11 n. 15. On its peculiarities cf. Syme 1958, 25; 125; Forni 1962, 13; Liebeschuetz 1966, 126; Ogilvie 1991, 1715–1716; Petersmann 1991, 1787; Beck 1998, 64; Sonnabend 2002, 143–145; Whitmarsh 2006, 307–310; Elisei 2008, 441; Sailor 2012, 38; Hägg 2012, 212; Audano 2015, 250; Audano 2023. But cf. also Soverini 2004, 13–14: "Nel complesso, più che a una sorta di commistione programmata di generi, mi limiterei a pensare alla consapevole scelta della forma biografica da parte di uno scrittore che però già sin d'ora manifesta i tratti inequivocabili di una vocazione prettamente storica, caratterizzata dalle esigenze artistico-letterarie, nonché dalle motivazioni e dagli interessi socio-politici [. . .] che caratterizzano l'impegno storiografico ad alto livello." Cf. also Fedeli 2013, 93–95.
142 Cf. Ogilvie 1991, 1718–1720 with further bibliography; Birley 2009, 49; Sailor 2012, 37.
143 Whitmarsh 2006.

logical reasons induced Tacitus to write this work,[144] it is worth underscoring that Whitmarsh's reading is very useful for understanding and explaining the ambiguities surrounding *Agr.* 21 and the occurrence of *humanitas* therein:

> Sequens hiems saluberrimis consiliis absumpta. Namque ut homines dispersi ac rudes eoque in bella faciles quieti et otio per uoluptates adsuescerent, hortari priuatim, adiuuare publice ut templa fora domos extruerent, laudando promptos, castigando segnes: ita honor et aemulatio pro necessitate erat. Iam uero principum filios liberalibus artibus erudire, et ingenia Britannorum studiis Gallorum anteferre, ut qui modo linguam Romanam abnuebant, eloquentiam concupiscerent. Inde etiam habitus nostri honor et frequens toga; paulatimque discessum ad delenimenta uitiorum, porticus et balinea et conuiuiorum elegantiam. Idque apud imperitos humanitas uocabatur, cum pars seruitutis esset. (*Agr.* 21)

> The following winter was taken up by measures of a most beneficial kind. His intention was, in fact, that people who lived in widely dispersed and primitive settlements and hence were naturally inclined to war should become accustomed to peace and quiet by the provision of amenities. Hence he gave encouragement to individuals and assistance to communities to build temples, market-places, and town houses. He praised those that responded promptly and censured the dilatory. As a result they began to compete with one another for his approval, instead of having to be compelled. Further, he educated the sons of the leading men in the liberal arts and he rated the natural talents of the Britons above the trained skills of the Gauls. The result was that those who just lately had been rejecting the Roman tongue now conceived a desire for eloquence. Thus even our style of dress came into favour and the toga was everywhere to be seen. Gradually, too, they went astray into the allurements of evil ways, colonnades and warm baths and elegant banquets. The Britons, who had had no experience of this, called it 'civilization' (*humanitas*), although it was a part of their enslavement. (trans. Birley 1999)

During the second year of his governorship in Britain, Agricola took pains to 'civilize' the native population in many ways: he helped them build temples, markets and houses, and also trained the sons of the Briton chieftains in the liberal arts. As a consequence, the Britons gradually began to aspire to Roman customs and comforts – the latter particularly dangerous, as they often result in vices. Then comes the interpretative issue which interests us, for Tacitus closes the paragraph with a sentence in which not only the meaning of the term *humanitas* needs determining, but also a pronoun like *id* – for what does this *idque* refer to? Before

---

144 Cf. Ogilvie 1991, 1715: "The 'Agricola' was Tacitus' first work and in it he was clearly feeling his way, both politically and stylistically. The result is that it is something of an uneven experiment, uneven in style." Cf. also Hanson 1991, 1743. For a diametrically opposite view cf. Turner 1997, 592: "The Agricola [. . .] emerges as the highly sophisticated work of a mature and capable author."

addressing this problem in greater detail, let us consider what is at stake in how we interpret this entire passage and the terms *id* and *humanitas* at its close.

Commenting on this passage, Woodman and Kraus rightly remark that this paragraph is "one of the most famous in T(acitus), perhaps in all Latin."[145] This will come as no surprise if one recalls another most celebrated Latin text, the lines of *Aeneid* 6 (851–853) where Anchises reminds the Romans of their main duty: *tu regere imperio populos, Romane, memento / hae tibi erunt artes, pacique imponere morem, / parcere subiectis et debellare superbos* ("You, who are Roman, recall how to govern mankind with your power. / These will be your special "Arts": the enforcement of peace as a habit, / Mercy for those cast down and relentless war upon proud men", trans. Ahl 2007). Yet statements – or even orders, as is the case with Vergil – of this kind sometimes raised the question as to whether this domination as it was put into practice was ethically legitimate and really beneficial for both ruler and ruled. In the case of *Agr.* 21, while scholars such as Birley speak of this piece in terms of the "classic passage in the surviving literature for state-sponsored Romanisation", thereby stressing Tacitus' pro-imperialist orientation, others – Lo Cascio for one – more cautiously limit themselves to claiming that here we meet the fundamental terms of the modern debate over Romanisation.[146] Whitmarsh is sceptical: "[I]t is questionable whether we should be thinking in terms of a single target, and (in contingency) a static, pellucid distinction between praise and blame."[147] As is evident, the answer to the question of Tacitus' attitude towards Romanisation in the *Agricola* is tightly linked to the interpretation of the term *humanitas* at the end of paragraph 21. My reading of this passage will end up corroborating Whitmarsh's general interpretation of the *Agricola*: *humanitas*, which is the term Tacitus employs to sum up all the elements of that paragraph, ultimately plays a neutral role; a positive or negative interpretation depends on the viewpoint from which we look at it, the Romans' or the Britons', because the text allows both.

First, let me try to determine which elements of Tacitus' description are subsumed under the word *humanitas*, or better, under the pronoun *id* (*Idque apud imperitos humanitas uocabatur*).[148] The neuter pronoun *id* with anaphoric reference to nouns of different gender is quite common in Latin.[149] At *Agr.* 21, since there is no neuter noun to which *id* could unmistakably refer, it is also clearly

---

145 Woodman/Kraus 2014, 199.
146 Birley 2005, 81; 2009, 57; Lo Cascio 2007, 75. On Romanisation in general cf. Scherr 2023, 17–18, with rich and updated bibliography on n. 46.
147 Whitmarsh 2006, 319.
148 Cf. also Della Calce/Mollea 2022, 135–136 on this passage.
149 Cf. *TLL* 7.2.472.12–45.

used in a collective way, but the extent to which it is collective is more difficult to determine. Unless we arbitrarily establish which components are included and which are left out, we must assume that *id* refers to the whole context, thereby including not only *delenimenta uitiorum* such as *porticus*, *balinea* and *conuiuia* – as some scholars have thought – but also *artes liberales*, *eloquentia* and *habitus*.[150] After all, we have already learnt that *artes liberales* and *eloquentia* are usual aspects of *humanitas*, and there can be little doubt that, alongside *habitus*, these aspects play an even more important role in culturally enslaving a people.

To begin with, if *artes liberales* and *eloquentia* are to be taken as a component of *humanitas* at *Agr.* 21, this implies that Tacitus also regarded this term as bearing educational connotations. In doing this, he distances himself from Seneca, but not so much from Cicero, contrary to current opinions.[151] As well as explicitly linking *humanitas* to the liberal studies in the *Pro Archia*, Cicero is in fact the first author whose use of the expression *artes liberales* is attested (*Inu.* 1.35), as I have remarked above.[152] Within the *Agricola*, the *artes liberales* not only recall Tacitus' father-in-law's upbringing and education at 4.2 (*per omnem honestarum artium cultum pueritiam adulescentiamque transegit*, "he passed his boyhood and youth in a complete training in liberal studies", trans. Birley 1999),[153] but are also evoked at. 2.2 (*expulsis insuper sapientiae professoribus atque omni bona arte in exilium acta*, "over and above this, the teachers of philosophy were expelled and all noble accomplishments driven into exile", trans. Birley 1999), and are the same *bonae artes* which had been forced into exile during (presumably) Domitian's reign.[154]

As for *eloquentia*, the 'quality or practice of fluent, apt, and effective speech' according to the *OLD*, it especially characterises the orators, and is in fact a recurrent word in Cicero's and Quntilian's oeuvre.[155] As is well known, in both these authors the good orator, in order to master *eloquentia*, must possess that superior

---

150 Liebeschuetz's 1966, 137 reading of this passage seems to imply this comprehensive interpretation of *humanitas*, and so does Whitmarsh 2006, 318, who translates *id* as 'Romanization'. *Contra* Haedicke 1975, 76; Høgel 2015, 73: "The sarcasm at work in this grim image of *humanitas* as nothing but a complacent cover for the surrender to the vices of civilisation now even found in the speech of the locals may be one of the reasons why Tacitus avoided the term altogether when writing of Romans." From the readings by Forni 1962, 175 and Soverini 2004, 204–205 it is difficult to find a clear answer to this issue. Cf. also Jens 1956, 337; Baldwin 1990; Scherr 2023, 222–223.
151 Cf. Benferhat 2011, 93–94. On Ciceronian *humanitas* cf. above, pp. 52–62.
152 Cf. above, p. 61.
153 D'Agostino 1962, 46.
154 Cf. Forni 1962, 88; D'Agostino 1962, 15. Soverini 2004, 115 speaks of a usually moral value of *bona ars* in Tacitus, but the context does not necessarily support his view.
155 Cf. *TLL* 5.2.408.42–43 (s.v. *eloquentia*): *frequentant imprimis Cic(ero), Quint(ilianus)*.

knowledge which only the *artes liberales* can provide. In the *Agricola*, Agricola's father was said to be *studio eloquentiae sapientiaeque notus* (4.1: "was noted for his devotion to eloquence and philosophy", trans. Birley 1999). But it is in the *Dialogus de oratoribus* that the term *eloquentia* becomes crucial for Tacitus. Like the *artes liberales*, *eloquentia* too was living through hard times, as is evident from the opening of the *Dialogus*: *Saepe ex me requiris, Iuste Fabi, cur, cum priora saecula tot eminentium oratorum ingeniis gloriaque floruerint, nostra potissimum aetas deserta et laude eloquentiae orbata uix nomen ipsum oratoris retineat* ("Dear Justus Fabius, – There is a question that you often put to me. How is it that, whereas former ages were so prolific of great orators, men of genius and renown, on our generation a signal blight has fallen: it lacks distinction in eloquence, and scarce retains so much as the name of 'orator'", trans. Peterson 1914). Yet despite being at times disregarded at home, the *artes liberales* and *eloquentia* evidently became a key factor in the process of Romanisation abroad. The spread of Latin language must have been central to this process. At *Agr.* 21 Tacitus considers *eloquentia* synonymous with mastery of the Latin language – *lingua Romana*, which "was the language which had spread with Roman power, and not a particular variety of that language restricted to Rome."[156] Cornelius Nepos' *Vita Attici* 4.1, discussed above, provides a close parallel for the association of *humanitas* with mastery of language.[157] As modern commentators point out with regard to Britain, the fact that both Latin language and literature were spreading in Tacitus' days is corroborated by Martial 11.13.5 (*dicitur et nostros cantare Britannia uersus*, "Britain too is said to sing our verses") and Juvenal 15.111 (*Gallia causidicos docuit facunda Britannos*, "eloquent Gaul taught British lawyers").[158] Granted, in ancient Rome education was not for everybody: *a fortiori*, it could not be for everybody in the provinces or among recently conquered peoples. Tacitus' clarification that Agricola's "civilizing efforts were aimed at the British chieftains and their sons" (*principum filios*) comes therefore as unsurprising.[159]

If the *artes liberales* and *eloquentia* undoubtedly played a crucial role, the acme of this process of civilization, that is Romanisation, is however represented by the Roman dress (*nostri habitus*) and especially by the *toga*, which more and more Britons began to wear (the *toga* is characterised as *frequens*). Virg. *Aen.* 1.282 and the success of this line in later authors make it clear that being *toga*-clad was synonymous with being Roman: *Romanos, rerum dominos gentemque togatam* ("Romans, that people in togas, the masters of all in existence", trans. Ahl

---

156 Adams 2003, 195. Cf. also Flobert 1988, 208.
157 Cf. above, pp. 62–63.
158 Cf. Ogilvie/Richmond 1967, 227; Soverini 2004, 203; Woodman/Kraus 2014, 202.
159 Garnsey 1978, 253. Further discussion in Lo Cascio 2007, 83–96.

2007).[160] In Vout's words, "to be *togatus* was to be actively involved in the workings of the state, whether a priest, an orator, a magistrate, a client or the emperor himself."[161] Yet once the acme has been reached, the onset of decline draws near. In a way, the fact that the *toga* spread all over the empire and was no longer prerogative of the Italian citizens of Rome may have contributed to its loss of social and ideological importance.[162] Of course this remains implicit in Tacitus' *frequens toga*, but right from the following sentence the possible negative aspects of *humanitas* are manifest.

It is true that porticoes (*porticus*), baths (*balinea*) and sumptuous banquets (*conuiuiorum elegantiam*) are not to be seen as vices in themselves (*uitia*). At *Ep.* 90.25 Seneca does not probably look kindly upon porticoes, but it must be borne in mind that such places gave birth to the philosophical school to which he belongs – *porticus* is the Latin for στοά. Likewise, banqueting can have beneficial effects: it is probably sufficient to mention the titles of works such as Plato's *Symposium* or Athenaeus' *Deipnosophists* (or *Banquet of the learned*) to give an idea of the philosophical and literary themes that can be touched upon while drinking and / or dining, although of course Trimalchio's dinner party in the *Satyrica* represents the other, that is negative, side to the same coin.[163]

Baths can be seen as a means of integration (and also of Romanisation) as well as "a prelude and preparation for [. . .] the banquet"; however, by the time of Tacitus they were also regarded as immoral venues.[164] Just to give a few examples, Seneca and Demetrius the Cynic disapproved of the luxurious lifestyle they came to symbolise, while Martial and Juvenal imply that mixed baths in particular were often frequented by loose women.[165] In a nutshell, even if they are not intrinsically vices, porticoes, baths and banquets certainly represent potential occasions for being immoral.[166] In this sense, Woodman and Kraus are right in pointing out that the genitive *uitiorum* "is not definitive or appositional ('enticing vices', viz. porticoes etc.) but objective or possessive ('enticements to vice')",

160 Cf. Imp. Aug. *Fr.* 35 Malcovati; Mart. 14.124.1; Suet. *Aug.* 40.5. Cf. Vout 1996, 213–216.
161 Vout 1996, 214. Cf. also Scherr 2023, 221: "Tacitus impliziert demnach mit *habitus* ganz bewusst nicht nur die Art der Kleidung, sondern es ist zugleich an römisches Wesen, römische Verhaltensweisen zu denken, was den zivilisatorischen Aspekt der Passage weiter unterstreicht."
162 On the social decline of the *toga* cf. Vout 1996, 216–218 with further bibliography.
163 For further bibliography as well as examples of pros and cons of banquets cf. Woodman/Kraus 2014, 205. The clarification 'drinking and / or dining' is necessary because the ancient Greek symposium came right after a banquet, but no longer involved eating.
164 Yegül 1992, 5. On the social importance of baths cf. Yegül 1992, 4; 30; Rimell 2015, 159–162.
165 Cf. Sen. *Ep.* 86.6–13; Philost. *VA* 4.42; Mart. 3.51, 11.47; Juv. 6.419–433 with Yegül 1992, 40–43 and Rimell 2015, 160–161.
166 Forni 1962, 175; Grimal 1991, 116; Soverini 2004, 204; Woodman/Kraus 2014, 206.

though their explanation "perhaps with the implication that *uitia* are not an inevitable consequence of the *delenimenta*" raises some doubts, especially in the light of their premises: "T(acitus) is distinguishing the buildings and banquets (*delenimenta*) from their immoral associations and demoralising effects (*uitiorum*)."[167] In other words, they do not seem to give *delenimenta* a pejorative meaning. Yet Benferhat has shown persuasively that right from its first occurrences in Republican Latin *delenimentum* always takes on some negative nuances, in that it always implies some deceit or intention to deceive.[168] Granted, compared to *uitia*, *delenimenta* are 'less' negative; they represent a previous step, so to speak. With regard to *Agr.* 21, therefore, the circle seems to square once we take it that *porticus, balinea* and *conuiuiorum elegantiam* are appositions of *delenimenta*, not of *uitiorum*. Thus, if on the one hand porticoes, baths and banquets are only potential occasions for being immoral, on the other hand Tacitus seems to imply that this potentiality is likely to materialise in Britain (in the same way as it had already done at Rome?). After all, these are the risks of 'civilization', as *humanitas* is usually translated at *Agr.* 21, and as Julius Caesar had already denounced at the opening of his *De bello Gallico*.[169] In Tacitus' view, to become Roman is not only to be able to speak perfect Latin or wear the *toga*, but also to be exposed to the blandishments of porticoes, baths and banquets. In other words, civilization is also a step towards possible corruption of the customs and thus towards decadence – and development is not always positive![170] The same myth of the noble savage that Tacitus fully exploits in the *Germania* also seems to shine through here. In a way, this is a variation upon the common theme of the *laudatio temporis acti*, according to which the (often idealised) past is far better than the present. Among other ancient authors, this topic was central to Tacitus' model Sallust, and returns in Ammianus.[171] Yet all this is not to say that *humanitas* has a negative connotation in the *Agricola*. As we have seen, none of the elements which constitute Tacitus' idea of *humanitas* are negative by themselves. Rather, we should speak of a broad meaning of the term *humanitas*, which includes neutral, that is neither positive nor negative, aspects of being Roman.[172] An exclusively negative sense should be – but is not necessarily – taken on by the term, and consequently, by the whole passage, from the non-Roman perspective of the Britons alone, for they do not realise that *humanitas* implies cultural slavery and is not necessarily syn-

---

167 Woodman/Kraus 2014, 204.
168 Benferhat 2011, 174–176.
169 On *humanitas* in Caesar cf. above, pp. 63–64.
170 Cf. Rutledge 2000, 85.
171 Cf. below, pp. 227–260.
172 Cf. Woolf 1998, 69–70.

onymous with progress.[173] On this occasion, the *Agricola*'s constant tension between pro- and anti-imperialist attitude, as argued by Whitmarsh, materialises in the different perspective from which to look at *humanitas*, the Romans' or the Britons'.[174]

According to Tacitus' narration, just one Briton would seem to realise the negative implications of Roman so-called *humanitas*, the chieftain Calgacus. The speech he delivers before his people prior to the Battle of Mons Graupius (*Agr.* 30–32) includes quite a few allusions to and criticisms of Roman imperialism.[175] Accordingly, and in addition to the references I mentioned at the outset of this section, scholars such as Liebeschuetz and Sailor have highlighted parallels between Calgacus' oration and *Agr.* 21 in pointing out the drawbacks of the Roman empire in Tacitus' view.[176] Rutledge has in turn maintained that both these texts are consistent in revealing the necessity of Roman imperialism, as they both show weaknesses of the Britons: *Agr.* 21 makes it clear that their 'civilization' actually leads to decadence, while Calgacus embodies too many anachronistic republican values, such as *libertas*.[177] This would mean that the Britons do not have the qualities to rule over their own land, and thus need an external ruler, that is, the Roman emperor. Nevertheless, I would again echo Whitmarsh, who argues that one of the main analogies between Calgacus' speech and *Agr.* 21 is that they both concern "identification and exposure of catachrestic signification, of *falsa nomina*":[178] *auferre trucidare rapere falsis nominibus imperium, atque ubi solitudinem faciunt, pacem appellant* ("They plunder, they butcher, they ravish, and call it by the lying name of 'empire'. They make a desert and call it 'peace'", trans. Birley 1999) of 30.6 is in dialectic relation with *Idque apud imperitos humanitas uocabatur, cum pars seruitutis esset* of 21.3.[179] Both passages therefore include two perspectives at the same time, the Romans' and the Britons', and it would be arbitrary to exclude either.

---

173 On *uocabatur* in this passage, cf. Soverini 2004, 205, with further examples: "il motivo della 'falsa definizione', per cui ad indicare una certa realtà viene impiegato un termine inadeguato e disviante, sembra particolarmente avvertito dalla sensibilità tacitiana." Cf. also D. Braund 1996, 161–165.
174 Whitmarsh 2006.
175 Cf. especially 30.1 and 30.7.
176 Liebeschuetz 1966, 136–137; Sailor 2012, 34. Cf. also Whitmarsh 2006, 318–319.
177 Rutledge 2000, 85–90.
178 Whitmarsh 2006, 318.
179 Cf. also Baroud 2023, 537.

3.2.2 The *Germania*

As said before, the second occurrence of *humanitas* in Tacitus is to be found in the *Germania*. Like the *Agricola*, it is a unique work which dates to 98 CE.[180] Its title in the manuscripts, *De origine et situ Germanorum*, evokes an ethnographic monograph, but this only applies to the first half of the work (chapters 1–27.1).[181] After describing the region and the physical and social features of its inhabitants, in the second half (27.2–46) Tacitus turns in fact to a survey of the peoples of Germania.[182]

Towards the end of the first half of the work, also through praising their hospitality, "Tacitus builds up his portrait of the Germani as the Roman other."[183] In this context, he says:

> Conuictibus et hospitiis non alia gens effusius indulget. Quemcumque mortalium arcere tecto nefas habetur; pro fortuna quisque apparatis epulis excipit. Cum defecere, qui modo hospes fuerat monstrator hospitii et comes; proximam domum non inuitati adeunt. Nec interest: pari humanitate accipiuntur. (21.2–3)

> No other people indulges more lavishly in feasting and entertainment. It is regarded as a sin to turn away any person from their house. Each according to his means receives guests with an elaborate meal. When his supplies have run out, the man who has been the host accompanies the guest to show him another lodging. They enter the next house even without an invitation. It makes no difference: they are received with equal warmth (*humanitate*). (trans. Birley 1999)

Although it is far from having the richness of meaning, but also of ambiguities, of the occurrence of *humanitas* in the *Agricola*, this one ultimately shares with the former the idea of civilization. In a way, it could also be said to be complementary to the *Agricola* instance, as it shows that the barbarians, whether they are Britons or Germani, do already possess an idea of civilization. Their idea is probably less sophisticated than the Romans', but for this same reason it is further from vice and more easily manageable. The barbarians possess genuine civilization which does not derive from the liberal arts or their dress, but is more natural, authentically human, at least within the boundaries and by the standards of their own

---

180 At 37.2 Tacitus refers to Trajan's second consulship (first half of 98 CE) and the context suggests that the historian is talking about a contemporary event. Cf. Rives 2012, 46 with further bibliography; Posadas 2023, 475.
181 Cf. Thomas 2009, 61.
182 On the issues concerning the genre and the style of this work cf. Thomas 2009, 61; *passim*; Rives 2012, 48–53; Posadas 2023, 475–477.
183 Rives 2012, 52.

society. Because of such genuineness and purity, here banquets are not seen as enticements to vice – or at least not to the same degree as in the *Agricola* – but as occasions in which *humanitas* towards fellow countrymen can be displayed. In view of all this, it is probably simplistic to reduce *humanitas* to an equivalent of *hospitalitas*, as the *TLL* entry suggests.[184] Here *humanitas* does take the shape of hospitality, but insofar as it is an offshoot of a more wide-ranging value, namely civilization. In the section on Gellius (and in Ammianus), we will see that and how this connection between *humanitas* and hospitality becomes clearer.

Tacitus' two earliest works thus show a much fuller use of the term *humanitas* in the *Agricola*, and a more restricted one in the *Germania*. In the case of *Agricola*, we could even state that *humanitas* has reached its highest level of meaningfulness in characterising the essence of the Romans: on the one hand, it contains the educational and rhetorical aspects embedded in the most pregnant Ciceronian occurrences of the term; on the other, it goes even beyond Cicero, including some possible less noble features and habits of the Roman people.[185] In contrast, the case of *Germania* proves that there can be a 'lower', 'more barbarian' level of *humanitas*, which is far from the Greek ideal of παιδεία, but at the same time is further from its potentially dangerous consequences. Tacitus must have seen how these dangerous consequences had materialised in first-century Roman society, and this may contribute to explaining why in the *Annales* and *Historiae* he avoided using the term *humanitas* in narrating the events from the end of Augustus' reign to Domitian's.

3.2.3 *Humanus* in Tacitus

But if Tacitus hardly uses *humanitas* in his works, he does use *humanus*. I agree with Benferhat that he did so because he perceived a significant difference in meaning between the noun and the adjective, a difference which emerges from the comparison between the occurrences of *humanitas* and those of *humanus*.[186] A closer look at the 45 instances of *humanus* – including a couple of cases of *inhumanus* – will make this clearer.

In most cases, *humanus* agrees with *adfectus, animus, corpus, cupido, effigies, genus, hostia, ingenium, infirmitas, ius, malignitas, memoria, modus, natura, ops,*

---

184 Cf. *TLL* 6.3.3082.24–25. Once more a precedent of this nuance of *humanitas* can be found in Cicero: cf. *TLL* 6.3.3082.19–24. For later uses cf. *TLL* 6.3.3082.26–55; Høgel 2015, 96.
185 On Ciceronian *humanitas* cf. above, pp. 52–62.
186 Benferhat 2011, 90.

os, res, sors, species, uox and thus simply conveys the idea of 'human' / 'of man', without any ethical, cultural or philanthropic implications.

In a couple of situations the adjective is used as a noun, in the common comparison / opposition between *humana* and *diuina*. The same (implicit) polarity can be found at *Ann.* 15.44, although here *humana consilia* might also imply that Nero, in paying attention to his people's needs while rebuilding Rome after the fire of July 64 CE, was inspired by philanthropic ideals: *Et haec quidem humanis consiliis prouidebantur. Mox petita dis piacula aditique Sybillae libri* ("Such were the provisions of human design. Later, atonements were sought, with consultation of the Sibyl's books", trans. Damon 2012). Nevertheless, the distance from the *Agricola* occurrence of *humanitas* remains immense.

As predictable, things change when it comes to *inhumanus*. At *Hist.* 2.70 Vitellius wants to tread the plains of Bedriacum to see the traces of his recent victory. The battlefield is ghastly to behold according to Tacitus' description, but *nec minus inhumana pars uiae quam Cremonenses lauru rosaque constrauerant, extructis altaribus caesisque uictimis regium in morem* ("no less callous (*inhumana*) was the part of the road which the people of Cremona had strewn with laurel and roses, after building altars and sacrificing victims in the manner appropriate for a king", trans. Wellesley/Ash 2009). At 3.83, Vitellians and Flavian forces, while fighting against each other on the streets of Rome, showed *inhumana securitas* ('inhuman indifference'). *Inhumanus* thus has a richer, that is ethical, meaning than *humanus*, because it really evokes the idea of what is unbecoming to a human being. But this is inevitable, since the negative prefix *in-* implies a form of judgement which makes of *inhumanus* no longer a simple relational adjective.

3.3 Suetonius: *Humanitas* as a Paradox in the *Vita Tiberii*

Our investigation into the use of *humanitas* in the Trajanic age ends with Gaius Suetonius Tranquillus. This is due to a chronological reason, for Suetonius flourished at the turn of the Trajanic and Hadrianic age. His *De uita duodecim Caesarum*, the largest and most famous extant part of his immense production as well as his only work to contain instances of *humanitas*, was in fact probably written between 119–122 CE, that is, at the beginning of the reign of Hadrian.[187] Yet the

---

[187] John the Lydian (*Mag.* 2.6) informs us that Suetonius' *Lives of the Caesars* were dedicated to Septicius Clarus as Praetorian prefect, so between 119–122 CE. Most scholars give credit to John the Lydian, but cf. also Townend 1959; Cizek 1977, 13 n. 39; Baldwin 1983, 2; 14; 47–51; Pausch 2004, 252–258; Power 2014b, 76–77. For an overview of Suetonius' lost works cf. Sonnabend 2002, 171; Vacher 2003², xxi–xxiv.

reason for including Suetonius in the Trajanic age is also that he belonged to the same cultural milieu as Tacitus and Pliny, and was certainly in close contact with the latter.[188] Moreover, as far as *humanitas* and concepts of value in general are concerned, it is worth recalling that Wallace-Hadrill draws a sharp parallel between Suetonius and Pliny the Younger, identifying in Pliny's already discussed *Panegyricus* 3.4 the "series of contrasting pairs of virtues and vices which cover very much the same ground as do Suetonius' pairs."[189] To recall it briefly, the first pair that Pliny mentions at *Pan.* 3.4 opposes *humanitas* to *superbia*, which Wallace-Hadrill translates and glosses thus: "humanity (equivalent to civility) and pride."[190] As fascinating as they may be, both the main statement and the parenthesis raise some doubts. To begin with, *humanitas* is extremely rare in Suetonius' extant oeuvre, as the term itself is only used twice in the *Vita Tiberii*;[191] nor is *ciuilitas* more frequent, appearing only at *Aug.* 51.1 and *Claud.* 35.1. Moreover, it is very hazardous to consider *ciuilitas* as an equivalent of *humanitas*. Not only are these two words never twinned in Latin, despite it being a language which makes ample use of synonymous doublets, but the very opposition of *humanitas* to *superbia* at *Pan.* 3.4 rules out that possibility: for how could pride (*superbia*) be seen as something opposite to civility?

On the contrary, along the lines I have been drawing in this chapter, especially in the introduction and the section on Tacitus, it is my contention that two arguments at least can be put forward to explain the rarity of *humanitas* in Suetonius' oeuvre. On the one hand, with Tacitus' case in mind, it does not seem rash to conjecture that this is at least partly due to the historical character of Suetonius' work, and to republican and early imperial historians' general avoidance of this term.[192] On the other hand – and this seems to me to be a perhaps stronger

---

188 Cf. Della Corte 1958, 77–113; Cizek 1977, 7–9; Baldwin 1983, 9–27; Gascou 1984, 735–736; Sonnabend 2002, 169–171; Duchêne 2020, 12–13. Furthermore, Baldwin 1983, 51 for one even proposes that "some, perhaps all, of the imperial biographies were composed and published by 117": cf. the previous footnote.

189 Wallace-Hadrill 1984, 155. On Pliny, *Pan.* 3.4 cf. above, pp. 87–88.

190 Wallace-Hadrill 1984, 155.

191 A third one in *Gram.* 14.2 is in fact within a Ciceronian letter to Atticus.

192 For the lack of *humanitas* in Roman historians cf. above, p. 116. One can object that Suetonius was a biographer rather than a historian. However, despite Plutarch's statement at *Alex.* 1.2 (οὔτε γὰρ ἱστορίας γράφομεν, ἀλλὰ βίους – "Nor do I write about history, but about lives"), the line between biography and history was generally blurred in antiquity. And, after all, Jerome himself called Suetonius a historian (*Chron. praef.* p. 6 Helm = p. 288 Roth). Cf. Wallace-Hadrill 1984, 8–10, who defines Suetonius a 'scholar'; Giua 1991, 3735 and n. 8; 3744–3745; Power 2014a, 1–2. Other scholars, such as Della Corte 1958, 203–230; Baldwin 1983, 66–100; Gascou 1984, 343–456, tend on the contrary to distinguish more clearly between history and biography, al-

point – we should not forget that, like Tacitus' major historical works, Suetonius' *Caesares* also deal with first-century emperors, and I have already reiterated more than once that *humanitas* does not seem to have been central to first-century Roman thought; nor was it among the emperors' most praised values. In the light of this, it might seem surprising that the only two instances of *humanitas* in Suetonius are to be found in the *Vita Tiberii*, the biography of an emperor who was by no means a positive model in Suetonius' view.[193] However, a closer analysis of these two occurrences will reveal that there is little room for surprise, for in Tiberius' reign there was only a lack, or at best, an appearance, of *humanitas*. Let us turn to the text in question.

Having praised the emperor's patience in the face of abuse and slander as well as his benevolent and 'democratic' behaviour towards the senate in the previous paragraph, at *Tib.* 29 Suetonius adds: *Atque haec eo notabiliora erant, quod ipse in appellandis uenerandisque et singulis et uniuersis prope excesserat humanitatis modum* ("And this was more remarkable because he himself almost exceeded politeness (*humanitas*) in addressing and paying his respects to individual senators and the senate as a whole", trans. Edwards 2000). As is often the case with *humanitas*, it is difficult to provide a translation which is utterly satisfying. 'Politeness' or 'courtesy' clearly make sense, but of course something is missing. The impression is that once more both the ideas of παιδεία and φιλανθρωπία are simultaneously expressed. The former is the precondition, as it were; the latter, which is far more evident, represents the practical manifestation, the kind and benevolent behaviour of a person of higher rank towards people of lower status.[194] What can be a little surprising, especially in the light of some negative readings of the *Vita Tiberii*, is that this emperor even exceeded the 'standard level' of *humanitas*.[195] But this simply means that a positive concept like *humani-*

---

though the latter recognises the historical value of the *Vitae Caesarum* (xii–xvi, 345, 457–674, 801–803), which is made clear right from the title, *Suétone Historien*.

193 Cf. Cizek 1977, 102–109; 148; Baldwin 1983, 252–253; Newbold 1984, 121–122; Gascou 1984, 696; Gunderson 2014, 141–145; Duchêne 2020, 101–115; 174–183. Nevertheless, according to Somville's 2002 arguments, Suetonius' description of Tiberius' life is not entirely negative. So when Cizek 1977, 155 claims that *humanitas* is a, perhaps the, criterion for distinguishing the good from the bad emperors, he is evidently speaking of his own idea of *humanitas*, not Suetonius'. Cf. also Cizek 1977, 195–197. Regarding the difficulties for understanding why some words are rare or are used in some *Vitae* alone, cf. the persuasive Baldwin 1983, 484–485, according to which, in the last analysis, there can be no reason for that, especially with words of little or no consequence.

194 On *humanitas* in this passage cf. also Vogt 1975, 150.

195 Cf. *e.g.* the reading by Gunderson 2014. However, according to other readings, *Tib.* 29 is entirely positive: cf. *e.g.* Cizek 1977, 96.

tas, if carried to excess, may seem to hide traces of its opposites, *inhumanitas* or *superbia*.

Other passages of this *Vita* may corroborate this interpretation. At *Tib.* 30, for instance, Suetonius ingeniously observes: *Quin etiam speciem libertatis quandam induxit conseruatis senatui ac magistratibus et maiestate pristina et potestate* ("Maintaining the traditional dignity and power of both senate and magistrates, he even introduced some appearance of a free state", trans. Edwards 2000). The overall message could appear to be positive, but the word *species* (semblance) insinuates serious doubts about Tiberius' true intention.[196] From paragraph 41 onwards then, there is no longer need of dissimulation, and at 42 Suetonius makes Tiberius' degeneration extremely clear:[197] *Ceterum secreti licentiam nanctus et quasi ciuitatis oculis remotis, cuncta simul uitia male diu dissimulata tandem profudit* ("Nevertheless, having obtained the licence afforded by seclusion, far from the eyes of the city, he finally gave in simultaneously to all the vices he had so long struggled to conceal", trans. Edwards 2000). In *Tib.* 50, in fact, the word *humanitas* itself bears its usually positive meaning, but the negative atmosphere is given by the fact that Suetonius is denouncing its lack: *Iuliae uxori tantum afuit ut relegatae, quod minimum est, offici aut humanitatis aliquid impertiret, ut ex constitutione patris uno oppido clausam domo quoque egredi et commercio hominum frui uetuerit* ("So far was he from showing his wife Julia, when she was in exile, a measure of respect and kindness – the least one might expect – that, when her father's orders confined her to a single town, he further forbade her to leave the house or to have any contact with other people", trans. Edwards 2000). The twin-

---

196 Cf. Gascou 1984, 720–721. On the contrary, Baldwin 1983, 263 believes that this is "a genuine compliment"; while Wallace-Hadrill 1984, 110 takes a sort of median position: "He [i.e. Suetonius] seems to approve vaguely of the 'sort of show of *libertas*' which Tiberius allowed the senate." On *libertas* in Suetonius cf. Baldwin 1983, 327–333; Wallace-Hadrill 1984, 110–112; 118. For the juxtaposition of *libertas* and *maiestas* cf. D'Aloja 2011, 67.

197 On paragraph 41 as a turning point in Suetonius' description of Tiberius cf. Bringmann 1971, 277; Döpp 1972, 451; Vogt 1975, 190; Cizek 1977, 136; Gascou 1984, 681; 691; Giua 1991, 3736; Duchêne 2020, 175. However, Giua 1991, 3736–3737 herself acknowledges that some negative aspects of Tiberius' nature can already be perceived in the first half of his biography. Cf. also Gascou 1984, 700–701. The cases of *humanitas* at 29 and of *speciem libertatis* at 30 seem to me to point in this same direction. Cf. also Bradley 1991, 3703 and n. 11, who then remarks: "towards Tiberius, Caligula, Nero and Domitian he [i.e. Suetonius] is unambiguously hostile" (3729). A different position in Bringmann 1971, 285: "Alle negativen Züge des Tiberius sind im letzten Abschnitt gesammelt, im ersten und im zweiten blieb dafür kein Raum." Cf. also Döpp 1972.

ning of *officium* and *humanitas* has a Ciceronian feel.[198] The phrasing at *Pro Flacco* 57 seems to be the closest to Suetonius:[199]

> Quid uos fieri censetis Trallibus? An id, quod Pergami? Nisi forte hae ciuitates existimari uolunt facilius una se epistula Mithridatis moueri impellique potuisse ut amicitiam populi Romani, fidem suam, iura omnia officii humanitatisque uiolarent, quam ut filium testimonio laederent cuius patrem armis pellendum a suis moenibus censuissent.

> What do you think happens at Tralles? Isn't it what happened at Pergamum? Unless perhaps these states wish it to be thought that they are more easily moved and could me more easily persuaded by a single letter of Mithridates to violate the friendship of the Roman people, their own loyalty, all the laws of duty and humanity (*offici humanitatisque*), than to injure by their testimony a son whose father they had voted to repel from their walls by force of arms. (trans. Lord 1953).

In his oratorical, emphatic tone, Cicero's accusation of violating all the laws of obligation and humanity (*iura omnia offici humanitatisque*) summarises and represents the climax of all violations, especially, as this is the case, when it comes to international relationships.[200] By contrast, the Suetonian occurrence pertains to the private sphere, which perhaps contributes to explaining why Suetonius' style is far less dignified and cutting; yet what he means by referring to this dittology is pretty much the same as in Cicero's *Pro Flacco*: all the laws of obligation and humanity would push Tiberius to have mercy upon his wife, but there is no room for humanity in this emperor's nature. In sum, it may sound a little paradoxical, but despite being the only *Vita* where the word *humanitas* appears, we must agree with Wallace-Hadrill 1984, 160 that "Suetonius' aim is not to explain the political crisis of Tiberius' reign but to compile a dossier of his *in*humanity"[201] (my emphasis).

---

198 On *officium* in this passage and in Suetonius in general cf. Vogt 1975, 242.

199 For other simultaneous instances of *officium* and *humanitas* cf. Cic. *Ver.* 2.2.118; *Phil.* 2.9; *Fam.* 3.1.1; 3.9.1; 11.27.8; 11.28.4; 16.4.2; *Att.* 6.1.1.

200 Cf. Mayer 1951, 147: "Die Begriffe [scil. *officium humanitasque*] sind zu einer einzigen Vorstellung unzertrennlich eng verschmolzen; h., an und für sich das generelle Wort, Menschlichkeit in weitesten Sinn, ist durch officium näher bestimmt im Sinne einer Gebundenheit an verpflichtende Gesetze und Normen, die die Beziehungen von einem Volk zum andern regeln, dadurch daß sie Vertrags- und Treubruch verbieten." J. Schneider 1964, 68–69 agrees with Mayer.

201 Wallace-Hadrill 1984, 160.

3.3.1 *Humanus* in Suetonius

Also Suetonius' use of *humanus* seems to have little connection with *humanitas*. To begin with, the *Vita Tiberii*, the only one to include instances of *humanitas*, has no instances of the adjective *humanus*. Indeed, the adjective is always used in its relational meaning, appearing alongside *fastigium, genus, habitus, ius, manus, ops, pes, ratio, res* and *species*. On one occasion it is substantivised and opposed to *diuinus* (*diuina atque humana*).

3.4 Conclusion

Like the end of the Neronian, that of the Domitianic era too imposed a revision of the rhetoric of power. *Clementia*, which Seneca had regarded as the virtue *par excellence* the good ruler should possess, was reinvented once after Nero's behaviour had invalidated its function, but Domitian gave it the final blow. As we saw in the introduction, figures do not allow us to go so far as to speak of a taboo word, but it is telling that its use in Tacitus seems to reveal the historian's hostility towards the concept of *clementia principis* and, what is more, aside from matters of interpretation, it is undeniable that this word is only used with reference to the age between Augustus' death and the early years of the Trajanic age, where what has come down to us of Tacitus' *Historiae* ends.

The rhetoric of works like Pliny the Younger's, which deal with present or future times rather than the historical past, reveal that there is no longer room for *clementia*, whereas there is a strong need to portray Trajan's as the beginning of an age that aspired to recall the idealised republican past. To this end, a Ciceronian-connoted value concept like *humanitas*, that was likely to remind people of the last fight for liberty during the republican age, must have worked very well, and it is for this very reason that in the Trajanic age *humanitas* became a core concept of value. In the case of Pliny, the fact that Cicero was also one of his most important stylistic models seems to explain why for example in his *Panegyricus* the term *humanitas* offers a striking, almost unrivaled, spectrum of nuances. Throughout the speech *humanitas* is first conceived of as an ontological value to be compared with *diuinitas*, then as an ethical one in opposition to *superbia*, and as a political one in association with *maiestas*. Furthermore, the instance of *studia humanitatis* explicitly sets Pliny's *humanitas* in the footsteps of Cicero's, and also makes explicit its educational dimension. Finally, a reference to Trajan's *humanitas* during banquets brings into play the social aspect of this value concept. But if the *Panegyricus* represented an official way of promoting *humanitas*, the *Epistulae* allowed Pliny to spread it among his friends and the upper echelons of Roman society, albeit in a more silent tone. The *Epistulae* thus provide not only further examples of the multi-facetedness of *humanitas*, but, most importantly, also reveal both that Pliny praised this virtue of Trajan in private contexts as well (cf. *Ep.* 6.31.14), and that, thanks to its peculiarity of transcending social class distinctions, *humanitas* could work at and across all levels of Roman society. It is for these very reasons that *humanitas* represented a possible and highly positive value to oppose to Rome's decadence under and immediately after Domitian's tyranny, a decadence which was also moral and that might result in the decadence of the arts and literature, as Pliny himself acknowledges.[202] From a backward perspective, we can ascertain that Pliny's strategy worked, for *humanitas* still played an important role in the Antonine age, and was again crucial three centuries later, when Theodosius I presented himself as a new Trajan. Yet the immediate success of this value concept also depended on Pliny's authoritative voice. In a period that was characterised by the presence of cultural circles which influenced Rome's life at all levels, Pliny's was certainly the most important one.[203] *Humanitas* and the other values (*temperamentum* or *moderatio*, *libertas*, and *amor* for instance)[204] he proclaimed in both his letters and the *Panegyricus* were therefore not only his own, but those embraced – or that Pliny hoped would be embraced – by a large part of the society, presumably by Trajan himself.[205]

That in the works by Tacitus and Suetonius that have come down to us there is little or no room for *humanitas* is consistent with the rhetoric of the times they portray, as we have seen. Accordingly, it is unsurprising that Suetonius associated the word *humanitas* just with Tiberius and just to remark that this emperor lacked, and only feigned, this value concept. Likewise, it cannot be surprising that in the *Annales* and *Historiae*, which were both composed late in Trajan's reign and deal with first-century history, Tacitus never employed *humanitas*. By contrast, he had employed the term *humanitas* in the works of the 98, the *Germania* and the *Agricola*, but it is tempting to regard both those occurrences as another way of criticising Domitian and his policy, even in the foreign field, where – from the Roman viewpoint – barbarians' traditional uncivilization turns out to be better than Roman civilization, or *humanitas*, if you prefer.

---

202 Cf. *e.g. Epp.* 2.14; 6.2.5–9; 3.18.9–10 and Trisoglio 1971, 421–422.

203 As Cizek 1989, 26 significantly remarks, Pliny is the only exponent of the age of Trajan whom Jerome cited (*Chron.* CCXXII Olymp., an XII = 109 CE). On Pliny's club cf. Cizek 1989, *passim*.

204 On the importance of all these values in addition to *humanitas* cf. Méthy 2007, *passim*. On *temperamentum* in particular, cf. Galimberti Biffino 2003. Broadly speaking, these values (or some of them) can also apply to Suetonius' thought: cf. Cizek 1977, 196; Gascou 1984, 722–735.

205 Cf. Soverini 1989, 545–548.

4 Trials and Educational Programmes: The Specialisation(s) of *Humanitas* in the Antonine Age

'Plinian' *humanitas* and its diffusion in the Trajanic age influenced Roman society in the years which followed. In this sense, statements like Dihle's leave little room for doubt, for according to the German scholar in the second century "administration and jurisdiction became increasingly humane or humanistic: any man who aspired to a military or an administrative office or to any kind of social standing had to prove a considerable degree of general education."[1] Dihle, or, better, his translator, seems to use 'humane' in the sense of 'humanistic', but, as I shall make clear in a moment, we could say with equal plausibility that the second century CE was also humane in philanthropic terms.[2] Thus, since both παιδεία and φιλανθρωπία, two fundamental components of Pliny's *humanitas*, played a major role in the culture of this century, it is highly likely that Pliny himself was one of the conveyors, if not the main one, of this message. After all, we must bear in mind that, not unlike his successors Mamertinus and Ausonius in the fourth century, Pliny must have used his *Panegyricus* also as a medium for official propaganda, as already remarked.[3] In the literary field in particular, we can best appreciate the success of *humanitas* in the long run, that is to say, in the Antonine age and its authors. For although the late fourth-century *Historia Augusta* twice attributes *humanitas* to Hadrian,[4] and some declamations and laws seem to allude to the *humanitas* of his reign,[5] the Hadrianic age, despite being characterised by general cultural prosperity, is usually seen as a period of literary decline, particularly in Latin, without prominent authors comparable to the earlier Tacitus and Pliny or the later Gellius and Apuleius.[6] But before providing an overview of the chapter and of its authors, let me briefly explain what allows us to speak of the second century, and of the Antonine age above all, as a 'humane' time.

---

1 Dihle 2013, 214–215.
2 As Gregor Vogt-Spira has kindly pointed out to me, Dihle's original German text actually speaks of an increasing *Humanisierung von Verwaltung und Rechtsprechung*.
3 Cf. above, p. 95. On the propagandistic role of late antique panegyrics cf. Castello 2010, 190; Cameron 2016[2], 136–137. Further below, p. 273.
4 On *humanitas* in the *Historia Augusta* cf. below, pp. 263–268.
5 Cf. below, pp. 194; 215.
6 On the decline of Latin literature in the Hadrianic age cf. for example the influential Steinmetz 1982, 1 and more recent biliography in Heusch 2011, 2 n. 3.

In the educational sense, two key factors make the second century 'humane': the general attention paid to the *artes liberales* and the related rise and success of the so-called Second Sophistic. Let us stick to literary sources. We have already mentioned the *artes liberales* and their relationship to *humanitas* both in the Cicero section in Chapter 2 and when discussing Tacitus' *Agricola* 21 in Chapter 3, as well as Pliny's statement *Si quando urbs nostra liberalibus studiis floruit, nunc maxime floret* (*Ep.* 1.10.1, that about Euphrates). However, it is only in Gellius' *Noctes Atticae* that the liberal arts are at the very core of the work as they had been in Varro's nine books *De disciplinis*, so much so that Mercklin rightly observed: "Sein [sc. Gellius'] Ideal war eine Enzyclopädie der freiesten Art nach Form und Umfang."[7] Grammar, Dialectic, Rhetoric, Geometry, Arithmetic, Astrology, Music and Medicine were in fact all important to Gellius' educational programme, as we shall see in more detail later.[8] Nor is Gellius unique from this standpoint, as he probably derived this view from his master Fronto,[9] and his contemporary Apuleius once wrote:

> Sapientis uiri super mensam celebre dictum est: 'prima', inquit, 'creterra ad sitim pertinet, secunda ad hilaritatem, tertia ad uoluptatem, quarta ad insaniam'. Verum enimuero Musarum creterra uersa uice quanto crebrior quantoque meracior, tanto propior ad animi sanitatem. Prima creterra litteratoris ruditatem eximit, secunda grammatici doctrina instruit, tertia rhetoris eloquentia armat. Hactenus a plerisque potatur. Ego et alias creterras Athenis bibi: poeticae conditam, geometriae limpidam, musicae dulcem, dialecticae austerulam, iam uero uniuersae philosophiae inexplebilem scilicet et nectaream. (*Flor.* 20.1-4)

> There is a famous saying of a wise man over dinner: "The first bowl," said he, "is for thirst, the second for cheer, the third for pleasure, the fourth for delirium." Not so the Muses' bowl: the more often drunk and the more strongly mixed, the more it promotes the health of the mind. The first bowl is the writing master's, and removes ignorance; the second is the schoolmaster's and provides learning; the third is the rhetorician's and arms with eloquence. Most drink no more than that: but *I* have drunk other bowls too in Athens – the aromatic one of poetry, the clear one of geometry, the sweet one of music, the slightly sharp one of dialectic, and of course the inexhaustible and sweet one of universal philosophy. (trans. Jones 2017)

Exact correspondence between Varro's *disciplinae*, Gellius' *artes* and the subjects mentioned by Apuleius is not to be expected. After all, what counts is that they all share the same quest for encyclopedic knowledge. Moreover, Athens and Greek culture play a fundamental role in fostering and enhancing such encyclopedic

---

7 Mercklin 1860, 694. Cf. also Pausch 2004, 150–163; Heusch 2011, 334–338.
8 Architecture, Varro's ninth *disciplina* seems to be of less interest to Gellius.
9 Cf. *e.g.* Heusch 2011, 337–338.

learning, as Apuleius' passage makes immediately clear, although the same message emerges from Gellius' *Noctes Atticae*.[10] Nor is this phenomenon limited to these two authors, for Roman society as a whole, and especially its elite, gradually became more and more bicultural and bilingual.[11]

Whether or not they can all be considered representatives of the Second Sophistic in strict terms, it is thanks to figures like Herodes Atticus, Favorinus, Aelius Aristides, Dio of Prusa or Apuleius that this superior bilingual culture established itself as the distinctive feature of the second century CE, especially of the Antonine age. Generally Greek by culture, these men were used to wandering all over the Empire to give public speeches and show off their learning. Superior knowledge, rhetoric, oratory and theatricality were their keywords. Quite inevitably, they made contact with Roman people, very often with members of the most prominent Roman families, sometimes even with the imperial one. Their appeal must have been irresistible, and their influence over Roman society clearly relevant. One of the personalities mentioned above, Herodes Atticus, who is also one of the most cited in Gellius' *Noctes Atticae*, even held the Consulate (143 CE).[12]

In the philanthropic sense, the best evidence in support of the 'humane' character of the second century CE comes from the field of law, where the so-called *humanior interpretatio iuris* reached its acme under the reign of Marcus Aurelius (161–180 CE).[13] This label simply means that laws and penalties generally became more lenient. The fact that the peak of this milder attitude is bound up with the person of the Philosopher-Emperor comes as no surprise, since Stoicism, the philosophy professed by Marcus Aurelius, safeguarded the rights of all human beings *qua* humans. Yet, if the role of Marcus must not be underestimated, lenient laws can also be seen as the arrival point of the cultural 'revolution' which began with Pliny and Trajan, and continued with the Second Sophistic. In other words, and to return to *humanitas*, in the long run *humanitas*-φιλανθρωπία (i.e. *humanior interpretatio iuris*) might also be interpreted as a consequence of *humanitas*-παιδεία (i.e. the central role of learning as a medium to moral excellence after Domitian).

Let me turn now to which authors on the Latin side reflected and contributed to creating the cultural and social climate I have sketched out – and how their *humanitas* relates to it.

---

10 Cf. Chapter 4.2: below, pp. 158–174.

11 Cf. D'Elia 1995, 58–59.

12 Cf. Dihle 2013, 2015: "The general spirit of the period is epitomised by the fact that in 143 AD, the Consulate was held jointly by M. Cornelius Fronto and Herodes Atticus, the two most renowned men of letters from the Latin and the Greek side respectively."

13 On *humanior interpretatio iuris* and *humanitas* in Roman law under Marcus Aurelius cf. *e.g.* D'Elia 1995, 41–43; De Pascali 2008; Costabile 2016, 193.

The chapter that follows starts off with Apuleius' revival of the judicial use of *humanitas*, which is not otherwise attested after Cicero and which evokes the aforementioned practice of *humanior interpretatio iuris*. Interestingly, this use of *humanitas* in Apuleius is not limited to the *Apologia*, but also plays a role in the *Metamorphoses*. I then move on to analysing a couple of significant instances of *humanus* in Apuleius' novel, where this adjective characterises some human features that either Lucius preserves after turning into an ass or reacquires during his process of retransformation into a man. The Apuleius section concludes with a focus on the *De Platone et eius dogmate*, the only 'purely' philosophical of his works where *humanitas* appears.

The second, longer chapter section is devoted to Aulus Gellius' *Noctes Atticae*. By analysing the instances of *humanitas* and by comparing them to some methodological premises that can be found in Gellius' preface, I seek to show the central role that *humanitas*, ultimately to be taken as encyclopedic learning, played in the educational programme he lays down in his work. Naturally, the famous passage of 13.17, which I have already mentioned several times as it is inevitably at the core of any research into *humanitas*, raises further questions that cannot be summarised here, but are given ample room both in the Gellius section and in other parts of the present work.

Finally, Fronto's rare use of the term *humanitas* throws further light on Gellius' exceptional, somehow revolutionary use of this term, at the same time corroborating Gellius' assertion that his contemporary did not give to *humanitas* the meaning of παιδεία, but favoured instead the meaning of φιλανθρωπία. In doing this, I also advance a speculative hypothesis, based on Fronto's own comments on the importance of word choice, as to why Fronto probably preferred other, more specific words to the polysemy and consequent ambiguity of *humanitas*.

4.1 *Humanitas* in the Courtroom: Apuleius

Apuleius of Madauros was a very versatile author. His extant works include an oration (*Apologia siue de magia*), a novel (*Metamorphoses siue asinus aureus*), excerpts of epideictic speeches (*Florida*), and philosophical treatises (*De deo Socratis, De Platone et eius dogmate, De mundo*).[14] In particular, two works stand out: the *Apologia*, the only entire judicial oration that has come down to us from imperial Latinity, and the *Metamorphoses*, the only complete work of prose fiction in Latin we possess. These are also the works which best reflect Apuleius' idea of

---

14 On his lost (and spurious) works cf. the survey in Gianotti 2004[2], 148–150.

humanitas and *humanus*. Two peculiarities will emerge. First, Apuleius mainly seems to link *humanitas* to the legal sphere, and exploits it for rhetorical purposes: this happens not only in the *Apologia*, but in the *Metamorphoses* as well. Secondly, given that the aspiration of Lucius-ass to reacquire his human appearance is at the core of the *Metamorphoses* from Book 4 onwards, the idea of humanness is present time and again throughout the story. However, this idea is exclusively expressed through the use of the adjective *humanus*, while the noun *humanitas* appears only once, and within a detour from the main plot, after Lucius' metamorphosis. But let us focus on the *Apologia* first.

4.1.1 The *Apologia*

Apuleius delivered the *Apologia* in his own defence about 158–159 CE.[15] The story, as is narrated by Apuleius, is quite simple: at his friend Pontianus' insistence, Apuleius marries Pontianus' mother Pudentilla, a wealthy widow who is significantly older than him. When Pontianus dies, Pudentilla's family, evidently resorting to a pretext, accuses Apuleius of having seduced her by magical means – hence the alternative title *De magia*[16] – in order to inherit her property after her death. We do not know for certain what the outcome of the trial was, but we infer that Apuleius probably demonstrated the inconsistency of the charge against him and was presumably acquitted.[17] It is true that the *Apologia* as we read it is almost certainly a re-elaborated version of the original speech he delivered,[18] but it nonetheless shows the absurdity of the accusation, mainly revealing that, according to Pudentilla's will, it was not Apuleius but her sons who stood to inherit her wealth.

As is usually the case with judicial orations, Apuleius' strategy needed to be twofold in order for his defence speech to work: on the one hand, he had to prove

---

15 The date of the trial is given by the date of Maximus' proconsulate: cf. relevant bibliography in Bradley 1997, 203 n.1. Modern scholarship has called into question the existence of this trial against Apuleius. In other words, some believe that this oration represents not only the literary revision of a true speech, but a literary work *tout court*. For a *status quaestionis* cf. Binternagel 2008, 9–20, with rich bibliography.
16 On the title of this oration cf. Costantini 2019, 2–4.
17 Cf. Costantini 2019, 7: "In addition to the triumphant tone which shines through his *Apologia*, the fact that the speech was later revised and published, the presence of statues to honour Apuleius' success alongside his career as rhetorician and priest in Carthage during the 160s AD, is strong evidence for his acquittal."
18 But cf. Gianotti 2004², 162: "Per quanto ritoccata con intenti letterari che potenziano i *colores* retorici e indulgono alle digressioni a effetto, la stesura a noi giunta dell'*Apologia* non ha perso il carattere di orazione giudiziaria cui è affidato il destino d'un imputato."

that the prosecution had no evidence against him; on the other hand, he sought to create an exclusive bond between the judge, that is the proconsul, and himself. What interests us here is the latter aspect of his strategy. Aware of his superior education, Apuleius mainly relied on it, believing this would be the common denominator between the proconsul Maximus and himself. The fact that Apuleius bombards Maximus, the audience (and today's readers) with citations from and allusions to ancient writers is ultimately due to his desire to display his extensive learning. Needless to say, times had changed and the golden age of Ciceronian oratory was just a memory, but Apuleius' emphasis on the importance of education and culture throughout the *Apologia* reminds us of Cicero's *Pro Archia*.[19] We have already seen in both the Cicero and the Pliny sections how the educational aspect of *humanitas* was central to this speech, and that Cicero exploited the polysemy of *humanitas* in the final *peroratio*.[20] The reader in search of this same educational and polysemic idea of *humanitas* in Apuleius' *De magia* would probably be disappointed. But in spite of the different nuances that the term takes on, in both orations *humanitas* is one of the qualities praised in the judges. Apuleius makes this clear at *Apol.* 35, when he rejects the accusation of using two marine animals, which he calls *ueretilla* and *uirginal* (probably to be identified with *balanus* and *pecten* respectively), for the sake of his erotic pleasure.[21] Finding this accusation ridiculous, he addresses Maximus as follows:

> Ne tu, Claudi Maxime, nimis patiens uir es et oppido proxima humanitate, qui hasce eorum argumentationes diu hercle perpessus sis; equidem, cum haec ab illis quasi grauia et uincibilia dicerentur, illorum stultitiam ridebam, tuam patientiam mirabar.

> Really, Claudius Maximus, you are a very patient man, and sympathethic (*proxima humanitate*) to the townspeople, to put up so very long with their arguments. Speaking for myself, I smiled at their stupidity and marveled at your patience when they mentioned such items as if they were grave and overwhelming. (trans. Jones 2017)

---

19 More generally, some scholars believe the *Apologia* to have a Ciceronian character: cf. Carbonero 1977; Harrison 2000, 44; 51; 2013, 41–42; May 2006, 75 and n. 15 for further bibliography. By contrast, Hijmans 1994 – 1727–1729 and 1762 in particular – Hunink 1997a; 1997b; 1998 seem to reject the idea that Apuleius is imitating one single model. On Cicero's use of *humanitas* in the *Pro Archia* cf. above, pp. 53–61. One of the aims of Costantini 2019 is to show that Apuleius' strategy must be "framed within a Platonic logic: Apuleius presents himself and the judge at the zenith of a Platonising hierarchy whereas the prosecutors lie at its base. Their spiritual vulgarity is the reason why they fail to understand the innocence of Apuleius, a true Socrates reborn as various scholars argue" (9).
20 Cf. above, pp. 59–60.
21 On these two fishes in the *Apologia* cf. Binternagel 2008, 61–63; Pellecchi 2012, 156–157 (with further bibliography); Costantini 2019, 112–119. The terms *uirginal* and *ueretilla* were probably coined by Apuleius himself: cf. Caracausi 1986–87, 169; Nicolini 2011, 132 n. 405.

Whoever aims at creating an exclusive bond also needs to create a category of those who are excluded from this bond. In the *Apologia*, not only the accusers, but also the inhabitants of Sabratha as a whole constitute this category. True, Apuleius scorns them because of their stupidity and lack of education (*illorum stultitiam ridebam*); nevertheless, he admires (and flatters) Maximus, whose *patientia* and *humanitas* enable him to tolerate their ignorance (*tuam patientiam mirabar*).[22] Even more than *humanitas*, *patientia* is the key term of this passage: as well as constituting the climactic point at the close of the sentence, it is evoked by the adjective *patiens* and the verb *perpessus sis*. But like *humanitas*, *patientia* is a value-term which is characterised by variability and ambivalence. Kaster claims: "It [scil. *patientia*] is a term that, more than any other Latin word I know, can be used to express either high praise or grave condemnation."[23] A survey of its instances reveals that it can correspond to dispositions such as endurance, patience, forbearance, but also passivity and submissiveness.[24] In other words, *patientia* is not necessarily a virtue. However, as Kaster 2002, 142 goes on to say,

> There was one category of free man in whom *patientia* was regularly praised and upon whom it was unhesitatingly urged, directly or by implication, as a virtue: that was the man whose superior power was beyond question [. . .] in whom *patientia* was above all the forbearance that stayed his hand and kept him from reaching out to crush his inferiors.[25]

This description fits our passage: no doubt the proconsul Maximus belongs to that category of powerful men, and no doubt Apuleius praises his *patientia*. But it is also the pairing with *humanitas* which leads us to understand *patientia* as forbearance; vice versa, *patientia* helps us better understand the meaning of *humanitas*.

Since Apuleius needs to widen the gap between Maximus and the throng, it would be counter-productive – and even outrageous – to claim that Maximus' *humanitas* is *proxima oppido* (very, perhaps too, close to the townspeople), if *humanitas* took on educational nuances as in Cicero's *Pro Archia*. Needless to say, neither a proconsul nor his education can be put on the same level as the throng. Conversely, *proxima oppido* strengthens the philanthropic idea that *humanitas* takes on here. But because of the uniqueness of the expression which originates from it, *proxima* was sometimes suspected of being a wrong *lectio*, in spite of both the manuscripts F and φ having this reading. By contrast, in the attempt to defend it, Butler and Owen maintained that this and two other instances of *proximus* in Apu-

---

22 Cf. Hunink 1997b, 113 on this passage: "One of the numerous examples of flattery of the judge."
23 Kaster 2002, 135.
24 Kaster 2002, 135. Cf. also *TLL* 10.1.708.55–10.1.716.27.
25 Kaster 2002, 142.

leius' *Apologia* are not to be seen as superlative, but as positive forms whose meaning would be 'easy, obvious, convenient'.[26] In support of their thesis they pointed out that a comparative *proximius* can be found in Ulpian *Dig.* 38.8.1.8 and Minucius Felix *Oct.* 19.2. Nowadays it is far easier for scholars to verify that the instances are actually many more, among which we can include Seneca, *Ep.* 108.16 (*abstinentiae proximiorem*) and, when the adjective is substantivised, Prisc. *Inst.* II 97, 15.[27] Yet it is my contention that *proxima* is really a superlative at *Apol.* 35. Despite the fact that the overall understanding of the passage does not depend on this issue, it must be noted that the context seems to suggest the presence of a superlative: *nimis patiens* makes in fact clear that Apuleius is talking about a behaviour and an attitude which are extraordinary and excessively tolerant and benevolent because they are undeserved. If in the following phrase *proxima* were taken as a simple, positive adjective, the tone of the sentence would be weakened, and Apuleius' wonder at Maximus' patience less comprehensible.

As for the juxtaposition of *patientia* and *humanitas*, we have already encountered it in a very short letter which Pliny sent to Trajan (10.106). In his article on *patientia*, Kaster does not mention *Apol.* 35, but he does mention this letter, where *humanitas* is for the first time placed in close relation with *patientia*.[28] Like Apuleius, Pliny needs to praise his superior addressee to gain his favour. And if *patientia* and *humanitas* enable Maximus to put up with the prosecution's unsubstantiated line of argument (*argumentationes*), these same virtues should lead Trajan to accept his soldiers' pleas (*precibus*). Trajan's positive response (10.107) confirms both the emperor's closeness to his army and the efficacy of the *patientia-humanitas* argument.

But in the *Apologia* there are other ways in which Apuleius exploits the *humanitas* argument to spotlight the boundary which separates Maximus and himself from his rivals and the inhabitants of Sabratha. At *Apol.* 86, while rebuking Pudentilla's son, who is guilty of divulging some of his mother's most private letters, he praises the different behaviour of the Athenians in an analogous situation:

> Athenienses quidem propter commune ius humanitatis ex captiuis epistulis Philippi Macedonis hostis sui unam epistulam, cum singulae publice legerentur, recitari prohibuerunt, quae erat ad uxorem Olympiadem conscripta.

> Now the Athenians observed the common laws of *humanitas* when they had intercepted their enemy Philip's letters. They had each of them read out in public, but prohibited the reading of one that he had written to his wife Olympias. (trans. Jones 2017)

---

26 Butler/Owen 1914, 24.
27 Cf. *TLL* 10.2.2040.74–2041.23 for a more detailed list.
28 Kaster 2002, 143. Cf. above, pp. 96–97.

The same anecdote is recorded by Plutarch, in the *Life of Demetrius* 22:[29]

καὶ τὴν Ἀθηναίων οὐκ ἐμιμήσαντο [*scil.* οἱ Ῥόδιοι] φιλανθρωπίαν, οἳ Φιλίππου πολεμοῦντος αὐτοῖς γραμματοφόρους ἑλόντες, τὰς μὲν ἄλλας ἀνέγνωσαν ἐπιστολάς, μόνην δὲ τὴν Ὀλυμπιάδος οὐκ ἔλυσαν, ἀλλ' ὥσπερ ἦν κατασεσημασμένη πρὸς ἐκεῖνον ἀπέστειλαν.

In this they [i.e. the Rhodians] did not imitate the considerate kindness of the Athenians, who, having captured Philip's letter-carriers when he was making war upon them, read all the other letters, indeed, but one of them, which was for Olympias, they would not open; instead, they sent it back to the king with its seal unbroken. (trans. Perrin 1920)

This story must have been well known in Plutarch's and Apuleius' day, so that to investigate whether the latter draws upon the former, if this were possible, would be of no consequence. Nevertheless it is striking that when the Greek author attributes this Athenian behaviour to their φιλανθρωπία, the Latin attributes it to their *ius humanitatis*.[30]

This expression, as I mentioned above, had been previously used by Cicero. We have already come across its occurrence at *Pro Flacco* 57, while dealing with Suetonius and the twinning of *officium* and *humanitas*, where *ius* appears in its plural form, *iura*.[31] Compare *Pro rege Deiotaro* 30: *Esto: concedatur haec quoque acerbitas et odii magnitudo: adeone, ut omnia uitae salutisque communis atque etiam humanitatis iura uiolentur?* ("Be it so: – let even this excess of bitterness and hatred be permitted. Was it to go to such an extent that all the laws of ordinary life and of common safety, and even of *humanitas*, are to be violated?", trans. Yonge 1913). As Gotoff puts it, here "Cicero maintains that Castor fails to adhere to the lowest code of conduct for civilized men."[32] The worst thing he does – *atque etiam* makes this clear – is in fact to violate every law of humanity. And to stress further the universality of this concept, Cicero pairs this expression with the adjective *communis*. Although in strict grammatical terms *communis*

---

29 On anecdotes in Apuleius' *De magia* cf. Binternagel 2008, 136–167 (148 on this very anecdote).

30 According to numerous sources (Sen. *Dial.* 4.23.4; Plin. *NH* 7.93–94 and Cass. Dio 41.63.5), Julius Caesar made something similar when burning, after refusing to open, the letter-boxes of the dead Pompey: interestingly, Seneca ascribes this behaviour to Caesar's *clementia*, Pliny to his *magnanimitas* and Cassius Dio to his φιλανθρωπία. Yet there is a fundamental difference between the two episodes: while the Athenians seem to be willing to respect Philip's privacy, Caesar's decision to burn the letters of his defeated rival is identified with his willingness to deny "himself access to material with which he [. . .] might otherwise persecute those implicated therein", as Howley 2017, 221 puts it. It is my contention that the uses of *ius humanitatis* in Apuleius and of *clementia* in Seneca mirror this behavioural difference, which instead vanishes in the Greek texts of Plutarch and Cassius Dio.

31 Cf. above, p. 131.

32 Gotoff 1993, 251.

goes with *salus* (*salutisque*) in this passage, at *Pro Flacco* 24 – the third and last occurrence of *ius humanitatis* in Cicero – it goes with *humanitas*, as in *Apologia* 86 (and as in the *Apologia*, *ius* is singular):

> Si quem infimo loco natum, nullo splendore uitae, nulla commendatione famae defenderem, tamen ciuem a ciuibus communis humanitatis iure ac misericordia deprecarer, ne ignotis testibus, ne incitatis, ne accusatoris consessoribus, conuiuis, contubernalibus, ne hominibus leuitate Graecis, crudelitate barbaris ciuem ac supplicem uestrum dederetis, ne periculosam imitationem exempli reliquis in posterum proderetis.

> If I were defending a man of low birth, of no distinction, with no reputation to commend him, but still a citizen, I would beg of you as citizens, in the name of the common law of *humanitas* and in the name of pity, not to surrender a citizen and your suppliant to unknown and suborned witnesses, the assistants, guests and intimates of the prosecutor, to men who are Greek in their fickleness and savages in their cruelty, lest you establish a dangerous precedent for others in after time. (trans. Lord 1953, slightly adapted)

In Apuleius' *De magia*, the presence of *communis*, in specifying that each and every Athenian possesses the idea(s) expressed by *ius humanitatis*, implies a widening of the gap between the civilized inhabitants of Athens, possibly the 'inventors' or 'founders' of *humanitas*, and the 'barbarians' of Sabratha, none of whom allegedly know *humanitas*.[33] In contrast, there is no hint of comparison in the Ciceronian occurrences, but again the adjective undoubtedly strengthens the bond within the civic community. This bond is neither innate in every man nor culturally established, but safeguarded by law (*ius*). In commenting on the passage under investigation, and on the phrase *commune ius humanitatis* in particular, Hunink has observed: "an expression referring to what is commonly called *ius gentium*, a judicial and philosophical concept which had become widespread in Apuleius' days."[34] Yet this statement raises some doubts. It is true that, as I have emphasised, such an expression mirrors the people's mentality, which regarded (milder and more humane) laws as a cornerstone of Roman society, especially in the Antonine age.[35] Nor is it due to chance that the phrase only appears in judicial contexts.[36] Technically speaking, however, Roman law did not include any formal

---

33 On the origins of *humanitas* cf. above, pp. 34–38.
34 Hunink 1997b, 211.
35 Cf. above, pp. 134–137.
36 Alongside the rarity of this phrase, this is the reason why statements such as "the notion of *humanitatis iura* is commonplace" (Gotoff 1993, 251) do not stand up to scrutiny. Analogously, I would not push the argument so far as to claim with Norden 1912, 59: "Da Apulejus den Ausdruck *commune ius humanitatis* nahezu wie ein Schlagwort gebraucht, dürfen wir annehmen, dass zu seiner Zeit die Idee des Weltbürgerrechtes eine feststehende geworden war." Cf. below for the second Apuleian occurrence of *commune ius humanitatis* in *Met.* 3.8.

ius humanitatis, and Hunink's reference to Gaius' *Institutiones* 1.1 only proves the existence of a 'formal' *ius gentium* and not the equivalence between *ius gentium* and *ius humanitatis*.[37] On the contrary, Gaius says that such a universal right is only called *ius gentium*, without allowing any other definition.[38] Moreover, given the undeniable relationship between Greek φιλανθρωπία and Latin *humanitas*, the comparison of *Apol.* 86 with Plutarch, *Demetr.* 22 rather confirms the philanthropic component which lies behind the expression *ius humanitatis* than this law being shared by all the peoples of the world.

But to clarify this issue further, let us open a brief parenthesis on the relationship between *ius* and the root *human-* in general. To express an idea which is analogous to that of *ius humanitatis*, Latin juridical texts like to resort, for example, to the formula *humanius est*, in which the comparative, as we have seen, is much apter than the positive *humanum* to render the complexity of the abstract noun.[39] After all the *ius humanum*, in which the positive form of the adjective appears, represents another major division in Roman right. At *Institutiones* 2.1-2, for example, Gaius writes:

> Superiore commentario de iure personarum exposuimus; modo uideamus de rebus: quae uel in nostro patrimonio sunt uel extra nostrum patrimonium habentur. Summa itaque rerum diuisio in duos articulos diducitur: nam aliae sunt diuini iuris, aliae humani.[40]

> In the former Commentary we explained the *ius* of persons; now let us consider the *ius* of things, which either form part of our property or do not form part of it. The principal divi-

---

37 Cf. Gaius 1.1: *Omnes populi, qui legibus et moribus reguntur, partim suo proprio, partim communi omnium hominum iure utuntur: nam quod quisque populus ipse sibi ius constituit, id ipsius proprium est uocaturque ius ciuile, quasi ius proprium ciuitatis; quod uero naturalis ratio inter omnes homines constituit, id apud omnes populos peraeque custoditur uocaturque ius gentium, quasi quo iure omnes gentes utuntur. Populus itaque Romanus partim suo proprio, partim communi omnium hominum iure utitur* ("All peoples who are ruled by laws and customs partly make use of their own *ius*, and partly have recourse to the *iura* which are common to all men; for what every people establishes as *ius* is their own and is called the *ius ciuile*, just as the *ius* of their own city; and what natural reason establishes among all men and is observed by all peoples alike, is called the *ius gentium*, as being the *ius* which all nations employ. Therefore the Roman people partly make use of their own *ius*, and partly avail themselves of the *ius* common to all men", trans. de Zulueta 1946).
38 Cf. also Justinian's *Digest* 1.1.1.4: *Ius gentium est quod gentes humanae utuntur*, where *humanae* is a simple relational adjective which means 'of man' and has nothing to do with the implications of the abstract *humanitas*.
39 On *humanius est* cf. Berger 1953, 489 and Pieri 2002, 373. This expression is also to be found in *Decl. min.* 279.5, on which cf. below, pp. 200–201. More generally on the relation between *humanitas* and *humanus/humanior* above, p. 22.
40 Justinian's *Digest* 1.8.1.1 reproduces Gaius' *Institutiones* 2.2 *verbatim*.

sion of things is under two heads, namely, those that are subject to divine right, and those that are subject to human right. (trans. de Zulueta 1946)

This opposition between *ius humanum* and *ius diuinum* must have been traditional and can already be found in Cicero's *De partitione oratoria* 129, not to mention the numerous passages by many authors in which we read of *diuina humanaque iura*. But it clearly implies that *humanum* takes on a pure relational meaning which at the same time excludes any sort of ethical implications or judgements, and only counterposes laws concerning human to laws concerning divine entities. *Ius humanitatis* and *ius humanum* are therefore two completely distinct concepts.

To return to Apuleius. In addition to the Athenians and Maximus – and, implicitly, Apuleius himself – the category of the 'chosen few' includes a fourth protagonist, Lollianus Avitus, Maximus' predecessor as proconsul. After he is merely named at *Apol.* 24, his presence in the *Apologia* becomes more significant from paragraph 94 onwards. Here, Apuleius provides examples that show against the claimants that he has always been in favour of and not against his stepsons. An example he gives is a letter of recommendation he wrote for Pontianus to Lollianus Avitus, 'seen as a climactic point in the case.'[41] Judging from Apuleius' account, the proconsul must have been very pleased to receive his letter:

> [h]is epistulis meis lectis pro sua eximia humanitate gratulatus Pontiano, quod cito [h]errorem suum correxisset, rescripsit mihi per eum quas litteras, di boni, qua doctrina, quo lepore, qua uerborum amoenitate simul et iucunditate, prorsus ut 'uir bonus dicendi peritus'. Scio te, Maxime, libenter eius litteras auditurum.

> On reading my letter, as the extraordinarily kind person he is, he congratulated Pontianus on having promptly corrected his mistake, and through him he sent back such a letter to me – heavens above – so cultivated, so elegant, in language both so charming and so pleasant, absolutely like "the good man skilled in speech" he is. I know, Maximus, that you will be glad to hear his letter. (trans. Jones 2017)

The error to which Apuleius refers here concerns his stepsons' misunderstanding: previously convinced that he would take advantage of his position and try to seize Pudentilla's property, they – or at least Pontianus – had by that time realised that this had not been the case. At any rate, what matters here is something else. As Harrison puts it: "It is of course a parallel for Avitus' successor Maximus' support for Apuleius in the case in progress; the panegyric pronounced on Avitus matches the praise of Maximus already frequently expressed in Apuleius' speech."[42] As we have seen, right from the beginning Apuleius displays his knowledge and erudition.

---

41 Harrison 2000, 83.
42 Harrison 2000, 83. Cf. also Hunink 1997b, 232.

On the one hand, this enhances his credibility as interpreter of the texts (letters, for instance) which will be read during the trial.[43] On the other – and it is worth stressing this again – "Apuleius seeks to develop a complicity between himself and Maximus", whose eulogy is mainly based on his philosophical knowledge and literary education, and sets the two of them apart from the throng.[44] In the passage under investigation Apuleius is thus simply including Maximus' predecessor in this exclusive relationship. Avitus' learning (*doctrina*) and charm of language (*lepos, uerborum amoenitas et iucunditas*) even make a *uir bonus dicendi peritus* of him. Moreover, it should not pass unnoticed that Apuleius is again showing off his own literary knowledge by quoting Cato the Elder's definition of the good orator, which clearly links the superior culture that a good orator ought to possess (*dicendi peritus*) to the moral sphere (*uir bonus*).[45] In a way, we might say that the idea of *humanitas*, in potentially implying both παιδεία and φιλανθρωπία, corresponds to this definition. Or, in other words, the idea of *humanitas* perfectly fits the orator. Accordingly, in general terms both *doctrina* and *lepos* could be closely related to *humanitas*.[46] But to what extent is this the case in the *Apologia*? While Avitus shows his *humanitas* in the act of congratulating Pontianus, who has understood that Apuleius is not to be seen as an enemy, he displays his *doctrina* and *lepos* in his own reply to Apuleius. For all their connections, these two episodes are distinct. As in the previous instances in the *Apologia*, here again *humanitas* is rather to be seen as having connotations of philanthropy. What is at stake in its use is Avitus' benevolence, not his education. Nevertheless, one may reasonably argue that his education lies behind his φιλανθρωπία. Granted, there is no evidence for this and such an interpretation would come into conflict with Apuleius' use of *humanitas* at *Apol.* 35 (where *humanitas* can hardly take on educational nuances), but the polysemy of *humanitas* does allow for this reading. The cases of Cicero and Pliny the Younger make this clear.[47] Regardless of this issue, it is evident that *humanitas* does play an important role in Apuleius' defence – perhaps not as a means of expressing education and knowledge, but along with (or as a consequence of) education and knowledge, *humanitas* is what brings together the civilized Athenians, the two proconsuls Maximus and Avitus, as well as, we might add, Apuleius himself, and what sets them apart from the common inhabitants of Sabratha and Apuleius' accusers. In

---

43 Noreña 2014, 40–41.

44 Harrison 2000, 46. Cf. also Sandy 1997, 132–133.

45 On this definition and other passages in which eloquence is closely linked to morality cf. Picone 1978, 150–151.

46 On *doctrina* and *humanitas* cf. above, pp. 62–63, *passim* and below, p. 167. The pair of *humanitas* with *lepos* is tipically Ciceronian: cf. *Prou.* 29; *De orat.* 2.270; 2.272; 3.29; *Fam.* 11.27.6.

47 Cf. above, Chapter 2.3 (on Cicero) and Chapter 3.1 (on Pliny the Younger).

other words, the *Apologia* is among the cases in which only an elite group of people can possess *humanitas*, though everybody can benefit from it. If Apuleius was actually acquitted, it was also thanks to his strategy and his careful use of *humanitas*.

4.1.2 The *Metamorphoses*

While in the *Apologia humanitas* is a weapon of exclusion, in the mock trial which takes place in Hypata during the Risus Festival (*Metamorphoses* 3), it becomes a double-edged sword. The protagonist Lucius, who is charged with voluntary manslaughter, immediately realises that, in the hope of being acquitted, he needs to win over the audience. Thus, he seeks to show that he too is part of the same community as the Hypatans: certainly not as a fellow citizen, but at least as a fellow human being. As Apuleius in the *Apologia*, though with the opposite aim in mind, Lucius also resorts to the *humanitas* argument in his defence speech, which van der Paardt refers to as an '*Apologia parua*'.[48] But his weapon backfires, for the witnesses for the prosecution seem to be able to use *humanitas* in a more sophisticated way, thereby reiterating Lucius' exclusion from the community. On the one hand, this mock trial corroborates the potential of the *humanitas* argument in the legal sphere, at least in Apuleius' view; on the other hand, the versatility of *humanitas* shows that this concept can be applied to opposite purposes, that is to create both exclusion and inclusion. Let us take a closer look at the texts.

While returning one night to his host Milo's house, Lucius, yet to be turned into a donkey, sees three robbers at the door. Being drunk, he does not hesitate to pull out his sword and kill the three of them. He then goes to bed. The following morning, when he gets up, the local magistrates are waiting to arrest and try him. Both during his journey to the courtroom and theatre, where the trial is eventually to take place, and during the trial itself, while Lucius is in despair, the crowd is laughing. The reason for this is eventually revealed: Lucius has not killed three men, but three wineskins that had been turned into men through a magic trick. In other words, having been the victim-protagonist of the Risus Festival which takes place every year at Hypata (Thessaly), Lucius has "served as patron of the Hypatans' community."[49]

---

48 Van der Paardt 1971, 63. Apart from the resemblance of these two speeches, on which cf. also May 2006, 182 and n.1 for further bibliography, Apuleius is believed to allude on several occasions to the *Apologia* in the *Metamorphoses*: cf. Mason 1983, 142–143; Harrison 2000, 9–10; 2013, 84 and n. 12 for further bibliography.
49 Habinek 1990, 54.

Apuleius' *Metamorphoses* is generally thought to be based on the lost *Metamorphoses* by the Greek Lucius of Patrae.[50] The relationship between the two – and the *Onos*, which is included in the Lucianic corpus – is disputed, but most scholars believe the Risus Festival, or the trial at the very least, to be originally Apuleian.[51] A survey of the use of *humanitas* within the trial of Hypata, and of the trial's interaction with the *Apologia* will also back up this view.

Lucius' defence begins at 3.4 and the judges' and people's *publica humanitas* is immediately invoked as the common value that should grant Lucius the right to defend himself even if the accusation seems to be incontestable:

> Nec ipse ignoro quam sit arduum trinis ciuium corporibus expositis eum qui caedis arguatur, quamuis uera dicat et de facto confiteatur ultro, tamen tantae multitudini quod sit innocens persuadere. Set si paulisper audientiam publica mihi tribuerit humanitas, facile uos edocebo me discrimen capitis non meo merito sed rationabilis indignationis euentu fortuito tantam criminis inuidiam frustra sustinere.

> I am not unaware how difficult it is, in the full display of the corpses of three citizens, for him who is accused of their murder, even though he speak the truth and voluntarily admit to the facts themselves, to persuade so large an audience that he is innocent. But if your public *humanitas* will briefly grant me a hearing, I shall easily convince you that I am not on trial for my life through any fault of my own, but rather, I am groundlessly suffering the great odium of the accusation as an accidental outcome of reasonable indignation. (trans. Hanson, adapted 1989)

Compared to Apuleius' *Apologia*, the different use of *humanitas* is immediately striking: while in the trial of Sabratha *humanitas* is seen as a prerogative of some people or social categories but not of its citizens, here *humanitas* is a quality which characterises the inhabitants of Hypata as a whole. This is much highlighted by the adjective *publica*, which also defines *humanitas* in [Quint.] *Decl.* 254.6 and 12, as al-

---

50 This has been the main strand of thought since Bürger 1887. An exception is represented by Bianco 1971, who believes that Apuleius' *Metamorphoses* derives directly from the *Onos*.

51 Cf. Perry 1923, 221; 1925, 253–254; Summers 1970, 511; Walsh 1970, 148; Bianco 1971, 49–63; May 2006, 188 and n. 19 for further bibliography, and a *status quaestionis* with further bibliography in De Trane 2009, 199. More sceptical Costantini 2021, 16: "The other surviving ass-novel, the *Onos*, does not preserve a comparable account of the Risus Festival (either the mock trial or the 'utricide'). Thus, it is impossible to ascertain whether this episode is entirely invented by Apuleius, or if he might have modelled it on the *Ur*-ass-novel or other traditions." More generally on the relationship between Apuleius' *Metamorphoses*, Lucius of Patrae's *Metamorphoses* and the *Onos* cf. Walsh 1970, 145–149; Bianco 1971; Mason 1978, 1–6; Scobie 1978, 43–46; Ciaffi 1983; James 1987, 7–16; Schlam 1992, 18–25; De Trane 2009, 15–22; Harrison 2013, 197–213 – on topographical differences – and 233; Tilg 2014, 1–18 and further bibliography in Harrison 1999, xxx.

ready noticed by van der Paardt, and [Quint.] *Decl. mai.* 6.3.[52] Set at the *exordium* of the oration, this phrase immediately shows that Lucius "has created his speech to the throng."[53] As for the meaning of *humanitas, publica* strengthens the idea of a bond that unites all human beings as such, a bond whose features Lucius clarifies later on.

The '*Apologia parua*', delivered by Lucius-protagonist and recounted by Lucius-narrator, is just over when Lucius-narrator reflects upon the results he hoped to have achieved:

> Haec profatus, rursum lacrimis obortis porrectisque in preces manibus per publicam misericordiam, per pignorum caritatem maestus tunc hos tunc illos deprecabar. Cumque iam humanitate commotos, misericordia fletuum affectos omnes satis crederem, [. . .] conspicio prorsus totum populum – risu cachinnabili diffluebant – nec secus illum bonum hospitem parentemque meum Milonem risu maximo dissolutum. (*Met.* 3.7)

> When I had finished this speech my tears welled up again and I stretched out my hands in supplication, sorrowfully begging now one group in the name of public mercy and now another for the love of their own dear children. When I felt sure that they had all been sufficiently stirred with human sympathy (*humanitas*) and moved by the pathos of my weeping, [. . .] I caught sight of the audience: absolutely the entire populace was dissolved in raucous laughter, and even my kind host and uncle, Milo, was broken up by a huge fit of laughing. (trans. Hanson 1989)

In the light of the previous passage at the outset of his defence speech, it becomes clear that in saying *cumque iam humanitate commotos, misericordia fletuum affectos omnes satis crederem*, Lucius is not only alluding to his bursting into tears and begging the judges and audience after the speech – after all, this would be quite an ingenuous pretension. More significantly, he is alluding to the tone and content of the speech itself, which right from the beginning was characterised by a plea for mercy. In this way, Lucius also reveals the key role he purposely assigned to *humanitas* in his oration. There can be no doubt that this was a stratagem: Frangoulidis clearly shows that the Hypatans are portrayed as a savage, cruel people throughout the *Metamorphoses*.[54] Given the evidence against him, as Apuleius in the *Apologia*, so Lucius in the '*Apologia parua*' thought flattery was the best weapon he had at hand.

---

52 Van der Paardt 1971, 51. The reading of the manuscripts is *audientiam publicam*. Gruter's emendation *publica*, which is thus made to agree with *humanitas*, is convincing. Haupt 1874, 243; Koch 1875, 637 and Van der Vliet 1885, 101 defended it without argument. As is clear from the main text, *publica humanitas* also appears elsewhere, while conversely, *audientia publica* never occurs in classical Latin.
53 Finkelpearl 1998, 89.
54 Frangoulidis 2008, 184–185.

On a linguistic level, this passage also helps us define Lucius' understanding of *humanitas*. Its affinity to *misericordia* is manifest: after characterising it through the adjective *publica* (*per publicam misericordiam*), which instead connoted *humanitas* at 3.4, Lucius even goes so far as to consider *humanitas* a synonym of *misericordia*. This is made clear by its use in the "asyndeton bimembre with rhetorical effect" *humanitate commotos, misericordia fletuum affectos*, where *humanitas* is used apparently to avoid the repetition of *misericordia*.[55] While the pairing of the verb *commoueo* with *misericordia* is in fact extremely common, especially in Ciceronian orations, it is never so tightly linked to *humanitas* before this Apuleian occurrence.[56] However, this does not imply that Apuleius (or his narrator Lucius) was the first to perceive a close relation between *humanitas* and *misericordia*. On the contrary, these two terms quite often appear together, mainly in Cicero, Seneca and Quintilian.[57] On occasion, *clementia* is also related to them.[58]

If on the one hand Lucius invokes *humanitas* as a defence instrument, on the other the widows of two of the three alleged corpses resort to the same argument to obtain vengeance. At 3.8, their theatrical reaction is as follows:

'Per publicam misericordiam, per commune ius humanitatis," aiunt "miseremini indigne caesorum iuuenum, nostraeque uiduitati ac solitudini de uindicta solacium date. Certe paruuli huius in primis annis destituti fortunis succurrite, et de latronis huius sanguine legibus uestris et disciplinae publicae litate.'

"In the name of public mercy," they cried, "in the name of the common rights of humanity (*per commune ius humanitatis*), have pity on these unjustly slaughtered youths and grant us the solace of vengeance in our widowhood and bereavement. At least succour the fortunes of this poor little child, orphaned in his earliest years, and make atonement to your laws and public order with that cut-throat's blood". (trans. Hanson 1989)

The opening of this speech echoes both Lucius' first words (*si paulisper audientiam publica mihi tribuerit humanitas*) and his reference in indirect speech to what he did and said right after delivering his oration (*per publicam misericordiam*). We might pinpoint just one significant difference: the widows prefer *ius*

---

55 Van der Paardt 1971, 66.
56 To quote just a few Ciceronian instances of *commoueo* with *misericordia*: *Verr.* 2.4.87; *Rab. perd.* 24; *Cluent.* 24; *Mur.* 65; *Deiot.* 40. One occurrence is also to be found in Quintilian 11.3.170.
57 Cic. *Cat.* 4.11; *Mur.* 6; *Flac.* 24 (where we have seen one of the rare occurrences of *ius humanitatis* appears); *Tusc.* 4.14.32; Quint. 6.1.22; Sen. *Ben.* 3.7.5, 5.20.5.
58 Cic. *Lig.* 29; *Rhet. Her.* 2.50; Sen. *Ben.* 6.29.1. On *misericordia* (and its relationship with *humanitas* and/or *clementia*) cf. Petré 1934; Borgo 1985, 29–30, in particular at n. 9. Yet I am sceptical about Borgo's claim that in Apuleius *misericordia* replaces *humanitas* as synonym of *clementia*: *Met.* 3.7 seems to contradict her.

humanitatis over the more banal *humanitas*. As well as suggesting lack of improvisation on the widows' part, the technicality and rarity of this expression, which we have already noticed at *Apol.* 86, reveal, more than the simple *humanitas*, the superior knowledge and the Latin education of the person speaking.[59] Or, to push this reasoning a step further, this use of *ius humanitatis* seems to unveil the author who lies behind the characters, Apuleius. Thanks to this expression, the widows not only resort to the same weapons that Lucius used, but they also try to make those weapons more effective. They achieve this through the tear-jerking presence of a child who has been made fatherless, allegedly, by Lucius' crime, and also by means of a more sympathetic vocabulary. In this respect, the pomposity of *per commune ius humanitatis* flatters the jury with their importance, and the adjective *commune* in particular contributes to Habinek's interpretation of the Hypatan festival "as a procedure whereby the community re-establishes its internal harmony and differentiates between its own civic identity and the world beyond its boundaries."[60] While at *Apol.* 86 *commune* helps oppose the civilized Athenians to the less civilized inhabitants of Sabratha, here it sets Lucius apart from the inhabitants of Hypata. But given the theatricality of the Risus Festival as a whole, readers are likely to suppose that the scene of the widows and their speech were not improvised. Fortunately for Lucius, the unveiling of the three wineskins brings about the end of the mock trial. The reader will never know whether Lucius would have been acquitted, but might imagine that in addition to the evidence against him, the widows' use of the *humanitas* argument would also have been more succesful than his.[61] We might add that in the framework of the Risus Festival the technicality of *ius humanitatis*, alongside Lucius' use of *humanitas*, also contributes to what Walsh calls "parody [. . .] of the procedure and characteristic speech of the law-court."[62] Certainly, this is facilitated by Lucius' skill as an orator, but even more by Apuleius'.[63] His oratorical experience as well as the same technical, typically Latin use of *humanitas* that we have also noticed in the

---

59 Cf. above, pp. 141–143. Cf. also Costantini 2021, 130: "Reprising the same terminology in different contexts may be seen as an attempt to engage in an oratorical competition between the parties involved in the lawsuit, as with Lucius' defence and the plaintiff's speech (IV.2). On the other hand, this also points to the stylistic uniformity of such Apuleian declamatory displays."

60 Habinek 1990, 54. On ritual and / or apotropaic interpretations of the mock trial cf. also De Trane 2009, 232–234.

61 After all, as De Trane 2009, 214 rightly remarks, neither his speech nor his pathetic gesticulation after the speech seem to allow Lucius the audience' sympathy: all people continuously laugh at him, but no one feels sorry for him.

62 Walsh 1970, 58. Cf. also Walsh 1970, 155; Finkelpearl 1998, 86–88; De Trane 2009, 211.

63 The importance of Lucius' oratorical skill within the mock trial is well highlighted by James 1987, 88. Cf. also De Trane 2009, 212–213.

Apologia may support the thesis according to which the Risus Festival, or the mock trial of Hypata at the very least, is originally Apuleian, that is to say that this episode was not present in Lucius of Patrae's *Metamorphoses*. Needless to say, the absence of the trial in the *Onos*, the only other work based on Lucius' *Metamorphoses* that has come down to us, is the best piece of evidence in favour of this theory.

After Lucius' 'acquittal' at the mock trial, the plot does not offer Apuleius further occasions for displaying his oratorical, legal mastery of the *humanitas* argument. However, *Metamorphoses* 3 somehow marks the true beginning of the story, for only towards the end of this book Lucius turns into an ass. From his metamorphosis onward, at the centre of the novel is a character who "is at great pains to demonstrate the persistence of *sensus humanus* within his bestial form."[64] The concept of humankind therefore becomes central, but the word *humanitas* seems to have little in common with this idea, and never appears to express it. Conversely, as Schlam's words suggest, the adjective *humanus* does play a role in this respect. However, since almost every book devoted to Apuleius' *Metamorphoses* deals, in a way or another, with the human and animal aspects of Lucius-turned-ass, here the focus will only be on two key cases where *humanus* bears special linguistic relevance.[65] These occurrences are also crucial in that they respectively mark the beginning and the end of Lucius' asinine life.

At *Met.* 3.26, Lucius-actor has just accidentally turned into an ass when Lucius-narrator reflects on what has happened: *Ego uero, quamquam perfectus asinus et pro Lucio iumentum, sensum tamen retinebam humanum* ("For my part, although I was a complete ass and a beast of burden instead of Lucius, I still retained my human intelligence", trans. Hanson 1989). The combination of *sensus* with *humanus* is uncommon, especially before Apuleius' day. It appears for the first time in Cicero's last works. At *Orator* 210 Cicero is warning lawyers to make prudent use of rhythmical style (*numerosa oratio*) in forensic speeches, as it might prevent the audience from feeling *humanus sensus*, that is, from being sympathetic. The phrase occurs again in *De diuinatione*, this time in its plural form *humanos sensus*. Cicero, both author and protagonist of *De diuinatione* Book 2, while contesting Cratippus' theories on divination, also says: *'Quid uero habet auctoritatis furor iste, quem 'diuinum' vocatis ut, quae sapiens non uideat, ea uideat insanus, et is qui humanos sensus amiserit diuinos adsecutus sit?'* ("But what weight is to be given to that frenzy of yours, which you term 'divine' and which enables the crazy man to see what the wise man does not see, and invests the

---

64 Schlam 1992, 100.
65 Cf. especially Schlam 1992, 99–112.

man who has lost human intelligence with the intelligence of gods?", trans. Falconer 1953) (2.110). The opposition between *humani* and *diuini sensus* alludes to the faculties which distinguish men from gods, first of all intelligence. Two further instances can be found within the Ciceronian corpus of letters, but in neither case is the author Cicero himself. Plancus defines the young Octavian's *sensus* as *moderatissimus* and *humanissimus*, presumably referring to the mildness of his character;[66] while the author of [*Ad Brutum* 26. 5 (1.17.5)] rhetorically asks: *quid enim tam alienum ab humanis sensibus est quam eum patris habere loco qui ne liberi quidem hominis numero sit?* ("What is more contrary to human feelings than to regard as a father one who does not even count as a free man", trans. Shackleton Bailey 2002). As for *humanus sensus* with animals, right at the beginning of his *Naturalis Historia* Book 8, Pliny the Elder claims: *Maximum est elephans proximumque humanis sensibus. Quippe intellectus illis sermonis patrii et imperiorum obedientia, officiorum quae didicere memoria, amoris et gloriae uoluptas* ("The largest land animal is the elephant, and it is the nearest to man in intelligence: it understands the language of its country and obeys orders, remembers duties that it has been taught, is pleased by affection and by marks of honour", trans. Rackham 1947),[67] from which we can infer that Pliny is thinking of *sensus* in terms of intelligence. Gellius then, in telling the story of the glorious death of Alexander the Great's horse, records that, after saving Alexander in a battle, Bucephalas *quasi cum sensus humani solacio animam expirauit* ("breathed his last, with indications of relief that were almost human", trans. Rolfe 1927).[68] However, the nearest passage to *Met.* 3.26 is probably to be found in the later Ampelius' *Liber Memorialis*, which probably dates to the third or fourth century CE. In the second section of this work, devoted to the zodiac signs, he says of the bull that *sensum humanum figura tauri continebat* ("preserved a human intelligence within a bull's aspect"). In writing his novel, Apuleius will have hardly thought about these parallels, but no doubt the nobility of those animals as well as the contexts in which they appear add to the light tone of Lucius' story when compared to the humility of an ass and the ridiculous episodes in which he is involved.

The second interesting case is instead offered by the combination of *humanus* with *somnus*, which never appears elsewhere in Classical Latin literature – nor is there an equivalent in the *Onos*, as rightly observed by Gianotti.[69] Later on in the story, at the beginning of Book 9, Lucius the ass is believed to have been infected with rabies, and his masters want therefore to murder him. Perceiving the danger

66 *Fam.* 10.24.5.
67 Plin. *HN* 8.1.
68 Gell. 5.2.4.
69 Gianotti 1986, 38 n. 16.

he is in, Lucius instinctively breaks into their bedroom. This turns out to be a place of safety, because instead of killing him, the masters simply lock the doors behind him. Being alone and having a bed at hand, Lucius can sleep a *somnus humanus* for the first time in a long while (*Met.* 9.2). Without further comments, Schlam points out that this event marks the beginning of Lucius' process of rehumanisation.[70] But to a Platonist like Apuleius, sleep (and, consequently, dreams) had a more profound significance linked to divine inspiration and prophetic powers.[71] An in-depth analysis of this topic would take us too far from our subject. Yet it is worth recalling that, according to Plato's *Republic*, sleep is probably the only thing which can equalise the sage and a despicable person. Or, to put it another way, sleep makes all men alike – just like death, which has always been considered tightly linked to sleep. This happens because in people who are asleep the non-rational part of the soul prevails over the rational.[72] This also means that people are more likely to be inspired by divine beings when asleep. But if sleep is close to death, awakening is synonymous with new birth. So, we might say that Lucius' *somnus humanus* is a prelude to his process of rehumanisation, which begins when he awakes from his human sleep and is completed when Isis appears to him in yet another dream later on in the story.

The true, physical retransformation of Lucius the ass into a human being only takes place in *Metamorphoses* 10. What paves the way for this retransformation is Lucius' fear of being killed by wild animals in the arena. As a new form of *spectaculum* for the crowd, the ass is to copulate with a murderess who has been condemned to the beasts in the arena. Lucius the ass fears that the beasts will surely attack him along with the woman, and so he decides to flee. He eventually reaches the shore of Cenchreae, where Isis appears to him in a dream and helps him reacquire his human shape.[73] But before all this, Lucius-narrator lingers over the story of the murderess for a while. The reason for her death sentence is that she has killed her husband's sister, believing her to be his mistress. The husband had always concealed that that woman was his sister (she was in fact his illegitimate sister, and he had only recently become aware of her existence). When the maiden was mature enough to get married, her mother – who was not able to provide her with a dowry – had no choice but to reveal the secret to her son and ask for his help, fearing his reaction:

---

70 Schlam 1992, 103.

71 On Apuleius' Platonism cf. below, pp. 156–158.

72 Cf. Pl. *Resp.* 571a–d.

73 On the fundamental meaning of this escape cf. Zimmerman 2000, 25 with further bibliography.

Sed pietatis spectatae iuuenis et matris obsequium et sororis officium religiose dispensat, et, arcanis domus uenerabilis silentii custodiae traditis, plebeiam facie tenus praetendens humanitatem, sic necessarium sanguinis sui munus aggreditur ut desolatam uicinam puellam parentumque praesidio uiduatam domus suae tutela receptaret, ac mox artissimo multumque sibi dilecto contubernali, largitus de proprio dotem, liberalissime traderet. (*Met.* 10.23)

With his exemplary sense of responsibility, the young man scrupulously discharged both his obligation to his mother and his duty to his sister. Entrusting the secrets of his respectable family to the safeguard of silence, and pretending on the surface to be acting out of common *humanitas*, he set about the task required by the ties of blood. He received the girl from the neighbours, abandoned without a parent's protection, into the guardianship of his own home; and he soon made an excellent marriage for her with one of his close and well-loved friends, supplying a generous dowry from his own resources. (Hanson 1989)

Astonishingly, the man's reaction was positive, and he even pretended to be acting out of *plebeia humanitas*. After Lucius' and the widows' judicial use of the concept, this is the fourth and last occurrence of *humanitas* in the *Metamorphoses*. Presuming that *humanitas* is mainly connoted as φιλανθρωπία, as we have seen to be usual in Apuleius, what does *plebeia* mean? As Zimmerman observes, this is the only occurrence of the adjective *plebeius* in Apuleius' oeuvre, and we might add that never before Apuleius is *humanitas* characterised as *plebeia*.[74] Two exegetical interpretations have been put forward: the *TLL* entry on *humanitas* explains this expression as *humanitas* '*in puellam pauperam*', that is to say 'towards a poor young woman'.[75] Conversely, the more recent entry on *plebeius* (*TLL* 10.1.2375.76–77), following Zimmerman, prefers the sense '*inter plebeios solita*', that is, 'the *humanitas* that ordinary people display toward each other', to borrow Zimmerman's words.[76] On balance, I find the second option to be more persuasive, especially because the first reading would run the risk of being contradictory. It is true that in the *Apologia humanitas* seems to end up being an elitist concept, but certainly not *prima facie*: while the proconsul Maximus is surely supposed to be able to grasp this thanks to his superior education – otherwise Apuleius' strategy would be ineffective right from the beginning – the throng would hardly follow Apuleius' sly arguments. On the contrary, there would be no reason for such a plan of action in this episode of *Metamorphoses* 10, and the presence of the adjective *plebeius* would impede this cunning, somehow implicit use of *humanitas* anyway. Moreover, *plebeius* does not properly mean *pauper*, and, read in this way, the phrase could imply a pejorative categorisation, which does not seem

---

74 Zimmerman 2000, 301.
75 *TLL* 6.3.3079.64.
76 Zimmerman 2000, 301.

to be apt here. Finally, it should be borne in mind that, generally speaking – and the case of Pliny the Younger in the previous chapter makes this clear – *humanitas* transcends social distinctions, and, unlike *clementia*, is not a prerogative of a person of higher rank towards one of lower. It is no coincidence that in his defence speech during the mock trial of *Metamorphoses* 3, Lucius relied on this very premise when he resorted to the *humanitas* argument and, making appeal to their common nature of equal human beings, sought to make the inhabitants of Hypata sympathetic to his miserable case.

4.1.3 The *De Platone et eius dogmate*

Given that the *Asclepius*, which will be discussed at the end of this book, is by now almost universally believed to be post-Apuleian, the term *humanitas* appears in only one more Apuleian work, the *De Platone et eius dogmate*. According to Dal Chiele, the *De Platone* is the most organic testament of Middle Platonism we have in Latin.[77] Along a post-Aristotelian tripartite structure, the two books which compose this treatise are devoted to physics and ethics – a third book, devoted to logic, is either unpreserved or was not written by the author despite his original project.[78] A third possibility then is that it is represented by the stand-alone Greek treatise Περὶ ἑρμηνείας, whose Apuleian authorship is nevertheless disputed.[79] Although *humanitas* does not seem to play a particularly significant role in this philosophical treatise, the two occurrences of the term here enlarge the scope of its application and throw further light on the possible nuances which *humanitas* can take on. Interestingly, we see that *humanitas* can also be employed to translate technical terms of ancient Greek physics. Sections 13–18 of Book 1 broadly focus on anthropology, and the end of section 16 deals in particular with those blood-vessels, *quas ad procreandum e regione ceruicum per medullas renum commeare et suscipi inguinum loco certum est et pulsu uenarum genitale seminium humanitatis exire* ("which proceed directly from the neck, through the inward parts

---

[77] Dal Chiele 2016, 16. A good synthesis of the main features of Middle Platonism can be found in D'Elia 1995, 88–89. For an in-depth analysis cf. instead Dillon 1996 – 306–340 on Apuleius. On Platonism in Apuleius cf. Moreschini 1978; Fletcher 2014.

[78] Cf. *Plat.* 1.4. Recently, Stover 2016 has suggested that the *Summarium librorum Platonis*, which R. Klibansky discovered in an Apuelian manuscript (*Vat. Reg. Lat.* 1572), should be identified with the *De Platone et eius dogmate*'s Book III. Regardless of the issue of the Apuleian authorship of this *Summarium* – its ascription to Apuleius has been challenged for example by Moreschini 2017 and Magnaldi 2017 – it does not contain any instances of *humanitas* and is therefore of no use to this research.

[79] Cf. the up-to-date state of research in Dal Chiele 2016, 16 n. 34.

of the kidneys, for the purposes of procreation, and which it is certain are received in the place where the groin is situated, and again depart from thence, as the generative seminary of human nature", trans. Taylor 1822). Neither the Plautine *seminium* nor the simpler *semen* are paired with *humanitas, humanus* or *homo* before this instance.[80] On the contrary, the phrase ἀνθρώπων / ἀνθρώπινον σπέρμα is quite common in Greek literature and was used by Plato himself (*Leg.* 853c). Given the nature of the treatise, it is therefore tempting to look to *seminium humanitatis* as a translation of ἀνθρώπινον σπέρμα. If on the one hand this implies for *humanitas* the acceptance of the tag *usu debilitato* put forward by the *TLL* entry (indeed *humanitas* seems to lose its polysemy and simply stand for *humanus*), on the other it gives a satisfactory explanation for the unusual meaning (at least in Apuleius) that the word takes on here.[81]

After dealing with physics in Book 1, Apuleius takes us back to the field of ethics in *De Platone* 2, so that the second and last occurrence of *humanitas* in this work is much more in tune with Apuleius' other instances of this word. 2.12-14 looks at the ideas of love and friendship, and, at some point, Apuleius recalls Plato's distinction between two kinds of friendship, one originating from pleasure (*uoluptas*), the other from necessity (*necessitas*). Seamlessly, the text continues as follows:

> Necessitudinum et liberorum amor naturae congruus est, ille alius abhorrens ab humanitatis clementia, qui uulgo amor dicitur, est adpetitus ardens, cuius instinctu per libidinem capti amatores corporum in eo quod uiderint totum hominem putant.

> And the love, indeed, of familiars and children is consentaneous to nature; but that which is abhorrent from the clemency of *humanitas*, and which is vulgarly called love, is an ardent appetite, by the libidinous stimulus of which, the lovers of body being captivated, think that the whole man consists in that which they behold. (trans. Taylor 1822, adapted)

Although the two terms are sometimes interrelated, nowhere else in Classical Latin does *clementia* depend on *humanitas*. Yet, the genitive *humanitatis* leaves little room for doubt: this is perhaps the clearest evidence that, at least to Apuleius' mind, *clementia* can by and large be seen as a hyponym of *humanitas*.[82] Dowling highlights the importance of *clementia* in Apuleius' *Metamorphoses* – where it is incidentally worth noting that the term *clementia* itself never appears –

---

80 Cf. Plaut. *Mil.* 1059. On Plautine vocabulary in Apuleius cf. Pasetti 2007.
81 Cf. *TLL* 6.3.3077.8–9.
82 On *clementia* and its relationship with *humanitas* cf. in particular above, pp. 40–44.

but ignores its presence in the philosophical works.[83] Judging from this passage, the impression is that this instance of *clementia* would confirm, and perhaps push a step further, Dowling's suggestion that "in the two centuries following the death of Nero, the definition of *clementia* continues to expand as the quality becomes ever more a part of [. . .] private ethics."[84] Indeed, here *clementia* is even related to *amor* and has nothing to do with the political contexts in which we have usually found it so far. Probably to avoid such a possible ambiguity, Apuleius decided to pair it with *humanitas*.

4.2 *Humanitas* at the Core of Aulus Gellius' Programme in the *Noctes Atticae*

Keulen has properly observed:

> Gellius' intellectual self-fashioning resembles Apuleius' self-presentation in the *Apology* as a man of *doctrina*, associating himself with the proconsul Claudius Maximus as belonging to the same Roman intellectual aristocracy, in contrast to the ignorant fools who had accused Apuleius.[85]

Yet in the case of Apuleius, we have also seen how *humanitas*, which has nothing to do with *doctrina* in his works, contributes to broadening the gap between people allegedly belonging to the same elite and people of lower rank. The same holds true for *humanitas* in Aulus Gellius, but with a striking difference: Gellius regarded *humanitas* as a concept closely related to *doctrina* and *eruditio*.[86] Evidence suggests, however, that the association of *humanitas* with *eruditio* was far from unanimous: Gellius more or less explicitly indicates that those who ignored this 'true', 'original' meaning of *humanitas* were half-educated (if not ignorant) people. The main targets of Gellius' polemic, as often in the *Noctes Atticae*, were probably not uneducated men but the allegedly learned grammarians.[87] The passage referred to, *Noctes Atticae* 13.17, is one I have already mentioned several

---

83 Dowling 2006, 254–255.
84 Dowling 2006, 220. Cf. also Dowling 2006, 228; *passim*. It is important to stress that Dowling's statement does not come into conflict with what I suggested in the introduction to Chapter 2 (pp. 46–47). On the contrary, this shift of the ideal of *clementia* into the ethical domain can be seen as a consequence of its weakening in the political sphere after Domitian. In other words, *clementia* lost its technical character.
85 Keulen 2009, 196.
86 Cf. below, pp. 159–160; 165; 169.
87 Cf. below, pp. 169–172.

times and is probably the most frequently cited text in modern discussions of Roman *humanitas*.[88] But despite the famous label 'Humanisme Gellien' coined by Marache and despite a chapter titled *Humanitas Gelliana* in a book by Beall, a thorough analysis of the various occurrences of *humanitas* in Gellius has not to my knowledge been undertaken, not even recently by Toledo Martin.[89] As the following section will show, *humanitas* is not only the protagonist of this famous 'article' – to borrow Stevenson's fitting definition for Gellian sections of the work[90] – of the *Noctes Atticae*, but is in fact a cornerstone of Gellius' cultural programme. To bridge this gap in scholarship, no other passage can provide a better starting point than *NA* 13.17 itself, which I now quote in full:

> 1. Qui uerba Latina fecerunt quique his probe usi sunt, humanitatem non id esse uoluerunt, quod uolgus existimat quodque a Graecis φιλανθρωπία dicitur et significat dexteritatem quandam beniuolentiamque erga omnis homines promiscam, sed humanitatem appellauerunt id propemodum quod Graeci παιδείαν uocant, nos eruditionem institutionemque in bonas artis dicimus. Quas qui sinceriter cupiunt adpetuntque, hi sunt uel maxime humanissimi. Huius enim scientiae cura et disciplina ex uniuersis animantibus uni homini datast idcircoque humanitas appellata est. 2. Sic igitur eo uerbo ueteres esse usos et cumprimis M. Varronem Marcumque Tullium omnes ferme libri declarant; quamobrem satis habui unum interim exemplum promere. 3. Itaque uerba posui Varronis e libro rerum humanarum primo, cuius principium hoc est: 'Praxiteles, qui propter artificium egregium nemini est paulum modo humaniori ignotus'. 4. 'Humaniori' inquit non ita, ut uulgo dicitur, facili et tractabili et beniuolo, tametsi rudis litterarum sit – hoc enim cum sententia nequaquam conuenit – sed eruditiori doctiorique, qui Praxitelem quid fuerit et ex libris et ex historia cognouerit.

> 1. Those who have spoken Latin and have used the language correctly do not give to the word *humanitas* the meaning which it is commonly thought to have, namely, what the Greeks call φιλανθρωπία, signifying a kind of friendly spirit and good-feeling towards all

---

88 Without (impossible) pretension of completeness, I list below some contributions dealing with the text in a way or another – the most significant to the purpose of the present work will instead be dealt with more thoroughly in due course: Lorenz 1914, 52; Jaeger 1946, xxiii and n.7; Pohlenz 1947, 451; Prete 1948, 10; 71; Riposati 1949, 247; Büchner 1961, 640 and n. 21; Maselli 1979, 53 and n. 98; Beall 1988, 74; 99–101; Hiltbrunner 1994a, 734; 1994b, 103 and n. 1; Bauman 2000, 20; Beall 2004, 217; Santini 2006, 72–74; Keulen 2009, 295; Stroh 2008, 539–540; Balbo 2012, 65; Ferrary 2014², 512 and n. 26; Høgel 2015, 44; Elice 2017, 253–256; 279–280; Leonardis 2018, 524–526; Mollea 2018, 147–149; 2023b, 4–6; Bettini 2019, 95–97; Boldrer 2021, 54–58.

89 Marache 1952, 251–257; Beall 1988; Toledo Martin 2021. Cf. also the sub-chapter 5.4 'Der Bildungsbegriff der ,Noctes Atticae': zwischen *honesta eruditio* and *humanitas*' in Heusch 2011. By 'Humanisme Gellien' Marache rather alludes to a philanthropic behaviour which has little, if anything, to do with Gellius' definition and use of the term *humanitas*.

90 Stevenson 2004. Howley 2018 opts instead for the label 'essays' to stress their nature of 'individual units' (3 n. 6).

men without distinction; but they gave to *humanitas* about the force of the Greek παιδεία; that is, what we call *eruditionem institutionemque in bonas artes*, or 'education and training in the liberal arts.' Those who earnestly desire and seek after these are most highly humanized. For the pursuit of that kind of knowledge, and the training given by it, have been granted to man alone of all the animals, and for that reason it is termed *humanitas*, or 'humanity.' 2. That it is in this sense that our earlier writers have used the word, and in particular Marcus Varro and Marcus Tullius, almost all the literature shows. 3. Therefore I have thought it sufficient for the present to give one single example. I have accordingly quoted the words of Varro from the first book of his *Human Antiquities*, beginning as follows: "Praxiteles, who, because of his surpassing art, is unknown to no one of any liberal culture (*humaniori*)." 4. He does not use *humanior* in its usual sense of 'good-natured, amiable, and kindly', although without knowledge of letters, for this meaning does not at all suit his thought; but in that of a man of 'some cultivation and education', who knew about Praxiteles both from books and from story. (trans. Rolfe 1927)

As is clear, Gellius' claims are mainly three. First, *humanitas* should mean παιδεία, that is to say *eruditio institutioque in bonas artes*, but the *uulgus* uses it as synonym of φιλανθρωπία, thereby signifying 'indiscriminate benevolence towards all other human beings'. Secondly, among animals, only man (*homo*) possesses *humanitas*, hence the etymology of the word. Thirdly, that the 'true' meaning of *humanitas* is παιδεία is guaranteed by two *auctoritates*, Cicero and Varro.

It goes without saying that these claims raise many questions, some of which have already been answered in previous chapters. Such is certainly the case with regard to the original meaning of *humanitas*: Gellius evidently opted for παιδεία, but we have abundant evidence that he was wrong. Furthermore, irrespective of the answer to this first question, Gellius' reference to παιδεία and φιλανθρωπία might seem to imply that *humanitas* has Greek origins. As we have seen in the Introduction, that of the origins of *humanitas* is an open question whose solution probably lies in keeping the comprehensive and polysemic idea of Roman *humanitas* distinct from its singular main components, which did originate in Ancient Greece. This is somehow linked to the problem of the etymology of *humanitas*, which Gellius derives – too simplistically – straight from *homo*. This issue too was dealt with in the Introduction.[91]

But some problems posed by Gellius' passage need to be dealt with in the light of Gellius' own oeuvre and of the world in which he lived. To begin with, is Gellius consistent in his own use of the term *humanitas*? And is it true that Gellius' contemporaries 'misused' the term? Also, what exactly is meant by the *uulgus*? In addition to all these questions, it will have not passed unnoticed the fact that Gellius gives in support of his claim an example in which the comparative

---

91 Cf. above, pp. 22; 45.

humanior rather than the noun *humanitas* or the simple adjective *humanus* is used. Clearly this is one of the most significant pieces of evidence in favour of the theory according to which the comparative *humanior* was considered much more suitable than the positive grade *humanus* to convey the idea of *humanitas*.[92] And although I have discussed this specific aspect of this and other related Gellian 'articles' elsewhere, I intend to reiterate my reasoning for the sake of completeness.[93] First, however, I will try to answer to the remaining questions, starting from that of Gellius' consistency or inconsistency. To do so, I will first consider other Gellian cases of *humanitas* and return to the fundamental passage of *Noctes Atticae* 13.17 at the end of this chapter section.

The first occurrence of *humanitas* I want to focus on is at 15.21, a very short 'article' focusing on the striking difference between Jupiter's and Neptune's sons. While Jupiter's sons are said to be models of virtue, wisdom and customs (*praestantissimos uirtute, prudentia, moribus*),[94] Neptune's sons, because they are born from the sea, are considered very fierce (*ferocissimos*), cruel (*inmanes*) and *alienos ab omni humanitate*.[95] On the basis of this passage some modern scholars have accused Gellius of being inconsistent. Thus Holford-Strevens trenchantly states that "the restriction of *humanitas* to learning in 13.17 is not observed" here (and elsewhere), but such a claim probably merits further investigation.[96] There is no denying that the preceding concepts of ferocity and cruelty do not instinctively evoke 'learning' when they are associated with *humanitas*, but they may well evoke something which is, so to speak, a consequence of learning, namely civilization.[97] Cyclopes, Cercyon, Sciron and the Laestrygonians, whether or not they can all be considered sons of Poseidon, are in fact characterised not only as fierce figures, but as outcasts, barbarian types which have yet to be reached by human civilization. This is certainly the case of the most famous Cyclopes, whose insolence and lack of laws – the latter in particular a cornerstone of civilization and Roman society – are already emphasised by Homer, while their ignorance and stupidity emerge from Euripides' *Cyclops*.[98] Along with the Laestrygonians,

---

92 Cf. above, p. 22.

93 Cf. Mollea 2023b, 4–9.

94 *Moribus* is Holford-Strevens 2020's reading, which follows Kronenberg 1910, while manuscripts read *uiribus*.

95 On monstruosity as a feature of Neptune's sons cf. Pease 1943.

96 Holford-Strevens 2003, 50 n. 24.

97 On *humanitas* as civilization cf. above, pp. 100–102, below, pp. 218–219, and *passim*.

98 Hom. *Od.* 9.106: Κυκλώπων δ' ἐς γαῖαν ὑπερφιάλων ἀθεμίστων ("in the land of the arrogant lawless Cyclopes"); Eur. *Cyc.* 173 (and *passim*): τὴν Κύκλωπος ἀμαθίαν ("the ignorance of the Cyclops"). Cf. also *agrestem* ('uncouth') *Cyclopa* of Hor. *Epist.* 2.2.125 and *ferus* ('savage') *Cyclops* of Sen. *Thy.* 582. On the fundamental importance of laws in Roman culture cf. also above, pp. 143–144.

they are also accused of inhospitality – another clear sign of incivility in the ancient world.[99] And the same holds true for Cercyon and Sciron, who according to the legend were both killed by the hero Theseus.[100] To sum up, this is probably not the clearest piece of evidence for Gellius' lack of consistency, as παιδεία, and thus *humanitas* in Gellius' terms, does evoke the idea of civilization.[101] Nevertheless, it is premature to reject Holford-Strevens' claim altogether.

Holford-Strevens also considers *Noctes Atticae* 16.12.5 as an instance of Gellius' failure to comply with his own definition of *humanitas*, but prudently adds "if this be a paraphrase."[102] Let us look first at the context. 16.12 is entirely devoted to discussing some alleged Greek etymologies of Latin words put forward by the grammarian Cloatius Verus.[103] The first etymologies seem to Gellius to be convincing, but at 16.12.5-6 he disapproves of the derivation of *faenerator* (usurer) from the verb φαίνεσθαι:

> Sed in libro quarto 'faenerator' inquit 'appellatus est quasi φαινεράτωρ ἀπὸ τοῦ φαίνεσθαι ἐπὶ τὸ χρηστότερον, quoniam id genus hominum speciem ostentent humanitatis et commodi esse uideantur inopibus nummos desiderantibus', 6. idque dixisse ait Hypsicraten quempiam grammaticum, cuius libri sane nobiles sunt super his quae a Graecis accepta sunt.

> But in his fourth book he says: "*Faenerator* is equivalent to φαινεράτωρ, meaning 'to appear at one's best', since that class of men present an appearance of *humanitas* and pretend to be accommodating to poor men who are in need of money"; and he declared that this was stated by Hypsicrates, a grammarian whose books on *Words Borrowed from the Greeks* are very well known. (trans. Rolfe 1927)

That *humanitas* has little to do with learning is evident, and is corroborated by *commodi esse uideantur inopibus nummos desiderantibus*. No doubt the idea of

---

99 Str. 1.2.9: καὶ γὰρ τὸν Αἴολον δυναστεῦσαί φασι τῶν περὶ τὴν Λιπάραν νήσων καὶ τῶν περὶ τὴν Αἴτνην καὶ Λεοντίνην Κύκλωπας καὶ Λαιστρυγόνας ἀξένους τινάς ("For instance, history says that Aeolus was once king over the islands about Lipara, and that the Cyclopes and the Laestrygonians, inhospitable peoples, were lords over the region about Aetna and Leontine", trans. Jones 1917).
100 Paus. 1.39.3: εἶναι δὲ ὁ Κερκυὼν λέγεται καὶ τὰ ἄλλα ἄδικος ἐς τοὺς ξένους καὶ παλαίειν οὐ βουλομένοις ("Cercyon is said to have treated strangers wickedly, especially in wrestling with them against their will", trans. Jones 1918); Mela 2.47: *ibi est Piraeus, Atheniensium portus, Scironia saxa saeuo quondam Scironis hospitio etiam nunc infamia* ("Piraeus, Athens' port, is there, as well as the Scironian Rocks, infamous once upon a time (and even today) for Sciron's savage hospitality", trans. Romer 1998). On Sciron cf. also Hyg. *Fab.* 38.4.
101 Swain 2004, 31.
102 Holford-Strevens 2003, 50 n. 24.
103 More on this etymology in Fögen 2000, 186–187.

φιλανθρωπία is far more suitable here, even though it is evoked because of its near-absence. As is the case with the already mentioned *speciem libertatis* of Suet. *Tib.* 30 in fact, *species* followed by an abstract noun indicating virtues or ideals reveals that there is only an appearance of that virtue or ideal.[104] As we have seen in the Suetonius passage, this construction serves to express the notion that there is only the appearance of freedom under Tiberius, while here, in the case of userer there is only an appearance of courtesy and altruism. In the case of users there is even worse, for they even show off (*ostentent*) their alleged φιλανθρωπία. Gellius' passage is unusual, as no one before had spoken of *humanitas* as a virtue that can be faked for the sake of ostentation (*ostentata humanitas*). Nor was the occurrence of *humanitas* as dependent on *species* very common by that time, despite being attested in Cicero's *Tusculanae disputationes* 4.32, where the soul of the gifted man is said to be also affected by disorders such as compassion (*misericordia*), distress (*aegritudo*) and fear (*metus*), which only at first sight have the semblance of humanity (*humanitatis* [. . .] *habent primam speciem*). We shall however find out that in the late fourth century Ammianus liked and recovered this expression to attack the large-scale simulation of *humanitas* in Roman society.[105]

Returning to Holford-Strevens' gloss, as is clear from his 2020 OCT edition, where '*faenerator . . . desiderantibus*' is printed in inverted commas, the suggestion is that we are dealing with a quotation, that is to say with lines not originally written by Gellius. Indeed, since Funaioli, this has been considered a fragment by Hypsicrates (*Fr.* 2 Funaioli) and consequently by Cloatius Verus (*Fr.* 1 Funaioli), who was quoting Hypsicrates.[106] Unfortunately, the difference between fragment (a text reported word for word from its exemplar) and testimony (a paraphrase of the model), which is crucial in this case, is not easily determined. On the contrary, the difficulty of knowing who the original author of these words is, is even doubled by the transmission from Hypsicrates to Cloatius Verus to Gellius. It is true that it would be enough for our aims to be sure that Gellius was accurately citing Cloatius Verus, but it is impossible to be certain of this. Accordingly, given these problems of authenticity and authorship, we cannot consider this passage as representative of Gellius' understanding of the word *humanitas* – in fact the unusual meaning attributed to *humanitas* here might well be due to the fact that the passage is a quotation.

---

104 Cf. above, p. 130.
105 Cf. below, pp. 245–247.
106 Funaioli 1907, 108; 468.

After the cases of Neptune's sons and of the *faenerator,* another passage where Gellius' consistency may be called into question is *Noctes Atticae* 18.10.8. Gellius recalls a visit to Herodes Atticus' country estate in Cephisia where he happened to fall ill and have a high fever. In describing Gellius' disease to his friends, the doctor confused vein with artery, causing them to question his expertise. This anecdote gives Gellius a chance for a tirade against those half-educated people who do not possess basic knowledge of the human body. To keep himself separated from this throng, Gellius proudly says:

> Quantum habui temporis subsiciui, medicinae quoque disciplinae libros attigi quos arbitrabar esse idoneos ad docendum. Et ex his cum alia pleraque ab isto humanitatis usu non aliena, tum de uenis quoque et arteriis didicisse uideor . . .

> Therefore I devoted such spare time as I had to dipping into those books on the art of medicine which I thought were suited to instruct me, and from them I seem to have learned, not only many other things which have to do with human experience (*humanitatis usu*), but also concerning veins and arteries . . . (trans. Rolfe 1927)

Once more, parallels with previous authors do not help here, for *humanitatis usus* never appears before Gellius. Instinctively one may think that this expression simply means 'need of human life' or 'human experience', but the presence of *isto* is significant. In this sentence *iste* only makes sense as an anaphoric reference, and, given that a common meaning of *usus* is 'usage', the easiest and perhaps most logical interpretation is that the whole phrase refers to *ad docendum,* thereby signifying "along with many other things which are not extraneous to such an educational usage." In any case, whether or not Astarita is right in extending this Gellian expression to all sciences (at least geography, physics and astronomy in addition to medicine), this is not to deny that the context is intrinsically and explicitly didactic.[107] The focus of the sentence is on the purpose clause *ad docendum,* and therefore the paideutic meaning of *humanitas* is particularly fitting.[108] (It would also be paradoxical for Gellius to misuse such an important term while blaming those who misuse words.) As well as revealing Gellius' wide cultural interests, this passage also epitomises the main aim of the *Noctes Atticae,* that is, to promote useful, encyclopedic

---

[107] Astarita 1993, 170. Cf. also Pieri 2002, 375: "Non è escluso che qui Gellio, riferendosi all'importanza di inserire qualche libro di medicina nella formazione dell'uomo colto, giochi anche con uno dei significati classici di *humanitas,* quello di παιδεία, sulla cui scarsa fortuna presso i contemporanei si era soffermato in un celebre passo delle *Noctes Atticae.*"
[108] This same interpretation seems implicitly to be endorsed by Beall 1988, 100. Cf. also Howley 2013, 11.

learning among his readers.[109] I will deal with this point in more detail later on in this chapter section.[110]

Paradoxical though it may seem, the clearest piece of evidence for Gellius' 'transgression' of the rule is to be found at 19.14.1, a passage which stresses the fundamental role played by Varro, the already mentioned *auctoritas* of 13.17, and Nigidius Figulus in educating humankind.[111] The text reads:

> *Aetas M. Ciceronis et C. Caesaris praestanti facundia uiros paucos habuit, doctrinarum autem multiformium uariarumque artium quibus humanitas erudita est columina habuit M. Varronem et P. Nigidium.*

> The time of Marcus Cicero and Gaius Caesar had few men of surpassing eloquence, but in encyclopaedic learning and in the varied sciences by which *humanitas* is enobled it possesses two towering figures in Marcus Varro and Publius Nigidius. (trans. Rolfe 1927)

If one recalls Gellius' definition of *humanitas* as *eruditio*, it is quite obvious that the meaning of the sentence cannot be the tautological 'by which learning / education / civilization is educated', which would sound even odder in Latin: *quibus eruditio erudita est*. Likewise, it is clear that *humanitas* has nothing to do with the 'faulty' meaning of φιλανθρωπία, but rather stands for 'humankind / human race'. However, although this occurrence of *humanitas* does not conform to Gellius' main statement at 13.17.1, it somehow does conform to the etymology of the noun he himself proposes when adding in the same paragraph *huius enim scientiae cura et disciplina ex uniuersis animantibus uni homini datast idcircoque humanitas appellata est*. Once it has been raised from barbarity to civilization thanks to education, humankind can at last merit its definition of *humanitas*.

Even though I have yet to investigate perhaps the two most important instances of Gellian *humanitas*, there is enough evidence to answer the question of Gellian consistency in using the term. Despite the objections raised in the previous pages against Holford-Strevens' accusation of inconsistency, I also think it unwise to support the opposite view that Gellius strictly obeyed the rule he himself laid down, as Beall instead proposes.[112] But if "to possess unitary meaning did not

---

[109] On the role of this passage (and of medicine in general) in Gellius' programme cf. Heusch 2011, 352–356. Cf. also Pausch 2004, 220–221.

[110] Cf. below, pp. 168–169. On encyclopedism in Ancient Greece and Rome cf. König/Woolf 2013 – 54–55 on Gellius.

[111] As Baldwin 1975, 76 rightly remarks, Varro and Nigidius Figulus appear together quite often in the *Noctes Atticae*.

[112] Beall 1988, 101: "The notion of *humanitas* in the *Attic Nights* is as rigidly subordinated to the liberal arts as Gellius' definition suggests."

imply that word had to mean the same thing on every occasion", as Vessey puts it, then Gellius was consistent.[113]

While the passages which I have analysed so far tell us something about Gellius' general consistency in using the term *humanitas* and also help us define his idea of this concept, taken in isolation they cannot help to answer the other questions I posed earlier, let alone show the centrality of *humanitas* to Gellius' educational programme. To this end, the text I shall analyse next, along with *NA* 13.17, is far more useful. At 9.3 Gellius praises King Philip II of Macedon, Alexander the Great's father, for not neglecting the Muses and liberal arts in wartime.[114] As a concrete example of Philip's refinement and wisdom, Gellius transcribes and translates into Latin his letter to Aristotle informing the philosopher of Alexander's birth.[115] According to Philip, this event could not have happened at a better time, for Alexander will still be able to benefit from the philosopher's fundamental teaching.[116] But before quoting the letter, he states:

> Is Philippus, cum in omni fere tempore negotiis belli uictoriisque adfectus exercitusque esset, a liberali tamen Musa et a studiis humanitatis numquam afuit, quin lepide comiterque pleraque et faceret et diceret.

> This Philip, although almost constantly busied and distracted by the labours and triumphs of war, yet never was a stranger to the Muse of the liberal arts and the pursuit of culture (*studiis humanitatis*), but his acts and words never lacked charm and refinement. (trans. Rolfe 1927)

If by resuscitating the rare expression *studia humanitatis*, Gellius pays homage to Cicero (and Pliny), he goes even further when creating a near-synonymous doublet through the addition of *liberalis Musa*,[117] an enigmatic expression that is not attested elsewhere in pre-Gellian literature. The passage suggests that *liberalis Musa* helps to strengthen and clarify further the meaning of *studia humanitatis*,

---

113 Vessey 1994, 1911. Cf. also Toledo Martin 2021, 169: "Quae cum ita sint, possumus conclūdere *Noctēs Atticās* esse hōc sēnsū opus hūmānissimum, quia pertinet ad haec omnia plurifāria et cōnfūsānea ex quibus rēs hūmānāe et hūmānitās cōnstant."

114 On Gellius' admiration for Philip cf. Marache 1952, 199.

115 On the rigour of Gellius' translation of Philip's Greek letter cf. Gamberale 1969, 100–104; Heusch 2011, 216 and n. 4. It is true that here the protagonist is Philip rather than Alexander, but nonetheless the exceptional role of Alexander in the *Noctes Atticae* is evident: according to Morgan 2004, 204, he is the only non-Roman hero in Gellius' work.

116 As Beall 1988, 95 remarks, when mentioning Alexander the Great, Gellius is usually interested in his education (cf. also *NA* 20.5 and 13.4).

117 *Musa* is the reading of a second hand of F (*codex Leouardiensis Prov. Bibl. van Friesland 55, saec. ix*); *mera* of F[1] and *mensa* of the other manuscripts make no sense.

thereby highlighting the importance of the liberal arts, especially to a statesman or, as is the case with Philip of Macedon, to a king.[118] This becomes all the more evident if one recalls that at *Praef.* 19 Gellius had banished from the *Noctes Atticae* those

> qui in lectitando <percontando> scribendo commentando numquam uoluptates, numquam labores ceperunt, nullas hoc genus uigilias uigilarunt neque ullis inter eiusdem Musae aemulos certationibus disceptationibusque elimati sunt.[119]

> who have never found pleasure nor busied themselves in reading, inquiring, writing and taking notes, who have never spent wakeful nights in such employments, who have never improved themselves by discussion and debate with rival followers of the same Muse, but are absorbed in the turmoil of business affairs. (trans. Rolfe 1927)

By naming a Muse again, Gellius somehow links this 'article' to one of the most programmatic sections of his *Preface*, at the same time implying that Philip and those like him are welcome readers of the *Noctes Atticae*. This leads us to further considerations.

It is striking that the subject of this Gellian passage is a ruler. While there has always been general agreement that Gellius' *Noctes Atticae* were addressed to a learned elite,[120] it has more recently been argued that the emperor too may have been a potential as well as exceptional addressee.[121] From this perspective, this passage would acquire further significance, in that it may be read as either indirect praise of the emperor for cultivating and fostering liberal studies or as an exhortation to (continue to) do so. Such an interpretation becomes particularly convincing if we assume, as most scholars do, that the *Noctes Atticae* were pub-

---

118 Cf. Lindermann 2006, 113: "Die Bildungsbegriffe beschreiben Philipp II. als einen König nach platonischem Vorbild, als Philosophen und Gelehrten." Also the association of *humanitas* and Muses can be found in Cicero. Compare Cic. *Tusc.* 5.66: *Cum Musis, id est cum humanitate et cum doctrina.*

119 On this passage cf. also Beall 2004, 220 and n. 50; Keulen 2004, 233–234; Gunderson 2009, 40–43. Cf. also *NA praef.* 13–14, with Gunderson 2009, 34: "Two sorts of readers are conjured: the one who knows too little and the one who knows too much; the anti-antiquarian and the already-antiquarian", though he later remarks that by *praef.* 19 it seems that the *commentarii* "are in fact only of interest to the already educated" (2009, 40).

120 Astarita 1993, 34; 206; Holford-Strevens 2003, 37; Swain 2004, 29 n. 88; Vardi 2004, 169; Morgan 2004, 199; Galimberti Biffino 2007, 930; Johnson 2010, 100–101.

121 Keulen 2009, 194; *passim. Contra* Howley 2018, 10–11: "But part of what makes the *NA* so provocative and interesting as artefact of Antonine Rome is the way it excludes the emperor, describing specifically activities that can only occur in his absence."

lished in the last years of Marcus Aurelius' reign or a little later.[122] Indeed, for all the wars and battles his reign witnessed, Marcus Aurelius no doubt also culti-vated the liberal arts, above all philosophy. Keulen seems convinced of this inter-pretation, but we should not rule out the possibility that Gellius might have had another emperor in mind, as "the only emperor named is Hadrian" and Antoni-nus Pius too respected men of culture.[123] Surely it would be odd if he did not have any, since at *Praef.* 12 he had clearly stated his aims in writing this book:

> Accepi quae aut ingenia prompta expeditaque ad honestae eruditionis cupidinem utiliumque artium contemplationem celeri facilique compendio ducerent, aut homines aliis iam uitae ne-gotiis occupatos a turpi certe agrestique rerum atque uerborum imperitia uindicarent.

> I took few items from them, confining myself to those which, by furnishing a quick and easy short-cut, might lead active and alert minds to a desire for independent learning and to the study of the useful arts, or would save those who are already fully occupied with the other duties of life from an ignorance of words and things which is assuredly shameful and boor-ish. (trans. Rolfe 1927)

If the section on Philip's letter is not meant to teach the fundamental importance of education and liberal studies to kings, emperors and statesmen in general, then it is not at all clear why Gellius chose to include this passage in his *Noctes Atticae*. Conversely, if it is meant to teach rulers, Keulen's allusion to a 'self-referential di-mension' of Philip's letter becomes particularly convincing.[124] By describing the re-lationship between Aristotle and Philip, Gellius would thus implicitly be drawing a comparison between the Greek philosopher and himself, thereby revealing once more those "aspirations to cultural authority expressed through his *Noctes Atticae*." All this takes us back to *NA* 13.17 and the kernel of discussion over Gellius' *humanitas*.

Very many scholars have worked on *NA* 13.17 in connection with Roman *hu-manitas*, but, aside from Beall and perhaps Heusch, they do not give sufficient emphasis to the role this text plays in understanding the importance of *humanitas* within Gellius' own oeuvre.[125] Whether or not the definition of *humanitas* as *eru-*

---

122 Cf. Holford-Strevens 1977, 101; 109: after 177 CE; 2003, 16–21: after 177 CE, but perhaps even a little after Marcus' death; Keulen 2009, 198; 235: between 177 and 180 CE. However, other scholars have opted for an earlier date, for example Marache 1952, 331–332: mid 150s; Astarita 1993, 14: before 161 CE.
123 Keulen 2009, 320; Baldwin 1975, 13. On Antoninus Pius' positive attitude towards learned men cf. Baldwin 1975, 96–97. D'Elia 1995, 50–52 shows how the Antonine dynasty all fostered cul-ture and the liberal arts, so that second-century Empire could be defined as 'enlightened monarchy.'
124 Keulen 2009, 320.
125 Beall 1988, 100; Heusch 2011, 373–376.

ditio institutioque in bonas artes merits consensus (which partly it does) it undoubtedly links this passage to Gellius' *Preface* and the aims he sets forth there. The aforementioned § 12 of the *Preface* is crucial.[126] Gellius' selection of material is said to be in keeping with his purpose of leading receptive and prompt minds to desire noble learning (*honestae eruditionis*) as well as to contemplate useful arts (*utiliumque artium*).[127] *Eruditio* and *utiles* (or *bonae / ingenuae*) *artes*, which Vessey regards as complementary,[128] are therefore the common denominator between Gellius' aims in the *Noctes Atticae* and his definition of *humanitas*. Or, in other words, fostering *humanitas* is one, if not *the*, aim of his *Noctes Atticae*.[129] Irrespective of the interpretation of the very word *humanitas* at 18.10.8 which has been proposed above, that passage contributes to defining Gellius' idea of useful learning, adding for example that it includes basic knowledge of medicine.[130] After all, as Beall puts it: "Gellius [. . .] expresses, perhaps better than most ancient writers, the full range of the *artes ingenuae* and their power to delight, improve, and elevate the mind."[131] 15.21, despite its brevity and apparent frivolity, is also important: the idea of civilization expressed there shows that Gellian *humanitas* denotes not only 'the *pursuit* of culture', as Kaster puts it with regard to 13.17, but also culture itself (and its products).[132] Likewise, *NA* 14.1 suggests some *auctoritates humanitas* should be built upon, especially Varro.[133] Cicero, not cited there, is instead cited at 13.17, and his role as fundamental *auctoritas* in the *Noctes Atticae* is beyond dispute.[134] And the concept of *auctoritas* as opposed to the concept of *ratio* (instead preferred by the grammarians) is fundamental to Gellius' educational pro-

---

126 Cf. Heusch 2011, 385.
127 Cf. Beall 1988, 100; Henry 1994, 1919.
128 Vessey 1994, 1898. Cf. also Heusch 2011, 372.
129 Cf. also Howley 2018, 32: "the work's most fundamental concerns the reading of books, the pursuit of knowledge, the consuming of stories."
130 On the importance of medicine to Gellius' encyclopedic programme cf. Heusch 2011, 352–356.
131 Beall 2004, 222.
132 Kaster 1986, 6. After all, it is true that Gellius himself claims that *Quas* [scil. (*eruditionem institutionemque in*) *bonas artes*] *qui sinceriter cupiunt adpetuntque, hi sunt uel maxime humanissimi*, but this by no means excludes the very achievement of education and instruction in the liberal arts from being called *humanitas* too.
133 One of the reason for Varro's success as exemplary model is probably due to its clearness. As Stevenson 2004, 155 puts it: "Gellius seems to feel little need to *explain* Varro; for the most part he simply reproduces relevant extracts."
134 Cf. mainly Santini 2006, a monograph entirely devoted to Cicero's role of *auctoritas* in the *Noctes Atticae*. Cf. also Galimberti-Biffino 2007, 937; Keulen 2009, 30 and n. 43.

gramme.[135] In other words, what counts in choosing the correct words and thus speaking good Latin is the canon of the best authors, above all Cicero and Varro.[136] But who can take on the burden of promoting *humanitas*? Apart from the *Preface*, at both 9.3 and 13.17 Gellius seems to propose himself as the perfect candidate who already embodies (t)his ideal of *humanitas*.[137] As Kaster puts it with regard to 13.17:

> In asserting his learning, against the 'common run', Gellius is simultaneously asserting the ethical qualities which his learning presupposes and which lead him to be *doctus*, as the *uulgus* is not. In the process of defining *humanitas*, he is claiming it for himself.[138]

While 9.3 also singles out (part of) the target audience to which *humanitas* should be of importance, that is rulers (and, probably, statesmen in general), 13.17 somehow represents the other side to the same coin, in that it contains explicit allusions to the enemies of *humanitas*, namely to those who are unaware of the concept to the point of not knowing the very meaning of the word. These people are the *uulgus* Gellius (and Kaster) speaks of, but what this *uulgus* consists of is disputed. Holford-Strevens maintains that "when Gellius states that the *uulgus* or *multitudo imperitorum* uses [. . .] *humanitas* 'learning' for φιλανθρωπία, [. . .] he means not that only the lower classes spoke thus, but that the usages are not found in pre-Augustan writers."[139] He then adds: "the *uulgus* that reads *amaro* at Verg. *Georg.* 2.247 (1.21. cap.) cannot be the teeming masses; cf. the *uulgus grammaticorum* of 2.21.6, 15.9.3. On the other hand, at 16.7.13 the term does denote the common people."[140] Less cautiously, Kaster says: "we must understand that by *uulgus* Gellius does not mean 'the mob', the general population: *humanitas* in any sense was probably not a common item in the vocabulary of the Roman tradesman or Italian peasant. [. . .] Here as elsewhere, Gellius uses *uulgus* to mean 'the common run of men', in the sense of 'the common run of educated men' – or, as he says on one occasion, the *uulgus semidoctum*, 'the common run of half-educated men'."[141] Both Holford-Strevens' and Kaster's claims can be questioned constructively, because they both resort to *petitiones principii*: the former in saying that Gellius means that "the usages are not found in pre-Augustan writers", the latter in taking for granted that

---

135 Maselli 1979, 34–35; Holford-Strevens 2003, 178; Lomanto/Garcea 2004, 50; Keulen 2009, 31–32; Gunderson 2009, 59. On *ratio* as the grammarians' favourite criterion cf. Maselli 1979, 32, who on the other hand maintains that Gellius is not utterly hostile to *ratio* (33).
136 On Gellius' favourite authors cf. Maselli 1979, 34–35; Astarita 1993, 15–16; Keulen 2009, 30 and n. 43.
137 On Gellius' self-candidature at 9.3 cf. above, p. 168.
138 Kaster 1986, 8.
139 Holford-Strevens 2003, 174–175.
140 Holford-Strevens 2003, 175 n. 15.
141 Kaster 1986, 8.

at 13.17 *uulgus* stands for "the common run of educated men". In fact, neither brings evidence in favour of his statement. On balance, Kaster's claim is a little hazardous in this form, but it nevertheless seems to hit the mark. Along the lines drawn throughout this chapter section, a comparison with Gellius' *Preface* may be decisive. I have already cited *praef.* 19 in connection with the Muses, which explicitly declares what kind of people are banished from the *Noctes Atticae*.[142] Similarly, § 20 identifies, in a provocative way, the polemical target of Gellius' work:[143]

> Atque etiam, quo sit quorundam male doctorum hominum scaeuitas et inuidentia irritatior, mutuabor ex Aristophanae choro anapaesta pauca, et quam ille homo festiuissimus fabulae suae spectandae legem dedit, eandem ego commentariis his legendis dabo, ut ea ne attingat neue adeat profestum et profanum uulgus a ludo musico diuersum. (There follow Ar. *Ra.* 354–356 and 369–371)

> Moreover, in order that the perversity and envy of certain half-educated men may be the more aroused, I shall borrow a few anapaests from a chorus of Aristophanes, and the conditions which that wittiest of men imposed for the viewing of his play, I shall lay down for the reading of these notes of mine: namely, that the profane and uninitiate throng, averse to the Muses' play, shall neither touch nor approach them. (trans. Rolfe 1927)

The epithet *male docti* clearly reveals that Gellius is referring to educated, or, better, half-educated men, and the same presumably holds true for the *profestum et profanum uolgus*, whose utterly uneducated men would hardly grasp the Horatian echo of *Odes* 3.1.1, let alone understand the Greek lines by Aristophanes.[144] Likewise, the 'lower classes' mentioned by Holford-Strevens would hardly understand Gellius' entire discussion of *humanitas* at 13.17, and, *a fortiori*, they would hardly appreciate the noble example in support of his claim taken from Varro's *Antiquitates rerum humanarum*. So, if Gellius' discussion of *humanitas* at 13.17 can be seen as the discussion of a keyword as well as an aim of his work (*praef.* 12), along the same lines the criticism of those who misuse this term (13.17.1) may be read as one of the several echoes (see the citation from Holford-Strevens above) of *praef.* 20. But there is also a further, external piece of evidence that may be brought in support of Kaster's claim. Maróti has argued persuasively that on a couple of inscriptions which probably date to Marcus Aurelius' reign the word

---

142 Cf. above, p. 167.
143 On Gellius' polemical attitude within the *Noctes Atticae* cf. Astarita 1993, 34.
144 The identification between *male docti homines* and *profestum et profanum uolgus* is explicitly stated by Vessey 1994, 1903.

humanitas stands for *omnia commoda*, that is, 'all comforts'.[145] These inscriptions are advertising plaques of baths offering a refreshment to their guests, and such an example of 'everyday' use of *humanitas* is hardly meant to evoke or reproduce the philosophic idea of φιλανθρωπία.

At this point, the question naturally arises as to whether Gellius' educated contemporaries, in the end at least partly to be identified with the grammarians, actually 'misused' the term *humanitas*.[146] The analysis of the instances of *humanitas* in Apuleius and Fronto – cf. the next chapter section on the latter – points towards a positive answer, and similar results can be inferred from grammatical texts. It is true that there is no trace of the word *humanitas* in the manuals by second-century grammarians such as Velius Longus, Quintus Terentius Scaurus or Flavius Caper. Nevertheless, in the Greek-Latin lexicon of the later *Hermeneumata Monacensia* for example, *humanitas* explicitly appears as the translation for φιλανθρωπία.[147] Accordingly, even though he is wrong in saying that this constitutes a misuse of the term, Gellius rightly highlights the prevalence of the idea of φιλανθρωπία in the contemporary use of the noun *humanitas*.[148]

---

145 Maróti (2002–2003). *CIL* XIV, 4015 (*IN [HIS] PRAEDIS AURELIAE FAUSTINIANAE BALINEUS LAVAT MORE URBICO ET OMNIS HUMANITAS PRAESTATUR*, "On these premises of Aurelia Faustiniana, there is a bathhouse: bathing in the style of the city, and all comforts are provided", trans. Kruschwitz 2015, adapted) and *AE* 1933, 49 (IN HIS PRAEDIIS COMINIORUM MONTANI ET FELICIANI IUN(IORIS) ET FELICIANI PATRIS EORUM BALNEU(M) ET OMNIS HUMANITAS URBICO MORE PRAEBETUR. "On these premises of the Cominius Family – Montanus, Felicianus Iunior, and Felicianus, their father – there is a bathhouse, and all comforts in the style of the city are provided", trans. Kruschwitz 2015, adapted).

146 On the grammarians as polemical target of Gellius' oeuvre cf. Marache 1952, 210–213; Maselli 1979, 31–32; 83, who correctly points out that Gellius' polemical target is the grammarians' teaching rather than the grammarians themselves; Astarita 1993, 204; Kaster 1997², 50–61; Vardi 2001, 50, who lists some grammarians whom Gellius 'spares'; Keulen 2009, 2; 28; Heusch 2011, 378; 383–384; Howley 2013, 10. It will not be superfluous to highlight that Vardy 2001, 53 adds that, because of their esoteric *Weltanschauung*, "experts in all disciplines are equally bad, and we should probably ascribe the relatively large proportion of grammarians among them to the fact that language and literature are the topics which most interest" Gellius.

147 On p. 162 col. a Goetz. According to Dickey 2012, 39, this lexicon was probably composed before 207 CE.

148 Following Cavazza 1996, 192–194 and Heusch 2011, 394–395, it is my contention that this equation does stand up to scrutiny, *pace* MacGregor 1982, 45 and Kaster 1986, 7.

4.2.1 *Humanus* in Gellius

As I have suggested above, Gellius' case is particularly revealing of the knowledge-able men's perception of the relationship between the noun *humanitas* and the adjective *humanus*.[149] Let me start the discourse yet again from *NA* 13.17. Kaster remarks that the comparative and superlative forms of *humanus* are used in *NA* 13.17, which would imply "that discrimination was the very business of the correct sense of *humanitas*: the distinction between men and beasts, of course, but also the distinction belonging to some men who, by dint of toil and application, were 'more human' than others."[150] However, we might rephrase this thought or even push it one step further to state that, according to Gellius, only the comparative and the superlative forms of *humanus* can express the idea embodied in the noun *humanitas*. It is sufficient to provide a survey of the Gellian instances of the positive forms of *humanus*. Not unlike the other authors we have analysed, Gellius too seems to use *humanus* to simply mean 'of man', in connection with nouns such as *opinio, uita, ius, natura, genitura, res, cupido, affectio, uox, fides, succidia, ingenium, genus, corpus, partus, sensus, uestigium, pudor, condicio, modus, ritus*.[151] Conversely, the adjective appears to be far more significant in Gellius' other occurrences of comparatives and superlatives. In addition to *maxime humanissimi* ("a phrase, with its double superlative, as extraordinary in Latin as in English"[152]) and *humaniori* in 13.17 (although this, taken from Varro, expands the question well beyond Gellius), there is one instance of *humanioris* at 19.12.7, and two other occurrences of superlatives, *humanissima* at 20.1.24 and *humanissimi* in the index written by Gellius himself (*capitula libri quinti decimi*, 21). At 19.12.7 Gellius is reporting a story, originally narrated by Herodes Atticus, of a Thracian who was fed up with his barbarian life and thus decided to migrate to more civilized lands (*in terras cultiores*), encouraged by his desire for a 'more human' life (*humanioris uitae cupidine*). That the idea of civilization is implied in this use of *humanior* is hardly deniable. The same holds true for *humanissimi* in the title of 15.21 (the passage opposing Jupiter's to Neptune's sons), which seems to reflect the allusions to civilization contained in that Gellian article.[153] On the contrary, at 20.1.24 a law is considered to be *huma-*

---

149 A more-in-depth discussion of what follows can be found in Mollea 2023b, 4–9.
150 Kaster 1986, 9.
151 Regarding *res humanae*, Astarita 1993, 204 remarks that in Gellius they include basic knowledge of physiology (cf. *NA* 18.10. 8 above), *officia* in general (cf. 2.7.15) and violent death (13.1.2).
152 Kaster 1986, 6.
153 The title reads: *Quod a poetis Iouis filii prudentissimi humanissimique, Neptuni autem ferocissimi et inhumanissimi traduntur* ("That by the poets the sons of Jupiter are represented as most wise and refined, but those of Neptune as very haughty and rude", trans. Rolfe 1927).

nissima, which rather evokes the idea of φιλανθρωπία. However, two clarifications are in order. First, this instance is in the form of reported speech (by the lawyer Sextus Caecilius), so this use might not be originally Gellian. Secondly and crucially, to claim that only the comparative and the superlative forms of *humanus* can imply the παιδεία-meaning of *humanitas* is radically different from saying that all comparatives and superlatives take on that meaning. In addition, one further, concluding observation can be added: despite disagreeing with *humanitas* having a moral meaning, Gellius' oeuvre, in so far as it is educational, must also be ethical.[154] Accordingly, as with Cicero or Pliny the Younger, it is somehow to be expected that the ideas of παιδεία and φιλανθρωπία become at times closer to one another, or even overlap.[155] After all, as Vardi puts it: "Gellius' view of learning and intellectual life preserves some distinctly Roman ideas of the gentleman-scholar in which he seems indebted to Cicero."[156] As my discussions have suggested, only the concept of *humanitas* can show how deep this ideological indebtedness really is.

4.3 Fronto: Are *eruditio in bonas artes* and φιλοστοργία Better than *Humanitas*?

To turn to Fronto after Gellius might seem counterintuitive, and not only because the former was surely older. As is well known from the *Noctes Atticae* in fact, Gellius esteemed Fronto and regarded him as an example to follow, even if Fronto was presumably not among Gellius' main, closer teachers.[157] Thus, both chronology and logic would *prima facie* suggest investigating Fronto's *humanitas* before Gellius'. Yet it is my contention that, in terms of *humanitas*, the distance between the two can only be appreciated once it has become clear how crucial this term was to Gellius' cultural programme. A clarification, which also serves as a methodological reminder, is in order. To claim that Gellius gave more importance and different nuances to the word *humanitas* is not to say that he gave more importance than Fronto to the concepts expressible by the word *humanitas*. It simply means that Gellius perceived the term as having different, that is, educational connotations, and as being more loaded, while Fronto seemed to prefer other expressions to refer to that same idea of παιδεία (and to that of φιλανθρωπία). But before investi-

---

154 Cf. Beall 1988, 86–93; Kaster 1997[2], 65–66; Swain 2004, 39; Morgan 2004, 187; Heusch 2011, 375; König/Woolf 2013, 55.
155 Cf. Heusch 2011, 396 n. 243.
156 Vardi 2004, 186.
157 Cf. *e.g.* Heusch 2011, 235.

gating some of these alternative expressions, let us turn to Fronto's instances of *humanitas* first.

Very little of what Fronto probably wrote in Latin has come down to us, but if Marache is right in claiming that the letters best represent his literary theory, such letters are apt to reveal the role that *humanitas* played in his oeuvre.[158] There are only two instances of the term in his epistolary collection, one in a letter addressed to the emperor Lucius Verus, and the other one in a letter to his friend Arrius Antoninus.[159]

On one day in Spring 161 CE, Lucius Verus and his master Fronto happened to visit Marcus Aurelius in the imperial palace, but at different times.[160] Consequently, they missed the chance to meet. Modern readers, who tend to suppose they met quite often, do not tend to see this episode as a problem – yet this assumption is mistaken. According to (a probable reconstruction of) the letter that Lucius Verus sent to Fronto on that occasion, they probably met very rarely: *Quin grauissimum stationis nostrae id esse arbitrer, quod ueniendi ad te adeo rari casus sunt uel desunt* (*Ad Verum Imp.* 1.11 = p. 114 Van den Hout: "Nay, I think it is the heaviest penalty of our position that I so seldom, if ever, have an opportunity of coming to you", trans. Haines 1919, slightly adapted).[161] In this very case then, the two had not seen each other for more than four months, as Fronto had spent this time in the countryside, probably in his Aurelian villa (*Ad Verum Imp.* 1.12.3 = p. 116 Van den Hout: *Nam ex hortis ego redii Romam ante diem quintum kal. April*, "For I returned from my gardens to Rome on March 28th", trans. Haines 1919).[162] This explains why the recently appointed co-ruler was so disappointed that he wrote a letter to Fronto expressing his sadness and frustration. In his response, Fronto sought to justify himself for not having informed Lucius Verus of his visit, but was also pleased by the content of Verus' letter:[163]

Neque tanto opere gauderem, si, cum ad te uenissem, summo cum honore a te appellatus essem, quam nunc gaudeo tanto me iurgio desideratum. Namque tu pro tua persingulari

---

158 Marache 1957, 19.

159 A third instance of *humanitas* in Fronto's *corpus* is actually to be found in a letter written by Lucius Verus (*Ad Verum Imp.* 1.1.3 = p. 108 Van den Hout): cf. below, p. 180.

160 On the date of this letter cf. Champlin 1980, 110; 134.

161 *Casus* is Van den Hout's 1988 plausible emendation for *solus*: cf. his apparatus criticus *ad loc.*

162 On Fronto's Aurelian villa and its identification with what he calls *horti* cf. Champlin 1980, 22–23.

163 On the importance of this exchange of letters for illuminating Fronto's friendship with Lucius Verus cf. Champlin 1980, 110–111.

> humanitate omnes nostri ordinis uiros, ubi praesto adsunt, honorifice adfaris, non omnes magno opere requiris absentes. (*Ad Verum Imp.* 1.12.1 = p. 115 Van den Hout)

> Nor should I be so greatly pleased, had I come to you and been welcomed by you with every honour, as I am now that you felt my absence enough to give me such a scolding. For while with your characteristic *humanitas* you give all members of our order, when they present themselves, an honourable welcome, yet it is not all of them about whom you make earnest enquiries when they are absent. (trans. Haines 1919)

The framework of a visit to the emperor, his co-emperor as addressee and the use of *humanitas* itself all contribute to remind us of a passage of Pliny's *Panegyric to Trajan* (49.5) upon which I have already touched.[164] In both cases *humanitas* points to the emperor's affability and courtesy towards his closest friends, and in both cases the tone is quite flattering. No doubt this is something to be expected in a panegyric, but not necessarily in a private letter.[165] Yet the presence of the *hapax persingulari* makes this flattery all the more evident.

If the first instance of Frontonian *humanitas* is probably not particularly significant in terms of its contribution to Fronto's thought, its meaning and context are at least clear. Unfortunately, this is not the case with the second and last occurrence of *humanitas* in Fronto's letters. In *Ad amic.* 2.8.2 = pp. 197–198 Van den Hout, Fronto is recommending a certain Baburiana, probably the victim of a judicial error, to the influential Arrius Antoninus.[166] If the common interpretation that can be inferred from the lacunose text is right, Fronto is stressing the reasons why he feels confident of recommending such a person when he says *tuae humanitati congruens uidebatur* ("It seemed in keeping with your *humanitas*", trans. Haines 1920). There is enough certainty that these words come at the end of a sentence, but unfortunately, if Van den Hout's computation is correct, 14 letters and one line cannot be read before that clause (*14 litt(eras) et unus uersus legi nequeunt*).[167] Right before this *lacuna*, there is a reference to Arrius Antoninus' regard for justice (*ita tamen ut ars maxima a<c> potissima sit iustitiae tuae ratio habenda*, "only so far however as is compatible above and before all with a regard for your justice", trans. Haines 1920), but too much is missing in between. However, given the context of a letter of recommendation, it seems reasonable to pro-

---

164 Cf. above, pp. 92–93. The passage reads: *non ipsum tempus epularum tuarum, cum frugalitas contrahat, extendit humanitas?* ("As for the length of your banquet, polite manners prolong what frugality cut short", trans. Radice 1975).
165 That Fronto's letters were not meant to be published is almost unanimously agreed: cf. Champlin 1980, 3; Fleury 2006, 30.
166 On Arrius Antoninus, probably consul in 170 CE, cf. Champlin 1980, 15; 34; Van den Hout 1999, 440 with rich bibliography. On this letter on behalf of Baburiana cf. also Champlin 1980, 70.
167 Van den Hout 1988 *ad loc.*

pose that *humanitas* refers to Arrius Antoninus' philanthropic qualities, which Fronto quite obviously praises.[168]

These two passages clearly show that Fronto's use of *humanitas* is far closer to the idea of φιλανθρωπία than to παιδεία. Granted, Gellius would have hardly appreciated these nuances of *humanitas*, but this is not to deny that *eruditio institutioque in bonas artes*, to recall Gellius' definition of *humanitas*, were dear to Fronto's educational programme. One example should be sufficient to prove this. In *Ad M. Caes.* 4.1.2 = pp. 53–54 Van den Hout, Fronto writes to his royal pupil: *Nam prius quam tibi aetas institutioni sufficiens adolesceret, iam tu perfectus atque omnibus bonis artibus absolutus: ante pubertatem uir bonus, ante togam uirilem dicendi peritus* ("For before you were old enough to be trained, you were already perfect and complete in all noble accomplishments, before adolescence a good man, before manhood a practised speaker", trans. Haines 1919). No doubt flattery is present in this passage, for Marcus does not even seem to need teachers, since nature has provided him with all necessary talents. But what interests us here is the joint presence of *institutio* and *bonae artes* on the one hand, and of the allusion to Cato's definition of *orator* as *uir bonus dicendi peritus* (which we have already encountered in Apuleius' *Apologia*) on the other hand.[169] Even more than in Apuleius, Cato's definition and the *bonae artes* link together the ethical and the educational sphere, thus suggesting that Fronto too possessed the most complete idea of *humanitas*, even if he did not call it by this name. At this point, one may ask why he did not name this principle *humanitas*. Unfortunately, unlike Gellius, Fronto is not interested in discussing the different meanings that the term *humanitas* can take on, so that this problem can only be tackled by resorting to *argumenta ex silentio*, which are bound to be speculative and tenuous. Nevertheless, I should like to propose my own hypothesis, however speculative it might be. As is well known, the study of Latin language was at the very heart of Fronto's interests, and the uncommon expertise he must have gained in this field earned him the appointment as Marcus Aurelius' official teacher of Latin oratory.[170] It is therefore no coincidence that one of Fronto's most important theoretical considerations about word choice in Latin language can be found in an early letter to Marcus Aurelius (*Ad M. Caes.* 4.3 = pp. 56–59 Van den Hout).[171] We might note two key elements of this famous text, which is unfortunately too long to be quoted in

---

168 In his commentary to this letter, Van den Hout 1999, 455 briefly glosses: "*humanitati*: 'fairness'."

169 Cf. above, pp. 145–146.

170 On Fronto's role as teacher of the emperors cf. Champlin 1980, 118–130.

171 It is usually dated 139 CE to 145 CE, with larger consense on 139 CE: cf. the *status quaestionis* in Van den Hout 1999, 150.

full here. First, the gifted author ought to look for *insperata atque inopinata uerba*, that is, words that a common author would probably not use in the same context.[172] At the same time, these words ought to be extremely clear in meaning so as not to run the risk of being misunderstood.[173] In Fronto, this criterion leads to a quest for archaisms.[174] Secondly and consequently, this ability to find the right word at the right time is Fronto's main criterion in listing his canon of the good authors, i.e. those authors who should be taken as models. Given the conditions, it is no surprise that these are in fact old and / or archaizing authors. Fronto mentions the elder Cato, Sallust, Plautus, Ennius, Coelius, Naevius, Lucretius, Accius, Caecilius, Laberius, Novius, Pomponius, Atta, Sisenna, Lucilius and, the exception which proves the rule, Cicero.[175] Unfortunately, most of them are only known in fragments; still, the word *humanitas* never appears in works of any of the aforementioned authors. One exception clearly stands out: Cicero. Fronto admires him, calling him *caput atque fons Romanae facundiae* ("the head and source of Roman eloquence", trans. Haines 1919) but also remarks: *uerum is mihi uidetur a quaerendis scupulosius uerbis procul afuisse* ("But he seems to me to have been far from disposed to search out words with especial care", trans. Haines 1919). In other words, as Marache states, "Cicéron est le seul qui ne doive pas l'estime de Fronton à la rareté de son vocabulaire."[176] Judging from the case of *humanitas*, a common Ciceronian word, nothing could be truer. But the problem with *humanitas*, as should by now be evident, is its ambiguity, its lack of univocality, clearly in contrast with Fronto's oratorical ideals. The fact then that none of Fronto's praised authors seem to have given any importance to this term can only have contributed to its underappreciation. Of course he would have used this word sometimes, as in the two instances that we have analysed, but surely he did not give to it as much weight as Gellius did.

In the light of this, it is quite surprising to come across studies devoting single chapters to Fronto's *humanitas*, such as that by Portalupi.[177] What is more, it is not at all clear what the scholar means by the title 'L'*humanitas* di Frontone'. She probably alludes to Fronto's humanity in its broadest, that is to say ambiguous, sense. Among other concepts and human virtues, sincerity, honesty, friendship, and even φιλοστοργία are mentioned, all values which have little to do with Gel-

---

172 On the key role of *insperata atque inopinata uerba* in Fronto's aesthetic ideals cf. Marache 1952, 145; 1957, 10.
173 Cf. Levi 1994, 291–292.
174 Marache 1952, 149. More on archaisms in Fronto in Portalupi 1961, 21–38.
175 For an in-depth analysis of this canon cf. Marache 1952, 155–179. Cf. also Steinmetz 1982, 184.
176 Marache 1952, 171. Cf. also Marache 1952, 144–145.
177 Portalupi 1961, 123–134.

lius' idea of *humanitas*. But the latter in particular is an extremely rare word in Latin literature, and only appears in Cicero's and Fronto's letters. Probably because of this rarity, much more than *humanitas*, φιλοστοργία seems to raise interest to Fronto, who dwells on its importance in a letter to Lucius Verus. Speaking of his friend Clarus, Fronto says:

> Nihil isto homine officiosius est, nihil modestius, nihil uerecundius. Liberalis etiam, si quid mihi credis, et in tanta tenuitate, quantum res patitur, largus. Simplicitas, castitas, ueritas, fides Romana plane, φιλοστοργία uero nescio an Romana; quippe qui nihil minus in tota mea uita Romae repperi quam hominem sincere φιλόστοργον: ut putem, quia reapse nemo sit Romae φιλόστοργος, ne nomen quidem huic uirtuti esse Romanum. (*Ad Verum Imp.* 1.6.7 = p. 111 Van den Hout)

> Nothing can be more conscientious than the man, nothing more reasonable, nothing more unassuming; generous also, if I am any authority, and considering the slenderness of his resources as openhanded as his means permit. His characteristics, simplicity, continence, truthfulness, an honour plainly Roman, a warmth of affection, however, possibly not Roman, for there is nothing of which my whole life through I have seen less at Rome than a man unfeignedly φιλόστοργος. The reason why there is not even a word for this virtue in our language must, I imagine, be, that in reality no one at Rome has any warm affection. (trans. Haines 1920)

It is no surprise that the high technicality of this Greek word, of which no Latin equivalent exists, fascinates Fronto. As Aubert points out, Fronto himself seeks to give the reader the chance to understand the exact meaning of φιλοστοργία by evoking values which are close to or parts of it.[178] This he does throughout the course of the entire letter, by mentioning values such as *familiaritas*, *amicitia*, *caritas*, *simplicitas*, *castitas*, *ueritas* and *fides*, none of which, taken alone, can correspond to φιλοστοργία. But it is also the case – and Aubert explicitly acknowledges this fact – that φιλοστοργία, indicating here the love of a living being for its offspring, is close to φιλανθρωπία (and consequently to *humanitas*), though it represents a more limited, more specific ideal than φιλανθρωπία.[179]

In conclusion, as for all other members of the Antonine elite, education, culture and παιδεία were central to Fronto: we might even claim that "the pursuit of learning was Fronto's chief and abiding passion, and [that] learning informs every aspect of his life."[180] The only difference between Gellius and Fronto is that Fronto does not name this learning *humanitas*. When he used the term *humanitas*, Fronto took it as referring to the general idea of φιλανθρωπία, although, in

---

178 Aubert 2011.
179 Aubert 2011. On φιλοστοργία in Fronto cf. also Lana 1966, 92.
180 Champlin 1980, 29. Cf. also Champlin 1980, 53.

line with his linguistic principles, he probably showed more interest in words which were at the same time less ordinary and more specific, such as, in particular, φιλοστοργία.

4.3.1 *Humanus* in Fronto (and Lucius Verus)

Humanus too crops up very rarely in Fronto's correspondence. Aside from the usual, irrelevant pairings with *amicitia, casus, consilium, corpus, cultus, genus* and *res* however, there are a couple of interesting occurrences.

On one occasion, for instance, *humanissimus* is, alongside *carissimus*, the adjective through which Lucius Verus greets Fronto in concluding a letter (*Ad Verum Imp.* 1.11 = p. 114 van den Hout). Although the use of superlatives is conventional in these circumstances, the context seems to suggest that *humanissimus* takes on a philanthropic dimension, that is, Fronto is regarded as very benevolent, very kind.

And to the same Lucius Verus we owe another interesting passage regarding the relationship between *humanitas* and *humanus*. For *Ad Verum Imp.* 1.1.3 = p. 108 van den Hout reads: *Adhibeo tibi deprecatores humanitatem ipsam, nam et delinquere humanum est et hominis maxime proprium*[181] *<ignoscere>* . . . ("I present to you as suppliants in my favour humanity herself, for even to offend is human, and it is man's peculiar privilege to pardon", trans. Haines 1920). This dramatic tone concludes what has come down to us of a comparatively long letter in which Lucius Verus only excuses himself for not writing letters to his master Fronto often enough. But this is also one of the very few circumstances where we find together *humanitas* and the adjective *humanus*.[182] Here *humanitas* is likely to be used in a collective way to design all men, and so is devoid of its cultural and ethical dimensions. And yet the positive grade *humanum* is used to stress man's attitude to making mistakes, while a superlative circumlocution (*hominis maxime proprium*) probably precedes a man's virtue, which should balance the whole sentence.

One instance can also be found of the expression *inhumanum est*, while the adverb *humanitus* appears once to refer to the misfortunes that can affect human beings. Finally, the substantivised *humana* is attested twice.

---

181 The text is interrupted by a *lacuna*.
182 For further simultaneous uses of *humanus* and *humanitas* cf. Mollea 2023b.

4.4 Conclusion

The Antonine age preserved the importance that *humanitas* had reacquired at the time of Trajan. In general terms, we can underscore two main differences, and at least partly ascribe them to the different genres to which the works of this age belonged. First, Antonine literary works display a less politically engaged use of *humanitas* (or less explicit in the case of Gellius). Secondly, all these authors refrained from exploiting, when not openly opposed, the polysemy of *humanitas*, each one preferring to stick to one main aspect of the word. These changes in the use of *humanitas* contribute to reflecting the socio-cultural novelties of the Antonine as opposed to the Trajanic age.

Apuleius' use of *humanitas*, for example, reflects the climate of the Second Sophistic, regardless of the appropriateness of defining Apuleius a sophist. The talent to manipulate the concept to his own advantage, making it evoke now exclusion (*Apologia*, the widows in the *Metamorphoses*) now inclusion (Lucius in the *Metamorphoses*), clearly reveals all his oratorical skills, and even reminds us of the sophists of the first generation, who were able to speak, with equal ability to persuade, both in favour of and against a given topic. But Apuleius also shows that philosophy had by that time reacquired the prestige that it had lost under Domitian, and *humanitas* is even employed to translate a philosophical technical term in the *De Platone et eius dogmate*.

More broadly, the revival of culture is perceptible in every section of Aulus Gellius' *Noctes Atticae*. In this encyclopedic work, *humanitas*, taken as Greek παι-δεία, is even at the heart of an educational programme which aims at combining the purity of the Latin language with the nobler Greek culture.[183] In doing so, Gellius also denounces the wrong ways of pursuing knowledge, embodied by the increasing category of those grammarians who had nothing to do with eminent figures of the past like Quintilian, and did not even know the true meaning of *humanitas*. Certainly Gellius did not include Varro, one of his models, in this category, despite the latter using the 'wrong' meaning of *humanitas*. This discrepancy is rather to be explained as a consequence of two theories of language which probably shared theoretical premises and aims, but, for all of Varro's influence on Gellius, took shape independently. This autonomy of judgement adds value to Gellius' personality as author, and, by extension, to the richness and variety of the Latin literature of the Antonine age, which is best represented by Apuleius' multifaceted oeuvre.

---

183 Cf. Heusch 2011, 397.

5 *Humanitas* in School: [Quintilian's] *Declamationes Minores* and *Maiores*

If Apuleius' *Apologia* is the sole entire judicial oration that has come down to us from Roman imperial age, this does not mean that classical Roman oratory was over. No doubt the fall of the republic and the consequent rise of the empire in the first century CE had struck a serious blow to both forensic and, even more, deliberative oratory, as testified by several authors.[1] And what is more for the aims of this book, such times coincided with the 'crisis' of *humanitas* and the success of *clementia* we have already dealt with.[2] Yet we shall see in later chapters that, from the end of the first century CE and in Pliny the Younger's footsteps, the epideictic genre (*genus demonstratiuum*) became quite successful thanks to the practice of composing and reciting panegyrics to praise emperors and imperial magistrates.[3] On some occasions then, *humanitas* played a significant role within the ideology of these eulogies. The persistence of the oratorical tradition was always guaranteed by the schools of declamation, from which also examples of deliberative and judicial oratory, albeit fictitious, have come down to us. This is testified to by two collections of declamations, known, because of their different length, as *Declamationes Minores* and *Declamationes Maiores*, which have been preserved under the prestigious name of Quintilian.

Because of the uncertainties surrounding the dating of both *Minor* and *Major Declamations*, I discuss the presence of *humanitas* in these two collections just after Apuleius, Gellius and Fronto. On the one hand, I do this on the grounds that the *Minores*, whose Quintilian's paternity is not excluded by scholars, are generally dated to the early second century CE at the latest, that is, close in time to Apu-

---

1 As Pernot 2005, 128 remarks, "the central text on this issue is the *Dialogus* of Tacitus." Yet, he also highlights that another strand of thought maintains that there was a renaissance of rhetoric during the first century of the imperial age. For a clear and well documented synthesis of this complex issue cf. Pernot 2005, 128–134, who concludes his discourse by saying that "the theme of eloquence's decline practically disappeared, apart from some late echoes, after the first century. The debate on this topic reflected the intellectual shock at the newness of the imperial regime. Once that was past, rhetoric evolved and prospered in a new setting with which contemporaries were comfortable."

2 Cf. above, pp. 40–44.

3 Cf. below, pp. 206; 225. Cf. MacDonald 2017, 781 *s.v.* Epideictic Rhetoric (Gk. *genos epideiktikon, panegyrikon;* L. *genus demonstratiuum*): "Rhetoric designed for display *(epideixis)* and public ceremony, often involving praise and blame; for Aristotle, one of the three principal genres of rhetoric."

leius;[4] on the other hand, because for the *Maiores*, which on the whole are later and date to the second and third centuries, Apuleius has been seen as the "riscontro più convincente."[5] Moreover, since Gellius accuses the improper use of *humanitas* by grammarians, it might be interesting to verify in the field how this word was used in school contexts.

As the occurrences of *humanitas* in these two collections are comparatively few – ten instances in the *Minor* and six in the *Major Declamations* – I have decided not to look into them in separate chapters.

Some further introduction to these two declamatory collections will be of help to address their relationship with *humanitas*.

5.1 The *Declamationes Minores*

The *Minor Declamations* are a sort of handbook targeted to students – and, why not? teachers – of the schools of rhetoric.[6] Its main aim was to train students in what was perhaps their most difficult exercise, the declamation. Declaiming meant to speak publicly, before their class and teacher, on a given topic. Excelling in this practice meant to be ready to speak in court. Two kinds of declamations have come down to us from antiquity: the *suasoriae*, "exercises requiring students to compose and perform imaginary deliberative speeches" and the *controuersiae*, "exercises requiring students to compose and perform imaginary forensic speeches."[7] All the minor declamations we possess today – 145 pieces of the original 338 – belong in the latter category. The presence of just ten occurrences of the word *humanitas* in this collection is by itself telling about the scarce value of this concept around the second century CE, especially as far as educational contexts are concerned. And the same goes for the *Major Declamations*. Add that, as we are about to see, the term takes on a rather monosemic meaning in these occurrences and it will be clear why Gellius blamed most of his contem-

---

4 On Quintilian as possible author of the *Minor Declamations* cf. Pasetti 2019, XXXV. The dating to the early second century is upheld, among others, by Stramaglia 1999, 24 and n. 6. Santorelli 2021b, xiii opts for the late first century.
5 Stramaglia 1999, 25. On the dating of the *Major Declamations* cf. the detailed and up-to-date Santorelli 2021a, which includes rich bibliographical discussion of previous hypotheses of dating and analyses each and every major declamation from the chronological viewpoint.
6 For a more detailed introduction to the *Minor Declamations* cf. Winterbottom 1984, XI–XXV and Pasetti 2019, XI–XXXVIII.
7 Both definitions are taken from MacDonald 2017 (790 and 779 respectively).

porary school teachers and tried to bring *humanitas* back to its past splendour and socio-cultural importance.

No other declamation more than *Decl. min.* 254 can be said to be built upon *humanitas*. Aside from the fact that the term itself appears four times within this short 'quasi-*suasoria*', as Winterbottom calls it, *humanitas* is the very principle which induces the petitioner to propose a bill for reinstating an exile in his community.[8] The latter had in fact come back to his city to say something about a plot to set up a tyranny, but, after the accused had been acquitted on a tied vote, he had to leave his city again. Hence the idea, developed throughout this declamation, of a bill to try to keep him in his homeland: *Non enim causa uictus est sed legibus, sed publica humanitate; quae quidem ipsa me in hoc exhortata est, ut rogationem ad uos de retinendo ciue ferrem in ciuitate tam misericorde* (254.6: "He was not defeated because of his case but because of the laws and the *humanitas* of the public – which itself urged me to propose to you a bill for keeping a citizen in so tender-hearted a community", trans. Shackleton Bailey 2006). The exile is said not to have been defeated by his case, but by the laws and *publica humanitas*. This rare pairing immediately reminds us of Apuleius' *Metamorphoses* discussed earlier on, and despite the small philological problem noticed there, this comparison might be telling as far as either the geographic or chronological setting of *Decl. min.* 254 is concerned.[9] Geography first.

On the base of judicial criteria, Wycisk has suggested that the story told in this declamation should take place in a Greek city.[10] Dimatteo stresses that this is anything but certain, and yet an expression like *publica humanitas*, which implies that *humanitas* is widespread within a community, would be particularly fitting for the Greek world, the ideological, often idealised 'homeland' of *humanitas* according to several influential Latin authors, as we have seen.[11] And the trial of Apuleius' *Metamorphoses* 3, like most part of that work, is set in Greece. Nor this should seem to be coming into conflict with what I have suggested in the Apuleius section, that is, that the presence of the *humanitas* argument in the mock trial of *Metamorphoses* 3 might account for the Apuleian originality of that entire episode.[12] For my claims are actually two: first, that the use of the *humanitas* argument is typically Roman, and secondly, that it is also typically Roman the 'idealised' belief that *humanitas* is or should be ontologically widespread, as it were, among Greeks.[13]

---

8 Winterbottom 1984, 319.
9 Cf. above, pp. 148–150.
10 Wycisk 2008, 198.
11 Dimatteo 2019, 261 n. 1. Cf. above, pp. 34–38.
12 Cf. above, pp. 151–152.
13 Cf. above, pp. 34–38.

On the other hand, an expression like *publica humanitas*, which only appears in judicial contexts, might also allude to an age whose laws are characterised by *humanitas*, as is the case of both the Hadrianic and Antonine ages.[14] The meaning of *humanitas* at 254.6 also points in this direction, since its philanthropic nuances, that once more make this text go hand in hand with Apuleius', are made clear by the adverb *misericorde* with which the sentence ends. That said, I am well aware that neither from a geographical nor from a chronological viewpoint the expression *publica humanitas* can be decisive, but might – and perhaps should – be taken into account in future discussions regarding the dating or geographical setting of *Decl. min.* 254.

Right from this very first instance, it is clear that *Decl. min* 254 and the Trial of Hypata of *Metamorphoses* 3 also share the argumentative use of *humanitas* as a double-edged sword. While in the case of Apuleius I have highlighted that the alleged widows echo Lucius' use of *humanitas* as defensive argument, turning it into a prosecutorial one, in *Decl. min.* 254 the same *humanitas*, which was the deciding argument for the prosecution leading the exile to conviction is turned into the argument on which the defender bases his speech. I am not sure, but all these analogies might also contribute to interpreting the Trial of Hypata as a parody of what happens in the declamatory schools, where one and the same argument can be equally used to two opposite ends.

To return to the text and deepen my analysis: the crucial role played by *humanitas* within *Decl. min.* 254 becomes even clearer on § 12, when the speaker ultimately reiterates the message of § 6: *Detulit adfectatae tyrannidis reum (ut pars iudicum putat) manifestum: impedimento publicae humanitatis uictus est* ("He charged a man clearly guilty of plotting to set up a tyranny (so half the jury thinks): he lost because public *humanitas* stood in his way", trans. Shackleton Bailey 2006). And the stress on the public character of this *humanitas* pops up again at 254.18, which reads: *Lex iubet eos absolui qui pares sententias tulerint. Inputabitis istud publicae misericordiae, inputabitis humanitati* ("The law orders that defendants who get half the votes are acquitted. You will set that to the score of public compassion, the score of *humanitas*", trans. Shackleton Bailey 2006). As is evident, especially through the comparison with § 6 and the anaphora of *inputabitis*, *misericordia* and *humanitas* are regarded as roughly synonyms here, and if on this occasion *publica* accords with *misericordia* and not with *humanitas* is just for the search of a *variatio*. Finally, the last instance of *humanitas* in this text

---

14 Cf. above, pp. 136–137; 215. Cf. Winterbottom 1984, 320 (regarding *legibus* at 254.6): "i.e. by the provision about equal votes leading to acquittal, a sign of the *humanitas* of the system."

again implies its being a double-edged sword – for the sake of clarity I quote § 19 in full:

> Quod si pares sententiae periculo prosunt, pro utroque sunt. An uero adfectatae tyrannidis reus absoluatur quoniam non plures pro accusatore quam pro reo sententiae fuerunt, hic qui †periculi qui exiliit† uel eandem uel etiam grauiorem poenam †experiretur†, non eandem experietur legis humanitatem?

> If equal votes favor the endangered, they are in favor of both. Or should a man charged with plotting to set up a tyranny be acquitted because the prosecution did not get more votes than the defense, and shall not he that <shared> the danger, that would have met with the same or even heavier punishment, meet with the same legal *humanitas*? (trans. Shackleton Bailey 2006)

Despite the textual uncertainties, the overall message, especially as far as the role of *humanitas* therein is concerned, seems to be clear: if a law is so mild that one whom half the population considered guilty of setting up a tyranny ends up being acquitted, *a fortiori* the same should apply to one who runs the risk of being convicted for the good of his hometown. And while I have remarked above that there is no hint of a *lex humanitatis* in the Roman Empire,[15] it is no doubt telling that this short text speaks two or three times of a *publica humanitas* and once of the *humanitas* of a law: that this declamation was written during a period in which the term *humanitas* was rhetorically in vogue, particularly in the judicial field, seems therefore to be likely.

Decl. min. 305 is thematically close to *Decl. min.* 254 and is about two exiles who are caught inside the borders of their hometown by a rich man. Forced to fight each other, they both die, and the rich man is charged with improper punishment. The role of *humanitas* in this declamation is restricted, as the term appears only once, in the narration: *Amplectebantur miseri pio furto extremum patriae solum, non mehercule scio an alicuius insidiis perducti, an aliqua humanitatis facie impulsi; nihil probare possum: ambo perierunt* (305.5: "The poor fellows embraced the edge of their country's soil with a patriotic cheat. Upon my word, I don't know whether they were led on by somebody's trickery or impelled by some show of *humanitas*. I can prove nothing: both are dead", trans. Shackleton Bailey 2006). Winterbottom rightly observes that "The 'show of kindness' makes no very strong contrast, for this too would be *insidiae*."[16] Yet if we look at this instance from the viewpoint of the history of *humanitas*, it is interesting in that it alludes to the notion of feigned *humanitas*, which appears rarely in Latin litera-

---

15 Cf. above, pp. 144–145.
16 Winterbottom 1984, 436.

ture and, when it does, in the form of *species* rather than *facies humanitatis*, as we have just noticed in Gellius.[17]

To a lesser yet important degree, *humanitas* plays a role in *Decl. min.* 273, where the noun appears twice at the beginning of the oration, contributing to "predisporre l'animo dei giudici in favore del garante",[18] as prescribed by the first *sermo*: *Priusquam uenimus ad causam, praeparare debebimus animum iudicis pro ipsa persona sponsoris* (273.1: "Before we come to the case, we shall need to prepare the judge's mind in favor of the actual persona of the sponsor", trans. Shackleton Bailey 2006). This case is about a man who catches his debtor in adultery and seizes all his property under the law. He then claims the debt from the sponsor, who rebuts.[19] The sponsor's speech begins with a self-referential appeal to both *humanitas* and *bonitas*: *Petitur a nobis pecunia quam non accepimus, non consumpsimus, non in ullum rerum nostrarum usum conuertimus. Etiam, cum istud periculum est sponsoris, miserabile est: bonitate labitur, humanitate conturbat* (273.2: "Money is claimed for us which we did not receive, did not spend, did not convert into any use pertaining to our affairs. Even when this is the risk a sponsor takes, it deserves pity; kindness is his undoing, *humanitas* bankrupts him", trans. Shackleton Bailey 2006). Santorelli rightly remarks that Quintilian himself (6.1.22) recommended that defenders should ascribe their clients' vicissitudes to their *bonitas, humanitas, misericordia*, the first passage in which *bonitas* and *humanitas* are paired together.[20] And yet the presence of the third element, *misericordia*, as well as the content of the message itself make it clear that this prescription dates back to the passage of the *Rhetorica ad Herennium* we have already touched upon above.[21] What is interesting in the light of these two precedents is the scholastic character of this use of *humanitas*: two oratorical treatises suggest mentioning this word at the beginning of a defensive speech and this is what the author of this declamation does: nothing more and nothing less. It is easy to notice how different are instead both Cicero's and Apuleius' polished, pervasive and at times polysemic uses of *humanitas* in their defensive orations.[22]

Also curious in this respect is the second instance of *humanitas* in *Decl. min.* 273, which comes just a couple of lines after the first one. Before addressing the heart of his argument, the sponsor says: *etiamnum ea quae humanitatis et consuetudinis gratia dici solent non omitto* (273.3: "Once again I shall not omit what is

---

17 Cf. the case of Gellius, above, pp. 162–163, and Ammianus, below, pp. 245–247.
18 Santorelli 2019, 380.
19 I have paraphrased here part of *Decl. min.* 273.1 following Shackleton Bailey's translation.
20 Santorelli 2019, 381.
21 Cf. above, pp. 50–52.
22 Cf. above, pp. 52–62 and pp. 138–156.

usually said for the sake of *humanitas* and custom", trans. Shackleton Bailey 2006). The twinning of *humanitas* and *consuetudo* is Ciceronian, as rightly observed by Santorelli, and might have echoed in the declamator's memory, but its meaning is not as clear here as it is in the Ciceronian instances.[23] Take for example the case of *Verrines* 2.1.65:[24] despite the law preventing it, Verres obliges the noble Philodamus to host one of his lackeys. Yet Philodamus, *posteaquam ius suum obtinere non potuit, ut humanitatem consuetudinemque suam retineret laborabat* ("after having failed to obtain what was his right, tried hard to preserve his usual *humanitas*", trans. Gildenhard 2011). And to pay homage to his guest he throws a sumptuous banquet. Here *humanitatem consuetudinemque* can easily be understood as an hendiadys: despite the injustice he suffered, Philodamus tried to preserve his customary (*consuetudo*) benevolent attitude towards guests (*humanitas*).[25] At *Decl. min.* 273.3 the presence of *consuetudo* does not raise any problems, because it makes sense that to ask some elementary questions such as *Debitorem appellasti? Cum ipso cui dederas pecuniam egisti?* ("Did you call upon the debtor? Did you broach it with the man to whom you had given the money?", trans. Shackleton Bailey 2006) can be considered usual. But what is the meaning of *humanitas*? I have difficulties seeing any philanthropic attitude or even a sort of kindness in questions that, for all their being customary, the defender ultimately asks his counterpart to conceal implicit accusations. This is why I would not rule out the possibility that the pairing of *consuetudo* and *humanitas* here is a kind of formula that the declamator uses irrespective of the exact meanings of the two. And this seems to me to be in tune with the scholastic use of the first occurrence of *humanitas* in this speech.

Two instances of *humanitas* also appear in *Decl. min.* 301, but their role is less structural, as it were. This case is about a rich man who accuses a poor man of fraud. Invited by the poor man to dinner, the rich man raped a girl whom the host had called a slave, while she was actually his own daughter. The girl demanded marriage under the law governing raped women and the rich man sued her father. The first instance of *humanitas* is to be found within the poor man's praise of the frugal dinner to which he invited the rich man. This passage is textually problematic and has induced scholars to put forward conjectures. In Winterbottom 1984 it reads thus:

---

23 Santorelli 2019, 381.
24 In the other Ciceronian instances, *humanitas* and *consuetudo* appear alongside other abstract concepts or elements: cf. *Rab.* 8 (*amicitiae uetustas* and *dignitas hominis*); *Vat.* 8 (*consilium* and *auxilium*); *Off.* 2.51 (*Vult hoc multitudo, patitur consuetudo, fert etiam humanitas* – on this passage cf. above, pp. 108–109) and *Fam.* 13.33.1 (*probitas*).
25 Cf. Gildenhard 2011, 110.

Inuitaui ad cenam – quae hic circumscriptio est? – pauper diuitem. Venisti. Ago gratias: ha-
buisti honorem, et illud humile limen intrasti, et adisti mensam, ad quam cum uenire coepi-
mus deos inuocamus. Alioqui †ius in me† humanitatis est nostra frugalitas, quae uobis
utique uelut refectionem quandam et quietem praebet. Inter uestras quoque epulas non
semper illa ponuntur peregrinis petita litoribus et siluis: aliquando haec uilia quae rure mit-
tuntur adhibetis, quae emere nos pauperes possumus. (*Decl. min.* 301.10)

I asked you to dinner (what fraud in that?), I poor, you rich. You came: I thank you. You did
me honor and you entered that humble threshold and you came to the table, which approaching we invoke the gods. There is a certain *humanitas* (thoughtfulness) in our frugality
[*Alicuius †in me† humanitatis est nostra frugalitas*]: it gives you folk a sort of recreation and
rest. In you rich men's banquets too, you don't always serve those items fetched from foreign seas and forests; sometimes you call upon these inexpensive products from the countryside, which we poor men can buy. (trans. and Latin in square brackets as in Sheckleton
Bailey 2006)

While no brilliant solution occurs to me on textual criteria, what we have so far
seen on *humanitas* might help us draw closer to a – hopefully satisfying – solution. The case of Pliny's *Panegyricus* 49.5, for example, has shown that *humanitas*
and *frugalitas* can be related to each other.[26] And the *Life of Didius Julianus* in the
Historia Augusta will show that *humanitas* understood as frugality was generally
considered one of the virtues of the good emperor.[27] Accordingly, in the case of
Decl. min. 301.10 my guess is that the context suggests that the poor man's *humanitas*, probably to be taken as courtesy, can only materialise in *frugalitas*, as there
is nothing else a poor man can offer to a rich when dining. Thus one possible
reading may be *Alioqui quiduis in me humanitatis est nostra frugalitas*, to be in-
tended "After all, frugality is all I have of *humanitas*." *Quid-* of *quiduis* might have
fallen because of haplography and *uis* can easily be mistaken for *ius*.[28]

The second instance of *humanitas* in this declamation appears within the
same argumentative part, on § 13. The poor man also rebuts the possible charge
that his daughter was part of the service, adding: *Nisi ueritus essem ne tibi inui-
diam fieri putares, nisi me frequenti humanitate in honore posuisses, ego ministras-
sem* ("If I had not been afraid of your thinking that I was embarrassing you, if
you had not done me honor with frequent *humanitas*, I would have been waiter",
trans. Shackleton Bailey 2006). In other words, poor families cannot afford any
servants, so they – the *pater familias* included – play the servant's role whenever
necessary. While the general message of this passage is clear, the meaning of *fre-*

---

26 Cf. above, pp. 92–93.
27 Cf. below, p. 268.
28 Andrea Balbo, *per litteras*, suggests: *Alioqui <quid> ius in me humanitatis est? Nostra frugalitas?*, to be taken as "What right of *humanitas* is there in myself? Our frugality?".

quenti humanitate is a little more nebulous. To begin with, the adjective *frequens* probably appears alongside *humanitas* here for the first time and the pairing is anyway extremely rare – we will come across another instance later on in Symmachus, where the context makes it clear that *humanitas* has to do with generosity.[29] Secondly, a little later on the poor man says: *non est circumscriptio quod interrogatus uerecunde respondi, et, cum mihi tecum coepisset nouus usus, erubui uideri sine ancilla* ("It is not fraud that I made a bashful answer when questioned and that when our familiarity had only just begun I was ashamed to be seen without a maid-servant", trans. Shackleton Bailey 2006). If the familiarity (*usus*) between the poor and the rich man is said to be recent (*nouus*), how can the poor man have benefited from the rich man's courtesies frequently, as suggested in Shackleton Bailey's translation? In the light of this, it is my contention that *frequens* should be understood here as carrying a meaning which is similar to that of the pairing *humanitas – consuetudo* we have already met at *Decl. min.* 273.3.[30] The poor man would therefore be alluding to the rich man's usual kind attitude towards men in general.

The case of *Decl. min.* 252 is of little interest to the discourse on *humanitas* itself, but, on the contrary, the sole instance of *humanitas* therein can help us improve the understanding of an uncertain passage. This declamation is based on the story of two girls, one poor and one rich, aspiring to some priesthood. Since the poor girl seems to prevail, the father of the other hopeful pays one of his parasites to rape her, being well aware that virgins alone can become priestesses. The poor girl's father thus sues the rich's and delivers the oration. The sole occurrence of *humanitas* is to be found in the poor man's *narratio* of the events, on § 14, here printed as in Winterbottom 1984:[31] *Nemo est tam adrogans sui aestimator ut accessurus ad comitia et periculum sortiturus humanitatis non malit sine aduersario esse.*[32] The apparent clarity of this passage is complicated by the very presence of *humanitatis*, which modern scholars usually take in conjunction with *periculum*, but thereby forming a nexus which is nowhere else attested in classical Latin. After all, it will be no coincidence that neither the entry on *humanitas* nor that on *periculum* in the *TLL* include it, and the presence of a verb like *sortior* is of no help (Shackleton Bailey 2006 does not hesitate to emend *sortiturus* in *subiturus*, which no doubt makes the text more idiomatic, but also *facilior*). In the light of all this, Ritter's decision of printing *inter cruces* from *et* to *humanitatis* would have perhaps

---

29 Cf. below, p. 309.
30 Cf. above, p. 188.
31 On the structure of this declamation cf. Santorelli 2019, 248–249.
32 For the English translation cf. below, p. 191.

merited more credit.[33] Yet following Winterbottom's edition, which does not raise any problems about this passage, Santorelli's recent Italian translation changes the ambiguity, but does not in itself solve it: "Nessuno presume così tanto di sé da non preferire l'assenza di avversari, quando intende presentarsi alle elezioni e sottoporsi a quel rischio che accomuna tutti gli uomini." And similarly reads Shackleton Bailey's English translation: "No one is so arrogant in his self-esteem that when he is about to go to the hustings and take a risk common to all men, he would not rather be unopposed." But what is the risk which all men share? As Santorelli explains in the commentary and Shackleton Bailey in a note, that of losing the elections, but first, not all men get involved in such a risky situation, and secondly, I am not sure *periculum sortiri* really means 'to take a risk', hence Shackleton Bailey's emendation to obtain this sense.[34] Either way, the fact that both translators feel the need to add interpretive details is telling about the opacity of this passage. And yet despite all this, it is my contention that the biggest problem – but also the solution – lies elsewhere. The thing is that, even admitting that *periculum sortiri / subire* alludes to the risk of defeat at the elections, the equation *humanitas* = *genus humanum* only appears late in Latin and is rather typical of Christian authors – the *TLL* entry gives *Decl. mai.* 8.3 as example of this use by pagan authors, but, as we will see later, the text of that passage is unsure too and I am much more inclined to believe that the meaning of *humanitas* is different there as it is here.[35] Accordingly, my feeling is that we should read *humanitate* instead of *humanitatis*. The text will therefore mean that no one is as presumptuous as to prefer, induced by the spirit of *humanitas*, to have competitors when he is about to stand for election and to have a trial. *Humanitas* would take on a meaning close to its philanthropic character we have already observed many times, thus referring to man's equity towards the others, even if these are rivals. Given the declamatory context then, I would be inclined to understanding *periculum* as a term pertaining to the judicial sphere and standing for 'trial', as is often the case in oratorical contexts from the *Rhetorica ad Herennium* onwards.[36] And the same goes for *aduersarius*, which perfectly fits both the political and judicial contexts.[37] In other words, we would face here two typical examples of situations in which nobody in ancient Rome would like to have a rival: an electoral campaign and a trial.

---

33 Ritter 1884, *ad loc.*
34 Santorelli 2019, 253; Shackleton Bailey 2006, 76 n. 7.
35 Cf. *TLL* 6.3.3076.60–3077.7 and Pieri 2002, 370–371. Cf. below, pp. 198–199.
36 Cf. *TLL* 10.1.14.62.10–42.
37 Cf. *TLL* 1.0.844.69–845.21 and 1.0.843.71–844.67 respectively.

5.2 The *Declamationes Maiores*

When we turn to the *Major Declamations* in search of the role of *humanitas* within this collection, what appears immediately clear is that there is no signifi- cant difference with the *Minor Declamations*, neither in quantitative nor in quali- tative terms. As we have seen with the previous collection, however, there are some occasions on which *humanitas* becomes relevant for some reason.

Like the *Minores*, the 19 *Declamationes Maiores* belong to the genre of the *controuersiae*, but these are – exceptionally – fully developed. As Santorelli ob- serves, they are "invaluable because they show how a student was expected to handle the themes, the recurring situations and arguments, the technical rules. And what is more, they lay bare the mistakes that were often made in the pro- cess."[38] Cleary, because of their reduced length, the *Minores* cannot hope to be so ambitious.

Four of the six occurrences of *humanitas* in the *Major Declamations* appear in two texts whose stylistic and thematic affinities have long been recognised, *Decl. mai.* 6 and 9.[39] In *Decl. mai.* 6, in particular, *humanitas* has been regarded as a cornerstone of the closing statement (although one instance is to be found in the introduction).[40] The context first. A man who had been kidnapped by pirates wrote to his wife and son for ramson. The wife had cried so much as to lose her eyesight. Being in constant need of help, she forbade his son from rescuing his father. The boy ignored his mother's order and saved his father by offering him- self as hostage. He then died and the pirates threw his corpse into the sea. As his body eventually reached his native shores, his father wanted to bury him, but his mother did not. The law which governs this *controuersia* says: *Qui in calamitate parentes deseruerit, insepultus abiciatur* ("A son who abandons his parents in mis- fortune is to be cast out unburied", trans. Winterbottom 2021). As can be easily deduced, the key value concept at stake is *pietas*,[41] and the problem is ultimately

---

38 Santorelli 2021b, xv. For a fuller introduction to the *Major Declamations* cf. Santorelli 2021b ix–xxxix; Stramaglia 2021 xxxix–lxxiii.

39 Ritter 1881, 167; Deratani 1927, 308 and, more recently, Krapinger 2007, 24; *passim*. The simi- larities between these two declamations have also induced scholars to date them to roughly the same time (usually the age of Hadrian) and to speculate that they were written by one and the same author: cf. Santorelli 2021a, 367; 371; 400; 410–412 (with up-to-date state of research).

40 Cf. Zinsmaier 2009, 51: "Zwar kommt er in der ganzen Deklamation namentlich nur zweimal vor, doch macht die Argumentation selbst deutlich, daß *humanitas* neben *pietas* einer der Eckpfeiler des Plädoyers ist."

41 Cf. Sussman 1995, 189: "A recurrent theme of this declamation is *pietas* [. . .] most commonly referring to the devotion between the father and the son." Cf. also Zinsmaier 2009, 48. On *pietas* in general cf. below, pp. 238–239.

whether the *pietas in patrem* is to prevail over the *pietas in matrem* or vice versa.[42] *Humanitas* becomes instead important when the burial itself is concerned. This is made clear right from its first occurrence on 3.3, when the corpse of the boy is seen to be lying on the shore: *conuenerunt etiam alieni parentes, totus in spectaculum populus effusus est, et ignoto quoque corpori publica humanitas quasi quasdam fecit exequias* ("The parents of other youths too have gathered there, the whole population has poured out to view the sight, and the *humanitas* of the public has given a sort of funeral even to the body of an unknown", trans. Winterbottom 2021). Once again when we meet the expression *publica humanitas* within an oratorical context the setting is likely to be Greek.[43] The novelty consists in what the *publica humanitas* encourages to do on this occasion, that is, to bury unknown corpses. As Pieri rightly remarks, Seneca was probably the first to ascribe this act to the spirit of *humanitas* – yet not *publica* and alongside *misericordia* – at *Ben.* 5.20.5.[44] Knowing the importance that entombment has always had in Western culture, it is unsurprising that Greek or Roman civilized men who find an unburied cadaver feel the need to give it a proper burial. And the second instance of *humanitas* in this declamation reiterates and puts in more explicit terms the same concept:

> Equidem, iudices, ut sentio, neminem non mortalium fauere hominis sepulturae conuenit, quia haec una res est, cuius exemplum ad omnes pertineat, ideoque non nisi ab ultimo parricidio exigitur poena trans hominem. Etiam si qua sunt iura, quae obstent, si tamen angustus saltem detur accessus, per quem intrare humanitas possit, uera clementia occasione contenta est. (*Decl. mai.* 6.10.4)

> Indeed, judges, in my opinion every mortal ought properly to favor a man's burial, because this is the one thing that sets a precedent for everyone; and hence it is only from the most horrible parricide that a penalty is exacted which goes beyond the living person. There are, maybe, legal rules that stand in the way; but if even a narrow window is available through which *humanitas* may enter, true mercy is happy to take the opportunity. (trans. Winterbottom 2021)

---

42 Cf. Sussman 1995, 190; Lentano 1999, 577.
43 Cf. Zinsmaier 2009, 17–18: "Die gewollt skizzenhafte Darstellung des Vorgeschehens in den *argumenta* macht es dem heutigen Leser schwer, dieses in einer bestimmten Zeit, an einem bestimmten Ort, in einem bestimmten Milieu anzusiedeln. Dennoch ist es möglich, aus der Fülle der stereotyp wiederkehrenden Motive als imaginären Schauplatz des Geschehens der meisten Kontroversienthemen eine Stadt zu abstrahieren, die in manchen Zügen an eine griechische Polis des 4. Jh. v. Chr. erinnert. Solche Charakteristika sind: die Freiheitsliebe der Bürger, die den Haß des Tyrannen auf sich zieht, Gesetze gegen *adfectata tyrannis*, Wunschprämien für Tyrannenmörder sowie das hohe Ansehen, das die tapfere Tat des Einzelnen genießt, verkörpert im Typus des *vir fortis* (ἀριστεύς)."
44 Pieri 2002, 372 n. 21.

When reading this passage, it is hard not to think about Creon and Antigone, with the former embodying positive laws (*iura*) and the latter that natural bond which unites all human beings as such (*humanitas*). Probably because of the judicial, however feigned, context of the declamation, the contrast between these two principles is not as stark as in Sophocles' tragedy, for instance. On the contrary, it rather looks as if *humanitas* should seep into laws whenever possible, a message that sounds particularly suited for ages such as that of Hadrian or the Antonine.[45]

In spite of the similarities with *Decl. mai.* 6, the use of *humanitas* in *Decl. mai.* 9 is rather different. As usual, a brief contextualisation first. A poor and a rich man are enemies, but their sons are close friends. When the son of the rich man is kidnapped by pirates, writes home for ransom and his father hesitates, the son of the poor man sets off to help him. After finding out that his friend has become a gladiator, the son of the poor man offers himself as substitute, but asks the son of the rich man to help his father in case he should die. He actually dies during the gladiatorial contest and the son of the rich man, once back home, finds the poor man in needy circumstances and helps him. The rich man thus disowns his son. The relevant law recites that *Abdicare et recusare liceat* ("It is to be lawful to disown and to challenge disownment", trans. Winterbottom 2021) and, as Dingel has put it: "Heute kann als erwiesen gelten, daß die *abdicatio* in der Form, wie die Deklamationen sie haben, als (auf griechischen Rechtbasierende) Fiktion anzusprechen ist."[46] The cultural context is likely to be yet again Greek, but on this occasion the uses of the *humanitas* argument do not seem to me to be relevant in this respect.

Both occurrences of *humanitas* are to be found in that part of the *argumentatio* which is usually called *refutatio*, when the opposing arguments are countered. While addressing the court, the son of the rich man says:

> Nec ignoro, iudices, quam male ista defensio de humano genere mereatur, si adeo nihil est per se misericordia, ut, nisi ulterior aliqua necessitas pudori uim fecerit, pro summo crimine damnanda sit minus necessaria humanitas. Ergo si alienum et ignotum, tamen, quae publica omnium mortalium quippe sub uno parente naturae cognatio est, hominem cibo forte iuuissem, poena dignum uideretur seruasse perituram animam et ignouisse rebus humanis et respectu communis omnium sortis uelut adorato numini [et] stipem posuisse fortunae? Si hoc crimen est, laudetur ergo crudelitas, nihil habeatur piratis lanistisque prudentius! Ferantur sane profutura humano generi duo exempla: intra tam breue tempus propter misericordiam alter abdicatus, alter occisus est. (*Decl. mai.* 9.15.6–16.1)

---

45 Cf. above, p. 134 and below, p. 215. Cf. also Pieri 2002, 373: "Nel citato esempio di *decl.* 6,10 la *humanitas* è confrontata con i *iura* e sembra indicare quelle leggi non scritte che regolano il codice etico degli uomini in quanto tali."
46 Dingel 1988, 116.

I am also aware, judges, how badly this defense deserves of the human race, if mercy is of so little intrinsic value that, unless some superior tie overwhelms one's sense of shame, less than unavoidable *humanitas* has to receive condemnation as a heinous crime. So, then, if I had given food to help a stranger, an unknown person, yet – for this is a relationship that binds everybody together as children of one parent, nature – a human being, it would seem to be a matter for punishment to have saved a life that would otherwise have been lost, to have made allowances for the vagaries of human life and, out of respect for the common lot of all, to (so to speak) have given alms to Fortune, as a deity we worship. If this is a crime, then let cruelty merit praise, and let nothing be thought wiser than pirates and managers of gladiators! Let two precedents be made known that will doubtless prove useful to humanity: within so short a time one man has been disowned, another killed – both for showing pity. (trans. Winterbottom 2021)

This first occurrence of *humanitas* would have sounded jarring to any listeners, because its unprecedented pairing with the adjective *necessaria* causes a contradiction in terms. For how can a concept like *humanitas*, which by definition should refer to a general benevolence towards the other, be restricted by other kinds of more specific ties? Recalling the just mentioned *necessitas, necessaria* is in fact to be taken as meaning 'connected by close ties of friendship, relationship.'[47] As Stramaglia puts it: "It would be inhuman to claim that kind behavior can be accounted for only if accorded for the sake of superior (i.e., specific, personal) ties with the person to be aided."[48] And this helps us highlight another aspect of *humanitas*. We have already observed that, unlike for example *clementia*, this concept does not necessarily imply any kind of hierarchical superiority on the part of the giver.[49] But now we should also exclude another kind of superiority, that which concerns familial, friendly or any other kind of specific relational bond: were it not yet clear enough, *humanitas per se* transcends any kind of tie which is not that which unites all human beings *qua* human, especially when its philanthropic aspect prevails, as the synonymous use with *misericordia* makes clear on this occasion.[50]

The way *Decl. mai.* 9 continues (*Ergo si alienum . . .*) corroborates this understanding of *humanitas* and, at the same time, makes explicit its contrast with *crudelitas*. The abstract concepts involved in this discourse, which starts in § 15 and ends at the beginning of § 16 (. . . *alter occisus est*), give origin to a circular composition – or imperfect chiasmus, if you like – whose argumentative efficacy is significant. For *misericordia* appears at the beginning (*si adeo nihil est per se misericordia*) and at the very end (*intra tam breue tempus propter misericordiam alter abdicatus,*

---

47 *OLD* s.v. *necessarius*[1], n. 6.
48 Stramaglia 2021, 214 n.72. Cf. also Krapinger 2007, 142 n. 295.
49 Cf. above, pp. 39–40; 82; *passim*.
50 On the relation between *humanitas* and *misericordia* cf. above, pp. 50–51; 149–150; 185.

alter occisus est), and is first followed by *humanitas* (*pro summo crimine damnanda sit minus necessaria humanitas*) and then preceded by *crudelitas* (*si hoc crimen est, laudetur ergo crudelitas*). From whatever rhetorical viewpoint we look at it, *crudelitas* is bound to lose: it has not the prominence that an initial or closing position can guarantee, nor is it quantitatively predominant, for *humanitas* is clearly used to reiterate the idea expressed by *misericordia* – hence the imperfection of the chiasmus. Tellingly, the contrast between *misericordia* and *crudelitas* follows in the footsteps of their simultaneous appearance in Quintilian's *Institutio oratoria* 5.10.27, where both abstract concepts are included within the places of arguments (*argumentorum loci*) and, more in detail, the cast of mind (*animi natura*): *animi natura, etenim auaritia, iracundia, misericordia, crudelitas, seueritas aliaque his similia adferunt fidem frequenter aut detrahunt, sicut uictus luxuriosus an frugi an sordidus quaeritur* ("Cast of mind, because avarice, irascibility, mercifulness, cruelty, severity, and the like often enhance or detract from credibility; one can ask, for instance, whether a man's lifestyle is luxurious, frugal, or miserly", trans. Russell 2001). But *crudelitas* is also opposed to *clementia*, such as in Seneca *De clementia* 2.4.1, where the Stoic philosopher offers his own definition of *crudelitas* (*Quid ergo obponitur clementiae? Crudelitas, quae nihil aliud est quam atrocitas animi in exigendis poenis*, "What, then, is the opposite of mercy? Cruelty, which is nothing other than grimness of mind in exacting punishment", trans. Cooper/Procopé 1995), or in Pliny the Younger's famous passage of *Panegyricus* 3.4 discussed above.[51] And as one would expect, *humanitas* makes no exception, being counterposed to *crudelitas* right from Cicero: at *Phil.* 11.8 Dolabella is said to be so *immemor humanitatis* [. . .] *ut suam insatiabilem crudelitatem exercuerit non solum in uiuo, sed etiam in mortuo* ("regardless of *humanitas* [. . .] as to practise his insatiable cruelty not only on the living, but even on the dead", trans. Ker 1957), while at *Ver.* 2.5.115 Sicilians *indigne ferunt illam clementiam mansuetudinemque nostri imperi in tantam crudelitatem inhumanitatemque esse conuersam* ("They were outraged that the mildness and gentleness of our rule had turned into such monstrous cruelty and inhumanity", trans. Berry 2006), where *crudelitas* goes hand in hand with the etymological opposite of *humanitas*, *inhumanitas*. What is more, we find in Cicero's *Pro Flacco misericordia* and *humanitas* opposed to *crudelitas* in the same passage in which we have also found the first instance of the expression *ius humanitatis*.[52]

In *Decl. mai.* 9.16.6 the son of the rich man goes on to portray his own character and expose his previous ambitions. In doing so, he mentions *humanitas* again: *iuuenis conceptus splendidis parentibus cum solum tam speciosae fortunae cre-*

---

51 Cf. also Sen. *Dial.* 4.13.2 (*De ira*) and Malaspina 2001, 390–391. Cf. above, pp. 87–88.
52 Cf. above, p. 143.

derem fructum posse prodesse et contra uarios mortalium casus quasi portum be-nignitatis aperire, concupiui quandam humanitatis ciuicam gloriam ("A youth born to noble parents, believing that the only benefit of so brilliant a fortune is to be able to help others and to open up, as it were, a harbor of kindness to the vary-ing chances of mortal men, I aspired to a kind of citizen's prize for *humanitas*", trans. Winterbottom 2021). As Winterbottom suggests, "this probably builds on the idea of the *corona ciuica*: a crown of oak leaves which one citizen gives to another who has saved his life in battle, in recognition of the preservation of his life and safety' (Gell. 5.6.11; trans. Rolfe)."[53] The presence of *benignitas*, roughly a synonym for *beneuolentia*, leaves little room for doubt that *humanitas* is once again to be understood, at least mainly, in philanthropic terms. But curiously, this is probably the first time that one is explicitly said to be aspiring to the glory of *humanitas*, while conversely *humanitas* and *gloria* are counterposed by Lactan-tius Placidus in his commentary to Statius' *Thebaid* 6.490 (*VICTVSQVE ET COL-LAVDATVS ABISSET quia praeposuit humanitatem gloriae ne cruentam uictoriam sortiretur, et uictus est cum favore*, "because he preferred *humanitas* over glory so as not to obtain a bloody victory. Accordingly, he was laudably defeated"). In this passage, Chromis, son of Heracles, is said to have preferred *humanitas* over glory: despite having the opportunity of defeating his enemy Hippodamus, who lies on the ground, he behaves mildly and ends up leaving the field vanquished (*uictus*) but at the same time praised of all (*collaudatus*).

That *humanitas* plays a key role in the *refutatio* of *Decl. mai.* 9 is also con-firmed by the sole occurrence of a superlative of (*in*)*humanus* in the two pseudo-Quintilian *corpora* of declamations. The son of the rich man lists the poor man's misfortunes and the superlative *inhumanissimus* rounds off the discourse, mark-ing its climactic point: *Post orbitatem, post egestatem quid amplius potest pati, nisi quod optat? Vlteriorne tibi aliqua ultio quaerenda est, aut aliquid rerum natura peius capit? Quis non te omnium mortalium inhumanissimum putet, si hoc aduer-sus inimicum tuum saltem optasti!* (9.18.5: "After bereavement, after poverty, what more can he suffer except what he wishes for? Do you have to look for a revenge that goes further than this? Does the whole world hold anything worse? Who would not think you the *inhumanissimum* of all mortals if you had even wished for such a thing to afflict your enemy?", trans. Winterbottom 2021). As what the poor man ultimately wishes for is death, nothing can be said to be more devoid of *humanitas* than to hope for something worse than death itself. By re-sorting to the etymological opposite of *humanitas*, the speaker thus recalls and

---

53 Cf. also Krapinger 2007, 145 n. 313.

brings to its climax the idea of cruelty already mentioned through the word *crudelitas* on § 15.

According to Pieri, the crucial role played by *humanitas* alongside *pietas* in *Decl. mai.* 6, as we have already observed, would be found in *Decl. mai.* 8 as well.[54] There is actually just one occurrence of the word *humanitas* in this declamation, but Pieri highlights that there are several occurrences of *homo* and of values which are antonyms of *humanitas*, such as *feritas* and *immanitas*.[55] As usual, providing some context will help understand why these concepts are at stake. This *controuersia* derives from the story of two twins who catch the same disease. When a doctor offers to cure one of the two by inspecting the vital organs of the other, their father accepts. Thus one brother dies and the other survives. Their mother then accuses the father of ill-treatment. It is therefore clear why *pietas* plays an important role and no doubt the same goes, broadly speaking, for *humanitas* as understood in the declamations so far investigated. In particular, the latter concept explicitly comes into play in the first *narratio*, when the mother starts to accuse most doctors' pretentious attitude towards her sons.[56] Unfortunately, this passage poses a textual issue – I quote it as in Stramaglia 2021:

> Iam tamen, iudices, de tam perdita pronuntiatione non querimur, quod aegros, quos sibi uidebantur explicare non posse, parentibus crediderunt; innocentior est simplicitas desperare, si remedia non noueris, et hanc ignorantiae malo probitatem, ut languorem quem nescias tantum neges posse sanari. Maximi tamen uirorum et quibus arti suae soluendo non sit humanitas, si sciebant hoc genus curationis et illud non indicare uoluerunt. (*Decl. mai.* 8.3.5–6)

> But now, judges, I am not complaining of such a despairing pronouncement, or that they left to the parents the fate of children whose sickness they thought they could not cure; it is more forgivable to express frank despair if you do not know the remedy, and I prefer the principled confession of ignorance that makes you restrict yourself to calling an illness incurable, when you cannot identify it. But they are the greatest of men, ones to whose art men of true *humanitas* could not but be in debt, if they knew this type of cure and yet would not reveal it. (trans. Winterbottom 2021)

Manuscripts read *artis suae soluendo non sit humanitas*, but the dative *arti* instead of the genitive *artis* is a conjecture by Obrecht, which Stramaglia prints in his edition. This choice has also been defended by Pieri, who translated "e per i quali il senso di umanità è insolvibile nei confronti della loro arte" and then explained: "Il primo dativo si spiegherebbe dunque come *dativus iudicantis*, mentre

---

54 Pieri 2002, 376.
55 Pieri 2002, 377. On *feritas* and *immanitas* cf. above, pp. 91–92 and 92 respectively.
56 Cf. the structure of this declamation proposed by Greco 1999, 15.

solo il secondo determinerebbe la locuzione *solvendo esse*."[57] Earlier, less economical conjectures had been proposed, but they understood *humanitas* as *genus humanum*, an equivalence that is generally rare and not elsewhere documented in the *Minor* and *Major Declamations*, as we are seeing.[58] Furthermore, as the same Pieri remarks, if that were the case, it would not be clear why all human beings should be grateful to doctors who were not able to impede the tragic death of one of the two twins.[59]

The last occurrence of the word *humanitas* within the *corpus* of the *Major Declamations* is at 15.3.1. *Major Declamations* 14 and 15 represent a rare example of antilogies, that is to say, two opposite (*in utramque partem*) speeches on one and the same issue.[60] The case in question concerns a prostitute who administers a potion to her lover in order to make him fall out of love. He then accuses her of poisoning him. *Decl. mai.* 14 is the client's speech, while *Decl. mai.* 15 is a speech in defense of the prostitute.

Unlike the previous instances of *humanitas* in the declamations, this one has little to do with the defensive strategy of the speaker. Found in the exordium (§ 3), it just comes up to characterise the prostitute's initial attitude towards her lover: *Postquam nihil miseratio, nihil proficiebat humanitas, temptauit asperitate discutere: poposcit, exclusit. Non defuerunt misero preces* ("After pity, after *humanitas* proved of no avail, she tried to shake him off by being tough. She made demands, she shut him out: but the wretched fellow was never short of entreaties", trans. Winterbottom 2021). As is evident, the woman sought to dissuade the man from courting her with milder means, but *miseratio* and *humanitas* failed, and she had to resort to *asperitas*. The rhetorical context as well as the structure of the period itself with the repetition *nihil . . . nihil* suggest that the second colon (*nihil proficiebat humanitas*) has no other purpose than to emphasise the same meaning of the first (*nihil miseratio*). It follows that the meaning of *humanitas*, as is often the case, is clarified by the term with which it is associated – *miseratio* on this occasion.[61] And *miseratio*, as the *Thesaurus Linguae Latinae* shows well, is both a cognate and a quasi-synonym for *misericordia*, which we have seen playing a key role alongside *humanitas* not only in other declamations, namely *Decl. min.* 254 and *Decl. mai.* 9, but also

---

57 Pieri 2002, 376.
58 See the state of research in Pieri 2002, 369–370. On the equivalence between *humanitas* and *genus humanum* cf. above, p. 191.
59 Cf. Pieri 2002, 376.
60 Cf. Longo 2008, 13.
61 We will find an analogous pairing of *humanitas* and *miseratio* in a letter by Symmachus: cf. below, pp. 312–313.

in the mock trial of Apuleius' *Metamorphoses* 3.[62] The main difference is that in *Decl. mai.* 15 both *humanitas* and *misericordia* play rather a narrative than argumentative role.

As is evident, the opposition between *humanitas* and *asperitas* makes even clearer the connotation of *humanitas* in this context. And it is hardly surprising that these two concepts had already been juxtaposed in oratorical context by Cicero, at *De oratore* 2.212:

> Sed est quaedam in his duobus generibus, quorum alterum lene, alterum uehemens esse uolumus, difficilis ad distinguendum similitudo; nam et ex illa lenitate, qua conciliamur eis, qui audiunt, ad hanc uim acerrimam, qua eosdem excitamus, influat oportet aliquid, et ex hac ui non numquam animi aliquid inflandum est illi lenitati; neque est ulla temperatior oratio quam illa, in qua asperitas contentionis oratoris ipsius humanitate conditur, remissio autem lenitatis quadam grauitate et contentione firmatur.

> Yet these two kinds of speaking, one of which should be gentle, the other vehement, show a certain similarity, which makes it difficult to keep them apart. For something of that gentleness, which wins us the favor of the audience, ought to flow into this vigorous forcefulness, by which we stir that same audience; and again from this forcefulness some spirit must sometimes animate that gentleness. No speech is better blended than one in which the sharpness of energetic passages is seasoned with the personal *humanitas* of the orator, while the relaxed attitude of gentleness is given strength by some weightiness and energy. (trans. May/Wisse 2001)

Cicero is treating the topic of *inuentio* and, in greater detail, how to handle *ethos* and *pathos*. The structure of this passage reveals the pairing of *uis* and *asperitas* against *lenitas* and *humanitas*. And tellingly, while a speech can be *asper*, the orator, *qua* man, should never lose his *humanitas*.

5.3 *Humanus* and Its Cognates

As usual, a final section is devoted to a survey of the adjective *humanus* and the adverbial forms.

Forms of superlative are not attested, but a comparative *humanius* appears in *Decl. min.* 279, which is about another case of *abdicatio*.[63] A father disowns his son, who took money from a rich man, caught with his wife, to let him go. The passage under investigation reads:

---

62 Cf. *TLL* 8.0.1112.37–83 on *miseratio*, and above, pp. 149–150, on *misericordia* and *humanitas* in Apuleius' *Metamorphoses*.
63 Cf. above, p. 194.

Loquatur maritus cum animo suo, loquatur cum adfectu suo, cum propria animi sui natura. Si propter hoc licet abdicare, istud quod fecit maritus non licet. Alioqui enim tolerabilius et certe humanius erat arbitrium uel occidendi adulteri uel accepta pecunia dimittendi transferri ad patres, quoniam certe leuius est uetare aliqua quam punire. (*Decl. min.* 279.5)

Let a husband consult his own mind, consult his own feelings, the particular nature of his mind. If it is lawful to disown for this, then what the husband did is not lawful. From another angle, it would be more tolerable and certainly *humanius* that the choice between killing an adulterer and taking money and letting him go were transferred to fathers, since it is certainly less drastic to forbid something than to punish it. (trans. Shackleton Bailey 2006)

Dimatteo rightly speaks of *humanitas* and highlights that this concept – but we should better say 'this' expression, that is, *humanius est* – is typical of juristic texts, something we have already seen in greater detail in the Apuleius section.[64] The presence of the comparative is by itself sufficient to rule out the hypothesis that the adjective is used with a pure relational meaning,[65] and the pairing with *tolerabilius*, another comparative, supports the view that the same *humanitas* met in the other declamations is at stake here. For no doubt a spirit of compassion and philanthropy is involved in this change of roles between father and son.

In addition to the already investigated instance of the superlative *inhumanissimus* in *Decl. mai.* 9.18, in the *Major Declamations* there is also one occurrence of the comparative of *inhumanus*. A mother tells his husband that she is used to seeing in dreams her dead son. The father therefore calls on a sorcerer and the mother stops dreaming of her son. Infuriate, she accuses her husband of illtreatment. Once again the accusation of lack of *humanitas* hits a father:

Misereor feminae, cuius inuidiae totum facinus ascribitur. Maritus sic filium inclusit, tamquam se inquietari mater ista quereretur. Igitur, iudices, nemo miretur si ad tam crudelem, ad tam immitem patrem umbra non uenit. Sciebat ubi lacrimas, ubi posset inuenire singultus, a quo magis desideraretur. Namque isti ferreum pectus et dura praecordia, nec sunt de orbitate sensus. Quid enim inhumanius patre, quid inueniri truculentius potest? (*Decl. mai.* 10.2.6–3.1)

I pity this woman, for it is to jealousy of her that this outrage is entirely due. Her husband has confined their son, as though his mother here were complaining about being disturbed! So, judges, let no one be surprised if the shade did not visit a father so cruel, so brutal. It knew where it could meet with tears, with sighs; it knew by whom it was more sorely missed. For this man has a breast clad in iron and a heart of flint: he does not feel his bereavement. What, in fact, can be found *inhumanius*, more callous than his father? (trans. Winterbottom 2021)

---

64 Dimatteo 2019, 415. Cf. above, pp. 144–145.
65 Cf. above, p. 22.

As in *Decl. mai.* 9, once again *humanitas* is opposed to *crudelitas* (*tam crudelem*), but the exceptional cruelty of this father is further emphasised by the presence of elements such as *ferreum pectus* and *dura praecordia*, or by a negative, albeit quite rare, concept like *truculentia*.[66] The image of the *dura praecordia* dates back to Ovid and Tibullus, but the closest parallel is likely to be Jerome's *Ep.* 14.3.2: *Non est nobis ferreum pectus nec dura praecordia, non ex silice natos Hyrcanae nutriere tigrides* ("We don't have a breast clad in iron and a heart of stone, nor were the Hircan tigers to nurture us, born from flint"), where the traditional topos of the Hyrcan tigers adds further to the savagery and barbarity of the subject in question.[67] Moreover, from the viewpoint of *humanitas*, elements such as these suggest an amplification of the concept of philanthropy in direction of the ampler idea of civilization, as we have already noticed several times in previous chapters.[68]

Something similar might happen in *Decl. mai.* 13.11.4, despite what we have observed on the striking difference usually lying between *ius humanitatis* and *ius humanum*.[69] The passage reads: *Barbarorum mos est populorum, quos procul omni iuris humani societate summotos proxime beluis natura efferauit* ("It is the custom of barbarous peoples, removed by nature far from any share in men's legal systems and reduced almost to the level of wild beast", trans. Winterbottom 2021). Although it is true that, as Winterbottom's translation suggests, *ius humanum* can simply indicate a legal system, the presence of wild beasts (*beluis*) leads to an opposition between civilization and barbarity that ultimately depends on the existence of human laws themselves. So the entire expression *omni iuris humani societate* does not seem to me to differ significantly from the Apuleian *commune ius humanitatis*.[70] This is perhaps too a small clue to call into question the fact that there is usually a conceptual difference between the comparative *humanior* and the positive *humanus*, but certainly on this occasion the author of the declamation must have played on the possible 'higher' meanings and implications that the etymological relatives of *humanus* have.[71]

---

[66] The first and sole occurrence of *truculentia* in republican Latin is, as one might expect, in Plautus' *Truculentus*, but then the term is not again attested until Tacitus (*Ann.* 2.24) and Apuleius (*Met.* 9.27; 36).

[67] On these elements, their parallels and further bibliographical references cf. C. Schneider 2013, 126–127.

[68] Cf. above, pp. 64; 123–126.

[69] Cf. above, pp. 143–145.

[70] Cf. above, p. 143.

[71] Cf. above, pp. 22–24.

In the remaining instances of both *corpora humanus* seems to have its common relational meaning and, as with other authors, it accords with nouns such as *accidentia, actus, aeuum, animus, calamitas, calliditas, cogitatio, condicio, consilium, discrimen, dolor, fragilitas, genus, infirmitas, ingenium, leuitas, manus, mens, metus, necessitas, oculi, opus, peccatum, pectus, persuasio, pignus, poena, ratio, religio, res, salus, sanguis, sanitas, scientia, sermo, seueritas, sollertia, spiritus, tormenta, uis, uiscera, uita* and *uitium*.

The expression *humanum est*, to be understood as 'it is characteristic of human beings', can be found at *Decl. min.* 260.15 and 335.11, while *inhumanum est*, which, as we have already observed, is no longer relational as it implies a sort of judgement, the idea that something is not worthy of man, appears at *Decl. min.* 311.10.[72] The same clearly goes for *inhumanus* in general, which is comparatively common in the declamations, appearing alongside *crudelitas, lex, munus* and *res*.

The adverb *humane* is not attested, but *inhumane* appears at *Decl. min.* 258.4; 273.4 and 336.14, and at *Decl. mai.* 13.13.3.

Eventually, in *Decl. mai.* 1.10.1 and 9.17.2 we also come across the substantivised *humana*.

5.4 Conclusion

As far as *humanitas* is concerned, some *Minor* and *Major declamations* set themselves in the path inaugurated by Cicero's orations and brought forward by Apuleius' *Apologia* and the fake trial of *Metamorphoses* 3. Yet the use of this argument in declamatory context generally appears as far more banal that in the aforementioned precedents. Granted, *humanitas* is used to characterise the behaviors and attitudes of some of the protagonists of these speeches, but in no case can we detect precise, refined strategies based on the unifying or separating power that this concept of value can have, unlike what we have observed for Apuleius and Cicero. Nor is *humanitas* explicitly attributed to judges as a form of *captatio beneuolentiae*. Compared with Cicero, the *humanitas* of the declamation also loses much, not to say all, of its polyphony, especially its educational, paedeutic component, and this fact would once again back up Gellius' assertion that his contemporaries ignored the true *humanitas*.[73] At the beginning of one of his books, Robert Kaster claims

---

72 On *inhumanus* in general cf. above, p. 45.
73 Cf. above, pp. 170–172.

that he chose "to concentrate on the *grammaticus*: a pivotal figure, about whom we know a good deal, but who has often been overshadowed in modern studies (as he was in antiquity) by his more conspicuous colleague, the rhetorician."[74] Yet from the angle of *humanitas*, by Gellius' standards at least, these rhetoricians do not turn out to be superior to their less conspicuous colleagues, the grammarians.

---

74 Kaster 1997[2], IX.

6 The Silent Third Century and Its Exception: Eumenius' *Oratio pro instaurandis scholis*

Unfortunately, like the case of the declamations has just shown, educational programmes such as Gellius', in which *humanitas* played a central role, soon faced hard times. Commodus' violent death in the late 192 CE marked the end of the Antonine age. There followed a comparatively short period of instability, until Septimius Severus seized power in June 193 CE. Since the formula of the 'adoptive principate' had been put into practice for the last time by Antoninus Pius, Septimius Severus inaugurated a new dynastic age, the Severan age. The assassination of the last member of this dynasty, Alexander Severus, in 235 CE, was another turning point in the history of Rome, for it marked the beginning of the so-called 'Crisis of the Third Century' (235–284 CE). This half-century saw no fewer than 26 claimants to the empire. Given the related climate of general disarray, it is no surprise that "little seems to have been written of any value", especially in the Latin west.[1] Nor was the situation significantly different during the Severan dynasty, under which only Greek authors like Cassius Dio, Philostratus or Herodian flourished. But when Diocletian stabilised the empire and created the 'tetrarchy', western literature began to recover, albeit gradually. As far as *humanitas* is concerned, there is however one significant case towards the end of the third century, and it is all the more interesting in that it is tightly connected to the cultural restoration which followed the crisis. The work referred to is Eumenius' *Oratio pro instaurandis scholis*, a panegyric probably delivered in 298 CE.[2] This chapter will analyse Eumenius' role as restorer of what is represented as the most complete and authentic, that is Ciceronian, sense of ancient *humanitas* after one of the darkest ages in the history of Rome.[3] Quite surprisingly, this aspect has usually been overlooked in Eumenian scholarship: Seager, in a contribution which is entirely devoted to the virtues in the *Panegyrici Latini*, completely neglects the role of *humanitas* in Eumenius' speech; similarly La Bua, in an article whose focus is on the importance of education and culture in Eumenius' speech, hardly mentions the term *humanitas*.[4]

---

1 Browning 1982, 684.
2 Some doubts over the exact date of Eumenius' panegyric have been raised by Nixon/Rodgers 1994, 148, according to whom any date between 297 and 299 CE would be possible. According to Barnes 1996, 541, it was composed after summer 298 CE. An overview of the various hypotheses can be found in Hostein 2012, 49–50. On the figure of Eumenius and his career cf. Hostein 2012, 154–157; *passim*.
3 On *humanitas* in Eumenius cf. also Mollea 2021.
4 Seager 1983; La Bua 2010.

I shall first contextualise this panegyric in both literary and historical terms. Given the brevity of Eumenius' oration and the crucial role that *humanitas* plays in it, my analysis will slightly differ from the previous chapters: instead of simply going through each and every instance of *humanitas*, I shall read the entire speech through the lens of *humanitas*. In doing this, I will show how *humanitas*, in perfect Ciceronian style, oscillates, roughly speaking, between the ideas of φιλανθρωπία and παιδεία, which also seem to overlap at times. Throughout, I will also spotlight how the *humanitas* topic closely links Eumenius to previous authors whose works I have already explored at length, namely Cicero's *Pro Archia*, Pliny's *Panegyricus*, Apuleius' *Apologia* and Gellius' *Noctes Atticae*.

The so-called *Panegyrici Latini* are a collection of twelve panegyrics dating, with the exception of Pliny's *Panegyric in praise of Trajan* we have already touched upon, from 289 CE to 389 CE.[5] Epideictic orations were usually written to thank the emperor(s) for bestowing some kind of honour upon the panegyrist himself or the civic community, or else to celebrate an important event. Either way, they heaped praise on the emperor(s). Eumenius' *Oratio pro instaurandis scholis*, which was actually delivered before an imperial governor, is the exception which proves the rule: praise of the (absent) emperors does emerge at times, but the aim of this oration is not to thank them for something they have already done, but to ask for their help in restoring the famous Maenian schools of Augustodunum (today's Autun) in central Gaul, which were prestigious schools of rhetoric presumably dating back at least to the principate of Tiberius: Tacitus is alluding to them when he describes the rebellion of Sacrovir (21 CE): *Augustodunum caput gentis armatis cohortibus Sacrouir occupauerat <ut> nobilissimam Galliarum subolem, liberalibus studiis ibi operatam, et eo pignore parentes propinquosque eorum adiungeret* ("Their capital Autun was held by Sacrovir with armed troops, as was the elite progeny of Gaul being educated there. Sacrovir's aim was to recruit – with these as hostages – their parents and relatives", trans. Damon 2012).[6] Unfortunately, Augustodunum was also at the centre of rebellions and wars in the centuries to come, in particular during the years of the Crisis of the third century. Eumenius' own panegyric reveals that the city had been gravely ruined, and so had the Maenian schools. When, by whom and how many times it had been attacked is a matter of dispute. Some believe that this was due to Tetricus, the last of the Gallic emperors, who besieged the city after its rebellion against the Gallic empire;[7] others impute the damages to the

---

5 On Pliny's *Panegyricus* cf. above, pp. 84–95.
6 Tac. *Ann.* 3.43.1.
7 Cf. Maguinness 1952, 97–98, who, in the wake of Galletier 1949, 111, believes that it was actually Victorinus to conquer the city; Rodgers 1989, 250–251; Rees 2002, 132–133 with further bibliography; La Bua 2010, 301.

invasion of the tribe of the Bagaudae.[8] The one possibility does not exclude the other.[9] In any case, Eumenius makes it clear that Augustodunum was still a building site when he delivered his speech about 298 CE.

Eumenius' panegyric opens in an interesting way: the orator excuses himself for delivering an unconventional speech. The reason for this, he goes on to explain, is that he is only a teacher of rhetoric, utterly unfamiliar with official, real orations. Nevertheless, his devotion to culture overcomes all his fears when the restoration of the Maenian schools is at stake (§ 1–3). These schools – Eumenius is sure – must be dear to the *principes* as well, for they have always cared about education and culture (3.2: *quibus optimarum artium celebratio grata atque iucunda est,* "to whom the praise of the finest arts are delightful and pleasing", trans. Rodgers 1994). Nor is the emphasis on the rulers' interest in cultural issues isolated, for Eumenius reiterates it several times throughout the speech, starting from 5.2 (*Cui enim umquam ueterum principum tantae fuit curae ut doctrinae atque eloquentiae studia florerent quantae his optimis et indulgentissimis dominis generis humani?* "Which of the ancient leaders ever cared so much that learning and the study of eloquence flourish as these, the best and kindest masters of the human race?", trans. Rodgers 1994) and 6. In the latter paragraph, Eumenius also becomes self-referential when he recalls that Constantius Chlorus has already appointed a (good) teacher of rhetoric for the Maenian schools: Eumenius himself. To cut a long story short, there can be no doubt that, under these presuppositions, the emperors will also foster the rebuilding of the schools. After all,

> Cui igitur est dubium quin diuina illa mens Caesaris, quae tanto studio praeceptorem huic conuentui iuuentutis elegit, etiam locum exercitii illius dedicatum instaurari atque exornari uelit, cum omnes omnium rerum sectatores atque fautores parum se satisfacere uoto et conscientiae suae credant, si non ipsarum quas appetunt gloriarum templa constituant? (6.4)

> Who could doubt, then, that the divine mind of Caesar, which chose a director with so much care for this gathering of youth, also wants the place devoted to its training to be restored and decorated, since all adherents and patrons of all things believe that they have hardly done justice to their vows and conscience if they do not erect temples in honor of those very attributes for which they wish to be praised? (trans. Rodgers 1994)

---

8 Cf. Lassandro 1973; Lassandro/Micunco 2000, 11; 20. Against Justus Lipsius' conjecture *Bagaudicae rebellionis* at 4.1 (manuscripts read *Batauicae rebellionis*), which Lassandro accepted, cf. Rodgers 1989, 253–254; Rodríguez Gervás 1991, 51; Nixon/Rodgers 1994, 154 n. 12 with further bibliography.
9 Cf. Rees 2002, 133.

At this point, given all this emphasis on school, teachers, *doctrina* and *eloquentia*, readers might expect that the first instance of *humanitas* in this oration would remind them of the nuances that the term takes on in Cicero's *Pro Archia*. Yet Eumenius introduces a glorious example of temples which were erected to praise virtues, and *humanitas* is said to be what prompted the Athenians to set up an altar to Mercy:[10] *Inde est quod Atheniensis humanitas aram Misericordiae instituit, quod Romani ducis animi magnitudo templum Virtutis et Honoris* (7.1: "This is the reason why the Athenians' *humanitas* set up an altar to Mercy, why a Roman general's greatness of spirit built a temple of Virtue and Honor", trans. Rodgers 1994). Even though we are by now accustomed to hearing of *Atheniensis humanitas*, in this case the expression is hardly to be taken as in the Ciceronian and Plinian instances that we saw in the Introduction, where *humanitas* clearly stands to evoke culture in its broadest sense, or even civilization.[11] Rather, it is closer to the Apuleian occurrence at *Apol.* 86, where the comparison with a Plutarchean passage shows the equation between *ius humanitatis* and φιλανθρωπία.[12] Here too *humanitas* seems to stand for φιλανθρωπία, and, as with the Apuleian case, this is made clear through a comparison with a Greek text dealing with the same episode. Compare Pausanias 1.17.1:

> Ἀθηναίοις δὲ ἐν τῇ ἀγορᾷ καὶ ἄλλα ἐστὶν οὐκ ἐς ἅπαντας ἐπίσημα καὶ Ἐλέου βωμός, ᾧ μά-
> λιστα θεῶν ἐς ἀνθρώπινον βίον καὶ μεταβολὰς πραγμάτων ὄντι ὠφελίμῳ μόνοι τιμὰς Ἑλλή-
> νων νέμουσιν Ἀθηναῖοι. τούτοις δὲ οὐ τὰ ἐς φιλανθρωπίαν μόνον καθέστηκεν, ἀλλὰ καὶ
> θεοὺς εὐσεβοῦσιν ἄλλων πλέον, καὶ γὰρ Αἰδοῦς σφισι βωμός ἐστι καὶ Φήμης καὶ Ὁρμῆς·

> In the Athenian market-place among the objects not generally known is an altar to Mercy, of all divinities the most useful in the life of mortals and in the vicissitudes of fortune, but honored by the Athenians alone among the Greeks. And they are conspicuous not only for their humanity but also for their devotion to religion. They have an altar to Shamefastness, one to Rumour and one to Effort. (trans. Jones 1918)

Certainly the clause τούτοις δὲ οὐ τὰ ἐς φιλανθρωπίαν μόνον καθέστηκεν parallels Eumenius' *Atheniensis humanitas*. The dedication of the temple to *Misericordia* also contributes to this interpretation of *humanitas*: as we have seen, the pairing of *misericordia* and *humanitas* is common in Latin, and it often leads to the two overlapping.[13] In a specular manner, φιλανθρωπία and ἔλεος tend to overlap in the text of Pausanias. And yet, for all this evidence, it is undeniable that the

---

10 Athens' altar to Mercy is cited several times in classical literature: cf. Klotz 1911, 541; Bessone 2009, 186 n. 3.
11 Cf. above, pp. 34–35.
12 Cf. above, pp. 141–142.
13 Cf. above, pp. 149–150.

Latin text maintains a different flavour from the Greek one, especially for a first-time reader unaware of these parallels: the continual attention to culture in Eumenius' panegyric in one way or another is reflected in the expression *Atheniensis humanitas*, while the Greek φιλανθρωπία is far less polysemic. Furthermore, it must not go unnoticed the fact that Eumenius would have found not *humanitas* or *misericordia*, but *clementia* associated with this altar towards the end of Statius' *Thebaid* (12.481–484): *urbe fuit media nulli concessa potentum / ara deum, mitis posuit Clementia sedem, / et miseri fecere sacram; sine supplice numquam / illa nouo, nulla damnauit uota repulsa* ("An altar once stood in the city center unoccupied by any god of power. There gentle Clemency had found her seat, made sacred by the misery of men. The goddess never lacked for supplicants; no prayer was ever censured or denied", trans. Ross 2004). On the one hand, this fact adds to Eumenius' willingness to imply a cultural dimension and to exploit in full the polysemy of *humanitas*; but on the other hand might be further evidence that *clementia*, especially as it emerges from Statius' oeuvre, was still a word to shun.[14]

After all, not only what precedes, but also the historical example that immediately follows the *ara Misericordiae* spotlights this link between *humanitas* and culture, literature in particular. Fulvius Nobilior is in fact said to have built the Temple of Hercules of the Muses (*Aedem Herculis Musarum*), because, among other reasons, "he was led by literature and his friendship for a great poet [i.e. Ennius]", trans. Rodgers 1994). By the same token, the emperor, who is Hercules' descendant, is said to cultivate the study of literature (*studium litterarum*) and even to consider it as the basis of all the virtues (8.2: *litteras omnium fundamenta esse uirtutum*). In sum, this emphasis on the importance of education and culture, which goes hand in hand with the necessity of rebuilding the Maenian schools, permeates the first half of the oration, until the end of § 10.

From § 11 onwards, Eumenius tackles the problem of how to finance this building operation. The solution he proposes is highly philanthropic on his part as well as being a bargain for the empire: Eumenius is in fact willing to use his own salary as a teacher of rhetoric, which amounts to 600,000 sesterces, to support the restoration of the Maenian schools:

> Hoc ego salarium, quantum ad honorem pertinet, adoratum accipio et in accepti ratione perscribo; sed expensum referre patriae meae cupio, et ad restitutionem huius operis, quoad usus poposcerit, destinare. Cuius uoluntatis meae ratio etsi adserenda non est, tamen sub hac tua humanitate et circumstantium exspectatione qua me audiri sentio aliquatenus prosequenda est.

---

14 Cf. also Mollea 2021, 73 and n. 16 for bibliography on *clementia* in Statius' *Thebaid*.

> This salary, as far as concerns the honor, I accept with reverence and enter into accounts received; but I wish to set the payment down under my native city, and to designate it for the rebuilding of this edifice, as long as necessity requires. Even if the reason for my choice need not be defended, yet because of your kindness (*humanitas*) and the expectation with which I am heard by the audience I feel that it ought to be described a little further. (trans. Rodgers 1994)

Not only the expectation of the audience (*circumstantium expectatione*), but also the governor's *humanitas* seem to demand clarification of Eumenius' offering. To some extent, this is to say that the *humanitas* of the governor is so important that it even determines the second half of Eumenius' oration. Indeed, the preposition *sub*, never to be found in direct connection with *humanitas* before Eumenius, strengthens the urgency of the matter. Yet to determine the exact meaning of *humanitas* here is not an easy task. Rodgers 1994 translates it as 'kindness', as translators often do when facing the problem of rendering *humanitas* into English. However, it is my belief that the word *humanitas* is rarely as polysemic as it is here and that the author is deliberately exploiting the ambiguity of the word; for Eumenius refers here to the *humanitas* of his main interlocutor, the governor in whose presence he is delivering his speech. Accordingly, there is little doubt that flattery is to be expected, and the ideas that the word *humanitas* can imply are perfectly suitable to this end. Given the recurring stress on the importance of literature and culture throughout the speech, the undoubtedly learned governor will have seen in the expression *tua humanitate* also an allusion to his superior education. But at the same time, Eumenius is appealing to his kindness, generosity, philanthropic disposition towards the city of Augustodunum and the orator himself.[15]

What is more, a few paragraphs later the governor would also learn that the Caesars possess that same *humanitas* which Eumenius has attributed to him. § 15.3 reads:

> Qui quod iubere possunt suadere dignantur et, cum uel tacitas eorum ac uultu tenus significatas uoluntates summi patris sequatur auctoritas, cuius nutum promissionem confirmantis totius mundi tremor sentit, ipsi tamen ultro imperandi potestatem cohortandi humanitate conciliant.

> They see fit to urge what they can command, although their wills, even unspoken and intimated only by their expression, are attended by the authority of the highest father Jupiter, whose nod the shaking of the entire world senses when he affirms a promise, yet the Em-

---

15 An analogous interpretation of this instance of *humanitas*, although probably expressed in less clear terms, can be found in Hostein 2012, 199.

perors of their own accord make the power of command agreeable by the kindness (*humanitas*) of persuasion. (trans. Rodgers 1994)

Eumenius had just read before the governor the letter through which Constantius had urged him to take the post of teacher of oratory of the Maenian schools, and what he stresses is the very fact of having been urged (14.4: *hortamur ut professionem oratoriam repetas*, "we urge you to resume the teaching of oratory", trans. Rodgers 1994) and not ordered to do so. Once more *humanitas* is central, as it is thanks to this philanthropic value that the emperor preferred exhortation (*cohortandi*) to orders (*imperandi*). Of course we could also conjecture, as with the previous instance of Eumenian *humanitas*, that the emperor's learning lies behind his kind behaviour: still, this must remain a conjecture, for the context does not explicitly allow this interpretation. Yet noteworthy here is the rare if not unique use of a gerund (*cohortandi*) which depends on *humanitas*, as well as the link between *humanitas* and exhortation, which will meet with the approval of later authors such as an anonymous panegyrist of Constantine (*Pan. Lat.* 12.14.1: *Studium et humanitas tua hortata est*) and Symmachus (*Ep.* 7.56: *tua nos hortatur humanitas*).[16] Linguistic arguments aside, we might also note that Eumenius' use of *humanitas* within the panegyric to an extent echoes Apuleius' technique in the *Apologia*, which in turn reminds us of Cicero's in the *Pro Archia*. Here as in the Apuleian oration *humanitas* is made to be a if not *the* component which binds together the protagonists of the speech, that is to say the direct addresse (the proconsul Maximus in Apuleius, the governor in Eumenius), personalities tightly connected with the addresses and who play a key role in the speeches (Maximus' predecessor Lollianus Avitus and the emperor Constantius), the Athenians who embody the highest level of civilization, and, implicitly, the orators themselves. For all the different nuances that the term *humanitas* takes on in these two authors, both Apuleius and Eumenius seem to resort to this concept as an oratorical strategy which can suggest identification within an elitist category of people as opposed to those who are excluded from this elite. But whereas for Apuleius *humanitas* served this purpose along with education and culture rather than as a part of them, Eumenius, setting himself in the tradition of Cicero, Pliny the Younger and Aulus Gellius, perceives *humanitas* as closely linked to παιδεία. More than in the instances which I have analysed so far, this becomes all the more clear towards the end of the panegyric, namely at § 19, which is perhaps the most important paragraph of the entire oration:

---

16 On this Symmachian occurrence cf. also below, p. 287.

1. Sed enim, Vir perfectissime, inter omnia quae uirtute principum ac felicitate recreantur, sint licet fortasse alia magnitudine atque utilitate potiora, nihil est tamen admirabilius hac liberalitate quam fouendis honorandisue litterarum studiis impartiunt. 2. Quippe, ut initio dixi, nulli umquam antehac principes pari cura belli munia et huiusmodi pacis ornamenta coluerunt. 3. Diuersissimus enim ad utramque sectam deflexus est, dispar natura mentium et discrepans in electione iudicium; ipsorum denique utrisque artibus praesidentium numinum dissoni monitus habitusque dissimiles. 4. Quo magis horum noua et incredibilis est uirtus et humanitas, qui inter tanta opera bellorum ad haec quoque litterarum exercitia respiciunt atque illum temporum statum quo, ut legimus, Romana res plurimum terra et mari ualuit, ita demum integrare putant, si non potentia sed etiam eloquentia Romana reuirescat.

But among all the things, Your Excellency, which are brought back into existence by the virtue and felicity of the rulers, although there may be others more important in size and utility, yet nothing is more worthy of admiration than the generosity which they share in fostering and honoring the study of literature. In fact, as I said at the beginning, no rulers have ever before bestowed equal care upon both the duties of war and the embellishment of this kind of peace. Each occupation requires a very different bent, natural abilities are not alike, and judgments vary in making a choice; finally the divinities presiding over each of these arts issue incompatible advice and their characters are discrepant. All the more novel and remarkable is the virtue and *humanitas* of these men, who in the midst of such extensive military operations are also concerned with these exercises in literature, and think that those conditions existing when, as we read, the Roman state was strongest by land and sea have at last been recreated, if not only Roman power but even Roman eloquence flourishes again. (trans. Rodgers 1994)

As Eumenius himself points out (*ut initio dixi*), his panegyric closes in ring-composition by returning to the importance of the liberal studies that the present emperors have always fostered. In particular, they stand out thanks to their ability to make two opposites coexist: wars on the one hand, literature and culture in general on the other hand. These two opposites, I argue, correspond to two different value-terms, *uirtus* and *humanitas*. § 19.4 is a consistent and rather long parallelism in which the first item of each clause refers to the first value mentioned at the head of the sentence (*uirtus*), while the second item refers to the second value (*humanitas*). Accordingly, signs of virtue are warlike deeds (*tanta opera bellorum*) and the restoration to a flourishing condition of the Roman power (*potentia . . . Romana reuirescat*); in contrast, literary exercises (*litterarum exercitia*) and the revival of Roman eloquence (*eloquentia Romana reuirescat*) are due to the emperors' *humanitas*. After all, that *uirtus* can be closely related to warfare is something we learn from the earliest Latin authors such as Ennius (*Ann.* 6.187–189 Skutsch) and Claudius Quadrigarius (*Ann. Fr.* 7 Peter), and it is summarised by the recurrent expression *uirtus bellica*.

As for *humanitas*, in claiming that "[Eumenius'] estimate of the value of literary studies is in the spirit of Cicero's *Pro Archia*",[17] Maguinness leads us to extend the comparison to this use of *humanitas* in the panegyric with Cicero's expression *studia humanitatis* at *Pro Archia* 3, a passage which I have already quoted in the Cicero section in Chapter 2, and quote here again for convenience:[18]

> Quaeso a uobis, ut in hac causa mihi detis hanc ueniam, accommodatam huic reo, uobis, quem ad modum spero, non molestam, ut me pro summo poëta atque eruditissimo homine dicentem, hoc concursu hominum litteratissimorum, hac uestra humanitate, hoc denique praetore exercente iudicium patiamini de studiis humanitatis ac litterarum paulo loqui liberius.[19]

> I beg of you that you will grant me an indulgence in this trial which is appropriate to this defendant here, and, I trust, not disagreeable to you – that you will allow me, speaking as I am on behalf of an eminent poet and a most learned man and before this crowd of highly educated people, this civilized jury, and such a praetor as is now presiding, to speak rather more freely on cultural and literary matters (*de studiis humanitatis ac litterarum*). (trans. Berry 2000)

The connection between *humanitas* and *litterarum exercitia* in Eumenius becomes perhaps more explicit in the light of this Ciceronian passage thanks to the repetition of the very term *humanitas* in a pair with *litterae* (*de studiis humanitatis ac litterarum*). But even more than the *Pro Archia*, another instance of *studia humanitatis*, that found in Aulus Gellius' *Noctes Atticae* 9.3 (analysed in the previous chapter) backs up the educational meaning of *humanitas* in Eumenius' panegyric 19.4. At 9.3 Gellius praises king Philip II of Macedon, Alexander the Great's father, for paying attention to the liberal arts in wartime. Thus, the extraordinary (*noua et incredibilis*) ability of Maximianus and Constantius Chlorus to honour literature and culture on account of their *humanitas* while succeeding in wars had at least one noble precedent, that of Philip, who, *cum in omni fere tempore negotiis belli uictoriisque adfectus exercitusque esset, a liberali tamen Musa et a studiis humanitatis numquam afuit* ("although almost constantly busied and distracted by the labours and triumphs of war, yet never was a stranger to the Muse of the liberal arts and the pursuit of culture", trans. Rolfe 1927).

Let us recap. As in Pliny the Younger's *Panegyricus* in praise of Trajan, Apuleius' *De apologia* and some declamations, we find in Eumenius' *Oratio pro instaurandis scholis* another oratorical example of the use of the *humanitas* argument in the Imperial age. As with the case of Pliny, or even more than there, it is not an

---

17 Cf. also Rodgers 1989, 249–250; Nixon/Rodgers 1994, 149; La Bua 2010, 309.
18 Maguinness 1952, 101.
19 On this passage cf. also Coşkun 2010, 82 (with further bibliography) and above, p. 55.

exaggeration to state that *humanitas* plays a, if not *the*, key role within Eumenius' speech. True, the higher number of occurrences in the *Panegyricus* lets us appreciate a wider range of nuances that Pliny gives to *humanitas*. Yet Eumenius displays cases where either the idea of φιλανθρωπία (7.1) or παιδεία (19.4) is clearly prominent, as well as more nuanced instances in which both ideas are in play (11.3 and 15.3). In doing this, Eumenius seems to echo Cicero's message and adjust it to his own case: as literary education and culture are futile if they do not enhance the soul and lead humans to better understand their condition as men among men, the emperors and Eumenius himself need to give proof of their superior education by taking care of the people's needs, among which the rebuilding of the Maenian schools takes pride of place. It is in fact thanks to these schools that literature and consequently culture and civilization, in a word, *humanitas*, can flourish again and perpetuate themselves.

Furthermore, from a political perspective, *humanitas* might be seen as a keyword that signals a return to a Golden Age after a period of crisis: funding the schools will allow the governor to display a virtue that the new emperors have themselves embraced and which signals a return to civilization after a period of darkness, a return that makes them closer to the Ciceronian age. The political differences between Cicero's age and theirs (republic vs. empire) are interestingly erased, and Cicero's *humanitas*, for all the changes in meanings and connotations it has witnessed, has once again become the ideal to which statesmen aspire.

7 The Age of Constantine and Another Exception: Firmicus Maternus' Civilization Without παιδεία in the *Mathesis*

Eumenius' appeal to governors' and emperors' *humanitas*, however isolated it probably was, apparently proved effective and forward-thinking. An investigation of the rhetoric of fourth-century legislation from Constantine onwards shows that most rulers decided to rely on *humanitas* to foster the renewal of the Roman Empire after the crisis of the third century.[1] Nor was this a novelty, for the legislation of Hadrian and the Antonine emperors had already been inspired by this value.[2] Yet the case of Constantine looks a little problematic. On the one hand, in fact, Justinian regards him as the first emperor to promote the ideal of *humanitas* in Roman legislation.[3] But on the other hand, Maranesi's chart on the virtues which are mentioned in the four Latin panegyrics addressed to Constantine induces us to suspect that *humanitas* did not play a relevant role during this emperor's reign and in his propaganda since the noun appears only twice, in *Pan.* 12 (9), whose author is unknown.[4] By contrast, other value concepts, especially *pietas* and *clementia*, "che sono vere e proprie marche di continuità comunicativa costantiniana", are referred to far more often and in all four 'Constantinian' panegyrics[5] – and there is no need to linger again on the official and media's role of this kind of compositions.[6] Whatever the true weight of *humanitas* in Constantine's intentions and concrete policy, we cannot but observe that it was not until the age of Theodosius I that both legal and literary sources reflected the pervasiveness of this concept.

---

1 Cf. for example Honig 1960, 6–7; Onida 2011–2012; Trisciuoglio 2018.

2 Cf. above, pp. 134; 194.

3 *Nou.* 89 *praef.*: *Naturalium nomen Romanae legislationi dudum non erat in studium, nec quaelibet circa hoc fuerat humanitas, sed tamquam alienigenum aliquid et omnino alienum a republica putabatur; a Constantini uero piae memoriae temporibus in constitutionum scriptum est libris* ("In former times, the attention of Roman legislation was not directed to natural children, nor was any *humanitas* manifested towards them, but their name was considered to a certain extent foreign to the Republic; but during the reign of Constantine, of pious memory, they were mentioned in the Books of Constitutions", trans. Scott 1932). Cf. also *Fragmenta Vaticana* 248, with Onida 2011–2012.

4 Maranesi 2013, 104.

5 Maranesi 2013, 105.

6 Cf. above, pp. 95 and 134.

7.1 Firmicus Maternus' *Mathesis*

To return to the pagan literature of the age of Constantine, the panegyrics aside, a partial exception to the rule as well as a curious literary case is represented by Firmicus Maternus' *Matheseos libri VIII*, "the most comprehensive – if not the most coherent – treatise on astrology from antiquity", probably published in 337 CE, when its dedicatee, Lollianus Mavortius, was proconsul of Africa and designated consul.[7] As Monat has shown, some contradictions that can be found throughout this text are probably due to its being the result of the compilation of different treatises of Alexandrine origins.[8] Yet this is not the only work of Firmicus which has come down to us, for we can also read the *De errore profanarum religionum*, presumably written after the author's conversion to Christianity.[9] As far as *humanitas* is concerned, a comparison between these two works reminds us of the case of Tacitus, where this noun appears only in one kind of works, namely the 'minor' *Agricola* and *Germania*, and not in the major historical works, the *Annales* and the *Historiae*.[10] For while in the *Mathesis* there are seven occurrences of *humanitas*, the *De errore* records none of it. Of course this can be simple coincidence, but the great importance Firmicus confers on abstract nouns ending in -*tas*, especially in the *De errore*, where they even "indicate the main topics and arguments of the book", might also suggest that the term *humanitas* sounded too little Christian to the ears of the converted astrologer.[11] And despite a fundamental, ontological difference between Firmicus' and Cicero's conceptions of *humanitas*, as also clearly emerges from the analysis of Firmicus' use of the adjective *humanus*, there is no denying that the seven occurrences of *humanitas* in the *Mathesis* really look Ciceronian, and therefore profoundly pagan, at first sight. And after Constans, Constantine's son, was elevated as Augustus of the West in 337 and imposed an authoritarian as well as repressive form of Christianity,[12] one

---

7 Cf. *PLRE* I 512–513; Sogno 2005, 167. On the dating of Firmicus' *Mathesis* cf. Monat 1992, 7 n. 1; Sogno 2005, 167 n.2.

8 Monat 1992, 15–20.

9 Cf. Monat 1992, 7: "La critique a maintenant écarté de façon définitive les difficultés minimes qui avaient empêché de reconnaître dans ces deux œvres la main d'un même auteur, encore païen quand il écrit la *Mathesis*, puis converti au christianisme." Cf. also Turcan 1982, 7–8 (with further bibliography); 15–17; Drake 1998, 135–136 and n. 12 for further bibliography. It is however to be stressed that in a later contribution Monat himself opens to the possibility that the *Mathesis* too might have been written after Firmicus' conversion to Christianity: cf. Monat 1999, 136.

10 Cf. above, pp. 115–127.

11 Sánchez Manzano 2017, 185, where there is also a long list of all abstract nouns ending in -*tas* which appear in the *De errore profanarum religionum*.

12 Cf. Woudhuysen 2018, 166–168.

cannot rule out the hypothesis that the absence of *humanitas* from the *De errore* may be due to the author's extreme care to eschew one of the terms which had more pagan connotations. Clearly this does not mean that the word *humanitas* was utterly banned under Constans, but it would not be too far off to think that a recently converted Christian became even stricter and more selective when it came to showing his orthodoxy at all levels.[13] After all, as Barnard puts it: "He had the typical intolerance of a convert, who is reborn and finds in his own past very little that is positive."[14] This attitude may even become a requirement, if Firmicus' acquaintance with emperor Constans became tighter and the *De errore* was meant to play a public, official role of propaganda, as suggested among others by Woudhuysen.[15] But at the time of the *Mathesis*, the situation appears to have been completely different, and *humanitas* was perfectly suitable for a pagan work destined to become "an explicit marker along the history of ideas."[16]

In the *Mathesis* the first instance of *humanitas* appears in Book 1, where Firmicus is at pains to show that celestial bodies influence men's habits and characters. Having said at 1.2.3 that all the people believe that "the Scythians are known for monstrous, savage cruelty" (*Scythae soli immanis feritatis crudelitate grassantur*; trans. Bram 1975), Firmicus rounds off his discourse by adding that, thanks to the stars, *et effrenata Scytharum rabies quacumque humanitatis clementia mitigatur* (1.10.12: "The unbridled fury of the Scythians is sometimes tempered by a certain clemency of *humanitas*", trans. Bram 1975). The juxtaposition of *rabies* and *humanitas* was already in Livy's episode of Pleminius, Scipio's *legatus* at Locri.[17] But while on that occasion *humanitas* was the norm and *rabies* the unusual aspect, here the situation is inverted, and *rabies* is the irrational equivalent of savagery and cruelty (*feritatis crudelitate*), through which the Scythians were characterised at the begin-

---

13 Cf. Monat 1992, 8: "Après la promulgation de la législation antipaïenne de Constant (341), il opère une conversion qui semble obéir surtout à des raisons d'opportunité"; and 9: "L'opportunisme et le ton parfois vengeur du *De errore* ne peuvent guère attirer de sympathies"; Hutchinson 2009, 200: "Firmicus might seem more committed to his career as a writer than to the inculcation of his beliefs: so one could infer when the pagan *Mathesis*, written before Constantine's death in May 337, is followed in the 340s by the ferociously anti-pagan *De Errore Profanarum Religionum*, written under the more militantly Christian Constans and Constantius II." Cf. also Turcan 1982, 23 and, more sceptically, Edwards 2015, 73 and Woudhuysen 2018, 168–169.
14 Barnard 1993, 98–99. Cf. also Turcan 1982, 23; Drake 1998.
15 Cf. Woudhuysen 2018, 172–177. This is however different from saying that the *De errore* inspired the emperor's legislation, as once believed: cf. Turcan 1982 n. 2 for a list of those who had this belief. Further discussion in Drake 1998.
16 Bram 1975, 3. Cf. also Gassman 2020, 56: "The result is a deeply religious and profoundly pagan work."
17 Cf. above, pp. 65–66.

ning of *Mathesis* 1. In other words, we face once again that opposition between civilization and barbarity which often crops up when speaking of *humanitas*, as we have already seen happening in particular in the cases of Caesar's *Bellum Gallicum* and Tacitus' *Agricola*.[18] Moreover, the extremely rare phrase *humanitatis clementia*, which we have already found in Apuleius' *De Platone* 2.14, clearly stresses the philanthropic aspect of *humanitas*, although the equivalence between *humanitatis clementia* and *amor*, 'love', which we see in the Apuleian instance, does not apply in Firmicus.[19] And yet, as in Apuleius, the expression itself is sufficient to show that Firmicus Maternus too regards *clementia* as a hyponym of *humanitas*, as something which springs from it.[20]

Despite all these parallels, right from this first occurrence of *humanitas* in the *Mathesis* it is necessary to highlight the crucial feature of Firmicus' conception of it, that is, his understanding *humanitas* as a civilization without παιδεία. Paradoxical as this may seem, it turns out to be logical and inevitable on closer inspection, for the presence or absence of *humanitas* in Firmicus' view depends on stars and planets, not on education and culture. The *clementia humanitatis* that can temper the Scythians' cruelty depends on the stars, and the same is true of the next instances of *humanitas* that we are about to encounter. Civilization, as well as the philanthropic attitude which can originate from it, is therefore understood as a gift of the stars and not as an achievement of humankind through education and learning.

This conception of *humanitas* as civilization becomes more evident in Book 3. Dealing with the birthday of the Universe, Firmicus says:

> Sed ut esset quod mathematici in genituris hominum sequerentur exemplum, ideo hanc quasi genituram mundi diuini uiri prudenti ratione finxerunt. Libet itaque diuinae istius compositionis explicare commenta, ut coniecturae istius admirabilis ratio magisterii studio pandatur. Voluerunt Lunam <ita> constituere, ut primum se Saturno coniungeret eique temporum traderet principatum; nec immerito, quia enim prima origo mundi inculta fuit et horrida et agresti conuersatione effera, et quia rudes hominis prima et incognita sibi uestigia lucis ingressos politae humanitatis ratio deserebat, Saturni hoc agreste et horridum tempus esse uoluerunt, ut ad imitationem huius sideris <in> initiis uitae constituta mortalitas agresti se conuersatione et inhumana feritatis exasperatione duraret. (3.1.10–11)

> The divine wise men of old invented this birthchart of the universe so that it would be an example for astrologers to follow in the charts of men. Therefore I would like to explain the rationale of that divine story. With good reason they located the Moon in such a way that she would first be related to Saturn and would give over to him the rulership of time. For in

---

18 Cf. above, pp. 64 and 118–124.
19 Cf. above, pp. 157–158.
20 Cf. above, p. 157.

the beginning the universe was rude and wild and savage because of its primitive way of life; and crude men who had just taken the first unfamiliar steps toward enlightenment lacked the prudence of polished *humanitas*. This rude and rustic time was allotted to Saturn so that human life in its beginning should seem to harden itself by uncivilized ferocity. (trans. Bram 1975, adapted)

While the phrase *inhumana feritatis exasperatio* recalls the just analysed case of Book 1, thereby putting the Scythians on the same level as the ancient, primitive men of the age of Saturn, *politae humanitatis ratio* opens to another dimension of *humanitas*, the Ciceronian flavour of which might induce one to take it as educational, but, in fact, it is not and it can only be defined, if at all, as rational. The parallel with *De republica* 1.28, discussed in the Ciceronian section, is emblematic: it is stated that only those who are refined by the arts pertaining to *humanitas* (*politi propriis humanitatis artibus*) are worthy of being called men.[21] Then, at *Pro Sestio* 92, Cicero claims: *Atque inter hanc uitam perpolitam humanitate et illam immanem nihil tam interest quam ius atque uis* ("Now, between life thus refined and humanized, and that life of savagery, nothing marks the difference so clearly as law and violence", trans. Gardner 1966). Firmicus' shares with the two Ciceronian passages the idea of smoothness (*politae, politi*), but while we have already seen that *artes* and *ius* are a cornerstone of the Roman idea of civilization as well as a consequence of education, Firmicus' *ratio* is once again a gift bestowed on man by the celestial vault.[22]

Although the Age of Saturn was not yet characterised by civilization, things got better when Jupiter and then Mars succeeded him:

Post Saturnum Iuppiter accepit temporum potestatem (nam huic secundo loco Luna coniungitur), ut deserto pristini squaloris horrore et agrestis conuersationis feritate seposita cultior uita hominum purgatis moribus redderetur. Tertio uero loco Marti se Luna coniungens ei temporum tradidit potestatem, ut rectum uitae iter ingressa mortalitas et iam humanitatis quadam moderatione composita omnia artium ac fabricationum ornamenta conciperet. (3.1.12)

After Saturn, Jupiter received the rulership of time, with the idea that the roughness of early times should be left behind and mankind be given a more cultivated mode of life. But in the third place the Moon joined herself to Mars, and gave him the rulership of time so that human life, entered on the right path and already instructed in *humanitas*, might learn arts and skills. (trans. Bram 1975)

---

21 Cf. above, pp. 49–50.
22 Cf. above, pp. 34–35. On the relationship between *humanitas* and *politus* cf. also *De or.* 2.72 and 2.154.

After the ideas of smoothness and *humanitas* mentioned at 3.1.11, the addition of the *artes* makes the parallel with Cicero's *De republica* more cogent, although once again a decisive difference must be noted. At *De republica* 1.28 Cicero says that only those men who thanks to the *artes* can possess *humanitas* are worthy of being so called, whereas in Firmicus' passage man is first given *humanitas* and only then can he learn arts and skills: the logic as well as the process are clearly inverted, but for a fourth-century author to resort to Ciceronian language in scientific as well as philosophical fields, especially when it comes to translations, is hardly surprising.[23]

These first three instances of *humanitas* in the *Mathesis* are therefore sufficient to show that Firmicus Maternus conceived this value concept in a way which on the surface reminded of Cicero, but on closer inspection shows a decisive ontological difference.

Three other instances are to be found in Book 5, which has not come down to us in its entirety. The part we can read deals with the signs and, in particular, with the ascendants. Mars is again linked to *humanitas* when appearing in the section which deals with those men who have the ascendant in the terms of Mercury (5.2.15: *Horoscopus in finibus Mercurii*). More in detail, the passage in question reads:

> Si uero Mars in ipsis partibus fuerit inuentus, et sit diurna genitura, faciet malos, malitiosos, malignos, et qui assiduis contentionibus certent, crudeles, temerarios, et qui nullis humanitatis rationibus mitigentur, clamosos, impudentes, insano furore praeposteros, et qui omnia uitio satietatis respuant, leues et qui ab omnibus facillimis persuasionibus transferantur, circumscriptores, carnifices, <et> qui omne facinus nefario mentis ardore concipiant. Si uero fuerit nocturna genitura, haec omnia ex aliqua parte mitescunt. (5.2.18)

> Mars found in these degrees in a diurnal chart will make the natives wicked, malevolent, constantly fighting, cruel, rash, softened by no feelings of *humanitas*, loud and shameless; they are insane with rage, spit on everything in a mood of vicious satiety, are fickle, easily persuaded to change their views-cheats, killers, given to every kind of crime. But in a nocturnal chart these evils are somewhat alleviated. (trans. Bram 1975)

The civilizing power of Mars that we have seen before becomes uncivilizing when it is in the degrees of Saturn. But regardless of this aspect, it is evident that this occurrence of *humanitas* is similar in meaning and nuances to that of *humanitatis clementia* of 1.10.12: the concepts of *crudelitas* and the like, which in both cases stand as opposite to *humanitas*, make this appear all the more clear.

The name of Saturn seems to crop up quite often with reference to Firmicus' uses of the noun *humanitas*, and this is hardly a coincidence: for we can see that

---

[23] Cf. above, pp. 49–50. That Cicero's *De republica* is one of Firmicus Maternus' sources has already been shown: cf. Montanari Caldini 1984.

he understands *humanitas* in his own sense of civilization, declining, according to each situation, with prevalence of the philanthropic or rational aspect, it is consistent that this noun appears when it comes to discussing the historical – or mythological in today's view – presence or absence of civilization, in regard to which the figure of Saturn poses itself as a sort of watershed. 5.3.15 is no exception, although *humanitas* is differently nuanced. All paragraph 5.3 deals with Saturn's influence on different signs and, in particular, at 5.3.15 Firmicus says: *Cum enim in tropicas Cancri uenerit partes Saturnus, tunc iacturam patrimonii faciet et in tantis angustiis constituet ut eos humanitas aliena sustentet. Tunc turbae, tunc seditiones, tunc erunt uaria uitae discrimina* ("When he comes to the tropical degrees of Cancer he indicates loss of inheritance and sets the native in such poverty that he must be maintained by a stranger's *humanitas*. Also riots, revolutions, and various crises are indicated", trans. Bram 1975). The context makes it clear that the philanthropic *humanitas* takes on the dimension of generosity, as we have seen happening in other circumstances. And yet the pairing with *aliena* is curiously rare: in Gellius' *Noctes Atticae* 15.21.1 we have come across a list of some mythical peoples who are *alien[i] ab omni humanitate*, but the context is completely different here and the prospective is inverted; moreover we are not used to hearing of a *humanitas* 'donated' by strangers in general.

There is instead no incompatibility between *humanitas* and Jupiter, as is evident from *Mathesis* 5.4.22. The discussion here concerns Jupiter in Sagittarius, and Firmicus says: *Sed qui sic habuerint Iouem, aliena patrimonia possidebunt. Erunt sane boni, apti ad omne humanitatis officium* ("Those who have Jupiter in this location will have possessions abroad. They will be of good character and trained in every kind of *humanitas*", trans. Bram 1975). The Ciceronian feel of this passage is remarkable. Even though there is probably no Ciceronian text which so closely associates *bonitas* with *humanitas* and *officium*, there is no need to linger on the importance of these three concepts in Cicero's political thought. But as far as the pairing of *humanitas* and *officium* is concerned, so as to best understand what Firmicus' message really is, it is worth recalling a part of a statement by Mayer which I have already quoted in the Suetonius section:

Die Begriffe [scil. *officium humanitasque*] sind zu einer einzigen Vorstellung unzertrennlich eng verschmolzen; h., an und für sich das generelle Wort, Menschlichkeit in weitesten Sinn, ist durch officium näher bestimmt im Sinne einer Gebundenheit an verpflichtende Gesetze und Normen.[24]

---

24 Mayer 1951, 147. On the relationship between *humanitas* and *officium* cf. above, pp. 130–131 and 142.

Mayer's discourse then continues with reference to international politics, but, if taken more generally and in the light of the influence of Ciceronian language on Firmicus, the message applies to the latter too, for there is obviously a close relationship between being *boni* and fulfilling the duties which bind all men together. After all, this is but another way to say that man, in order to be considered *bonus*, must obey by all the rules and laws which makes him worthy of being so called.

The last instance of *humanitas* in the *Mathesis* is to be found in its final book, Book 8. Section 8.10 is about Leo, and at its beginning Firmicus claims:

> In I. parte Leonis oritur Canicula quae a Graecis Sirios dicitur. Quicumque hoc sidere oriente nati fuerint effrenatos animos ad omne studium praeposteri facinoris applicabunt. Erunt etiam ab omni humanitatis gratia separati, et qui libenter omnia uiolentiae studia sectentur, furiosi, iracundi, terribiles, minaces, <et> quos omnes homines et oderint pariter et metuant. (8.10.1)

> In the first degree of Leo rises Canicula, the smaller Dog-star whom the Greeks call *Sirios*. Whoever are born with this star rising will apply a maddened brain to every kind of monstrous crime. They will be separated from all feelings of *humanitas* and seek out violent deeds. They will be raving, wrathful, fearsome, and threatening, and be both hated and feared by everyone. (trans. Bram 1975)

Saturn and, to a lesser degree, Mars are therefore not the only ones to show some incompatibility – albeit not always – with *humanitas*, for this can also be the case of Leo. The opposition between *humanitas* on the one hand and *uiolentia, furia, ira*, and the like on the other hand definitely confirms that Firmicus' understanding of *humanitas* as civilization is consistent throughout the entire course of its *Mathesis*. Despite the profound difference which I have highlighted, the Ciceronian influence in this respect is outwardly undeniable and clearly adds to the pagan perception of this value concept in Firmicus' mind. Accordingly, whether it is for opportunistic or for ideological reasons, when Christian orthodoxy became stricter under Constans it would have been natural for Firmicus utterly to avoid employing this word in a text like the *De errore profanarum religionum*, which he published after his conversion. Whether by God himself or by the emperor or one from his entourage, like St. Jerome, more than St. Jerome, Firmicus will have feared to be reproached: "*Ciceronianus es, non Christianus*" ("You are Ciceronian rather than Christian").[25]

---

25 Jer. *Ep.* 22.30.4.

7.2 *Humanus* in Firmicus' *Mathesis*

Firmicus' 'uniqueness' as far as his conception of *humanitas* is concerned is also revealed by his uses, in the *Mathesis*, of the adjective *humanus*, which also confirm his understanding of *humanitas* as civilization without παιδεία. For Firmicus' oeuvre does not show instances of comparatives or superlatives of *humanus*, and in its positive form the adjective usually appears, as in most other authors, in conjunction with nouns such as *casus, conciliatio, conuersatio, corpus, cruor, fragilitas, gens, genus, iudicium, lex, mors, natura, ratio, res, sanguis, signum* and *uox*.

Yet two kinds of pairings are interesting. The first one is that with *signum*, which is typical of the *Mathesis* and is used when zodiac signs are referred to man and not, for example, to other animals.[26] More characteristic as well as more important not only with regard to Firmicus but more generally in the light of what I have been saying about the relationship between *humanitas* and the adjective from which it derives, are those instances in which *humanus*, implicitly or explicitly, in its positive grade, is said of *homo*.[27] For it is clear that on these occasions the adjective *humanus* means 'humane' and has a philanthropic connotation, and this might seem to come into conflict with the theory that the comparatives and superlatives of *humanus* are much more suitable than the positive *humanus* to render the idea of *humanitas* as a mixture of παιδεία and φιλανθρωπία. Yet despite appearances, Firmicus' case ends up strengthening rather than weakening this theory. It is in fact to be stressed that, as with the instances of *humanitas*, in all these occurrences of *humanus* Firmicus speaks of a concept that utterly disregards the educational aspect, which, as should be evident by now, is one of the two key components which enable men to realise themselves most fully. In other words, the comparatives and superlatives of *humanus* imply an upgrade that can only be achieved through education, and this cannot be the case of Firmicus.

---

26 Cf. *e.g.* Firm. *Math.* 3.3.11: *In humanis enim signis* [. . .] *In quadrupedis uero signis* . . .

27 Cf. *e.g.* Firm. *Math.* 4.19.32: *Si Sol cum domino geniturae hac qua diximus, fuerit radiatione coniunctus, cum ceteris quae dominus geniturae dederit, haec etiam a Sole pro naturae suae potestatibus conferuntur. Facit itaque homines plenos fidei, sed inflatos superbiae spiritu subleuatos, sapientes et omnia [spiritu] aequa putantes, moderatione compositos, humanos, religiosos et qui patres suos integro semper <amore colant>* ("If the Sun is in conjunction with the ruler of the chart, together with other things which the ruler contributes, these also are indicated according to the power of his nature: the Sun makes men full of responsibility but raised up with inflated pride, wise, moderate, humane, pious; they always respect their fathers", trans. Bram 1975). Cf. also *Math.* 5.1.16; 5.3.17; 5.3.28; 5.3.39.

8 *Humanitas* in the Thedosian Age: The Reproposition of the Trajanic Pattern?

While, despite the paucity of pagan sources in Latin for the age of Constantine, during the first part of the fourth century the argument *humanitas* seems to have been little exploited in socio-political context, things change when we move towards the second half of the fourth century and the Theodosian age in particular. At the beginning of the previous chapter I have already stressed that scholars usually agree that *humanitas* played an important role in fourth-century legislation. And yet the rhetoric of laws is one thing, the people's perception of the emperors is another, and the two do not necessarily run in parallel.[1] In other words, the presence of the term in numerous laws does not imply that the judges' and emperors' behaviours concretely followed the path of *humanitas*. Laws are projected into the future, but we need to turn to historiography for a backward perspective on, and evaluation of, people and events. Latin fourth-century pagan literature includes only one great historian, Ammianus Marcellinus. His *Res Gestae*, which end with the Roman defeat of Hadrianople in 378 CE, were completed after 395, in the Theodosian age. What has come down to us, which forms the narration of the events from 353 to 378, shows that Ammianus gave much importance to *humanitas* in all its facets. Yet he perceived that period as devoid of *humanitas*, a value which was mostly feigned, especially by emperors. His strategy is opposite to that of Tacitus (and rather reminds us of Suetonius): while Tacitus avoided using the term with reference to periods and emperors which neglected *humanitas*, Ammianus explicitly laments its absence and denounces its simulation. What unites Ammianus and Tacitus, however, are the socio-political contexts in which these two historians wrote, and which explain their special care towards the word *humanitas*. Both the Trajanic and the Theodosian age did not simply promulgate laws (apparently) inspired by *humanitas*, but exalted it as a complex cluster of values which can create a special bond between the emperor and his subjects, and across (and within) different levels of Roman society. The two historians thus exalted 'in negative' the *humanitas* of the ages in which they wrote by spotlighting the lack of *humanitas* in previous times. And even if we look at those who are usually considered the 'minor' historians of the fourth century, namely Eutropius, Aurelius Victor and the author of the *Epitome de Caesaribus*, or also the author(s) of a series of imperial biographies which taken together fall

---

1 On the propagandistic use in late imperial legislation of concepts like *humanitas* cf. Girotti 2017, 17.

under the name of *Historia Augusta*, the situation does not seem to differ so much.[2] Evidently, this trend is the reverse of that used by the writers who exalt *humanitas* in the positive: we saw in Chapter 3 that, in the case of Trajan's Rome, Pliny the Younger was the main supporter and disseminator of this ideal; his main counterpart in the Theodosian age was Symmachus, slightly anticipated by Ausonius.

We learn from various sources that Theodosius explicitly presented himself as a new Trajan, and allegedly went so far as to fabricate proof of his blood relationship with him.[3] And if Theodosius was the new Trajan, Symmachus was the new Pliny. Thus, the first half of this last chapter will be devoted to the *humanitas* of Ammianus and the other historians, and the second half to that of Ausonius and Symmachus. Whereas in the case of Ausonius' *Gratiarum actio* to Gratian we can simply appreciate a return to the praise of an emperor (also) through the concept of *humanitas*, which furthermore recovers its educational dimension, for Symmachus *humanitas* is really crucial. As with Pliny, *humanitas* emerges from his correspondence as a binding value within Roman society. Pliny aimed to foster the rebirth of Rome after Domitian's tyranny, but Symmachus' goal was just as difficult: he wanted to preserve intact the prestige and power of the traditional senatorial class, which was at that time seriously threatened by multiple factors. The fourth century had been characterised by social mobility, with a great deal of people of humble origins – even barbarians – reaching the highest military and administrative offices. In addition, the success of Christianity would undermine the traditional values on which Roman *nobilitas* had long relied.[4] In this context, the defeat of Hadrianople could have been perceived as the deathblow, marking the end of the Roman empire as well as of its traditional structure and society. Thus, also through the traditional, not to say patriotic, *humanitas*, Symmachus sought to maintain and reinforce the network of relationships which had once

---

2 Cf. Lizzi Testa 2022, xii: "In Rome, in the second half of the fourth century, a cultured senatorial nobility again dictated its own exegesis of recent events, both because many of its members were involved, and because Theodosius I did not want skeletons in his closet while he was in the process of founding a new dynasty", and 81.
3 Cf. Claud. 8.18–29; Them. *Or.* 16.202d–205a and 19.229b; Oros. *Hist.* 7.34.1–3. There is also an extensive comparison between Theodosius and Trajan – favourable to the former – in the *Epitome de Caesaribus* (48). Cf. also Paul. Diac. *Hist. Rom.* 12.5 and the *Scholia Vallicelliana* (Whatmough 1925, 140), with Stover/Woudhuysen 2023, 171–172. Although Theodosius is the most often compared to Trajan, "the notion of Trajan as predecessor for new emperors to surpass recurs in various locations", as B. Gibson/Rees 2013, 157 remark, mentioning for example the case of Tacitus in the *Historia Augusta* (*Tac.* 8.5).
4 Some bibliographical references to these issues can be found in the general Introduction, above pp. 5–6.

made up the backbone of Roman society, the *ordo senatorius*.[5] In this respect, it is telling that Symmachus employs *humanitas* so many times – to our knowledge, only Cicero among pagan authors had used the term more often – but only in letters which date after the battle of Hadrianople and Theodosius' appearance on the political stage early in 379 CE.[6] Indeed, the deeper we dive in the Theodosian age, the more frequently Symmachus uses the term *humanitas*, so much so that his letters seem to confirm Marcone's claim that *humanitas* is a sign of the new (i.e. Theodosian) times.[7]

One clarification needs to be made straight away. Given the common image of Theodosius as the promoter, or even the emblem, of Christianity, one might see a contradiction in presenting the pagan Symmachus' *humanitas*, the unifying value of the senatorial class, as a value which was shared by Theodosius himself. Yet Theodosius' religious policy was not always – and not everywhere – so strict, let alone in the city of Rome, and in any case all his interventions in the religious sphere were motivated by socio-political convenience rather than by theological principles.[8] In particular, he needed to preserve social stability, especially after Hadrianople. In the Eastern empire, his legislation aimed at smoothing disagreements and conflicts between different Christian sects, neglecting the traditional opposition between pagans and Christians. That in principle he had nothing against pagans is further proved by his appointing several pagan aristocrats to the highest public offices, as is the case, for instance, with Flavius Eutolmius Tatianus, who became praetorian prefect of the East. In the western part of the empire, where Symmachus lived, the importance of pagan aristocracy was even greater, especially in Rome, and Theodosius was well aware of this, so much so that Symmachus himself could reach the consulate (391 CE). As Errington puts it, "[t]here is no sign of any religious dimension to Theodosius's political activities there [i.e. in Rome]. His attitude was conciliatory, for he knew well enough that without the support of the Roman aristocrats [most of whom were still pagan] a new government in Italy would have a hard time achieving that traditional political consensus among the ruling classes without which no Italian government

---

5 Cf. Brown 1971, 121: "The most vocal patriots of the late fourth century were resolute pagans." On the political importance of Roman senators during the fourth century cf. Lizzi Testa 2022, xiii–xv, 263–264 and *passim*.

6 Yet "Symmachus' correspondence extends from 364 till 402", as Matthews 1975, 7 rightly remarks.

7 Marcone 1987, 26 – with reference to the Theodosian age: "Segno dei tempi è l'*humanitas* [. . .], il fondamentale valore dell'età celebrato in ogni tipo di documenti."

8 For a detailed description of Theodosius' (religious) policy cf. Errington 2006, 212–259.

could function satisfactorily."[9] By functioning as the glue holding Rome's senatorial class together, Symmachus' *humanitas* was therefore perfectly fitting to Theodosius' policy.

8.1 Absent and Feigned *Humanitas*: Ammianus' Perspective on the Decline of the Empire

Ammianus concludes his *Res Gestae* by resorting to the following statement: *Haec ut miles quondam et Graecus, a principatu Caesaris Neruae exorsus ad usque Valentis interitum, pro uirium explicaui mensura* (31.16.9: "These events, from the principate of the emperor Nerva to the death of Valens, I, a former soldier and a Greek, have set forth to the measure of my ability", trans. Rolfe 1986).[10] Regardless of the fact that these words are to be taken as a declaration of modesty or, on the contrary, of pride, there is no doubt that the self-referential phrase *ut miles quondam et Graecus* is key to our understanding of his personality and historiographical method.[11] In judging the content of his work, his viewpoint, style, vocabulary and so forth, we need therefore to bear in mind two points: first, that he was a Greek writing in Latin, and second, that he was (or had been) a career soldier. As a non-native Latin author, he must have looked for a model to imitate, and it comes as no surprise that he mainly found this model in Cicero.[12] As a soldier who was at times a direct protagonist of the events he narrates, it is to be expected that he paid much attention to the behaviour and moral values of rulers, high-ranking military officers and powerful men and women in general.[13] And, what is more, he had in-

---

9 Errington 2006, 242. Cf. also Brown 1971, 121; Lizzi Testa 2022, 94. A brief survey on the different positions of scholars concerning the relationship between pagans and Christians in the late fourth century can be found in Gassman 2020, 165–166.

10 Calboli 1974, 74 and Matthews 1989, 461 among others regard Ammianus' statement as an expression of modesty, and so seems to do Mazzoli 2012, 66–67, although he then (70–72) stresses Ammianus' criticism of Roman habits, to which the historian opposes his Greek, nobler origins. *Contra*, Barnes 1998, 65; Den Boeft *et al.* 2018, 298; Piatti 2019 rather think of a declaration of pride – cf. *e.g.* Piatti's translation: "Come un soldato d'altri tempi e in quanto greco . . ." (p. 35).

11 On the meaning(s) of *ut miles quondam et Graecus* cf. Camus 1967, 23; Sabbah 1978, 532–537; 597; Barnes 1998, 65 and nn. 1 and 2; 79–80; Kelly 2008, 103 and n. 203; Den Boeft *et al.* 2018, 297–299. Further bibliography in Rohrbacher 2002, 24.

12 Cf. Camus 1967, 60–68; Sabbah 1978, 72–75; 352; 596–597; Salemme 1989, 40; 63; Mazzoli 2012, 68.

13 On the moral character of Ammianus's work cf. Rosen 1982, 117–130; Seager 1986, *passim*; Brandt 1999, 13–14; *passim*; Wieber-Scariot 1999, 27; Drijvers/Hunt 1999, 4–5; Zugravu 2018, 344–345; 355–356.

sight into a reality that others would not have been able to see as closely. In addition to the cultural context in which he wrote, these two criteria also account for Ammianus' extensive use of *humanitas,* a word with Ciceronian connotations whose multifacetedness is very apt to portray different aspects of people's nature. In this respect, Ammianus distances himself from two major Roman historiographers in Sallust and Tacitus, who, as we have seen, usually avoided using the word.[14] After all, despite setting himself in the footsteps of Tacitus (*a principatu Caesaris Neruae,* where Tacitus' *Historiae* ended), in many respects Ammianus' work reminds us more of previous Greek than Roman historians, and the use of *humanitas* is no exception.[15] Philologists of Wilhelmine Germany already understood – as Barnes rightly brought back to light – the 'essential Greekness' of Ammianus' thought, and this is also mirrored in his use of *humanitas-*φιλανθρωπία as a sovereign virtue (or *Herrschertugend,* to borrow a German term).[16] Aside from Ammianus in fact, φιλανθρωπία *qua* sovereign virtue is accorded far more space in Greek historical thought than its equivalent *humanitas* is accorded in Roman, as also a survey of *humanitas* in fourth-century minor historians will confirm.[17] Although this perspective might seem to have the limitation of equating Ammianus' conception of *humanitas* with the Greek φιλανθρωπία, thereby oversimplifying the versatility of the Latin word (of which we are by now well aware), we will see in this chapter that Ammianus pays far more attention to this philanthropic aspect of *humanitas,* without however neglecting its educational and cultural components.[18]

I will first look into the instances in which Ammianus uses *humanitas* to characterise imperial virtue or links it to emperors. The analysis of these passages will bring into play both the role that Ammianus accorded to the education of emperors and statesmen, and the relationship between *humanitas* and foreigners

---

14 Cf. more generally Seager 1986, 36: "Of the moderate virtues prized by Ammianus, most are found much more rarely, if at all, in Tacitus."

15 The extent to which Ammianus was influenced by Tacitus is debated. Among the scholars who have brought to light the affinities between the two of them or at least Ammianus' willingness to continue Tacitus' work we can name Thompson 1947, 17; Camus 1967, 70–73; Momigliano 1974, 1398; Sabbah 1978, 565; 596–598, who at the same time also emphasises Ammianus' affinities with Greek authors and mentality (cf. note below); Fornara 1992; Brandt 1999, 19. More hesitant are Matthews 1989, 32; Barnes 1998, 192–193 – with a concise state of research, who yet spotlights some parallels between the two (193–195); Kelly 2008, 175–177.

16 Barnes 1998, viii; 67–68. On Ammianus' 'Greekness' cf. also Thompson 1947, 16; Sabbah 1978, 376; 536; 596. Further bibliography and an overview in Barnes 1998, 69–71.

17 Brandt 1999, 140–141. Cf. also Chapter 8.2 below.

18 *Pace* Girotti 2017, 21 and *passim,* according to whom for Ammianus the value *humanitas* "non ha nulla a che vedere con la *philantropia* [sic], ma è per lo più connesso alla *paideia.*" More in detail on the structural weakness of Girotti 2017 cf. Mollea 2018a.

or barbarians. However, as we will see, several of these cases describe *humanitas* as feigned; hence, investigation of instances of *simulata humanitas* or *species humanitatis* will be in order. I will then consider the significant role that *humanitas* plays in Ammianus' two digressions on Rome, and how this value can be related to noble women or astrologers. Finally, I shall provide an overview of Ammianus' use of the adjective *humanus*.

8.1.1 *Humanitas* in the *Res Gestae*

Let me start with those instances where *humanitas* is associated with emperors. The relationship is quite complex. To begin with, Ammianus never uses the word *humanitas* in relation to Julian the Apostate, *pace* Selem and De Jonge.[19] This is striking, because Julian emerges as Ammianus' favourite ruler.[20] Of course his exclusion from the category of *humanitas*-gifted rulers is not to be overstated, for neither is he accused of lacking in this virtue, nor, on the other hand, does this mean that *humanitas* is not important to Ammianus. Yet, from a rhetorical point of view, it is significant that the term *humanitas* is only linked to the emperors whose overall portraits emerge as negative from Ammianus' narration.

The first case in point is Julian's (losing) opponent Constantius, whom Ammianus presents as claiming twice that he possesses *humanitas*. The passage (*Res Gestae* 14.10) is quite a long chapter recounting the drawing up of a peace deal between the Romans and the Alemanni. The Alemanni were devastating Gallic lands close to the Roman province, and Constantius therefore decided to move against them. *Res Gestae* recount that, as the Roman army arrived in their territories, the Alemanni begged for pardon and peace. The emperor was well aware of the possible benefits deriving from peace, but also knew it was difficult for him to justify his decision not to fight, especially after forcing the soldiers into exhausting marches. He thus resolved to pass the ball to them, at least apparently: in fact, he addressed them with a persuasive speech in which he clearly revealed his intentions (14.10.11–15). The oration, as it is given by Ammianus, ends thus:

> In summa tamquam arbitros uos, quid suadetis, opperior ut princeps tranquillus temperanter adhibere modum allapsa felicitate decernens. Non enim inertiae, sed modestiae humanitatique, mihi credite, hoc, quod recte consultum est assignabitur. (14.10.15)

> In short, I await your decision as arbiters, as it were, being myself convinced as a peace-loving prince, that it is best temperately to show moderation while prosperity is with us.

---

19 Selem 1964, 150; De Jonge 1980, 308.
20 On the relationship between *humanitas* and the emperor Julian cf. also below, pp. 239–240.

> For, believe me, such righteous conduct will be attributed, not to lack of spirit, but to discretion and *humanitas*. (trans. Rolfe 1935)

Opting for peace, says Constantius, would be seen as a sign of moderation, intellectual poise and humanity, not of inactivity or passiveness. This message seems to be inspired not only by Constantius' willingness to counter his reputation for cruelty but also by common sense, and yet in what follows (14.10.16) Ammianus does not miss the chance to throw some discredit on the emperor by stating that the army only voted for peace because they mistrusted Constantius' war skills.[21] After the Ciceronian model of the *Pro Archia*, which was followed by Lucius' speech in *Metamorphoses* 3 and Eumenius' panegyric, we face here another case where the *humanitas* argument appears within the *peroratio* of an oration. This time, however, *humanitas* is paired with *modestia* and opposed to *inertia*. This triangular relation *humanitas-modestia* vs. *inertia* is significant to understanding Ammianus' view of *humanitas*, for it invites us to nuance Brandt's claim that for Ammianus *humanitas* is subordinate to *temperantia*.[22] Brandt rightly concludes from the general meaning of this passage that *humanitas*, here used in reference to the Romans' mild use of force, can only be gained if the ruler subordinates his own feelings and interests to those of his army and people, and shows some *modestia*.[23] This ultimately explains the meaning of its pairing with *modestia*. However, this does not necessarily mean (*pace* Brandt) that *humanitas* must be subordinated to *temperantia*. In fact, a closer look at the passage, and more specifically at the association of *humanitas* with *modestia*, seems to contradict this claim.

In discussing 14.10.15, Brandt argues that this relationship between moderation (*Maß*) and humanity (*Menschlichkeit*) appears quite often in Cicero, and in support of his statement he refers to *Leg. Man.* 13; *Mur.* 66; *Phil.* 13.36 and *Sen.* 7.[24] However, in three of these Ciceronian passages (*Mur.* 66; *Phil.* 13.36; *Sen.* 7) it is the word *moderatio*, rather than *modestia*, that is associated with *humanitas*; in the fourth case (*Leg. Man.* 13) then, *humanitas* is linked to *mansuetudo* and *temperantia*, and *modestia* is once again absent. It is true that at *Tusc.* 3.16 *temperantia*, *moderatio* and *modestia* appear together in one sentence, but this does not

---

21 On Constantius' bad reputation during his life cf. Whitby 1999, who at 70 claims: "The evidence for Constantius' harshness was undoubtedly improved after his death, but it was still a reputation that had to be countered during his life since mildness and mercy were important imperial virtues."

22 Brandt 1999, 140. Apart from the quick survey by Seager 1986, 20–22 and the unconvincing Girotti 2017, Brandt's is to my knowledge the only study to allow significant space to Ammianus' use of *humanitas*.

23 Brandt 1999, 140.

24 Brandt 1999, 140 n. 124.

mean that they are interchangeable, let alone synonymous. Nor does this allow for the conclusion that one virtue is subordinated to the other. On the contrary, both syntax and content indicate that they are considered to be of equal importance. Accordingly, even if one accepted the equivalence between *moderatio* and *modestia*, there is no reason why *modestia*, and consequently *humanitas*, should be seen as hyponyms of *temperantia*. Compare Cicero's *Leg. Man.* 36, where *humanitas* and *temperantia* are clearly put on the same level, or even *Leg. Man.* 13 mentioned by Brandt himself.[25] If we do not restrict our scope to Ciceronian texts, the same holds true for a Ciceronian author like Pliny the Younger, whom we have seen claiming in the *Panegyricus*: *Diuinitatem principis nostri, an humanitatem temperantiam facilitatem, ut amor et gaudium tulit, celebrare uniuersi solemus?* (2.7: "What about us? Is it the divine nature of our prince or his *humanitas*, his moderation and his courtesy which joy and affection prompt us to celebrate in a single voice?", trans. Radice 1975).[26] If we then recall Seneca's *Letter* 88 discussed above, it will appear clear that he explicitly regarded *temperantia* and *humanitas* as two different values providing different benefits.[27] But it is also the very relationship put forward here at 14.10.15 which dissuades us from looking for rigid classifications of value concepts, especially in the case of *humanitas*. It is sufficient to compare the opposition between *inertia* and *humanitas* to yet another Plinian passage already discussed, *Pan.* 3.5, where *humanitas* is opposed to *superbia*, and *inertia* to *labor*. Closer to Ammianus is instead a passage of the

---

25 Cic. *Leg. Man.* 36: *Ac primum quanta innocentia debent esse imperatores, quanta deinde in omnibus rebus temperantia, quanta fide, quanta facilitate, quanto ingenio, quanta humanitate!* ("In the first place, what integrity commanders should have; then what moderation in everything they do, what good faith, what graciousness, what intelligence, what humanity!", trans. Berry 2006).

26 Cf. above, pp. 85–86.

27 On *humanitas* in Seneca cf. above, pp. 67–71. Sen. *Ep.* 88.29–30: *Temperantia uoluptatibus imperat, alias odit atque abigit, alias dispensat et ad sanum modum redigit nec umquam ad illas propter ipsas uenit; scit optimum esse modum cupitorum non quantum uelis, sed quantum debeas sumere. Humanitas uetat superbum esse aduersus socios, uetat amarum; uerbis, rebus, adfectibus comem se facilemque omnibus praestat; nullum alienum malum putat, bonum autem suum ideo maxime quod alicui bono futurum est amat* ("Take self-control, the quality which takes command of the pleasures; some she dismisses out of hand, unable to tolerate them; others she merely regulates, ensuring that they are brought within healthy limits; never approaching pleasures for their own sake, she realizes that the ideal limit with things you desire is not the amount you would like to but the amount you ought to take. *Humanitas* is the quality which stops one being arrogant towards one's fellows, or being acrimonious. In words, in actions, in emotions she reveals herself as kind and good-natured towards all. To her the troubles of anyone else are her own, and anything that benefits herself she welcomes primarily because it will be of benefit to someone else", trans. Campbell 1969)

Rhetorica ad Herennium, in which we find the same opposition between the negative *inertia* and the positive *modestia: quam ille modestiam dicet esse, eam nos inertiam et dissolutam neglegentiam esse dicemus* (3.6: "what he declares to be temperance we shall declare to be inaction and lax indifference", trans. Caplan 1954).[28] In sum, neither the context nor previous instances of the concepts of value involved in Amm. Marc. 14.10.15 justify Brandt's taxonomy and, specifically, the claim that Ammianus subordinates *humanitas* to *temperantia*. Rather, all these combinations of *humanitas* with other values, and its opposition to faults like *inertia,* confirm the need to investigate each and every occurrence of *humanitas* as an ever-evolving nexus of interrelated connotations that are also influenced by the presence of other words which are ethically connoted.

When we turn to the second passage where Constantius invokes *humanitas* within a speech, we immediately realise that Ammianus established an interesting dialectical relationship between the two occurrences. 21.13.10–15 features the *contio* that the emperor delivered in front of his army before the decisive battle against Julian (which did not take place eventually). To begin with, the external narrator Ammianus recounts that Constantius, caught between two fires, is hesitant as to what course of action to take: should he concentrate all his forces against the 'inner' enemy Julian, or would it be better to send part of the army to monitor the Persians' movements? In the end, he opts for the latter solution, but does so – Ammianus seems to rejoice in making this clear – "in order not to be blamed for his inactivity."[29] As in the preceding instance at 14.10.15, Ammianus once again alludes to Constantius' unwillingness to show *inertia* towards external enemies. However, while in that case the *inertia* was replaced by the nobler *humanitas,* which fortunately prevented war, at 21.13.10 that same *humanitas* is regarded by the emperor as the error which has too long put off an inevitable war:

> Sollicitus semper, ne quid re leui uel uerbo committam inculpatae parum congruens honestati, utque cautus nauigandi magister clauos pro fluctuum motibus erigens vel inclinans compellor nunc apud uos, amantissimi uiri, confiteri meos errores, quin potius, si dici liceat uerum, humanitatem, quam credidi negotiis communibus profuturam.

> Being always careful by no act or word, however slight, to allow myself to do anything inconsistent with faultless honour, and like a cautious steerman putting my helm up or down according to the movements of the waves, I am now constrained, dearly beloved soldiers, to confess to you my mistake, or rather (if I may be allowed to use the right word) my *humanitas,* which I believed would be profitable to the interests of all. (trans. Rolfe 1940)

---

28 On *humanitas* in the *Rhetorica ad Herennium* cf. above, pp. 50–52.
29 Amm. Marc. 21.13.3.

Here Constantius realises that what had been his main merit at 14.10.15, that is, his tendency to subordinate his own good to that of others, has turned out to be a double-edged sword in this case. Symptomatic, in this sense, is the fact that *humanitas*, which had been the key element of his *peroratio* at 14.10.15 as well as the last and most important feeling he tried to instill in his soldiers so as to persuade them not to fight, has now become the first element of his *introductio*, the basis, so to speak, on which to build an oration aimed at encouraging the soldiers' minds. Constantius' premature death will prevent the slaughter in a field battle, but it is telling that the entire chapter 13 of Book 21 is full of negative presages for himself and his army. Accordingly, if on the one hand Kelly is right in giving credit to Constantius for recognising (albeit a little too late, we might add) the validity of the negative *exemplum* of Gallus (cf. 21.13.11 with 15.8.2) and therefore for admitting his previous errors of judgement, on the other hand, Constantius' biggest error turns out paradoxically to be his having considered *humanitas* as an error.[30] So in both these two passages *humanitas* carries the idea of 'restraint', but Ammianus' narration adds irony to these events: in the first case, Constantius' *humanitas* is presented as insincere, but leading to a positive outcome; in the second, it is presented as possibly genuine, but the emperor did not persist in his moderate behaviour, and this led to a negative outcome. Both passages underline the incompatibility between *humanitas* and Constantius.

From this standpoint however, the case of Constantius is not unique within the *Res Gestae*, for one more time Ammianus features a case where *humanitas* is regarded – again wrongly, judging by the historian's tone – as a value leading to a negative result or behaviour. Towards the beginning of book 29, the historian tells of the numerous plots against the emperor Valens' life. Despite all being unsuccessful, these plots made the emperor obsessive and indiscriminately cruel:

> Inexpiabile illud erat, quod regaliter turgidus, pari eodemque iure, nihil inter se distantibus meritis, nocentes innocentesque maligna insectatione uolucriter perurgebat, ut dum adhuc dubitaretur de crimine, imperatore non dubitante de poena, damnatos se quidam prius discerent quam suspectos. (29.1.18)

> But it was inexcusable that, with despotic anger, he was swift to assail with malicious persecution guilty under one and the same law, making no distinction in their deserts; so that while there was still doubt about the crime the emperor had made up his mind about the penalty, and some learned that they had been condemned to death before knowing that they were under suspicion. (trans. Rolfe 1986)

---

30 Kelly 2008, 287.

And as if that were not enough,

> Adolescebat autem obstinatum eius propositum admouente stimulos auaritia et sua et eorum, qui tunc in regia uersabantur, nouos hiatus aperientium et, si qua humanitatis fuisset mentio rara, hanc appellantium tarditatem. (29.1.19)

> This persistent purpose of his increased, spurred on as it was both by his own greed and that of persons who frequented the court at that time, and opened the way to fresh desires – and if any mention of *humanitas* was made – which rarely happened – called it slackness. (trans. Rolfe 1986)

In sum, the emperor's entourage even worsened Valens' own greed and vices in general,[31] so much that they went so far as to call *humanitas* 'slowness' – and it is worth noting that in Latin *tarditas* stands for both slowness of movement and slowness of intellect. Like *error* at 21.13.10, *tarditas* makes an unusual pairing when associated with *humanitas*, and, in broader terms, when seen as the dark side of a virtue. Cicero's *tenth Philippic* probably provides the closest parallel: *Itaque illi ipsi si qui sunt qui tarditatem Bruti reprehendant tamen idem moderationem patientiamque mirantur* (10.14: "Therefore the very persons – if any such there be – who censure the slowness of Brutus, yet at the same time admire his moderation and patience", trans. Ker 1957). The opposition between *tarditas* on the one hand and *moderatio* and *patientia* on the other hand seems to be posed in less explicit terms than that between *tarditas* and *humanitas.* Yet in the light of the close relationship between *humanitas* and *moderatio* already observed in Ammianus, and between *humanitas* and *patientia* already noticed several times in other authors, Valens ends up being implicitly compared to Caesar's assassin Brutus. From the standpoint of Ammianus' conception of *humanitas* then, the parallel of *Phil.* 10.14 clearly contributes to spotlighting the Ciceronian influence on Ammianus' language and worldview, and to illustrating the way he uses Ciceronian terminology to present Roman emperors as either bad or good rulers. But to return to 29.1.19: clearly on this occasion Valens did not (and evidently could not because of his courtiers!) display any *humanitas*, but earlier in the *Res Gestae* he had done so, as the next passage shows.

Section 12 of book 27 narrates the critical political situation in Armenia after Julian's death and a later peace agreement between the Persian king Shapur and

---

31 Cf. Den Boeft *et al.* 2013, 33 for other passages where Ammianus refers or alludes to Valens' greed, or to the vices of courtiers in general. According to Selem 1964, 149, 29.1.19 is one of those passages which reveal Ammianus' concern for (and probably dislike of) the rising category of wealthy courtiers who would threaten the privileges of the traditional aristocracy. More extensively on greed in Ammianus Brandt 1999, 402–412.

the young emperor Jovian. The passage explains that Shapur ignored the terms of the peace treaty, imprisoned the Armenian king Arsaces, then killed and replaced him with two Armenian defectors called Cylaces and Arrabannes. The two of them however broke their allegiance again and conspired with Arsaces' wife and son against Shapur. In doing so, they obviously looked for the Romans' help. In fact, Arsaces' young son Papa was even housed by Valens:

> Arsacis filium Papam suadente matre cum paucis e munimento digressum susceptumque imperator Valens apud Neocaesaream morari praecepit, urbem Polemoniaci Ponti notissimam, liberali uictu curandum et cultu. Qua humanitate Cylaces et Arrabannes illecti missis oratoribus ad Valentem auxilium eundemque Papam sibi regem tribui poposcerunt. (27.12.9)

> Papa, son of Arsaces, at the persuasion of his mother, had departed with a few followers from the fortified town and been received by the emperor Valens, who advised that he stay a while at Neocaesarea, a well-known city of Pontus Polemoniacus, where he was to receive liberal support and education. This act of *humanitas* encouraged Cylaces and Arrabannes to send envoys to Valens to ask that he aid them and give them the said Papa as their king. (trans. Rolfe 1986)

Evidently, unlike the case of 29.1.19, in this context Valens' *humanitas* could hardly fall under the definition of mercy, for Papa cannot be considered a spared enemy. In fact, Armenian royalty were not Roman enemies at that time, and at any rate Valens did not limit himself to sparing him. No doubt this instance of *humanitas* shares with the previous one the broad idea of φιλανθρωπία, but it is quite differently nuanced. The presence of the phrase *liberali uictu curandum et cultu* is highly significant. The twinning of *uictus* and *cultus* is very common in Latin literature, particularly in Cicero and Gellius.[32] The jurist Ulpian explicitly links them when defining *uictus*: *Verbo "uictus" continentur, quae esui potuique cultuique corporis quaeque ad uiuendum homini necessaria sunt. Vestem quoque uictus habere uicem Labeo ait* (*Dig.* 50.16.43: "Food, drink, the care of the body, and everything necessary to human life is embraced in the term 'maintenance'. Labeo says that maintenance also includes clothing", trans. Scott 1932). But while the emphasis of *uictus* is on the most material and individual aspects of human life (food, drink, and even clothes), *cultus* has a broader meaning, which often implies the notions of culture and education.[33] On one famous occasion in particular, the same notion is expressed through the association of *cultus* with *humanitas*: *horum omnium fortissimi sunt Belgae, propterea quod a cultu atque humanitate prouinciae longissime absunt*

---

32 Ammianus' good knowledge of Gellius' oeuvre has already been spotlighted in modern scholarship: cf. Sabbah 1978, 517–518; Kelly 2008, 192–203.

33 On *cultus* cf. the relevant entry in the *TLL*, especially 4.0.1324.70–80.

(Caes. *BGall.* 1.1.3: "Of all these, the Belgae are the bravest, for they are furthest away from the civilization and *humanitas* of the Province", trans. Hammond 1996, slightly adapted).[34] And the same holds true in Ammianus' passage, for Papa was most likely about fifteen years old by the time of his stay at Valens' court, and needed therefore not only room and board but also education. In providing him with both, Valens thus displayed more than mere benevolence or kindness, but also awareness of the importance of instruction for young nobles probably destined to rule one day. *Humanitas* is likely to epitomise all these feelings here. As we have seen, such an awareness is most likely to be expected from people who already possess a high level of education, but Ammianus shows us that that is not always the case. From Valens' final obituary, in fact, we learn that he was not well educated (31.14.5: *nec bellicis nec liberalibus studiis eruditus*, "was trained neither in the art of war nor in liberal studies", trans. Rolfe 1986). In other words, the *humanitas* he displays on this occasion probably originates from his regret for not having benefited from others' *humanitas*. At any rate, this episode, almost unique in Valens' life, seems to be the exception which proves the rule. As well as being rare (cf. *mentio rara* of 29.1.19), Valens' *humanitas* must have been short-lasting, for one paragraph later (27.12.10) Ammianus informs his readers that Papa was then brought back to Armenia by the Roman general Terentius. Nevertheless, someone else later appealed to Valens' *humanitas*.

Book 31, the last one of Ammianus' *Res Gestae*, recounts both the events which led to the epochal battle of Hadrianople and the battle itself, where Valens lost his life. The uninterrupted pressure that Goth tribes, often suffering from shortage of food, had long exerted on the north-eastern borders of the Empire was becoming unbearable, and the Romans, in order to avoid bloody conflicts, were often forced to let them in (more or less) peacefully. To this sort of 'welcoming' attitude of the emperor Ammianus refers at 31.4.12:

> Per hos dies interea etiam Videricus Greuthungorum rex cum Alatheo et Safrace, quorum arbitrio regebatur, itemque Farnobio propinquans Histri marginibus, ut simili susciperetur humanitate, obsecrauit imperatorem legatis propere missis.

> During these days also Videricus, king of the Greuthungi, accompanied by Alatheus and Saphrax, by whose will he was ruled, and also by Farnobius, coming near to the banks of the Danube, hastily sent envoys and besought the emperor that he might be received with like *humanitas*. (trans. Rolfe 1986)

Previous examples of Valens' *humanitas*, which we might understand here as humanitarian aid more than simple hospitality, had evidently persuaded the Greu-

---

34 On this Caesarian passage cf. above, p. 64, and also below, pp. 256–257.

thungi that they could take advantage of the same benefits already granted to other Goth tribes. Yet, as with Constantius, it looks as if there is always some incompatibility between Valens and *humanitas*: the phrase *simili* [. . .] *humanitate* makes it clear that right before this episode there had been other occasions on which Valens had displayed a similar attitude, but Ammianus had not employed the word *humanitas*. By contrast, every time Ammianus associates this concept with this emperor, he is quick to underline that Valens' displays of *humanitas* are short-lived and are generally followed by a change of attitude. Showing *humanitas* towards internal enemies is rare and seen as a flaw (29.1.19); when shown towards a young foreign prince it is short-lasting (27.12.9), and when it comes to the Greuthungi there is no room at all for *humanitas*: *Quibus, ut communi rei conducere uidebatur, repudiatis* (31.4.13: "These envoys were rejected, as the interests of the state seemed to demand", trans. Rolfe 1986).[35] In sum, the fact that Ammianus attributes the term *humanitas* to Valens no less than three times does not help mitigate the negative image that the historian gives of this emperor throughout the *Res Gestae*, and which culminates in his obituary (31.14.5–8).[36] On the contrary, Valens' incoherent and inconsistent use of *humanitas* ends up adding to his negative portrayal.

Yet in general terms, as Sabbah has observed, the figure of Valens emerges as more positive than Ammianus' treatment of his brother and colleague Valentinian.[37] This is particularly true in the context of *humanitas*, for Valentinian's fault is aggravated by the fact that he did not follow the path of *humanitas* despite having *exempla* of it – a reasoning that Ammianus could have applied to many other emperors.[38] The long passage is worth quoting in full:

> Atquin potuit exempla multa contueri maiorum et imitari peregrina atque interna humanitatis et pietatis, quas sapientes consanguineas uirtutum esse definiunt bonas. E quibus haec sufficiet poni: Artaxerxes, Persarum ille rex potentissimus, quem Macrochira membri unius longitudo commemorauit, suppliciorum uarietates, quas natio semper exercuit cruda, lenitate genuina castigans tiaras ad uicem capitum quibusdam noxiis amputabat et, ne secaret aures more regio pro delictis, ex galeris fila pendentia praecidebat. Quae temperantia

---

morum ita tolerabilem eum fecit et uerecundum, ut adnitentibus cunctis multos et mirabiles actus impleret Graecis scriptoribus celebratos. (30.8.4)

And yet he could have contemplated many examples of the men of old, and might have imitated native and foreign instances of *humanitas* and righteous mercy, which philosophers call the kind sisters of the virtues. Of these it will suffice to mention the following. Artaxerxes, that mighty king of the Persians, whom the length of one of his limbs made known as Macrochir, with inborn mildness corrected various punishments which that cruel nation had always practised, by sometimes cutting off the turbans of the guilty, in lieu of their heads; and instead of cutting of men's ears for various offences, as was the habit of the kings, he shared off threads hanging from their head-coverings. This moderation of character so won for him the contentment and respect of his subjects, that through their unanimous support he accomplished many noteworthy deeds, which are celebrated by the Greek writers. (trans. Rolfe 1986)

A close reading of this passage confirms that in Ammianus' taxonomy *humanitas* is not subordinated to *temperantia*.[39] Ammianus' argument is as follows: first, Valentinian must have known good examples of *humanitas* and *pietas*; secondly, the case of Artaxerxes stands out among these examples; thirdly, Artaxerxes' *temperantia* (*morum*) was even celebrated by Greek writers. Here Ammianus clearly equates *temperantia* with the pair *humanitas-pietas*, rather than subordinate *humanitas* to *temperantia*. In the light of what I said above about the relationship between *temperantia* and *humanitas* in other authors (above all, Cicero), Ammianus seems to use *temperantia* and *humanitas* as synonyms. More specifically, the twinning of *humanitas* with *pietas* helps these two polysemic words clarify each other, thereby allowing the reader to understand that *humanitas* carries a connotation of philanthropy. Briefly, there is neither need nor reason to assume that in Ammianus' view *humanitas* is subordinated to *temperantia*. By contrast, my interpretation perfectly fits Brandt's treatment of *pietas* in Ammianus. According to him, in fact, the historian mainly gives *pietas* philanthropic connotations, the same that can also be carried by *humanitas*.[40] In this respect, and in regard to the pairing of *pietas* with *humanitas* in particular, 30.8.4 makes all the more clear that Ammianus distances himself from previous authors like Cicero, who had instead connected *pietas* and *humanitas* to refer to two very distinct values.[41] To discuss *pietas* at length would require another book, so I limit myself to a couple of considerations. At *De inuentione* 2.66 Cicero broadly defines *pietas* as *quae erga patriam aut parentes aut alios sanguine coniunctos officium conseruare moneat* ("what warns us to keep our obli-

---

39 Cf. above, pp. 230–231. *Contra*, Brandt 1999, 140.
40 Brandt 1999, 147.
41 For the joint presence of *pietas* and *humanitas* within a sentence cf. *e.g.* Cic. *Verr.* 2.2.97; 2.4.12; *Planc.* 96; *Off.* 3.41; *Att.* 6.3.8; 11.17.1; Quint. *Inst.* 6 *praef.* 10; Sen. *Dial.* 4.28.2.

gations to our country or parents or other kin", trans. Hubbell 1949, slightly adapted) and Hellegouarc'h, quoting Cicero, *Phil.* 14.29, stresses how its meaning is close to *fides*, although the latter generally concerns the legal sphere, while *pietas* rather concerns the religious sphere.[42] When applied to politics then, *pietas* becomes linked to the idea of *patria* and, even more, of patriotism.[43] What is most remarkable, however, is the fact that, unlike Ammianus' use at 30.8.4 for instance, *pietas*, like often *clementia*, usually implies an upward relationship, from a person of lower rank towards an entity of higher rank, whether it is a person or a god. Conversely, Ammianus' understanding of *pietas* tends to resemble the Christian conception of piety, and it is possible that he was affected by Christian language more in this respect than in that of *humanitas*, where no significant variation in meaning and context is detectable in comparison with previous pagan authors, as we are seeing. After all, as Kelly puts it: "[Ammianus] is far more at home in the language of Christianity than he appears."[44]

The case of Valentinian at 30.8.4 as well as the last two instances of *humanitas* with regard to Valens open the door to further investigations. First, we have seen that Valens' concern for Papa's education can hardly originate from the emperor's own education. So to what extent is education important to rulers, and can it be called *humanitas* in Ammianus' oeuvre? Secondly, both 27.12.9 and 31.4.12 bring into play Roman *humanitas* towards barbarians, while 30.8.4 seems to imply that the Persian king Artaxerxes, unlike Valentinian, possessed *humanitas*. So what is this relationship like? And can barbarians also possess and show *humanitas* by Ammianus' time? Let me start with the first issue.

Camus probably stressed more than others the importance that Ammianus attaches to education and culture, and went so far as to claim that Ammianus' love for Julian mainly derives from this emperor's exceptional *Bildung*.[45] Along the same lines a few years earlier Selem had maintained that Ammianus admired Julian's *humanitas*.[46] Given that Ammianus never uses the word *humanitas* in relation to Julian, as I mentioned above, Selem's point is that Ammianus loved Julian because of his ability to reconcile culture and morality. The combination of these two aspects is of particular relevance, for Blockley rightly stated: "Education, though it is an aid to and perhaps a prerequisite for virtue, does not, in Am-

---

42 Hellegouarc'h 1963, 276.
43 Hellegouarc'h 1963, 278. More generally on *pietas* cf. Schröder 2012.
44 Kelly 2008, 157. Ammianus' attitude towards Christianity is an open and very debated question. For an overview cf. Neri 1985, 25–70; Wittchow 2001, 185. Cf. also Barnes 1998, 90–94.
45 Camus 1967, 55. On the importance of education for Ammianus in general cf. also Camus 1967, 108–109 and 129.
46 Selem 1964, 150. Along the same lines De Jonge 1980, 308: cf. above, p. 229.

mianus' eyes, automatically confer it."[47] The validity of such an assertion, which undoubtedly concerns rulers first, is corroborated by passages such as 27.6.9:

> Vt enim mihi uideri solet mores eius et appetitus licet nondum maturos saepe pensanti, ineunte adolescentia, quoniam humanitate et studiis disciplinarum sollertium expolitus, librabit suffragiis puris merita recte secusue factorum.

> For as I am wont to think, when I consider, as I often do, his character and his inclinations, although they are not yet fully developed: when he enters on the years of youth, since he has been instructed in the liberal arts and in the pursuit of skilful accomplishments, he will weigh with impartial justice the value of right and wrong actions. (trans. Rolfe 1986)

This excerpt is taken from the investiture speech which Valentinian delivered before his troops when he appointed his young son Gratian to the rank of Augustus.[48] That *humanitas* is educationally connoted is made all the more clear by its twinning with *studiis* (*disciplinarum sollertium*), a phrase which basically reproduces the formulaic expression *studia humanitatis*.[49] What is striking, however, is the fact that the emperor does not only emphasise his son's knowledge, the result of Ausonius' teachings, but also regards this knowledge as the precondition for Gratian's future ability to distinguish right from wrong.[50] To answer to the first question posed above: education, as long as it is not an end in itself, is important to rulers, and Ammianus also calls it *humanitas*. The case of the aspiring emperor Theodorus provides another example in this sense. The episode of which he is protagonist is the same we have already touched upon when highlighting Valens' and his courtiers' lack of clemency towards conspirators (or alleged conspirators) at the opening of book 29. As we know, Valens was always obsessed by the idea of suffering conspiracies, and tended to give credit to informers. In the case of Theodorus, a defendant named Fidustius declared that an oracle had outlined the profile of the future emperor, who would be an *optimus princeps*. And when it came to unveiling his name:

> Atque cunctantibus, quisnam ea tempestate omnibus uigore animi antistaret, uisus est aliis excellere Theodorus secundum inter notarios adeptus iam gradum. Et erat re uera ita ut opinati sunt. Namque antiquitus claro genere in Galliis natus et liberaliter educatus a primis pueritiae rudimentis modestia, prudentia, humanitate, gratia, litteris ornatissimus semper officio locoque, quem retinebat, superior uidebatur altis humilibusque iuxta acceptus. So-

---

47 Blockley 1975, 160.
48 On imperial speeches in Ammianus cf. De Bonfils 1986, 29–32 – 30–31 on Valentinian's speech.
49 On *studia humanitatis* cf. above, pp. 57–59; 61; 90; 166–167.
50 On Ausonius and Gratian cf. below, pp. 269–273.

lusque paene omnium erat, cuius linguam non infrenem, sed dispicientem, quae loqueretur, nullius claudebat periculi metus. (29.1.8)

And while they were in doubt who there was at that time that was superior to all in strength of character, it seemed to them that Theodorus surpassed all others; he had already gained second rank among the secretaries, and was in fact such a man as they thought him. For he was born of a clan famous in olden times in Gaul, liberally educated from earliest childhood, and so eminent for his modesty, good sense, refinement (*humanitate*), charm, and learning that he always seemed superior to every office and rank that he was holding, and was dear alike to high and low. He was also almost the only man whose mouth was closed by no fear of danger, since he bridled his tongue and reflected on what he was going to say. (trans. Rolfe 1986)

This passage is telling in several respects. To begin with, *humanitas* is placed in the middle of a list of values which includes *modestia* and *prudentia* on the one hand and *gratia* and *litteris* on the other. We have already seen that Ammianus associated *modestia* with *humanitas*, and that it basically stands for restraint.[51] The case of *prudentia* is a little more complex. More than once Cicero defines it as "that which allows us to distinguish good from evil."[52] And Hellegouarc'h rightly notices that while in the professional sphere *prudentia* refers to the ability, derived from experience and study, to do a job, in politics it evokes practical experience as opposed to theory.[53] He thus concludes, following Cicero, that *prudentia* is a fundamental virtue for any statesman.[54] *Gratia* is even more polysemic. In the Republican age, it can refer to the esteem, respect and influence of the statesman, but more broadly it is associated with the idea of friendship.[55] Since *litteris* is self-explanatory, Brandt's comment – albeit interpreted in a different way from his – seems particularly apt to describe the bridging role of *humanitas* in this context:

Berücksichtigt man die Wortstellung – *humanitas* steht zwischen *prudentia* und *gratia*, verbindet also sozusagen den dianoethischen Bereich (*prudentia*) mit dem ethischen (*gratia* bei dem Mitmenschen als Resultat charakterlicher Liebenswürdigkeit) – dann wird klar, daß der Ausdruck hier etwas wie geistig-moralische Bildung bezeichnet.[56]

---

51 Cf. above, pp. 230–231.
52 Cf. *Inu. rhet.* 2.160; *Nat. D.* 3.38, and Hellegouarc'h 1963, 256 n. 10 for further references.
53 Hellegouarc'h 1963, 257. Cf. Hellegouarc'h 1963, 257 nn. 3 and 5 for references to ancient passages.
54 Cf. Hellegouarc'h 1963, 257 n. 8 for the Ciceronian passages corroborating this statement. More on *prudentia* in Ammianus in Brandt 1999, 108–119.
55 Cf. Hellegouarc'h 1963, 204–206.
56 Brandt 1999, 134 n. 75.

In other words, we face here one of those cases where the boundary between the παιδεία- and the φιλανθρωπία-meaning of *humanitas* is particularly fluid, so much so that it becomes hard to say which one prevails over the other. In fact, while the proximity of expressions such as *liberaliter educatus, prudentia* and *litteris ornatissimus* incline us toward the educational aspect,[57] the association of *humanitas* with *modestia* and *gratia ornatissimus* as well as the fact that people belonging to both the higher and the lower classes of Roman society liked Theodorus (*altis humilibusque iuxta acceptus*) rather stress its philanthropic connotation.[58] What is certain, however, is that, in Ammianus' view, a good emperor should possess both cultural and moral qualities, hence his admiration for Theodorus: *uisus est aliis excellere Theodorus . . . . Et erat re uera ita ut opinati sunt.* Hence, also, Ammianus' dislike of Valens, who not only lacked these qualities, but even killed someone who did possess them and could therefore have been a better ruler than himself, Theodorus.

So much for the role of *humanitas*-education with regard to rulers. Let me now turn to the second question posed by 27.12.9, 30.8.4 and 31.4.12, that is to say, the relationship between *humanitas* and foreigners in Ammianus' work. The passages just referred to show that Roman *humanitas* can be expected from and accorded to barbarians. The close of Book 18, however, portrays a different situation, for this time Ammianus presents the Persian king Shapur as displaying *humanitas* during the siege of Nisibis:

> Inuentas tamen alias quoque uirgines Christiano ritu cultui diuino sacratas custodiri intactas et religioni seruire solito more nullo uetante praecepit lenitudinem profecto in tempore simulans, ut omnes, quos antehac diritate crudelitateque terrebat, sponte sua metu remoto uenirent exemplis recentibus docti humanitate eum et moribus iam placidis magnitudinem temperasse fortunae. (18.10.4)

> Yet finding that there were others also who were maidens and consecrated to divine service according to the Christian custom, he ordered that they be kept uninjured and allowed to practise their religion in their wonted manner without any opposition; thus he made a pretence of mildness for the time, to the end that all whom he had heretofore terrified by his harshness and cruelty might lay aside their fear and come to him of their own volition, when they learned from recent instances that he now tempered the greatness of his fortune with *humanitas* and gracious deportment. (trans. Rolfe 1935)

---

57 On the other hand, it must be stressed that *prudentia* in Ammianus can also be independent of education: cf. 14.6.1 with Brandt 1999, 112.

58 In view of this, it is not clear why Brandt 1999, 134 and n. 75 endeavours to prove that at 29.1.8 the idea of *humanitas* as *Bildung* is almost exclusive. In speaking of a 'geistig-moralische Bildung' in fact, he inevitably links the idea of education expressed by *Bildung* to the moral aspects (*moralische*) well epitomised by the φιλανθρωπία component of *humanitas*.

From a linguistic perspective, *humanitas* is opposed here to *diritas* (frightfulness) and *crudelitas* (cruelty). *Diritas* appears eleven times in Ammianus, but is generally a rare occurrence in classical Latin literature. This explains why we have no instance of *humanitas* being paired with that term. In contrast, *crudelitas* is far more common, and also appears elsewhere in opposition to *humanitas*, as we have already seen.[59]

Yet the most interesting aspect of *humanitas* in this passage is that, alongside the instance of 30.8.4 discussed above, it brings into play the status of the Persians: worst of the barbarians or forefathers of the Graeco-Roman cultural tradition? Scholarship is divided on this question, and the analysis of these two passages cannot hope to solve the problem once and for all.[60] All it can do is suggest a new point of view from which to address this issue, the diachronic perspective. The two Persian kings to whom Ammianus attributes *humanitas* belong in fact to two different epochs: Shapur, a 'suitable' rival of Constantius in the recent and inglorious past, and Artaxerxes in a more remote and idealised age. This difference is reflected in their opposite level of *humanitas*: while at 18.10.4 Shapur's *humanitas* is only feigned, as is clear from the phrase *lenitudinem . . . simulans*, at 30.8.4 Artaxerxes is even regarded as an *exemplum* of *humanitas*. Regarding the latter, by saying that this Artaxerxes was surnamed 'long-handed' (*Macrochir*), Ammianus makes it clear that he is referring to Artaxerxes I, the fifth king of Persia, who reigned from 465 BCE to 424 BCE. Despite the doubts raised by De Romilly, Plutarch records at the very opening of the *Life* of Artaxerxes' grandson, Artaxerxes II 'Mindful', that he was famous in antiquity for his mildness of character and clemency: Ὁ μὲν πρῶτος Ἀρτοξέρξης, τῶν ἐν Πέρσαις βασιλέων πρᾳότητι καὶ μεγαλοψυχίᾳ πρωτεύσας, Μακρόχειρ ἐπεκαλεῖτο, τὴν δεξιὰν μείζονα τῆς ἑτέρας ἔχων, Ξέρξου δ' ἦν υἱός (1.1: "The first Artaxerxes, preëminent among the kings of

---

59 Cf. above, pp. 195–196.

60 Cf. *e.g.* Drijvers 1999, 176: "For the Romans Parthia was an *alter orbis*. This other world represented eveything which was not Roman [. . .] This barbarian is portrayed as the negative embodiment of Graeco-Roman values and ideals, where social life fails to comply with the norms of Graeco-Roman society", and the opposite opinion of Matthews 1989, 140, who commented upon Julian's Persian campaign by saying that this "was a journey to the origins of civilisation itself, to a land of ancient culture fully equal in material resources and complexity of social organisation to the Classical Near East of Ammianus' birth and upbringing. [. . .] For Ammianus, Mesopotamia was in a sense the natural extension of the Classical world." It is perhaps worth specifying that Parthia and Persia are often (mis)used as synonyms, as made clear by Drijvers 1999, 177: "One aspect of Rome's ideology of Parthia is that no distinction is made between Medes, Persians, Parthians and other orientals." As a result, modern scholars often pick the name they prefer, without paying too much attention to the differences, which are particularly relevant in chronological terms.

Persia for gentleness and magnanimity, was surnamed Longimanus, because his right hand was longer than his left, and was the son of Xerxes", trans. Perrin 1926).[61] The term φιλανθρωπία does not appear in this passage, but, alongside it and ἐπιείκεια, πραότης is one of the aptest Greek words to denote the idea of mildness ('douceur'), as De Romilly has shown.[62] Moreover, in the case of Plutarch, πραότης often appears together with φιλανθρωπία.[63] Plutarch's attestation therefore confirms the paradigmatic character of Artaxerxes I's behaviour, and explains why Ammianus also attributed to a Persian king a value which is usually the prerogative of Romans or, at most, of Greeks. The same does not hold for the almost contemporary Shapur, although his simulated *humanitas* ultimately puts him on the same level as his Roman counterpart(s). In other words, when it comes to *humanitas* Ammianus fixes chronological rather than ethnic boundaries. Here as elsewhere in Ammianus, the so-called practice of the *laudatio temporis acti* shines through, and, aside from very few exceptions, statesmen and rulers, whether they are Roman or not, can hardly equal the (moral) values of their ancestors. In this respect, the two Roman digressions are particularly significant, as we will see shortly.

Both the cases of Shapur and Valens also spotlight Ammianus' treatment of the dangers in feigning *humanitas*. In this respect, a case in point is 29.6.5: some time during his reign, Valentinian decided to fortify the Danubian borders in the land of the Quadi, who quite expectedly did not appreciate this policy. Works proceeded slowly at first, but things changed when Marcellianus was put in command in that area. In particular, to crush any forms of opposition, Marcellianus traitorously killed the Quadi's king Gabinius, "the only savage who is credited with moderation" in Ammianus' work:[64]

> Denique Gabinium regem, ne quid nouaretur, modeste poscentem, ut assensurus humanitate simulata cum aliis ad conuiuium corrogauit, quem digredientem post epulas hospitalis officii sanctitate nefarie uiolata trucidari securum fecit.

> Finally, when king Gabinius mildly asked that no new step should be taken, he pretended that he would assent, and with feigned *humanitas* invited the king with others to a banquet. But as Gabinius was departing after the feast and suspected no treachery, Marcellianus, with abominable violation of the sacred duties of hospitality, had him murdered. (trans. Rolfe 1986)

---

61 De Romilly 2011², 286 n. 2.
62 De Romilly 2011², 37; *passim.* Cfr. also Della Calce 2023, 21–23.
63 Cf. De Romilly 2011², 278 and n. 2.
64 Seager 1986, 68.

Displaying all his contempt for Marcellianus' behaviour, Ammianus openly speaks of *simulata humanitate*, an expression which cannot be found elsewhere in previous Latin literature. Ammianus evidently represents deceit as a vice that is traditionally attributed to foreigners, but that Roman commanders should always avoid. The teaching of Livy's *Ab Vrbe condita* is echoed here. Yet the situation is even worse, for not only does Marcellianus resort to deceit, but he even violates a kind of sacred law of the ancient world, that of hospitality.[65] This latter ideal is clearly linked to *humanitas* in the passage under investigation, but, as usual, the polysemy of *humanitas* transcends the mere meaning of *hospitalitas*. In fact, if we look at the previous paragraph (29.6.4), we find that Marcellianus' nature is characterised by haughtiness through the expression *intempestiue turgens*, which evokes the same idea as *superbia*: as we have seen, *superbia* can be used, together with the rare *inhumanitas*, to denote the opposite of *humanitas*.[66] Accordingly, in simulating *humanitas* Marcellianus is not only displaying his faked sense of hospitality, but he is also endeavouring to hide his arrogant, haughty nature.

The same idea of feigned *humanitas* is expressed through the expression *species humanitatis*, which we have already encountered in Gellius' conceptualisation of *humanitas*.[67] I remarked on that occasion that this phrase is rare in Latin literature, but Ammianus is the exception to the rule, for two out of 17 occurrences of *humanitas* in his work are preceded by *species*. The first instance is at 25.8.1. About the first half of Book 25 tells of Julian's last days of life during the Persian campaign, but from 25.5 onwards the new emperor Jovian becomes the unfortunate protagonist of the events. As this war is turning into a nightmare for the Romans, Jovian, fearing that he might be deposed, accepts peace terms that Ammianus regards as dishonourable.[68] As well as saying *Quibus exitiale aliud accessit et impium* (25.7.12: "To these conditions there was added another which was destructive and impious", trans. Rolfe 1940), the historian begins section 25.8 by speaking of *pax specie humanitatis indulta* ("the peace granted under pretence of *humanitas*", trans. Rolfe 1940, slightly adapted), thereby echoing the content of the speech (indirectly referred by Ammianus) of the Persian ambassadors at 25.7.6: *Condiciones autem ferebant difficiles et perplexas fingentes humanorum respectu reliquias exercitus redire sinere clementissimum regem, si, quae iubet, impleuerit cum primatibus Caesar* ("Nevertheless, they offered conditions which were difficult and involved, for they pretended that, with respect to human prin-

---

65 On hospitality as a cornerstone of (Roman) civilization cf. above, pp. 16 and 126.
66 Cf. above, pp. 44–45.
67 Cf. above, pp. 162–163.
68 For the sake of clarity, this is the same peace agreement I have already mentioned when analysing Valens' *humanitas* towards barbarians at 27.12.9.

ciples, the most merciful of kings would allow the remnants of the army to return, if the emperor and his most distinguished generals would comply with his demands", trans. Rolfe 1940, adapted). The idea of simulation is expressed by *specie* at 25.8.1 and by *fingentes* at 25.7.6, whereas *humanitatis* recalls, etymologically at least, *humanorum respectu*. But 25.7.6 also makes a connection between *humanorum respectu* and the idea of clemency (*clementissimum regem*). In this context, the expression *specie humanitatis* is likely to express the same idea of simulated clemency.[69] After all, Ammianus speaks of *pax indulta*, where the participle of *indulgeo* ('to grant as a favour, concede', but also 'to be lenient') implies superiority on the part of those who concede peace, and we know that *clementia* is more apt a noun than *humanitas* to evoke a unilateral, downward relationship between people of higher and people of lower rank or condition. From a more rhetorical standpoint then, although Ammianus concedes that this further case of feigned *humanitas* is not literally associated with Jovian, we once again get the sense that in his view *humanitas*, especially when it is linked to emperors, has too many obscure sides for it to be ascribed to a model emperor like Julian.

The second instance of *species humanitatis* can be found towards the epilogue of the *Res Gestae*, at 31.5.7. We are on the threshold of the battle of Hadrianople, and the Thuringii, driven by hunger and lack of means, and mistreated by the Romans, rebel against Valens. The scenario is as follows: while the Goth kings Alavivus and Fritigernus are banqueting together with some Roman officials at Marcianopolis (Thracia), some barbarians try to enter the city in search of food, but are warded off. A bloody riot ensues, leading the Roman Lupicinus to slaughter the guards who are awaiting Alavivus and Fritigernus. As the news reaches the Goths who are by then besieging the city, the situation risks taking a turn for the worse, but Fritigernus comes up with a cunning idea:

> Vtque erat Fritigernus expediti consilii, ueritus, ne teneretur obsidis uice cum ceteris, exclamauit grauiore pugnandum exitio, ni ipse ad leniendum uulgus sineretur exire cum sociis, quod arbitratum humanitatis specie ductores suos occisos in tumultum exarsit. Hocque impetrato egressi omnes exceptique cum plausu et gaudiis ascensis equis volarunt moturi incitamenta diuersa bellorum.

> And since Fritigern was quickwitted and feared that he might be held with the rest as a hostage, he cried out that they would have to fight with heavy loss of life, unless he himself were allowed to go out with his companions to quiet the people, who, believing that their leaders had been slain under pretence of friendly entertainment (*humanitatis specie*), had blazed out into turbulence. And when this request was granted, they all departed. They

---

69 The phrase *clementiae specie* (ablative) is used by Cicero, for instance, with reference to Julius Caesar's despotic power at *Phil.* 2.116, on which cf. Angel 2008, 119–120.

were received with applause and rejoicing, and mounting horses hastened away, to set in motion the various incitements that lead to wars. (trans. Rolfe 1986)

The connotations of this occurrence of *species humanitatis* are significantly different from the previous case: here the ideas of courtesy and hospitality seem to prevail over the notion of clemency. However, what is interesting about this passage is that it represents another Ammianean instance of feigned or missed *humanitas* in the relationship between Romans and barbarians. This is actually only a potential instance of simulation on the Romans' part: indeed, it rather reveals Fritigernus' than the Romans' predisposition to treachery. Ammianus' narration nowhere suggests that the Romans had invited the Goth kings to the banquet with the intent of ambushing them, nor do we know if an ambush would have actually taken place had Fritigernus not come up with his idea. In any case, there is no denying that, on the surface at least, this passage also highlights the extent to which Ammianus liked to allude to the infidelity of some Roman officials or emperors.

To recap, we have so far seen how Ammianus uses the word *humanitas*, both in its educational and above all philanthropic dimensions, in relation to emperors or other powerful men. We have also noticed that Ammianus often uses it when he describes the relationship between Romans and non-Romans, one of the clearest contexts in which it emerges that *humanitas* can be feigned.

Three no less interesting fields in which *humanitas* appears are yet to be investigated: *humanitas* in the two excursuses on Rome, *humanitas* with regard to women, and *humanitas* and astrologers. To some degree, in all these cases Ammianus continues to articulate the opposition between civilization and barbarism. Let me procede in order.

Towards the conclusion of his study, Seager claims:

> If any one element deserves to be singled out as fundamental to Ammianus's perception of men and events, it is perhaps the antithesis between civilization and barbarism. [. . .] Ammianus saw barbarism in all its manifestations, both external and internal, as the ultimate threat to the Roman way of life.[70]

We might add that Ammianus' use of *humanitas* helps him articulate the notion that the lack of civilization is key to understanding Roman society, for the numerous cases we have already observed ultimately show that, when they lack *humanitas*, the Romans are on the same – low – level as barbarians. In this respect, despite the completely different socio-cultural context, the parallel with Cicero's un-

---

[70] Seager 1986, 131. Cf. also Seager 1986, 68. The numerous acts of violence disseminated across Ammianus' work also account for this opposition between civilization and barbarism: cf. Zugravu 2018, 349.

derstanding and political use of *humanitas* is striking.[71] Ammianus' two 'Roman digressions', and his use of *humanitas* therein, represent the litmus test: if even Rome is no longer the 'abode of all virtues' (*uirtutum omnium domicilium*) and her aristocracy no longer lives up to their duties, then it is unsurprising that the empire as a whole is degenerating. Compare 14.6.21:

> Illud autem non dubitatur, quod cum esset aliquando uirtutum omnium domicilium Roma ingenuos aduenas plerique nobilium ut Homerici bacarum suauitate Lotophagi humanitatis multiformibus officiis retentabant.

> Furthermore, there is no doubt that when once upon a time Rome was the abode of all the virtues, many of the nobles detained here foreigners of free birth by many kindly attentions (*humanitatis multiformibus officiis*), as the Lotus-eaters of Homer did by the sweetness of their fruits. (trans. Rolfe 1935)

When reading a passage like this, it is easy for scholars to claim that Ammianus betrays his rancour towards Rome here, for he would be among the foreigners who were expelled during the famine of 383 or 384 CE mentioned at 14.6.19. Yet this, together with the notion that Ammianus would be treated badly by the citizens of the *Vrbs* during his stay there, is pure speculation.[72] What is certain from this and other passages, however, is that Ammianus believes Rome to have been the guiding light for the entire ancient world as long as virtues were cultivated: *humanitas* must have played a key role among or in addition to these virtues. In this sense, it is hard to tell exactly what Ammianus means by the expression *humanitatis multiformibus officiis*. We saw in the Suetonius section that the twinning of *humanitas* and *officium* is rather common, and in that very passage *iura omnia offici humanitatisque* stands for 'all the laws of obligation and humanity'. Yet here, significantly, *humanitas* is not on the same level as *officia*, but depends on it. An analogous construction can be found in Quintilian's *Institutio oratoria*:

> Frequentabunt uero eius [*scil.* oratoris] domum optimi iuuenes more ueterum et uere dicendi uiam uelut ex oraculo petent. Hos ille formabit quasi eloquentiae parens, et ut uetus gubernator litora et portus et quae tempestatium signa, quid secundis flatibus quid aduersis

---

71 On Cicero's political use of *humanitas* cf. above, pp. 52–54.
72 On the extent of the autobiographical character of Ammianus' attitude towards Rome cf. the sceptical Kelly 2008, 132–135; 141, who denies that the historian was among those who had been expelled. Also Momigliano 1974, 1396, while remarking that the two Roman excursuses presume Ammianus' good knowledge of Rome, is hesitant to admit his expulsion from the city. Further support to this theory is brought by Rees 1999, who shows the affinities between Ammianus' Roman digressions and Juvenal's *Satires*. Cf. also Den Hengst 2007, 167–177; Matacotta 2010, 303–304. By contrast, Thompson 1947, 14; Matthews 1989, 13; Sogno 2006, 33 are more inclined to admit Ammianus' personal involvement in the events and his expulsion from the City.

ratio poscat docebit, non humanitatis solum communi ductus officio, sed amore quodam ope-
ris: nemo enim minui uelit id in quo maximus fuit. Quid porro est honestius quam docere
quod optime scias? (12.11.5–6)

Promising young men will frequent his house, as in the old days, and learn the road to true
oratory from him as from an oracle. The father of eloquence will educate them, and, like a
veteran pilot, teach them the coasts and the harbours and the signs of the weather, what
reason prescribes when the wind is fair and what when it is contrary. His motive will be
not only the common duty of *humanitas*, but a love of the work, for no one likes to see the
field diminished in which he was once supreme. And what occupation is more honourable
than teaching what you know best? (trans. Russell 2001)

In Ammianus' passage *humanitas* is probably differently nuanced, because the
hospitable aspect largely prevails over the educational one which shines through
Quintilian's text. Yet in both these cases the philanthropic component is there,
and I would suggest that *officium humanitatis* is comparable to *ius humanitatis*, in
that they both evoke the idea that *humanitas* is an obligation towards fellow
human beings. In Ammianus, moreover, the Homeric similitude seems to suggest
that in Rome's early history *humanitas* used to result in something particularly
pleasant and appealing (cf. *bacarum suauitate*), but also multifarious (*multiformibus officiis*). In other words, the versatility of the term *humanitas* would be reflected in the multiple ways it could be performed.

Moreover, as in other passages we have already encountered, within this context of hospitality *humanitas* serves to measure the level of civilization of a given
people, namely the Romans, the only one for which this ideal should be taken for
granted. In addition, given Rome's duty (*officium*) to impose 'civilization' on the
world, it goes without saying that the most appropriate situation in which to display *humanitas* is towards non-Romans, as in this case. Yet Ammianus later laments that this noble Roman custom belongs to the past: *Nunc uero inanes flatus
quorundam uile esse, quidquid extra urbis pomerium nascitur, aestimant praeter
orbos et caelibes nec credi potest, qua obsequiorum diuersitate coluntur homines
sine liberis Romae* (14.6.22: "But now the vain arrogance of some men regards everything born outside the pomerium of our city as worthless, except the childless
and unwedded; and it is beyond belief with what various kinds of obsequiousness
men without children are courted at Rome", trans. Rolfe 1935). The pessimistic
message aside, it is also worth noting here that *flatus* recalls the idea of haughtiness traditionally opposed to *humanitas*.[73]

In the second Roman digression (Book 28), Ammianus uses the term *humanitas* to stigmatise the way in which the Roman notion of civilization is understood

---

73 Cf. also above in this section, p. 245.

by the inhabitants of Rome. Here Ammianus appears to argue – rather polemically – that their understanding of culture is determined by trivial matters such as the baths that they frequent, the kind of water they use or the house in which they live:

> Ex his quidam, cum salutari pectoribus oppositis coeperunt, osculanda capita in modum taurorum minacium obliquantes adulatoribus offerunt genua sauianda uel manus id illis sufficere ad beate uiuendum existimantes et abundare omni cultu humanitatis peregrinum putantes, cuius forte etiam gratia sunt obligati, interrogatum, quibus thermis utatur aut aquis aut ad quam successerit domum. (28.4.10)

> Some of these men, when one begins to salute them breast to breast, like menacing bulls turn to one side their heads, where they should be kissed, and offer their flatterers their knees to kiss or their hands, thinking that quite enough to ensure them a happy life; and they believe that a stranger is given an abundance of all the duties of *humanitas*, even though the great men may perhaps be under obligation to him, if he is asked what hot baths or waters he uses, or at what house he has been put up. (trans. Rolfe 1986)

In view of this passage, it appears clear that Ammianus' Rome is again (or still?) threatened by the risks of 'Roman civilization' under the slogan of *humanitas*, as denounced by Tacitus in *Agricola* 21.[74] In particular, the baths – as a breeding ground for corruption and vice – are the common denominator between the two texts.[75] But we have gone one step further here, because Ammianus implies that baths have now become a diagnostic factor in establishing who possesses or does not possess *humanitas*.[76] Or, to put it another way, baths represent an element of inclusion or exclusion within the city of Rome's community, and, by extension, of the very idea of Romanness. Whether you are a Roman or not, Ammianus seems to imply, what counts is that you can talk at length about baths and thermal waters, and Rome's nobility will welcome you into their elitist community. Given the general context of the passage and the expression *cultu humanitatis*, Ammianus is clearly thinking of *humanitas* in the broader terms of civilization rather than as mere kindness. We have already noticed the same connection between *cultus* and *humanitas* in the case of Valens' attitude towards the Armenian Papa.[77] While here the link is even closer because of the dependence of the genitive *humanitatis* on *cultus*, it is clear that in both cases *humanitas* takes on a strong educational and

---

74 On Tacitus' *Agr.* 21 cf. above, pp. 118–124.

75 Cf. Tac. *Agr.* 21: *paulatimque discessum ad delenimenta uitiorum, porticus et balinea et con-uiuiorum elegantiam.* On this passage cf. above, pp. 122–123.

76 A similar idea can be found with reference to Neronian Rome in Seneca's *Epist.* 86, but without the term *humanitas* appearing there: cf. Rimell 2013.

77 Cf. above, pp. 235–236.

cultural component. The passage also hints again at the idea of feigned *humanitas*, implying that foreigners can simulate *humanitas* by simply showing off their knowledge of the refinements of baths. It also implies that the notion of *humanitas* is now founded upon trivial non-values, and reiterates the concept that when they lack or feign *humanitas*, Romans and non-Romans, whether they are barbarians or simple foreigners, are similarly uncultured. As Seager has emphasised, when it comes to possessing or not possessing virtues, there is one major difference between Romans and non-Romans: the Romans alone are reprimanded by Ammianus for lacking these values.[78] This is also the case in Ammianus' use of *humanitas*: the Romans should be culturally, historically, even naturally perhaps, bound up with this ideal. Valentinian's obituary, as we have seen, is a case in point.[79]

Judging from the two excursuses on Rome and from Ammianus' use of *humanitas* within them, Rome therefore emerges as the mirror of an empire in which fundamental values (education, culture, hospitality, clemency, all of which can also fall under the category of *humanitas*) are about to collapse, and this decline in turn explains the political troubles of the Empire. In other words, the decline of *humanitas* is used here to explain why the Roman empire is undergoing a decline which culminates in the defeat of Hadrianople. Some exceptions to this value crisis clearly existed, such as the case of the prefect of the city of Rome Olybrius, another protagonist of the second Roman digression. Thanks to this prefect, the opening of this section bodes well, although the digression soon turns into a list of the vices which affected Rome's nobility and plebs. Ammianus says of him:

> Diu multumque a negotiis discussus urbanis adigente cumulo foris gestorum ad ea strictim exsequenda regrediar exorsus ab Olybrii praefectura tranquilla nimis et leni, qui numquam ab humanitatis statu deiectus sollicitus erat et anxius, ne quid usquam factum eius asperum inueniretur aut dictum, calumniarum acerrimus insectator, fisci lucra, unde poterat, circumcidens, iustorum iniustorumque distinctor et arbiter plenus in subiectos admodum temperatus. (28.4.1)

> After long lasting and serious dispersion from affairs in Rome, constrained by the great mass of foreign events, I shall return to a brief account of these, beginning with the prefecture of Olybrius, which was exceedingly peaceful and mild; for he never allowed himself to be turned from humane conduct (*ab humanitatis statu*), but was careful and anxious that no word or act of his should ever be found harsh. He severely punished calumny, cut down the profits of the privy-purse wherever it was possible, fully and impartially distinguished justice from injustice, and showed himself most lenient towards those whom he governed. (trans. Rolfe 1986)

---

78 Seager 1986, 21; 68.
79 Cf. above, p. 236.

Olybrius' prefecture (369–370 CE) is regarded as extremely tranquil (*ab . . . praefectura tranquilla nimis et leni*) for the very reason that he never abandoned the path of *humanitas*. *Humanitas* is conceived here as human benevolence towards others, mainly subordinates. But it is also interesting that in this case *humanitas* is treated as a permanent condition (*statu*) of its possessor, a condition which quite exceptionally was neither affected by the climate of moral decadence nor by Olybrius' own vices. In particular, Olybrius had one major vice – he devoted all his private life to luxury – but this did not have any repercussions on public life (cf. 28.4.3).[80] Unfortunately for Rome, the same cannot be said of his successor Ampelius, whose behaviour and policy induce Ammianus to claim:

> Quae probra aliaque his maiora dissimulatione iugi neglecta ita effrenatius exarserunt, ut nec Epimenides ille Cretensis, si fabularum ritu ab inferis excitatus redisset ad nostra, solus purgare sufficeret Romam; tanta plerosque labes insanabilium flagitiorum oppressit. (28.4.5)

> These shameful acts, and others worse than these, had, by being constantly overlooked, blazed up to such unbridled heights that not even that celebrated Cretan Epimenides, if, after the manner of myth, he had been called up from the lower world and returned to our times, would have been able single-handed to purify Rome; such was the stain of incurable sins that had overwhelmed most people. (trans. Rolfe 1986)

With these biting comments on the moral condition of Roman society, we can conclude our brief survey on *humanitas* in Ammianus' digressions on Rome, and focus our attention on the extant opening of the *Res Gestae*, Book 14.1. More specifically, I would like to explore one of the episodes of what Wieber-Scariot aptly calls the 'Gallus-Constantina-Tragödie', referring to Ammianus' presentation of Constantina as an antiheroine in the narration of a story that recalls classical tragedies.[81] For Ammianus, the wife of the Caesar Constantius Gallus, Constantina, was the antimodel of the Roman *matrona*, as we see from the very beginning of Book 14, where Ammianus first tells of Gallus' cruelty, and then adds:[82]

> Cuius [*scil.* Galli] acerbitati uxor graue accesserat incentiuum germanitate Augusti turgida supra modum, quam Hanniballiano regi fratris filio antehac Constantinus iunxerat pater, Megaera quaedam mortalis, inflammatrix saeuientis assidua, humani cruoris auida nihil mitius quam maritus. (14.1.2)

---

80 More generally on the virtues and vices of the prefects of Rome cf. Drexler 1974, 13–18.
81 Wieber-Scariot 1999, 76 and *passim*.
82 For an in-depth study of Constantina's negative role in the *Res Gestae* cf. Wieber-Scariot 1999, 74–195. On her and his husband's negative portraits in Ammianus cf. also Barnes 1998, 120–121 and 129–132.

> To his cruelty his wife was besides a serious incentive, a woman beyond measure presumptuous because of her kinship to the emperor, and previously joined in marriage by her father Constantine with his brother's son, King Hanniballianus. She, a Megaera in mortal guise, constantly aroused the savagery of Gallus, being as insatiable as he in her thirst for human blood. (trans. Rolfe 1935)

Among the crimes they are accused of, the indiscriminate condemnation of citizens takes pride of place. Under their domination even whistleblowers were superfluous: the Caesar and his wife were not concerned with keeping up appearances, and many people were put to death in total non-compliance with human and divine laws (14.1.4–5). They wanted to be aware of everything happening and went so far as to send out malicious men to collect intelligence in every corner of Antioch (14.1.6). As Ammianus makes it clear, Constantina's role in all this was decisive:

> Adolescebat autem obstinatum propositum erga haec et similia multa scrutandi stimulos admouente regina, quae abrupte mariti fortunas trudebat in exitium praeceps, cum eum potius lenitate feminea ad ueritatis humanitatisque uiam reducere utilia suadendo deberet. (14.1.8)

> Moreover, his fixed purpose of ferreting out these and many similar things increased, spurred on by the queen, who pushed her husband's fortunes headlong to sheer ruin, when she ought rather, with womanly gentleness, to have recalled him by helpful counsel to the path of truth and *humanitas*. (trans. Rolfe 1935)

Instead of bringing her husband back to the path of truth and *humanitas* thanks to her presumed womanly mildness, Constantina even encouraged him in his faults. What is interesting about this passage is the unique triangular relationship between *lenitas*, *humanitas* and *ueritas*. Despite the potential connections of their meanings, *lenitas* ('mildness, gentleness, clemency') and *humanitas* rarely appear together, although they do in Ciceronian texts.[83] Their relation to *ueritas* is less clear, probably because the very meaning of *ueritas* in this context is ambiguous: we do not know whether Ammianus uses *ueritas* to allude to the fact that Gallus should respect the truthfulness of the events instead of inventing charges and condemning at will, or if he uses *ueritas* to evoke the 'adherence to standards of honesty, uprightness, sincerity' that should characterise a good ruler.[84] Since *ueritas* ought to be a consequence of *lenitas*, the second option is probably preferable, although the context also allows for the first possibility. The noun *ueritas* in fact, like *humanitas*, can have multiple meanings, a polysemy which opens up

---

[83] Cf. *De or.* 2.212 (with regard to the tone of orations) and *Fam.* 13.1.4. But cf. above in this section the case of Artaxerses, where *lenitas* can be seen as a sort of halfway point between *humanitas* and *temperantia.*
[84] Cf. *OLD* s.v. *ueritas.*

two possible interpretations. Conversely, *humanitas* appears to be less polysemic than in most other situations, and the deciding factor is again the presence of *lenitas*, which clearly involves ethics, that is, a philanthropic feeling, rather than education. Ammianus blames Constantina for her lack of *lenitas*, a virtue that women usually possess (*feminea*), in the same way as he blames those powerful, Roman men who do not possess *humanitas* and other virtues. Moreover, if later on in his oeuvre the laudatory portrait of the only other woman to be described at length, Constantius' second wife Eusebia, counterbalances the situation, Ammianus had already reminded the reader (while speaking of Constantina) that virtuous empresses had existed and had mitigated the crimes of their husbands: *cum eum potius lenitate feminea ad ueritatis humanitatisque uiam reducere utilia suadendo deberet, ut in Gordianorum actibus factitasse Maximini truculenti illius imperatoris rettulimus coniugem* (14.1.8: "when she ought rather, with womanly gentleness, to have recalled him by helpful counsel to the path of truth and *humanitas*, after the manner of the wife of that savage emperor Maximinus, as we have related in our account of the acts of the Gordians", trans. Rolfe 1935).[85]

Finally, let us look at *humanitas* in regard to astrologers (with, in the background, once again the emperor Valens). The protagonist is actually only one astrologer (*mathematicus*), a certain Heliodorus. What is striking about this figure is the fact that the royal court and Ammianus display opposite attitudes towards him: while Valens and his courtiers love him, Ammianus repeatedly expresses his contempt.[86] His main argument is that Heliodorus' official role at court was to predict the future, but in practice this turned into inventing accusations against whomever the emperor disliked. The question is, what benefits did he gain from such a behaviour? Ammianus is clear:

> Inter fragores tot ruinarum Heliodorus, tartareus ille malorum omnium cum Palladio fabricator, mathematicus, ut memorat uulgus, colloquiis ex aula regia praepigneratus abstrusis iam funebres aculeos exsertabat omni humanitatis inuitamento ad prodenda, quae sciret uel fingeret, lacessitus. Nam et sollicitius cibo mundissimo fouebatur et ad largiendum pelicibus merebat aes collaticium graue. (29.2.6–7)

> Amid the crash of so many ruins Heliodorus, that hellish contriver with Palladius of all evils, being a mathematician (in the parlance of the vulgar) and pledged by secret instructions from the imperial court, after he had been cajoled by every enticement of *humanitas* to induce him to reveal what he knew or could invent, how put forth his deadly stings. For he was most solicitously pampered with the choicest foods, and earned a great amount of contributed money for presents to his concubines. (trans. Rolfe 1986)

---

85 On the positive role of Eusebia in Ammianus' *Res Gestae* cf. Wieber-Scariot 1999, 197–284.
86 On Ammianus' bad attitude towards Heliodorus cf. *e.g.* 29.2.9.

Omni humanitatis inuitamento: all the seductions of *humanitas* which the emperor could offer him induced Heliodorus to play his dirty role. But what does *humanitas* mean in this context? Brandt is rather oblique in this respect, and generally alludes to *Gastfreundlichkeit*, hospitality.[87] This idea is clearly implied, but the explicit reference to refined food (*cibo mundissimo*) suggests that the interpretation can be pushed a little further. Although the association of *humanitas* and *inuitamentum* does not occur elsewhere in classical Latin, a passage in Petronius' *Satyrica* has something close to it:

> Non recessit tamen miles, sed eadem exhortatione temptauit dare mulierculae cibum, donec ancilla uini odore corrupta primum ipsa porrexit ad humanitatem inuitantis uictam manum, deinde refecta potione et cibo expugnare dominae pertinaciam coepit et "quid proderit" inquit "hoc tibi, si soluta inedia fueris, si te uiuam sepelieris, si antequam fata poscant, indemnatum spiritum effuderis? (*Sat.* 111.10–11)

> Still the soldier did not withdraw, but with the same encouragement tried to press some food on her servant, until the maid was seduced by the fragrance of the wine. She first extended her own hand, overcome by the *humanitas* of the invitation, and once she was refreshed by the drink and food, began to lay siege to her mistress' obstinacy, and said: "What will this benefit you, if you faint from hunger, if you bury yourself alive, if you breathe out your innocent life before the Fates summon it?" (trans. Schmeling 2020)

In the story of the widow of Ephesus,[88] the reaction of the widow's handmaid to the soldier's offer of wine and food is of particular interest for this study: as with the case of Heliodorus, here too there is a close relation between food, *humanitas* and the idea of seducing through food (*inuitantis*).[89] Commenting on this instance of *humanitas* at *Satyrica* 111, Høgel says: "This may be a rhetorical manner of expression,

---

87 Brandt 1999, 136 n. 88 and 137.
88 Here is the account of the story according to Colton 1975, 35: "An Ephesian matron, famous for her chastity, was stricken with such grief after the demise of her husband that she remained in his tomb, bent on starving herself to death. Her only attendant was a devoted maidservant. Some thieves were crucified near the tomb, and a soldier was posted to guard the crosses. At night, having heard groans and seen a light, the soldier entered the tomb and offered the mourning widow food and sympathy. The widow ignored his kindness, but the maidservant accepted the nourishment. Later she induced her mistress to partake of the food. The soldier, enamored of the beautiful widow, burned to win her hand. Implored by maidservant not to struggle against love, the widow finally yielded to the soldier. During his absence from his post, one of the bodies of the executed thieves disappeared from its cross. Fearing that he would be punished for neglecting his duty, the soldier was on the point of taking his own life when the widow saved him by having the body of her late husband removed from the coffin and fastened to the unoccupied cross."
89 On this and the other instances of *humanitas* in Petronius cf. specifically Ebersbach 1993.

the *humanitas* being a sort of metonymy for the meal, but it is a usage that caught on."[90] This passage of Ammianus provides an excellent example of this later usage.

8.1.2 *Humanus* in the *Res Gestae*

Brandt has rightly remarked that Ammianus never employs the noun *humanitas* simply to mean 'of man', or to point to human nature or mankind.[91] He also shows that when Ammianus wishes to express the notion 'human', he resorts to a noun followed by the adjective *humanus*, such as the usual *casus, corpus, cruor, hostia, manus, mens, modus, mos, necessitas, prospectus, ratio, res, sanguis, sensus, uis, uisio* and *uultus.* This indicates that, as in the case of other authors, there is no complete overlap between the noun *humanitas* and the adjective *humanus*. In addition, one may notice that the neuter is substantivised four times, and that there are no instances of superlatives. There are however two occurrences of the comparative, and in both cases it accompanies the noun *cultus*, which we have already seen to be at times linked to *humanitas* in Ammianus' oeuvre.[92] Of particular interest to our research into the concept of *humanitas* is the instance at 15.11.4, on which I have already lingered elsewhere:[93]

> Horum omnium [*scil.* Gallorum, Belgarum et Aquitanorum] apud ueteres Belgae dicebantur esse fortissimi ea propter, quod ab humaniore cultu longe discreti nec aduenticiis effeminati deliciis diu cum transrhenanis certauere Germanis.

> Of all these nations the Belgae had the reputation in the ancient writers of being the most valiant, for the reason that being far removed from civilised life (*ab humaniore cultu*) and not made effeminate by imported luxuries, they warred for a long time with the Germans across the Rhine. (trans. Rolfe 1935)

That this passage echoes Caesar's *De Bello Gallico* 1.1, analysed above, is beyond question:[94]

> Horum omnium [*scil.* Belgarum, Aquitanorum et Gallorum] fortissimi sunt Belgae, propterea quod a cultu atque humanitate prouinciae longissime absunt, minimeque ad eos mercatores saepe commeant atque ea quae ad effeminandos animos pertinent important,

---

90 Høgel 2015, 76.
91 Brandt 1999, 134 and n. 74.
92 On the relationship between *humanitas* and *cultus* in Ammianus cf. above, pp. 235 and 250.
93 Cf. Mollea 2023b, 13–15.
94 Cf. above, pp. 64 and 235.

proximique sunt Germanis, qui trans Rhenum incolunt, quibuscum continenter bellum gerunt.

Of all these, the Belgae are the bravest, for they are furthest away from the civilization and *humanitas* of the Province. Merchants very rarely travel to them or import such goods as make men's courage weak and womanish. They live, moreover, in close proximity to the Germans who inhabit the land across the Rhine, and they are continually at war with them. (trans. Hammond 1996, slightly adapted)

Whether Ammianus directly depends on Caesar or not is of little importance in this context, for an intermediate source would need to be very close to both texts from a terminological point of view.[95] What counts are the elements these two texts share: they both acknowledge that the Belgae are the most courageous people in Gaul, and they agree on the reasons for this – the Belgae are sufficiently removed from civilization and, therefore, from the risk of becoming effeminate. Moreover, they are (or used to be) in constant war with the bellicose Germans. Our focus is clearly on the relationship between the expressions *ab humaniore cultu* of Ammianus and *a cultu atque humanitate* of Caesar. First, given that Ammianus elsewhere employs the pair *humanitas-cultus*, his preference for the comparative of *humanus* followed by the noun *cultus* can hardly be regarded as a stylistic choice. Instead, it rather shows that all these expressions sounded almost synonymous to him. Secondly and crucially, Ammianus does not resort to the positive form of *humanus*, but to the comparative: as we have already seen in several authors, it looks as if the comparative (and the superlative) is far more suitable to convey the nuances of the noun *humanitas*, especially when its educational and cultural aspects are at stake.

The second instance of *humanior cultus* in the *Res Gestae* seems to confirm this. Book 24.1 describes Julian's entrance into Assyria and his burning of the city of Anathas. Despite this fact, the emperor showed his clemency towards its citizens, as Ammianus does not forget to remark:

et statim munimento omni incenso Pusaeus eius praefectus, dux Aegypti postea, honore tribunatus affectus est. Reliqui uero cum caritatibus suis et supellectili humaniore cultu ad Syriacam ciuitatem Chalcida transmissi sunt. (24.1.9)

At once the whole fortress was set on fire; Pusaeus, its commander, later a general in Egypt, was given the rank of tribune. As for the rest, they were treated kindly, and with their families and possessions were sent to Chalcis, a city of Syria. (trans. Rolfe 1940)

---

95 Barnes 1998, 98 for one stresses that Ammianus's dependence on Caesar is not necessarily direct. Cf. also Vergin 2013, 76.

Unfortunately, we do not have other Latin sources for establishing comparisons. Nevertheless, some observations are in order. To begin with, it is evident that there is no second term of comparison after the comparative. Technically speaking, *humaniore* is therefore an absolute comparative. But what would its meaning be? The Loeb translation by Rolfe, as we have just seen, reads: "they were treated kindly", thereby overcoming all problems. Nor, to pick another example, is Selem's Italian translation better: "ricevettero un trattamento corretto." In my view, the main problem of both these translations does not lie in the fact that they do not render the comparative, but that they neglect the idea of culture and civilization, and, as a consequence, of philanthropy carried by *humaniore*. In other words, what the text means is that the inhabitants of Anathas were treated in respect of the civic norms of their own and of the human community. Thus the main function of the comparative is to bring into play the ideal of *humanitas* rather than to express the intensity of a behaviour or feeling.

One more occurrence of the adjective *humanus* seems worth a look, that at 21.6.4. Speaking of Constantius' third marriage, Ammianus does not miss the opportunity to reiterate his admiration for the emperor's second wife, Eusebia:[96]

> Eodem tempore Faustinam nomine sortitus est coniugem amissa iam pridem Eusebia, cuius fratres erant Eusebius et Hypatius consulares, corporis morumque pulchritudine pluribus antistante et in culmine tam celso humana, cuius fauore iustissimo exemptum periculis declaratumque Caesarem rettulimus Iulianum.

> At that same time Constantius took to wife Faustina, having long since lost Eusebia, sister of the ex-consuls Eusebius and Hypatius, a lady distinguished before many others for beauty of person and of character, and kindly in spite of her lofty station, through whose well-deserved favour (as I have shown) Julian was saved from dangers and declared Caesar. (trans. Rolfe 1940)

She is described as *humana* despite her lofty condition (*in culmine tam celso*), a contrast that might remind us of Pliny the Younger's portrait of Trajan in the *Panegyricus*.[97] After all, like *superbia*, *culmen* is also etymologically linked to the idea of a superior position or condition – it is sufficient to remark that the English 'hill' has its same root.[98] Accordingly, like Trajan, Eusebia maintained her human and humane attitude even though, thanks to her royal, upper condition, she could have shown haughtiness on several occasions.

---

96 Cf. above, p. 254.
97 Cf. above, pp. 87–88.
98 Cf. Ernout/Meillet 2001⁴ s.v. *collis*.

8.1.3 Conclusion

To recap. As far as *humanitas* is concerned, Ammianus represents both continuity and break with the tradition preceding him. There is continuity, because in terms of the nuances *humanitas* takes on within his oeuvre he does not ultimately differ from previous authors such as Eumenius, Gellius or Apuleius, and at times we find echoes of Ciceronian, Caesarian and even Petronian uses of the word. Ammianus appears to have assimilated the polysemy that *humanitas* had been enriching from the beginnings of its history in Republican Rome until his day: the Ciceronian educational component is there; the ethical idea of philanthropy, which also materialises in hospitality, is there; the nobler ideal of civilization resulting from the two previous aspects is there as well. At times then, Ammianus' *humanitas* is even associated with the earthly notion of food.

Yet Ammianus' *humanitas* also implies a break with the tradition, because he is the first historian writing in Latin to make relatively abundant use of this concept. This second aspect might be explained in different ways. To begin with, the socio-political context in which Ammianus wrote seems to have conferred great importance to the concept of *humanitas*, as the section on Symmachus will reveal in greater detail. Judging from Ammianus' narration, this can also be regarded as an hoped-for reaction to the violence which characterised immediately previous times at all levels and in all forms.[99]

Moreover, in the centuries from Tacitus to Ammianus Latin changed significantly in many respects, not least in style, so that by the fourth century CE historians would hardly feel the need to distance themselves from Cicero and from rhetorical style and vocabulary in general. On the contrary, as Sabbah puts it: "Ammien a voulu être le Polybe, le Tacite et le Suétone de son temps, sans renoncer à en être aussi un parfait orateur" – the fact that Cicero was the model *par excellence* of the perfect orator is implicit in this statement.[100] Moreover, as I emphasised in the introduction to this section, we must bear in mind that Latin was not Ammianus' mother tongue, and, if he had to look for a model to follow, no one more than Cicero better represented Latin prose.

Then come the questions of Ammianus' military profession and of his more or less direct role in the events he narrates. By this I mean to reiterate what scholarship has already shown, at least in broad terms: that is, his tendency to judge events from an ethical standpoint – and we have seen in the very many instances

---

99 Cf. Zugravu 2018, 378: "Ammiano [. . .] è stato [. . .] anche il testimone di un'epoca violenta, in cui dominava un'atmosfera di horror, di insicurezza e sospetto, di terrore onnipresente [. . .] e di sofferenza generalizzata."
100 Sabbah 1978, 598.

in which *humanitas* also implies philanthropic connotations that in his oeuvre this word almost always takes on ethical nuances. The main objects of his moral judgement are, as one would expect, powerful men and emperors in particular – which explains why *humanitas* is mostly linked to these figures. In Ammianus' work *humanitas* is regarded as a founding value of Roman society, and it must be for this very reason that the historian is very keen on denouncing every distortion or lack of it. Julian aside, almost all the other emperors mentioned by Ammianus distorted *humanitas*, and this fault becomes extremely serious when there is evidence that they were aware of the importance of this value and deliberately did not behave accordingly. This puts them on the same level as barbarians, and, to some degree, contributes to explaining Rome's gradual decadence, which, in Ammianus' narration, reached its nadir with the battle of Hadrianople.

8.2 *Humanitas* in the Minor Roman Historians of the Fourth Century

Aside from the great Ammianus Marcellinus, what has come down to us of fourth-century Latin historiography shuns long and detailed narrations in the tradition of the Greek Herodotus and Thucydides or the Latin Livy and Tacitus.[101] True, our perception is also influenced by the fact that the *Annales* of Virius Nichomacus Flavianus and, possibly, other works of a larger scope have perished.[102] Nevertheless, there is no denying that these were often replaced by brief historical accounts to which we usually refer today by the name of *Epitomes* or *Breuiaria*.[103] When they deal with the imperial age, epitomes also tend to show a biographical structure, which reflects the authors' understanding of the history of this time as marked by the succession of different emperors.[104] Taking at its most extreme this principle, we come across the *Historia Augusta*, a work which consists of 30 imperial biographies, from Hadrian to Carus, Carinus and Numerian, that is, from 117 to 285 CE. My analysis, inevitably quick because of the paucity of occurrences of *humanitas* and *humanus* in these works, will first deal with the breviaries and then with the *Historia Augusta*.

---

101 Cf. Brown 1971, 115: "It appeared that in the fourth century the mantle of Tacitus could fall only on the shoulders of a Greek such as Ammianus."
102 Cf. Bonamente 2003, 85–86.
103 The differences between *Epitome* and *Breuiarium* as highlighted in modern scholarship are of little interest in this context: for a survey and some bibliographical references cf. Banchich 2008, 305–306; Stover/Woudhuysen 2023, 44–71.
104 Cf. Banchich 2008, 305.

8.2.1 The Breviaries: Eutropius, Aurelius Victor and the *Epitome de Caesaribus*

In spite of their own different characteristics, Eutropius' *Breuiarium*, Aurelius Victor's *Historiae abbreuiatae* and the *Epitome de Caesaribus* seem to share one general purpose, that is, "to propose the continuity of the history of Rome in its ethical values, political institutions and military prestige as a model for the state of the empire and its future security."[105] Yet because of their conciseness and general tendency to privilege facts and anecdotes over ideological and cultural considerations, it cannot be surprising that there is very little trace of a value concept like *humanitas* in the epitomators. This is not to deny that also works like Eutropius' or Aurelius Victor's reveal a moralising view of history as well as their authors' overall opinion regarding emperors, but simply they do not specifically linger on each and every emperor's virtues and flows.[106]

Eutropius' *Breuiarium ab Vrbe condita*, composed after 369 CE[107] and dedicated to emperor Valens, counts no occurrences of *humanitas* and only three of *humanus* (twice in accordance with *genus*, once with *memoria*). This happens despite the fact that the *Breuiarium* displays a rather biographical structure in its second part, the one devoted to the imperial age, where also vices and virtues of the emperors are listed.[108] To some extent, this might be seen as the most explicit way to say that there was not at all room for *humanitas* in the imperial age. But the noun does not appear in the narration of the republican age either and also the other concept which has often been mentioned for its dialectic relationship with *humanitas*, namely *clementia*, only appears twice in Eutropius, on both occasions in the section on emperor Hadrian – although what the epitomator says is that Hadrian was not renowned for his clemency (8.7.1: *Non magnam clementiae gloriam habuit*).[109] In the light of this, it is perhaps safer to presume that Eutropius eschews altogether the word *humanitas* because it does not belong in the noblest historiographical tradition.[110]

Things change very little when it comes to Aurelius Victor's *Historiae abbreuiatae*, written about 359–360 CE.[111] One sole occurrence of *humanitas* can be

---

105 Bonamente 2003, 85. More in detail on the aims of Eutropius' *Breuiarium* cf. Bird 1993, xix–xx.
106 Cf. Banchich 2008, 305.
107 Cf. Bird 1993, xiii.
108 Cf. Bird 1993, xx–xxiii.
109 More generally on Eutropius' sceptical, not to say negative, view of Hadrian's policy cf. Bird 1993, xxi–xxii.
110 Cf. above, p. 116.
111 Cf. Dufraigne 1975, xv–xvii; Stover/Woudhuysen 2023, 25–27.

found in one of the final chapters of this short epitome, on 39.26. Chapter 39 very concisely summarises the period from Diocletian's until Constantius' and Galerius' accession to the throne. Aurelius Victor mentions the noun *humanitas* when speaking of the Illyrian origins of the three of them as well as of Maximian. He says: *His sane omnibus Illyricum patria fuit: qui, quamquam humanitatis parum, ruris tamen ac militiae miseriis imbuti satis optimi reipublicae fuere* ("Illyricum was actually the native land of all of them: so although they were deficient in *humanitas*, they had nevertheless been sufficiently schooled by the hardships of the countryside and of military service to be the best men for the state", trans. Bird 1994). The context is clear: to possess *humanitas* would be best for those who are to govern and yet their experience on the field compensates for this lack. The contrast between *humanitas* and *rus* therefore reveals that Aurelius Victor conceives the former in educational terms, and this is little surprising in the light of the importance that this author generally acknowledges to education and culture.[112] On the other hand, we cannot but ascertain that, as is often the case with Ammianus, Aurelius Victor resorts to the noun *humanitas* to denounce its lack.

Humanus is rare too in the *Historiae abbreuiatae*, appearing with *genus* and *mens*, and standing alone as substantivised adjective with reference to the noun *memoria* to mean 'of mankind' (39.15: *post memoriam humani*). The fourth and last instance is instead a little more complex and has brought editors to make conjectures. The passage in question, taken from § 5, devoted to Nero, in Nickbakht/ Scardino 2021 reads thus: *namque ubi mentem inuaserint uitia, nequaquam uerecundiae †externis societate humanius† datur, peccandi consuetudo noua et eo dulciora affectans ad extremum in suos agit. Humanius* is the *lectio* of P, while the other manuscript, O, reads *extenis societate humani*. Nickbakht/Scardino's apparatus criticus lists a considerable amount of conjectures, including the one which convinces me the most, *humana ius* proposed by Pierre Dufraigne in his 1975 edition. *Humana* would therefore go with *societas* and the meaning of the sentence would be: "For, in fact, when vices have entered the mind, in no way are strangers accorded that law of respect imposed by the human community, and habitual sinning, which leads to novel and therefore sweeter pleasures, finally turns them to their own family" (trans. Bird 1994, adapted).

In the light of the importance of *humanitas* in the Theodosian age, as testified to by Symmachus' oeuvre and Pacatus' panegyric, it is a little surprising that neither the noun *humanitas* nor the comparative or superlative of *humanus* appear

---

112 Cf. Dufraigne 1975, xviii; Bird 1984, 71–80. Bonamente 2003, 90 claims: "With regard to culture and rhetorical education, they are, in Aurelius Victor's opinion, an indispensable basis for the making of princes, even taking as an example Cyrus the Great." Further bibliography in Bird 1984, 149 n. 1.

in the *Epitome de Caesaribus*. This work, which has come down to us as an epitome of Aurelius Victor's *Historiae abbreuiatae* but that in fact shows its independence on several levels, for example extending the narration until Theodosius,
presents the latter in quite a laudatory tone, but nowhere speaks of *humanitas*.[113]
Humanus does appear, but in its simple relational meaning in accordance with
conuersatio, genus, ius and *res*.

8.2.2 The *Historia Augusta*

A work of its own, the *Historia Augusta* is surrounded by so many problems that
any discussions on the role of *humanitas* therein need to be very careful and pro-
visional. While it is by now usually agreed that it was written by a single author
who resorts to six different pseudonyms[114] – although who this author was is anything but certain – its dating still oscillates between 361 and 430 CE.[115] As is obvious, that of the dating in particular is a very relevant problem, as it affects the
overall message and interpretation of the *Historia Augusta*.[116] Furthermore, numerous doubts have been expressed about its genre (history, biography, work of
fiction or something else?) and, consequently, about its reliability.[117] What it is
worth highlighting, however, is that on various occasions the *Historia Augusta*, in
Suetonius' *De vita Caesarum* footsteps,[118] stresses the importance of *mores* and
uirtutes, to be preferred over *acta*.[119]

In the light of these premises, I limit myself to some first remarks, tacitly implying that the *Historia Augusta* can be dated to the late fourth century and there-

---

113 The date of composition of the *Epitome* is disputed and it has recently been suggested that it
was written by Paul the Deacon in the eight century: cf. Stover/Woudhuysen 2023, *passim* on this
issue.
114 Cf. Dessau 1889; Adams 1972; Marriott 1979; Birley 2006, 19; Fedeli 2014, 10–11; Stover/
Kestemont 2016, 154; Gasti 2020, 94. *Contra* Tse *et al.* 1998; Den Hengst 2010².
115 Cf. Paschoud 2002 (after 389); Birley 2006, 19 (after 395); Cameron 2011, 772 (between 361 and
385); Fedeli 2014, 11.
116 Cf. Momigliano 1954, 27.
117 Cf. Momigliano 1954, 25–26; Birley 2006, 23–28; Pausch 2010; Fedeli 2014, 11–12; Stover/
Kestemont 2016, 143; Gasti 2020, 94–95.
118 Cf. Chazal 2021, 17–19 on the structural similarities between Suetonius' *De uita Caesarum*
and the *Historia Augusta*. Furthermore, as Momigliano 1954, 24, Fedeli 2014, 10 and Stover/
Kestemont 2016, 144 remark, the *Historia Augusta* might have begun with the lives of Nerva
and Trajan, that would be now lost, in order to continue Suetonius' oeuvre. Birley 2006,
21–22 (n. 13 for further bibliography) is sceptical on this point.
119 Cf. *Auid. Cass.* 3.1; *Max. et Balb.* 4.5; *Aurel.* 22.4, with discussion in Savino 2017, 239 and n. 12.
Cf. also Fedeli 2014, 11; 13.

fore be of relevance to this study. The occurrences of *humanitas* are only four, and on two occasions the noun appears in the *Life of Hadrian*, which on the one hand is in tune with what we have seen about the general climate of his reign and legislation, but on the other hand might come into conflict with Eutropius' denying clemency to this emperor. To begin with, we need to show that the philanthropic side of *humanitas* prevails in its instances of the *Life of Hadrian*, and that its association with *clementia* is therefore pertinent. In *Hadr.* 10.8 we read: *De militum etiam aetatibus iudicabat, ne quis aut minor quam uirtus posceret, aut maior quam pateretur humanitas, in castris contra morem ueterem uersaretur, agebatque, ut sibi semper noti esse<nt>, et eorum numerus sciretur* ("Furthermore, with regard to length of military service he issued an order that no one should violate ancient usage by being in the service at an earlier age than his strength warranted, or at a more advanced one than *humanitas* permitted. He made it a point to be acquainted with the soldiers and to know their numbers", trans. Magie 1921). The two comparative structures (*minor . . . posceret, maior . . . humanitas*) clearly oppose *humanitas* to *uirtus*, but the meaning of *humanitas* is completely different from the Eumenian case in which we found the same juxtaposition. While on that occasion the term signalled the importance that both the emperor and the governor of the *prouincia Lugdunensis* conferred to culture as well as to military prowess, the cultural aspect of *humanitas* does not seem to shine through here.[120] By contrast, the text might open up to two possible interpretations – or, perhaps more probably in the light of the intrinsic polysemy of *humanitas*, has a double message to convey – depending on who the concrete referent of such *humanitas* is, whether the soldier or the emperor. There is in fact no doubt that *uirtus* refers to the soldier's value or strength, and, given the symmetrical structure of the sentence, the same might go for *humanitas*. If this were the case, *humanitas* then would mean 'human nature', and the overall message would be that Hadrian wanted soldiers to be mature enough to know the true meaning of virtue and military value, but not so old that their bodies were no longer in good shape. Yet, taken in broader terms and perhaps more intuitive at first glance, *humanitas* can refer to the emperor's respect towards old men, who would be spared and exempted from military service. In other words, the emperor's own *humanitas* would set the limit to the enlistment. In this latter sense, the noun would be connoted in philanthropic terms and therefore closer in meaning to *clementia*. But I reiterate that am not sure the text asks the reader to choose between the two options: after all, both would be good reasons for not having too

---

120 Cf. above, pp. 212–213.

old soldiers in the army, and the polysemy of *humanitas* encourages this twofold reading.

The context of the second occurrence of *humanitas* in the *Life of Hadrian* is utterly different, and is likely to remind us of passages of Pliny's panegyric in praise of Trajan where the emperor is said to be easy-going in social situations.[121] *Hadr.* 20.1 reads: *In conloquiis etiam humillimorum ciuilissimus fuit, detestans eos, qui sibi han<c> uoluptatem humanitatis quasi seruantes fastigium principis inuiderent* ("Most democratic in his conversations, even with the very humble, he denounced all who, in the belief that they were thereby maintaining the imperial dignity, begrudged him the pleasure of such *humanitas*", trans. Magie 1921). Like Pliny's Trajan, Hadrian is praised for his friendliness with humble people, which makes him *ciuilissimus*, indirectly associating two concepts like *ciuilitas* and *humanitas* that, as we have seen before, do not usually appear together.[122] And clearly this implies that *humanitas* can be understood as a form of benevolence towards people of lower rank.

Now that it has been made clear that the two instances of *humanitas* in relation to Hadrian have something to do with the idea of *clementia*, which is itself attributed to Hadrian at *Hadr.* 5.5, we can return to the issue of the possible discrepancy between the author of the *Historia Augusta*'s and Eutropius' representations of this emperor. This inconsistency has not escaped the attention of modern scholars, and, as far as the idea of clemency is concerned, Chazal has recently included it among the elements that would reveal the author of the *Historia Augusta*'s willingness to portray Hadrian as an ambiguous figure, neither utterly positive nor negative, despite 'officially' including him in the list of the *boni*.[123] In support of his claim, Chazal observes that Latin historians and biographers – Suetonius for one – are not new to attributing *clementia* to the first years of reign of emperors who then turn out to be fierce.[124] I am sceptical. While I have no difficulties admitting that Hadrian's portrait in the *Historia Augusta* can reveal dark sides of this emperor, this does not seem to be the case of *clementia* and analogous concepts. The two instances of *humanitas* are undoubtedly positive in this respect and the same goes for the occurrence of *clementia* at 5.5: none of these seem therefore to open up to the practice of doublespeak we have observed earlier on in Pliny's sec-

---

121 Cf. *e.g.* Plin. *Pan.* 49.5; 71.6: above, pp. 92–94.
122 Cf. above, p. 128.
123 Cf. Chazal 2021, 120. The opposition between *boni* and *mali principes* is regarded as the best evidence of Pliny's *Panegyricus*' influence on the *Historia Augusta* by Burgersdijk 2013. On the influence of Pliny's and the other panegyrics on the *Historia Augusta* cf. also Paschoud 2002.
124 Cf. Chazal 2021, 120–125.

tion.[125] The oxymoronic doublet *saeuus clemens* of *Hadr.* 14.11 might raise questions about Hadrian's clemency, but if one looks deeper at the context, one notices that the long list of contradictory adjectives has the aim of emphasising the final message that Hadrian was generally inconsistent and unpredictable in his behaviours than questioning all the virtues mentioned: *Idem seuerus laetus, comis grauis, lasciuus cunctator, tenax liberalis, <simplex> simulator, saeuus clemens et semper in omnibus uarius* ("He was, in the same person, austere and genial, dignified and playful, dilatory and quick to act, niggardly and generous, deceitful and straightforward, cruel and merciful, and always in all things changeable", trans. Magie 1921). Accordingly, with regard to Hadrian's idea of clemency and philanthropy, the author of the *Historia Augusta* seems to distance himself from Eutropius and put Hadrian's reign in the footsteps of his predecessor Trajan's, during which we know *humanitas* was important. And it would not be too far off to think that, in case the *Historia Augusta*, or the *Life of Hadrian* at least, was written during the Theodosian age, its author might have wanted to exalt in Hadrian, Trajan's successor, that same *humanitas* that acquired (or was acquiring) new importance under Theodosius (or his successors).[126]

Likewise, Hadrian's *humanitas* is consistent with the other emperors' lack of it. When the term crops up again in the *Historia Augusta*, in the *Life of Caracalla* 4.2, it is only to stress its absence even in front of cadavers: *Occisus est etiam eius* [scil. *Caracalli*] *iussu Patru<in>us ante templum diui Pii, tractaque sunt eorum per plateam cadauera sine aliqua humanitatis reuerentia* ("Patruinus, too, was slain by his order, and that in front of the Temple of the Deified Pius, and his body as well as Papinian's were dragged about through the streets without any regard for *humanitas*", trans. Magie 1921). The context recalls a declamatory one we have seen above, but, more generally, it is by now unsurprising that respect before the dead is a requisite of *humanitas*, whether it is understood more broadly as civilization or more specifically as benevolence towards the other.[127]

The last occurrence of *humanitas* in the *Historia Augusta* is to be found in the section on Trebellianus in the *Lives of the Thirty Pretenders*. Yet it does not refer to Trebellianus nor to any other emperor in particular, but to emperors in general, and, perhaps more important, the author explicitly says that such *humanitas* is offered but never accepted; in other words, it does not materialise. Read *Tyr. Trig.* 26.5: *Neque tamen postea Isauri timore, ne in eos Gallienus s<a>euire<t>, ad*

---

125 On the practice of doublespeak in imperial literature cf. above, pp. 86–87.

126 Also consider that Trajan and Nerva are among the very few first-century emperors to be considered *boni* in the *Historia Augusta*: *Per Neruam atque Traianum usque ad Marcum solito melior* (*Car.* 3.3); cf. Bonamente 2010, 77–82; Savino 2017, VIII; 129–130.

127 Cf. above, pp. 193–194.

aequalitatem perduci quauis principum humanitate potuerunt ("Never afterwards, however, was it possible to persuade the Isaurians, fearing that Gallienus might vent his anger upon them, to come down to the level ground, not even by any offer of *humanitas* on the part of the emperors", trans. Magie 1932). After proclaiming himself emperor among the Isaurians, Trebellianus "had betaken himself into the inmost and safest parts of Isauria, where he was protected by the natural difficulty of the ground and by the mountains" (26.3, trans. Magie 1932). However Gallienus sent his general Camsisoleus against Trebellianus, who went down to the plains, was defeated and killed. This is why the Isaurians did not want to leave their mountains again after that defeat, and it is logical that they rejected the offering of *humanitas*, because, as the *Historia Augusta* continues to narrate, "after the time of Trebellianus they have been considered barbarians" (26.6: *post Trebellianum pro barbaris habentur*; trans. Magie 1932, adapted). The incompatibility is therefore not between *humanitas* and emperors on this occasion, but between *humanitas* and barbarians, along the lines of another pattern with which we are familiar.

The author of the *Historia Augusta*'s conception of *humanitas* as closely bound to *clementia* is further proved by a passage in the *Life of Aurelian* where we find the sole occurrence of the comparative *humanior* in the entire work. *Aur.* 25.1 reads: *Recepta T[h]yana Antiochiam proposita omnibus inpunitate breui apud Dafnem certamine optinuit atque inde praeceptis, quantum probatur, uenerabilis uiri Apollonii parens humanior atque clementior fuit* ("After thus recovering Tyana, Aurelian, by means of a brief engagement near Daphne, gained possession of Antioch, having promised forgiveness to all; and thereupon, obeying, as far as is known, the injunctions of that venerated man, Apollonius, he acted with greater kindness and mercy", trans. Magie 1932). The fact that Aurelian became benevolent only upon Apollonius' exhortation does not plead in his favour, but what interests us the most is, on the one hand, that *humanior atque clementior* appears as a synonymous doublet and thus specifies at best the sense of *humanior* in this context; and on the other hand, that the author had no real necessity to resort to comparative forms since there is no second object of comparison. In my view, the comparative *humanior* is therefore used to stress its bond with *humanitas*, while *clementior*, which was not at all necessary since *clemens* is not a relational adjective, serves the stylistic purpose of balancing the doublet.

The superlative of *humanus* appears instead twice in the *Historia Augusta*. Pertinax, one who is considered a *bonus princeps*,[128] is said to be *mitissimus et humanissimus*, where the doublet with the superlative of *mitis* makes it clear

---

128 Cf. Savino 2017, 127–129.

once again that the philanthropic dimension largely prevails in the *Historia Augusta*'s understanding of *humanitas*.[129] And *mitissimus* as well as *humanissimus* also apply to Didius Julianus, whom Pertinax always considered a colleague and successor, as in fact he was.[130] Yet *mitissimus* appears at 4.8 and is highly significant as it refers to Didius' entire reign (*totoque imperii sui tempore mitissimus fuit*), while *humanissimus* is limited to banquets at 9.2 (*humanissimus ad conuiuia*).[131] Whereas at Pliny's *Panegyricus* 49.5 *humanitas* compensates for *frugalitas*, the former permitting to prolong the banquets that the latter would cut short, there is no doubt that *humanissimus ad conuiuia* said of Didius means that he was sober during banquets, for the author wants to counter what people often say of this emperor – wrongly – namely that he was gluttonous (9.1: *Obiecta sane sunt Iuliano haec: quod gulosus fuisset*). These two characteristics, as well as what the author of the *Historia Augusta* says of Didius at 3.8–10 and 9.1–2, seem to me to make a good emperor of him, and I do not understand why Savino lists him among bad emperors.[132]

As for the positive *humanus*, it appears – without particular relevance – alongside *fragilitas, genus, hostia, ius, mos, oratio, orbis, positio, res, sanguis, species, stercus*.

8.3 *Humanitas* Back Again: Ausonius' *Gratiarum actio*

The great renaissance of *humanitas* under Theodosius I – however rhetorical and a means to an end it might have been – was slightly anticipated by Ausonius' *Gratiarum actio*. The great poet delivered this formal oration in the imperial palace at Trier in the second half of 379 CE.[133] Like Pliny's *panegyric* to Trajan and Mamertinus' to Julian, Ausonius' speech too was composed to thank the emperor for appointing its author to consulship.[134] Having been accused of lack of original-

129 Curiously, Hadrian, Aurelian and Pertinax also share noble physical descriptions in the *Historia Augusta*, and Fedeli 2014, 14 maintains that these are among the very rare cases in which the physical aspect "riflette una maestosa solennità, consona alla somma carica."
130 Cf. *Did. Jul.* 2.3.
131 On frugality during banquets as a virtue, and its lack as a flaw, in the *Historia Augusta* cf. Fedeli 2014, 23–25; Chazal 2021, 82; 205–214, who on p. 206 remarks, "la sobriété des moeurs caractérise le bon prince."
132 Cf. Savino 2017, 127.
133 Cf. Green 1991, 537; Balbo 2018, 159 n.1.
134 Cf. Grilli, 1982, 140; Green 1991, 537; Castello 2010, 190; Gómez-Santamaría 2015, 660; Balbo 2018, 159 n.1. On the differences between panegyric and *gratiarum actio* cf. Balbo 2018, 160–163.

ity[135] – which is after all something to be expected from this kind of compositions –, Ausonius' *Gratiarum actio* has more recently attracted scholars' attention
thanks to its rhetorical features and, above all, due to the light it may throw on
Theodosius I's accession to the throne and the historical-political climate after the
defeat of Hadrianople. At the same time, this text is revealing of Ausonius' self-
esteem and of his own political ambitions, mainly deriving from his having been
Gratian's mentor right from the future emperor's youth.[136] These being the premises, it should not be surprising that the first occurrence of *humanitas* we meet in
this oration has (also) to do with the emperor's education and culture.[137] After all,
if Ammianus deserves credit, Valentinian himself, when presenting his son Gratian to his army, had praised the young emperor's *humanitas* as prerequisite for
his other virtues.[138]

Accordingly, when in chapter 5 of his *gratiarum actio* Ausonius tries to answer on what grounds Gratian has bestowed such a great honour on him, since
the emperor's response seems to be that he was in debt to Ausonius,[139] the discourse quite inevitably shifts to education:

> Quid autem mihi debes, gratissime imperator? (Patitur enim humanitas tua, ut praeter re-
> gias uirtutes priuata appellatione lauderis)? Quid tu mihi debes? Et contra quid non ego tibi
> debeo? Anne quod docui? Hoc ego possum uerius retorquere, dignum me habitum, qui do-
> cerem; tot facundia doctrinaque praestantes inclinata in me dignatione praeteritos, ut esset
> quem tu matura iam aetate succinctum per omnes honorum gradus festinata bonitate
> proueheres; timere ut uidereris, ne in me uita deficeret, dum tibi adhuc aliquid, quod de-
> beres praestare, superesset. (5.24)

> But what do you owe me, most gracious Emperor – for your *humanitas* permits me to set
> aside your kingly qualities and use this familiar form of complimentary address? What do
> you owe me? And on the other side, what do I not owe you? Is it because I was your tutor? I
> can turn this about and say more exactly that I was deemed worthy to teach you; that so
> many men superior to me in eloquence and learning were passed over; that the honourable
> choice fell upon me, in order that you might have a man equipped with ripe years whom
> your impetuous generosity might advance through all the stages of a distinguished career;
> and that you seemed to fear that my life might fail while there still remained unbestowed
> something which you ought to bestow. (trans. Evelyn-White 1921)

---

135 Green 1991, 537.
136 Cf. B. Gibson 2018, 282; 287.
137 On the importance of culture in the *gratiarum actio* cf. Balbo 2015; Balbo 2018, 175–177.
138 Cf. above, p. 240.
139 On the importance of Ausonius quoting Gratian's own words on this occasion cf. B. Gibson
2018, 283.

Lolli has rightly highlighted that the epithet *gratissime* is a play on word with Gratian, the emperor's name, and has emphasised that Ausonius' freedom of speech on this occasion is due to his familiarity with the emperor, a feeling which is subsumed in the word *humanitas*.[140] Without denying that this occurrence of the word *humanitas* might have this implication, it is my contention that Ausonius' mastery of language is even more sublime here and exploits the polysemy of *humanitas*. First, if we assume that here *humanitas* also takes on an educational component, it will become clear why the emperor cannot take offence and, on the contrary, inevitably understands the pun. For will not one who loves playing with language and poetry, as is evident from works like the *Technopaegnion* or the *Griphus ternarii numeri*, have tried to pass this habit down to his pupil? Will not the education he has always imparted to Gratian have also been based on irony? Secondly, by saying that it is thanks to his *humanitas* that Gratian also accepts being praised for private qualities, Ausonius is actually praising another of his private qualities, *humanitas* itself. Thirdly, in chapter 6.27 Ausonius reiterates the expression *priuata appellatio* by resorting to an epithet which far more than *gratitudo* is closer to *humanitas*: *Scis enim, imperator doctissime (rursum enim utar laude priuata)* ("You know, most learned Emperor (for once again I will use a personal mode of complimentary address)", trans. Evelyn-White 1921). And were all this not enough, at the very beginning of chapter 6 Ausonius mentions and quotes Cicero, the first to fully exploit the polyphony of *humanitas*.[141] Yet there is perhaps a closer parallel than Cicero: Eumenius, because the same simultaneous praise of official virtues and *humanitas* also characterises the *Oratio pro instaurandis scholis*, as we have seen.[142] As Green has noticed, however, it would be difficult for Ausonius to linger over military virtues just after the defeat of Hadrianople.[143]

Despite this first occurrence of *humanitas* and the relevance of its implications, the reader who continues reading this oration will not come across this noun again until the final chapters; nor will they find numerous or significant occurrences of the adjective *humanus*. Other value concepts, such as *fortitudo*,

---

140 Lolli 2006, 717. Cf. also Gómez-Santamaría 2015, 662; B. Gibson 2018, 281: "Ausonius turns the expression of public thanks which it is customary for a consul to offer into a means for exploring his individual association with the emperor."

141 On Cicero in the *Gratiarum actio* cf. Green 1991, 538; Balbo 2015, 17–18; Balbo 2018, 174 and, above all, Balbo 2013. On this passage in particular cf. Balbo 2018, 177–178.

142 On further parallels between Ausonius' *Gratiarum actio* and Eumenius' *Panegyricus dictus Augustoduni* cf. Sivan 2004², 17. On Eumenius cf. above, pp. 205–214.

143 Green 1991, 538. Cf. also Jussen 2019, 268–269.

prouidentia, bonitas and *clementia* are mentioned, and *pietas* and *liberalitas* take the lead.[144]

This is not to deny, however, the general importance of *humanitas,* as is evident from its two close occurrences in a rhetorically pivotal point like the end of the speech.[145] Furthermore, these two instances reveal different nuances when compared to the first one.

In chapter 16 Ausonius is still praising Gratian's generosity (*liberalitas*), and in the final section makes a comparison between the present emperor and the Antonines:

> Antoninorum [comitas] fuit etiam in Germanicorum cohorte amicorum et legionibus familiaris humanitas, sed ego nolo beneuolentiam tuam aliorum collatione praecellere; abundant in te ea bonitatis et uirtutis exempla, quae sequi cupiat uentura posteritas et si rerum natura pateretur, adscribi sibi uoluisset antiquitas. (16.75)

> The intimate *humanitas* of the Antonines was also exhibited towards the Germans, in their suite of friends and in their legions. But I do not care to extol your benevolences by comparing others. You furnish a host of such instances of goodness and virtue as generations to come will long to imitate, and as ages past would have wished, did the nature of things allow, to have attributed to themselves. (trans. Evelyn-White 1921, adapted)

I have accepted here Green's text, despite not being completely convinced by the deletion of *comitas.*[146] Fortunately, the sense of *humanitas* does not seem to be much affected by the text one decides to print. For *humanitas* is regarded as *familiaris* and immediately afterwards is substituted by *beneuolentia,* one of the very words by which Gellius identified his contemporaries' misuse of *humanitas.* That this word is employed in its philanthropic meaning is rarely as clear as it is here. What is interesting are the categories towards which the Antonines are explicitly said to have shown their *humanitas,* that is, barbarians and soldiers, or, better, barbarian soldiers. To back up Ausonius' statement, Green refers to Fronto's *Ad M. Caes.* 4.1, in which "Fronto instructs Marcus how to treat his *cohors amicorum*", but at the same time remarks: "It is unlikely, however, that even Pius, in whose reign the Germans were relatively quiet, had Germans among his *amici.*"[147] Regardless,

---

144 Cf. Grilli 1982, 147; Lolli 2006, 721–722; Raimondi 2008, 162–163; Castello 2010, 199; 204; Balbo 2018, 168–170; 179.
145 It must also be borne in mind that "l'elogio [scil. di Graziano] diventa però il tema centrale a partire dal paragrafo 61, in cui esso tocca anche le caratteristiche più comuni, quelle che emergono nella vita quotidiana, senza occuparsi solo di quelle di particolare rilievo." (Balbo 2018, 170).
146 For a synthesis of the textual issues concerning this passage cf. Green 1991, 552.
147 Green 1991, 552.

what counts is that Gratian is portrayed as not inferior to them in this respect; on the contrary, he too will be an example for future generations of governors.

The message becomes even stronger a few lines later, when the comparison is drawn between Gratian and Trajan, the emperor to whom Theodosius looked as the model *par excellence*. The connection with the previous paragraph is explicit because, after saying that he does not want to praise Gratian through comparison with other emperors (*aliorum collatione*), Ausonius seems to reverse his decision:

> Necesse est tamen aliquid comparari, ut possit intellegi, bona nostra quo praestent. Aegrotantes amicos Traianus uisere solebat: hactenus in eo comitas praedicanda est. Tu et uisere solitus et mederi praebes ministros, instruis cibos, fomenta dispensas, sumptum adicis medellarum, consolaris adfectos, reualescentibus gratularis. In quot uias de una eius humanitate progrederis! (17.76)

> Nevertheless, some comparison must be made in order to make clear the superiority of our blessings. Trajan was in the habit of visiting his friends when they were sick: so far we may grant that he had a considerate nature. Your practice is both to visit and to heal them: you provide them with attendants, you order their diet, you prescribe medicines, you furnish the cost of remedies, you comfort them in their pain, and you congratulate them on their recovery. See in how many ways you show advance beyond Trajan's single form of *humanitas*! (trans. Evelyn-White 1921)

Green has highlighted that this Trajanic habit of visiting his friends and soldiers is first praised in Pliny's *Panegyricus* 13, a passage where neither *comitas* nor *humanitas* are mentioned, but on the centrality of the latter throughout the entire Plinian eulogy of Trajan I have lingered at length earlier.[148] In claiming that Gratian's *humanitas* even surpassed Trajan's, Ausonius speaks of the latter's *una humanitas* compared to the multifaceted of Gratian. In context, Ausonius alludes to the fact that, in addition to visiting them, Gratian also heals sick friends, behaving like a doctor.[149] This must have been an exaggeration in any case, but if we broaden the horizons and look at Pliny's multifaceted understanding and presentation of Trajan's *humanitas* – much more polyphonic than Gratian's in the *Gratiarum actio* – it will become all the more clear that rhetoric far prevails over reality, as always with panegyrics.[150]

---

[148] Green 1991, 552. Cf. also B. Gibson 2018, 275; Jussen 2019, 268. On *humanitas* in Pliny's *Panegyricus* cf. above, pp. 84–95.

[149] Cf. Lolli 2006, 718; Raimondi 2008, 163.

[150] Cf. Aug. *Conf.* 6.6.9: to compose panegyrics meant *recitare imperatori laudes, quibus plura mentirer et mentienti faueretur ab scientibus* ("to recite the praises of the emperor, in which I was to tell many lies, by which lies favor was to be gained from those who knew [the truth]", trans. Bourke 1953 – the reference to this passage is in Grilli 1982, 141).

Whether Theodosius I's accession to the throne was promoted by Ausonius and his faction, or, on the contrary, was opposed by them, requires the analysis of so many points that would lead us too far from the scope of this research.[151] Yet a fact which concerns both the *Gratiarum actio* and this research on *humanitas* might be relevant in this respect: this official speech, in which Ausonius is inevitably (also?) "portavoce della propaganda ufficiale del potere",[152] ends by focusing on the presence of the pairing *humanitas* – Trajan, two elements which are key to Theodosius' policy of renewal, as we have seen.[153] But how to interpret this? Is this but a coincidence or is Ausonius resorting to one of his rhetorical strategies, when not play on words, to allude to Theodosius and the beginning of his political propaganda without naming him? And, if the latter were the case, what would his aim be? To claim that Gratian's *humanitas* is superior to Theodosius' as it is superior to Trajan's, his *alter ego*? Or is Ausonius trying to warn his pupil Gratian against Theodosius? I am not sure a satisfying answer can be found at the current state of research. What seems to me to be clear, however, is that after Hadrianople and the difficult – in many respects – central part of the fourth century, as it emerges from Ammianus' narration,[154] times were mature for the comeback of *humanitas*.

8.4 Defending Roman Nobility: *Humanitas* and Networking in the Work of Symmachus

In the following epigraph, Matacotta alludes to one of the main reasons why it would be fitting to conclude a study on *humanitas* in pagan Latin literature with Quintus Aurelius Symmachus, namely his watershed role during the transition years between paganism and Christianity:

> But Symmachus' last years must have been troubled by a suffering that he endured as a cross to bear silently, and that never shines through his correspondence. If it is true that his son-in-law Nicomachus Flavianus Jr. had to convert to the Christian faith in order to obtain his political rehabilitation after joining the regime of the usurper Eugenius, then Symmachus must have been tormented until the day of his death by the thought that his descend-

---

151 Cf. Raimondi 2008, 156–158 and Castello 2010, 193–205, both with a clear state of research and rich bibliography on this issue.
152 Castello 2010, 190.
153 Cf. above, pp. 224–227. Despite not mentioning *humanitas*, Balbo 2018, 169 stresses that Ausonius' list of virtues in the *gratiarum actio* sets Gratian in the wake of Trajan and Hadrian.
154 Cf. above, pp. 227–260.

274 — 8 *Humanitas* in the Thedosian Age: The Reproposition of the Trajanic Pattern?

ants would be educated in the new religion, and that his fight proved as futile as his life was useless.[155]

To be sure, the Italian scholar probably overstated the case when presenting Symmachus as a fundamentalist pagan who opposed Christianity, since the tone of the very many letters which he wrote to pagans rather indicates the opposite.[156] Yet our focus should be on Matacotta's emphasis on the idea that future generations would receive a Christian education. Despite showing respect for Christianity and despite having several Christian friends, Symmachus defended Roman traditional education and its value system.[157] This clearly emerges from his struggle with Ambrose over the Altar of Victory (384 CE), which is perhaps the most famous of the last pagan attempts to resist the imposition of Christianity, and explains why he is one of the protagonists of Cameron's *The Last Pagans of Rome*.[158] Furthermore, Symmachus very often employed the traditional Roman concept of *humanitas* in his writings, and only Cicero, among pagans, makes more use of the term.

In view of these premises, it is no surprise that Cicero and Pliny the Younger are the classical authors to whom Symmachus is usually compared. Yet modern scholars have not sufficiently explored the links between their conceptions of *humanitas* and that of Symmachus, and have limited themselves to pointing out stylistic affinities, commonality of genres as well as vague similarities of thought.[159]

---

155 Matacotta 2010, 377.
156 Cf. Cristo 1974, 43–51; Sogno 2006, 50. Further bibliography in Klein 1971, 161 n. 1.
157 Cf. Cavuoto-Denis 2023, 37: "Il fut une personnalité complexe, dont l'obstination pour la Romanité traditionelle [. . .] est souvent touchante."
158 Cameron 2011. But cf. Brown 2012, 101: "Symmachus was what we now call a 'pagan.' He has even been acclaimed by modern scholars as one of the 'last pagans' of Rome. It might be more accurate to call him the 'first pagan.' He was the first member of the Roman nobility whom we can see adjusting to an unprecedented situation."
159 Already his contemporaries compared Symmachus to Cicero and/or Pliny, especially on the grounds of his oratorical skills: cf. Macr. *Sat.* 5.1.7; Prud. *C. Symm.* 1.633–634 with Klein 1971, 68; Matthews 1974, 66; Cracco Ruggini 1986, 102; Matacotta 2010, 376; Kelly 2013, 261–262. Moreover, also some modern scholars regard Cicero and Pliny as the epistolographic models of Symmachus: cf. Matacotta 2010, 247 and the relevant bibliography in Kelly 2013, 263 n. 4. By contrast, Kelly 2013, 263–269 spotlights the significant differences between Symmachus' and Pliny's letters, while admitting that there are more analogies between Symmachus' oeuvre and Pliny's *Panegyricus* (269–274). Other scholars stress Cicero's, Pliny's and Symmachus' common view of poetry: cf. Cracco Ruggini 1986, 114 and n. 54. On the similarities, not only of thought, between Symmachus and Cicero cf. Klein 1971, 59–60; 68; 103; 106; Cameron 2011, 357. On analogies and differences between Symmachus and Pliny cf. Cameron 2011, 360–361; 415, who concludes: "Tempting as it might seem to suppose that Symmachus saw himself as the Pliny of his age, the truth is that Pliny was more to the taste of Jerome and Ambrose" (416). Yet it is my contention that the present

Two exceptions are the studies by Klein and Marcone.[160] Klein devotes a short section to Symmachus' *Humanität* (67–76), but his study does not provide an in-depth discussion of the concept, and is founded on a limited number of occurrences of the word. Similarly, Marcone recognises the importance of *humanitas* in the Theodosian age and its recurrent use in Symmachus' writings, but, given the nature of his work – a commentary on Book 4 of the *Letters* – he cannot investigate its nuances in detail.[161] Accordingly, a coherent picture of Symmachus' own conceptualisation of the word *humanitas* remains a *desideratum*.

8.4.1 Symmachus' *Humanitas*

Symmachus uses the word *humanitas* 45 times in his writings, three times in the *Orationes*, five times in the *Relationes* and 37 times in the *Epistulae*. What is more, he uses this noun in an unprecedented – with the obvious exception of Cicero – variety of contexts.[162] This is not only due to Cicero's influence over his style and thought, but also to Symmachus' habit of using words that could take on a vast range of meanings (and, conversely, to his love for concepts which could be indicated by a variety of quasi-synonymous words).[163] As we see, the common denominator of all the occurrences of *humanitas* to be found in his work is the cultural and social background that each of these instances presupposes. This is not new, for we have already seen many times that *humanitas* often implies adherence to a set of norms or customs which are shared by a more or less large collectivity as opposed to those who are excluded from it. Just to recall a couple of examples discussed at length in the course of this research, in Apuleius' *De magia, humanitas* is used in a judicial context to create an elitist bond between the judge, his predecessor and the accused Apuleius, which sets them apart from the uncultivated inhabitants of Sabratha;[164] by contrast, we saw instances where Tacitus and Ammianus used *humanitas* to establish a distinction between Romans and Non-Romans, to paraphrase Veyne's famous article.[165] What is new in Symmachus, however, is that *humanitas* seems to encapsulate the code of conduct of

---

study on Symmachus' *humanitas* will reveal the profundity of the ideological relationship between Symmachus and Pliny.

160 Klein 1971 and Marcone 1987.
161 Marcone 1987, 26–28.
162 On Cicero's *humanitas* cf. above, pp. 52–62.
163 Cf. Matacotta 2010, 359; 373–374.
164 Cf. above, pp. 138–147.
165 Veyne 1993.

the senatorial order, without necessarily implying any outward-directed opposition. *Humanitas* is one of the means through which Symmachus aimed to remind his fellow senators of their social habits and duties, in the hope of preserving (or restoring) the features of a social class whose very survival was threatened by the continual changes to the socio-political structure of the Roman empire.[166] But at the same time, such a concept, which we have seen to be socially transversal by definition, was of no obstacle to the maintenance of good relationships with Roman common people.[167] As well as having other secondary aspects, in his view *humanitas* becomes therefore an incitement to write letters, to introduce and/or recommend people – two major means to keep social and political relationships alive;[168] it is linked to other crucial values like *pietas, caritas, religio* and *hospitalitas*, and of course to the παιδεία which all noble men ought to possess;[169] it has peculiar traits of concreteness, and can obviously be an imperial characteristic too. Probably this social, and consequently political, use of *humanitas* links Symmachus to Pliny the Younger and Cicero more than any other aspect.

I shall start by looking at the role which *humanitas* plays as a stimulus to exchange letters between friends. As will soon become clear, the boundary between this kind of letter, the so-called *salutatoria*, and letters of recommendation (*commendaticiae*), practically the only two categories of Symmachian letters, is sometimes blurred by *humanitas* itself, because this very concept encourages the

---

166 On the perilous status of the senate in Symmachus' days cf. Poglio 2007, xiii–xxxii; *passim*; Brown 2012, 98.

167 Cf. Matthews 1974, 72–73. This interpretation of the role of Symmachian *humanitas* seems to be compatible with the recent suggestion by Cavuoto-Denis 2023 that Symmachus' socio-political programme addresses the entire nobility. Cf. in particular Cavuoto-Denis 2023, 48–49: "Symmaque [. . .] s'adresse autant aux vieilles familles de l'Empire qu'à cette nouvelle élite (bureaucratique, étrangère, militaire), pour qui il n'a pas la même admiration, notamment intellectuelle. L'omniprésence de la classe sénatoriale sous toutes ses formes, incluant d'anciens sénateurs et de jeunes gens nouvellement cooptés au sein de l'Ordre, des femmes et des militaires ou encore de hauts fonctionnaires de l'Empire, n'est pas anodine et constitue, à notre avis, la réelle idéologie symmachéenne."

168 Cf. Sogno 2006, 88: "Letter writing is also a fundamentally political activity", and Roda 1986, 184–188; 201–202 who rightly observes that letters of recommendation end up benefitting not only the recommendee, but also the recommender. Cf. also Cracco Ruggini 1986, 109; Brown 2012, 97; 100–101.

169 Cf. Lizzi Testa 2022, 44: "[I]t is clear that the cultural wealth – beyond movable and immovable property – of some members of the late fourth-century senatorial aristocracy was still significant. It was an important component of the central political role the senatorial aristocracy played."

extension of friendships, whereby friends are recommended to other friends.[170] I will therefore investigate this bridging role of *humanitas* as well as those *commendaticiae* in which Symmachus leverages the *humanitas* argument to persuade his interlocutors to support his recommendees.[171] I will then move on to those instances where *humanitas* is regarded as an imperial virtue and, by extension, as a value which characterises an entire age, as emerges from the expressions *humanitas saeculi / temporum*. These occurrences are to be found not only in the *Epistulae*, but also in the *Relationes* and *Orationes*. After focusing on these functional roles of *humanitas*, in the second and shorter part of this sub-chapter I will change tack and investigate some more isolated cases which help us to define better Symmachus' extremely multifaceted conception of *humanitas*.

From as many as five letters *humanitas* explicitly emerges as the main value by virtue of which letters should be written to maintain friendships.[172] The short *Ep.* 7.98 is symptomatic, for it is entirely devoted to this issue:[173]

> Iamdudum desiderabam litteras tuas: nunc inmodica animi gratulatione suscepi. Debita igitur reuerentia et amore respondens adicio postulatum, ut in reliquum frequentare digneris munus optabile quod sponte tribuisti. Sed in hac postulatione non opus est conmorari. Neque enim petitio mea debet elicere quod tua promittit humanitas. Vale.

> I have long been awaiting a letter from you: now I have received it with immense joy. Thus with due reverence and obeying my love for you, I reply and add the following request, that in the future you will send me more frequently those desirable gifts that you have spontaneously accorded to me on this occasion. But there is no need to linger on this request. Indeed, my request does not need to ask for what your *humanitas* guarantees. Farewell.

In expressing his delight at receiving a letter from Longinianus, who probably occupied the prestigious post of *comes priuatarum largitionum* at that time, Symmachus takes the opportunity to urge his friend to send him more frequent letters in

---

170 On the topics as well as for a classification of Symmachus' letters cf. Matthews 1974, 61–63; Callu 2003, 24–25; Sogno 2006, 63. Matacotta 2010, 358 is emblematic: "L'argomento più trattato nelle lettere è costituito, appunto, dalle lettere". Cf. also Matthews 1974, 64, reiterated in Matthews 1975, 7: "[I]n the great majority of cases, the letters are nothing but the mere performance of *amicitia*, its pure administration." Also *honestas* and *dignitas* play a crucial role in Symmachus' letters of recommendation: cf. Cavuoto-Denis 2023, 52–53; 59 and *passim*.

171 As Roda 1986, 177 observes, the *commendatio* is the most recurrent element in Symmachus' letters. Cf. also Brugisser 1993, 273–330.

172 On writing letters as an *officium* in Symmachus (and not only) cf. Brugisser 1993, 4–16; Cavuoto-Denis 2023, 113–114.

173 Cf. Matthews 1975, 7: "Symmachus only rarely admits spontaneity to his letters, and he often conveys no information at all."

future.[174] In an unmistakably adulatory tone, he then closes the letter by adding that his exhortation is superfluous, because Longinianus' *humanitas* will undoubtedly make this happen.

The same applies to *Ep.* 2.88, which is addressed, like all the letters in Book 2, to Symmachus' dear friend and daughter's father-in-law Flavianus the Elder.[175] Compared to *Ep.* 7.98, the slight difference is that this letter has some content beyond the mere request of sending along more letters, that is, Symmachus congratulates Flavianus on a new prestigious appointment:[176]

> Et honore tui, quo nunc auctus es, et continuo in me amore delector. Volo igitur ut communia pignora curae mihi esse non dubites, quae magis merita tua quam scripta commendant. Supererat, ut adsiduum stili tui munus exposcerem; sed redundantis est operae bona spontanea postulare, ne meus stilus extorquere uideatur quod tui animi spondet humanitas. Vale.

> I take pleasure both from the appointment that has now raised you and the love you keep showing towards myself. I therefore want you not to doubt that I take care of our protégé, whom your merits recommend more than your letters. But there was just one thing left to me to do, that is, to ask for frequent gifts from your stylus. Although it is superfluous to ask for goods that are voluntary and I do not want that my stylus seems to extort what your heart's *humanitas* promises. Farewell.

The logic of *Epp.* 7.98 and 2.88 is inverted in *Ep.* 3.65, which does not express a hope for the future, but already acknowledges the merits of Ricomeres, apparently a good friend of Symmachus' and one who held several prestigious military posts.[177] His *humanitas* has always prompted him to write to Symmachus, who in turns feels obliged to pay back *humanitas* in the same way:

> Scio praestantem animum tuum salutis meae et reuersionis indicia cupide, ut amicitia postulat, opperiri, et ideo expectationi tuae reuectus in patriam satisfeci, meque agere ex sententia atque esse memorem tuae circa nos humanitatis insinuo; simulque deprecor ut adfectionem quam mihi et praesenti dependere et absenti dignatus es polliceri, litterarum munere, quotiens usus tulerit, non grauueris augere. Vale.

> I know that your outstanding feelings fervently desire news, as friendship requires, on my health as well as on my return. That's because, once back to my homeland, I decided to satisfy your impatience: I inform you that it is going satisfactorily and that I remember well

---

174 On Longinianus' career cf. *PLRE II* 686–687.

175 On Flavianus the Elder, his political role as well as on his relationship with Symmachus cf. Matacotta 2010, 226–240; Cavuoto-Denis 2023, 83–89. Cf. also below, pp. 285; 287; 292–293.

176 The date of this letter as well as the nature of the appointment it mentions are uncertain: for more details and bibliography cf. Cecconi 2002, 424–425.

177 Cf. *PLRE I* 765–766.

your *humanitas* towards myself. And at the same time I beg that it will not be too much of a trouble for you to increase the number of the epistolary gifts whenever possible: these have revealed the affection you feel for me when I am present and promise to me when I am absent. Farewell.

Along the same lines Symmachus writes to a certain Eusebius (probably):[178]

Conpertum habeo quolibet honorum culmine animum tuum non solere mutari — quidquid enim bene meritis honestatis accedit, id solutum magis uidetur esse quam praestitum —, et ideo mirari me ac stupere confiteor cur tanta uirtute atque humanitate praeditus iampridem circa me munere litterarum [causis occupationis] abstineas. Quod ego etsi occupatione magis quam uoluntate arbitrer accidisse, tamen orare non desino ut censuram tuam nostri memorem frequens sermo declaret. Vale. (*Ep.* 8.1)

It is clear to me that your feelings do not usually depend on the rank of the public office you hold – indeed, any honourable action that has increased your merits seems to be a reward rather than a loan. Accordingly, I must admit that I am surprised and startled that, given such a great virtue and *humanitas* of yours, you have not been sending your epistolary gifts to me for long time. And although I think this is due to your being busy rather than to your willingness, I nonetheless keep begging that a frequent correspondence proves that your office is mindful of myself. Farewell.

Compared with the previous *Epp.* 7.98, 2.88 and 3.65, *Ep.* 8.1 looks like the other side of the same coin: despite possessing *humanitas* – and also *uirtus*! – Eusebius seems to ignore it, abstaining from sending letters to Symmachus, to the latter's surprise (*et ideo mirari me ac stupere confiteor*). Like Longinianus, Eusebius does not avoid Symmachus' exhortation to write more often, although he seems to be excused on account of his noble but time-consuming duties (*honorum culmine . . . occupatione magis quam uoluntate*).

The identity of Eusebius is unclear, although he was probably someone of a high social class. It is interesting to note, however, that in other instances the association of *uirtus* with *humanitas* is made to refer to cultural and military values respectively, *uirtus* preserving its original function of indicating the quality *par excellence* of the good soldier or general. This is certainly the case of Eumenius' *Oratio pro instaurandis scholis* we investigated earlier on,[179] and in Symmachus we find another passage where the pairing of *uirtus* and *humanitas* concerns a

---

178 The name of the addressee of this letter is not in the manuscripts. Seeck 1883, CXCI dates the letter to 396 and, following in his footsteps, Callu 2003, 113 n.1 integrates *<Eusebio?>*, identifying him with the *uir inlustris iudex praetorianus* of *Ep.* 6.12.2, possibly the same Eusebius who received *Ep.* 9.55 (cf. *PLRE I* 306–307 – Eusebius 32). Cf. also Ruta 2023, 29–30.
179 Cf. above, pp. 205–214.

famous general.[180] Accordingly, one might speculate that Eusebius too was renowned for his military prowess, even if we do not have sufficient evidence to
prove this. After all, the same expression *uirtute et / atque humanitate* is also attested with a broader meaning since Caesar's and Cicero's day: it condenses the
qualities of a well-educated, honest and noble man, who knows the social norms
which regulate the world in which he lives.[181] Either way, there is little doubt that
this occurrence of *humanitas* brings into play cultural aspects which transcend
the mere sense of benevolence and rather evoke the idea of παιδεία-based *humanitas*. Further instances of *humanitas* with this meaning will be investigated in
the second part of this chapter, but the next example might well fall into the
same category.[182]

In another similar context, Symmachus uses *humanitas* to excuse his close
friend and excellent poet Ausonius at *Ep.* 1.18, especially if Callu is right in linking
this letter with Ausonius' role of Praetorian prefect, either of Gaul (377 CE) or of
Gaul, Italy and Africa (378–379 CE):[183]

> Ego etsi continuis litteris honorem tuum celebrare possem, non satis mihi uiderer, proquam
> res postulat, fungi debitum meum: tantum abest ut operam tibi adsiduitatis exprobrem. Sed
> ut hoc meae uerecundiae conpetit, item tuae humanitatis est studium nostrum pari gratia
> sustinere. Animaduerte quo tendat summa uerborum meorum: iamdudum nihil tribuis
> quod legamus. Totum me, inquies, emancipauit sibi cura praetorii. Verum est: potiris merito
> summa iudicia, sed maximas ingenii tui uires fortuna magna non onerat. Proinde etiam his
> rebus adtende, quae ita occupatis nihil molestiae adferunt, ut ipsas molestias plerumque
> solentur. Vale.

> Even if I were able to celebrate the honor of your appointment by a succession of letters, I
> would not be satisfied that I was sufficiently fulfilling my obligation as the occasion de-
> mands; so far am I from reproaching you for your diligent efforts in your new office. But, as
> such a course befits my sense of propriety, so it is due to your *humanitas* to support my
> devotion with equal goodwill. Notice where the gist of my words is leading; for some time
> now you have given me nothing to read. You will say, "The concerns of the praetorian pre-
> fecture have claimed me entirely for themselves." It is true; you deservedly have the right
> to make judgments about most important matters. But great good fortune does not weigh
> heavily on the very great resources of your talent. Be attentive, then, to these matters,
> which are no trouble for busy people but often in fact provide solace from troubles. Fare-
> well. (trans. Salzman/Roberts 2011)

---

180 On the second Symmachian occurrence of the expression *uirtute et humanitate* cf. below,
pp. 307–308.
181 Cf. *e.g.* Caes. *BGall.* 1.47.4; Cic. *Planc.* 58; *Lig.* 12; *De or.* 3.1; *Fam.* 14.1.
182 Cf. below, pp. 306–308.
183 Callu 2003, 83 n. 1. On this letter and its dating cf. also Salzman 2011, 53–54.

Given the identity of the recipient, Symmachus might well be referring here not to letters, but to literary works: the practice of sending recently composed literary pieces to good friends for them to read and comment upon was well-established by that time.[184] This would explain why Symmachus is referring to Ausonius' *maximas ingenii tui uires*, an expression that would be strange if it only referred to letter writing. In this case, *humanitas* would no longer refer to a vague feeling of benevolence, but to the love of literature Symmachus and Ausonius shared. After all, in the wake of his models, which included Cicero and Pliny the Younger, at times Symmachus too seems to attribute educational, literary and cultural nuances to *humanitas*, as we will see in greater detail below, and the same is certainly true of Ausonius, as we have already noticed.[185]

If we return to *humanitas* as a stimulus to exchange letters, we must acknowledge that in this respect Symmachus cannot be accused of inconsistency. Judging from what he says in the short *Ep.* 7.84, he practises what he preaches: *Primam mihi scribendi causam religio fecit, ut amicitia nostra litteris excolatur; secundam suggessit humanitas, ut uiro optimo Thalasso familiari meo tua concilietur adfectio.* ("The first stimulus to writing came from a religious feeling, which induced me to cultivate our friendship by means of letters. *Humanitas* came second, to suggest that your affection for myself may be extended to the excellent Thalassus, a friend of mine"). The addressee is yet again an important statesman, Messalla Avienus, Praetorian prefect of Italy and Africa in 399–400 and one of the protagonists of Macrobius' *Saturnalia*, to whom Symmachus sent a few letters (now in Book 7).[186] However, this time Symmachus regards *religio* as the first impulse (*primam . . . causam*) which induces him to exchange letters with Messalla; *humanitas* comes second (*secundam*). It is interesting that here Symmachus clearly distinguishes the different aims of *religio* and *humanitas*: thanks to the former, he is led to cultivate his friendship with Messalla, whereas the latter invites him to extend the friendship to a third person. This clearly suggests that *humanitas* has also to do with recommendation, but I shall look at this aspect in greater detail later. For the moment, let me dwell a little longer on the relationship between *religio* and *humanitas*, an association / opposition which we have not yet encountered.

As Roda rightly observes, *religio* is one of Symmachus' most employed words to indicate the mutual duties of friendship, especially with regard to the exchange of letters.[187] Yet its meaning probably merits closer inspection given the problematic and discussed etymology of *religio*, and that Symmachus himself also used

---

184 Cf. the example of Pliny's letters: above, pp. 101–105.
185 Cf. below, pp. 306–308 and above, pp. 269–273.
186 Cf. *PLRE II* 760–761 – Messalla Avienus 3 and Callu 2003, 164.
187 Roda 1981, 199.

this word with other meanings.[188] In *De natura deorum* 2.71–72, Cicero makes a clear distinction between *religio* and *superstitio*: *superstitiosi* are those who spend their days praying and making sacrifices in order for their sons to outlive them, while *religiosi* refer to those who diligently reconsider and re-read (Latin *re-lego*), as it were, everything related to the cult of the gods.[189] It follows that *superstitio* is negative while *religio* is positively connoted, and – more importantly for the purpose of the present study – that Cicero connects *religio* to the verb *relego*. This is quite different from what we see in Lactantius and Servius, who, in the tradition of Lucretius, make *religio* derive from *religo* (to bind fast), as though religion were literally that which binds people to god(s).[190] In the case of *Ep.* 7.84, both the idea of creating a bond and the notion of continuing to re-read or revise (a relationship) are present in Symmachus, although *religio* is probably used in a broader, less technical context. To be sure, what *religio* confers to friendship is an aura of sacredness, which Symmachus could already find in Cicero's *De inuentione* 2.168:

> Amicitiarum autem ratio, quoniam partim sunt religionibus iunctae, partim non sunt, et quia partim ueteres sunt, partim nouae, partim ab illorum, partim ab nostro beneficio profectae, partim utiliores, partim minus utiles, ex causarum dignitatibus, ex temporum opportunitatibus, ex officiis, ex religionibus, ex uetustatibus habebitur.

> In as much as some friendships are related to religious scruples, and some not, and some are old and some new, some arise from a kindness done to us by others, and some from our

---

188 Cf. Ernout/Meillet 2001[4], s.v. *religio*; Gothóni 1994, both with further bibliography. Gothóni endorses Cicero's etymology. On the meanings which *religio* takes on in Symmachus' oeuvre cf. Matacotta 2010, 374.

189 *Non enim philosophi solum uerum etiam maiores nostri superstitionem a religione separauerunt. Nam qui totos dies precabantur et immolabant, ut sibi sui liberi superstites essent, superstitiosi sunt appellati, quod nomen patuit postea latius; qui autem omnia quae ad cultum deorum pertinerent diligenter retractarent et tamquam relegerent, <hi> sunt dicti religiosi ex relegendo, elegantes ex eligendo, ex diligendo diligentes, ex intellegendo intellegentes; his enim in uerbis omnibus inest uis legendi eadem quae in religioso. Ita factum est in superstitioso et religioso alterum uitii nomen alterum laudis* ("For religion has been distinguished from superstition not only by philosophers but by our ancestors. Persons who spent whole days in prayer and sacrifice to ensure that their children should outlive them were termed 'superstitious' (from *superstes*, a survivor), and the word later acquired a wider application. Those on the other hand who carefully reviewed and so to speak retraced all the lore of ritual were called 'religious' from *relegere* (to retrace or re-read), like 'elegant' from *eligere* (to select), 'diligent' from *diligere* (to care for), 'intelligent' from *intellegere* (to understand); for all these words contain the same sense of 'picking out' (*legere*) that is present in 'religious'. Hence 'superstitious' and 'religious' came to be terms of censure and approval respectively", trans. Rackham 1967).

190 Cf. Lact. *Diu. Inst.* 4.28.2; Serv. *Aen.* 8.349; Lucr. 1.931.

own services to them, an examination of their nature will involve a consideration of the value of causes, the suitableness of times and occasion, moral obligation, religious duties, and length of time. (trans. Hubbell 1949)

Cicero does not expand on this topic – that is not the aim of a rhetorical treatise like *De inuentione* after all – but this passage is sufficient for us to verify that he considered that there was a tight connection between *amicitia* and *religio*. This idea is backed up by Quintilian, who, in stating that the perfect orator should not be afraid of other people and therefore needs to be accustomed to social life right from his birth, speaks of lifelong friendships in terms of *religiosa quadam necessitudine inbutae* ('imbued with a certain religious bond').[191]

But what about *humanitas*? In his commentary on Cicero's *Somnium Scipionis* 1.8.7, the fifth-century author Macrobius writes: *de iustitia ueniunt innocentia, amicitia, concordia, pietas, religio, affectus, humanitas* ("From justice derive innocence, friendship, concord, *pietas*, *religio*, affection, *humanitas*"). He thus unites several concepts, including *religio*, *amicitia* and *humanitas*, and claims that they all derive from justice (*de iustitia ueniunt*), surely meaning to say that justice is a general precondition for all these value concepts to exist, and not that it is a sort of hyperonym, let alone a more important value within a ranking. Yet Macrobius was not the first to link *humanitas* and *religio*. If we recall the texts dealing with the 'Athenian' origin of *humanitas*, we will perhaps also remember that *humanitas* was seen as only one of a series of discoveries that the Romans imported from the Greeks. Another one was *religio*.[192]

Given the emphasis on *humanitas* as a stimulus to write letters in Symmachus' thought and in the light of the above reasoning on *religio*, let me now return to Symmachus' *Ep.* 7.84. The concomitant use of *religio* and *humanitas* has an adulatory purpose: because of its sacred implications which adorn Symmachus' friendship with Messalla, *religio* is superior to *humanitas*. While *religio* confers a sort of divine status to a human relationship, as is the case with *amicitia*, *humanitas* stops at the very human level of recommendations. But the opposition is clearly specious, for neither is there evidence of any ontological superiority of *religio* over *humanitas*, nor does Symmachus regard *humanitas* as an insufficient reason for cultivating friendships.

An analogous case within an analogous context is provided by the opposition between *humanitas* and *caritas*. The close of *Ep.* 9.90, one of the very many letters of Book 9 whose addressee is unknown, reads:

---

191 Quint. *Inst.* 1.2.20.
192 Cf. Cic. *Flac.* 62; Plin. *Ep.* 8.24.2 (above, pp. 35–37).

Non inuideo poscentibus testimonia uel suffragia tua, sed ualidior est amicitiae causa quam gratiae. Precarias epistulas postpone legitimis. His frequentius caritas studeat, illas nonnumquam praestet humanitas. Vale.

I do not envy those who ask for your testimony or approbation, but friendship is stronger a reason than favour. Letters obtained by prayer must come after the genuine ones. May affection encourage to write genuine letters more often! May *humanitas* guarantee letters obtained by prayer from time to time. Farewell.

Caritas should lead one to write letters to friends more often, whereas *humanitas* yet again lies at a lower level, that of letters of recommendation. It is worth noting the appropriateness of linking *caritas* to friendship in this situation. Compare Cicero, *Partitiones Oratoriae* 88:

Amicitiae autem caritate et amore cernuntur; nam cum deorum tum parentum patriaeque cultus eorumque hominum qui aut sapientia aut opibus excellunt ad caritatem referri solet, coniuges autem et liberi et fratres et alii quos usus familiaritasque coniunxit, quamquam etiam caritate ipsa, tamen amore maxime continentur.

Friendships are manifested by esteem and by affection. Respect for the gods and for parents and country and for those persons who are eminent for wisdom or for wealth is customarily classed under esteem, whereas wives and children and brothers and other persons attached to us by association and familiarity are bound to us partly it is true by actual esteem but chiefly by affection. (trans. Rackham 1960)

As Hellegouarc'h glosses: "Il semble donc que la juxtaposition de *amor* et *caritas* ait pour but de distinguer deux sortes d'affections: l'affection naturelle que l'on éprouve pour des parents ou des amis intimes pour laquelle *amor* constitue le terme adéquat et celle qui s'applique à des êtres qui sont plus éloignés de nous au point de vue des relations naturelles."[193] Accordingly, when one is only a friend and not a relative, as seems to be the case with the addressee of this Symmachian letter, *caritas* is more appropriate than *amor* to define the feeling upon which this relation of friendship is based.

Yet *Ep.* 4.48 and 2.43 testify both to the inadequacy of the opposition between *humanitas* and *religio* / *caritas* and to the flexibility of Symmachus' use of concepts of value. Symmachus wrote *Ep.* 4.48 to Minervius, the *comes sacrarum largitionum* for the West in 398/399, after 398 CE.[194] Its purpose is to support Bassus' petition in favour of his sister, who reclaims a fleeing slave. The opening reads: *Litteras nonnullis humanitate praestamus: has autem domino et fratri meo Basso qui sororis fortunas tuetur, iusto amore detulimus* ("To some people we grant a letter induced by

---

193 Hellegouarc'h 1963, 148.
194 On Minervius cf. *PLRE I* 603 (Minervius 2).

our *humanitas*, but legitimate love made me accord this letter to Bassus, my brother and a gentleman, who defends his sister's wealth"). On this occasion Symmachus opposes *iustus amor* instead of the 'expected' *caritas* to *humanitas*, but, despite according greater value to the former, regards the latter as a sufficient reason to write letters of recommendation. After all, this is utterly unsurprising in the light of what he says when recommending Flavius Sexio to Flavianus the Elder at *Ep.* 2.43:[195] *Est humanitatis et consuetudinis tuae aliis quoque placitos amore dignari* ("It is part of the *humanitas* habitual to your nature, to honour with your affection those whom others have found congenial", trans. Matthews 1974). Not only does the opposition between *humanitas* and *amor* vanish, but Flavianus' usual *humanitas* – *humanitatis et consuetudinis* is to be taken as an hendiadys – even becomes the premise for his *amor* towards Sexio. On the one hand, this is a symptom of the ductility of both *humanitas* and *amor*, but the presence of *amor* instead of a weaker concept like, for example, *caritas*, probably strengthens Symmachus' request by suggesting that a very close friendship should grow between the two. If, in the wake of Vera, Cecconi is right in supposing that Symmachus' aim is to support Sexio's admission to the senate and, consequently, to expand his control over the senatorial order, then he would have good reasons to resort to such loaded words in this letter.[196]

The 'bridging' role of *humanitas* we have noticed in the last four Symmachian occurrences of this term is summed up and formulated as a sort of moral law by Symmachus himself in *Ep.* 4.73, sent between 386–387 CE to the then Praetorian prefect of Italy and Illyricum Eusignius:[197]

> Facio quod suadet humanitas, ut amicitiae tuae uiros bonae frugis adiungam. Horum unus est Felix honorabilis gradu atque exercitatione militiae, cui si quid amoris inpenderis, ad meam gratiam pertinebit. Vale. (*Ep.* 4.73)

> I do what *humanitas* persuades me to do: I add honest men to your friends. One of them is Felix, honourable for his rank and his service in the army. I will be grateful if you devote some affection to him.

An important caveat needs to be made here: friendships must only be extended to other virtuous men (*bonae frugis*).

---

195 More on Sexio and on the political function of this letter in Cecconi 2002, 291–295. On Sexio cf. also *PLRE I* 838.
196 Vera 1979, 402–403; Cecconi 2002, 294–295.
197 On the date of this letter and on Eusignius cf. Marcone 1987, 105 and *PLRE I* 309–310 respectively.

In all the five last letters (7.84, 9.90, 4.48, 2.43 and 4.73), we should notice the indirect effect of *humanitas*: it persuades Symmachus to write to a friend, but on behalf or in favour of a third person who is dear to him. More broadly, in the light of what we have seen so far about Symmachus' *humanitas*, we can say that it operates at two levels: at a higher one, as a means to preserve friendship between two people (*Epp.* 1.18, 7.98, and 8.1); at a lower one, as an opportunity – with evident utilitarian purposes – to extend to a third party the existing friendship between sender and addressee (*Epp.* 7.84, 9.90, 4.48, 2.43 and 4.73).[198]

This last argument prompts us to turn our attention to the use of *humanitas* within Symmachus' many letters of recommendation. Before doing so, I want to discuss briefly one last case in which *humanitas* has to do with the exchange of letters between friends. This instance is of particular interest because it might seem to invert, perhaps even contradict, the trend I have sketched so far. The beginning of *Ep.* 5.13, which is addressed to Theodorus, reads:[199]

> Iampridem nihil scribis. Aequum esset huic culpae talionem reponi: sed ego arbitror imitanda non esse quae doleas, et animo persuadeo alias potius interuenisse causas officii differendi quam residem uoluntatem. Quamquam uereor ne factum tuum haec ipsa grauet humanitas. Nam qui mihi pro te satisfacio, ostendo nihil me tale meruisse.

> You have not written to me for a long time. Given such a fault, it would be right to resort to a retaliation, but I believe that hurtful actions are not to be imitated. Also, I convince myself that other reasons than your idle willingness intervened to cause the delay of your duty. Nevertheless I fear that this same *humanitas* might aggravate the situation. Indeed, in excusing yourself in your place, I reveal that I did not merit it.

Interestingly, the same value which Symmachus regards several times as a major stimulus to write letters to friends can now excuse those who do not do so. But far from being a contradiction or a sign of inconsistency, this is simply a further clue to understanding the versatility of *humanitas*. Indeed, *humanitas* is here conceived as the virtue which urges one to try to understand a friend's problems, without judging them negatively. In other words, from whatever point of view it is considered, *humanitas* remains for Symmachus fundamental within a relation of friendship.

Whereas so far *humanitas* has worked as an incitement to write letters, in the case of letters of recommendation it can also play a more central role. This mainly happens through the shift of the possessor of *humanitas*, from the sender to the addressee – notice that Symmachus speaks very often of *humanitas tua* on

---

198 On these two levels cf. also Roda 1986, 184.
199 On Theodorus cf. *PLRE I* 901–902 (Flauius Mallius Theodorus 27); Rivolta Tiberga 1992, 93–96.

these occasions. Instead of being the value which encourages the recommender to present his recommendee's case, it becomes the element that should persuade the recommender's friend to take the recommendee's case to heart and support it. Symmachus enunciates this principle in clear terms at the opening of *Ep.* 2.70, addressed to Flavianus the Elder (*Humanitatis interest commendationem deferre poscentibus*, "It is typical of *humanitas* to accord a recommendation to those who ask for it"), as well as at the beginning of *Ep.* 7.56, probably addressed to Hadrian (*Tua nos hortatur humanitas opem poscentibus non negare*, "Your *humanitas* urges us not to deny help to those who ask for it").[200] As one would expect, an immediate consequence is an implicit increase in the level of adulation. Two letters from Book 7 and four letters from Book 5 illustrate this.

Ep. 7.34 to Symmachus' relative Atticus Maximus plays a sort of 'bridging role' with the previous category of letters which extend friendships.[201] The logic is simply inverted, for friendship – if it can be defined as such – is extended only once a recommendee's request has been satisfied:

> Salutationis honorificentiam praelocutus Gaetulici agentis in rebus exequor postulatum, qui a te iustum fauorem per me optat adipisci. Humanitatis tuae est amplecti probabilem uoluntatem numerumque eorum qui te iure suspiciunt adiectione noui cultoris augere. Vale. (*Ep.* 7.34)

> After paying the homage of the salutation, I support the request of the *agens in rebus* Getulicus, who desires to get a deserved favour from you thanks to my intercession. It is typical of your *humanitas* to embrace commendable desires as well as to increase the number of those who rightly venerate you through the addition of a new worshipper.

The short *Ep.* 5.31 is addressed to Magnillus, who throughout his career held the prestigious posts of Governor of Liguria and *Vicarius Africae*.[202] Without providing much detail, it generally recommends an unnamed woman who was on good terms with the apparently esteemed philosopher Asclepiades:[203]

> Propinquam sancti Asclepiadis philosophi absque litteris meis abire par non fuit: nam illius merita poposcerunt ut ad curaturam praeclari uiri pertinens tuo patrocinio traderetur. Pro quo non arbitror ambitu longae orationis utendum, cum eam humanitati tuae contemplatio parentis sine cuiusquam petitione commendet. Vale

> It would have been unfit to let a relative of the venerable philosopher Asclepiades go away without a letter of mine. In fact, her merits required that you accord your protection to

---

200 On Flavianus the Elder cf. above, pp. 278 and 285; on Hadrian cf. below, p. 294.
201 On Atticus cf. *PLRE I* 586–587 (Nonius Atticus Maximus 34).
202 Cf. *PLRE I* 533.
203 On Asclepiades cf. *PLRE I* 114 (Asclepiades 4).

someone who is object of care of such an illustrious man. To this end, I do not think that I need to resort to the circumlocutions of a long speech, since the contemplation of her relative recommends her to your *humanitas* without the need of anyone's request. Farewell.

In another letter, Symmachus pairs *humanitas* with *patrocinium*. Here he recommends the *agens in rebus* Julian to Patruinus, an influential figure of the Palatine administration in the last years of the fourth century thanks to his familiarity with Stilicho:[204] *Iuliani agentis in rebus modestiam noui, natales probo, doleo fortunam; fatalibus enim malis diu et grauiter exhaustus est. Sed credo cum eo omnia in gratiam esse reditura, si tuo patrocinio et humanitate foueatur.* (*Ep.* 7.107: "I know the *agens in rebus* Julian's temperateness, I approve of his origins, I am sorry about his condition: he has long been tormented by deadly misfortunes. But I believe everything will get better again if your protection and *humanitas* support him"). Although the lack of context does not allow us to understand fully the meaning of *patrocinium*, we can see here as in the previous *Ep.* 5.31 that the term means protection in general, without implying the technical references to legal defence that it often took on. Symmachus' other occurrences of this word confirm this.[205]

At a slightly higher level of detail, *Ep.* 5.60, probably written between 396 and 398 CE, informs us that Symmachus is recommending a certain Turasius, apparently victim of an unjust verdict, to the *humanitas* of Florus Paternus, the then *comes sacrarum largitionum* for the West.[206] The close of the letter reads: *Tuere igitur aequa poscentem et humanitatis tuae latius extende famam quae incrementis maximis cumulabitur, si Turasio per te secunda successerint. Vale* ("So defend one who asks for just things, and extend further the reputation of your *humanitas*. This will increase up to the maximum if thanks to you Turasius gets good results. Farewell"). It is worth highlighting here the close relationship Symmachus establishes between *humanitas* and *aequitas*: Paternus' fame for *humanitas* will increase because, by supporting someone who is making a fair request (*aequa poscentem*), he is on the right side of the controversy.[207] Interestingly, this is a variation upon the theme of the relationship between *humanitas* and *iustitia*

---

204 Cf. Callu 2003, 184.

205 Cf. *Ep.* 2.63; 2.70; 2.74; 2.76.1; 3.37; 4.38.1; 5.41; 7.42; 9.35; 9.57; *Rel.* 3.3; 28.4. By contrast, when Symmachus wants to specify that *patrocinium* concerns the judicial sphere, either the context is explicit (*Rel.* 19.7; 30.2) or he pairs *patrocinium* with terms like *iustitia* (*Ep.* 2.91.1; 4.28.1).

206 Cf. *PLRE I* 671–672 (Paternus 6).

207 Cf. Mantovani 2017, 22: "In tutte le sue applicazioni, dunque, *aequus* è accompagnato da un carico semantico legato dall'idea di uguaglianza, di corrispondenza, di proporzione, di equilibrio."

which we have already discussed when looking into Pliny's *humanitas*.[208] To re-call it briefly: at *Ep.* 9.5.1 Pliny praises Calestrius Tiro for reconciling *humanitas* and *iustitia* during his administration of Baetica. Likewise, we noticed there that Cicero regarded *humanitas* and *iustitia* as two of the main virtues which best fit the head judge during a trial.[209] A similar case is illustrated by Ulpian, who claimed that *aequitatem* [. . .] *ante oculos habere debet iudex* ("The judge must have equity before his eyes").[210] Symmachus is once again setting himself in the tradition of his two greater 'models'. This is especially true of Cicero, one of the very few authors to link *humanitas* with *aequitas,* as does Symmachus, and not only with *iustitia.* Among the instances of this pairing, at *Verr.* 2.2.86 *humanitas* and *aequitas* characterise the personality of Scipio Aemilianus when dealing with the restoration of Himera's independence.[211] Or, if we look for a judicial context, at *Flac.* 78 Cicero uses a letter by his brother Quintus as evidence in the trial, and, in order to corroborate the content of this letter, he speaks of *litteras plenissimas humanitatis et aequitatis* ("a letter utterly full of *humanitas* and *aequitas*").[212]

The fifth instance is represented by *Ep.* 5.41, which is the longest of the three and is addressed to the higher-ranked figure, Flavius Neoterius, who was Praeto-rian prefect of the East in 380–381, Praetorian prefect of Italy in 385, and Praeto-rian prefect of Gaul in 390, before holding the consulship in 390 CE.[213] The letter, comparatively detailed and probably dated to 382,[214] recounts the vicissitudes of

---

208 On *aequitas* cf. the up-to-date, well-documented and clear overview by Mantovani 2017. Fur-ther bibliography, especially on its use in legal studies, in Mantovani 2017, 19 n. 7. On the relation-ship between *aequitas* and *iustitia* cf. Vogt-Spira 2014 and again Mantovani 2017, 51–53, whose caveat on pp. 38–39 deserves to be quoted: "Il nesso fra *iustitia* (come equivalente della greca δικαιοσύνη) e *aequitas* resta peraltro problematico, nel senso che a volte i due termini sembrano usati sinonimicamente o come un'endiadi, altre volte le nozioni vengono considerate affini, ma distinte."
209 Cf. above, pp. 97–98. More on the relation between *humanitas, iustitia,* judges and tribunals in Symmachus below, pp. 312–313.
210 *Dig.* 13.4.4.1.
211 According to Cicero's narration, Scipio Aemilianus thought that, in order to preserve Rome's glory, the then Carthaginian Himera should be given back to the Sicilians after Carthage's defeat.
212 On the pairing of *humanitas* and *aequitas* cf. also *Off.* 2.19; Caes. *BCiu.* 3.20.2, and, above all, Vitruvius' *De architectura* 9 *praef.* 2: *e quibus* [scil. *philosophis*] *qui a teneris aetatibus doctrina-rum abundantia satiantur, optimos habent sapientiae sensus, instituunt ciuitatibus humanitatis mores, aequa iura, leges, quibus absentibus nulla potest esse ciuitas incolumis* ("And those who from an early age enjoy an abundance of learning develop the best judgment, and in their cities they have established civilized customs, equal justice, and those laws without which no commu-nity can exist safely", trans. Rowland 1999).
213 *PLRE I* 623.
214 Cf. Callu 2003, 180 n. 2.

the advocate Epictetus, who was disbarred by the then consularis of Syria Carterius for slandering his opponent Sabinus.[215] In order to obtain Epictetus' reinstatement, Symmachus resorted to a twofold strategy. As well as writing to Carterius directly (*Ep.* 9.31), he also wrote to the more influential Neoterius, asking him to uphold Epictetus' case. To make his case stronger, Symmachus invokes *humanitas* to not only excuse him on the grounds of his excessive passion and sympathy with the defendant, but also to show that Epictetus was dear to a great deal of clients, who now needed and missed him:

> Nunc illa clientium turba unius fortuito insultat errori; quod ne diu maneat, tua praestabit humanitas. Satis datum est correctioni, nunc ingenium tuum respice. Illud causa meruerit, hoc tribue lenitati. Scio inlustrem uirum praefectum praetorio his quoque litteris tuis prompte esse cessurum. (*Ep.* 5.41.2)

> A crowd of clients is insulting the fortuitous mistake of one man alone, but your *humanitas* will ensure that this will not last for long. Punishment has been given ample room; now consider your attitude: the occasion required the former, but now accord mildness to your disposition. I am sure that the Praetorian prefect, that illustrious man, will be ready to surrender to this letter if it also on your behalf.

Despite the obvious affinity between *humanitas* and *lenitas* ('mildness', 'clemency'), here we find the unusual pairing of these two values. *Lenitas* can be regarded as a value which is quite close to *clementia*, which we have seen to be in turn linked to *humanitas*.[216] Cicero also paired the two in a letter to Memmius, stating that *lenitas* can originate from *humanitas*:

> Quod si ita est et si iam tua plane nihil interest, uelim, si qua offensiuncula facta est animi tui peruersitate aliquorum (noui enim gentem illam), des te ad lenitatem uel propter summam <tuam> humanitatem uel etiam honoris mei causa. (*Fam.* 13.1.4)

> If that is so, and it is now of absolutely no importance to you, I should like you, if your feelings have been ever so slightly hurt by the wrong-headedness of certain persons (I know that coterie), to allow yourself to incline towards leniency, whether because of your own exceptional *humanitas*, or even as a compliment to myself. (trans. Glynn Williams 1965)

In Symmachus' *Ep.* 5.41.2 going from *humanitas* to *lenitas* is not as straightforward as in Cicero, but in the end the relationship between the two holds tight. The impression is that, as in the case of *clementia*, *lenitas* is more specific than

---

215 We are informed of the role of Carterius thanks to another letter on the same issue which Symmachus sent to Carterius himself (*Ep.* 9.31).
216 Hellegouarc'h 1963 does not devote an independent section to *lenitas*, but only mentions it twice (261 and 263 n. 10) when discussing *clementia*.

humanitas, for it is restricted to the category of the subordinates. To put it differently and state again one of the fundamental principles of *humanitas*: while *humanitas* transcends social class distinctions and thus induces, or should induce, all true human beings to respect the 'sacred' bond which ties them together by nature, *lenitas* rather appears as one of its offspring, that which leads a higher-ranked person to show mildness towards one who is junior to them – in this respect its meaning is close to *clementia*.

One last occurrence of this category of *humanitas* merits special attention, for it enlarges the category of the recommendees to include the entire senatorial order, to which Symmachus belonged and which he famously defined as 'the better part of mankind' (*pars melior humani generis*).[217] *Ep.* 5.65, like *Ep.* 5.60, was probably written to Paternus when he was *comes sacrarum largitionum*. It deals with the problem of the high custom duties imposed on some exotic animals (in this specific instance, bears) which recently appointed quaestors and praetors had to purchase when organising inaugural games. As this 'plague' had afflicted or would afflict all senators one day, Symmachus wrote: *Quaeso igitur ut humanitatem quae inter uirtutes tuas prima est, nostri ordinis editoribus dignanter inpertias et ursorum transuectionem cupiditati mancipum subtrahas* ("I therefore ask that you courteously bestow *humanitas*, which takes pride of place among your virtues, on those from our order who have organised the games, and that you save the transport of the bears from the greed of the contractors"). Two points must be stressed. First, in comparison with the use of *humanitas* in the previous Symmachian letters of recommendation, here the social rank of the recommendees cannot be lower than that of the person to whom they are recommended – the only difference being in the privileged but fixed-term post held by Paternus. Secondly, by making appeal to Paternus' *humanitas*, and by regarding it as Paternus' most important virtue, on this occasion Symmachus seems to display a conception of *uirtus* and *humanitas* that is different from that developed in *Ep.* 8.1 and *Ep.* 2.16.[218] Yet it must be borne in mind that the singular *uirtus* usually has its own meaning(s), while the plural *uirtutes*, especially in classical and later Latin, collectively indicates all possible virtues.[219]

To summarise, in all the cases we have seen so far the *humanitas* of the recommender and the *humanitas* of the person to whom one is recommended are two

---

217 *Ep.* 1.52. Cf. also *Or.* 6.1 and *Or.* 8.3. As Chastagnol 1986, 73 puts it: "Aussi bien dans ses Lettres et ses Relationes que dans ses Discours, Symmaque nous apparaît d'emblée comme le représent-ant-type du Sénat, le sénateur par excellence."
218 On *Ep.* 2.16 cf. below, pp. 307–308.
219 Cf. Hellegouarc'h 1963, 245 and, above all, McDonnell 2006, 128–134. On the meanings of vir-tue cf. also Balmaceda 2017, 14–47.

sides of the same coin. As well as pointing to the flattering character that *humanitas* can take on – an aspect we have encountered in numerous examples throughout this study – the latter side of this polarity also testifies to the transitivity and reciprocity of this concept of value, which is in turn linked with its potential universal nature. It is therefore unsurprising to find that *humanitas* can also refer to the recommendation itself, as happens in the short *Ep.* 9.56, in which Felix asks Symmachus to recommend him to a certain Geminianus:[220] *Felix cum et domus tuae cultor esse diceret et humanitatem commendationis meae amicis interuenientibus postularet, desiderio eius familiarem paginam non negaui* ("Since Felix claims to be a worshipper of your house and asks for the *humanitas* of my recommendation through the intercession of friends, I did not refuse the friendly page that he desired"). The clarification *amicis interuenientibus* ('through the mediation of some common friends') is telling not only because it illustrates once again the relationship between *humanitas* and friendship, but also because it gives us yet another indication of that late-fourth-century network of recommendations in which *humanitas* played a central role. This urges us to broaden the compass of *humanitas* to expressions like *humanitas saeculi* or *humanitas temporum.*

The *humanitas*-topic within Symmachus' letters of recommendation has not been completely covered yet. From three letters in particular (*Epp.* 4.19, 5.39 and 7.49) that of recommendation emerges as a practice which does not find its roots in the *humanitas* of the recommender or else of his addressee, but in the spirit of *humanitas* which characterised the time in which Symmachus and his contemporaries lived. This is something we have already touched upon briefly when introducing *humanitas* in the fourth century CE and the recurrent use of the term in the legislation of the time.[221] But while Ammianus' work induces us to question the veracity of most fourth-century emperors' *humanitas*, Symmachus appears to be sincere in maintaining several times that the late fourth century was indeed a time of *humanitas*.

Ep. 4.19, probably written early in 395 CE, is tightly connected with the destiny of Symmachus' own family. When the usurper Eugenius seized power after Valentinian II's death in 392 CE and tried to re-establish Rome's traditional religion, Flavianus the Elder, whom I have already mentioned a couple of times, was one of Eugenius' main supporters, becoming his Praetorian prefect and also consul *sine collega* (in 394 CE). After Eugenius' defeat in the decisive battle of the Frigidus (5–6 September 394 CE), Theodosius demanded that Flavianus' salary as Praetorian prefect of Eugenius be given back. As Flavianus had committed suicide a few

---

220 Probably Erius Fanius Geminianus, on whom cf. *PLRE I* 389.
221 Cf. above, p. 226.

days after the Frigidus, the demand passed on to his son, Flavianus the Younger.[222] However, as Symmachus says when upholding Flavianus the Younger's case in the letter to Protadius, brother of the then *quaestor sacri palatii* Florentinus, Flavianus the Younger did not have the amount of money requested and thus begged for Theodosius' mercy.[223] In this context, Symmachus addresses Protadius as follows: *Fac igitur, si quid in te opis est, ut adflictae domui pia temporum parcat humanitas* (*Ep.* 4.19.2: "Make sure, if you have any power, that the righteous *humanitas* of this period spares this shattered household"). To avoid the tragic possibility that Flavianus the Younger may turn to a usurer in his desperate search for money, Symmachus invokes the *pia temporum humanitas*, that is to say, he asks for Protadius' help in the same spirit of *humanitas* which Theodosius has restored. It is therefore clear that *humanitas* has increasingly become an abstracted and transcendent concept, and is no longer an exclusively human characteristic. The role of the emperor(s) and of their entourage in disseminating this ideal has caused *humanitas* to become a value that people could perceive in the air. As we learn from *Ep.* 5.47, Symmachus succeeded in his intention and obtained for his son-in-law a reduction of the sanctions.[224]

An analogous situation is found in *Ep.* 5.39, which probably dates to 390 CE, when, as we saw earlier, the addressee Neoterius was both Praetorian prefect of Gaul and consul.[225] On this occasion Symmachus recommended a certain Alexander, who had fallen from grace presumably after joining the usurper Maximus' cause.[226] Relying on Neoterius' and, consequently, on Theodosius' forgiveness, Alexander hoped to have his rank of tribune and notary reinstated after Maximus' defeat (388 CE). Symmachus' letter closes thus: *Facile est enim ut sub tam pio gubernatore rei p. infortunia hominum saeculi uincat humanitas. Vale* ("It is in fact easy under such a pious ruler of the State that the *humanitas* of the age gets the better of men's misfortunes"). Instead of *humanitas temporum* we find here *humanitas saeculi*, but the meaning is pretty much the same. Indeed, the tie between *humanitas* and the ruling emperor becomes even stronger, for in such contexts the term *saeculum* is used to indicate the reign of a given emperor.[227] The *saecu-*

---

222 On Flavianus the Younger cf. Matacotta 2010, 240–243; Cavuoto-Denis 2023, 84–89.

223 On Protadius cf. *PLRE I* 751–752 (Protadius 1).

224 On the historical context of *Ep.* 4.19 as well as on Flavianus the Younger's difficult economic situation after the battle of the Frigidus cf. Marcone 1987, 59–60. On this specific issue of Flavianus the Younger cf. also below, pp. 295–296.

225 On the dating cf. Rivolta Tiberga 1992, 146. On Neoterius cf. above, pp. 289–290.

226 On this Alexander cf. Rivolta Tiberga 1992, 144.

227 For more details on Symmachus' and previous authors' (Pliny above all!) use of *saeculum* to indicate the reign of an emperor cf. Kelly 2013, 284–285.

lum alluded to is clearly the age of Theodosius, and even if the expression 'pious / faithful pilot' (*pio gubernatore*) refers to Neoterius, a broader adulation towards Theodosius, as in *Ep.* 4.19, is not missing, and is again conveyed through the use of *humanitas.*

As well as speaking one more time of *humanitas saeculi* with reference to the age of Theodosius in one of his *Relationes*, as we shall see in detail shortly, Symmachus once employs this expression in regard to the reign of Theodosius' son and successor Honorius. This occurs in *Ep.* 7.49, the dating of which is uncertain (perhaps 401–402?), but whose addressee is likely to be the Hadrian mentioned in *Ep.* 6.34, who held more than once the prefecture of Italy and Africa under Honorius.[228] Symmachus writes in support of his nephew, probably victim of an injustice that would affect his wealth, and once again he invokes the *humanitas saeculi* as the ideal which should lead Hadrian to approve his request: *Negotii autem genus de humanitate saeculi exspectat auxilium, cuius qualitas uirtutibus tuis precum lectione pandetur* ("This kind of business waits for the aid from the *humanitas* of this age. And the quality of this aid will be revealed by your virtues when reading the requests"). The relation between *humanitas* and *uirtus* which we have already observed many times is here mediated by *auxilium*.[229] Symmachus' argument goes as follows: the climate of *humanitas* typical of the age morally obliges one to grant help in that situation; the (high) quality of the help given will be the consequence of the (excellent) virtues of Hadrian. To put it more directly, an abstract, conceptual, quasi-transcendent *humanitas* fosters the exercise of virtues.

The *humanitas* which Symmachus praises in, and requests from, his interlocutors, and which he himself sometimes displays when recommending people is thus a general characteristic of one of the imperial periods during which he lived, the Theodosian age.[230] As I remarked above, this also emerges from the dating of Symmachus' uses of the word *humanitas*. I did not dwell too long on the meaning of the word *humanitas* itself in all these instances, but it should have emerged quite clearly from the contexts that it mainly evokes philanthropic attitudes, usually towards people of lower status who are experiencing hard times. The cases of *humanitas temporum* and *humanitas saeculi* then imply that the climate of an age reflects the personality of the ruler. In other words, if the late fourth century is said to be characterised by benevolence and humanity, this is probably because

---

228 Cf. *PLRE I* 406 (Hadrianus 2). On the dating and address of this and other letters from Book 7 (42–59) cf. the state of research in Callu 2003, 179–180. The suggestion that this block of letters is addressed to this Hadrian was first put forward by Bonney 1975.

229 On *humanitas* and *uirtus* cf. above, pp. 212–213; 279–280.

230 By the label 'Thedosian age' I also include here the reigns of Theodosius' sons Arcadius and Honorius.

the policy of those who ruled at that time was shaped around those values. In the case of Symmachus we have explicit evidence for this, for also emperors and imperial rescripts are linked to the word *humanitas*.

On one occasion in particular Symmachus reveals that he perceives a very close connection between the *humanitas* of the *saeculum* and that of the emperor. Or, more precisely, that he regards the two as equivalent. Symmachus deals with the problem of Flavianus the Younger's restitution of his father's 'illegitimate' salary as Praetorian prefect of Eugenius not only in the already investigated *Ep.* 4.19, but also in *Ep.* 4.51. The addressee of this letter, which dates to 395 CE like *Ep.* 4.19, is the *quaestor sacri palatii* Florentinus. In the first half of the letter Symmachus simply explains the issue in detail – and it is not worth dwelling again upon it – but the second part merits attention:

> Ergo per te ac tui similes amoliri postulat inminentem ruinam. Nec res inpetratione difficilis est. Nam quod plerisque sua inuidia laborantibus imperialis remisit humanitas, id patris nomine postulatum multo aequior uenia relaxabit. Proficiet ista concessio etiam temporum gloriae, si quod beneficiis principis deerat, pius successor adiecerit. Vale.

> Accordingly, he asks that the catastrophe which threatens him be avoided thanks to your and your fellow noblemen's intercession. Nor is this difficult to obtain. Indeed, if you ask for it in the name of a father, the emperor's indulgence will concede far more fairly what the *humanitas* of the emperor has remitted to the very many who were victims of their own envy. This concession will also add to the glory of the age, if a pious successor makes up for those merits which the previous emperor lacked. Farewell.

We need to focus on three intertwined aspects: the replacement of *humanitas temporum* of *Ep.* 4.19 with *imperialis humanitas*, the relation between the latter expression and *temporum gloria*, and Honorius' and Stilicho's continuation of Theodosius' clement policy.

Compared to *humanitas temporum* or *humanitas saeculi*, *imperialis humanitas* sounds more direct. The emperor's merits and his personal role as purveyor of this ideal are explicitly acknowledged. And even though the pairing of *humanitas* with the adjective *imperialis* is almost unique, it is perhaps unsurprising that, especially in the case of living rulers, *humanitas* is mainly linked with the term *imperator* or its cognates in panegyrics. With regard to the same Theodosius, of particular relevance is what Drepanius says at *Pan. Lat.* 2.20: *humanitas inquam, quae tam clara in imperatore quam rara est* ("a kindliness, I might say, that is as remarkable in an Emperor as it is rare", trans. Nixon 1994).[231] But, as we know, *humanitas* had also been attributed to other fourth-century emperors like Con-

---

[231] On the occurrences of *humanitas* in Drepanius' panegyric cf. Rees 2023, 295–296.

stantine, Gratian and, much earlier, to Trajan in Pliny's *Panegyricus*, the model for all panegyrics which would follow.[232]

On the other hand the larger notion of period or age remains, and the fact that the acts deriving from the emperor's *humanitas* contribute to the glory of the age (*temporum gloria*) has the result of making explicit the obvious: the ruler determines the political and social climate of his reign, as well as its rhetoric. But the reference to Honorius as continuer of his father's policy adds a deeper message: in the case of very good rulers, like Theodosius, their policies may even determine their successors'. In other words, a *saeculum* does not necessarily end with an emperor's death. Theodosius dies without *humanitas* being his exclusive prerogative. His philanthropic attitude has affected his contemporaries and also his successors, so much so that what had been his former *imperialis humanitas* has now become the *humanitas* of an entire generation, and, more precisely, the *humanitas* which glorifies an entire age (*temporum gloria*).

At this point, although the *Epistulae* have much else to say about Symmachus' *humanitas*, I want to turn to his *Relationes*. As with Pliny the Younger, we are fortunate enough to possess both private and official writings by Symmachus. And as with Pliny the Younger, the key (and true) social and political role played by the idea of *humanitas* best emerges from its being used consistently in both kinds of writings.

The 49 *Relationes* are reports which Symmachus sent as *praefectus Vrbis* to some or all the members of the imperial college between 384 and 385 CE. They deal with different matters related to the city of Rome, and their aim is either to inform the emperors of current affairs or to ask them for advice on particular issues (or both). According to Callu, the *Relationes* cover four areas: the most important one concerns the administration of the City and Symmachus' role of *praefectus Vrbis* therein (17); then follow reports on judicial (12) and social (11) matters, while 9 are about politico-religious affairs.[233]

Within some of these *relationes* we encounter instances of both *humanitas* with reference to the emperor and *humanitas* in regard to the *saeculum*. Let me first focus on the latter. *Rel.* 9, a 'social' report in Callu's classification,[234] is addressed to both Theodosius and Arcadius, and tells of the equestrian statues that the Senate dedicated to the emperor's father, Flavius Theodosius, (officially) to thank Theodosius for some imperial gifts (chariot races and theatrical plays)

---

232 Cf. *Pan. Lat.* 12.14.1; 3.28.2; Aus. *Grat. act.* 24, and Plin. *Pan.* 24.2, on which cf. also above, pp. 269–270; 90.
233 Callu 2009, li–lii. For an introduction to the *Relationes* cf. also Barrow 1973, 15–19; Cavuoto-Denis 2023, 277–327.
234 Callu 2009, lii n. 5.

which he had recently bestowed on Rome, thereby making Rome's inhabitants enthusiastic and bringing the City back to its past splendour.[235] After this long *captatio beneuolentiae*, towards the end of the letter Symmachus does not miss the chance to ask the emperors to have more food sent to Rome – we must bear in mind that in 384 CE Rome was hit by famine.[236]

> Fecistis ut Vrbs cana luxuriet in primam reducta laetitiam et uer illud quondam uigentis aetatis. Audeo iam sperare potiora: mittetis etiam regiam classem quae annonariis copiis augeat deuotae plebis alimoniam. Hanc uero in Tiberinis ostiis mixtus Populo Senatus excipiet; uenerabimur tamquam sacras puppes quae felicia onera Aegyptiae frugis inuexerint. Non sunt auara uota quae saeculi excitauit humanitas: de exemplis uenit ista fiducia; magna sumendo maiora praesumimus. (*Rel.* 9.7)

> Your efforts have made a city grey with age flourish again, have restored it to its original luxuriance and to the springtime of its earlier years of vigour. I hopefully await still better things; you are going to send a royal fleet to augment with plentiful supplies of corn the free maintenance of a devoted people. This fleet senate and people together will welcome in the entrances to the Tiber: we shall revere as almost sacred the ships which will have brought in their bountiful cargoes of the crops of Egypt. It is not greed that inspires the desires which the *humanitas* of the age has aroused; rather, the precedents you have set are the source of our confident expectations; because we have received so much we anticipate even more. (trans. Barrow 1973)

The *humanitas saeculi* appears therefore as a sufficient reason for being certain that the people's hopes will be fulfilled. Despite Vera's remarks, there is no denying that the level of flattery is high, but at the same time it is evident that *humanitas* is given a central role.[237] Furthermore, the clarification that such a trust relies on previous examples of the emperor's *humanitas* accounts for the presence of an expression like *humanitas saeculi*, for it is taken for granted that this value has long been characterising the policy of Theodosius by this time.

And not only of Theodosius. We have just seen that his son and successor Honorius too was affected by this philanthropic attitude, and the same holds true for Valentinian II, the then Augustus of the West. And if the case of Honorius tes-

---

235 According to Vera 1979, esp. 394–395, the dedication of statues to Theodosius' father was part of a broader political project aimed at strenghtening the relationship between Theodosius and the Senate of Rome, i.e. the Western part of the empire.

236 On this famine cf. the section on Ammianus (above, p. 248), and below, p. 310.

237 Vera 1979, 383: "Certamente, i due motivi, quello dell'onore concesso a Flavio Teodosio e quello della richiesta di aiuti annonari, si saldano senza tracce visibili di sutura sotto l'abile penna di Simmaco. Tuttavia, non è da presumersi una rozza proposizione utilitaristica, in chiave di do ut des, nel conferimento delle statue e nella richiesta di approvvigionamenti. Diciamo semplicemente che il clima instauratosi avrebbe facilitato l'accoglimento dei voti del senato."

tifies to the chronological duration of *humanitas*, its being related to Valentinian II is all the more important in that it shows that *humanitas* was one of the political and cultural values, and thus attitudes, that bound together eastern and western policies of the time. But the case can be put in more detailed terms: if we accept the well-documented and convincing thesis that it was Theodosius' aim to try to manage to have great influence on western emperors, and on Valentinian II in particular,[238] then the spread of *humanitas* in the West is to be seen as one of the aspects in which Theodosius' policy materialised all over the empire.

One example of Valentinian II's *humanitas* occurs at *Rel.* 41.1, where this value, being the value of an emperor, is even called *sacra*. This 'judicial' report dealing with a case of succession is actually addressed to the entire imperial college, but the context makes it undoubtedly clear that *humanitas* only refers to Valentinian:

> Certum atque dilucidum est nihil esse tam familiare legibus quam Vestra decreta, Domini Imperatores Valentiniane, Theodosi et Arcadi inclyti, uictores ac triumphatores semper Augusti, sed executorum praua interpretatio, dum supplicantibus fauet, plerumque iussa corrumpit. Statuerat receptus in caelum germanus Numinis Vestri, cum Marcianus dudum protector Aggareae bona tamquam uacantia postulasset, ut, si ea hereditas scriptum successorem uel legitimum non haberet, in ius fisci tamquam domino nuda concederet; tunc insinuato per rationalem patrimonii modo opperiretur petitor, quid ei sacra deferret humanitas.

> It is certain and transparently clear that nothing is so akin to the laws as your decrees, my Lords Emperors, but a wrong-headed interpretation of them by those who carry them out often perverts your commands by showing favour to litigants. Your Divinities' brother now received into heaven had given his decision when Marcianus, in former time a *protector*, asked for the property of Aggarea as being property without an owner; he had ordered that, if the inheritance had no heir nominated in the will and no legitimate successor, it should pass, as lacking an owner, into the jurisdiction of the fisc; then, when the *rationalis* had provided information about the extent of the estate, the suppliant should wait to see what the Emperor in his *humanitas* would grant him. (trans. Barrow 1973)

In this passage, Symmachus' reference to Gratian's brother (*germanus Numinis Vestri*) links *humanitas* to Valentinian II. Less idealistic than usual, here the emperor's *humanitas* is measured in money and nothing else. If we bear in mind the (para)etymological relation of *humanitas* with man (*homo*), its rare pairing with the adjective *sacra* ('sacred', 'holy') might seem striking, and even oxymoronic – compare also the opposition between *humanitas* and *diuinitas* we saw in Pliny

---

238 Cf. Vera 1979.

the Younger's *Panegyricus*.[239] Yet in ancient Latin the pairing of *homo* with *sacer* indicated a man "which might be violated without any *nefas*: a man whom anyone might slay with impunity."[240] The expression *sacer esto* was in fact a curse, "and the *homo sacer* on whom this curse falls is an outcast, a banned man, tabooed, dangerous."[241] By Theodosius' time, however, *sacer* was already commonly used to designate members of the imperial house: if on the one hand the term was no longer given particular emphasis, on the other hand its association with emperors testified to their implicit divine nature.[242]

Indeed, on one other occasion Symmachus even speaks of the *humanitas* of a sacred rescript (*rescripti sacri humanitate*).[243] The emperor is likely to be once again the addressee of the message, and the context is once again a 'judicial' *relatio*, the short 39. This instance of *humanitas* further testifies to the pervasiveness of this word in the socio-political climate of the age, so much so that even a document is said to possess *humanitas* – granted, because the rescript embodies the emperor's will as well as his benevolent attitude.

One more time Symmachus attributes *humanitas* to Valentinian II, and this occurs again in an official report, *Relatio* 14. This text is of particular interest because it brings into play a very important social category of Symmachus' day, the guilds. Due to compelling military needs, the emperor had ordered all Roman guilds to hand over to the Treasury an unspecified number of horses. But at the guilds' insistent request and probably even lockout threat, Symmachus refused to obey the emperor's order.[244] The aim of his report to Valentinian is therefore to ask the emperor to withdraw or change his order. To persuade him, Symmachus also resorts to an example featuring Valentinian I, Valentinian II's father, as protagonist. According to his account, Valentinian I found himself in an analogous situation, but withdrew an order at the people's protest. *Humanitas* is once again located at a strategic point, at the close of the letter:

> Quod si adiciantur insolita, forsitan consueta cessabunt. Quare paternum Clementiae Tuae ingerimus exemplum. Praetuli oraculum quod pius successor imiteris. Oro atque obsecro ne Populum quem triumphantes saepe ueneramini ceteris urbibus conferatis. Dabit fortuna

239 Cf. above, p. 85. On the original meaning of *sacer* and its connection with gods cf. Warde Fowler 1911.
240 Warde Fowler 1911, 58, with reference to Macrobius, *Sat.* 3.7.3.
241 Warde Fowler 1911, 58. The bibliography on *homo sacer* is vast: cf. above all Agamben 1995.
242 Cf. *OLD* s.v. *sacer*, 7 and, above all, Hiltbrunner 1968.
243 *Rel.* 39.3.
244 More details on this episode in Matacotta 2010, 310–312, according to whom Symmachus' decision reveals that he feared the Roman people more than the emperor. Cf. also Sogno 2006, 39–40 on this *relatio* as well as on the guilds and their role in Symmachus' Rome.

melior quidquid castrensis usus efflagitat; humanitatis merito necessitas Vestra sedabitur. (*Rel.* 14.4)

Now, if services to which they are unaccustomed are added, there is a risk that those to which they are already accustomed will languish. That is why we impress on you his pronouncement which it is for you to imitate as his dutiful successor. I beg and beseech you not to equate with all other cities the people whom in your triumphs you have often regarded with respect. Fortune will improve and will give you what the requirements of the imperial administration demand; if you show *humanitas*, it will win your alleviation of your present needs. (trans. Barrow 1973)

On this occasion we encounter another new pairing, or better, a new opposition: *humanitas* vs. *necessitas*.[245] As usual, *humanitas* appears as the winning force, but in this very case this value ought to be as strong as to prevail even over imperial military obligations and needs. If it indeed prevailed, we do not know, for the outcome of this matter is uncertain. What is certain however is that Symmachus must have regarded *humanitas* as a very powerful and reliable value, and one which could also be effective on Valentinian II.

Aside from one other occurrence at which I shall look later, in the *Relationes* *humanitas* has therefore first and foremost to do with the emperors' behaviours and with the political climate of the time. As Symmachus was prefect of Rome, it is obvious that he primarily addressed his official reports to the Augustus of the West, Valentinian II. But what really matters is that, as in the case of Pliny, in both the *Relationes* and the *Epistulae* there is evidence that *humanitas* was used with political purposes at both official and private level.

One further, yet speculative argument, given the paucity of material to investigate, may be made in favour of the official return of *humanitas* only after Theodosius'accession. This is provided by Symmachus' other official writings which have come down to us, the *Orationes*. Symmachus' fame among his contemporaries, and more generally in late antiquity, was mainly due to his oratorical skills.[246] Unfortunately, very little of his oratorical production is extant, and in all likelihood all the eight preserved orations can be dated before 377 CE.[247] Of these eight speeches, only three are panegyrics that Symmachus delivered on emperors, and, what is more, they are lacunose. He delivered *Or.* 1 and 2 on Valentinian I, and *Or.* 3 on Gratian. They all date about 369–370 CE. Contrary to the cases of Pliny's *Panegyricus* on Trajan and, albeit on a smaller scale, of Drepanius' on Theodosius,

---

245 But cf. *necessaria humanitas* of *Decl. mai.* 9.15.6: above, pp. 195–196.
246 Cf. above, pp. 274–275.
247 On the dating of Symmachus' *Orationes* cf. Seeck 1883, ix–x; Cristo 1974, 38–39. More generally on the *Orationes* cf. Cavuoto-Denis 2023, 329–381.

none of them include the noun *humanitas*.[248] But on the other hand, this is consistent with Ammianus' treatment of *humanitas* with regard to the emperors whom we encounter in his historical work, especially in the case of Valentinian I, who despite knowing good examples of *humanitas* never possessed it.[249] Of course other somewhat similar virtues can be praised in panegyrics, like for example *clementia*, but the impression is that *humanitas* preserved a less standardised meaning – while *clementia* had by that time also become part of the emperor's official titulature.[250] Moreover, Sogno's investigation of the virtues of Valentinian I that Symmachus praises in his two surviving orations is revealing, for no moral virtue seems to be applied to this emperor.[251]

To return to *humanitas*, judging from Symmachus' writings, it looks as if before Theodosius *humanitas* was rather the prerogative of the Senate, while only after Theodosius the emperors shared this senatorial value; or better, vice versa. *Or.* 4, which probably dates to 376 CE, is symptomatic: *humanitas* is used twice to refer to the Senate, while *clementia* is attributed to the emperors. Let us look at the relevant passage more closely. This oration is known as *Pro patre*, for Symmachus delivered it to thank both emperors and Senate for appointing his father Avianus Symmachus to the ordinary consulship for 377 CE.[252] In the first extant paragraph the opposition between the Senate's *humanitas* and the emperors' *clementia* is explicit. The one led the Senate to ask for this appointment, the other persuaded the emperors to grant it:

> <Si quis miratus cur post patris mei grauissimam orationem ego quoque susceperim> dicendi munus et gratulationis uerba protulerim, secum reputet quantos huius beneficii habeamus auctores – humanitatem uestram qui postulastis, clementiam principum qui dederunt – desinet profecto mirari non unum pro consulatu gratias agere, quem tam multos uideat detulisse. (*Or.* 4.1)

> If anyone wonders that after my father's impressive oration I too have decided to give a speech and express words of gratitude, they just need to reflect on the importance of the sources of this gift – the *humanitas* of you who have asked for it, the *clementia* of the Emperors who have accorded it – and no doubt they will stop wondering that one sole person

---

248 On Pliny's *humanitas* cf. above, pp. 83–115. In Drepanius' panegyric there are overall three occurrences of *humanitas*, two at 20.2 and one at 20.5: cf. Rees 2023, 295–296.
249 Cf. above, p. 237.
250 On *clementia* in late antiquity cf. also above, pp. 264–265. On its presence in imperial titulature cf. Dowling 2006, 234–235. Cf. also below, pp. 302–304.
251 Cf. Sogno 2006, 15–17. The praised virtues are *patientia* (to be taken as endurance of extreme weather or geographical conditions), *industria*, warfare skills, *prouidentia*.
252 More on this oration in Pabst 1989, 159–163; Sogno 2006, 25; Matacotta 2010, 203; Cavuoto-Denis 2023, 352–371.

> cannot express adequate thanks for a consulate which has been conferred by so many people.

The problem is the extent to which we can speak of a true opposition between *humanitas* and *clementia* in this passage.[253] As we have already seen, it is quite common to find these two values together.[254] But on most occasions they are clearly used to strengthen one and the same idea of benevolence. At other times instead they are on two different levels, *humanitas* representing a universal value that each and every man can show towards a fellow human being, and *clementia* being the prerogative of a higher-ranked person towards an inferior.[255] This Symmachian occurrence may well belong to this second category: the senators are on the same hierarchical level as Avianus Symmachus, and thus *humanitas* is the right way to call the attitude which they display; by contrast, the emperors are senior to him, and *clementia* sounds more appropriate to emphasise this distance. It looks as though, in contrast to the tendency of the age, *clementia* as used here maintains its weighty connotations as well as its original characteristics of one-sided value, which are further emphasised by its comparison with *humanitas*.[256] But even more importantly, once again Symmachus' *Weltanschauung* reveals striking analogies with Pliny the Younger's. As we saw towards the beginning of this study, to stress Trajan's distance from his predecessors, and above all Domitian, Pliny preferred to praise his *humanitas* rather than his *clementia*, with the very aim of spotlighting his being a man among men rather than a tyrant.[257] The same is true of Symmachus: before the accession of Theodosius, *humanitas* could hardly be attributed to emperors, who at best possessed *clementia*. More generally, Symmachus employs the noun *clementia* very rarely (six times in the *Epistulae* and three in the *Orationes*) if we exclude from this calculation the 45 occurrences of *Clementia Vestra / Tua* with which he addresses the imperial college in the *Relationes*, and which, I stress, testify again to the weakening of its meaning. In the end we can say that two equivalences hold: Symmachus corresponds to Pliny, Theodosius corresponds to Trajan. Theoretically, despite the fact that the meanings of *humanitas*

---

253 Indeed Kelly 2013, 282 maintains that there is unanimity between senate and emperor at the beginning of this oration.
254 Cf. especially above, pp. 157–158.
255 Cf. above, pp. 39–40.
256 On the general evolution of *clementia* in the imperial period cf. Dowling 2006, 234: "There is compelling evidence that in the imperial period clemency transcends boundaries of class and patronage and is found at all levels of Roman society, even among equals."
257 Cf. above, p. 85.

and *clementia* can overlap, at least partly, in Pliny's footsteps Symmachus seems to show that word choice matters, and matters greatly.

Only one exception might seem to stand out, *Ep.* 4.4, which merits attention because of its role in modern Symmachian scholarship. It was addressed in 399 CE to Stilicho, who at that time was probably the most powerful man in the Roman empire, to thank him for Flavianus the Younger's appointment to the urban prefecture. Unlike most Symmachian letters, *Ep.* 4.4 is unfortunately too long to be quoted in full, so I limit myself to reproducing part of § 2:

> Maius quiddam est honorem restituere quam dedisse; illud enim fieri fortuna consentit, hoc contra ipsam praestat humanitas. Praemiserat alia exempla clementiae receptus caelo principum parens et Flaviano meo multa casibus detracta reddiderat: reservatus est unus et potissimus bonitatis titulus heredi, quem magnitudinis tuae monitu paternis beneficiis d. n. Honorius adiecit interpretatus scilicet diuo principi tempus non animum defuisse. Nunc perfecta sunt a successore consimili interrupta fato clementiae. (*Ep.* 4.4.2)

> Reestablishing an honour is more important than bestowing it, for while one thing happens in agreement with fate, in the other case *humanitas* prevails over fate. The father of our Emperors, who is now embraced in Heaven, gave other examples of his *clementia* and gave back to my dear Flavianus a lot of things of which he had been deprived by fate. A unique as well as most powerful sign of goodness has been reserved for his heir: on your Greatness' advice, our Lord Honorius has added it to the benefits granted by his father, rightly judging that the divine Emperor had lacked time rather than willingness. Now his very similar successor has accomplished the *clementia* which had been interrupted by fate.

Its commentator Marcone, in regarding this letter as crucial to understanding the policy of continuity between Theodosius and his successors, claims: "La ep. 4 è il documento più significativo di questa prospettiva ideologica: a Onorio riconosce il merito di aver seguito gli *exempla clementiae* paterni e di aver sentito il dovere di recare a compimento quanto era stato interrotto dal destino."[258] Yet here and in previous passages Marcone seems to overestimate the importance of *clementia* as it emerges from Symmachus' oeuvre, probably because he goes too far in establishing a complete overlap between *humanitas* and *clementia*. Indeed, on page 26 he had (more correctly) emphasised the role of *humanitas* as mirror of the Theodosian age. But it is not only the low rate of occurrences of *clementia* that contradicts his thesis, but the very context in which *clementia* appears twice at *Ep.* 4.4.2.[259] We must bear in mind that Honorius gave back to Flavianus an office which he had already held under the 'reign' of the usurper Eugenius in 394 CE.[260]

---

[258] Marcone 1987, 28.
[259] This, as it seems to me, emerges well from the reading of this letter provided by Matacotta 2010, 242–243.
[260] Cf. Marcone 1987, 39.

But siding with a usurper was a grave fault which usually implied the death penalty. Yet the new appointment clearly proves that Flavianus had been forgiven by Honorius by 399 CE. Hence the need to praise the emperor's *clementia*, because this is the most proper way to describe the behaviour of a higher-ranking person who would have the right to condemn someone but prefers to spare him. Indeed, as a way of introducing his praise, Symmachus first underscores the importance of *humanitas* in restoring Flavianus to his role, but then the context requires more technicality, and also more flattery. Accordingly, I find it risky to confer general validity to a principle which Symmachus applies to a particular case, and which does not allow for placing *clementia* on the same level as *humanitas* in his value system.

But to return to *Or.* 4, Symmachus mentions the Senate's *humanitas* once more, this time echoing Cicero rather than Pliny: *Noua sunt quae adgredimur, sed uestra humanitas auctor est inusitata faciendi* (*Or.* 4.2:"What I am going to do is something novel, but your *humanitas* encourages to do something unusual"). The unusual (*inusitata*) practice Symmachus refers to is his delivery of this very oration to thank Senate and emperors for bestowing an honour not on the person speaking themselves, but on someone else, his father. In regarding the Senate's *humanitas* as the mainspring of his action, he calls to mind Cicero's *Pro Archia* – § 3 in particular – as a token of its influence on future uses of the *humanitas* argument in oratorical contexts.[261] But while on previous occasions our interest mainly lay on the expression *studia humanitatis*, now *uestra* (i.e. the judges') *humanitas* is crucial, for this is one of the main reasons why the judges should allow Cicero to resort to an oratorical genre which probably had no precedents (*hoc uti genere dicendi quod non modo a consuetudine iudiciorum uerum etiam a forensi sermone abhorreat*, "I should be using a manner of speaking which is out of keeping not only with the tradition of the courts but also with the customary style of forensic pleading", trans. Berry 2000). So we are dealing with two oratorical contexts out of character and both facilitated by *humanitas*. Symmachus' instance, however, looks like a variation upon a theme, for it also shows differences from the Ciceronian case. One in particular: while Cicero hopes that the judges will display their *humanitas* – and his tone strategically takes this as a given – Symmachus delivers his oration because the senators have already given proof of theirs towards his father. On a linguistic level then, there is little evidence that this Symmachian occurrence of *humanitas* is as educationally nuanced as the Ciceronian ones in the *Pro Archia*.

---

261 On Cicero's *Pro Archia* cf. above, pp. 54–60.

One last occurrence of *humanitas* in the *Orationes* is to be found in *Or. 7 Pro Synesio*, which, like the *Pro patre*, was presumably delivered before the senate.[262] According to Sogno, this is one "of the most revealing documents concerning the process of *adlectio*, by which new members of non-senatorial birth gained access to the senate."[263] Moreover, this speech summarises "the ideal prerequisites of a candidate to be admitted into the *amplissimus ordo*."[264] In the light of this and of what emerged from the *Pro patre*, it will probably come as no surprise that *humanitas* is one of the virtues at which Synesius, the new senator in question, aims:

> Pendet circa illum sollicitae domus pietas, sed ipse de se exigit quidquid omnium sibi humanitas relaxauit. Iam uideo, Iuliane, causas consultissimae placiditatis tuae: tali filio magis securus es quam remissus. (*Or.* 7.5)

> The affection of an anxious family floats over him, but he requires from himself the *humanitas* that people usually acknowledge to him. I can see, Julian, the reason of your very careful placidity: with a son like this you are more untroubled than relaxed.

The first and major part of the chapter primarily focused on the political and utilitarian role played by *humanitas* in Symmachus' oeuvre and in Roman society during the reigns from Valentinian I to Arcadius and Honorius, with great emphasis being placed on the watershed policy of Theodosius I. In this context, I looked at how *humanitas* contributes to explaining Symmachus' action and the Theodosian age. With this aim in mind I also took pains to specify the political and administrative posts held by Symmachus' interlocutors, in order to underscore further the existence of a network of high-ranked people which determined the public life of the age and which was based on certain common values.[265] I now turn my attention to how Symmachus' work can help us further understand the myriad nuances that *humanitas* can take on as well as the countless contexts in which we can encounter it. Needless to say, this differentiation has practical purposes, but there is obviously a high level of overlap. The first part itself also testifies to the persistence of the philanthropic connotations of *humanitas* and, to a lesser degree, of its educational and cultural meaning. By the same token, this second half will deal with occurrences of *humanitas* which are set in identical or similar social contexts to the previous ones.

---

262 Sogno 2006, 26.
263 Sogno 2006, 26.
264 Sogno 2006, 28.
265 Cf. Sogno 2006, 88: "The purpose of letter writing is not primarily the communication of information but the formation and preservation of ties of friendships in a world where distances made visits if not impossible then certainly difficult."

Let me start with those instances which provide further confirmation that Symmachus' conception of *humanitas* is comparable to that of Cicero and Pliny the Younger. As we noticed in passing earlier on, Symmachus, like his two models, believes that *humanitas* potentially has educational components, that is to say, that it is, or can be, related to the Greek concept of παιδεία. In Symmachus however this does not emerge as clearly as in other authors where we encountered expressions like *studia humanitatis*. At times he seems to have reached a level of assimilation in which the Greek concepts of παιδεία and φιλανθρωπία are simultaneously present but hardly distinguishable from one another. This might be the case in *Ep.* 1.18 to Ausonius, as we saw earlier, and best emerges in more personal letters addressed to his close friend Flavianus the Elder, another person of letters.[266] On two occasions Symmachus sends him letters of recommendation in favour of literati using *humanitas* as leverage. At first sight, *humanitas* is used in the same way and with the same meaning as in the other letters of recommendation investigated above.[267] Yet we must bear in mind two points. First, Symmachus was often cryptic in his letters and took much for granted. Secondly, it is not always sufficient to focus our attention on the sender: the identity of the recipient also affects the content of a letter. Before pushing this reasoning further, let us look at the texts:

> Pro optimis uiris quisquis interuenit, non magis illorum uidetur iuuare commodum quam suum commendare iudicium. Quare in eo quod fratris mei Maximi desideria litteris prosequor, non tam illi usui <sum>, quam mihi laudi est. Est enim uita atque eruditione liberalium disciplinarum pariter insignis neque ulli praestantium philosophorum secundus ac propterea tua familiaritate dignissimus. Cuius tibi negotia cum in rem missus absoluerit, quaeso ut humanitate, qua clarus es, iustas petitiones ingrauato auxilio prosequaris. Vale. (*Ep.* 2.29)

> Whoever intervenes in favour of excellent men seems to support their interests no less than recommend his own judgement. This is why whenever I accompany with a letter my brother Maximus' requests I am of use to him no less than of praise to myself. He is in fact distinguished for his life as well as for his erudition in the liberal disciplines; he is not inferior to the most outstanding philosophers and, for these reasons, he is absolutely worthy of your friendship. Once his envoy for this business has made you clear the situation, I beg, in the name of that *humanitas* for which you are famous, that you offer to him your increased help to satisfy his legitimate requests. Farewell.

> Vt habitus et crinis indicio est, Serapammon litterarum peritiam pollicetur, cuius si se meminisset exortem, nunquam philosophis congruentem sumpsisset ornatum. Sed de hoc uestra aestimatio sit, qui talium rerum profitemini notionem. Mihi religio fuit non negare uerba

---

266 On Flavianus' literary works cf. Matacotta 2010, 239–240.
267 Cf. above, pp. 286–294 in particular.

poscenti. Facies rem morum tuorum, si ope atque humanitate fortunam peregrinantis adiuueris. Vale. (*Ep.* 2.61)

Judging from his outfit and hairstyle, Serapammon must be a seasoned literatus. For if he had thought of lacking in knowledge, he would have never put on clothes similar to those of the philosophers. But I leave it to you to appreciate it or not, since you claim to be an expert on this kind of things. My respect towards him has obliged me not to deny these words for which he asked. You will do something in keeping with your habits if you help a man coming from far away with your support and *humanitas*. Farewell.

Both these letters emphasise the erudition and the literary skills that the recommendees possess (*eruditione liberalium disciplinarum . . . insignis* and *litterarum peritiam pollicetur*), thereby implying that this is the common denominator between Flavianus and themselves.[268] Thus, when a man of letters of a certain standing like Flavianus was asked to support their causes on these grounds and was reminded of the *humanitas* for which he was famous (*humanitate, qua clarus es*), it is easy to imagine that he will have taken it as a more or less flattering appeal to his culture rather than to his mere benevolence. Nor is it sensible to think that a man like Symmachus, who knew Cicero and his oratorical strategies almost by heart, resorted by accident to a multifaceted value like *humanitas* on these two occasions.

One further occurrence where *humanitas* seems to be educationally and culturally connoted can be found in Symmachus' *Epistulae*, and yet again within a letter addressed to Flavianus the Elder. The beginning of *Ep.* 2.16 reads: *Si necdum filii mei Nicasii laudabiles mores et honestum institutum didicisti, accipe pro eo locupletissimum uadimonium, meum Promotum uirtute et humanitate conspicuum* ("If you have not yet learnt of the laudable behaviour and noble customs of my son Nicasius, take this very rich deposit in place of him: this is my dear Promotus, famous for his virtue and *humanitas*"). We have already found the twinning of *uirtus* and *humanitas* at *Ep.* 8.1, and already on that occasion I suggested that *humanitas* is likely to be related to education. Here three further elements can be added to the argumentation I put forward then. First and foremost, as Cecconi shows well, Promotus must have been a great general:[269] this fact allows us to link *uirtus* to his military skills, and, consequently, *humanitas* to his respect for culture, along the same and more proper lines observed in Eumenius' panegyric.[270] Secondly, the addressee is still Flavianus the Elder, which means that it

---

268 On these letters' attention for liberal arts, philosophy and those who pursue them, as well as for the relationship between *Ep.* 2.29 and *Ep.* 2.61 cf. Cecconi 2002, 235–239; 349–351.
269 Cecconi 2002, 192–193 (with further bibliography).
270 Cf. above, pp. 212–213.

might be an effective strategy to recommend a person for his uncommon culture, this time leaving it implicit that love for culture is what unites the two of them. Thirdly and conversely, it would make little sense in this general context if the stress were on the philanthropic aspect of *humanitas*, for how could this have significant consequences for Flavianus' opinion of him?

Ep. 8.1 and *Ep.* 2.16 thus portray two valiant men, who were probably military leaders and whose skills and values are synthesized in the formula *uirtute et humanitate*. But on other occasions Symmachus connects *humanitas* with more specific virtues or abstract concepts. We have seen for instance that it can be opposed to *caritas* and *religio* when it comes to differentiating between letters of recommendation and intimate letters among friends, or else it can be paired with *aequitas* or *lenitas* when its meaning needs to be clarified further.[271] At *Ep.* 7.116 instead *humanitas* is what enables one to understand who merits *benignitas* and *misericordia*, and on which occasions. The letter's opening reads: *Scis pro insita tibi humanitate quid paruulis et parentum suffragio destitutis benignitatis ac misericordiae debeatur* ("Thanks to your innate *humanitas* you know what kind of benevolence and compassion is due to the young people who have been deprived of their parents' aid"). The context is well known, that of inheritance after the death of one's parents. Once again Symmachus asks for the help of an influential person, Patruinus, *comes sacrarum largitionum* for the West from 401 to 408 CE.[272] Those in need of help are the sons of a certain Severus, probably to identify with Valerius Severus (*PLRE I* 837 – Valerius Severus 29). As for the relation between *humanitas*, *misericordia* and *benignitas*, a distinction is required. We have seen, especially while looking into Apuleius' use of *humanitas*, that the meanings of *humanitas* and *misericordia* can even overlap sometimes. More interesting is the unusual pairing with *benignitas*, which sounds very appropriate in the case in question. As Hellegouarc'h illustrates well, *benignitas* is that virtue which induces people to bestow gifts.[273] In this respect, it is similar to *beneficentia*, the value by which benefits (*beneficia*) are bestowed. By presenting *humanitas* as the origin of *misericordia* and *benignitas*, Symmachus thus implies that at times it is not enough to have a benevolent and clement attitude (*misericordia*), but concrete acts (*benignitas*) are necessary. This example clearly contributes to make explicit an aspect of concreteness which is often only implicit in the notion of *humanitas*, but that in Symmachus' oeuvre is not unique, as the following examples show.

---

271 Cf. above, pp. 281–285; 288–291.
272 Cf. *PLRE II* 843–844.
273 Hellegouarc'h 1963, 217–218.

An analogous situation of inheritance is portrayed in *Rel.* 41, which deals with the problem of the *delatores*, those who denounced (ostensible) vacant goods to the public administration in the hope of seeing these goods bestowed on themselves. Without looking in detail into this *relatio*, I only notice that *humanitas* refers to the *testator*'s generosity (41.3: *nihil de testatore humanitatis exigeret*), although the amount of money in question is very low. Its meaning is therefore very close to the previous occurrence of *humanitas* at *Ep.* 7.116.

Along the same lines is to be set the short *Ep.* 9.65 to Alevius, in all likelihood an addresse of unusual low rank:[274]

> Vehiculi rotae cuius debeant esse mensurae linea missa testabitur. Superest ut omne carpentum adfabre et firmis compaginibus explicetur. Si parte pretii ad hoc opus est, quod dandum scripseris iubebo numerari. Humanitas xeniorum tuorum debet esse moderatior: religio enim animis potius quam muneribus aestimatur. Vale.

> The sketch I am sending to you will make it clear of what size the wheel of the carriage needs to be. Now we have to put together the whole wagon skilfully and with a firm structure. If you need an advance payment for this, write to me how much it amounts to and I will have it paid. The *humanitas* of your gifts must be more sober: affection is shown by one's attitude rather than one's gifts. Farewell.

While I note in passing that we face here another instance of *religio* with reference to the maintenance of friendship,[275] our focus goes on *humanitas xeniorum tuorum*. If in *Ep.* 7.116 the relationship between *humanitas* and gifts is indirect, in *Ep.* 9.65 it is clearly direct, and it looks as if the gifts themselves become vehicles of this ideal.

The same direct relationship between *humanitas* and gifts is found in *Ep.* 9.82, in which Symmachus thanks the unknown addressee of this letter for sending him fruits from his Marsican orchards. The short message closes with an Homeric echo: *Faciet frequens humanitas tua ut saepe alias in Marsos bona Phaeacum translata celebremus* ("Your frequent *humanitas* will make sure that we often celebrate the fruits of the Faiakes transplanted among the Marsi").[276]

To remain in the domain of concreteness, we learn from Symmachus that *humanitas* can even accelerate an oil delivery. Judging from *Ep.* 9.58, there had long been an office responsible for the supply of African oil in Formia.[277] But at the time when Symmachus sent this letter to the *praefectus annonae* Caecilianus to

---

274 Cf. Roda 1981, 197.
275 Cf. above, pp. 281–283.
276 Cf. Hom. *Od.* 7.114–126. For a list of the Homeric echoes in Symmachus cf. Roda 1981, 213 – with further bibliography.
277 More details and relevant bibliography in Roda 1981, 191–192.

ask for his intervention, probably between 396 and 397 CE, there must have been some delay in the delivery which might harm Formia's inhabitants.

A much more serious situation is portrayed in *Ep.* 4.74, written in 383 CE and addressed to Eusignius, the then proconsul of Africa.[278] This letter testifies to the poor harvest and to the ensuing harsh conditions suffered by the African provinces. Further, it envisages a real famine for the following year, the famous famine recounted by Ammianus, which would cause the expulsion of foreigners from Rome.[279] Under the circumstances, Symmachus urges Eusignius to help the provincial peoples by showing all his *humanitas*:

> Iure igitur ad aeternorum principum prouidentiam prouincialium sollicitudo confugit. Interea dum maior ab illis salubritas petitur, humanitas tua foueat exhaustos et tamquam particeps doloris alieni persuadeat laborantibus sibi accidisse, quidquid prouinciae pertulerunt. (*Ep.* 4.74.2)

> With good reason therefore the anxiety of the residents of the provinces has induced them to make appeal to the foresight of the eternal emperors. In the meantime, while better health is required to them, may your *humanitas* soothe the exhausted and, by seeming to take part in their suffering, convince them that you too have experienced what the provinces have suffered.

Rather than referring to material, concrete help, which is instead expected from the imperial college (*dum maior ab illis salubritas petitur*), here *humanitas* implies and requires emotional involvement on Eusignius' part. Crucial is the innovative relationship between *humanitas* and *dolor* (*alienus*), never to be found in pagan Latin authors before Symmachus. The idea is that the people should feel that their governors share their pains and sorrows. Ever since Tertullian there existed in Latin a more technical term to name this feeling: *compassio* (*cum + patior*), a calque from the Greek συμπάθεια. But a search for *compassio* in the *Thesaurus Linguae Latinae* reveals that this word remained the prerogative of Christian authors.[280] Accordingly, it looks as if this occurrence of *humanitas* was to some extent influenced by Christian thought, but at the same time Symmachus endeavoured to keep this hidden. He did so by avoiding a Christian term and by reinvesting a traditional pagan one like *humanitas* with new nuances.

Once more in Symmachus' writings *humanitas* is explicitly connected with *dolor*. *Ep.* 3.88 is addressed to Rufinus, one of Symmachus' most influential friends. A committed Christian, he was *magister officiorum* of Theodosius from

---

278 On Eusignius cf. also above, p. 285.
279 Cf. above, pp. 248 and 297.
280 *TLL* 3.2022.84–2023.69.

388 to 392 CE, consul in 392 and Praetorian prefect of the East from 392 to 395.[281] The letter in question concerns the death of a common acquaintance of theirs whose identity remains obscure, a man with whom Symmachus was clearly on bad terms, so much so that he had first thought of not speaking of his death at all – hence Rufinus' reproach.[282] In Symmachus' view, another sort of 'law of *humanitas*' recommended such a behaviour:[283] *Scis humanitatis hanc esse rationem, ut parum probatis et ante discordibus ad uicem doloris quem mors incutere solet, reuerentiam saltem silentii deferamus* (*Ep.* 3.88.1: "You know that this is the principle of *humanitas*: instead of the sorrow which death usually causes, we need at least to concede the deference of silence to those whom we did not approve of and who were not dear to us"). While I note in passing that the expression *humanitatis ratio* echoes Cicero,[284] the content merits more attention: contrary to the African provincials in the previous case, this dead man does not deserve his *dolor* to be shared by Symmachus; at most, *humanitas* grants him the deference of silence (*reuerentiam . . . silentii*). In other words, the comparison between *Ep.* 4.74 and *Ep.* 3.88 shows that *humanitas* calls for sympathy only when the victim is worthy of it, and not always indiscriminately.

The ideas of culture, concreteness and relation with other concepts of value which we have observed in the previous instances of *humanitas* in some ways come together at *Ep.* 6.21, which is addressed to both Symmachus' daughter and her husband Flavianus the Younger. The young couple was used to spending most of the year in Campania, either at Baiae or in the Phlegraean Fields. When the sons of Symmachus' friend Entrechius had to prolong their stay in Campania due to bad weather conditions, Symmachus thus asked his son-in-law to take care of them: *Quapropter dum nauigatio intractabilis est, in oris Campaniae paulisper haerebunt; sed ne peregrinationis amara sustineant, humanitas uestra praestabit* ("Accordingly, as long as navigation is impossible, they will spend some time on the shores of Campania. But your *humanitas* will make sure that they will not suffer the bitterness of the travel").[285] The impression is that the broad concept of benevolent attitude becomes more specific, evoking the idea of hospitality that we have already seen to be at times associated with, if not conveyed by, *humani-*

---

281 Cf. *PLRE I* 778–781 – Rufinus 18.
282 Cf. Pellizzari 1998, 241–242 for more details and bibliography on this letter. On Symmachus' attitude in this letter as well as towards other people with whom he was on bad terms cf. Matthews 1986, 174–175.
283 On a previous Symmachian instance of *humanitas* treated as a kind of law cf. above, p. 285.
284 Cf. Cic. *Quinct.* 97; *Verr.* 2.2.97; 2.4.120; *Rab. perd.* 2; *Mur.* 66.
285 On this letter cf. Marcone 1983, 93–94.

tas.[286] The major difference between this and the previous instances observed in Petronius, in Tacitus' *Germania* or in Gellius 15.21 is that educational and cultural implications remain more in the background here.[287]

In the last few pages I have gathered some Symmachian occurrences of *humanitas* which are barely related to one another, not to say unrelated, and which do not seem to fit well in the categories I drew up in the main part of this chapter. They nonetheless contribute to our understanding of Symmachus' extremely multifaceted view of *humanitas*, for example by underscoring its concreteness, its cultural components, its malleability (on its own and in relation with other concepts of value).

Before turning to Symmachus' use of the adjective *humanus*, I should now like to conclude my overview of *humanitas* by spotlighting a final aspect which further suggests that Symmachus' *humanitas* engages consciously with a long-lasting tradition which seemingly began with Cicero: the use of *humanitas* in judicial contexts. Curiously, in Symmachus this occurs in letters, not in orations. Three letters from Book 7 (*Epp.* 7.81, 7.83 and 7.89), all addressed about 399 CE to the then Praetorian prefect of Italy Messalla, deal with one and the same trial, the protagonist of which is Symmachus' friend Jucundus.[288] *Ep.* 7.81 provides the introduction to the story: Jucundus has been summoned to Milan to face a trial on unspecified charges concerning private matters. Yet he is ill, and therefore Symmachus asks Messalla to relocate the trial to Rome. His first request must not have been very effective, for Symmachus reiterates it with a more incisive tone in *Ep.* 7.89, which I quote in full:

> Iamdudum litteras meas in manus tuas credo perlatas, quibus allegaui, quod iudiciis adprobatum est, amicum meum Iucundum quamquam tui examinis cupidum per ualetudinem non posse proficisci. Huius in dies morbus augescit et ideo repeto postulatum ne incidat inuidiam contumaciae qui miserationem meretur. Et sane ciuili causae nihil decerpet humanitas, si ad uicarium uestrum transferatis examen. Nam pariter et laboranti detrahetur iniuria et negotio finis eueniet. Vale.

> I believe that my letter has been in your hands for a while now. I appended to it the notification, approved by the court, according to which my friend Jucundus, despite looking forward to being examined by you, was not able to leave because of his indisposition. His disease worsens day after day and I therefore beg you again that one who deserves pity will not fall victim of a judgement by default. To be sure, your *humanitas* will not diminish the effectiveness of the civil trial, if you delegate the examination to your substitute. Indeed, at

---

286 Cf. above, pp. 126; 162; 245; 251.
287 Cf. above, pp. 255; 125–126; 161–162.
288 On Messalla cf. above, p. 281.

the same time a suffering man will be saved from an injustice and we will put an end to this affair. Farewell.

As far as *humanitas* is concerned, the message may be summed up as follows: *humanitas* does not obstruct justice. This same principle was probably implicit in Pliny the Younger's *Ep.* 9.5.1, where the proconsul of Baetica Calestrius Tiro was praised for administering justice with *humanitas* (*iustitiam tuam prouincialibus multa humanitate commendas*).[289] Here the impression is that *humanitas* is used to avoid the repetition of *miseratio* in the previous sentence, and we have already noticed the same rhetorical technique with the same equivalence between the two words in *Decl. mai.* 15.3 (*postquam nihil miseratio, nihil proficiebat humanitas, temptauit asperitate discutere.*)[290]

Unlike *Ep.* 7.81, Symmachus' second letter to Messalla probably achieved some results and persuaded the Praetorian prefect to accept Symmachus' request. Yet bureaucratic difficulties must have cropped up, and Symmachus decided to send yet another letter to Messalla, *Ep.* 7.83, in which he revealed his upset over the event. The letter ends thus: *Inpensius igitur quaeso ut uicarii foro saepe in his iudiciis agitata causa reddatur, quando hoc et sacrae litterae imperant et iudiciorum non refutat humanitas. Vale.* ("I therefore beg you with more ardour that this case, which has until now taken place in the local court, be transferred to your substitute: the sacred letter prescribes this and the *humanitas* of the tribunals does not deny it. Farewell"). Regardless of the outcome of the Jucundus affair, which is unknown and at any rate would be of scarce interest to this study, Symmachus' rhetorical strategy merits some attention. Being placed at the end of the letter, *humanitas* assumes great emphasis, especially because it is here said to be possessed by the courts themselves (*iudiciorum*). Compared to the more common instances in which *humanitas* is praised in, or expected from, some judges, as exemplified by Cicero's *Pro Archia*, the shift is significant. Symmachus' statement appears to have objective and universal validity, for *humanitas* is regarded as the value which all tribunals possess. Whether this happened by accident or not, it certainly symbolises, and goes hand in hand with, the policy of *humanitas* applied to laws, which we have seen characterising a major part of the legislation of the fourth century CE.

---

289 Cf. above, pp. 97–98.
290 Cf. above, pp. 199–200.

8.4.2 *Humanus* in Symmachus

Symmachus' use of *humanus* confirms that there is a substantial difference between the multifacetedness of the noun and the relative flatness of the adjective. Exceptionally, he employs the adjective less often (29 times) than the noun (37 times), and in most cases *humanus* is paired with the usual nouns we have already encountered in the previous authors simply to mean 'of man'. Thus, as many as 9 times it goes with *genus*, three times with *ingenium*, twice with *sensus*, and only once with *caput, casus, consilium, cunctatio, fortuna, gaudium, natura, ops, oratio, sanguis, uerbum* and *uox*. Moreover, we find two instances of the substantivised neuter plural *humana* to indicate the 'human things'. There are no occurrences of comparatives and there is only one superlative: *humanissimum* at *Ep.* 5.8.1. The addressee is the same Theodorus we have encountered as the recipient of Symmachus' *Ep.* 5.13, and the superlative, which is closer to the meaning of the noun *humanitas* as usual, refers to the good practice of writing letters to friends. In particular, it goes with *inceptum* ('undertaking') in the sentence: *Gaudeo mihi sermonis tui primitias contigisse et inpendio postulo ut humanissimum inceptum religiosa cura non deserat* ("I am glad that I have received the first fruits of this dialogue and very much beg that your scrupulous care will not abandon this very kind undertaking"). The topic is by now well known, and one in which the role of *humanitas* is crucial, at least to Symmachus.[291]

8.4.3 Conclusion

As with the cases of Cicero and Pliny the Younger, two main aspects characterise Symmachus' *humanitas*: its pervasiveness across all his written works and its polysemy (although, as far as the latter is concerned, Symmachus comes slightly second). Nor should this come as surprising, for Symmachus' intent, despite the long time which separates him from his two models, was pretty much the same: he needed a unifying factor to defend (his conception of) Roman society during a period which threatened its stability and even its survival, and *humanitas* was perfectly fitting to this end. In the name of *humanitas*, in fact, Symmachus writes letters to maintain and extend relations of friendship, thereby reinforcing the internal bond among the members of the senate. And yet the often exalted transversal nature of *humanitas* also allows him to extend this bond upwards, to the emperor(s), and downwards, to members of the other social classes whom he regards as possibly useful to his – and

---

291 Cf. above, pp. 277–285.

Theodosius' – political project. The variety of addressees of Symmachus' letters, *relationes* and orations as well as of the other people involved in his discourses is good evidence of this strategy.

8.5 *Humanitas* in the Theodosian Age: Final Remarks

In the context of Theodosius I's effort to save and restore the Roman Empire after Hadrianople, and of his related willingness to appear as a new Trajan, the use of *humanitas* by Ausonius and Symmachus on the one hand, and of Ammianus and the 'minor' historians on the other hand revived the Trajanic pattern embodied by Pliny the Younger, Tacitus and Suetonius. Like Pliny, Symmachus fostered the spread of *humanitas* as a unifying value within the upper echelons of Roman society; like Tacitus and Suetonius, Ammianus and the other historians spotlighted the lack of this value during the reigns of previous emperors. After all, it is unsurprising that historians do not deal with ruling sovereigns, for as Lizzi Testa 2022 has remarked in commenting Ammianus' closure of the *Res Gestae*, "the final sentence alludes to the tradition that historians should leave the ruling emperor to panegyrists."[292]

Through his correspondence in particular, Symmachus' willingness to preserve and extend the network of senators emerges clearly. A senator of the noblest birth himself, Symmachus was thereby trying to defend Rome's as well as his own interests. Christians, barbarians as well as the increasing social mobility might represent serious threats to the senatorial class and, by extension, to the traditional structures of the Empire. In this socio-political climate, the concept of *humanitas* becomes much more than an incitement to write letters: as a well-established Roman value, it served to forge, foster and preserve links with other members of the *ordo senatorius* without at the same time compromising the relationships with the other social classes. Invoking a Ciceronian value takes on a strong cultural and political meaning: let us, through our profoundly Roman *humanitas*, remain Romans! Despite his Christian orientation, Theodosius must have understood the importance of this message and of having Rome's pagan ar-

---

292 Lizzi Testa 2022, 128. Ammianus' *Res Gestae* end thus: *Scribant reliqua potiores, aetate et doctrinis florentes. Quod id (si libuerit) aggressuros, procudere linguas ad maiores moneo stilos* ("The rest may be written by abler men, who are in the prime of life and learning. But if they chose to undertake such a task, I advise them to forge their tongues to the loftier style", trans. Rolfe 1986). Cf. also Lizzi Testa 2022, 130: "Ammianus was [. . .] following a well-known literary tradition, being conscious that the denigration of the previous emperor helped to exalt the one currently in power."

istocracy on his side. In this, as in many other respects, he also influenced the policy of his two sons and successors, Arcadius and Honorius. This explains why it is legitimate to refer to his, and his sons', reign as an age of *humanitas*, as Symmachus himself does more than once.

The importance of *humanitas* not only to Symmachus', but to the Theodosian age's socio-political thinking is confirmed by Ammianus' extraordinary interest in this value concept; or, more precisely, by his stressing that most previous fourth-century emperors, with the sole exception of Julian, had neglected this fundamental value.[293] Moreover, Ammianus explicitly attacks the aristocracy of the city of Rome for ignoring the true, traditional aspects of *humanitas* as civilization. Their frivolity – it is implied – was contributing heavily to the decadence of Rome. Also from this point of view, it comes therefore as unsurprising that Symmachus relied on *humanitas* to try to bring back the senatorial class to the splendour of its glorious past.

---

[293] It goes without saying that this conclusion is based upon Ammianus' extant books and might be differently nuanced if the first thirteen books of his *Historiae* had come down to us.

9 Back (or Forward?) to the Ontological Origins of *Humanitas*: The *Asclepius*

Despite its title, this book does not conclude with Symmachus, but with a Hermetic work called *Asclepius*, whose author is unknown. As we have seen, Symmachus serves the purpose of closing the circle which starts with Pliny the Younger, thereby connecting the ideology and political rhetoric of the Trajanic with that of the Theodosian Age. But the *Asclepius* is even more radical a watershed, especially as far as the history of *humanitas* is concerned. As I will show, it takes *humanitas* forward, rather than back, to its essence, to the essence of man,[1] basically ignoring all its previous major history from Cicero to Symmachus, and resulting in a new understanding of the term which probably evolves from a scant use attested earlier primarily in Seneca among the authors and works which have come down to us.[2]

9.1 *Humanitas* in the *Asclepius*

While in the case of Seneca the rejection of Ciceronian *humanitas* is likely to have to do with the socio-political context of the middle I century CE, as we have seen, the *Asclepius* ignores politics and its rhetoric altogether; what interests the author of this work is theosophy, and in this respect alone can the language of the Stoic philosopher Seneca be relevant to him. The *Asclepius* is a text of opposition to Christianity, but at the same time it contains elements which Christian and Medieval authors liked very much. Moreschini has best summarised all this:

> The *Asclepius* [. . .] with its theosophy, with its *pietas* and gnosis, with its exaltation of human dignity, furnished the Latin West of the late Imperial Age with the text and the certainty that were otherwise missing for non-Christians. The non-Christian reader found in the *Asclepius* the pagan equivalent of Christianity: revelation, gnosis, and the salvation reserved for the just. [. . .] Christianity, which ended up winning out over paganism precisely in the fourth century, also had good reason to find the *Asclepius*'s doctrines interesting – a certain kind of Christianity, that is.[3]

---

1 Cf. Festugière 1991[2], 28: "Il carattere proprio di tale o talaltra mistica, deriva dalla natura particolare della miseria provata. Angoscia metafisica = contemplazione di Dio Fonte dell'Essere. Sentimento del male terreno = contemplazione degli astri, accordo della ragione umana con la Ragione immanente al cosmo; o, al contrario, mediante una fuga totale lontano dal mondo, unione a un Dio ultramondano grazie alla quale 'l'uomo essenziale' ritorna alla propria origine."
2 On the influence of Stoicism on the *Asclepius* cf. Moreschini 1985, *passim*.
3 Moreschini 2011, 73. Cf. also Moreschini 1985, 9; 41; 117–119.

As the *Asclepius* is ultimately also a reflection on man,[4] it is no surprise that the word *humanitas* and the adjective *humanus* crop up quite often – although there are no occurrences of either the comparative or the superlative of *humanus*. What is surprising is that in all the eleven instances in this work the word *humanitas* points to the idea of human nature – although the discourse is far less banal than it might appear at first sight. In this respect, the *Asclepius* plays a bridging role between paganism and Christianity, and despite the doubts concerning its dating, it appears as particular fitting to close this study on pagan *humanitas* between the second and fourth centuries.

The *Asclepius* "constitutes a literary genre – theosophical treatise-*cum*-revelation – without parallel in the Latin context."[5] It is the entirely preserved Latin translation of an unpreserved Greek Hermetic text titled Λόγος τέλειος, 'Perfect discourse'. Transmitted alongside Apuleius' philosophical works, its Apuleian authorship has usually been denied and, on the basis of testimonies by Lactantius and Augustine,[6] it is usually dated to the second half of the fourth century, possibly the Theodosian Age.[7] It features a dialogue between god Hermes Trismegistus, Asclepius, Tat and Hammon – although the discourse is in fact brought forward by Hermes Trismegistus alone. Three closely interrelated topics are at its core: man, God and the world.[8] Given all these peculiarities, it comes as no surprise the fact that also the vocabulary of this work – and not only as far as the noun *humanitas* is concerned – is one of its own.[9]

As for *humanitas*, I am not aware of studies devoted to it, but Horsfall Scotti, in a paper where she tries to reject Hunink's theory of the Apuleian authorship of the *Asclepius*, recalls that Bosscha had mentioned the term *humanitas*, when understood as 'human race', among those singular linguistic elements that the *Asclepius* shares with Apuleius, or, better, with De *Platone et eius dogmate* 1.16.[10]

---

4 Cf. Parri 2005, 203: "ciò che anima l'*Asclepius* è, per usare un'espressione di Nikolaj Berdjaev, un bisogno di antropodicea, di giustificazione dell'uomo."
5 Moreschini 2011, 53. Cf. also Parri 2005, 202–203. Moreschini 1985, 81 speaks of a *mysterium*: "L'*Asclepius*, dunque, è la rivelazione di un *mysterium*, che l'iniziato apprende, ottenendo così la gnosi." Cf. also Moreschini 1985, 83.
6 On Lactantius and Hermetism cf. in particular Moreschini 1985, 27–41; 2011, 35–47; on Augustine and Hermetism Moreschini 1985, 43–46.
7 Cf. Moreschini 1985, 10; 71–73; Horsfall Scotti 2000; Rochette 2003, 68; 92–95; Moreschini 2011, 2; 49, all containing references to previous bibliography. The latest to uphold the Apuleian authorship of the *Asclepius* is to the best of my knowledge Hunink 1996.
8 Cf. Parri 2005, 189: "Schematicamente l'insegnamento di Ermete ha per oggetto l'uomo, il mondo e Dio. I tre ambiti di indagine non sono separati né separabili."
9 Cf. Bertolini 1985, 1152.
10 Cf. Horsfall Scotti 2000, 399–400 (against Hunink 1996).

Horsfall Scotti objects that this is no decisive parallel, for *humanitas* would stand for 'human race' also at *Decl. mai.* 8.3 and in Tertullian.[11] Yet, if, following Pieri, my previous discussion of *humanitas* at *Decl. mai.* 8.3 hits the mark, *humanitas* means something else than *genus humanum*.[12] Likewise, the case of Apuleius' *De Platone* 1.16 is no plain parallel, especially if *seminium humanitatis* is the translation of the Greek ἀνθρώπινον σπέρμα: of course in this instance *humanitas* means something like 'human nature', but in a sort of technical expression which is hardly comparable to different uses of the term *humanitas*.[13] As for Tertullian, the study of his use of the term *humanitas* is beyond the scope of this work – and at first sight would require an in-depth analysis – but it is sufficient to look at *Aduersus Marcionem* 2.27.2 to find confirmation of *humanitas* understood as 'human nature'.[14] In sum, while it appears quite clear that the meaning of *humanitas* cannot be used either against or in favour of the Apuleian authorship of the *Asclepius*, what *humanitas* really means in and to the *Asclepius* still lacks an answer, and it is to these two questions that I now turn.

In the course of this book, we have been seeing how the history of pagan *humanitas* from the first uses of the word until the Theodosian age is ultimately that of a dialectic between the concepts of παιδεία and φιλανθρωπία. That this is not the case of the *Asclepius* appears as crystal clear right from its first two occurrences, on § 4:

Supradicta autem genera inhabitant usque ad loca specierum, quarum omnium rerum inmortales sunt species. Species enim pars est generis, ut homo humanitatis, quam necesse est sequi qualitatem generis sui. Vnde efficitur ut, quamuis omnia genera inmortalia sint, species non omnes inmortales. Diuinitatis enim genus et ipsum et species inmortales sunt. Reliquorum genera, quorum aeternitas est generis, quamuis per species occidat, nascendi

---

11 Cf. Horsfall Scotti 2000, 400.

12 Cf. Pieri 2002 and above, pp. 198–199.

13 Cf. above, pp. 156–158.

14 *De isto pluribus retractarem, si cum ethnicis agerem, – quamquam et cum haereticis non multo diuersa congressio – sed quatenus et ipsi deum in figura et in reliquo ordine humanae condicionis deuersatum iam credidistis, non exigetis utique diutius persuaderi deum conformasse semetipsum humanitati, sed de uestra fide reuincimini* ("Of this I might have discoursed at greater length if I had been treating with heathens – although even with heretics the method of attack is not very different. But seeing that you yourselves have already stated your belief that a god has dwelt in human shape and in all the rest of what belongs to man's estate, you will assuredly not demand any further persuasion that God has in fact made himself conformable to human condition, but are confuted by virtue of your own creed", trans. Evans 1972). Further analysis also merit the other instances from Christian texts which are listed in the *TLL* entry on *humanitas*: cf. 3076.60–3077.7.

fecunditate seruatur, ideoque species mortales sunt, <genera non sunt>, ut homo mortalis sit, inmortalis humanitas.

The aforesaid kinds, however, dwell as far as the places that belong to its forms, and the forms of all these things are immortal. Now a form is part of a kind, as a human is of *humanitas*, and it must follow the quality of its kind. Whence, although all kinds are immortal, it happens that not all forms are immortal. In the case of divinity, both kind and form are immortal. The fertility of coming to be preserves the kinds of other things, where eternity belongs to the kind even though the forms perish. Thus, there are mortal forms, (but not kinds,) so that a human is mortal and *humanitas* immortal. (trans. Copenhaver 1992)

In both these two instances *humanitas* is regarded as a *genus*, but what does this mean? As far as I know, the most detailed answer about the meaning of *genus* in the *Asclepius* has been given by Marco Bertolini, who analyses it in close relationship with *species*:

> *Genus* conosce nell'*Asclepius*, come *species* e *forma*, un uso prevalentemente tecnico: non è casuale infatti che il termine, nella maggior parte delle attestazioni, compaia, sempre in rapporto a *species*, nella sezione dell'opera costituita dai capp. 3–5, dedicata ai concetti di εἶδος e di γένος e ai loro reciproci rapporti. Di fronte a *species*-εἶδος, impiegato in tale contesto, come abbiamo visto, per indicare la forma sensibile individuale, particolare modificazione di una forma sensibile di base, e quindi l'essere individuale caratterizzato da qualità specifiche, *genus* è impiegato, come costante traduzione di γένος, in riferimento alla specie, al genere determinato da caratteristiche e qualità comuni a tutti gli individui che ne fanno parte.[15]

In what follows, Bertolini highlights that the relationship between *genus* and *species* corresponds to that between *soliditas* and *particulae*, and brings as an example the very passage *Species enim pars est generis ut homo humanitatis* already quoted above.[16] The obvious consequence is that at *Asclepius* 4 *humanitas* is synonymous with *genus humanum*. But the parallel with Seneca's 'Platonic' *Epistula ad Lucilium* 65.7, rightly brought to light by Ilaria Parri, leads one to think that by *genus humanum* the author of the *Asclepius* does not refer to all human beings, but to their nature, to the very idea of man *qua* man.[17] Read Seneca: *Itaque homines quidem pereunt, ipsa autem humanitas, ad quam homo effingitur, permanet.* The message is clearly the same as in the final part of *Asclepius* 4 (*ideoque species mortales sunt, <genera non sunt>, ut homo mortalis sit, inmortalis humanitas*), and this cannot mean that all men, when taken together, are immortal; rather, it

---

15 Bertolini 1985, 1206. For further details on species in the *Asclepius* cf. Bertolini 1985, 1200–1206. But consider also the caveat by Moreschini 1985, 114: "la discussione sulla *species* e sul *genus* [. . .] è tra le più confuse che si trovino nell'*Asclepius*."
16 Cf. Bertolini 1985, 1206–1207.
17 Cf. Parri 2005, 43 and n. 107.

means that the idea of man is immortal. Let me try to clarify this difference through an example. Theoretically, like all other animal species, man can die out; yet the idea of man would survive anyway, as is the case with dinosaurs, which are extinct but of which we all have an idea in our minds.

There is more. *Asclepius* 4 and Seneca's *Epistula* 65.7 also put in explicit terms the relationship between *homo* and *humanitas*. *Asclepius* 4, in particular, reverses the etymological relationship we have observed in the Introduction:[18] ontologically, in fact, the *genus humanitas* precedes the *species homo*; the *particula* derives from the *soliditas*.

If we continue reading the *Asclepius*, we find out, significantly, that this *humanitas* is an excellent *genus*. Despite the fact that it is not conceived in either philanthropic or educational terms, it ends up being characterised by those same elements which define it when understood as civilization. Compare *Asclepius* 8:

> Modo autem dico mortalia non aquam et terram, quae duo de quattuor elementis subiecit natura hominibus, sed ea, quae ab hominibus aut in his aut de his fiunt, aut ipsius terrae cultus, pascuae, aedificatio, portus, nauigationes, communicationes, commodationes alternae, qui est humanitatis inter se firmissimus nexus et mundi partis, quae est aquae et terrae; quae pars terrena mundi artium disciplinarumque cognitione atque usu seruatur, sine quibus mundum deus noluit esse perfectum.

> Just now, in speaking about mortal things, I mean to speak not about water and earth, those two of the four elements that nature has made subject to humans, but about what humans make of those elements or in them – agriculture, pasturage, building, harbors, navigation, social intercourse, reciprocal exchange – the strongest bond among humans (*humanitas*) or between humanity (*humanitas*) and the parts of the world that are water and earth. Learning the arts and sciences and using them preserves this earthly part of the world; god willed it that the world would be incomplete without them. (trans. Copenhaver 1992)

Terrae cultus evokes the idea of agriculture, as is the case of *fruges* in Cicero's *Pro Flacco* 62 and Pliny's *Epistula* 8.24.2; *aedificatio* echoes Vitruvius' *De Architectura* 2.1.6, while *communicationes* and *commodationes* can be compared to *porticus et balinea et conuiuiorum elegantiam* of Tacitus' *Agricola* 21: in all these passages the aforementioned elements are regarded as characteristic of *humanitas* understood in its conception of civilization.[19] Tellingly, however, these are conceptual, not verbal correspondences. *Asclepius* 8 does not reveal any explicit references to those texts, but at the same time *humanitas* is a common denominator. The fact that the *Asclepius* is a translation of a Greek text might play a relevant role in this respect and a comparison with its model would be valuable. Unfortunately this is

---

18 Cf. above, pp. 22–24.
19 Cf. above, pp. 34–37; 65; 122–123.

not possible, and although we do possess some excerpts of the Greek text which was probably at the basis of the *Asclepius*, in no circumstances can a comparison be drawn with the passages in which the noun *humanitas* appears.[20] But while the independence of *Asclepius* 8 from the Latin tradition appears to be evident, the fact remains that what the Latin tradition considered to be the key elements in defining the idea of *humanitas* as civilization, in a fourth-century Latin transla-tion of a Hermetic Greek text those same elements represent the *humanitatis inter se firmissimus nexus*, that is, the strongest bond of human nature. One has therefore the impression that things have come full circle: while republican and early imperial authors took pains to outline the model of man – generally the Roman man – worthy of being so called only once he has internalised the noblest *humanitas*, the author of the *Asclepius* seems to take all this as fulfilled, so much so that the noun *humanitas* can now be used to describe the community of men – though not exactly *all* men –[21] as such, because now man is in principle worthy of being so called.[22] And those elements which had first represented targets to be achieved in order to realise the noblest *humanitas* have now become the concrete proof that such *humanitas* has been realised. By contrast, the Christian view is quite different, as is well highlighted by Parri:

> L'operare umano nel mondo contrassegna nel racconto genesiaco l'espiazione per la disob-bedienza a Dio. Al contrario, per l'uomo dell'*Asclepius* dedicarsi all'agricoltura e all'edifica-zione di case e ripari non è conseguenza di una punizione, ma esprime l'aderenza al disegno divino, poiché Dio non volle che il mondo fosse perfetto senza le «arti» umane.[23]

In the light of this, the fact that *humanitas* is regarded as half divine – something which would usually be very surprising in other authors and contexts – is likely to look unsurprising in the *Asclepius*. This is explicitly stated at *Asclepius* 10: *hu-manitas ex parte diuina, ex alia parte effecta mortalis est* ("humankind is divine in one part, in another part mortal", trans. Copenhaver 1992). And as if this were not enough, *Asclepius* 22 adds:

> Denique et bonum hominem et qui posset inmortalis esse ex utraque natura conposuit, diuina atque mortali, et sic conpositum est per uoluntatem dei hominem constitutum esse meliorem et diis,[24] qui sunt ex sola inmortali natura formati, et omnium mortalium.

---

20 For the Greek parallels of the *Asclepius* cf. Rochette 2003. Cf. also Moreschini 1985, 79–80.

21 Cf. below, pp. 324–325.

22 Cf. Moreschini 1985, 85: "L'ermetismo dell'*Asclepius* ha eliminato quasi completamente ogni aspetto della svalutazione dell'uomo in quanto tale e del mondo in cui egli abita, ed è giunto ad una visione ottimistica della personalità umana e delle sue capacità."

23 Parri 2005, 212.

24 Cf. Parri 2005, 216: "L'affermazione che l'uomo è *melior et diis* è radicale e rivelatrice."

In short, god made mankind good and capable of immortality through his two natures, divine and mortal, and so god willed the arrangement whereby mankind was ordained to be better than the gods, who were formed only from the immortal nature, and better than all other mortals as well. (trans. Copenhaver 1992)

It is sufficient to recall Cicero's *De oratore* 2.86 discussed above to make it clear to what a great extent the *Asclepius* distances itself from the Roman traditional view of the relationship between *humanitas* and *diuinitas*.[25] Nor can the case of the *Asclepius* be compared with Pliny's *Panegyricus* 2.7, where the superiority of *humanitas* to *diuinitas* is a consequence of preferring an emperor like Trajan, who considered himself a man, over a tyrant like Domitian, who instead regarded himself as a god.[26] *A fortiori*, as one can easily imagine, this message of the *Asclepius* is utterly incompatible with the Christian religion.[27] By contrast, once again it is Seneca's understanding of *humanitas* to appear closer to that of the *Asclepius*, so much so that Laudizi even claims that in some respect for Seneca "l'uomo e la sua *humanitas* sono accomunati a Dio".[28] But why this glorification of man and *humanitas* in the *Asclepius*? On what basis does it rely?

Asclepius 23 can be of help:

Et quoniam de cognatione et consortio hominum deorumque nobis indicitur sermo, potestatem hominis, o Asclepi, uimque cognosce. Dominus et pater uel, quod est summum, deus ut effector est deorum caelestium, ita homo fictor est deorum, qui in templis sunt humana proximitate contenti, et non solum inluminatur uerum etiam inluminat. Nec solum ad deum proficit, uerum etiam conformat deos. [. . .] Nec inmerito miraculo dignus est, qui est omnium maximus. Deorum genus omnium confessione manifestum est de mundissima parte naturae esse prognatum signaque eorum sola quasi capita pro omnibus esse. Species uero deorum, quas conformat humanitas, ex utraque natura conformatae sunt; ex diuina, quae est purior multoque diuinior, et ex ea, quae intra homines est, id est ex materia, qua fuerint fabricatae, et non solum capitibus solis sed membris omnibus totoque corpore figurantur. Ita humanitas semper memor naturae et originis suae in illa diuinitatis imitatione perseuerat, ut, sicuti pater ac dominus, ut sui similes essent, deos fecit aeternos, ita humanitas deos suos ex sui uultus similitudine figuraret.

And since this discourse proclaims to us the kinship and association between humans and gods, Asclepius, you must recognize mankind's power and strength. Just as the master and father – or god, to use his most august name – is maker of the heavenly gods, so it is mankind who fashions the temple gods who are content to be near to humans. Not only is mankind glorified; he glorifies as well. He not only advances toward god; he also makes the gods

---

25 Cf. above, p. 85.
26 Cf. above, p. 85.
27 An example is given by the relationship between *humanitas* and God in Ennodius' writings, on which cf. Mollea 2022b, 71–74.
28 Laudizi 2021, 341.

strong. [. . .] Mankind certainly deserves admiration, as the greatest of all beings. All plainly admit that the race of gods sprang from the cleanest part of nature and that their signs are like heads that stand for the whole being. But the figures of gods that *humanitas* form have been formed of both natures – from the divine, which is purer and more divine by far, and from the material of which they are built, whose nature falls short of the human – and they represent not only the heads but all the limbs and the whole body. Always mindful of its nature and origin, *humanitas* persists in imitating divinity, representing its gods in semblance of its own features, just as the father and master made his gods eternal to resemble him. (trans. Copenhaver 1992)

Man, because he erects statues of the gods, is put on the same level as the *summus deus*, the superior God who makes the heavenly gods.[29] It is thanks to this demiurgic talent that man is said to be *miraculus digno*.[30] After all, the simulacra he makes are not empty statues, but they are "ensouled and conscious, rilled with spirit and doing great deeds; statues that foreknow the future and predict it by lots, by prophecy, by dreams and by many other means; statues that make people ill and cure them, bringing them pain and pleasure as each deserves" (trans. Copenhaver 1992).[31] But do all men comply with this requirement? An answer had already been given at *Asclepius* 9: *Aliqui ipsique ergo paucissimi pura mente praediti sortiti sunt caeli suspiciendi uenerabilem curam* ("Some very small number of these humans, endowed with pure mind, have been allotted the honored duty of looking up to heaven", trans. Copenhaver 1992), and is now reiterated at the beginning of § 23: *Sed de hominibus istud dictum paucis sit pia mente praeditis. De uitiosis uero nihil dicendum est, ne sanctissimus sermo eorum contemplatione uioletur* ("But one may say this only of the few people endowed with faithful mind. Of the vice-ridden say nothing, lest we profane this most holy discourse by considering them", trans. Copenhaver 1992). The expression *pia mente* is crucial, for it makes it clear that *humanitas*, that is, human nature, is comparable, even superior to god as long as it is led by *pietas*, namely that "atteggiamento spirituale di base da cui è determinata e caratterizzata la vita dell'uomo conforme alla volontà

---

29 Cf. Moreschini 1985, 99: "Vi è, dunque, per l'autore ermetico un primo dio, che è al di sopra degli altri dèi minori: ebbene, questa gerarchia dell'essere divino è sostanzialmente quella della cultura monoteistica della tarda età imperiale." Cf. also Moreschini 1985, 107–112.

30 Cf. Moreschini 1985, 43–44; 112–113; Parri 2005, 113–115. More generally on the relationship between man and god(s) in the Hermetic thought in Festugière 1991², 19–22.

31 *Asclep.* 24: *Statuas animatas sensu et spiritu plenas tantaque facientes et talia, statuas futurorum praescias eaque sorte, uate, somniis multisque aliis rebus praedicentes, inbecillitates hominibus facientes easque curantes, tristitiamque laetitiamque pro meritis.*

divina"[32] – and one can easily notice how in the *Asclepius* not only *humanitas* and *pietas*, but also the relationship between the two of them is utterly different from what we have seen in previous authors and works.[33]

At the same time, § 23 makes it clear that the 'revolutionary' understanding of *humanitas* in the *Asclepius* also goes through the revaluation of corporeality.[34] From *Asclepius* 8 we already know that god made man corporeal so that he could contemplate and preside over the material substances.[35] The addition of § 23 is that it is man's artfulness, at best expressed in erecting divine statues, to play the bridging role between God and the material world: because he is half material and can handle the material substance, man can build statues; but it is because his best part is divine (*diuina, quae est purior multoque diuinior*) that he looks at the gods and erects statues which represent gods.[36]

The next step concerns man's happiness. Given these premises, it follows that man can be happy if and only if he can grasp the divine. This he can do thanks to the *sensus*, the equivalent of the Greek νοῦς,[37] although only very few men possess it:[38]

Sensus autem, quo dono caelesti sola felix sit humanitas – neque enim omnes, sed pauci, quorum ita mens est, ut tanti beneficii capax esse possit; ut enim sole mundus, ita mens humana isto clarescit lumine et eo amplius; nam sol quicquid inluminat, aliquando terrae et lunae interiectu interueniente nocte eius priuatur lumine – sensus autem cum semel fuerit animae commixtus humanae, fit una ex bene coalescente commixtione materia, ita ut numquam huiusmodi mentes caliginum inpediantur erroribus. (*Asclep.* 18)

But consciousness, the heavenly gift that is happiness for *humanitas* alone (not all humans, but only the few who have the mind to contain so great a bounty – as the sun lights up the world, so the human mind shines with the light of consciousness, but it is greater, for what-

---

32 Bertolini 1985, 1153. It is also worth noticing that, especially in Lactantius' interpretation of the Hermetic thought, *pietas* ultimately corresponds to γνῶσις: Moreschini 1985, 38.
33 On *pietas* and its relation to *humanitas* cf. above, pp. 192–193; 237–239. On *pietas* in the *Asclepius* cf. Bertolini 1985, 1152–1157.
34 Cf. Moreschini 1985, 86; Parri 2005, 226.
35 *Asclep.* 8: *Ergo, ut tantus et bonus* [scil. *Deus*], *esse uoluit alium qui illum, quem ex se fecerat, intueri potuisset, simulque et rationis imitatorem et diligentiae facit hominem.*
36 Cf. Moreschini 1985, 112–113: "L'uomo si serve della sostanza divina e più pura, da una parte, e della materia vera e propria, dall'altra (cap. 23): questo significa che l'uomo ha il potere – e in questo aspetto la natura umana raggiunge, per qualche verso, la magia – di 'creare' un dio, attirando la forza divina entro la statua che egli stesso costruisce."
37 Cf. Bertolini 1985, 1177. On this kind of νοῦς / *sensus* cf. also Moreschini 1985, 87–88; 107–109; Festugière 1991[2], 28–29; 41.
38 Cf. Moreschini 1985, 89: "Anche nell'*Asclepius*, come generalmente nell'ermetismo, il risvolto esoterico è assai forte."

ever the sun illuminates is sometimes deprived of its light by the interposition of earth and moon and the intervening night), consciousness, once coupled with the human soul, becomes one material in the closely joined coupling, so that minds of this sort are never obstructed by the errors of darkness. (trans. Copenhaver 1992)

Once again it is clear that, when he speaks of *humanitas*, the author of the *Asclepius* does not refer to all men, but to man's nature, actually to his highest nature. After all, neither *pietas* nor *sensus* are ever-lasting, once and for all acquired possessions, as is clear from Hermes' Egyptian example at *Asclepius* 25:

> Quid fles, o Asclepi? Et his amplius multoque deterius ipsa Aegyptus suadebitur inbueturque peioribus malis, quae sancta quondam, diuinitatis amantissima, deorum in terras suae religionis merito sola deductio, sanctitatis et pietatis magistra, erit maximae crudelitatis exemplum.

> Asclepius, why do you weep? Egypt herself will be persuaded to deeds much wickeder than these, and she will be steeped in evils far worse. A land once holy, most loving of divinity, by reason of her reverence the only land on earth where the gods settled, she who taught holiness and fidelity will be an example of utter cruelty. (trans. Copenhaver 1992, slightly adapted)

Predictably, the consequence is that the gods withdraw from men:

> Fit deorum ab hominibus dolenda secessio; soli nocentes angeli remanent, qui humanitate commixti ad omnia audaciae mala miseros manu iniecta conpellunt, in bella, in rapinas, in fraudes et in omnia quae sunt animarum naturae contraria. (*Asclep.* 25)

> How mournful when the gods withdraw from mankind! Only the baleful angels remain to mingle with humans (*humanitas*), seizing the wretches and driving them to every outrageous crime – war, looting, trickery and all that is contrary to the nature of souls. (trans. Copenhaver 1992)

The ostensible plainness of this occurrence of *humanitas* actually puts it in striking contrast with its previous instances in the *Asclepius*. We had so far experienced that *humanitas* means 'human (highest and noblest) nature', that which only very few men really possess. On the contrary, on this occasion it comes to indicate all men in general, thereby becoming synonymous with what other authors call *genus humanum*.[39] The watershed is marked by the withdrawal of *hu-*

---

39 It is necessary to specify 'other authors', because *genus*, as we have seen, is a technical term in the *Asclepius*. This is confirmed by the comparison between *Asclep.* 4 discussed above and *Asclep.* 35, where we come across *hominum genus* used as a synonym of *humanitas* as mostly understood in the *Asclepius*: *Et quamuis unumquodque animalis genus omnem generis sui possideat formam, in eadem forma singula tamen sui dissimilia sunt, ut hominum genus, quamuis sit*

manitas from god: as long as it possesses its divine half, the noblest *humanitas* persists, although it does not concern all men; but once it separates itself from god, *humanitas* loses its highest understanding and indicates all men. From quality to quantity: now the label *humanitas* includes all men, but their value is significant inferior. After all, to return to the beginning of *Asclepius* 25, this is the inevitable result of the loss of *diuinitatis amor, religio, sanctitas* and *pietas*, those values which, as we by now know, constitute the backbone of the utmost conception of *humanitas* in the *Asclepius*.

The Egyptian excursus also induces Hermes Trismegistus to investigate further the nature of the "gods who are considered earthly" (§ 38: *deorum qui terreni habentur*, trans. Copenhaver 1992), that is to say, those who reside in the statues built by men. Hermes explains:

> Constat, o Asclepi, de herbis, de lapidibus et de aromatibus diuinitatis naturalem uim in se habentibus. Et propter hanc causam sacrificiis frequentibus oblectantur, hymnis et laudibus et dulcissimis sonis in modum caelestis harmoniae concinentibus, ut illud, quod caeleste est, †caelestius† et frequentatione inlectum in idola possit laetum, humanitatis patiens, longa durare per tempora. Sic deorum fictor est homo. (*Asclep.* 38)

> It comes from a mixture of plants, stones and spices, Asclepius, that have in them a natural power of divinity. And this is why those gods are entertained with constant sacrifices, with hymns, praises and sweet sounds in tune with heaven's harmony: so that the heavenly ingredient enticed into the idol by constant communication with heaven may gladly endure its long stay among humankind. Thus does man fashion his gods. (trans. Copenhaver 1992)

Asclepius 25 has shown a trend inversion: the concept of *humanitas* itself has not changed, but is thenceforth seen in negative conditions, as a limitation. § 38 follows along these lines, so much so that we even hear of a *humanitas* that needs to be endured. This is something surprising: while it is to be expected that *humanitas* can be the active subject of a verb like *patior*, that is to say, *humanitas* can be the value thanks to which something is permitted, limited or endured,[40] to say that *humanitas* is a burden to be bore reverses the viewpoint. In Seneca's *Ep.* 4.10 we do come across the expression *humanitatem pati*, but the context is utterly different and *humanitas* is even regarded as *contumeliosa*, 'insulting', 'disrespectful', because it refers to the haughty generosity of the rich and mighty towards those

---

uniforme, ut homo dinosci ex aspectu possit, singuli tamem in eadem forma sui dissimiles sunt ("And although each kind of living thing possesses the whole form of its kind, within that same form each of them differs from the other: for example, although mankind is one in form, so that a human can be distinguished on sight, each person within the same form differs from the others", trans. Copenhaver 1992).

40 Cf. Cic. *Off.* 2.19; *Fam.* 10.5.3; Sen. *Ep.* 65.7.

who beg for something to eat or drink. Clearly this is not the meaning of *humanitas* at *Asclepius* 38. Rather, we notice that from the ontological revaluation of man we have already observed in some passages of the *Asclepius*, we shift here to his depreciation, especially when the focus is on his earthly aspects, and this is likely to remind us of the Christian view of man.

The last occurrence of *humanitas* in the *Asclepius* also alludes to man's fragility. Yet on this occasion *humanitas* does not concern the theosophical discourse developed throughout the course of this work; it concerns Hermes Trismegistus himself as the speaker of this discourse. He says:

> Dictum est uobis de singulis, ut humanitas potuit, ut uoluit permisitque diuinitas. Restat hoc solum nobis, ut benedicentes deum orantesque ad curam corporis redeamus. Satis enim nos de diuinis rebus tractantes uelut animi pabulis saturauimus. (*Asclep.* 40)

> I have told you everything that a human being (*humanitas*) could say, with god's willingness and permission. Blessing god and praying, it remains for us only to return to the care of the body. We have dealt enough with theology, and we souls have eaten our fill, so to speak. (trans. Copenhaver 1992)

The contrast between *humanitas* and *diuinitas* is no longer looked at from an ontological viewpoint, but is put in terms of a difference between possibility and will. Once the philosophical discourse is over, it is no longer about looking for what men and gods have in common: man does what his limits permit him to do; god does whatever he wants and sets the limits to man's agency. Eventually, this gap ends up affecting Hermes Trismegistus and his role of spokesperson of the Hermetic thought to the Latin speaking community. Scholars have always noticed the structural difficulties posed by the *Asclepius*, but, as Moreschini has put it with particular reference to this work: "I trattati ermetici sono l'espressione di quel sentimento religioso e di quella irrazionalità che caratterizzano la civiltà tardo-antica, e manifestano anche nella struttura letteraria l'abbandono delle forme tradizionali di pensiero."[41] Hermes' reference to the limits posed by his *humanitas* looks therefore to be nothing but the author's attempt to excuse himself for having difficulty in explaining a matter that would rather require divine skill.

---

41 Moreschini 1985, 78. Cf. more generally on this issue Moreschini 1985, 74–78; 2011, 56–57; Parri 2005, 16–20.

9.2 *Humanus* in the *Asclepius*

The use of the adjective *humanus* within the *Asclepius* is in tune with the singular understanding of *humanitas* which emerges from this work. The absence of any relationship between *humanitas* and the Greek concepts of παιδεία and φιλανθρωπία is paralleled by the lack of any forms of comparative or superlative of the adjective *humanus*.[42]

The positive grade *humanus* is instead used often, as one would expect, and with reference to *anima, animal, genus, gratulatio, intellegentia, lex, mens, natura, proximitas* and *sensus*.

Humana is then used as substantivised adjective to mean 'human things', while *humani* also appears to indicate the category of men.

9.3 Conclusion

This analysis has showed that *humanitas* plays a key role in the *Asclepius*. As one of the main focuses of this work is on man, the term *humanitas* is mostly used to indicate man's highest, noblest nature, the one which only those men who honour and take inspiration from God and resort to the principles of *pietas* and *religio* can achieve. But when the bond with the divine is lost, the noun *humanitas*, like the *Asclepius*' conception of man, is no longer that noble, and it comes to indicate man alongside all his weaknesses. What is evident is that the *humanitas* of the *Asclepius* distances itself both from the long tradition that looked at *humanitas* in terms of a relationship between παιδεία and φιλανθρωπία, and from those occurrences of the term *humanitas* which indicate all men as such, irrespective of their quality.

---

42 At *Asclep.* 5 the expression *amantes hominum* appears to be a calque of the Greek φιλάνθρωπος and this fact seems to confirm that the author of the *Asclepius* does not understand the word *humanitas* as a translation of the Greek φιλανθρωπία.

10 Pagan *Humanitas* in the Imperial Age: Concluding Remarks

At the beginning of his study on the perceptions and representations of Roman republican age during the first century of the Empire, Gowing claims:

> While it may be historically practical and neat to mark the end of the Republic and the beginning of the Principate with the assassination of Julius Caesar in 44 BC or the battle of Actium in 31 BC, it took well over a century for the idea and the ideals of the Republic to be purged from the Roman imagination and memory (though they would never be purged entirely).[1]

No doubt *humanitas* is one of those originally republican ideals that "would never be purged entirely", at least until the late fourth century CE. On the contrary, the main novelty of this book is to have revealed how important the concept of *humanitas* was in some periods of the imperial age, often by the very fact of evoking a socio-political climate which had characterised the last fight for freedom under the Republic. This is certainly the case of the Trajanic as well as of the Theodosian age, where Pliny's and Symmachus' use of *humanitas* both in official works like the panegyrics or the *relationes* served the purpose of spreading the idea that new eras had begun, inspired by ideals such as *humanitas*, which should guarantee more respect of human dignity than the ages that had just ended. In short, once again after Cicero, *humanitas* was used as a programmatic and propaganda word. To this end a significant contribution also came from historical works such as those of Tacitus, Ammianus, or the other fourth-century minor historians which belonged to the same ages as Pliny and Symmachus, and which characterised previous times as lacking *humanitas*. It is true that our sources are limited, and those which I have taken into account in this study are mainly literary; yet Pliny's and Symmachus' letters above all are likely to express not only their own values, but also those embraced by the social class to which they belonged – or at least by its majority –, namely, the senatorial class, which came second after the emperor in terms of socio-political influence.

The reasons why Pliny and Symmachus resorted to *humanitas* as a binding value do not only lie however in what the term echoed from an historical viewpoint, but also in the multifacetedness of its meanings. Regardless of the doubts raised by today's linguists on its etymology, in ancient times, from Cicero and Gellius on, the noun *humanitas* was linked to *homo*, 'human being', thus focusing on man and representing the fulfilment of human nature: in this respect, it is telling

---

1 Gowing 2005, 3.

that comparatives and superlatives of *humanus,* as this book has contributed to show, are preferred over its positive grade to render *humanitas.* The focus on man is the deciding factor in the political uses of *humanitas,* as the idea that is conveyed is that all human beings are potentially involved in reciprocal relationships. Thus, although in the end Pliny and Symmachus used *humanitas* to strengthen the bonds within the social classes to which they belonged, the notion itself potentially transcended class distinctions and could therefore also work to bridge gaps upwards, with the emperor, and downwards, with the equestrian order and the lower echelons of Roman society. After all, it is for this very reason that Cicero had given pride of place to this value concept, as it was probably the aptest to foster his idea of *consensus omnium bonorum,* the political harmony of all good men, which, in Cicero's view, would save the Roman republic from destruction. So that all good men, irrespective of their initial social conditions, might play an important role for the *res publica, humanitas* needed to be something which could be acquired, for example through the study of the liberal arts: hence its connotation of παιδεία. At the same time, education could not be an end in itself, but had to elevate man from an ethical viewpoint: hence its connotation of φιλανθρωπία. Pliny and, in his footsteps, Symmachus understood the potential benefits deriving from this polysemy of the term and exploited it as Cicero had done. Eumenius and Ausonius, so far as we can understand from the few occurrences of *humanitas* in their works, did something similar, albeit on a smaller scale.

After all, if we think of the other value or abstract concepts which we have seen are sometimes mentioned alongside *humanitas* or instead of it, we understand even better why Pliny's and Symmachus' choices fell upon it. Take for example *clementia.* Even leaving aside the 'tyrannical' connotation it probably acquired after its public uses during the reigns of Nero and Domitian – which is likely to explain the decrease of frequency of its instances in the aftermath of their reigns, as the charts in the Introduction have shown –, the term itself presupposes a downward relationship between the condition of its bestower and that of its recipient. As a consequence, this cannot be presented as a socially transversal, let alone as a potentially egalitarian concept, not to say that it lacks the educational component, and therefore the polysemy, of *humanitas.* Or take also *urbanitas,* another value concept which is sometimes linked to *humanitas.* It can share with some occurrences of *humanitas* the idea of 'refinement', but the term itself evokes *urbs,* a city, if not *Vrbs,* the city *par excellence,* namely Rome, thereby implying the opposition between the educated, civilized, polished inhabitants of big cities, Rome especially, and the less educated, less civilized and less polished inhabitants of the countryside. As is evident, this concept too would hardly be even potentially socially inclusive. By the same token, a word like *doctrina* necessarily implies education, but does not imply an ethical connotation, and the exclusion of the moral component would be too much of a loss in the political field.

The comparison with these abstract concepts – but the list could be brought forward – also contributes to explaining why *humanitas* can be used with reference to non-Romans (and non-Greeks), as in Tacitus and Ammianus. Despite the fact that the Romans usually regarded themselves as the best in the world, and therefore usually considered *humanitas* one of their distinctive qualities on which they prided themselves, this is not necessarily so, as Tacitus shows both in the *Agricola* and *Germania*, where only two occurrences of the term are sufficient to call into question not only the idea of exporting civilization, but the Roman idea of civilization itself: the *humanitas* of the barbarians could be less barbaric than that of the Romans. The instance at *Agricola* 21.3, in particular, is perfect to show that the polysemy of *humanitas* results in its ambiguity and polyvalency: depending on what notions (the primary παιδεία and φιλανθρωπία, and their offshoots 'refinement', Latin language, attire, etc.) one includes or excludes, and in what measure they are perceived as present in each and every occurrence of the term, *humanitas* can be understood in one way or another. And this in turn explains why at times we find *humanitas* alongside other words which serve to explain better its meaning, at other times not: it depends on the author's willingness to be clear or, vice versa, to exploit the polysemy and ambiguity of *humanitas*.

Granted, another way to be clear about one's own understanding of *humanitas* is to spell it out, as Gellius does in the famous passage of *Noctes Atticae* 13.17, although in the end the cultural programme he wants to promote inevitably acquires an ethical component as well. Gellius' political influence during the Antonine age was not as high as that of Pliny and Symmachus in the Trajanic and Theodosian ages respectively, and yet he fights his battle against those who did not seem to understand, and therefore appreciate, the true value of *humanitas*. Indeed, if we look at [Quintilian's] *Declamationes Minores* and *Maiores*, we can better understand Gellius' criticism.

On the other hand, since public oratory suffered a crisis in the imperial age, as revealed by Quintilian, and by Tacitus in the *Dialogus*, it was probably to be expected that the Ciceronian use of *humanitas* in oratorical contexts would lose some of its weight: it looks as if *humanitas* was still used as an argument because of its illustrious tradition, but the educational component and the broader sociopolitical and cultural programme it implied in Cicero were out of place, and consequently its effectiveness decreased. This eventually resulted – at least in schools and during the second century CE – in the impoverishment of the polysemy of *humanitas* noted by Gellius, which Apuleius' fake trial in *Metamorphoses* 3 and the *Apologia* seem to confirm – although Apuleius' argumentative use of *humanitas* is far more elaborated than that in the declamations.

Taken to the extreme, the fact that some potential components can be left out from occurrences of *humanitas* leads to the case of Firmicus Maternus, where we encounter a kind of civilization which surprisingly disregards education in that it depends on the stars and their influence. And the benevolent attitude some men or peoples sometimes show is again due to the stars.

Even more a radical reinterpretation of *humanitas* is offered by the *Asclepius*, which goes as far as to intertwine the human quality *par excellence* with what is apparently at its farthest from it, *diuinitas*. As we have seen, the *Asclepius* stands out for its uniqueness, since it seems to ignore the long history of *humanitas* as well as all its socio-political implications. And yet the noun itself is employed very often to indicate man's highest nature, which only human beings inspired by God can achieve. If the divine bond is lost, the noun *humanitas* loses most of its ennobling meaning and comes to indicate man with all his weaknesses. In reinvesting *humanitas* with this fluid meaning, which oscillates between a more and a less noble understanding of man, the author of the *Asclepius* therefore obtains the paradoxical result of summing up the entire history of *humanitas* while neglecting it altogether: it is sufficient to substitute the 'divine' with the liberal arts to understand that, not unlike Cicero in the *Pro Archia*, he shows man the path through which he can realise himself.

But perhaps most important, the relationship between *humanitas* and *diuinitas* which emerges from the *Asclepius* enables us to complete the picture involving *humanitas* and the abstract concepts which are ontologically closest to it. The opposition of *humanitas* to *superbia* and/or *diuinitas* we observed in Pliny the Younger's *Panegyricus* now seems to appear clearer, for we end up facing a sort of triangle (or rather an asymmetric square), with *diuinitas* and *superbia* representing its upper vertices: right from their etymologies, which connect them with gods, they evoke attitudes which are hierarchically superior to what is allowed to man, but *diuinitas* indicates the positive side, that is, the inevitable possession of higher qualities, whereas *superbia* the negative one, namely the superior behaviour of those who regard themselves as better than others. At the base of the triangle lies *humanitas*, but it actually needs to be split into two: one, altogether positive, stands in opposition to *superbia*; the other, being opposed to *diuinitas*, indicates man's nature, which is inevitably inferior to god's, but not necessarily negative. It is therefore in its socio-political and cultural dimension, which abundantly prevails in the Latin authors I have investigated in this book, that *humanitas* is defined by the notions of παιδεία, φιλανθρωπία and their offshoots, the ones which are considered the best to counter *superbia*. This discourse, and the relationship between *humanitas* and *diuinitas* in particular, is likely to be of great importance to Christian thought, and should be the focus of another book.

Appendices

Abbreviations

L&S   C.T. Lewis, C. Short, *A New Latin Dictionary*, New York – Oxford 1991.

LSJ   *A Greek-English Lexicon*, compiled by H.G. Liddell and R. Scott. Revised and augmented throughout by Sir H.S. Jones [. . .], Oxford 1996.

OLD   *Oxford Latin Dictionary*, Oxford 1968.

PLRE I   A.H.M. Jones, J.R. Martindale, J. Morris, *The Prosopography of the Later Roman Empire*, Vol. I, A.D. 260–395, Cambridge 1971.

PLRE II   J.R. Martindale, *The Prosopography of the Later Roman Empire*, Vol. II, A.D. 395–527, Cambridge 1980.

TLL   *Thesaurus Linguae Latinae* editus auctoritate et consilio Academiarum quinque Germanicarum Berolinensis, Gottingensis, Lipsiensis, Monacensis, Vindobonensis, voll. I–. . ., Leipzig 1900. . . (also available online).

Bibliography

Journal abbreviations are those of *L'Année philologique*.

Adams 1972: James N. Adams, *On the Authorship of the Historia Augusta*, in: "CQ" 22, 1, 186–194.

Adams 2003: James N. Adams, Romanitas *and the Latin Language*, in: "CQ" 53, 1, 184–205.

Agamben 1995: Giorgio Agamben, Homo sacer. *Il potere sovrano e la nuda vita*, Torino.

Altman 2009: William H.F. Altman, *Womanly Humanism in Cicero's* Tusculan Disputations, in: "TAPhA" 139, 407–441.

Altman 2016: William H.F. Altman, *The Revival of Platonism in Cicero's Late Philosophy*. Platonis aemulus *and the Invention of Cicero*, Lanham.

Anderson 1993: Graham Anderson, *The Second Sophistic: a Cultural Phenomenon in the Roman World*, London – New York.

Angel 2008: Natalie Angel, Clementia *and* Beneficium *in the Second Philippic*, in: Tom Stevenson and Marcus Wilson (eds.), *Cicero's Philippics. History, Rhetoric and Ideology*, West Harbour (Auckland), 114–130.

Astarita 1993: Maria L. Astarita, *La cultura nelle "Noctes Atticae"*, Catania.

Aubert 2011: Sophie Aubert, *La φιλοστοργία chez Fronton, une vertu sans équivalent latin?*, in: "Aitia" [Online]1, http://journals.openedition.org/aitia/179.

Audano 2015: Sergio Audano, *Sopravvivere senza l'Aldilà: la* consolatio *laica di Tacito nell'*Agricola, in: Cristina Pepe and Gabriella Moretti (eds.), *Le parole dopo la morte. Forme e funzioni della retorica funeraria nella tradizione greca e romana*, Trento, 245–288.

Audano 2023: Sergio Audano, *De vita Agricolae*, in: Pagán 2023, 331–335.

Baker 2015: Patrick Baker, *Italian Renaissance Humanism in the Mirror*, Cambridge.

Balbo 2012: Andrea Balbo, Humanitas *in Imperial Age. Some Reflections on Seneca and Quintilian*, in: "The Journal of Greco-Roman Studies" 47, 63–94.

Balbo 2013: Andrea Balbo, *Sulla presenza ciceroniana nella* Gratiarum Actio *di Ausonio*, in: "Aevum" 87, 1, 157–168.

Balbo 2015: Andrea Balbo, *"Classici" nell'oratoria tardoantica: riflessioni sul ruolo dei riferimenti letterari nella* Gratiarum Actio *di Ausonio*, in: "C&C" 10, 15–32.

Balbo 2018: Andrea Balbo, *Ausonio oratore. Tecniche argomentative e prassi retorica nella* gratiarum actio, in: Étienne Wolff (ed.), *Ausone en 2015: Bilan et nouvelles perspectives*, Paris, 159–182.

Baldwin 1975: Barry Baldwin, *Studies in Aulus Gellius*, Lawrence (KS).

Baldwin 1983: Barry Baldwin, *Suetonius*, Amsterdam.

Baldwin 1990: Barry Baldwin, *Tacitus*, *"Agricola" 21: an Explanation*, in: "Mnemosyne" 43, 3, 455–456.

Balmaceda 2017: Catalina Balmaceda, Virtus Romana. *Politics and Morality in the Roman Historians*, Chapel Hill (NC).

Banchich 2008: Thomas M. Banchich, *The Epitomizing Tradition in Late Antiquity*, in: John Marincola (ed.), *A Companion to Greek and Roman Historiography*, Malden (MA) – Oxford – Victoria, 305–311.

Baraz 2020: Yelena Baraz, *Reading Roman Pride*, Oxford – New York.

Barnard 1993: Leslie W. Barnard, *L'intolleranza negli apologisti cristiani con speciale riguardo a Firmico Materno*, in: Pier F. Beatrice (ed.), *L'intolleranza cristiana nei confronti dei pagani*, Bologna, 79–99.

Barnes 1996: Timothy D. Barnes, *Emperors, Panegyrics, Prefects, Provinces and Palaces (284–317)*, in: "JRA" 9, 532–552.

Barnes 1998: Timothy D. Barnes, *Ammianus Marcellinus and the Representation of Historical Reality*, Ithaca – London.

Baroud 2023: George Baroud, *Ideology*, in: Pagán 2023, 536–539.

Barrow 1973: Reginald H. Barrow, *Prefect and Emperor. The* Relationes *of Symmachus. A.D. 384*, Oxford.

Bartsch 1994: Shadi Bartsch, *Actors in the Audience*, Cambridge (MA).

Bartsch 2006: Shadi Bartsch, *The Mirror of the Self. Sexuality, Self-Knowledge, and the Gaze in the Early Roman Empire*, Chicago – London.

Bauman 2000: Richard A. Bauman, *Human Rights in Ancient Rome*, London – New York.

Beall 1988: Stephen M. Beall, Civilis eruditio: *Style and Content in the "Attic Nights" of Aulus Gellius*, Berkeley (diss.).

Beall 2004, Stephen M. Beall, *Gellian Humanism Revisited*, in: Holford-Strevens/Vardi 2004, 206–222.

Beck 1998: Jan-Wilhelm Beck, *"Germania" – "Agricola": Zwei Kapitel zu Tacitus' zwei kleinen Schriften. Untersuchungen zu ihrer Intention und Datierung sowie zur Entwicklung ihres Verfassers*, Hildesheim – Zürich – New York.

Benferhat 2011: Yasmina Benferhat, *Du bon usage de la douceur en politique dans l'œuvre de Tacite*, Paris.

Benoist/Gangloff 2019: Stéphane Benoist and Anne Gangloff, *Culture politique impériale et pratique de la justice: Regards croisés sur la figure du prince "injuste"*, in: Olivier Hekster and Koenraad Verboven (eds.), *The Impact of Justice on the Roman Empire. Proceedings of the Thirteenth Workshop of the International Network Impact of Empire (Gent, June 21–24, 2017)*, Leiden – Boston, 19–48.

Berger 1953: Adolf Berger, *Encyclopedic Dictionary of Roman Law*, Philadelphia (PA).

Berger/Fontaine/Schmidt 2020a: Jean-Denis Berger, Jacques Fontaine and Peter L. Schmidt (eds.), *Die Literatur im Zeitalter des Theodosius (374–430 n. Chr.). Erster Teil. Fachprosa, Dichtung, Kunstprosa*, München.

Berger/Fontaine/Schmidt 2020b: Jean-Denis Berger, Jacques Fontaine and Peter L. Schmidt (eds.), *Die Literatur im Zeitalter des Theodosius (374–430 n. Chr.). Zweiter Teil. Christliche Prosa*, München.

Bertolini 1985: Marco Bertolini, *Sul lessico filosofico dell'*Asclepius, in: "ASNP" 3, 15, 4, 1151–1209.

Bessone 2009: Federica Bessone, Clementia *e* philanthrōpia. *Atene e Roma nel finale della Tebaide*, in: "MD" 62, 179–214.

Bessone 2011: Federica Bessone, *La* Tebaide *di Stazio. Epica e potere*, Pisa – Roma.

Bettini 2019: Maurizio Bettini, *Homo sum. Essere "umani" nel mondo antico*, Torino.

Bianco 1971: Gerardo Bianco, *La fonte greca delle metamorfosi di Apuleio*, Brescia.

Binns 1974: James W. Binns (ed.), *Latin Literature of the Fourth Century*, Oxford – New York.

Binternagel 2008: Alexandra Binternagel, *Lobreden, Anekdoten, Zitate – Argumentationstaktiken in der Verteidigungsrede des Apuleius*, Hamburg.

Bird 1984: Harry W. Bird, *Sextus Aurelius Victor. A Historiographical Study*, Liverpool.

Bird 1993: Harry W. Bird, *Eutropius: Breviarium*, Liverpool.

Birley 2005: Anthony R. Birley, *The Roman Government of Britain*, Oxford – New York.

Birley 2006: Anthony R. Birley, *Rewriting second- and third-century history in late antique Rome: the Historia Augusta*, in: "Classica" 19, 1, 19–29.

Birley 2009: Anthony R. Birley, *The Agricola*, in: Woodman 2009, 47–58.

Blair 2019: Stephen Blair, *The Beast in His Den. The* domus Flavia *and the Rhetoric of Enclosure in Pliny's Panegyricus*, in: "Maia" 71, 2, 429–439.

Blockley 1975: Roger C. Blockley, *Ammianus Marcellinus: A Study of his Historiographical and Political Thought*, Bruxelles.

Blundell 1986: Sue Blundell, *The Origins of Civilization in Greek and Roman Thought*, Beckenham.

Bodel 2015: John Bodel, *The Publication of Pliny's Letters*, in: Ilaria Marchesi (ed.), *Pliny the Book-Maker: Betting on Posterity in the Epistles*, Oxford, 14–108.

Boissier 1906: Gaston Boissier, *À propos d'un mot latin. Comment les Romains ont connu l'humanité*, in: "Revue des deux mondes" 36, 5, 762–786.

Boissier 1907: Gaston Boissier, *À propos d'un mot latin. Comment les Romains ont connu l'humanité*, in: "Revue des deux mondes" 37, 5, 82–116.

Boldrer 2021: Francesca Boldrer, *L'humanitas nella letteratura latina arcaica: le interpretazioni nell'epica e nella commedia e il giudizio di Gellio*, in: Maria Bambozzi (ed.), *Paradigmi d'identità. Tradurre e interpretare i* classici, Ancona, 53–76.

Bolisani 1961–62: Ettore Bolisani, *Nel XIX centenario della nascita di Plinio il giovane: la sua* humanitas, in: "Atti dell'Istituto Veneto di scienze, lettere ed arti" 120, 59–79.

Bonamente 2003: Giorgio Bonamente, *Chapter Three. Minor Latin Historians of the Fourth Century A.D.*, in: Gabriele Marasco (ed.), *Greek and Roman Historiography in Late Antiquity. Fourth to Sixth Century A.D.*, Leiden – Boston, 85–125.

Bonamente 2010: Giorgio Bonamente, Optimi principes-divi *nell'*Historia Augusta, in: Lavinia Galli Milić and Nicole Hecquet-Noti (eds.), *Historiae Augustae Colloquium Genevense in honorem F. Paschoud septuagenarii: les traditions historiographiques de l'Antiquité tardive: idéologie, fiction, réalité*, Bari, 63–82.

Bonelli 1994: Guido Bonelli, *Plinio il Giovane e la schiavitù: Considerazioni e precisazioni*, in: "QUCC" 48, 3, 141–148.

Bonney 1975: Robert Bonney, *A New Friend for Symmachus?*, in: "Historia" 24, 357–374.

Borgo 1985: Antonella Borgo, Clementia*: studio di un campo semantico*, in: "Vichiana" 14, 25–73.

Boyancé 1970a: Pierre Boyancé, *Sur les origines péripatéticiennes de l'*humanitas, in: Walter Wimmel (ed.), *Forschungen zur römischen Literatur. Festschrift zum 60. Geburtstag von Karl Büchner*, Wiesbaden, 21–30.

Boyancé 1970b: Pierre Boyancé, *Études sur l'humanisme cicéronien*, Bruxelles.

Boyle 2003: Anthony J. Boyle, *Introduction: Reading Flavian Rome*, in: Anthony J. Boyle and William J. Dominik (eds.), *Flavian Rome: Culture, Image, Text*, Leiden – Boston, 1–67.

Bradley 1991: Keith R. Bradley, *The Imperial Ideal in Suetonius' 'Caesares'*, in: "ANRW" II, 33, 5, 3701–3732.

Bradley 1997: Keith R. Bradley, *Law, Magic, and Culture in the* Apologia *of Apuleius*, in: "Phoenix" 51, 2, 203–223.

Bram 1975: Jean R. Bram, *Ancient astrology. Theory and practice. Matheseos libri VIII*, Park Ridge (NJ).

Brandt 1999: Axel Brandt, *Moralische Werte in den Res Gestae des Ammianus Marcellinus*, Göttingen.

D. Braund 1996: David Braund, *Ruling Roman Britain: Kings, Queens, Governors and Emperors from Julius Caesar to Agricola*, London.

S. Braund 1996: Susanna M. Braund, *The Solitary Feast: a Contradiction in Terms?*, in: "BICS" 41, 37–52.

S. Braund 1997: Susanna M. Braund, *Roman Assimilation of the Other*: Humanitas *at Rome*, in: "AClass" 40, 15–32.

S. Braund 2009: Susanna M. Braund, *Seneca. De Clementia*, Oxford – New York.

S. Braund 2012²: Susanna M. Braund, *Praise and Protreptic in Early Imperial Panegyric: Cicero, Seneca, Pliny*, in: Rees 2012, 85–108 [= Susanna M. Braund, *Praise and Protreptic in Early Imperial Panegyric: Cicero, Seneca, Pliny*, in: Mary Whitby (ed.), *The Propaganda of Power*, Leiden 1998, 53–76].

Bringmann 1971: Klaus Bringmann, *Zur Tiberiusbiographie Suetons*, in: "RhM" 114, 3, 268–285.

Brown 1971: Peter Brown, *The World of Late Antiquity. From Marcus Aurelius to Muhammad*, London.

Brown 2012: Peter Brown, *Through the Eye of a Needle. Wealth, the Fall of Rome, and the Making of Christianity in the West, 350–550 AD*, Princeton – Oxford.

Browning 1982: Robert Browning, *Later Principate. Introductory*, in: Edward J. Kenney (ed.), *The Cambridge History of Classical Literature. II. Latin Literature*, Cambridge, 681–691.

Bruggisser 1993: Philippe Bruggisser, *Symmaque ou le rituel épistolaire de l'amitié littéraire. Recherches sur le premier livre de la correspondance*, Fribourg.

Büchner 1949: Karl Büchner, *Die Atticusvita des Cornelius Nepos*, in: "Gymnasium" 56, 100–121.

Büchner 1958: Karl Büchner, *Humanitas Horatiana A.P. 1 – 37*, in: "AClass" 1, 64–71.

Büchner 1961: Karl Büchner, *Humanum und humanitas in der römischen Welt*, in: "Studium generale" 14, 636–646.

Bürger 1887: Karl Bürger, *De Lucio Patrensi sive De ratione inter asinum q. f. lucianeum Apuleique Metamorphoses intercedente*, Berlin (diss.).

Burgersdijk 2013: Diederik W.P. Burgersdijk, *Pliny's* Panegyricus *and the* Historia Augusta, in: "Arethusa" 46, 2, 289–312.

Burgersdijk/Ross 2018: Diederik W.P. Burgersdijk and Alan J. Ross (eds.), *Imagining Emperors in the Later Roman Empire*, Leiden – Boston.

Burgess 1972: John F. Burgess, *Statius' Altar of Mercy*, in: "CQ" 22, 339–349.

Bury 1989: Ernst Bury 1989, *Humanitas als Lebensaufgabe. Prolegomena zu einer Neukonzeption der Lektüre der Plinius-Briefe*, in: "AU" 1, 89, 42–64.

Busti 2019: Francesco Busti, "Ab Iove princeps". *Traiano figlio di Giove*, in: "Maia" 71, 2, 266–279.

Bütler 1970: Hans-Peter Bütler, *Die geistige Welt des jüngeren Plinius. Studien zur Thematik seiner Briefe*, Heidelberg.

Butler/Owen 1914: Harold E. Butler and Arthur S. Owen, *Apulei Apologia sive Pro se de magia liber*, Oxford.

Calboli 1974: Gualtiero Calboli, *La credibilità di Ammiano Marcellino e la sua arte espositiva*, in: "BSL" 4, 67–103.

Callu 2003: Jean-Pierre Callu, *Symmaque. Correspondance. Tome I. Livres I et II*, Paris.

Callu 2009: Jean-Pierre Callu, *Symmaque. Tome V. Discours – Rapports*, Paris.

Cameron 2011: Alan Cameron, *The Last Pagans of Rome*, Oxford – New York.

Cameron 2016²: Alan Cameron, *Wandering Poets and Other Essays on Late Greek Literature and Philosophy*, Oxford – New York.

Camus 1967: Pierre-Marie Camus, *Ammien Marcellin, témoin des courants culturels et religieux à la fin du IVᵉ siècle*, Paris.

Caracausi 1986–87: Ebe Caracausi, *Gli hapax nell'Apologia di Apuleio*, in: "AAPal" 7, 153–184.

Carbonero 1977: Oreste Carbonero, *Analogie e rapporti fra la difesa ciceroniana del poeta Archia ed il processo per la magia di Lucio Apuleio*, in: "Sileno" 3, 245–254.

Casapulla 2019: Vincenzo Casapulla, "Nihil quale ante dicamus". *Il* Panegirico *di Plinio e i suoi modelli*, in: "Maia" 71, 2, 323–338.

Castello 2010: Maria G. Castello, *La crisi dell'impero e la frantumazione dell'illusione di rinascita. La* Gratiarum Actio *di Decimo Magno Ausonio*, in: "Historia" 59, 2, 189–205.

Cavarzere 2011: Alberto Cavarzere, *Gli arcani dell'oratore. Alcuni appunti sull'*actio *dei Romani*, Roma – Padova.

Cavazza 1996: Franco Cavazza, *Aulo Gellio. Le notti attiche. Libro XIII*, Bologna.

Cavuoto-Denis 2023: Nicolas Cavuoto-Denis, Vsus scribendi. *Le projet littéraire de Symmaque dans les Lettres, les Discours et les Rapports*, Turnhout.

Cecconi 2002: Giovanni A. Cecconi, *Commento storico al libro II dell'Epistolario di Q. Aurelio Simmaco*, Pisa.

Champlin 1980: Edward Champlin, *Fronto and Antonine Rome*, Cambridge (MA).

Chantraine 1968: Pierre Chantraine, *Dictionnaire étymologique de la langue grecque. Histoire des mots. Tome I. A – Δ*, Paris.

Chantraine 1974: Pierre Chantraine, *Dictionnaire étymologique de la langue grecque. Histoire des mots. Tome III. Λ – Π*, Paris.

Charlesworth 1937: Martin P. Charlesworth, *The Virtues of the Roman Emperor. Propaganda and the Creation of Belief*, London.

Chastagnol 1986: André Chastagnol, *Le Sénat dans l'OEuvre de Symmaque*, in: Paschoud 1986, 73–96.

Ciaffi 1983: Vincenzo Ciaffi, *Il romanzo di Apuleio e i modelli greci*, Bologna.

Cizek 1977: Eugen Cizek, *Structures et idéologie dans "Les Vies des Douze Césars" de Suétone*, Bucureşti – Paris.

Cizek 1989: Eugen Cizek, *La littérature et les cercles culturels et politiques à l'époque de Trajan*, in: "ANRW" II.33.1, 3–35.

Coleman 1990: Kathleen M. Coleman, *Latin Literature after AD 96: Change or Continuity?*, in: "AJAH" 15, 19–39.

Colton 1975: Robert E. Colton, *The Story of the Widow of Ephesus in Petronius and La Fontaine*, in: "CJ" 71, 1, 35–52.

Comerci 1994: Giuseppe Comerci, Humanitas, liberalitas, aequitas: *nuova paideia e mediazione sociale negli* Adelphoe *di Terenzio*, in: "BSL" 24, 3–44.

Conte 1994: Gian Biagio Conte, *Latin Literature. A History*, Baltimore and London.

Coşkun 2010: Altay Coşkun, *Cicero und das römische Bürgerrecht: die Verteidigung des Dichters Archias*, Göttingen.

Costabile 2016: Felice Costabile, *Temi e problemi dell'evoluzione storica del diritto pubblico romano*, Torino.

Costantini 2019: Leonardo Costantini, *Magic in Apuleius'* Apologia. *Understanding the Charges and the Forensic Strategies in Apuleius' Speech*, Berlin – Boston.

Costantini 2021: Leonardo Costantini, *Apuleius Madaurensis. Metamorphoses. Book III*, Leiden – Boston.

Cova 1972: Pier V. Cova, *Arte allusiva e stilizzazione retorica nelle lettere di Plinio: A proposito di VI, 31, 16–17; II, 6; VIII, 16; VIII, 24; VIII, 33, 10*, in: "Aevum" 46, 1/2, 16–36.

Cova 1978: Pier V. Cova, *Lo stoico imperfetto. Un'immagine minore dell'uomo politico nella letteratura latina del principato*, Napoli.

Cracco Ruggini 1986: Lelia Cracco Ruggini, *Simmaco*: Otia e Negotia *di classe, fra conservazione e rinnovamento*, in: Paschoud 1986, 97–116.

Cristo 1974: Stuart Cristo, *Quintus Aurelius Symmachus. A Political and Social Biography*, New York (diss.).

D'Agostino 1962: Vittorio D'Agostino, *Cornelii Taciti De vita et moribus Iulii Agricolae liber*, Torino.

Dal Chiele 2016: Elisa Dal Chiele, *Apuleio. De Platone et eius dogmate. Vita e pensiero di Platone*, Bologna.

D'Aloja 2011: Chiara D'Aloja, *Sensi e attribuzioni del concetto di* maiestas, Lecce.

De Bonfils 1986: Giovanni de Bonfils, *Ammiano Marcellino e l'imperatore*, Bari.

D'Elia 1995: Salvatore D'Elia, *Una monarchia illuminata. La cultura nell'età degli Antonini*, Napoli.

Della Calce 2023: Elisa Della Calce, Mos uetustissimus – *Tito Livio e la percezione della clemenza*, Berlin – Boston.

Della Calce/Mollea 2022: Elisa Della Calce and Simone Mollea, Humanitas *liviana e* imperium Romanum*: una relazione possibile*, in: Pauline Duchêne, Charles Guittard, Marine Miquel, Mathilde Simon and Étienne Wolff (eds.), *Relire Tite-Live, 2000 ans après. Actes du colloque tenu à l'Université Paris Nanterre et à l'École Normale Supérieure de Paris (5 et 6 octobre 2017)*, Bordeaux, 133–142.

Della Calce/Mollea 2023: Elisa Della Calce and Simone Mollea, *Per uno stato modello: l'*humanitas *come antidoto all'odio nel* De republica *ciceroniano*, in: Francesca Alesse and Lorenzo Giovannetti (eds.), *Le metamorfosi dell'odio. Percorso interdisciplinare tra storia, filosofia, letteratura*, Torino, 123–144.

Della Corte 1958: Francesco Della Corte, *Svetonio eques Romanus*, Milano – Varese.

Den Boeft *et al.* 2013: Jan den Boeft, Jan W. Drijvers, Daniël den Hengst and Hans C. Teitler, *Philological and Historical Commentary on Ammianus Marcellinus XXIX*, Leiden –Boston.

Den Boeft *et al.* 2018: Jan den Boeft, Daniël den Hengst, Hans C. Teitler and Jan W. Drijvers, *Philological and Historical Commentary on Ammianus Marcellinus XXXI*, Leiden –Boston.

Den Hengst 2007: Daniel den Hengst, *Literary Aspects of Ammianus' Second Digression on Rome*, in: Jan den Boeft, Jan W. Drijvers, Daniel den Hengst and Hans C. Teitler (eds.), *Ammianus after Julian. The Reign of Valentinian and Valens in Books 26–31 of the* Res Gestae, Leiden, 159–179.

Den Hengst, 2010[2]: Daniel den Hengst, *The Discussion of Authorship*, in: Diederik W.P. Burgersdijk and Joop A. van Waarden (eds.), *Emperors and Historiography. Collected Essays on the Literature of the Roman Empire by Daniël den Hengst*, Leiden-Boston, 177–185 [= in: Giorgio Bonamente and François Paschoud (eds.), *Historiae Augustae Colloquium Perusinum*, Bari 2002, 187–195].

De Jonge 1980: Pieter de Jonge, *Philological and Historical Commentary on Ammianus Marcellinus XVIII*, Groningen.

De Pascali 2008: Nicola De Pascali, Ratione humanitatis. *Significati e implicazioni di un concetto nella legislazione di Marco Aurelio*, in: "Ostraka" 17, 1–2, 35–68.

Deratani 1927: Nikolaj F. Deratani, *De rhetorum Romanorum declamationibus. II: Quaestiones ad originem maiorum, quae sub nomine Quintiliani feruntur, declamationum pertinentes*, in: "RPh" 3, 1, 289–310.

De Romilly, 2011[2]: Jacqueline de Romilly, *La douceur dans la pensée grecque*, Paris [1st ed. 1979].

Dessau 1889: Hermann Dessau, *Über Zeit und Persönlichkeit der* Scriptores Historiae Augustae, in: "Hermes" 24, 337–392.

De Trane 2009: Ginetta De Trane, *Scrittura e intertestualità nelle* Metamorfosi *di Apuleio*, Lecce.

De Vaan 2008: Michiel de Vaan, *Etymological Dictionary of Latin and the other Italic Languages*, Leiden – Boston.

Dickey 2012: Eleanor Dickey, *The Colloquia of the Hermeneumata Pseudodositheana. Volume I. Colloquia Monacensia-Einsidlensia, Leidense-Stephani, and Stephani*, Cambridge.

Dihle 2013: Albrecht Dihle, *Greek and Latin Literature of the Roman Empire. From Augustus to Justinian*, Abingdon – New York [1st ed. München 1989].

Dillon 1996: John M. Dillon, *The Middle Platonists: 80 B.C. to A.D. 220*, Ithaca (NY).

Dimatteo 2019: Giuseppe Dimatteo, *Decl. min. 254 and 279*, in: Pasetti *et al.* 2019, 260–271; 412–419.

Dingel 1988: Joachim Dingel, Scholastica materia. *Untersuchungen zu den* Declamationes minores *und der* Institutio oratoria *Quintilians*, Berlin – New York.

Dowling 2006: Melissa B. Dowling, *Clemency & Cruelty in the Roman World*, Ann Arbor (MI).

Döpp 1972: Siegmar Döpp, *Zum Aufbau der Tiberius-Vita Suetons*, in: "Hermes" 100, 3, 444–460.

Drake 1998: Harold A. Drake, *Firmicus Maternus and the Politics of Conversion*, in: Gareth Schmeling and Jon D. Mikalson, *Qui miscuit utile dulci. Festschrift Essays for Paul Lachlan MacKendrick*, Wauconda (Illinois), 133–150.

Drake 2016[2]: Harold A. Drake, *Introduction. Gauging Violence in Late Antiquity*, in: Harold A. Drake (ed.), *Violence in Late Antiquity. Perceptions and Practices*, London – New York, 1–11 [1st ed. 2006].

Drexler 1956: Hans Drexler, *Maiestas*, in: "Aevum" 30, 3, 195–212.

Drexler 1974: Hans Drexler, *Ammianstudien*, Hildesheim.

Drijvers 1999: Jan W. Drijvers, *Ammianus Marcellinus' Image of Arsaces and Early Parthian History*, in: Drijvers/Hunt 1999, 171–182.

Drijvers/Hunt 1999: Jan W. Drijvers and David Hunt (eds.), *The Late Roman World and Its Historian. Interpreting Ammianus Marcellinus*, London – New York.

Duchêne 2020: Pauline Duchêne, *Comment écrire sur les empereurs? Les procédés historiographiques de Tacite et Suétone*, Bordeaux.

Dufraigne 1975: Pierre Dufraigne, *Aurélius Victor. Livre des Césars*, Paris.

Dutsch 2002: Dorota Dutsch, *Towards a Grammar of Gesture: a Comparison between the types of hand movements of the actor in Quintilian's Institutio Oratoria 11.3.85–184*, in: "Gesture" 2, 265–287.

Dyck 1996: Andrew R. Dyck, *A Commentary on Cicero*, De Officiis, Ann Arbor.

Ebersbach 1993: Volker Ebersbach, *Die humanitas des Petronius oder Diagnose eines gesellschaftlichen Verfalls*, in: Barbara Kühnert, Volker Riedel and Rismag Gordesiani (eds.), *Prinzipat und Kultur im 1. und 2. Jahrhundert*, Bonn, 192–202.

Edelstein 1967: Ludwig Edelstein, *The Idea of Progress in Classical Antiquity*, Baltimore.

Edwards 2015: Mark Edwards, *Religions of the Constantinian Empire*, Oxford – New York.

Elice 2017: Martina Elice, *Per la storia di humanitas nella letteratura latina fino alla prima età imperiale*, in: "Incontri di Filologia Classica" 15 (2015–2016), 253–295.

Elisei 2008: Chiara Elisei, *Agricola primus inventor e la retorica della conquista*, in: Paolo Arduini, Sergio Audano, Alberto Borghini, Alberto Cavarzere, Giancarlo Mazzoli, Guido Paduano e Alessandro Russo (eds.), *Studi offerti ad Alessandro Perutelli*, Roma, 441–449.

Ernout/Meillet 2001[4]: Alfred Ernout and Antoine Meillet, *Dictionnaire Étymologique de la langue latine. Histoire des mots*, Paris.

Errington 2006: Robert M. Errington, *Roman Imperial Policy from Julian to Theodosius*, Chapel Hill (NC).

Fantham 1982: Elaine Fantham, *Quintilian on Performance: Traditional and Personal Elements in Institutio 11.3*, in: "Phoenix" 36, 3, 243–263.

Fedeli 2013: Paolo Fedeli, *L'occhio indiscreto del biografo (prima parte)*, in: "Argos" 36, 83–112.

Fedeli 2014: Paolo Fedeli, *L'occhio indiscreto del biografo (seconda parte)*, in: "Argos" 37, 9–30.

Feldherr 2019: Andrew Feldherr, *Out of the Past. Pliny's Panegyricus and Roman Historiography*, in: "Maia" 71, 2, 380–411.

Ferrary 2014[2]: Jean-Louis Ferrary, *Philhellénisme et impérialisme. Aspects idéologiques de la conquête romaine du monde hellénistique*, Roma.

Festugière 1949: André J. Festugière, *La révélation d'Hermès Trismégiste II: le dieu cosmique*, Paris.

Festugière 1991[2]: André J. Festugière, Ermetismo e mistica pagana, Genova [1st or. ed. *Hermétisme et mystique païenne*, Paris, 1967].

Finkelpearl 1998: Ellen D. Finkelpearl, *Metamorphoses of Language in Apuleius. A Study of Allusion in the Novel*, Ann Arbor (MI).

Fletcher 2014: Richard Fletcher, *Apuleius' Platonism. The Impersonation of Philosophy*, Cambridge.

Fleury 2006: Pascale Fleury, *Lectures de Fronton: un rhéteur latin à l'époque de la Seconde Sophistique*, Paris.

Flobert 1988: Pierre Flobert, Lingua Latina *et* lingua Romana*: purisme, administration et Invasions Barbares*, in: "Ktema" 13, 205–212.

Fögen 2000: Thorsten Fögen, Patrii sermonis egestas. *Einstellungen lateinischer Autoren zu ihrer Muttersprache*, München – Leipzig.

Fornara 1992: Charles W. Fornara, *Studies in Ammianus Marcellinus. II: Ammianus' Knowledge and Use of Greek and Latin Literature*, in: "Historia" 41, 4, 420–438.

Forni 1962: Giovanni Forni, *Taciti De vita Iulii Agricolae*, Roma.

Frangoulidis 2008: Stavros Frangoulidis, *Witches, Isis and Narrative. Approaches to Magic in Apuleius' "Metamorphoses"*, Berlin – New York.

Funaioli 1907: Gino Funaioli, *Grammaticae Romanae Fragmenta*, Leipzig.

Galimberti Biffino 2003: Giovanna Galimberti Biffino, *Il* temperamentum *e l'uomo ideale dell'età traianea*, in: Luigi Castagna and Eckard Lefèvre (eds.), *Plinius der Jüngere und seine Zeit*, München – Leipzig, 173–187.

Galimberti Biffino 2007: Giovanna Galimberti Biffino, Loquere uerbis praesentibus *(1, 10, 4): il criterio 'dell'elegantia' in Gellio*, in: "Latomus" 66, 4, 929–941.

Galletier 1949: Édouard Galletier, *Panégyriques latins. Tome I (I-V)*, Paris.

Gamberale 1969: Leopoldo Gamberale, *La traduzione in Gellio*, Roma.

Gamberini 1983: Federico Gamberini, *Stylistic Theory and Practice in the Younger Pliny*, Hildesheim – Zürich – New York.

Gardner 1970: David D. Gardner, *A Frequency Dictionary of Classical Latin Words* (Stanford PhD Dissertation).

Garnsey 1978: Peter D.A. Garnsey, *Rome's African Empire under the Principate*, in: Peter D.A. Garnsey and Charles Whittaker (eds.), *Imperialism in the Ancient World*, Cambridge, 223–254.

Gascou 1984: Jacques Gascou, *Suétone historien*, Roma.

Gassman 2020: Mattias P. Gassman, *Worshippers of the Gods. Debating Paganism in the Fourth-Century Roman West*, Oxford – New York.

Gasti 2020: Fabio Gasti, *La letteratura tardolatina. Un profilo storico (secoli III-VII d.C.)*, Roma.

Geisthardt 2015: Johannes M. Geisthardt, *Zwischen Princeps und Res Publica. Tacitus, Plinius und die senatorische Selbstdarstellung in der Hohen Kaiserzeit*, Stuttgart.

Giacomelli/Givone 2019: Alberto Giacomelli and Sergio Givone, *Introduzione*, in: Alberto Giacomelli and Sergio Givone (eds.), *Umanesimo, Humanismus, Humanisme. Filosofie dell'umano fra Rinascimento e contemporaneità*, "paradosso" 2019, 2, 9–12.

Gianotti 1986: Gian F. Gianotti, *'Romanzo' e ideologia. Studi sulle* Metamorfosi *di Apuleio*, Napoli.

Gianotti 2004[2]: Gian F. Gianotti, *Per una rilettura delle opere di Apuleio*, in: Giuseppina Magnaldi and Gian F. Gianotti (eds.), *Apuleio. Storia del testo e interpretazioni*, Alessandria, 141–182.

B. Gibson 2005: Bruce Gibson, *The High Empire*: AD *69–200*, in: Stephen Harrison (ed.), *A Companion to Latin Literature*, Malden – Oxford – Victoria, 69–79.

B. Gibson 2011: Bruce Gibson, *Contemporary contexts*, in: Roche 2011, 104–124.

B. Gibson 2018: Bruce Gibson, *Gratitude to Gratian: Ausonius' Thanksgiving for His Consulship*, in: Burgersdijk/Ross 2018, 270–288.

B. Gibson 2019: Bruce Gibson, *Trajan the Panegyrist. Pliny, paneg. 69–75*, in: "Maia" 71, 2, 249–265.

B. Gibson/Rees 2013: Bruce Gibson and Roger Rees, *Introduction: Pliny the Younger in Late Antiquity*, in: "Arethusa" 46, 2, 141–165.

R. Gibson: Roy K. Gibson, *Pliny on the Nile. Panegyricus 29–32*, in: "Maia" 71, 2, 447–466.

R. Gibson/Morello 2012: Roy K. Gibson and Ruth Morello, *Reading the Letters of Pliny the Younger. An Introduction*, Cambridge.

Gildenhard 2010: Ingo Gildenhard, *Creative Eloquence: The Construction of Reality in Cicero's Speeches*, Oxford – New York.

Gildenhard 2011: Ingo Gildenhard, *Cicero, Against Verres, 2.1.53–86*, Cambridge.

Girotti 2017: Beatrice Girotti, *Assolutismo e dialettica del potere nella corte tardoantica. La corte di Ammiano Marcellino (parte 1)*, Milano.

Giua 1991: Maria A. Giua, *Una lettura della biografia svetoniana di Tiberio*, in: "ANRW" II.33.5, 3733–3747.

Giustiniani 1985: Vito R. Giustiniani, *Homo, humanus, and the Meanings of 'Humanism'*, in: "Journal of the History of Ideas" 46, 2, 167–195.

Gómez-Santamaría 2015: *Autorrepresentación del orador en las* Gratiarum Actiones *consulares de época imperial*, in: Jesús de la Villa Polo, Patricia Cañizares Ferriz and Emma Falque Rey (eds.), Ianua Classicorum. *Temas y formas del Mundo Clásico. Actas del XIII Congreso Español de Estudios Clásicos*, Madrid, 659–666.

Gothóni 1994: René Gothóni, *Religio and Superstitio Reconsidered*, in: "Archiv für Religionspsychologie" 21, 1, 37–46.

Gotoff 1993: Harold C. Gotoff, *Cicero's Caesarian Speeches. A Stylistic Commentary*, Chapel Hill (NC) – London.

Gowing 2005: Alain M. Gowing, *Empire and Memory. The Representation of the Roman Republic in Imperial Culture*, Cambridge – New York.

Greco 1999: Lorenzo Greco, *Introduzione*, in: Antonio Stramaglia, *[Quintiliano]. I gemelli malati: un caso di vivisezione (Declamazioni maggiori, 8)*, Cassino, 3–21.

Green 1991: Roger P.H. Green, *The Works of Ausonius*, Oxford – New York – Toronto.

Grilli 1982: Alberto Grilli, *Ausonio: il mondo dell'impero e della corte*, in: "Antichità Altoadriatiche" 22, 139–150.

Grimal 1991: Pierre Grimal, *Tacito*, Milano [1st ed. Paris 1990].

Guarneri Citati 1927: Andrea Guarneri Citati, *Indice delle parole, frasi e costrutti ritenuti indizio di interpolazione nei testi giuridici romani*, Milano.

Gunderson 2009: Erik Gunderson, *Nox Philologiae. Aulus Gellius and the Fantasy of the Roman Library*, Madison (WI).

Gunderson 2014: Erik Gunderson, *E.g. Augustus: exemplum in the Augustus and Tiberius*, in: Power/ Gibson 2014, 130–145.

Habinek 1990: Thomas N. Habinek, *Lucius' Rite of Passage*, in: "MD" 25, 49–69.

Haedicke 1975: Walter Haedicke, *Nur ein Tacitus-Kapitel. Agricola 21*, in: "AU" 18, 3, 74–77.

Hägg 2012: Tomas Hägg, *The Art of Biography in Antiquity*, New York.

Hall 2004: Jon Hall, *Cicero and Quintilian on the Oratorical Use of hand Gestures*, in: "CQ" 54, 1, 143–160.

Hanson 1991: William S. Hanson, *Tacitus' 'Agricola': an Archaeological and Historical Study*, in: "ANRW" II.33.3, 1741–1784.

Harder 1929: Richard Harder, *Über Ciceros Schrift Somnium Scipionis*, Halle.

Harder 1934: Richard Harder, *Nachträgliches zu humanitas*, in: "Hermes" 69, 1, 64–74.

Harrison 1999: Stephen J. Harrison, *Introduction: Twentieth-Century Scholarship on the Roman Novel*, in: Stephen J. Harrison (ed.), *Oxford Readings in The Roman Novel*, New York, xi–xl.

Harrison 2000: Stephen J. Harrison, *Apuleius: a Latin Sophist*, Oxford.

Harrison 2013: Stephen J. Harrison, *Framing the Ass. Literary Texture in Apuleius'* Metamorphoses, Oxford.

Haupt 1874: Maurice Haupt, *Coniectanea*, in: "Hermes" 8, 3, 241–256.

Havelock 1963: Eric A. Havelock, *Preface to Plato*, Cambridge (MA) – London.

Hellegouarc'h 1963: Joseph Hellegouarc'h, *Le vocabulaire latin des relations et des partis politiques sous la république*, Paris.

Henry 1994: Madeleine M. Henry, *On the Aims and Purposes of Aulus Gellius'* Noctes Atticae, in: "ANRW" II.34.2, 1918–1941.

Hershkowitz 1995: Debra Hershkowitz, *Pliny the Poet*, in: "G&R" 42, 2, 168–181.

Heusch 2011: Christine Heusch, *Die Macht der* memoria. Die,Noctes Atticae' *des Aulus Gellius im Licht der Erinnerungskultur des 2. Jahrhunderts n. Chr.*, Berlin – New York.

Hijmans 1994: Benjamin L. Hijmans Jr., *Apuleius Orator*: Pro se de Magia *and* Florida, in: "ANRW" II.34.2, 1708–1784.

Hijmans/van der Paardt 1978: Benjamin L. Hijmans Jr. and Rudi T. van der Paardt (eds.), *Aspects of Apuleius' Golden Ass*, Groningen.

Hiltbrunner 1968: Otto Hiltbrunner, *Die Heiligkeit des Kaisers. (Zur Geschichte des Begriffs* sacer*)*, in: "Frühmittelalterliche Studien" 2, 1–30.

Hiltbrunner 1994a: Otto Hiltbrunner, *Humanitas (φιλανθρωπία)*, in: "Reallexikon für Antike und Christentum" 16, 711–752.

Hiltbrunner 1994b: Otto Hiltbrunner, *Humanitas und Philanthropia: zum Unterschied sozial-ethischer Begriffe im Osten und Westen des Kaiserreiches*, in: "Archeologia Moldovei" 17, 103–107.

Hoffer 1999: Stanley E. Hoffer, *The Anxieties of Pliny the Younger*, New York.

Høgel 2015: Christian Høgel, *The Human and the Humane. Humanity as Argument from Cicero to Erasmus*, Göttingen – Taipei.

Høgel 2019: Christian Høgel, Humanitas*: Universalism, equivocation, and basic criterion*, in: Andrea Balbo and Jaewon Ahn (eds.), *Confucius and Cicero. Old Ideas for a New World, New Ideas for an Old World*, Berlin – Boston, 129–139.

Holford-Strevens 1977: Leofranc Holford-Strevens, *Towards a Chronology of Aulus Gellius*, in: "Latomus" 36, 1, 93–109.

Holford-Strevens 2003: Leofranc Holford-Strevens, *Aulus Gellius*: an Antonine Scholar and his Achievement, Oxford – New York.

Holford-Strevens/Vardi 2004: Leofranc Holford-Strevens and Amiel Vardi (eds.), *The World of Aulus Gellius*, Oxford – New York.

Honig 1960: Richard M. Honig, *Humanitas und Rhetorik in spätrömischen Kaisergesetzen. Studien zur Gesinnungsgrundlage des Dominats*, Göttingen.

Hopkins 1978: Keith Hopkins, *Conquerors and Slaves*, Cambridge.

Horsfall Scotti 2000: Mariateresa Horsfall Scotti, *The* Asclepius*: Thoughts on a Re-Opened Debate*, in: "VChr" 54, 4, 396–416.

Hostein 2012: Antony Hostein, *La cité et l'empereur. Les Éduens dans l'Empire romain d'après les Panégyriques latins*, Paris.

Howley 2013: Joseph A. Howley, *Why Read the Jurists? Aulus Gellius on Reading Across Disciplines*, in: Paul J. du Plessis (ed.), *New Frontiers: Law and Society in the Roman World*, Edinburgh, 9–30.

Howley 2017: Joseph A. Howley, *Book-Burning and the Uses of Writing in Ancient Rome: Destructive Practice between Literature and Document*, in: "JRS" 107, 213–236.

Howley 2018: Joseph A. Howley, *Aulus Gellius and Roman Reading Culture. Text, Presence, and Imperial Knowledge in the* Noctes Atticae, Cambridge.

Hügli/Kipfer 1989: Anton Hügli and Daniel Kipfer, *Philanthropie*, in: Joachim Ritter and Karlfried Gründer (eds.), *Historisches Wörterbuch der Philosophie. Band 7: P–Q*, Basel, 543–548.

Hunink 1996: Vincent Hunink, *Apuleius and the "Asclepius"*, in: "VChr" 50, 3, 288–308.

Hunink 1997a: Vincent Hunink, *Apuleius of Madauros. Pro Se de Magia (Apologia). Volume I. Introduction, Text, Bibliography, Indexes*, Amsterdam.

Hunink 1997b: Vincent Hunink, *Apuleius of Madauros. Pro Se de Magia (Apologia). Volume II. Commentary*, Amsterdam.

Hunink 1998: Vincent Hunink, *Comedy in Apuleius'* Apology, in: "Groningen Colloquia on the Novel" 9, 97–113.

Hutchinson 2009: Gregory O. Hutchinson, *Read the Instructions: Didactic Poetry and Didactic Prose*, in: "CQ" 59, 1, 196–211.

Innes 2011: Doreen C. Innes, *The* Panegyricus *and rhetorical theory*, in: Roche 2011, 67–84.

Jaeger 1946[3]: Werner Jaeger, *Paideia. The Ideals of Greek Culture*, Oxford [1st ed. *Paideia. Die Formung des griechischen Menschen*, 3 voll., Berlin, 1934, 1944 and 1947].

James 1987: Paula James, *Unity in Diversity. A Study of Apuleius'* Metamorphoses *with Particular Reference to the Narrator's Art of Transformation and the Metamorphosis Motif in the Tale of Cupid and Psyche*, Hildesheim – Zürich – New York.

Janka 2015: Markus Janka, *Plinius und die Poesie. Von der Freizeitdichtung zur Literaturtheorie*, in: "Gymnasium" 122, 6, 597–618.

Jens 1956: Walter Jens, *Libertas bei Tacitus*, in: "Hermes" 84, 3, 331–352.

Jocelyn 1973: Henry D. Jocelyn, *Homo sum: humani nil a me alienum puto. (Terence*, Heauton timorumenos *77)*, in: "Antichthon" 7, 14–46.

Johnson 2010: William A. Johnson, *Readers and Reading Culture in the High Roman Empire: A Study of Elite Communities*, Oxford – New York.

Jussen 2019: Dennis Jussen, *Enduring the Dust of Mars: The Expectation of Military Leadership in Panegyric to the Child-Emperor Gratian*, in: "Arethusa" 52, 3, 253–273.

Kaster 1986: Robert A. Kaster, Humanitas *and Roman Education*, in: "SStor" 9, 5–15.

Kaster 1997[2]: Robert A. Kaster, *Guardians of Language: The Grammarian and Society in Late Antiquity*, Berkeley – Los Angeles – London [1st ed. 1988].

Kaster 2002: Robert A. Kaster, *The Taxonomy of Patience, or When is 'Patientia' Not a Virtue?*, in: "CPh" 97, 2, 133–144.

Kelly 2008: Gavin Kelly, *Ammianus Marcellinus: the Allusive Historian*, Cambridge – New York.

Kelly 2013: Gavin Kelly, *Pliny and Symmachus*, in: "Arethusa" 46, 2, 261–287.

Keulen 2004: Wytse Keulen, *Gellius, Apuleius, and Satire on the Intellectual*, in: Holford-Strevens/Vardi 2004, 223–245.

Keulen 2009: Wytse Keulen, *Gellius the Satirist: Roman Cultural Authority in Attic Nights*, Leiden – Boston.

Klein 1971: Richard Klein, *Symmachus. Eine tragische Gestalt des ausgehenden Heidentums*, Darmstadt.

Klingner 1947: Friedrich Klingner, *Humanität und humanitas*, in: *Beiträge zur geistigen Ueberlieferung*, Godesberg, 1–52.

Klingner 1952[2]: Friedrich Klingner, *Römische Geisteswelt*, I, Wiesbaden.

Klotz 1911: Alfred Klotz, *Studien zu den Panegyrici Latini*, in: "RhM" 66, 513–572.

Koch 1875: Hanz-Albrecht Koch, *Zu Apulejus*, in: "RhM" 30, 637–640.

Kohl 1992: Benjamin G. Kohl, *The changing concept of the* studia humanitatis *in the early Renaissance*, in: "Renaissance Studies" 6, 2, 185–209.

König/Whitton 2018: Alice König and Christopher Whitton, *Introduction*, in: Alice König and Christopher Whitton (eds.), *Roman Literature under Nerva, Trajan and Hadrian*, Cambridge, 1–34.

König/Woolf 2013: Jason König and Greg Woolf, *Encyclopaedism in the Roman Empire*, in: Jason König and Greg Woolf (eds.), *Encyclopaedism from Antiquity to the Renaissance*, Cambridge, 23–63.

Konstan 2005: David Konstan, *Clemency as a Virtue*, in: "CPh" 100, 4, 337–346.

Kraner/Dittenberger/Meusel 1960: Friedrich Kraner, Wilhelm Dittenberger and Heinrich Meusel, *C. Iulii Caesaris Commentarii de bello Gallico*, Erster Band, Berlin.

Krapinger 2007: Gernot Krapinger, *[Quintilian] Der Gladiator (Grössere Deklamationen, 9)*, Cassino.

Kristeller 1961[2]: Paul O. Kristeller, *Renaissance Thought. The Classic, Scholastic, and Humanistic Strains*, New York – Evanston – London.

La Bua 2010: Giuseppe La Bua, *Patronage and Education in Third-Century Gaul: Eumenius' Panegyric for the Restoration of the Schools*, in: "Journal of Late Antiquity" 3, 2, 300–315.

Lacey 1970: Walter K. Lacey, *Boni Atque Improbi*, in: "G&R" 17, 1, 3–16.

Lana 1955: Italo Lana, *Lucio Anneo Seneca*, Torino.

Lana 1966: Italo Lana, Simplicitas, philostorghía e curiositas *nella letteratura latina del II secolo d.C.*, in: "Cultura e scuola" 18, 90–94.

Lassandro 1973: Domenico Lassandro, *Batavica* o *Bagaudica rebellio?*, in: "GIF" 4, 1973, 300–308.

Lassandro/Micunco 2000: Domenico Lassandro and Giuseppe Micunco, *Panegirici Latini*, Torino.

Laudizi 2021: Giovanni Laudizi, *La nozione di* humanitas *nelle* Epistulae morales *di Seneca*, in: *Lucrezio, Seneca e noi. Studi per Ivano Dionigi*, Bologna, 337–344.

Lefèvre 1994: Eckard Lefèvre, *Terenz' und Menanders Heautontimorumenos*, München.

Lefèvre 2009: Eckard Lefèvre, *Vom Römertum zum Ästhetizismus. Studien zu den Briefen des jüngeren Plinius*, Berlin – New York.

Leigh 2004: Matthew Leigh, *The* Pro Caelio *and Comedy*, in: "CPh" 99, 4, 300–335.

Leigh 2013: Matthew Leigh, *From* Polypragmon *to* Curiosus. *Ancient Concepts of Curious and Meddlesome Behaviour*, Oxford.

Lentano 1999: Mario Lentano, *La declamazione latina. Rassegna di studi e stato delle questioni (1989–1998)*, in: "BSL" 29, 571–621.

Leonardis 2018: Irene Leonardis, *L'*Humanitas, *secondo Varrone. La memoria della stirpe umana*, in: "Athenaeum" 106, 2, 516–532.

Levene 1997: David S. Levene, *God and Man in the Classical Latin Panegyric*, in: "PCPhS" 43, 66–103.

Levi 1994: Mario A. Levi, *Ricerche su Frontone*, Roma.

Liebeschuetz 1966: Wolfgang Liebeschuetz, *The Theme of Liberty in the Agricola of Tacitus*, in: "CQ" 16, 1, 126–139.

Lindermann 2006: Jens-Olaf Lindermann, *Aulus Gellius Noctes Atticae, Buch 9: Kommentar*, Berlin.

Lipps 1967: Peter Lipps, *Humanitas in der frühen Kaiserzeit. Begriff und Vorstellung*, Freiburg im Breisgau.

Lizzi Testa 2022: Rita Lizzi Testa, *Christian Emperors and Roman Elites in Late Antiquity*, Abingdon – New York.

Lo Cascio 2007: Elio Lo Cascio, *I valori romani tradizionali e le culture delle periferie dell'Impero*, in: "Athenaeum" 95, 75–96.

Lolli 2006: Massimo Lolli, *Ausonius: die* Gratiarum actio ad Gratianum imperatorem *und "De maiestatis laudibus". Lobrede auf den Herrscher oder auf den Lehrer?*, in: "Latomus" 65, 3, 707–726.

Lomanto/Garcea 2004: Valeria Lomanto and Alessandro Garcea, *Gellius and Fronto on Loanwords and Literary Models: Their Evaluation of Laberius*, in Holford-Strevens/Vardi 2004, 41–64.

Longo 2008: Giovanna Longo, *[Quintiliano] La pozione dell'odio (*Declamazioni maggiori, *14–15)*, Cassino.

Lorenz 1914: Siegfried Lorenz, *De progressu notionis philanthropias*, Leipzig.

MacDonald 2017: Michael J. MacDonald (ed.), *The Oxford Handbook of Rhetorical Studies*, Oxford – New York.

MacGregor 1982: Alexander P. MacGregor, Dexteritas *and* Humanitas: Gellius 13.17.1 and Livy 37.7.15, in: "CPh" 77, 1, 42–48.

Magnaldi 2017: Giuseppina Magnaldi, review of Stover 2016, in: "ExClass" 21, 367–376.

Maguinness 1952: William S. Maguinness, *Eumenius of Autun*, in: "G&R" 21, 63, 97–103.

Maguinness 2012[2]: William S. Maguinness, *Locutions and Formulae of the Latin Panegyrists*, in: Rees 2012, 265–288 [= *Hermathena* 23, 48, 1933, 117–138].

Malaspina 2001: Ermanno Malaspina, *L. Annaei Senecae De clementia libri duo*, Alessandria.

Malaspina 2003: Ermanno Malaspina, *La teoria politica del* De clementia: *un inevitabile fallimento?*, in: Arturo De Vivo and Elio Lo Cascio (eds.), *Seneca uomo politico e l'età di Claudio e di Nerone*, Bari, 139–157.

Malaspina 2009: Ermanno Malaspina, *La clemenza*, in: Luciano De Biasi, Anna M. Ferrero, Ermanno Malaspina and Dionigi Vottero (eds.), *Lucio Anneo Seneca. Opere, vol. V*, Torino, 7–299.

Malaspina 2019: Ermanno Malaspina, *Euphratès, Artémidore et ceux* qui sapientiae studium habitu corporis praeferunt (Ep., I, 22, 6)*: la place de la philosophie dans la culture de Pline*, in: Sophie Aubert-Baillot, Charles Guérin and Sébastien Morlet (eds.), *La philosophie des non-philosophes dans l'Empire romain du I^e au IIIe siècle*, Paris, 121–156.

Maltby 1991: Robert Maltby, *A Lexicon of Ancient Latin Etymologies*, Leeds.

Mantovani 2017: Dario Mantovani, L'*aequitas romana: una nozione in cerca di equilibrio*, in: "Antiquorum philosophia" 11, 15–60.

Manuwald 2011: Gesine Manuwald, *Ciceronian praise as a step towards Pliny's* Panegyricus, in: Roche 2011, 85–103.

Marache 1952: René Marache, *La critique littéraire de langue latine et le développement du goût archaïsant au IIe siècle de notre ère*, Rennes.

Marache 1957: René Marache, *Mots nouveaux et mots archaïques chez Fronton et Aulu-Gelle*, Paris.

Maranesi 2013: Alessandro Maranesi, Consensus *e* virtutes *nella prima età costantiniana*, in: "Aevum" 87, 1, 99–112.

Marchesi 2008: Ilaria Marchesi, *The Art of Pliny's Letters. A Poetic of Allusion in the Private Correspondence*, New York.

Marcone 1983: Arnaldo Marcone, *Commento storico al libro VI dell'epistolario di Q. Aurelio Simmaco*, Pisa.

Marcone 1987: Arnaldo Marcone, *Commento storico al libro IV dell'epistolario di Q. Aurelio Simmaco*, Pisa.

Markus 1974: Robert A. Markus, *Paganism, Christianity and the Latin Classics in the Fourth Century*, in: Binns 1974, 1–21.

Maróti 2002–2003: Egon Maróti, *Omnis humanitas*, in: "ACD" 38–39, 277–280.

Marriott 1979: Ian Marriott, *The authorship of the* Historia Augusta. *Two computer studies*, in: "JRS" 69, 65–77.

Marrou 1948: Henri-Irénée Marrou, *Histoire de l'éducation dans l'Antiquité. Tome II. Le monde romain*, Paris.

Maselli 1979: Giorgio Maselli, *Lingua e scuola in Gellio grammatico*, Lecce.

Mason 1978: Hugh J. Mason, Fabula Graecanica*: Apuleius and his Greek Sources*, in: Hijmans/van der Paardt 1978, 1–16.

Mason 1983: Hugh J. Mason, *The Distinction of Lucius in Apuleius'* Metamorphoses, in: "Phoenix" 37, 2, 135–143.

Matacotta 2010: Dante Matacotta, *Simmaco. L'antagonista di Sant'Ambrogio*, Forlì.

Matthews 1974: John F. Matthews, *The Letters of Symmachus*, in: Binns 1974, 58–99.

Matthews 1975: John F. Matthews, *Western Aristocracies and Imperial Court A.D. 364–425*, Oxford – New York.

Matthews 1986: John F. Matthews, *Symmachus and His Enemies*, in: Paschoud 1986, 163–175.

Matthews 1989: John F. Matthews, *The Roman Empire of Ammianus Marcellinus*, Baltimore.

May 2006: Regine May, *Apuleius and Drama. The Ass on Stage*, Oxford.

Mayer 1951: Josef Mayer, *Humanitas bei Cicero*, Freiburg (diss.).

Mazzoli 2012: Giancarlo Mazzoli, *Piani della memoria nelle* Res gestae *di Ammiano Marcellino*, in: Lucio Cristante and Tommaso Mazzoli (eds.), *Il calamo della memoria. Riuso di testi e mestiere letterario nella tarda antichità*, vol. 5, 61–74.

McDonnell 2006: Myles McDonnell, *Roman Manliness.* Virtus *and the Roman Republic*, Cambridge.

Meillet 1921: Antoine Meillet, *Linguistique historique et linguistique générale*, Paris.

Mercklin 1860: Ludwig Mercklin, *Die Citiermethode und Quellenbenutzung des A. Gellius in den* Noctes Atticae, in: "Jahrbuch für classische Philologie Suppl." 3, 2, 633–710.

Merrill 1919: Elmer T. Merrill, *Selected Letters of the Younger Pliny*, London [1st ed. 1903].

Méthy 2007: Nicole Méthy, *Les lettres de Pline le Jeune. Une représentation de l'homme*, Paris.

Mineo 2006: Bernard Mineo, *Tite-Live et l'histoire de Rome*, Paris.

Miraglia 2019: Luigi Miraglia, *L'umanesimo e i suoi "princìpi primi"*, in: Alberto Giacomelli and Sergio Givone (eds.), *Umanesimo, Humanismus, Humanisme. Filosofie dell'umano fra Rinascimento e contemporaneità*, "paradosso" 2019, 2, 13–36.

Mollea 2016: Simone Mollea, review of Høgel 2015, in: "BMCR" 2016.02.31.

Mollea 2018a: Simone Mollea, review of Girotti 2017, in: "Ciceroniana On Line" 2, 2, 317–324.

Mollea 2018b: Simone Mollea, *Aulus Gellius' definition of* humanitas, *Aelius Aristides and Willem Canter*, in: Alberto F. Araújo, Custódia Martins, Henrique M. Carvalho, José P. Serra and Justino Magalhães (eds.), *Paideia &* Humanitas. *Formar e educar ontem e hoje*, Ribeirão, 147–156.

Mollea 2019: Simone Mollea, Naturales Quaestiones *4a* Praef. *20 And* Ep. *34.2: Approaching the Chronology and Non-Fictional Nature of Seneca's Epistulae Morales*, in: "CQ" 69, 1, 319–334.

Mollea 2021: Simone Mollea, *Un interessante caso di* humanitas *in età imperiale: l'*Oratio pro instaurandis scholis *di Eumenio*, in: "BSL" 51, 1, 71–80.

Mollea 2022a: Simone Mollea, Humanitas *dei giudici, colpevolezza dell'imputato in alcune orazioni ciceroniane?*, in: Andrea Balbo (ed.), *Atti del Convegno "Da Cicerone al Digesto: interazioni fra oratoria giudiziaria, retorica e diritto tra l'età repubblicana e imperiale"* (Università di Torino, 22–23 novembre 2021), "Ciceroniana Online" 6, 2, 233–257.

Mollea 2022b: Simone Mollea, *Ennodio e l'*humanitas: *tra romanità e cristianesimo*, in: Fabio Gasti (ed.), *Ennodio di Pavia: cultura, letteratura e stile tra V e VI secolo*, Firenze, 69–82.

Mollea 2023a: Simone Mollea, Voluntas, virtutes *e* otium. *Seneca*, Epistulae ad Lucilium *67 e 68. Introduzione, traduzione e commento*, Alessandria.

Mollea 2023b: Simone Mollea, *Did Fully Fledged* humanitas *Exist before the Ciceronian Age? A Study on the Relation between* humanus, *its Comparative and Superlative, and the Noun* humanitas, in: "Mnemosyne" (2023) online, 1–21 [= 77, 2, 2024, 283–303].

Mollea 2023c: Simone Mollea, *Cicerone (e Simmaco). Tra* humanitas, amicitia, *contagio e lettere*, in: "Altre Modernità" 12, 39–52.

Momigliano 1954: Arnaldo Momigliano, *An Unsolved Problem of Historical Forgery: The* Scriptores Historiae Augustae, in: "JWI" 17, 1, 22–46.

Momigliano 1974: Arnaldo Momigliano, *The Lonely Historian Ammianus Marcellinus*, in: "ASNP" 3, 4, 4, 1393–1407.

Monat 1992: Pierre Monat, *Firmicus Maternus. Mathesis. Tome 1, livres 1 et 2*, Paris.

Monat 1999: Pierre Monat, *Astrologie et pouvoir: les subtilités de Firmicus Maternus*, in: Elisabeth Smadja and Evelyne Geny (eds.), *Pouvoir, divination et prédestination dans le monde antique*, Besançon, 133–136.

Montanari Caldini 1984: Roberta Montanari Caldini, *Cicerone, Firmico e la dittatura di Scipione Emiliano*, in: "Prometheus" 10, 1, 19–32.

Moreschini 1978: Claudio Moreschini, *Apuleio e il platonismo*, Firenze.

Moreschini 1985: Claudio Moreschini, *Dall'*Asclepius *al* Crater Hermetis. *Studi sull'ermetismo latino tardo-antico e rinascimentale*, Pisa.

Moreschini 2011: Claudio Moreschini, Hermes Christianus. *The Intermingling of Hermetic Piety and Christian Thought*, Turnhout.

Moreschini 2017: Claudio Moreschini, review of Stover 2016, in: "BMCR" 2017.03.31.

Morgan 2004: Teresa Morgan, *Educational Values*, in: Holford-Strevens/Vardi 2004, 187–205.

Müller 2003: Reimar Müller, *Die Entdeckung der Kultur: antike Theorien über Ursprung und Entwicklung der Kultur von Homer bis Seneca*, Düsseldorf.

Narducci 1981: Emanuele Narducci, *La* humanitas *come ideologia dell'adattamento*, in: Mario Labate and Emanuele Narducci, *Mobilità dei modelli etici e relativismo dei valori: il personaggio di Attico*, in: Andrea Giardina and Aldo Schiavone (eds.), *Società romana e produzione schiavistica, III: Modelli etici, diritto e trasformazioni sociali*, Bari, 175–182.

Neri 1985: Valerio Neri, *Ammiano e il Cristianesimo. Religione e politica nelle* Res gestae *di Ammiano Marcellino*, Bologna.

Nesholm 2010: Erika J. Nesholm, *Language and Artistry in Cicero's* Pro Archia, in: "CW" 103, 4, 477–490.

Newbold 1984: Ronald F. Newbold, *Suetonius' Boundaries*, in: "Latomus" 43, 1, 118–132.

Nicolini 2011: Lara Nicolini, *Ad (l)usum lectoris. Etimologia e giochi di parole in Apuleio*, Bologna.

Nikolaïdis 1980: Anastasios G. Nikolaïdis, *A Note on the Relationship between* philanthropía *and* humanitas, in: "Platon" 22/23, 350–355.

Nixon/Rodgers 1994: Charles E.V. Nixon and Barbara S. Rodgers, *In Praise of Later Roman Emperors. The Panegyrici latini*, Berkeley – Los Angeles – Oxford.

Nocchi 2013: Francesca Romana Nocchi, *Tecniche teatrali e formazione dell'oratore in Quintiliano*, Berlin – Boston.

Norden 1912: Fritz Norden, *Apulejus von Madaura und das römische Privatrecht*, Leipzig –Berlin.

Noreña 2014: Carlos F. Noreña, *Authority and Subjectivity in the 'Apology'*, in: Benjamin T. Lee, Ellen Finkelpearl, Luca Graverini and Alessandro Barchiesi (eds.), *Apuleius and Africa*, London, 35–51.

Nussbaum 1971: Gerry B. Nussbaum, *A Study of Odes I 37 and 38. The Psychology of Conflict and Horace's* Humanitas, in: "Arethusa" 4, 1, 91–97.

Nybakken 1939: Oscar E. Nybakken, *Humanitas Romana*, in: "TAPhA" 70, 396–413.

Ogilvie 1991: Robert M. Ogilvie (1991), *An Interim Report on Tacitus' Agricola*, in: "ANRW" II.33.3, 1714–1740.

Ogilvie/Richmond 1967: Robert M. Ogilvie and Ian Richmond, *Cornelii Taciti De vita Agricolae*, Oxford.

Onida 2011–2012: Pietro P. Onida, *Per lo studio delle costituzioni imperiali in Sardegna*: cursus publicus *e* humanitas *costantiniana*, in: "Diritto@Storia" 10 (https://www.dirittoestoria.it/10/Tradizione-Romana/Onida-Costantino-costituzioni-imperiali-Sardegna.htm).

Oniga 2009: Renato Oniga, *Contro la post-religione. Per un nuovo umanesimo cristiano*, Verona.

Oniga 2016: Renato Oniga, *La genesi del concetto di* humanitas *nella commedia latina arcaica*, in: Fabiana Di Brazzà, Ilvano Caliaro, Roberto Norbedo, Renzo Rabboni and Matteo Venier (eds.), *Le carte e i discepoli. Studi in onore di Claudio Griggio*, Udine, 21–30.

Pabst 1989: Angela Pabst, *Reden*: Q. Aurelius Symmachus, Darmstadt.

Pagán 2012: Victoria E. Pagán (ed.), *A Companion to Tacitus*, Malden – Oxford – Chichester.

Pagán 2023: Victoria E. Pagán (ed.), *The Tacitus Encyclopedia*, II vol., Hoboken (NJ)-Chichester.

Pagnotta 2022: Fausto Pagnotta, *Cicerone e la* Societas hominum. *Contesto e funzioni di un concetto politico*, Sesto San Giovanni.

Panoussi 2009: Vassiliki Panoussi, *Roman Cultural Identity in Cicero's* Pro Archia, in: Eleni Karamalengou and Eugenia D. Makrygianni (eds.), Ἀντιφίλησις. *Studies on Classical, Byzantine and Modern Greek Literature and Culture. In Honour of John-Teophanes A. Papademetriou*, Stuttgart, 516–523.

Parri 2005: Ilaria Parri, *La via filosofica di Ermete. Studio sull'*Asclepius, Firenze.

Paschoud 1986: François Paschoud (ed.), *Colloque genévois sur Symmaque: à l'occasion du mille six centième anniversaire du conflit de l'autel de la Victoire*, Paris.

Paschoud 2002: François Paschoud, *Les* Panégyriques latins *et l'*Histoire Auguste: *quelques réflexions*, in: Pol Defosse (ed.), *Hommages à Carl Deroux. II. Prose et linguistique, Médecine*, Bruxelles, 347–356.

Pasetti 2007: Lucia Pasetti, *Plauto in Apuleio*, Bologna.

Pasetti 2019: Lucia Pasetti, *Introduzione*, in: Pasetti *et al.* 2019, IX–XXXVIII.

Pasetti *et al.* 2019: Lucia Pasetti, Alfredo Casamento, Giuseppe Dimatteo, Gernot Krapinger, Biagio Santorelli and Chiara Valenzano, *Le* Declamazioni minori *attribuite a Quintiliano. I (244–292)*, Bologna.

Pausch 2004: Dennis Pausch, *Biographie und Bildungskultur. Personendarstellungen bei Plinius dem Jüngeren, Gellius und Sueton*, Berlin – New York.

Pausch 2010: Dennis Pausch, Libellus non tam diserte quam fideliter scriptus? *Unreliable Narration in the* Historia Augusta, in: "AncNarr" 8, 115–135.

Pease 1943: Arthur S. Pease, *The Son of Neptune*, in: "HSCP" 54, 69–82.

Pellecchi 2012: Luigi Pellecchi, Innocentia eloquentia est. *Analisi giuridica dell'*Apologia *di Apuleio*, Como.

Pellizzari 1998: Andrea Pellizzari, *Commento storico al libro III dell'Epistolario di Q. Aurelio Simmaco*, Pisa.

Pernot 2005: Laurent Pernot, *Rhetoric in Antiquity*, Washington D.C.

Perry 1923: Ben E. Perry, *Some Aspects of the Literary Art of Apuleius in the Metamorphoses*, in: "TAPhA" 54, 196–227.

Perry 1925: Ben E. Perry, *On Apuleius'* Metamorphoses *II, 31 – III, 20*, in: "AJPh" 46, 3, 253–262.

Petersmann 1991: Gerhard Petersmann, *Der 'Agricola' des Tacitus. Versuch einer Deutung*, in: "ANRW" II.33.3, 1785–1806.

Petré 1934: Hélène Petré, Misericordia. *Histoire du mot et de l'idée du paganisme au christianisme*, in: "REL" 12, 376–389.

Pfeiffer 1931: Rudolf Pfeiffer, *Humanitas Erasmiana*, Leipzig.

Piantadosi 2014: Steven T. Piantadosi, *Zipf's word frequency law in natural language: A critical review and future directions*, in: "Psychonomic Bulletin & Review" 21, 1112–1130.

Piatti 2019: Federico Piatti, *Un sigillum enigmatico*: Amm. XXXI, 16, 9, in: "Gilgameš" 2, 2, 28–40.

Picone 1978: Giusto Picone, *L'eloquenza di Plinio: teoria e prassi*, Palermo.

Pieri 2002: Bruna Pieri, *I medici e la* humanitas *(Ps. Quint.* decl. *8,3)*, in: "Paideia" 57, 369–378.

Poglio 2007: Federico A. Poglio (2007), *Gruppi di potere nella Roma tardoantica (350–395 d.C.)*, Torino.

Pohlenz 1947: Max Pohlenz, *Der hellenische Mensch*, Göttingen.

Portalupi 1961: Felicita Portalupi, *Marco Cornelio Frontone*, Torino.

Posadas 2023: Juan L. Posadas, *Germania*, in: Pagán 2023, 474–478.

Power 2014a: Tristan Power, *Introduction: The Originality of Suetonius*, in: Power/Gibson 2014, 1–18.

Power 2014b: Tristan Power, *The Endings of Suetonius' Caesars*, in Power/Gibson 2014, 58–77.

Power/Gibson 2014: Tristan Power and Roy K. Gibson (eds.), *Suetonius the Biographer: Studies in Roman Lives*, New York.

Prete 1944: Sesto Prete, *Der Begriff " humanitas " in der römischen Komödie*, Köln.

Prete 1948: Sesto Prete, *"Humanus" nella letteratura arcaica latina*, Milano.

Prost 2006: François Prost, Humanitas: *originalité d'un concept cicéronien*, in: "L'art du comprendre" 15, *Philosophies de l'humanisme*, 31–46.

Pultrová 2019: Lucie Pultrová, *Correlation between the gradability of Latin adjectives and the ability to form qualitative abstract nouns*, in: Zdeněk Žabokrtský, Magda Ševčíková, Eleonora Litta and Marco Passarotti (eds.), *Proceedings of the Second International Workshop on Resources and Tools for Derivational Morphology*, Praha, 25–34.

Pultrová 2022: Lucie Pultrová, *The Category of Comparison in Latin*, Leiden – Boston.

Radice 1968: Betty Radice, *Pliny and the* Panegyricus, in: "G&R" 15, 2, 166–172.

Raimondi 2008: Milena Raimondi, *Ausonio e l'elezione di Teodosio I*, in: "Aevum" 82, 1, 155–178.

Rees 1999: Roger Rees, *Ammianus Satiricus*, in: Drijvers/Hunt 1999, 141–155.

Rees 2001: Roger Rees, *To Be and Not to Be: Pliny's Paradoxical Trajan*, in: "BICS" 45, 149–168.

Rees 2002: Roger Rees, *Layers of Loyalty in Latin Panegyric. AD 289–307*, New York.

Rees 2012: Roger Rees (ed.), *Latin Panegyric*, New York.

Rees 2014: Roger Rees, *Adopting the Emperor: Pliny's Praise-giving as Cultural Appropriation*, in: Roger Rees and Jesper M. Madsen (eds.), *Roman Rule in Greek and Latin Writing: Double Vision*, Leiden – Boston, 105–123.

Rees 2023: Roger Rees, *A Commentary on Panegyrici Latini II (12)*, Cambridge.

Reeve 1996: Michael D. Reeve, *Classical Scholarship*, in: Jill Kraye (ed.), *The Cambridge Companion to Renaissance Humanism*, New York, 19–46.

Reitzenstein 1907: Richard Reitzenstein, *Werden und Wesen der Humanität im Altertum*, Straßburg.

Rieks 1967: Rudolf Rieks, *Homo, humanus, humanitas. Zur Humanität in der lateinischen Literatur des ersten nachchristlichen Jahrhunderts*, München.

Rimell 2013: Victoria Rimell, *The Best a Man Can Get: Grooming Scipio in Seneca Epistle 86*, in: "CPh" 108, 1, 1–20.

Rimell 2015: Victoria Rimell, *The Closure of Space in Roman Poetics: Empire's Inward Turn*, Cambridge.

Riposati 1949: Benedetto Riposati, *Varrone e Cicerone maestri di umanità*, in: "Aevum" 23, 3, 246–266.

Ritter 1884: Constantin Ritter, *M. Fabii Quintiliani Declamationes quae supersunt CXLV*, Leipzig.

Rives 2012: James B. Rives, *Germania*, in: Pagán 2012, 45–61.

Rivolta Tiberga 1992: Paola Rivolta Tiberga, *Commento storico al libro V dell'Epistolario di Q. Aurelio Simmaco*, Pisa.

Roche 2011: Paul A. Roche (ed.), *Pliny's Praise: the* Panegyricus *in the Roman World*, Cambridge – New York.

Rochette 2003: Bruno Rochette, *Un cas peu connu de traduction du grec en latin: l'"Asclepius" du* Corpus Hermeticum, in: "CCG" 14, 67–96.

Roda 1981: Sergio Roda, *Commento storico al libro IX dell'Epistolario di Q. Aurelio Simmaco*, Pisa.

Roda 1986: Sergio Roda, *Polifunzionalità della lettera* commendaticia: *teoria e prassi nell'epistolario simmachiano*, in: Paschoud 1986, 177–207.

Rodgers 1989: Barbara S. Rodgers, *Eumenius of Augustodunum*, in: "AncSoc" 20, 249–266.

Rodríguez Gervás 1991: Manuel J. Rodríguez Gervás, *Propaganda política y opinión pública en los panegíricos latinos del bajo imperio*, Salamanca.

Rohrbacher 2002: David S. Rohrbacher, *The Historians of Late Antiquity*, London.

Roller 1998: Matthew Roller, *Pliny's Catullus: The Politics of Literary Appropriation*, in: "TAPhA" 128, 265–304.

Romano 2014: Elisa Romano, *Umanesimo e Humanities. Passato nel presente*, in: "ClassicoContemporaneo" 0, 42–55.

Rosen 1982: Klaus Rosen, *Ammianus Marcellinus*, Darmstadt.

Ruta 2023: Alessio Ruta, *Quinto Aurelio Simmaco. Epistularum liber VIII*, Alessandria.

Rutledge 2000: Steven H. Rutledge, *Tacitus in Tartan: Textual Colonization and Expansionist Discourse in the* Agricola, in: "Helios" 27, 1, 75–95.

Sabbah 1978: Guy Sabbah, *La méthode d'Ammien Marcellin. Recherches sur la construction du discours historique dans les* Res gestae, Paris.

Sage 1990: Michael M. Sage, *Tacitus' Historical Works: A Survey and Appraisal*, in: "ANRW" II.33.2, 851–1030.

Sailor 2012: Dylan Sailor, *The Agricola*, in: Pagán 2012, 23–44.

Sailor 2023: Dylan Sailor, *Agricola (Iulius Agricola, Gnaeus)*, in: Pagán 2023, 27–31.

Salemme 1989: Carmelo Salemme, *Similitudini nella storia. Un capitolo su Ammiano Marcellino*, Napoli.

Salzman 2011: Michele R. Salzman, *The Letters of Symmachus: Book 1*, Atlanta.

Sánchez Manzano 2017: María Asunción Sánchez Manzano, *Lexicon and style in the works attributed to Firmicus Maternus*, in: "Pallas" 103, 181–189.

Sandy 1997: Gerald Sandy, *The Greek World of Apuleius. Apuleius and the Second Sophistic*, Leiden – New York – Köln.

Santini 2006: Piero Santini, *L'auctoritas linguistica di Cicerone nelle "Notti Attiche" di Gellio*, Napoli.

Santorelli 2019: Biagio Santorelli, *Decl. min. 252 and 27*, in: Pasetti *et al.* 2019, 247–255; 379–384.

Santorelli 2021a: Biagio Santorelli, *Datazione e paternità delle* Declamazioni maggiori *pseudo-quintilianee*, in: Andrea Lovato, Antonio Stramaglia and Giusto Traina, *Le* declamazioni maggiori *pseudo-quintilianee nella Roma imperiale*, Berlin – Boston, 361–429.

Santorelli 2021b: Biagio Santorelli, *General Introduction*, §§ 1–4, in: Stramaglia *et al.* 2021, ix–xxxix.

Schadewaldt 1973: Wolfgang Schadewaldt, *Humanitas Romana*, in: "ANRW" I.4, 43–62.

Schanz 1959[2]: Martin Schanz, *Geschichte der römischen Literatur bis zum Gesetzgebungswerk des Kaisers Justinian. Vierter Teil. Die römische Literatur von Constantin bis zum Gesetzgebungswerk Justinians. Erster Band. Die Literatur des vierten Jahrhunderts*, München.

Scherr 2023: Jonas Scherr, *Die Zivilisierung der Barbaren. Eine Diskursgeschichte von Cicero bis Cassius Dio*, Berlin – Boston.

Schlam 1992: Carl C. Schlam, *The Metamorphoses of Apuleius. On Making an Ass of Oneself*, London.

C. Schneider 2013: Catherine Schneider, *[Quintilien] Le tombeau ensorcelé (Grandes déclamations, 10)*, Cassino.

J. Schneider 1964: P. Josef Schneider, *Untersuchungen über das Verhältnis von humanitas zu Recht und Gerechtigkeit bei Cicero*, Freiburg im Breisgau (diss.).

Schneidewin 1897: Max Schneidewin, *Die antike Humanität*, Berlin.

Schröder 2012: Bianca J. Schröder, *Römische* pietas – *kein universelles Postulat*, in: "Gymnasium" 119, 4, 335–358.

Schulz 1934: Fritz Schulz, *Prinzipien des römischen Rechts*, München.

Scobie 1978: Alexander Scobie, *The Structure of Apuleius'* Metamorphoses, in: Hijmans/van der Paardt 1978, 43–62.

Seager 1983: Robin Seager, *Some Imperial Virtues in the Latin Prose Panegyrics. The Demands of Propaganda and the Dynamics of Literary Composition*, in: "Papers of the Liverpool Latin Seminar" 4, 129–165.

Seager 1986: Robin Seager, *Ammianus Marcellinus. Seven Studies in His Language and Thought*, Columbia (MI).

Seeck 1883: Otto Seeck, *Q. Aurelii Symmachi quae supersunt*, Berlin.

Selem 1964: Antonio Selem, *Ammiano Marcellino e i problemi sociali del suo tempo*, in: "ASNP" 33, 1, 147–153.

Sellmair 1948: Josef Sellmair, *Humanitas Christiana. Geschichte des christlichen Humanismus*, München.

Shackleton Bailey 2006: David R. Shackleton Bailey, *[Quintilian]. The Lesser Declamations*. 2 Volumes, Cambridge (MA) – London.

Sherwin-White 1966: Andrew N. Sherwin-White, *The Letters of Pliny: A Historical and Social Commentary*, Oxford.

Sivan 2004[2]: Hagith Sivan, *Ausonius of Bordeaux. Genesis of a Gallic aristocracy*, London – New York.

Snell 1953[2]: Bruno Snell, *The Discovery of the Mind. The Greek Origins of European Thought*, Cambridge (MA) [1st ed. *Die Entdeckung des Geistes. Studien zur Entstehung des europaïschen Denkens bei den Griechen*, Hamburg, 1947].

Sogno 2005: Cristiana Sogno, *Astrology, Morality, the Emperor, and the Law in Firmicus Maternus' Mathesis*, in: "ICS" 30, 167–176.

Sogno 2006: Cristiana Sogno, *Q. Aurelius Symmachus: a Political Biography*, Ann Arbor (MI).

Sola 2016: Giancarla Sola, *La formazione originaria. Paideia, humanitas, perfectio, dignitas hominis, Bildung*, Milano.

Somville 2002: Pierre Somville, *Psychographie de Tibère*, in: "AC" 71, 85–92.

Sonnabend 2002: Holger Sonnabend, *Geschichte der antiken Biographie. Von Isokrates bis zur Historia Augusta*, Stuttgart – Weimar.

Soverini 1989: Paolo Soverini, *Impero e imperatori nell'opera di Plinio il Giovane: Aspetti e problemi del rapporto con Domiziano e Traiano*, in: "ANRW" II.33.1, 515–554.

Soverini 2004: Paolo Soverini, *Cornelio Tacito. Agricola. Introduzione, testo critico, traduzione e commento*, Alessandria.

Spinelli 2022: Tommaso Spinelli, *The Diachronic Frequency of Latin Words. A Computational Dictionary. Volume I (A/AB–Azymus)*, Heidelberg.

Steinmetz 1982: Peter Steinmetz, *Untersuchungen zur römischen Literatur des zweiten Jahrhunderts nach Christi Geburt*, Wiesbaden.

Stevenson 2004: Andrew J. Stevenson, *Gellius and the Roman Antiquarian Tradition*, in: Holford-Strevens/Vardi 2004, 118–155.

Stover 2016: Justin A. Stover, *A New Work by Apuleius: The Lost Third Book of the 'De Platone'*, Oxford – New York.

Stover/Kestemont 2016: Justin A. Stover and Mike Kestemont, *The Author of the* Historia Augusta*: Two New Computational Studies*, in: "BICS" 59, 2, 140–157.

Stover/Woudhuysen 2023: Justin A. Stover and George Woudhuysen, *The Lost History of Sextus Aurelius Victor*, Edinburgh.

Stramaglia 1999: Antonio Stramaglia, *[Quintiliano] I gemelli malati: un caso di vivisezione (*Declamazioni maggiori*, 8)*, Cassino.

Stramaglia 2021: Antonio Stramaglia, *General Introduction. §§ 5–8*, in: Stramaglia *et al.* 2021, xxxix–lxxiii.

Stramaglia *et al.* 2021: Antonio Stramaglia, Michael Winterbottom and Biagio Santorelli, *Quintilian. The Major Declamations*, 3 volumes, Cambridge (MA) – London.

Strasburger 1966: Hermann Strasburger, *Der 'Scipionenkreis'*, in: "Hermes" 94, 1, 60–72.

Stroh 2008: Wilfried Stroh, *De origine uocum humanitatis et humanismi*, in: "Gymnasium" 115, 6, 535–571.

Strunk 2017: Thomas E. Strunk, *History after Liberty. Tacitus on Tyrants, Sycophants, and Republicans*, Ann Arbor (MI).

Sulek 2010: Marty Sulek, *On the Classical Meaning of Philanthrôpía*, in: "Nonprofit and Voluntary Sector Quarterly" 39, 3, 385–408.

Summers 1970: Richard G. Summers, *Roman Justice and Apuleius' Metamorphoses*, in: "TAPhA" 101, 511–531.

Sussman 1995: Lewis A. Sussman, *Sons and Fathers in the* Major Declamations *Ascribed to Quintilian*, in: "Rhetorica" 13, 2, 179–192.

Swain 2004: Simon Swain, *Bilingualism and Biculturalism in Antonine Rome: Apuleius, Fronto, and Gellius*, in: Holford-Strevens/Vardi 2004, 3–40.

Syme 1958: Ronald Syme, *Tacitus*, Oxford.

Tempest 2020: Kathryn Tempest, *Cicero's* Artes Liberales *and the Liberal Arts*, in: "Ciceroniana Online" 4, 2, 479–500.

Thomas 2009: Richard F. Thomas, *The Germania as Literary Text*, in: Woodman 2009, 59–72.

Thompson 1947: Edward A. Thompson, *The Historical Work of Ammianus Marcellinus*, Cambridge.

Tilg 2014: Stefan Tilg, *Apuleius'* Metamorphoses. *A Study in Roman Fiction*, Oxford.

Toledo Martin 2021: Rogelio Toledo Martin, *Lucubrationes Gellianae, sive quem in modum Gellius usus sit vocabulo quod est* humanitas *et quantum intersit inter eius usum et eius definitionem*, in: Antonio María Martín Rodríguez (ed.), Linguisticae Dissertationes. *Current Perspectives on Latin Grammar, Lexicon and Pragmatics. Selected Papers from the 20th International Colloquium on Latin Linguistics (Las Palmas de Gran Canaria, Spain, June 17–21, 2019)*, Madrid, 161–170.

Toussaint 2008: Stéphane Toussaint, *Humanismes/Antihumanismes de Ficin à Heidegger. I.* Humanitas *et Rentabilité*, Paris.

Townend 1959: Gavin B. Townend, *The Date of Composition of Suetonius' Caesares*, in: "CQ" 9, 2, 285–293.

Traina 1969[3]: Alfonso Traina, *Comoedia. Antologia della palliata*, Padova [1st ed. 1960].

Trisciuoglio 2018: Andrea Trisciuoglio, *Humanitas e cura delle esigenze umane nel Codice Teodosiano*, in: "Ius Romanum" 2, 349–357.

Trisoglio 1971: Francesco Trisoglio, *L'elemento meditativo nell'epistolario di Plinio il giovane*, in: *Fons Perennis. Saggi critici di Filologia Classica raccolti in onore del Prof. Vittorio D'Agostino*, Torino.

Tromp de Ruiter 1931: Solko Tromp de Ruiter, *De vocis quae est ΦΙΛΑΝΘΡΩΠΙΑ significatione atque usu*, in: "Mnemosyne" 59, 3, 271–306.

Tse *et al.* 1998: Emily K. Tse, Fiona J. Tweedie and Bernard D. Frischer, *Unravelling the Purple Thread: Function Word Variability and the* Scriptores Historiae Augustae, in: "Literary and Linguistic Computing" 13, 141–149.

Tuck 2016: Steven L. Tuck, *Imperial Image-Making*, in: Zissos 2016a, 109–128.

Turcan 1982: Robert Turcan, *Firmicus Maternus. L'erreur des religions païennes*, Paris.

Turner 1997: Andrew J. Turner, *Approaches to Tacitus'* Agricola, in: "Latomus" 56, 3, 582–593.

Tylor 1871: Edward B. Tylor, *Primitive Culture: Researches into the Development of Mythology, Philosophy, Religion, Art, and Custom*, London.

Vacher 2003[2]: Marie-Claude Vacher, *Suétone. Grammariens et rhétheurs*, Paris [1st ed. 1993].

Van den Hout 1988: Michael P.J. van den Hout, *M. Cornelii Frontonis* Epistulae, Leipzig.

Van den Hout 1999: Michael P.J. van den Hout, *A Commentary on the Letters of M. Cornelius Fronto*, Leiden – Boston.

Van der Paardt 1971: Rudi T. van der Paardt, *L. Apuleius Madaurensis. The Metamorphoses. A Commentary on Book III with Text and Introduction*, Amsterdam.

Van der Vliet 1885: Johannes van der Vliet, *Ad Apulei* Metamorphoses, in: "RPh" 9, 100–102.

Vardi 2001: Amiel Vardi, *Gellius against the Professors*, in: "ZPE" 137, 41–54.

Vardi 2004: Amiel Vardi, *Genre, Conventions, and Cultural Programme in Gellius'* Noctes Atticae, in: Holford-Strevens/Vardi 2004, 159–186.

Vera 1979: Domenico Vera, *Le statue del senato di Roma in onore di Flavio Teodosio e l'equilibrio dei poteri imperiali in età teodosiana*, in: "Athenaeum" 57, 381–403.

Vergin 2013: Wiebke Vergin, *Das Imperium Romanum und seine Gegenwelten: Die geographisch-ethnographischen Exkurse in den Res Gestae des Ammianus* Marcellinus, Berlin – Boston.

Vesperini 2015: Pierre Vesperini, *Le sens d'*humanitas *à Rome*, in: "Mélanges de l'École française de Rome – Antiquité" [En ligne], 127–1 | 2015, mis en ligne le 09 juin 2015, consulté le 25 mars 2019. URL: http://journals.openedition.org/mefra/2768; DOI : 10.4000/mefra.2768.

Vessey 1994: David W.T. Vessey, *Aulus Gellius and the Cult of the Past*, in: "ANRW" II.34.2, 1863–1917.

Veyne 1993: Paul Veyne, Humanitas: Romans and Non-Romans, in: Andrea Giardina (ed.), The Romans, Chicago, 342–369.

Vogt 1975: Wolfgang Vogt, C. Suetonius Tranquillus. Vita Tiberii. Kommentar, Würzburg (diss.).

Vogt-Spira 2014: Gregor Vogt-Spira, "Ehrenhaft leben – niemanden verletzen – jedem das Seine gewähren". Der Gerechtigkeitsdiskurs in Rom zwischen Tradition, Ethik und Recht, in: Gert Melville, Gregor Vogt-Spira and Mirko Breitenstein (eds.), Gerechtigkeit, Köln – Weimar – Wien, 40–57.

Volk 2021: Katharina Volk, The Roman Republic of Letters. Scholarship, Philosophy, and Politics in the Age of Cicero and Caesar, Princeton – Oxford.

Von Albrecht 1969: Michael von Albrecht, Das Prooemium von Ciceros Rede pro Archia poeta und das Problem der Zweckmäßigkeit der argumentatio extra causam, in: "Gymnasium" 76, 419–429.

Vout 1996: Caroline Vout, The Myth of the Toga: Understanding the History of Roman Dress, in: "G&R" 43, 2, 204–220.

Walde/Hofmann 1938: Alois Walde and Johann B. Hofmann, Lateinisches etymologisches Wörterbuch, Heidelberg.

Wallace-Hadrill 1982: Andrew Wallace-Hadrill, Civilis Princeps: Between Citizen and King, in: "JRS" 72, 32–48.

Wallace-Hadrill 1984: Andrew Wallace-Hadrill, Suetonius. The Scholar and His Caesars, New Haven.

Walsh 1970: Patrick G. Walsh, The Roman Novel. The 'Satyricon' of Petronius and the 'Metamorphoses' of Apuleius, Cambridge.

Warde Fowler 1911: William Warde Fowler, The Original Meaning of the Word Sacer, in: "JRS" 1, 57–63.

Whatmough 1925: Joshua Whatmough, Scholia in Isidori Etymologias Vallicelliana, in: "Archivum Latinitatis Medii Aevi" 2, 134–169.

Whitby 1999: Michael Whitby, Images of Constantius, in: Drijvers/Hunt 1999, 68–78.

Whitmarsh 2006: Tim Whitmarsh, This In-Between Book: Language, Politics and Genre in the Agricola, in: Brian McGing and Judith Mossman (eds.), The Limits of Ancient Biography, Swansea, 305–333.

Whitton 2019: Christopher Whitton, The Art of Self-Imitation in Pliny (and the Date of the Panegyricus), in: "Maia" 71, 2, 339–379.

Wieber-Scariot 1999: Anja Wieber-Scariot, Zwischen Polemik und Panegyrik: Frauen des Kaiserhauses und Herrscherinnen des Ostens in den Res Gestae des Ammianus Marcellinus, Trier.

Winterbottom 1984: Michael Winterbottom, The Minor Declamations ascribed to Quintilian, Berlin – New York.

Winterbottom 1994: Michael Winterbottom, M. Tulli Ciceronis De officiis, Oxford.

Wittchow 2001: Frank Wittchow, Exemplarisches Erzählen bei Ammianus Marcellinus: Episode, Exemplum, Anekdote, München.

Wood 2019: Clem Wood, Pliny's Paneg. 82–88 and Trajanic Literature and Culture, in: "Maia" 71, 2, 280–289.

Woodman 2009: Anthony J. Woodman (ed.), The Cambridge Companion to Tacitus, New York.

Woodman/Kraus 2014: Anthony J. Woodman and Christina S. Kraus, Tacitus. Agricola, Cambridge.

Woolf 1998: Gregory Woolf, Becoming Roman. The Origins of Provincial Civilization in Gaul, Cambridge.

Woudhuysen 2018: George Woudhuysen, Uncovering Constans' Image, in: Burgersdijk/Ross 2018, 158–182.

Wycisk 2008: Tonia Wycisk, "Quidquid in foro fieri potest": Studien zum römishen Recht bei Quintilian, Berlin.

Yegül 1992: Fikret K. Yegül, Baths and Bathing in Classical Antiquity, Cambridge (MA).

Zago 2012: Giovanni Zago, Sapienza filosofica e cultura materiale. Posidonio e le altre fonti dell'Epistola 90 di Seneca, Bologna.

Zetzel 2022: James E. G. Zetzel, *The Lost Republic. Cicero's* De oratore *and* De re publica, New York – Oxford.

Zimmerman 2000: Maaike Zimmerman, *Apuleius Madaurensis, Metamorphoses. Book X: Text, Introduction and Commentary*, Groningen.

Zinsmaier 2009: Thomas Zinsmaier, *[Quintilian] Die Hände der blinden Mutter (*Größere Deklamationen, *6)*, Cassino.

Zissos 2016a: Andrew Zissos (ed.), *A Companion to the Flavian Age of Imperial Rome*, Chichester – Malden (MA).

Zissos 2016b: Andrew Zissos, *The Flavian Legacy*, in: Zissos 2016a, 487–514.

Zucker 1928: Friedrich Zucker, *Plinius epist. VIII 24 – ein Denkmal antiker Humanität*, in: "Philologus" 84, 209–232.

Zugravu 2018: Nelu Zugravu, *Ammiano Marcellino e la cultura della violenza*, in: Eduard Nemeth (ed.), *Violence in Prehistory and Antiquity*, Kaiserslautern – Mehlingen, 337–401.

Index Locorum

Index Rerum

Index Nominum